MW00617589

The Oxford Series on India–China Studies

Series Editors
Prasenjit Duara, Tansen Sen, and Anand A. Yang

The Oxford Series on India–China Studies aims to develop an interdisciplinary corpus of research on historical and contemporary relations between India and China, as well as comparative studies of the two nations. It provides a multi-disciplinary site to bring together studies that go beyond the current obsession with strategic and geo-political, economic, or environmental issues and comparisons between India and China, thereby opening up spaces for a consolidated body of literature devoted to a holistic understanding of India–China relations from national, regional, and global perspectives. It will include broadly four categories of works: first, studies on India–China relations—economic, commercial, cultural, political—in historical and/or contemporary times; second, translations of key primary works from India and China, such as accounts and travelogues of Buddhist monks; third, translations of contemporary writings in the Chinese language into English, focusing on India–China relations; and lastly, works in progress that address research areas as yet unaddressed. Consolidating new scholarship that will enrich the field of India–China studies, this series aims to open up channels of greater dialogue between the two Asian giants.

Prasenjit Duara is Oscar Tang Chair of East Asian Studies, Duke University, Durham, North Carolina, USA.

Tansen Sen is Professor, History; Director, Center for Global Asia, NYU Shanghai, China; and Global Network Professor, NYU, New York, USA.

Anand A. Yang is Walker Family Endowed Professor, History, and Professor, International Studies, Henry M. Jackson School of International Studies, University of Washington, Seattle, USA.

'This is a fine collection of historical case studies detailing interactions between India and China in the colonial and post-colonial periods. It provides a window into India–China entanglements through intimate accounts based on primary sources in a range of languages. The volume offers the reader a much-needed history of the connections between two societies that will determine the world's future.'

'This superb volume explores modern India–China connections unbounded by the constraints of previously postulated national and temporal frameworks. By focusing on global trends instead, the essays in this collection trace India–China connections through a truly exciting array of people, ideas, and texts. The Introduction is an excellent primer on the growing field of India–China studies.'

'This collection of essays is an invaluable and timely addition to our knowledge of the cultural connections between India and China in the colonial and early post-colonial eras. At a time of heightened political and military rivalry, it is especially important to remember the wider political and cultural contexts of the relations between these two giant neighbours.'

'This volume represents a refreshing and long overdue reappraisal of the connections between China and India in the modern era. Thematically expansive and methodologically diverse, the fourteen essays here—authored by a fetching blend of established and rising stars—offer rich empirical and conceptual insights, taking us well past the now-tired tropes of civilization, nation-state, and pan-Asianism. Essential reading for anyone invested in the study of trans-cultural Asia and in the defining relationship of the so-called "Asian century".'

Beyond Pan-Asianism

Connecting China and India, 1840s–1960s

Edited by
Tansen Sen
and
Brian Tsui

OXFORD
UNIVERSITY PRESS

OXFORD
UNIVERSITY PRESS

Oxford University Press is a department of the University of Oxford.
It furthers the University's objective of excellence in research, scholarship,
and education by publishing worldwide. Oxford is a registered trademark of
Oxford University Press in the UK and in certain other countries.

Published in India by
Oxford University Press
22 Workspace, 2nd Floor, 1/22 Asaf Ali Road, New Delhi 110 002, India

© Oxford University Press 2021

The moral rights of the authors have been asserted.

First Edition published in 2021

ISBN-13 (print edition): 978-0-19-012911-8
ISBN-10 (print edition): 0-19-012911-5

ISBN-13 (eBook): 978-0-19-099212-5
ISBN-10 (eBook): 0-19-099212-3

Typeset in ScalaPro 10/13
by The Graphics Solution, New Delhi 110 092
Printed in India by Rakmo Press, New Delhi 110 020

Contents

Figures and Tables

Figures

Tables

Acknowledgements

We thank the Chiang Ching-kuo Foundation for International Scholarly Exchange, Taipei, Taiwan, for supporting our work. Without its very generous financial support for our three-year research project, 'Beyond Pan-Asianism: China–India Connections, 1911–1949', this volume would not have materialized.

We thank institutions that hosted meetings and helped shape this volume. They include Academia Historica, Taiwan; the Australian National University; Fudan University, China; The Hong Kong Polytechnic University, China; and New York University Shanghai, China. We do hope that solidarity between academics across nations, a phenomenon that sustains the work that we do, will continue to solidify.

We appreciate the comments and suggestions of the two anonymous reviewers, which made several sections of the volume, particularly the Introduction, much stronger with respect to content and analysis. Our gratitude also goes to Prasenjit Duara for writing the Epilogue to the volume.

We would also like to thank Barun Sarkar and his team at Oxford University Press, especially Moutushi Mukherjee and Smita Mathur, for seeing the publication process through efficiently and expeditiously.

Introduction

TANSEN SEN AND BRIAN TSUI

The essays in this volume describe the manifold ways in which China, India, and their respective societies were connected from the 1840s to the 1960s. This period witnessed the inexorable rise and terminal decline of *Pax Britannica* in Asia, the blooming of anti-colonial movements of various ideological hues, and the spread and entrenchment of the nation-state system across the world. This layered legacy looms large in the relations between Chinese and Indian societies in the twenty-first century. Euro-American imperialism figured as much more than the backdrop against which China and India interacted. Practitioners of global history (Armitage 2013; Bayly 2004; Osterhammel 2014) attribute to Western imperialism the dissemination of the inter-state system that originated in Europe, whose attendant procedures, norms, and codes still largely organize how present-day India and China interact with one another and with the rest of the world. Aside from the institutional setting of the modern world, processes of imperial expansion—movement of peoples, weapons, goods, and capital—tied China and India together in globalizing networks that stretched across multiple continents. In addition, attempts to overcome and dislodge imperialist rule engendered imaginaries, proposals, and institutions that brought together Indian and Chinese figures, both historical and fictional. From opium trade and Sikh presence in Shanghai's international settlement to nationalism and literary imaginations, stories of modern China–India interactions can hardly begin without taking colonialism and interrogations of empire seriously. Beyond the pan-Asianist, anti-colonialist interactions between intellectuals and political activists, and the celebration of 'brotherly' relations in the 1950s, this volume suggests that China engaged with the South Asian subcontinent and vice versa in more ambiguous terms.

This Introduction outlines four key aspects that help situate the chapters in this volume, chapters that examine China–India connections through multiple angles and in different phases of entanglement. It starts with an overview of some of the main players, events, and organizations that shaped and fostered these connections between the 1840s and the 1960s. Second, it explains the concept of pan-Asianism that strings the chapters together, not because all chapters address this notion, but because they demonstrate the need to understand the period under study beyond idealist perceptions of Asian unity. Third, the Introduction questions the use of fixed periodizations and geographically constrained understandings of China–India interactions. Here, the complexities of political transitions, the various roles of mediators, the shortcomings of artificial temporalities, and the limitations of nation-state frameworks are addressed. Fourth, the Introduction highlights some of the methodological concerns related to studying issues in China–India interactions, focusing in particular on the notion of 'China/India as method' proposed by the Taiwanese scholar Chen Kuan-hsing (陳光興). The final section of the Introduction briefly summarizes the chapters that follow and describes how they fit into the collection's overall conceptualization.

Entanglements in a Period of Vicissitudes

After several centuries of Buddhist and commercial exchanges (Liu 1988; Sen 2003), connections between China and India were gradually reset during the post-fifteenth century period due to the dominance of European colonial powers over the routes that linked the two regions. New networks of religious connections emerged with the arrival of Jesuit missionaries in ports occupied by the Portuguese, and new commodities entered the stream of commercial exchanges as a result of the British demand for Chinese tea, which they traded for Indian opium (Liu 2020; Sen 2017). Additionally, British probing of the Tibetan frontier, starting from the late eighteenth century, shaped a complex set of geopolitical relations with the Qing Empire and the subsequent Kuomintang (KMT) government in China (Mosca 2013; Sen 2020). These networks were used not only by the European colonial powers, but also by Kashmiri and Parsi traders, Cantonese carpenters, and Hakka labourers who carved out their own unique commercial, migratory, and anti-colonial links between different regions of China and India.

The Opium War and the subsequent signing of the Treaty of Nanjing between the Qing Empire and the British in 1842 augmented many of these connections while at the same time introducing new avenues of contacts, exchanges, and mutual learning as China and India went through multiple phases of turmoil, conflict, and anti-colonial resistance over the next century. One of the key facets of these connections was the appearance of several eyewitness accounts and travelogues written by Chinese and Indians during the second half of the nineteenth century. These included the writings of the Qing officials Huang Maocai (黃楙材) (1843–90) and Ma Jianzhong (馬建忠) (1845–1900), who were dispatched in the 1870s and 1880s to assess the military threat from the British in India. There was also the famous intellectual Kang Youwei (康有為) (1858–1927), who escaped to India in 1901 after the failure of his reform movement in China. Kang wrote about his travels in India as well as his views on Indian society and political structure.[1]

The views of India and Indians expressed in the writings of these Chinese visitors tallied with the contemporary discourse on India as a 'lost/vanquished nation' (*wangguo* [亡國]), that is, an ancient civilization that had succumbed to a European colonial power.[2] This perception hardened and became widespread in the early twentieth-century China, when the British employed Sikhs to police the concession areas in cities such as Shanghai, Tianjin, and Wuhan. The depiction of these Sikh policemen as a symbol of Indian capitulation to their European masters became ubiquitous in Chinese newspapers and popular publications, leading to the coining of the pejorative term 'Red-head Asan' (*hongtou asan* [紅頭阿三]) for Indians more generally.[3] It was at this moment that writings on China by Indians also started appearing in several languages. Thakur Gadadhar Singh and Ashutosh Roy were part of the British Army that fought the Boxers at the turn of the nineteenth century, and they wrote about their experiences in Hindi and Bengali, respectively.[4] Singh in particular offered a complex view of British expansion in India and China and underscored the entangled histories and fates of the two countries (Yang 2017).[5] There were other Indians in China during this early period, such as Indumadhav Mullick and Benoy Kumar Sarkar, who also wrote about their travels or discussed issues that placed India and China in comparative perspectives (Sen 2007).[6]

Some of these intellectual ponderings, which avoided engaging with perceptions of Indians among 'lowbrow' circles in China, became intimately entangled with the emergence of the idea of pan-Asianism articulated by the Japanese scholar Okakura Tenshin in 1903. His idea of 'Asia as One' quickly took root with several Indian and Chinese scholars, particularly those based in Japan. Pan-Asianism identified a civilizational connection between China, India, and Japan prior to the arrival of the European colonial powers, one that should be revived in the twentieth century.[7] In 1907, inspired by this ideology, one Chinese scholar in Japan called Zhang Taiyan (章太炎) (1869–1936) asked rhetorically, 'Are not our three countries like a folding fan?' He then described this triangular bonding as: 'India is the paper; China is the bamboo frame; and Japan is the pivot linking these two handles' (Shimada 1990: 80).[8]

Rabindranath Tagore, the Indian Nobel laureate and proponent of the pan-Asian concept, met Okakura twice before the latter's death in 1913. Tagore was initially receptive, but then grew concerned about the Japan-centric vision that Okakura was promoting.[9] The same was eventually true of Zhang Taiyan, who, as discussed later, discovered Japan's imperialistic agenda embedded in the idea outlined by Okakura. In fact, in the 1930s, Okakura's ideas were ultimately integrated into the militaristic concept known as the Greater East Asia Co-Prosperity Sphere (Dai Tōa Kyōeiken [大東亜共栄圏]).[10] Thus, in 1924, when Tagore visited China,[11] an altered idea of pan-Asianism developed that centred on the cultural connections between China and India.

Santiniketan, a site about 200 km from Calcutta (now Kolkata), became the hub where this new concept of pan-Asianism was 'put into action'. Already in 1921, Tagore had established an educational institution known as Visva-Bharati in Santiniketan, which adopted the motto, 'Where the world makes a home in a single nest'. Since its inauguration, Tagore had planned to set up a centre for China studies in this 'nest'. However, it was only in 1937, after several years of fund-raising efforts, that an institution called Cheena Bhavana (The Chinese Hall) was established at Visva-Bharati. Tagore's literary works and Visva-Bharati appealed to a wide range of Chinese scholars, artists, and even political leaders, several of whom visited him in Santiniketan. In addition to Chinese writers such as Xu Zhimo (徐志摩) (1897–1931) and Xie Bingxin (謝冰心) (1900–99), who were deeply influenced by Tagore's writings, painters such as Gao Jianfu (高劍父) (1879–1951) and Xu Beihong (徐悲鴻) (1895–1953), and KMT leaders Chiang Kai-shek (蔣介石) (1887–1975) and Dai Jitao (戴季陶) (1891–1949), met with Tagore in India. A key person in these interactions was Tan Yunshan (譚雲山) (1898–1983), who went to Santiniketan in 1928 and eventually convinced the KMT to fund the establishment of Cheena Bhavana. It was also his connections that brought renowned Chinese scholars and KMT representatives to Santiniketan.[12]

The visits of the KMT representatives to Santiniketan were pri-marily associated with the attempt to convince Indian independence leaders to join the British in the war against the Japanese occupa-tion of China. Jawaharlal Nehru (1889–1964) was one of the main figures in the Indian independence movement who had close con-nections with KMT leaders, members of the Chinese Communist Party, and Soong Ching-ling ([宋慶齡] Song Qingling), the wife of the late Sun Yat-sen (1866–1925). During the 1930s and 1940s, the Indian National Congress (INC) launched several initiatives to sup-port the Chinese in their war against the Japanese. This included the observation of a 'China Day' in India, the dispatch of a medical mission in 1938, and Nehru's visit to China in 1939.[13] For their part, the Chinese side funded educational exchanges between the two countries, voiced support for the Indian independence move-ment, and sent 'Goodwill Missions' to meet with Indian leaders such as Mohandas Gandhi (1869–1948), Nehru, and Muhammad Ali Jinnah (1876–1948).[14] This mutual logistical and moral support against colonialism continued through to the end of the Second World War.

The post-War period, which witnessed Indian independence and the establishment of the People's Republic of China (PRC) after a brutal civil war between the KMT and the Chinese Communist Party, was marked by a significant restructuring of political relations between China and India. Issues related to the status of Tibet, border demarcation, and the national identities of migrant communities complicated these relations. These complications surfaced during the Asian Relations Conference, held in Delhi in March–April 1947. A separate invitation to Tibet to participate in this conference, organized by the Indian Council for World Affairs at the behest of the interim prime minister, Jawaharlal Nehru, drew strong protests from KMT officials, who threatened to withdraw. This also created distrust of Nehru among many KMT officials and the leaders of the Chinese Communist Party, who believed that the Indian leader planned to continue the British policy of not fully recognizing Tibet as a sovereign part of China (Sen 2017). This view persisted until the signing of an 'Agreement on Trade and Intercourse between the Tibet region of China and India' (also known as the 'Panchsheel Treaty') in 1954, which recognized Tibet as an integral part of China.

Despite the signing of the aforementioned treaty, the frequent exchanges of cultural delegations, mutual visits by political leaders, and the revival of the ideals connected with pan-Asianism, disagreements over how to demarcate the border persisted during the 1950s. The status of Indian and Chinese migrant communities living in different parts of the Republic of India (ROI) and the PRC also remained unclear. In the early 1950s, for example, the Khache, descendants of Kashmiri Muslim traders residing in Tibet, asserted their 'Indian' identity and demanded that they be allowed to 'return' to India (Atwill 2018). Similarly, Chinese migrants in India who had settled in Bengal, Assam, and elsewhere since the eighteenth century struggled to determine their national identities. Some of them opted to accept PRC passports, which were offered by Chinese diplomatic missions in India. Many others remained stateless as the ROI drafted citizenship laws that left little room for Chinese settlers and their descendants to acquire Indian citizenship. When disagreements over the demarcation of the border led to a brief war between the ROI and the PRC in 1962, collateral damage was inflicted on Chinese living in India. Many, including those born in India and those of mixed heritage, were deported, while others were interned in detention centres across the country for over five years.[15] By the mid-1960s, the ties between China and India had completely unravelled.

Pan-Asianism and beyond

The diverse intellectual and literary musings of the Chinese and Indians mentioned earlier often envisaged the transcendence of Euro-America's political and epistemological domination. They ran parallel to, or were interwoven with, interactions between revolutionary parties. Transnational solidarity, as one dimension of Chinese nationalism, brought radicalized Chinese intellectuals into communion with their counterparts from India and across Asia. Projects such as the Asia Solidarity Association attracted anarchists, socialists, and nationalists based in Tokyo, the epicentre of radical thought for China, India, and many other colonized Asian countries in the early twentieth-century. Successors to this 1907 intellectual experiment in Asian unity, as Rebecca Karl (2002) remarks, were varied and were made to serve both revolutionary and conservative political agendas. The most problematic and intensively scrutinized iterations of regional solidarity are those that lent themselves to Japanese imperialism or directly endorsed it. Prominent Japanese pan-Asianist intellectuals (Hotta 2007; Saaler and Koshmann 2007; Tankha 2006), whose ideas were themselves often messy and hard to pin down, embraced the Japanese state's intrusion into the continent because it appealed to anti-colonialism, fraternity among Asian peoples, and transcendence of the liberal international order. Yet, it is increasingly clear from other works (Aydin 2007; Duara 2003; Saaler and Szpilman 2011) that Asianist thoughts were far from being confined to the Japanese Empire. In his study of Gadhadar Singh's sympathetic account of the Boxer Rebellion, Anand Yang (2017) shows that notions of pan-Asian affinity had currency among readerships beyond the Indian elite. Singh brought his perspective on India's subjugation to British rule to bear in his reading of the Boxers and criticized the barbaric violence that Western forces imposed on China in the name of civilization. Like better known Indian writers, Singh related to the Chinese as fellow victims of colonialism, the world order into which Asia was inducted at gunpoint.

Indeed, while perhaps not nearly as recognizable as a distinct strain of thought as it was in Japan, the ideas that Asians confronted common enemies, faced similar challenges, and charted futures unshackled by Euro-centric socio-political and epistemological systems were shared across China and India. In the first half of the twentieth century, as recent works demonstrate, pan-Asianism in one form or another informed China's and India's engagements with one another and with other societies in the region. Its palatability to activists from a wide political spectrum was helped by pan-Asianism's inherent ambiguity. As Sven Saaler and Christopher Szpilman (2011) observe, pan-Asianist ideals, even though entangled with Japanese imperialist ambitions, held appeal in India and Southeast Asia, as these societies seldom found themselves on the receiving end of Japan's predatory behaviour. In India, Carolien Stolte (2013) argues, Asianism represented a rich, diverse tradition and was by no means an import from East Asia. It encompassed contradictory viewpoints, some converging with the nationalist agenda and some working against the nation-state as a model for the South Asian subcontinent's future. In China, which suffered a great deal of Japanese aggression relatively early, intellectuals took pains to discriminate between militarist appropriations of Asianist thoughts and their emancipatory variants. In addition, some individuals advocated transnational affinities on internationalist and/or Global Southern terms, which typically also included regions beyond Asia. Li Dazhao (李大钊) (1889–1927), one of China's earliest communists, proposed 'New Asianism' as a superior alternative to both Japanese-led domination of Asia and capitalist globalization spearheaded by the West (Smith 2014: 248). The universalism in these positions—in form but not in content, of course—was not dissimilar to the most sophisticated strains of Japanese pan-Asianism. For renowned Kyoto School philosophers such as Nishida Kitarō (西田幾多郎) (1870–1945) and Miki Kiyoshi (三木清) (1897–1945), 'Asia', 'Greater Asia', and the 'Orient' (Tōyō [東洋]) were not just regionalist, geographical concepts, but ones that represented an intervention of world historical significance.[16] 'Asia', in the late 1930s and the 1940s, was the site from which a new world order transcending Western modernity was to be launched (Yamamuro 2001).

The chapters that follow reinforce the historical entanglement of China and India in global trends as a central narrative framework.

They both echo and go beyond the pan-Asianist perimeters that much existing scholarship adopts in understanding China's and India's interactions with other societies both within and outside Asia. Even those studies that do not evoke the specific history of colonial-era pan-Asianist discourse often rely implicitly on the tenets of Asian solidarity or oneness as the dominant mode of crafting and recognizing China–India interactions. Moving beyond such assumptions requires exploring different archives and examining a wider cast of characters beyond the usual categories of political leaders and intellectual elites. In contrast to other volumes on China–India relations, which focus on the inter-state dimension, this volume addresses interconnectivity at multiple levels and dimensions. As a result, the various chapters bring both historiographical and literary perspectives to bear in examining a diverse array of primary sources, from archival records and newspapers to fiction and philosophical treatises. As well as furthering the dialogue between historians and literary scholars, the interdisciplinary approach enshrined in this volume results in a more nuanced picture of India–China connectedness. Diplomats and politicians are by no means ignored, but contributors see writers, intellectuals, entrepreneurs, traders, intelligence officers, and spies as equally important mediators between the two societies. Together, this volume shows how pan-Asianism can be a productive angle through which China–India interactions can be conceptualized, particularly at the level of elites and the nationalist movements in the two countries.

In terms of literary, philosophical, religious, and realpolitik thinking and practices, however, the chapters in the present volume also suggest that pan-Asianism informs but does not necessarily define or exhaust stories of China–Indian interaction. International migration, religious commitments, literary and philosophical imaginations, geopolitical rivalries, and nation-state building cannot be understood exclusively under the rubrics of pan-Asianist solidarity. In some instances, particularly when state interests were involved, suspicions trumped camaraderie. Without dismissing its significance, one needs to look beyond pan-Asianism to account for the ambiguities, complexities, and contradictions that plagued China–India interactions throughout the late nineteenth and twentieth centuries.

One of the contributions made by this volume is that it delves extensively and systematically into archival documents held by institutions in Asia, particularly in India and Taiwan. Some of the sources we have consulted are discussed in the concluding chapter of this book. Aside from documents held and curated by the state, this volume also pays attention to materials that have largely escaped absorption by public archives.

Contextualizing China–India Connections

Although most of the chapters in this volume pertain to the period before the emergence of the ROI in 1947 and the PRC in 1949, the volume does not make hard temporal distinctions based on political changes. This choice to de-emphasize periodization echoes the volume's title, *Beyond Pan-Asianism*, which attempts to encapsulate the nuances within and beyond the shared anti-colonial sentiments that linked Indian independence with the Chinese revolution. As the chapters by Reinhardt and Sen show, several aspects of India–China connections continued or become more comprehensible if no strict timeframes associated with political transitions are imposed on what were multifaceted and complex interactions between the two regions. The same is true of the earlier period, for the collapse of the Qing Empire in 1911, a watershed moment in Chinese history, did not significantly alter Indian and Chinese writings about each other's countries (see the chapters in the first two sections of this volume). The interactions between India and China were always fluid, transcending artificial temporalities and geographical constructs, and functioning at multiple levels, from the geopolitics of nation-states to the mobilities of their subalterns.

This volume also puts into relief the pertinence of China–India interactions in the colonial and hence global context (Osterhammel and Petersson 2005: 69–79). It should be stressed that while bilateral ties and comparisons do feature prominently in many of the chapters, they are stories not just of two countries and their relationship, but of supranational trends and developments of global significance. In particular, this volume contributes to historiographical investigations that recontextualize China's modern developments in respect of the hegemony of capitalist modernity. Prasenjit Duara (1995) has highlighted the ways in which the institution of the nation-state, along with the cult of linear progress, came to exercise the minds of Chinese and

Indian thinkers and political activists. He observes how, in both societies, the quest for national subjectivity often colluded with colonial epistemology, resulting in an exclusionary and repressive modernity that was shared across Asia and beyond as it underwent decolonization. James Hevia (2003) demonstrates that China was incorporated into Britain's Asian Empire, with its centre in India, even though notionally it remained, or indeed was forced to become, a sovereign state. Throughout the latter half of the nineteenth century, imperialist warfare, looting, and treaty-making rendered China a subservient part of *Pax Britannica*. Focusing also on the British Empire in China, Robert Bickers (2015) convincingly shows that, from trade and policing to movements of people and the security of the British Empire in Asia, India and China were inextricably tied together. Homing in on the Qing perspective, Matthew Mosca (2013) traces the enormous importance of British India's emergence in reconfiguring China's geopolitical outlook. Western imperialism prompted officials and thinkers to treat realms beyond the Qing in ways that resembled modern state-to-state interactions. British imperialism, with its appeals to free trade, civilization, and religiously inflected ideologies of progress, make capitalist imperialism much more palpable through state-led warfare and treaty-making. Interactions between China and India, and their epistemological underpinnings, thus entered a new phase.

Of equal importance, and in even more diverse ways, were the efforts to link China, India, and the rest of the world together in ways that challenged the hegemony of capitalist imperialism. Through imperialist violence, by the second half of the nineteenth century, the global inter-state system had replaced the 'archaic globalization' of loosely organized universalist polities. Nationalist agitations often contained internationalist sentiments that interrogated hardening geopolitical boundaries and challenged the confines of the nation-state's sovereign rights (Bayly 2004). Intellectual historian Wang Hui (2015: 4–7) identifies the convergence of nationalism and social revolution or socialist nation-building as the hallmark of Asia's 'short twentieth century'. If imperialism, monarchical rule, and military conquest were the leitmotifs of the nineteenth century, nationhood and the people's sovereignty were those of the twentieth century. Unlike nineteenth-century nationalist movements, which were wedded to the bourgeois social order, the Chinese revolution and the

Indian freedom struggle were anti-systemic movements (Wallerstein 2002) in the sense that they posed challenges to the Western imperialist presence and, in varying degrees, questioned capitalist modernity. These movements mobilized populations, created links, and shared agendas across national borders, eventually constituting the mainstay of Asian political economies in the postcolonial era.[17]

It is appropriate that nationalist and socialist movements, including the more transient ones that formed concrete links between diasporic communities in China and India (Cao 2017; Deepak 2001; Thampi 2005; Zhang 2015), should occupy scholarly attention. In the mid-1920s, internationalist activism, particularly that inspired by the Communist International (Comintern) through the League against Imperialism (Prashad 2007), brought nationalist parties into dialogue with one another. After the 12 April coup of 1927, which marked the end of communist participation in China's national revolution, the KMT state harnessed revolutionary mechanisms to pursue industrialization and social goals within a largely capitalist framework while appealing to a vague promise to overcome the liberal inter-state order. It sought cooperation with other Asian nationalist movements, citing civilizational discourses of immanent spiritual affinities, including the INC, which had earned itself a mass following and influence (Tsui 2018). As the Second Sino-Japanese War morphed into the Pacific War with Tokyo's expansion into British and US possessions in Asia, the ways in which the elites in Nationalist China and India's independence movement positioned themselves in relation to the 'Greater East Asia' project took centre stage. This happened as these figures recalibrated their nationalist aspirations and their discomfort with capitalism, while Japan's 'imperial regionalism' (Duara 2010) promised an autarkic Asia-wide bloc freed from Western domination. Much about these histories can now be unearthed from state-maintained archives in mainland China, Taiwan, India, and the United Kingdom. However, inasmuch as India's interactions with China are concerned and vice versa, sources held by depositories in Asia remain underexplored.

China/India as Method

One aim of the present volume is to demonstrate that instances of interaction outside formal diplomacy merit serious, critical examination. It therefore takes a small but essential step towards conceptualizing China–India connections more widely than hitherto. The highly idealistic and controversial notion of a 'Himalaya Sphere' aside (Tan 2015), not much effort has been spent in ruminating on the possibilities and limitations of thinking about China and India as connected societies or in comparative terms.[18] One notable exception is the India–China Summit on Social Thought, held in Shanghai in 2010, which resulted in a Chinese-language volume. The event's main organizer, Chen Kuan-hsing (2014), a pioneer of the inter-Asia cultural studies movement, opined that thinking about the similarities and differences between India and China could point to visions beyond those defined by nation-state developmentalism. Beholden to socio-political models offered by 'advanced' countries in Europe and North America, Chinese intellectuals, among whom Chen counts himself, were able to use India as 'method', that is, to take seriously the South Asian country's modern experience in order to re-examine their own assumptions about China and the rest of the world. In particular, he brings up India's ethno-linguistic diversity and shows how it resulted in a polity distinct from a typical nation-state in the European sense, with a common language, the predominance of national parties, and a highly centralized government system. He also observes that for many Indian intellectuals, China's socialist experiments and empowerment of women were matters of much greater interest than whether or when the size of China's economy managed to surpass Euro-America's. Thinking about India critically allows China to interrogate its fetish—hegemonic since the 'Reform and Opening Up' period—for catching up with Euro-America and creating a social order built around state-led industrialization. Such an enterprise would open up possibilities for alternative visions of global social order distinct from that of the capitalist modernity that prevails in the West.[19]

Chen's musings on India and Asia (2010) as 'method' are inspired by the famed Japanese historian of China Mizoguchi Yūzō, whose many books include the influential *Hōhō to shite no Chūgoku* (方法 としての中国) [*China as Method*] (1989). An expert in intellectual developments in late imperial China, Mizoguchi (2004) traces the genesis of the Chinese socialist revolution to the Ming–Qing transition, that is, to the late sixteenth to early seventeenth century. He argues that mutual aid, reciprocity, and a willingness to take care of the young and the weak—hallmarks of the clan communities that began to thrive amidst economic upheaval of the late Ming—laid the intellectual foundations for the socialist revolution. Rather than impediments to modernity, Mizoguchi counterintuitively proposes that China's supposedly premodern social networks and popular ethical norms contributed to it. However, his intervention is not an empirical but methodological one: instead of mobilizing concepts derived from Europe to assess China, scholars would do well to map dynamics that are internal to China to study the country *and* the rest of the world. Rather than taking the European experience as the universal norm against which China is measured,[20] categories internal to and derived from Chinese history should be used to examine other societies. Mizoguchi's challenge has been reissued by Chen, who calls on scholars to learn from the experiences of civil societies across Asia in order to produce knowledge that defies Cold War categories. Deploying China or India as 'method' is explicitly normative, a move that engages histories with a view to challenging the epistemological framework—underpinned by the ideological and great power rivalries of the Cold War—under which relations between China, India, and other Asian societies are understood and described.[21]

Exploring Alternatives

The present volume does not advocate deploying China or India as 'method', even though we welcome it as one potentially productive way through which China–India connections can be narrated. Some of the chapters in this volume do indeed converge with the 'China/India as method' approach. Sidelining both colonial states and nation-states, they unearth literary tropes and philosophical concepts to demonstrate how they were attempts to imagine alternatives to global imperialism and capitalism. Other contributors are more circumspect, suggesting that state-driven geopolitical designs and desires to overcome the nation-state system—whether expressed through pan-Asianism or the 'China/India as method' ideal—cannot be neatly demarcated. Indeed, this volume does not impose a singular methodological programme, but instead allows multiple approaches and archival sources to guide us in questioning narratives that have dominated how we think about China, India, and their connectedness.

Specifically, the first part of the volume looks at the ways in which Chinese writers attempted to undermine imported colonial doctrines by engaging with different meanings of India: India as synonymous with its religions or mythologies, India as a colonized realm, India as accomplice to the colonizer. The three chapters in the section 'Epistemological Interventions' examine a trove of literary texts which feature the Indian policeman, the critique of the Hegelian perception of time that emerges from the writings of Zhang Taiyan, and the imagination of a Sino-Indian tropology in works by Xu Dishan. Adhira Mangalagiri argues that, through the figure of the Indian policeman, Chinese writers articulated an anti-colonial discourse that subverted and exceeded static notions of colonizer/colonized and self/other imposed by colonial epistemologies. Gal Gvili shows how Xu Dishan's engagement with Indian mythology and religions in his fiction extends to a critique of imperialist epistemologies, particularly Social Darwinism, then prevalent in China. As for Zhang Taiyan, according to Viren Murthy, the Chinese revolutionary's critique of imperialist epistemologies, including Hegelian visions of progressive history, hinged upon a hypothetical China–India alliance that transcended a Japanese-led pan-Asianism. Together, the three essays offer a different methodology for engaging with China–India connectedness. They propose to examine expressions of rhetorical, figurative, and thematic engagements with India in Chinese literature as a moment when the imagination of connectivity enabled the production of new epistemologies that profoundly challenge the more familiar Republican-era understandings of history, colonialism, and the role of literature in national transformations.

The second section of the volume, 'Encounters and Images', focuses on how China was represented in Indian writings and vice versa. These three chapters eloquently demonstrate that China and India already appeared regularly in each other's print media at the turn of the twentieth century. Images of the two countries that circulated in the burgeoning urban market for books and periodicals in the late nineteenth and early twentieth centuries left a strong imprint on how the two countries understood one another in subsequent decades. Zhang Ke studies late Qing travel writings on India, which, despite superficial similarities with their early modern predecessors, represented a new genre tied to imperial China's uneasy transformation into a nation-state in the shadow of Western imperialism. To Chinese travellers, India featured not as a culture or the birthplace of Buddhism, but as a concrete polity governed under the auspices of British colonialism. Zhang argues that Chinese travel writings are not about India or even China per se, but about the triangulated relationship between China, British India, and the British Empire as a whole. From the Indian side, Kamal Sheel and Anand Yang delve into writings in the vernacular Indian languages of Hindi, Bengali, and Urdu to show that popular perceptions of China at the turn of the twentieth century were predominately favourable and sympathetic. Just as the Tokyo-based Chinese revolutionary Zhang Taiyan's affinity with India and Indian culture informed his anti-imperialist, internationalist nationalism (Lin 2018), Sheel and Yang draw attention to contemporary expressions in India of regionalist affinities with China that are not beholden to the strictures of the nation-state model. Although often expressed in the language of cultural and civilizational commonalities, Yang remarks aptly that the basis of China–India solidarity rested not so much on the two societies' romanticized pasts as on their shared predicament at the receiving end of imperialist violence. Before regionalist pan-Asianist movements became deeply embroiled in state-led geostrategic manoeuvring, evocations of transnational solidarity begat the potential for forms of China–India connectedness that challenged the capitalist nation-state order.

Section III, 'Cultures and Mediators', continues the stories the previous section has already charted out by tracing concrete instances of dialogue and exchange facilitated by twentieth-century governmental, intellectual, and religious networks. It shows how ideas that emerged since the onslaught of Western imperialism in the late nineteenth and early twentieth centuries were actuated in subsequent practices of China–India interactions. Observing how Rabindranath Tagore's interactions with China were overshadowed in subsequent scholarship by the controversy he stirred up during his 1924 visit to the country, Yu-Ting Lee recounts a little-studied episode to show that his engagement with Chinese intellectuals was not confined to his (in) famous celebration of Eastern civilization. The rather obscure conversation the famed Chinese philosopher Feng Youlan (馮友蘭) (1895– 1990) had with Tagore in 1920, when the former was a student at Columbia University, serves to reorient readers' attention to the poet's humanistic thought. After 1924, Tagore's humanism, from which his life-long criticism of the nation-state system derived, was reduced to an East/West binary in the Chinese context and recognized as conservatism. This (mis)understanding—or 'provincialization', as Lee puts it—of Tagorean thought persists in present-day scholarship on the poet's engagement with China. Adding another twist to Tagore's complicated legacy in China–India connections, Brian Tsui charts the extraordinary career of the poet's Chinese protégé, Tan Yunshan. Enamoured by Tagore's adoration of Eastern spirituality and sweeping critique of industrial modernity, Tan found himself negotiating strenuously between his self-identity as a scholar inheriting Tagore's enterprise and the KMT's identification of his network in India as a geopolitical tool. In the end, Tan's investment in a seemingly apolitical pan-Asian cultural unity converged with Nationalist China's anti-communist, anti-Japanese pan-Asianism, which was torn between allegiance to Western allies and support for anti-colonial agitation. Homing in on the building of a gurdwara in Hong Kong in 1901, Yin Cao examines how the British Empire brought the evangelical Singh Sabha Movement from its home in Punjab to China and beyond when the Sikhs began to be recruited to fuel imperial adventures at the turn of the twentieth century. Janice Hyeju Jeong's chapter questions the Chinese Islamic Goodwill Missions's (Chinese) nationalist credentials by highlighting their transnational and heterogeneous connections across the Islamic world, arguing that the Second World War strengthened, rather than weakened, the cosmopolitan networks of Chinese Muslims. Together, the chapters in Section III demonstrate how turn-of-the-twentieth-century iterations of pan-Asianist identities came into conflict with, deviated from, or simply failed to take account of the hard realities of state-building and war-making enterprises that incorporated China and India as parts of their centre stages.

The section 'Building and Challenging Imperial Networks' addresses the ways in which China and India's imbrications within the British Empire and its associated networks of transport, trade, migration, and settlement provided a vast range of spaces within which new identities, alliances, and solidarities between the two countries could be imagined and produced. It takes fully on board the building and dismantling of Euro-American empires in Asia as the most significant developments inspiring interactions between China and India. Madhavi Thampi's chapter shows how the treaty ports and other Chinese cities provided both refuges for anti-colonial Indian activists and sites of recruitment for these movements from among their Indian populations. She extends Cao's story of British imperial expansion in Asia from the Indian subcontinent to China, but focuses on how the colonized fought back against their colonial overlords. Population-wise, the Indian diaspora in China was small, but its political militancy was energized by exposure to ideologies such as socialism, anti-imperialism, and pan-Asianism. The pronounced internationalism of Indian nationalists in China informed the longevity and specificity of their anti-British political pursuit, which encompassed an anti-colonialism built into an idea of a just world order. In studying the development of the Nationalist government's intelligence on and policies towards India during the Second World War, Liao Wen-shuo's essay reveals the desire of the members of KMT to work with the Indian nationalist movement without disrupting their alliance with Britain, as well as the stereotypes and misunderstandings that emerged from these very same efforts. It demonstrates that, even while China was struggling to defend itself from the Japanese imperialist onslaught, the Nationalist government became adept at balancing its anti-colonial devotions with its inclusion in an international order still dominated by the Western imperial powers. Anne Reinhardt's essay explains how not only the shipping networks that linked China and India but also the shipping system inaugurated in both places by British interests in the nineteenth century presented indigenous shipping entrepreneurs with parallel obstacles as nationalist entrepreneurs sought to challenge foreign dominance in Chinese and Indian waters from the 1920s to the 1950s. She homes in on shipping nationalism as the common denominator between indigenous entrepreneurs in India and China respectively as they transitioned from foreign-dominated economies to those presided over by postcolonial regimes. She also draws attention to the shared conditions that confronted Walchand Hirachand (1882–1953) and Lu Zuofu (盧作孚) (1893–1952), as well as the little-acknowledged structural connections between the two countries under a global economic system. Tansen Sen brings the story up to the 1960s. Focusing on the border town Kalimpong and the individuals who were suspected to be Chinese spies, he stresses the continuities between colonial and postcolonial state concerns and the arbitrariness of national categories such as 'Chinese', 'Indian,' and 'Tibetan'. He also introduces material from multiple archives and demonstrates the need to examine these important, albeit rarely utilized, sources. Together, the essays in this section chronicle the shifting and multifaceted patterns of China–India interactions as the two countries were transformed from colonial subjects into fledgling nation-states.

The interconnected nature of China and India under British hegemony in Asia was as diverse in its varieties as the extent to which it presented challenges to the reigning imperialist, capitalist order. Some ties, like those of the Sikh diaspora, were, initially at least, contingent on British imperial expansion. Others presented radical, albeit subtle, critiques of the ideological assumptions of Empire. Still others were anticipatory of Asia's postcolonial order, even while also exhibiting a desire to transcend the nation-state system. The decades that followed the 1940s would see anti-colonial agitation in India turn the country into a formidable nation-state, while a much stronger state emerged in China than the one presided over by the Nationalists. Much like other anti-systemic movements, the parties that governed the ROI and the PRC during the Cold War period mixed nationalist and socialist commitments. Moreover, as in the case of their counterparts elsewhere, both the Indian and Chinese movements eventually found themselves cutting back on their radical militancy and promises of social transformation. In place of popular mobilization, bureaucratic and hierarchical norms held sway (Wallerstein 2002), as statist principles and the mantra of national security became hegemonic. Transnational movements of people and goods, tolerated under the (semi)colonial order presided over by the British, were ironically eroded in postcolonial Asia as borders hardened and geostrategic concerns assumed the priority in nation-states with competing claims to territorial rights. As Tansen Sen (2017: 478) remarks, while appealing to grand civilizational discourses of unity and amity, nation-states imposed 'monitored, managed, and restrictive people-to-people connections'. After the Cold War, nation-states in Asia have encouraged greater, but by no means unregulated flows of capital, knowledge, goods, culture, and labour. However, the increased porosity of national borders and the intermingling of cultures were far from being emancipatory. Instead, they were corollaries, engineered by the nation-states themselves, of neoliberal governmentality and capital valorization (Duara 2010: 979–83).

The present volume therefore retraces episodes in the entangling of the two communities from the two modern national or colonial states and those who traversed them. It highlights the fact that modern China–India ties went beyond, if not challenged, the capitalist nation-state system, but also reinforced it. In this sense, Prasenjit Duara is most astute in describing this volume as one that exemplifies the circulatory nature of histories that confounds linear national processes. We hope that our collective endeavour will invite future works that continue our discussion on the efficacy and limits of pan-Asianism and on using China or India as 'method' in understanding and conceptualizing the historical connections between the two societies and their neighbours across Asia.

Notes

1. On these Chinese writers, see the essay by Zhang Ke in this volume.
2. See Karl (2002) on Chinese views of *wangguo* and their perception of India within that context.
3. In addition to the works of Jackson (2012) and Cao (2018), see also Chapter 1 by Adhira Mangalagiri and Chapter 9 by Yin Cao in this volume on the presence and perception of the Sikhs in China.
4. See Yang (2017) for an English translation of the work and a reprint of Roy's (2013) Bengali edition.
5. The views of Gadadhar Singh are also discussed in Chapter 5 by Kamal Sheel in this volume.
6. For a detailed discussion of various Indian groups in China between 1800 and 1949, see Thampi (2005).
7. For a comprehensive collection of writings related to pan-Asianism, see Saaler and Szpilman (2011). China–India interactions within the context of pan-Asianism are discussed in Sen (2017).
8. For a detailed discussion of Zhang Taiyan in the context of China–India interactions, see Chapter 3 by Viren Murthy in this volume.
9. The relationship between Tagore and Okakura is examined in Bharucha (2006).
10. A recent study of the Greater East Asia Co-Prosperity Sphere is Yellen (2019).

11. There are several studies of Tagore's visit to China in 1924. The two most influential works are Hay (1970) and Das (1993). See also Chapter 7 on Tagore by Yu-Ting Lee in this volume.

12. On the role of Cheena Bhavana in fostering interactions between China and India, see Tsui (2010), Sen (2017), and Chapter 8 by Brian Tsui in this volume.

13. See Sen (2020) for interactions between China and India between 1937 and 1949. On the relationship between Chiang Kai-shek and Nehru, including their visits to India and China respectively, see Samarani (2005) and Yang (2014). Their political connections during the Second World War period are explored in Chapter 12 by Liao Wen-shuo in this volume.

14. While the Buddhist 'Goodwill Mission' led by the monk Taixu is discussed in Sen (2017), Janice Hyeju Jeong examines the Chinese Muslim 'Goodwill Mission' to India in Chapter 10 in this volume.

15. On the experience of the Chinese community in India during the late 1950s and early 1960s, see Cohen and Leng (1972), Banerjee (2017), and Chapter 14 by Tansen Sen in this volume.

16. The Kyoto School in Japan was a loose umbrella encompassing Japanese philosophers conversant with Western, particularly continental, philosophy. The right wing of the Kyoto School was infamous for its acceptance of the Japanese state's military adventurism.

17. This is not the place to examine the ways in which the socialist state in China after 1949 and India's postcolonial state after 1947 were similar to or different from one another. Remarkably, given the vastly disparate ideological resources on which they respectively drew, assessments converge (Chibber 2003; Cumings 1999; Meisner 1999) regarding what the two regimes achieved, namely state-led development that laid the basis for industrial capitalism.

18. On issues with methods and conceptualization of China–India topic within the context of state of China–India studies, see Sen (forthcoming).

19. Recent works by Ghosh (2017), Duara and Perry (2018), and Liu (2019, 2020) have also proposed new and innovative ways of examining the connections between India and China. The contributions to this volume seek to add to this recent discourse on conceptualizing and producing a methodological framework for examining the connections and comparisons between India and China.

20. This has been done to some extent by Pollock and Elman (2018).

21. A recent volume on early modern China and India (Pollock and Elman 2018) echoes Mizoguchi in proposing a strategy of 'cosmopolitan comparison' in order to decentre Western categories, even as it self-consciously,

and not without some discomfort, inherits a mode of scholarship steeped in colonial epistemology.

References

Armitage, David. 2013. *Foundations of Modern International Thought.* Cambridge: Cambridge University Press.

Atwill, David. 2018. *Islamic Shangri-La: Inter-Asian Relations and Lhasa's Muslim Communities, 1600 to 1960.* Oakland: University of California Press.

Aydin, Cemil. 2007. *The Politics of Anti-Westernism in Asia: Visions of World Order in Pan-Islamic and Pan-Asian Thought.* New York: Columbia University Press.

Banerjee, Payal. 2017. 'The Chinese in India: Internment, Nationalism, and the Embodied Imprints of State Action'. In Amit R. Das Gupta and Lorenz M. Lüthi (eds), *The Sino-Indian War of 1962: New Perspectives*, pp. 215–32. London: Routledge.

Bayly, C.A. 2004. *The Birth of the Modern World, 1780–1914.* Oxford: Blackwell.

Bharucha, Rustom. 2006. *Another Asia: Rabindranath Tagore and Okakura Tenshin.* New Delhi: Oxford University Press.

Bickers, Robert. 2015. 'Britain and China, and India, 1830s–1947'. In Robert Bickers and Jonathan J. Howlett (eds), *Britain and China, 1840-1970: Empire, Finance and War*, pp. 58–83. Abingdon, Oxon: Routledge.

Cao, Yin. 2017. *From Policemen to Revolutionaries: A Sikh Diaspora in Global Shanghai, 1885–1945.* Leiden: Brill.

Chen Kuan-hsing (陳光興). 2010. *Asia as Method: Toward Deimperialization.* Durham, NC: Duke University Press.

———. 2014. 'Xu: jinxingshi zhong de "Xitian Zhongtu" jihua' (序： 進行式 中的 "西天中土" 計劃) ['Preface: West Heavens, a Project in Progress']. In Chang Tsong-zung, Chen Kuan-hsing and Gao Shiming (eds), *Cong Xitian dao Zhongtu: Yin-Zhong shehui sixiang duihua* (從西天到中土：印中社會 思想對話) [*India–China Summit on Social Thought*], pp. 1–9. Shanghai: Shanghai renmin chubanshe.

Chibber, Vivek. 2003. *Locked in Place: State-Building and Late Industrialization in India.* Princeton: Princeton University Press.

Cohen, Jerome A. and Leng Shao-chuan. 1972. 'The Sino-Indian Dispute over the Internment and Detention of Chinese in India'. In Jerome A. Cohen (ed.), *China's Practice of International Law*, pp. 268–320. Cambridge: Cambridge University Press.

Cumings, Bruce. 1999. *Parallax Visions: Making Sense of American–East Asian Relations at the End of the Century.* Durham, NC: Duke University Press.

Das, Sisir Kumar. 1993. 'The Controversial Guest: Tagore in China'. *China Report* 29 (3): 237–73.

Deepak, B.R. 2001. *India–China Relations in the First Half of the Twentieth Century*. New Delhi: A.P.H. Publishing.

Duara, Prasenjit. 1995. *Rescuing History from the Nation: Questioning Narratives of Modern China*. Chicago: The University of Chicago Press.

———. 2003. *Sovereignty and Authenticity: Manchukuo and the East Asian Modern*. Lanham MD: Rowan & Littlefield.

———. 2010. 'Asia Redux: Conceptualizing a Region for Our Times'. *The Journal of Asian Studies* 69 (4): 963–83.

Duara, Prasenjit and Elizabeth J. Perry. 2018. 'Beyond Regimes: An Introduction'. In Prasenjit Duara and Elizabeth J. Perry (eds), *Beyond Regimes: China and India Compared*, pp. 1–27. Cambridge, Mass.: Harvard University Asia Center.

Ghosh, Arunabh. 2017. 'Before 1962: The Case for 1950s China-India History'. *The Journal of Asian Studies* 76 (3): 697–727.

Hay, Stephen N. 1970. *Asian Ideas of East and West: Tagore and His Critics in Japan, China, and India*. Cambridge, Mass.: Harvard University Press.

Hevia, James L. 2003. *English Lessons: The Pedagogy of Imperialism in Nineteenth-Century China*. Durham, NC: Duke University Press.

Hotta, Eri. 2007. *Pan-Asianism and Japan's War 1931–1945*. New York: Palgrave Macmillan.

Jackson, Isabella. 2012. 'The Raj on Nanjing Road: Sikh Policemen in Treaty-Port Shanghai'. *Modern Asian Studies* 46 (6): 1672–704.

Karl, Rebecca E. 2002. *Staging the World: Chinese Nationalism at the Turn of the Twentieth Century*. Durham, NC: Duke University Press.

Lin Shaoyang (林少陽). 2018. *Dingge yiwen – Qingji geming yu Zhang Taiyan 'fugu' de xin wenhua yundong* (鼎革以文—清季革命與章太炎「復古」的新文化運動) [*Revolution by Means of Culture: The Late Qing Revolution and Zhang Taiyan from 1900 to 1911*]. Shanghai: Shanghai renmin chubanshe.

Liu, Andrew B. 2019. 'Production, Circulation, and Accumulation: The Historiographies of Capitalism in China and South Asia'. *The Journal of Asian Studies* 78 (4): 767–88.

———. 2020. *Tea War: A History of Capitalism in China and India*. New Haven: Yale University Press.

Liu Xinru. 1988. *Ancient India and Ancient China*. Delhi: Oxford University Press.

Meisner, Maurice. 1999. *Mao's China and After: A History of the People's Republic*. New York: Free Press.

Mizoguchi Yūzō (溝口雄三). 1989. *Hōhō to shite no Chūgoku* (方法としての中国) [*China as Method*]. Tokyo: Tōkyō daigaku shuppankai.

————. 2004. *Chūgoku no shōgeki* (中国の衝撃) [*China's Impact*]. Tokyo: Tōkyō daigaku shuppankai.

Mosca, Matthew W. 2013. *From Frontier Policy to Foreign Policy: The Question of India and the Transformation of Geopolitics in Qing China*. Stanford: Stanford University Press.

Osterhammel, Jürgen. 2014. *The Transformation of the World: A Global History of the Nineteenth Century*. Princeton: Princeton University Press.

Osterhammel, Jürgen and Niels Petersson. 2005. *Globalization: A Short History*. Princeton: Princeton University Press.

Pollock, Sheldon and Benjamin Elman. 2018. *What China and India Once Were: The Pasts That May Shape the Global Future*. New York: Columbia University Press.

Prashad, Vijay. 2007. *The Darker Nations: A People's History of the Third World*. New York: The New Press.

Roy, Ashutosh. 2013. *Amar Chin-probas* [*My Travels in China*]. Kolkata: Jadavpur University.

Saaler, Sven and J. Victor Koschmann (eds). 2007. *Pan-Asianism in Modern Japanese History: Colonialism, Regionalism and Borders*. New York: Routledge.

Saaler, Sven and Christopher W.A. Szpilman (eds). 2011. *Pan-Asianism: A Documentary History*, 2 Vols. Lanham, MD.: Rowan & Littlefield.

Samarani, Guido. 2005. 'Shaping the Future of Asia: Chiang Kai-shek, Nehru and China–India Relations during the Second World War Period'. Working Papers in Contemporary Asian Studies, No. 11, Centre for East and South-East Asian Studies, Lund University, Sweden.

Sen, Narayan C. 2007. 'China as Viewed by Two Early Bengali Travellers: The Travel Accounts of Indumadhav Mullick and Benoy Kumar Sarkar'. *China Report* 43 (3): 465–84.

Sen, Tansen. 2003. *Buddhism, Diplomacy, and Trade: The Realignment of Sino-Indian Relations, 600–1400*. Honolulu: University of Hawai'i Press.

————. 2017. *India, China, and the World: A Connected History*. Lanham: Rowman & Littlefield.

————. 2020. 'Relations between the Republic of China and India, 1937–1949'. In Kanti Bajpai, Manjari Chatterjee Miller, and Selina Ho (eds), *Routledge Handbook on China–India Relations*, pp. 63–86. London: Routledge.

————. Forthcoming. 'China–India Studies: Emergence, Development, and State of the Field'. *The Journal of Asian Studies*.

Shimada Kenji. 1990. *Pioneer of the Chinese Revolution: Zhang Binglin and Confucianism*. Translated by Joshua A. Fogel. Stanford: Stanford University Press.

Smith, Craig Anthony. 2014. 'Constructing Chinese Asianism: Intellectual Writings on East Asian Regionalism (1896–1924)'. PhD dissertation, The University of British Columbia, Vancouver, Canada.

Stolte, Carolien Margaretha. 2013. 'Orienting India: Interwar Internationalism in an Asian Inflection, 1917–1937'. PhD dissertation, Leiden University, The Netherlands.

Tan Chung. 2015. *Himalaya Calling: The Origins of China and India.* Hackensack, N.J.: World Century.

Tankha, Brij. 2006. *Kita Ikki and the Making of Modern Japan: A Vision of Empire.* Kent: Global Oriental.

Thampi, Madhavi. 2005. *Indians in China, 1800–1949.* New Delhi: Manohar.

Tsui, Brian. 2010. 'The Plea for Asia—Tan Yunshan, Pan-Asianism and Sino–Indian Relations'. *China Report* 46 (4): 353–70.

———. 2018. *China's Conservative Revolution: The Quest for a New Order, 1927–1949.* Cambridge: Cambridge University Press.

Wallerstein, Immanuel. 2002. 'New Revolts against the System'. *New Left Review* (18): 29–39.

Wang Hui (汪暉). 2015. *Duan ershi shiji: Zhongguo geming yu zhengzhi de luoji* (短二十世紀：中國革命與政治的邏輯) [*Short Twentieth Century: The Logic of Chinese Revolution and Politics*]. Hong Kong: Oxford University Press.

Yamamuro Shin'ichi (山室信一). 2001. *Jindai Riben de dongbei Ya quyu zhixu gouxiang* (近代日本的東北亞區域秩序構想) [*Modern Japan's Imaginations of Northeast Asian Regional Order*]. Taipei: Zhongyang yanjiu yuan dongbei Ya quyu yanjiu.

Yang, Anand A. (ed.). 2017. *Thirteen Months in China: A Subaltern Indian and the Colonial World.* Translated by Anand A. Yang, Kamal Sheel, and Ranjana Sheel. New Delhi: Oxford University Press.

Yang Tianshi. 2014. 'Chiang Kai-shek and Jawaharlal Nehru'. In Hans van de Ven, Diana Lary, and Stephen MacKinnon (eds), *Negotiating China's Destiny in World War II*, pp. 127–40. Stanford: Stanford University Press.

Yellen, Jeremy A. 2019. *The Greater East Asia Co-Prosperity Sphere: When Total Empire Met Total War.* Ithaca: Cornell University Press.

Zhang Xing. 2015. *The Chinese Community in Calcutta: Preservation and Change.* Halle: Universitätsverlag Halle-Wittenberg.

SECTION I

EPISTEMOLOGICAL INTERVENTIONS

1

Slave of the Colonizer

The Indian Policeman in Chinese Literature[*]

ADHIRA MANGALAGIRI

His face as dark as coal, wrapped up in a beard and red turban,
Stupid like cattle, prodded along; he stands shamelessly before us.
Such a tall, huge, strong man, yet, now his nation has fallen and he is
only a slave,
We should learn from his example and immediately expose our own
societal ignorance.

                                                            Diedie (1913: 34)

The poet Diedie ([喋喋] 'Chatterbox') dedicates this 1913 quatrain to colonial China's Indian policemen, wielders of the arms of the British Empire and enforcers of colonial law on the streets of China's treaty ports. Diedie renders a figure riddled with contradiction: The Indian policeman is at once intimidating and

---

[*] Unless stated otherwise, all translations from Chinese to English in this chapter are the author's.

'stupid'; strong yet weak; a colonizer himself colonized. This critique of the policeman, moreover, quickly turns on itself: The concluding line reveals the poem's primary object of scrutiny to be not the Indian 'other', but the Chinese self. The Indian policeman, in this literary iteration, blurs those distinctions so characteristic of the Manichean colonial world: between colonized and colonizer, self and 'other'.

Upon closer examination, the poem reveals yet another interpretive layer. 'Mocking the Indian Policeman' appeared in *Huaji zazhi* (滑稽雜誌) [*The Comical Journal*], a Suzhou journal printed in 1913–14 and committed to publishing humorous materials in line with what Christopher Rea (2015) has termed the 'age of irreverence' in modern Chinese popular culture. A reader flipping through the journal would have read Diedie's seemingly heavy criticism of the 'shameless' Indian policeman in a humorous, light-hearted tone. Humour enables the reader to momentarily disarm the Indian, stripping the policeman of his ability to victimize and framing him, instead, as the victim of ridicule. The poem's instruction to learn from the policeman's example provides another strategy for prevailing over the oppressor since the policeman becomes a means in service of enlightening the Chinese self. In this way, the poem beckons identification with the policeman in the same gesture as it enables the reader to imaginatively subvert the policeman's violence. Again, the poem exemplifies the power-inflected contradictory pulls of writing the Indian policeman.

This study investigates the Indian policeman as he appears in Chinese literary form.[1] Diedie's quatrain is one among a wealth of Chinese poems, short stories, and novels that feature the Indian policeman in a variety of literary constellations. Such texts have remained overlooked, scattered among the profusion of Chinese literary journals and newspapers that circulated in Shanghai between 1900 and 1940.[2] The figure of the Indian policeman threads these texts together, producing a subsection of modern Chinese literature centrally concerned with China's colonial condition. In bringing this lost archive to light, this chapter charts the development of the literary Indian policeman through the early decades of the twentieth century. I trace the ways in which Chinese writers engaged this figure—and through him, ideas of India—as a creative means to express colonial anxieties and anti-colonial sentiment.

During the first decades of the twentieth century, heated debates on how to retain China's national autonomy in a colonial world, how to cultivate a modern national consciousness, and the role of the West in China's modernization centrally shaped normative ideas of literature. As writers experimented with the capacity of literature to drive societal change, literary practice and readers' tastes rapidly shifted from the late Qing explosion of 'new fiction' genres, to the May Fourth insistence on vernacular literature, to Marxist-inflected ideas of revolutionary literature in the late 1920s. The Indian police-man captured writers' imaginations at each historical juncture, and as a result, this Indian figure evolved along with shifting literary tides. The dynamic ability of this figure to at once signify contradictory modes of being—self and 'other', colonizer and colonized, old and new, comrade and enemy—meant that he posed an epistemological challenge, frustrating familiar categories and representational con-ventions. Yet, the challenge of apprehending this unknowable figure in literary form also endowed him with creative malleability and inter-pretive openness, making him an ideal literary vehicle through which to navigate, shape, and participate in literary debates of the day. As the texts I discuss suggest, attempts to fix the Indian policeman in literary form only highlight the figure's multiplicity of meaning and reveal the limits of conceptualizing India's position in the Chinese literary imagination within narrow categories of political relation.

Along with the other chapters in Section I of this volume, then, this chapter studies the ways in which grappling with the epistemo-logical challenge of thinking India opened possibilities for Chinese writers to reconceptualize China–India literary relation beyond the discursive paradigm of dominant pan-Asianist thought. Departing from chapters in Section II, which discuss Chinese encounters with the ontological realities of India, this chapter reads the Indian police-man as a figurative device borne out of and embedded within Chinese literary practice. While literary engagements emerged in relation (and often, in reaction) to the actual Indians stationed in colonial China, I study the Indian policeman not in his own right but as a literary figure giving expression to evolving discourses of China's colonial experience. Doing so reveals the range of possibilities engaging ideas of India opened up for Chinese writers, far exceeding the binary poles of solidarity/resistance and friendship/enmity. Writers and readers harnessed these creative possibilities to produce a corpus of Chinese fiction that foregrounds China's colonial condition and tells the story of modern Chinese literature's development anew from the perspective of an unlikely Indian interlocutor.

India in Colonial Chinese Discourse

Although writings on India enjoy a long history in the Chinese cultural sphere, the colonial condition of the early twentieth century endowed India with a position of heightened significance in Chinese intellectual discourse.[3] At the time, India was not the only colony that figured in debates on how best to resist colonization and retain national autonomy in China's journey towards modernity. In addition to India, intellectuals closely monitored developments in the Philippines, South Africa, Poland, Egypt, Turkey, Vietnam, Manchuria, and a host of other sites in the colonial world (Karl 2002b: 16). Yet, India stood apart in the Chinese cultural imagination of the time—a crucial point often overlooked in studies of late Qing transnationalism. This discursive centrality resulted both from ideas of India circulating in Chinese intellectual circles, and from the crisscrossing colonial networks that brought Chinese and Indians into unprecedented encounters, often from opposing sides of the colonizer/colonized divide.

As several chapters in this volume discuss, Kang Youwei's (康有為) (1858–1927) writings on India proved seminal in late Qing debates on how to best adapt the Qing state to the demands of the modern world.[4] Kang famously positioned India as a negative example for China. The two countries were commensurate enough, he argued, that India's colonization could portend China's impending fall. But China had one significant advantage: by looking to India and learning from its mistakes, China could still implement those reforms necessary for fending off colonization. Kang and his contemporaries often evoked this idea of India as a cautionary tale through the metaphor of India as the 'front-car' (qianche [前車]). On the railroad track of history, the metaphor ran, China and India seemed to be positioned on commensurate paths heading in similar directions, and only by acknowledging this foundational sameness could China strive towards a different future and diverge from its destined historical fate of following India's footsteps into colonization.

Kang employs the 'front-car' metaphor in a 1902 open letter to fellow reformers on China's susceptibility to colonization. The letter responded to those scholars who, referring to the ongoing division of the Balkans and other Western regions, had called for provincialization or fragmentation as a viable option for China. Kang disagreed. India's colonization, he argued, stemmed precisely from the fragmented and internally combative nature of its many independent domains under Mughal rule, and such disunity had weakened its ability to mount a strong defence in the face of British colonization. Given the commensurable historical, geographical, societal, and political circumstances of China and India, a similar provincialization of China would surely result in its colonization.[5] Throughout the essay, Kang warns his reader against inciting revolution in the name of internal divisions in China: 'Revolution? [Provincial] Independence? That path is sure to lead to colonization and slavehood! ... [I]f you, my compatriots, do not want colonization, then do not follow the example of India's provincial revolution and independence' (Kang [1902] 1998: 335). Kang's framing of India as the colony most commensurate with China and therefore most capable of indicating China's future proved popular, and intellectuals increasingly positioned India as uniquely capable of foretelling China's fate in the colonial world.

A second factor contributed to the singular position of India at the forefront of Chinese intellectual debates on colonialism: the physical presence of Indian policemen on the streets of Chinese treaty ports. Recent scholarship has importantly documented the historical processes that led to Indians serving the British in China.[6] Briefly, in the 1880s, following the success of the Hong Kong Police Force's Sikh Branch, the British colonial administration supported the incorporation of Indians into the British-run Shanghai Municipal Police (SMP). Formal recruiting of Indians into the SMP began in 1884, first locally from Shanghai's Indian population and later directly from Punjab. The number of Indian policemen in the SMP, estimated to have reached 3,000 at its peak, rapidly grew until British control in Shanghai was officially dissolved in the wake of the Second World War in 1943. The Indian population in Shanghai then gradually dispersed: some were posted to other parts of the British Empire, some were repatriated to India, and others joined in Indian nationalist or Axis-led anti-British movements (Jackson 2012).

Given the nature of colonial intervention in Chinese treaty ports, scholars have found it useful to analyse China's colonial condition under the rubric of semi-colonialism. Shu-mei Shih (2001), for example, has argued that the presence of pockets of extraterritoriality governed by multiple colonial powers—most prominently, Britain, Germany, France, Japan, Russia, and USA—in cooperation and competition with each other engendered unique Chinese ideological, political, and cultural formations that do not align with experiences of formal colonialism (as in India). The mosaic of colonial enclaves produced a fragmentary and diffused colonial presence in China, resulting in an 'ambivalence toward colonialism' (Shih 2001: 36). One factor in such ambivalence involved a bifurcated 'split in the concept of the West' between an attractive, desirable metropolitan West and an undesirable colonial West (Shih 2001: 36). In addition, Shih argues, because Chinese 'native culture' had been 'deconstructed' by thinkers who sought to overthrow tradition in favour of modernity, an idea of 'tradition' no longer existed as epistemologically distinct from the colonial realm and so could not serve unproblematically as a site of resistance (Shih 2001: 37). As a result, in colonial China, 'it was difficult to target the enemy clearly' and 'articulating resistance [proved] difficult' (Shih 2001: 37).

In this semi-colonial landscape, the figure of the Indian policeman gains significance. On the streets of Shanghai, the West as colonizer remained largely invisible, obscured by the flashy and alluring signs of the metropolitan West. Instead, the Indian policeman, a daily oppressor of the Chinese in Shanghai's International Settlement, fulfilled the role of the colonial enemy. His intimidating appearance—turban, long moustache and beard, large stature, baton in hand—made for an instantly identifiable and hyper-visible sign of colonial jurisdiction and governance. And because he policed everyday crimes such as traffic violations and petty thefts, the Indian policeman embodied the face and facet of colonial administration with which Chinese citizens had the most direct interaction. As writers sought to overcome the difficulties Shih describes, of targeting a single enemy and articulating anti-colonial resistance, the Indian policeman discursively took on the role of colonial enemy.

Yet, the Indian policeman inhabited this role of colonial enemy uncomfortably. Viewed at once as a proxy colonizer and a colonized being himself, he sparked a form of resistance founded upon self-identification. The weight of an intellectual tradition that had long asserted a foundational sameness between China and India, combined with the particular challenges of targeting the Western colonizer and voicing resistance under semi-colonization, gave rise to the Chinese literary trope of the Indian policeman. Given the popularity of this figure as the literary vehicle of choice in engaging ideas of colonialism, the Chinese colonial condition found its clearest literary articulation not in opposition to a (Western) colonizer, but in mediation through a fellow (Indian) colonized being. Rendering the Indian policeman in literary form afforded writers creative possibilities to exceed the China–West axis and the reified poles of solidarity/resistance in expressing colonial anxieties and staging protest.

The Concept of Wangguo Nu

A 1904 novel, *Fenge hou zhi wuren* (分割後之吾人) [*My People after Partition*] by Xu Zhuodai (徐卓呆) (1880–1958), presents an early example of how Chinese literary engagements with colonialism inhered within depictions of the Indian policeman. Xu penned the novel during his days in Japan as a foreign student of physical education (1902–5), some years before he burst onto the Shanghai cultural scene as 'Charlie Chaplin of the East' (Rea 2019).[7] *My People* was published serially in the popular journal *Jiangsu* (江蘇) printed in Tokyo by an association of overseas students from Jiangsu province. The novel ranks as the first text Xu authored under the penname Zhuodai, a tongue-in-cheek moniker simultaneously connoting greatness and stupidity (Rea 2019: 10–11). The penname alludes to the farcical tone and sharp wit Xu would soon become well known for, and indeed, *My People* bears signs of this literary style in its incipiency, marking Xu's transition from an overtly political literary persona into a master of comedy. The year before *My People*, Xu's novel *Mingri zhi guafen* (明日之瓜分) [*Tomorrow's Partition*] (1903) appeared in the same journal under the penname Guazi (瓜子).[8] *Tomorrow's Partition* takes on the theme of confronting China's impending division by foreign powers, critiquing China's blind complacency in allowing the colonizers in. Expanding on the same theme, *My People* picks up where the earlier

novel ends by imagining the aftermath of partition in a China already
subjected to colonial rule.

My People opens with its protagonist, Huang Shibiao (黃士表)
(literally, 'yellow scholarly model'), a Han Chinese from Jiangsu, reading news of China's dire circumstances following the invasion of the
Eight-Nation Alliance (the foreign powers that sent troops to quell the
Boxer Uprising of 1900). Huang Shibiao dozes off and is awoken by
a tap on his shoulder. An old man named Huang Xuanchu (黃軒初)
has appeared and offers to give Huang Shibiao a tour of the 'terrible
sights of colonized China' (Xu 1904, No. 8: 128). The reader realizes
that Huang Shibiao has 'awoken' to a dystopian dream of China's
future under colonization. The novel goes on to paint vivid scenes of
the Chinese people's fate as colonized people living under the yoke of
foreign rule.

In one such scene, Huang Shibiao and the old man are walking
along, discussing the high colonial taxes and the common man's hardships, when they happen upon a group of black-faced and turbaned
Indian policemen marching to the orders of a British man. The old
man explains that these are colonized Indians, nothing but slaves
(Xu 1904, No. 8: 134). Xu's characterization of the Indian policemen
as colonized slaves evokes the concept of *wangguo nu* (亡國奴). By
the end of the nineteenth century, wangguo nu—literally, 'slave of
the lost/vanquished nation'—had become a ubiquitous term to convey slavishness under colonization. The term 'wangguo' predates
Western presence in China, its history extending back centuries
when it referred to a lost or conquered state during dynastic change
(Karl 2002a: 217). In the context of late Qing discourse, wangguo
immediately signified colonization, with the Indian policeman commonly figuring as the quintessential slave (*nu*) given his perceived
complicity in carrying out the colonizer's dirty work in China.[9] As in
Diedie's poem mentioned earlier, writers quickly became accustomed
to denouncing the Indian policeman as a colonized slave; the epithet
'wangguo nu' fulfilled the dual purpose of expressing contempt for
the Indian and the colonial apparatus he stood for while also asserting
China's relative (albeit precarious) autonomy in the colonial world.

The 'wangguo nu' concept emerges as a central preoccupation
in *My People*. In order to depict a post-partition Chinese landscape,
Xu effects a deeper, discursive transformation of the 'wangguo nu'

concept's system of reference. *My People* rewrites wangguo nu as capable not only of drawing a contrast between the colonized slave and the still-autonomous Chinese, as in its popular usage, but also to articulate an equivalence between the two. Xu opens up the wangguo nu's referential capacity by harnessing the figure of the Indian policeman, the exemplary colonized slave. In the novel's construction of a fallen China, depicting the Indian policeman proves a powerful literary strategy for positioning the Chinese subject not as separate from or in opposition to but as a colonized slave himself.

To this end, Xu writes a series of interactions between Huang Shibiao and the Indian policeman, crafted to displace the idea of wangguo nu from the category of 'other' and into that of 'self'. A crucial scene unfolds in a teashop where Huang Shibiao and the old man retreat for a bite to eat. As they discuss the high price of food (again, a consequence of the inhumane taxes the British impose), an Indian man enters: 'his stature was short and his face was yellow with a red cloth wrapped around his head ... upon closer examination, he didn't look Indian at all' (Xu 1904, No. 9/10: 235). Confused, Huang Shibiao asks where the man is from and is surprised to learn that he is indeed Chinese. 'Why are you dressed in this way?' Huang Shibiao asks (Xu 1904, No. 9/10: 235). 'Don't you know?' the man replies, 'the British have ordered that our clothing must now change, we must dress like the Indians' (Xu 1904, No. 9/10: 235). Huang Shibiao is dumbstruck. Soon after, he leaves the teashop to find a sea of people dressed like the Indian wangguo nu. This image of Indian policeman and Chinese subject as indistinguishable from each other literalizes Xu's resignification of wangguo nu. As this realization sinks in, Huang Shibiao declares, 'I, Huang Shibiao, vow that one day I will finally take revenge on this great enemy' (Xu 1904, No. 9/10: 235).

The notion of Chinese and Indian blending into one elicits terror, what Karl has termed the 'terror of doubling' in her discussion of *My People*, 'the immanence of Chinese as a "lost people" evoked by the fearful plausibility of interchangeability of Chinese and Indians' (Karl 2002b: 159–63). This is not a union of Chinese and Indian in solidarity, but nor does this gesture entail rupture or hostile estrangement. The hybrid image of a single body that appears both Chinese and Indian (yellow skin and Indian turban) signals a closeness experienced on the most intimate of scales, that of the body. This closeness amplifies the terrifying nature of the encounter thereby precipitating the novel's pedagogical imperative to jolt its reader out of the lull of complacency, as literalized in Huang Shibiao's vow of revenge. Shibiao's (and the reader's) urge to resist this merging of Chinese and Indian further emphasizes the fleeting, strained quality of a China–India unity that finds expression as an object of rebellion, only in the imaginary dreamscape of a fictional text and only in the hope that this unity never venture into the realm of the real. Echoing Kang's 'front-car' rhetoric, the hybrid wangguo nu furnishes a provisional China–India sameness necessary for arousing the desire for divergence.

My People takes its project—of refiguring wangguo nu to signify the Chinese self—a step further. The Indian wangguo nu's enslavement granted him the power to oppress other colonized beings, making him complacent in his own colonization. A fallen China could not afford such passivity. To avoid this pitfall, Xu casts the colonized Chinese as even more enslaved than the lowly Indian. When Huang Shibiao first observes the marching policemen, he asks about the British officer standing behind them. The old man replies:

> 'This is the Police Chief.' Shibiao asked, 'Why do they not appoint an Indian as the Chief?' The old man answered, 'The reason is that they are Indians, they are a colonized people, nothing more than slaves. How could they be allowed to work in a position of authority? Ah! Indian people have lost their nation, yet they can hold a wooden baton and stand at the traffic junctions, wielding the power of the British, bullying, scaring, and ridiculing us. Although our compatriots are colonized, do not think that you can now bully others; you will still be bullied by others. At least Indians can still serve as the British's slavish beasts of burden. I'm afraid that our people cannot even be such slavish beasts.' Upon hearing this, Shibiao couldn't help but cry. (Xu 1904, No. 8: 134)

Here, the old man frames the colonized Chinese as oppressed not by the colonizer but by the colonizer's slave. The Chinese wangguo nu, then, becomes the slave of a slave. This theme recurs throughout, such as when Huang Shibiao witnesses two Indian policemen brutally kicking an elderly Chinese woman to the ground while wrongfully accusing her of causing a commotion (Xu 1904, No. 9/10: 244). The Chinese surpasses the Indian as the most wretched of the colonized people, further entrenching the Chinese subject within the concept of wangguo nu.

My People does not afford its reader the relief of awakening from Huang Shibiao's nightmare or witnessing his act of revenge. The novel ends abruptly after its first five chapters; the remaining parts never made it to print.[10] The novel's incompleteness leaves Huang Shibiao trapped in his nightmare, tasking the reader, instead, with the imperative of awakening. As the political potential of imagining oneness between the Chinese subject and Indian wangguo nu gained increased literary recognition, Xu's endeavour found completion in the various literary experiments with the Indian policeman that writers conducted in the years to come.

Twin Souls

In early March of 1907, the popular Shanghai-based newspaper *Shenbao* (申報) issued an apology to its readers. *Shenbao* would no longer carry the novel that the newspaper had published in instalments over the past week.[11] A new novel by the same writer would now take its place, a 'bizarre and bewildering' tale titled *Shuang linghun* (雙靈魂) [*Twin Souls*]. The novel would be written in an allegorical style, like that of Zhuangzi, with the aim of 'awakening the nation's soul' (*Shenbao* 1907: 18). As promised, the newspaper's 1907 spring issues published *Twin Souls* in twenty-four instalments over the course of a month. The novel tells the story of an Indian policeman, Jing Erya (警爾亞) (literally, 'police of Asia'), whose soul transfers into the body of a Chinese student, Huang Zuhan (黃祖漢) (literally, 'yellow descendent of the Han'). *Twin Souls* chronicles the adventures of its titular figure—a man whose body contains within it two souls, one Chinese and one Indian—each vying for dominance over the other.

The novel opens with Jing's death. One snowy night in Shanghai, in the course of a dramatic chase, Jing is shot by a gang of bandits. His body falls to the ground. Huang bumps into Jing at the precise moment of the latter's death, just as the soul is departing Jing's body. Huang experiences a jolt of fright and shock, a cold sensation washes over him. At this moment, unbeknownst to both Huang and Jing, Jing's Indian soul transfers into Huang's Chinese body. The Chinese and Indian souls remain unaware that they are now housed within a single body and Jing never realizes that he has died. As the souls cyclically gain and cede control of Huang's body, the body (with a Chinese external appearance) alternates between acting out the life of an Indian policeman and that of a Chinese student. These fluctuations occur without warning, resulting in the following sorry scene in which this body bearing twin souls paces back and forth, one moment towards Jing's police station on a road bearing a 'Western' name (Pike Road), and the next towards Huang's home on a road with a 'native' Chinese name (Fuzhou Road):

> This one body, then, held two souls. Its consciousness had also split in two. Suddenly, for a moment, he would think of his name as Huang Zuhan. But the next moment, he would think he was Jing Erya. For a moment he would walk northwest, wanting to return to Pike Road. But the next second, he would suddenly start walking southeast, wanting to return to Fuzhou Road. And so, at this time, his thought and actions were chaotic, as though in a dream. He walked back and forth between the two ends of the bridge, like a butterfly caught in a spider's web, unable to escape. (Yadong 1907, No. 3: 19)

The twin-souled man remains trapped between the status of 'foreigner' and 'Chinese' in colonial Shanghai, a city that otherwise drew clear spatial and administrative demarcations between the areas under foreign jurisdiction and those under Chinese control. The twin-souled body frustrates such categories. In a series of comic incidents, for example, he salutes a passing British officer in English (much to the officer's confusion), while the next moment he frequents a local shop and orders breakfast in Chinese.

After several such episodes of confusion, Huang/Jing is admitted to a hospital in the International Settlement where a doctor finally diagnoses his twin-souled condition. The British doctor, however, fails to find a cure. Huang's desperate parents attempt a number of alternative methods to exorcise Jing's soul from Huang's body, including traditional Chinese medical remedies, folk shamanistic rituals, religious appeals, but to no avail. Finally, they take the twin-souled man to a 'Universal Scientific Research Centre', where scientists from a host of Western nations descend upon him to offer various scientific solutions.

By the end of the novel, all attempts prove futile. Both Chinese traditional medicine and the Western natural sciences fail to cure Huang. An educationist by the name of Jili ([基立], meaning 'foundational'), president of the Research Centre, concludes that no external scientific cure can return to Huang autonomy over his body. For the Chinese soul to triumph, he must strengthen himself through self-education and thereby shield himself from Jing's onslaughts. If he does so, 'it will not be difficult to cultivate [*peizhi* (培植)] his Chinese soul and gradually defeat his Indian soul' (Yadong 1907, No. 24: 18).

Shenbao printed each instalment of *Twin Souls* with the subtitle 'yuyan xiaoshuo' (寓言小説) ['allegorical fiction'], in line with the description of the novel in the initial advertisement. True to this description, the novel lends itself to a clear allegorical interpretation in which Jing's invasion and occupancy of Huang's body stands for the foreign powers' colonial presence in China. This condition, the author argues, can only be rectified intrinsically through education and a self-motivated strengthening of a national consciousness, not by some externally enforceable cure borrowed from the West. Throughout, the novel provides explicit encouragement for its interpretation as a national allegory, voicing the familiar late Qing anxiety over China's increasingly colonized nature. In one such instance, when Jing's soul gains control over Huang's body, the narrative pauses, as is characteristic in late Qing fiction, to inject the following authorial aside: 'I can see the daily diminishing of the nation's soul, while the foreign [*ke* (客)] soul is increasingly aroused and flourishes. Alas!' (Yadong 1907, No. 10: 19).

The novel's rejection of Western science in favour of Chinese knowledge and ethics as providing a cure for the afflicted national soul finds further corroboration in the author's biographical details. Although *Twin Souls* appeared in *Shenbao* anonymously, the novel was later attributed to Peng Yu (彭俞) (1876–1946) under the penname Yadong Pofo (亞東破佛).[12] Originally from Zhejiang province, Peng moved to Shanghai in 1906 where he published a series of novels and short fiction, including *Twin Souls*, while working at small printing houses to earn his living.[13] Around the age of forty, and on the recommendation of his friend the philosopher Ma Yifu (馬一浮) (1883–1967), Peng entered the Hupao temple near Hangzhou to study Buddhist and Daoist classics, eventually becoming a monk there. He re-entered secular life in 1928 and resumed his literary career in Shanghai until his death.[14] Peng's interest in traditional Chinese forms of knowledge, which later led him to pursue a study of the classics as a monk, clearly informed his literary practice in *Twin Souls*.

As a national allegory, *Twin Souls* fits comfortably with the newspaper *Shenbao*'s programme. Founded in 1872 by the British merchant Ernest Major in Shanghai's International Settlement, the Chinese-language *Shenbao* modelled itself in opposition to the Qing court's official gazette, the main source of news at the time (Mittler 2004: 3). Unlike the gazette, which selectively conveyed voices of elites and those pieces of news officials deemed appropriate for dissemination, *Shenbao* prided itself as a vehicle for public opinion, debate, and entertainment in service of its 'double agenda of general enlightenment and progressive change' (Mittler 2004: 18). *Shenbao* described its mission in its inaugural issue as providing 'the "newest" and most "up-to-date" knowledge, in order to "renew the people"' (Mittler 2004: 15). Accordingly, *Twin Souls*'s publication in *Shenbao* would have amplified for readers the novel's express intention to 'awaken the nation's soul' (as advertised in the initial announcement), with the invaded body's quest for autonomy unambiguously signalling the nation's plight under colonization.

Twin Souls performs its symbolic, allegorical function somewhat paradoxically through an intensely material construction of and meditation on the site of the body. Take, for example, the novel's detailed explanation of how a single body can come to contain two souls. According to the canonical Chinese medical text *Huangdi neijing* (黃帝內經), the narrator explains, the soul resides within the liver. When a person suffers a fright, the gate to the soul's abode can suddenly open, whereupon the soul can escape from the liver, travel through the spine up to the brain, and exit the body through the 'skull-gate' which has now also opened as a result of the fright.[15] The frightened shock Huang experienced upon bumping into Jing caused the former's soul to fall out of his liver, but just as Huang's soul travelled towards the skull-gate, Jing's soul rushed in through it. At that moment, the chilly conditions of the snowy night (to which Huang's internal organs were now exposed given the opening in his skull) caused Huang's muscles to contract, closing the gate and trapping both Chinese and Indian souls within Huang's body. Both souls then followed the spinal path back to the liver and resided therein (Yadong

1907, No. 2: 18). This minutely detailed and, according to the medical text quoted, seemingly plausible explanation of the twin-souled condition literalizes the symbolic capacity of a protagonist who appears at once as an abstracted allegory and as a real, material being. In this way, the novel pulls the reader outwards onto the conceptual scale of the nation at the same time as it draws the reader into the innards of the substantial body.

The allegorized nation's identity crisis under colonization similarly inheres within the site of the body as the twin-souled man struggles to recognize himself while under Jing's control. Forced to confront his body in a mirror, the man's confusion echoes the dissonance and disorientation of consolidating a national consciousness while under foreign rule:

> The doctor asked his attendant to bring a mirror. He placed the mirror in front of Huang Zuhan. Huang peered in the mirror and was panic-stricken. He said, 'I am Jing Erya! How could I have suddenly changed into a Chinese person? Ah! How can this be, how can this be ...' The doctor said, 'This body is not yours. Do you believe me now?' With great disbelief, Huang looked in the mirror again. After a while, he suddenly asked, now speaking in Chinese, 'Why are you making me look in a mirror?' (Yadong 1907, No. 9: 18)

The souls struggle to come to terms with a body each feels alienated from. Huang is a stranger in his own body, while Jing, who later carefully examines the yellow colour of his skin and newly shortened stature, encounters his body as belonging to someone else. Heightened attention to and detailed descriptions of the body's physical attributes and material specificity seem to contradict the novel's self-professed recommendation to read it symbolically. In heeding this direction, the readerly labour involved in resisting the lure of the literal and in constantly abstracting into allegory lies at the heart of the novel's educational ambition of cultivating the national soul as the only viable path to decolonization. Training the reader in abstraction inculcates a participation in the formation of a collective national consciousness; the novel, thus, performs its moral.

Shuttling its reader between the scales of the abstract and the concrete, the novel's anti-colonial sensibility emerges as an aspirational yet embodied practice mediated through the lived experience of the ontological body. Since the Chinese body is reigned over by one soul at a time (usually by Huang's in the morning and Jing's in the afternoon), when Jing is dominant, the Chinese body performs the motions of a colonized British subject and experiences on a bodily register the conditions of Indian colonial oppression. In one scene, Huang/Jing is taken to the police station, ironically the very police station where Jing used to work before his death. Jing holds control over the body at this point, but because he outwardly appears to be a Chinese man, another Indian policeman (Jing's former colleague) promptly throws him into a prison cell. Jing cries out to the police-man in an 'Indian language':

> 'We have lost our nation, and our people have been stamped out! How can you not feel any compatriotism towards me and still imprison me?' The [British] inspector overheard him say this. Furious, he rushed into the cell and began beating [Jing] with a baton. Whenever British peo-ple hear the Indian policemen conversing in their local language, the British at once start to beat them up, for they fear that this may spark [Indian] nationalism. (Yadong 1907, No. 4: 19)

This prison scene instigates a radical reordering of the conven-tional demarcations of colonizer/colonized in Shanghai that posi-tioned the Indian proxy colonizer and Chinese subject on opposing sides of the divide. Here, inhabiting a hybrid body allows both the Chinese and the Indian to experience the other's colonial condition, giving rise to an otherwise impossible realization of shared coloni-zation. Furthermore, this realization occurs in the throes of layered conflict between Chinese and Indian: Huang and Jing compete to gain control over the Chinese body, the Indian prison guard unjustly imprisons the Chinese, the British inspector mistakenly beats the Chinese body while intending to punish the Indian. This tangled web of antagonistic relations unexpectedly enables the Chinese body to verbalize a position of sameness with the Indian policeman—he utters the Indian's words: we (wobei [我輩]) have lost our nation, we are compatriots. The sound of these words incites the British's ire. As he beats the prisoner, it is the Chinese body that receives the colonizer's abuse and endures the physical pain that, we are told, was meant to be inflicted on the Indian for his subversive use of the 'Indian language'. And just as Huang bears the British colonizer's violence, Jing, now imprisoned by his compatriot, is subject to the Indian policeman's exercise of power over the Chinese.

Later on, an interrogator interviews the prisoner, unaware that Huang's soul has regained control over the body. Confused by the conflicting answers he receives from the prisoner who now claims to be a Chinese student, the interrogator raises his baton at Huang. Huang cries out, 'You British are praised as the most civilized in the world, yet you use your power to punish and force people to submit to you!' (Yadong 1907, No. 5: 19). Here, Huang articulates Jing's protest: Inverting the colonial logic of the white man's civilizing mission, he accuses the British of barbarism for perpetuating the violence that facilitates and bolsters their colonial rule. Yet, the possibility of solidarity between Chinese and Indian crumbles with the realization that Huang's vocalized combativeness with the British only underscores Jing's silence, a sign of the Indian wangguo nu's slavishness and complacency. Huang's outcry performs Jing's rebellion at the same time as it highlights Jing's impotence in voicing his own protest. The experience of viscerally sharing in and bearing witness to the other's colonial subjugation makes possible a joint anti-colonial critique animated by difference, one that positions Chinese and Indian as together opposing a shared colonizer in the same gesture as it rejects equation between the Chinese and Indian's colonial conditions.

After the twin-souled man arrives at the Research Centre, the remaining nine chapters are comprised of the scientists' lengthy speeches elaborating cures for the twin-souled condition based on Western scientific and medical discourses of the day ranging from hypnosis to optical physics.[16] These chapters position Chinese patient and Western cures in a binary relation that obscures the particularly non-Western, Indian characteristic of the ailment afflicting Huang. And yet, it is precisely this Indian-ness that drives forward the novel's plot, with the Indian policeman's dual capacity to signify both colonizer and colonized offering a wealth of entertaining possibilities with which to stir the reader's imagination. As a literary device, the Indian policeman facilitates the novel's scalar navigation of the figurative and the visceral, thereby enacting just as pedagogical a function as the novel's later, more explicitly instructive, chapters. The 'awakening' enacted here is the formation of a national consciousness that comes into view neither wholly in opposition to a colonizer nor in complete

solidarity with a fellow colonized being. The twinning of Indian and
Chinese souls figures a national consciousness animated by a constant negotiation between selves and others, multiply conceived, born
of suspension between the poles of sameness and difference, gravitat-
ing at once towards neither and both.

The Hongtou Asan

In the early decades of Republican China, the term *hongtou asan* (紅頭
阿三) (meaning 'red-headed asan') gained popularity as the preferred
moniker for the Indian policeman, marking an ebbing and refiguring
of the late Qing concept of wangguo nu and its attendant 'front-car'
rhetoric. Hongtou asan was likely already in colloquial use (as *hong-
dou ase* in the Shanghai dialect), but increasingly appeared in print
in the 1920s following May Fourth calls to vernacularize literary writing. Unlike wangguo nu, the mere utterance of which immediately
communicated a denunciation of the policeman, taken on its own,
the term 'hongtou asan' appeared neutral: 'hongtou' visually marked
the red turban the policemen wore as part of their uniforms, while
'asan' remained semantically ambiguous. The uncertain origins of
asan soon proved a popular topic of discussion in Shanghai's newspapers and journals and possible definitions accompanied the term's
increased frequency in print. As writers explored hypotheses of asan's
etymological roots, their attempts to narrativize the term endowed it
with political and emotive heft.

Three possible explanations of asan/ase emerged as the most
commonly cited and in each case, writers harnessed the search for
etymological roots as a means to inflect the act of naming the Indian
policeman with political resonance. The first theory suggested that
asan derived from 'aye, sir' a phrase that the policemen were often
heard repeating to their British superiors. Linking asan to 'aye, sir'
evoked Shanghai's colonial power dynamics by depicting the Indian
policeman as obsequiously obeying British orders (Shi Jiu 1935: 5).
A 1923 vignette outlines a second theory which traces asan to 'Ah!
Sir', presented as a common greeting in English. This explains, the
vignette reads, why the Indian asan responds happily to a name otherwise reserved for monkeys. The policeman is not insulted because
ase sounds to him like 'Ah! Sir' and so he thinks passers-by are simply

saying 'Hey, Mister!' to greet him. Asan proves an apt name since like the monkey (that often featured in Shanghai's street performances), the Indian nods eagerly in his oblivion, unable to understand that he is the target of mockery (Cheng 1923: 61). A third explanation links asan to *disan* ([第三], meaning 'the third'), emphasizing the lowly rank the Indian policeman occupies in the British colonial hierarchy (*Shiyong Yingwen banyuekan* [實用英文半月刊] 1937: 49). Again, defining asan afforded writers an opportunity to endow the empty signifier with political charge and anti-colonial critique.

A 1927 short story titled 'Hongtou Asan' (紅頭阿三) ['Red-Headed Asan'], published in a Shanghai students' magazine, dramatizes the political and literary stakes of naming the policeman.[17] Written from the policeman's perspective, the story opens with his lament: ever since he has arrived in China, all he hears are the sounds of people mocking him. He senses hatred from the rickshaw pullers and pedestrians on 'N Street' in 'S City' (Shanghai's Nanjing Street) when they shout 'hongtou asan' at him, but struggles to understand what these four characters mean. One day, following an unpleasant incident with a rickshaw rider who yells 'Get lost, hongtou asan', he has an epiphany. He cries out, 'I understand now! You hateful Chinese, I understand now! You condemn me as a wangguo nu! But you shouldn't get too complacent. Soon you, too, will become a hongtou asan!' (Chen 1927: 40). Conjoining hongtou asan and wangguo nu revitalizes the late Qing rhetoric and mobilizes the latter term's capacity to enact a mirror-like function; the Indian's acknowledgement of his own colonization facilitates a warning of China's impending fall.

The story recalls this older rhetoric in order to critique it. The policeman's realization links the colloquial hongtou asan, a distinctly verbal utterance (indeed, the short story opens with the phrase between quotation marks, visually highlighting its orality), with the older, more literary formulation of wangguo nu. This conceptual manoeuver alludes to the literary debates of the time on the appropriate linguistic register of literature. May Fourth debates crystallized the binary between the vernacular (*baihua* [白話]) and classical (*wenyan* [文言]) modes of writing, with proponents urging writers to break the shackles of tradition and modernize literature by writing in the vernacular. The Indian policeman's struggle to define himself unfolds in dialogue with this ongoing negotiation of literary identity in the Chinese cultural sphere, with the condemnation of wangguo nu evoking here both late Qing anti-colonialism and May Fourth iconoclasm. The second half of the story fixates on the Indian's internal thoughts as he mourns his nation's colonization and yearns to overcome his wangguo nu characteristic; these thoughts appear in an idiom remarkably consonant with May Fourth appeals for China to expel its backward traditions in order to rise as a modern nation. Melodramatically grieving his weak nation, the policeman cries, 'My nation has been conquered and extinguished. Ah! Motherland, why don't you fight back? Because of your cowardice, your people are everywhere mistreated by others!' (Chen 1927: 40). The story ends with the policeman weeping at the edge of the Huangpu river. 'Ah! Motherland', he sighs, 'my vast yet weak and cowardly motherland, from today onwards I forsake you! ... I wish you all—my compatriots—oh how I wish, one day soon, you could all wash away from your heads these three words: wangguo nu' (Chen 1927: 41). The policeman's voice drowns in the sounds of the river.

Written in the vernacular baihua, the story's depiction of the hongtou asan's grief and shame for his motherland's weakness immediately echoes the trope of 'national humiliation' in May Fourth literature.[18] The protests on 4 May 1919 broke out in large part as a response to what students considered China's humiliation during the negotiation of the Versailles Peace Treaty, which awarded parts of China to Japan. This preoccupation with national humiliation grew into a larger literary concern with China's failure to modernize, resulting in a host of short stories with protagonists who personified China's perceived powerlessness and grieved the nation's failures. Yu Dafu's canonical short story 'Chenlun' (沉淪) ['Sinking'] (1921) exemplifies this trend: The impotent and afflicted antihero famously proclaims 'O China, my China ... I wish you could grow rich and strong soon! Many, many of your children are still suffering' before the narrative leaves him at the edge of the sea, contemplating (and perhaps committing) suicide (Lau 2007: 55).[19] Explicitly echoing Yu Dafu's celebrated story, down to its ambiguously suicidal ending, 'Hongtou Asan' inscribes the Indian policeman in May Fourth discourse at the same time as it frames the Indian's anguish of colonization in terms familiar to the Chinese reader and legible within acclaimed literary conventions of the time. While the story opens with the Indian policeman as the object of

Chinese hatred and a pathetic product of India's colonization, by the end, the hongtou asan reveals himself as none other than the May Fourth antihero. A text that appears on its surface to denounce the Indian policeman aesthetically positions the hongtou asan and May Fourth protagonist as sharing in each other's national shame.

May Thirtieth Literature

The spring months of 1925 witnessed strikes and protests against working conditions in Shanghai's foreign (mostly Japanese) owned mills and factories. The death of a Chinese worker during a protest at a Japanese factory in mid-May further stoked the workers' anger and drew radical students to the International Settlement where they delivered speeches and distributed pamphlets against foreign intervention in China. As students joined in the workers' protests, the express target of protest expanded beyond working conditions in foreign-owned factories to, more broadly, the 'unjust nature of imperialism' (Wasserstrom 1991: 63). Unrest and conflict brewed beneath the surface of daily life in colonial Shanghai, finally erupting on 30 May, when protestors gathered outside the International Settlement's police station to demand the release of students who had been arrested shortly beforehand. Faced with a sea of angry but allegedly peaceful protestors, the foreign police (of the SMP) opened fire on the masses, fatally wounding several students and workers. Eyewitness reports of pools of blood spreading across the streets of the International Settlement painted a horrifying image. Chinese newspapers held the Indian policemen responsible for the fatalities, accusing them of blindly carrying out unjust and inhumane British orders to brutalize and open fire on the unarmed protestors.

Over the following months, this massacre, as it came to be known in the Chinese public sphere, fuelled a nationwide movement. The events of 30 May unleashed a new wave of Chinese hatred towards the already despised Indian policeman. As the perpetrator of bloodshed on 30 May, the Indian policeman came to symbolize the evils of foreign rule in China and protestors often evoked the policeman as an object of dissent. Literary depictions of the May Thirtieth massacre invariably featured the Indian policeman violently containing the protests (Fried 2004). Ba Jin's (巴金) 1931 novel, *Siqu de taiyang* (死去

的太陽) [*The Setting Sun*], for instance, offers a detailed semi-fictional account of the protests: The protagonist Wu Yangqing witnesses a 'massive Indian policeman grabbing his classmate by the collar', a Western policeman 'viciously' beating up a student, and 'a stream of fresh, red blood streaming down [the student's] face' (Ba Jin 1931: 6). Such literary engagements helped keep alive the memory of the events on 30 May 1925 and the Indian policeman's role in the massacre as the May Thirtieth Movement grew into what scholars have characterized as the first organized mass movement explicitly against the intervention of foreign powers in China.[20]

May Thirtieth discourse took shape alongside the crisis of communist survival following the Kuomintang's anti-communist purge in 1927. As Marxist theory permeated the literary sphere via the Soviet Union and Japan, leftist writers (and the literary societies they were affiliated with) launched public debates on the definition and practice of 'revolutionary literature'. Shanghai's consecutive massacres—on 30 May 1925 and on 12 April 1927 when Jiang Jieshi (Chiang Kai-shek) ordered the killing of thousands in Shanghai—yoked together the Indian policeman with literary explorations of a communist revolutionary consciousness. As a result, the controversial figure of the Indian policeman offered leftist writers a literary site of contestation: in writing the Indian policeman, proponents of rival literary schools crafted their visions for the form revolutionary literature ought to take.

Two prominent figures in Shanghai's literary circles, Jiang Guangci (蔣光慈) (1901–31) and Yang Cunren (楊邨人) (1901–55), experimented with casting the Indian as a sympathetic comrade, writing against the dominant portrayal of the policeman as despicable and violent, and extending to him a Marxist-inflected notion of solidarity. In 1928, Jiang and Yang, together with other like-minded writers, founded the Sun Society (Taiyang She [太陽社]), a literary group closely aligned with the Chinese Communist Party which prioritized the utility of literature in realizing proletarian revolution.[21] Members of the society called for literary practice to break from aesthetic concerns and melancholic portrayals of tormented individuals (as in writings of the older May Fourth generation) and instead to empower the oppressed masses by sparking revolutionary consciousness and promoting the bright future revolution would bring.

Yang's story, titled 'Hongtou Asan' and published in 1930, tells of a Chinese man who visits the International Settlement courthouse (the Mixed Court) to observe the trial of his two revolutionary friends. In the courtroom, the narrator sits among a group of Indian policemen. As he awaits the turn of his friends' trial, the hongtou asan seated beside him whispers (in broken English) 'Do you come to see the school-boy?' (Yang 1930: 12). Taken aback, the narrator looks up to find an Indian policeman with 'extremely kind and friendly eyes' (Yang 1930: 13). The two proceed to engage in a surreptitious conversation (again rendered in English):

'Yes, I come to see my friends ... Yesterday my friends ... had not come back home ... So I come to see them. Do you know what was matter with them?'
'The school-boy is good, the policeman is bad!' ...
'Is the school-boy good?'
'Yes, school boy is good. You know we cannot go back home. The Englishman is bad. So very bad.' (Yang 1930: 13)

The Indian policeman's expression of solidarity with the Chinese protestor (the 'school boy') and criticism of the British colonizer have a profound impact on the narrator. He is 'immediately moved by [the hongtou asan]. The pain of those weak peoples who are oppressed by the imperialists immediately rises in [his] heart, as though [he], too, is a hongtou asan' (Yang 1930: 14). The story ends on an optimistic note, with the narrator convinced that his encounter with the Indian policeman is proof that the colonized peoples, '[his] brothers, have all risen up' (Yang 1930: 15). Unlike earlier texts that fictionalized oneness with the Indian policeman in the hope that this similarity would not be actualized and that China would avoid following India's path into colonization, in this May Thirtieth climate, Yang explores the emancipatory potential of identifying with the Indian policeman and together striving for revolution. The image of the Chinese man as himself a hongtou asan issues a call to arms, not against but alongside the Indian.

Jiang's 1929 short story 'Asan' appeared in the inaugural issue of *Tuohuangzhe* (拓荒者) [*Pioneer*], the journal of the League of Left-Wing Writers founded in 1930 following a CCP-ordered truce between former rivals, Lu Xun and the Sun and Creation Societies.[22] Narrated from the Indian policeman's point of view, the story tells the tale of Asan, an Indian policeman, who ends up arrested by the British and put behind bars. In the days prior, Asan had arrested the student protestors who would gather in the International Settlement to distribute red and green leaflets and chant slogans. Asan did not understand what the students were protesting or what 'Bolshevik' meant, a term his British superiors often used to label the protestors as loathsome. One day, Asan dutifully arrests a student distributing fliers, but as he hauls his prisoner away, the student says to him, 'Friend, we are all oppressed people! We want China's liberation, and freedom for China's poor. Why do you oppose us? Is it that you have forgotten your motherland? We should unite' (Jiang 1930: 59). The student's words have an immediate effect on Asan: '[A] small wave began to stir in his mind: China's liberation ... India ... the British ...' (Jiang 1930: 59–60). He sets his prisoner free. As Asan realizes the connection between his own colonization and the student's call for Chinese revolution, Jiang constructs an expansive, collective form of revolutionary consciousness that redraws the lines of conflict, replacing the colonizer/colonized divide with one between the (capitalist) imperialists and the oppressed. The rearranged categories of class antagonism make possible new solidarities.

A British chief witnesses the exchange with the Chinese student and reprimands Asan. 'You, too, are a Bolshevik', the chief says before throwing Asan behind bars (Jiang 1930: 60). 'Asan, having never understood what a Bolshevik is, and never dreaming that he could be called one, was now dragged into the jail like any other prisoner' (Jiang 1930: 61). As he thinks back to his mistreatment at the hands of the British, 'he finally understood what Bolshevik means' (Jiang 1930: 61). Demonstrating the power of literature to cultivate revolutionary consciousness in the most unlikely, anti-revolutionary of figures, Jiang inverts the epiphany Yang's narrator undergoes; here, it is the hongtou asan who voices sameness with the Chinese protestor.

Jiang and Yang received caustic critique for their favourable portrayals of the Indian policeman, likely due in equal parts to the widespread hatred for the policeman and the fragmentation of Shanghai's literary sphere into various camps. Critics accused such portrayals of attempting to recuperate the Indian policeman from his villainous role in the May Thirtieth massacre. In a highly satirical essay, one critic, Jin Xuan (錦軒), writes: '[I]t appears that the hongtou asan has recently come into some good luck. Unbelievably, he has been praised by some benevolent Chinese heroes upholding justice. They say that, in the blink of an eye, the hongtou asan is capable of gaining awareness, of understanding, and of rising up' (Jin 1930: 46). Jin Xuan goes on to ridicule the absurdity of the instantaneous emotional transformations in the stories by Jiang and Yang, finding it ludicrous that the Indian policeman could be capable of expressing any political convictions. He concludes that if China is to rise up one day, it will not be due to such fanciful and unrealistic writing.

Intolerance towards the idea of the Indian policeman as an imagined comrade-in-arms meant that this literary figure continued to carry out an unfixable function in constant fluctuation, as though suspended in the pull towards multiple poles. The Indian policeman could be neither wholly friend nor enemy; moments of antagonist clash aesthetically generated both solidarity and rebellion. Mao Dun's (茅盾) (1896–1981) well-known 1930 novel *Hong* (虹) [*Rainbow*] stages precisely such an encounter between the Indian policeman and its protagonist, Mei. The novel's dramatic climax depicts Mei participating in a students' protest (based on May Thirtieth). The previous night, Mei's group leader had instructed her to refrain from violence during the protests and to strictly follow orders of non-resistance (*wudikang* [無抵抗]) (Mao Dun 1930: 224). Not one to play by the rules, Mei feels restricted by these orders but decides to follow them for the sake of the larger cause. Entering into the protesting masses, Mei initially joins in the scripted chants. Then, suddenly, she comes face-to-face with an Indian policeman: 'A massive Indian policeman blazed before her eyes. Like a demon, he charged towards her' (Mao Dun 1930: 265). At this moment, Mei bursts into a rage:

'Nonresistance?' This word flashed through her mind. Immediately, with even more force, she roared out, 'People of China, come together! Let's attack these murderous bandits—Ah! You colonized slaves!' As though they were stones, she flung her last few words at the Indian policeman, who was now charging straight towards her. (Mao Dun 1930: 265)

Mei adamantly expresses—and, indeed, is able to express—her true political convictions only once she encounters the Indian policeman. Throughout the novel, Mei struggles to reconcile her romantic and political interests, and repeatedly fails to construct a political identity as distinct from that of the men she admires.[23] But in the moment when she physically collides with the Indian policeman, she breaks free, violating the order of non-resistance. No longer constrained by the orders or influence of others, she is now unrestrained and violent. Mei finally articulates a politics of her own.

What is it about coming face-to-face with the Indian policeman that causes Mei to erupt? Mei's reaction is triggered by a flicker of self-recognition in the policeman's image. Mei hurls the insult of 'colonized slaves' not only at the policeman, but also at the part of herself reflected in the Indian's subjugation. This self-image can manifest only in the clash with the policeman. Although Mao Dun, known for his naturalistic realism, renders this scene in terms quite different from Yang's, the characters' epiphanies mirror each other. Like Yang's protagonist, Mei realizes that she, too, is a 'colonized slave', and it is this split-second twinning of selves that enables her to voice her protest. And, when interpreted intertextually, the trace of Jiang's awakened Asan informs a reading of Mao Dun's policeman. In precipitating Mei's rebellion and participating in her resistance, the policeman is no longer a mere silent aggressor, but becomes constitutive of Mei's new self. In this way, Mei's call to arms voices both her own protest, as well as the silent echo of the Indian policeman's unarticulated resistance.

In May Thirtieth discourse, the literary Indian policeman emerged as an active participant in the crafting of revolutionary literature, both in his ability to spark Chinese protest as the object of rebellion and in the promise that he could aesthetically join in such outcry. Literary experiments with the Indian policeman illuminate a collaborative undertow, drawing the Chinese protestor and Indian policeman together in expressions of protest, precisely during a historical moment that marked the height of antagonism between Chinese and Indian actors in Shanghai.

The Gandhian Policeman

With a new revolutionary consciousness pervading the nation following the May Thirtieth movement, Chinese news sources increasingly reported on independence movements unfolding across the colonial world. Through the 1920s, the Chinese print media—publications associated with communists and nationalists alike—had a long-standing interest in reporting Gandhi's freedom movement under-way in India, with intellectuals vigorously debating Gandhi's view of modernity and civilization as well as the merits and feasibility of his revolutionary vision (Wang 2018: 149–68). In March 1930, Chinese newspapers carried news of the 'Dandi March', a 240-mile journey Gandhi undertook on foot, with thousands joining along the way, in resistance to (or non-cooperation with) the colonial Indian govern-ment's monopoly on salt production and the tax levied on salt. The Dandi March announced Gandhi's ability to mobilize thousands across class-based and other social divides, in open nonviolent rebel-lion against British rule and towards a common goal of Swaraj (self-rule). News of such developments in India soon travelled to China, and Chinese journals and newspapers published numerous articles on and photographs of the Dandi March.[24]

Gandhi's growing presence in the Chinese literary sphere gave rise to a paradox: Among the most popular Indian figures in literary discourse, on one extreme lay the Indian policeman as the ultimate colonized slave, and, on the other extreme was Gandhi, the harbinger of revolution and saviour of the Indian people. In critique of popular discourses that relegated these figures to two different, discordant ideas of India, some Chinese writers sought to reconcile contradic-tory images by writing the Indian figure as simultaneously deplorable and exemplary.[25] A popular strategy to this end involved endowing the Indian policeman with a Gandhian revolutionary consciousness. Such a strategy had the added benefit of avoiding harsh criticism of the kind directed at Yang and Jiang. Writers could now circumvent explicitly expressing solidarity with the Indian and burdening the Chinese communist with the task of enlightening the policeman. The fictionalized Gandhian policeman avoided such unpopular literary trends while still achieving the intended effect of recuperating the policeman from his widespread disrepute and presenting him as a fellow colonized subject alongside the Chinese.

A 1930 short story, 'Yinbu zhi si' (印捕之死) ['Death of an Indian Policeman'] by Pan Jienong (潘子農) (1909–93), features an Indian policeman named Gan Kexin (甘克辛), whose very name foreshad-ows the conceptual joining together of Gandhi and the policeman:

The character *gan* alludes to the Chinese transliteration of 'Gandhi' (Gandi [甘地]), and the character *xin* to Chinese renditions of 'Singh', a common surname among the Indian policemen. Gan is stationed in X City, based on Shanghai's International Settlement and described as a police state entirely under British control. One day, the British chief orders Gan to aid him in arresting X City's revolutionary Indians who have gathered to discuss Gandhi's Dandi March. Gan knows these revolutionary Indians well. They are members of the National Salvation Association (Jiuguohui [救國會]), founded by the Indians of X City in support of Gandhi's anti-British movement. In the past, Gan had himself participated in the association, helping others evade arrest. This time, however, he has no choice but to arrest the association's members. Facing this predicament, 'he experienced the extent of the British people's viciousness. It is not enough that they slaughter Indian people ... they make Indian people arrest their own innocent compatriots and revolutionary visionaries' (Pan 1930: 38).

Later, as Gan escorts two Indian revolutionaries to the police station, he experiences incredible internal turmoil. He knows that disobeying orders will result in punishment, even death. He compares the value of his own life with that of the two revolutionary Indian youths he has arrested. Finally, with the cause of the nation in his heart, he sets his prisoners free. Just as expected, the British chief beats Gan until he is bloody. Ultimately, Gan voices his confession in explicitly anti-colonial terms. He cries out, '[E]ver since you British destroyed our peoples, not a day passes without us Indians having to live in an abyss of suffering. That is why our motherland's visionary and hero, Gandhi, leads our independence movement against all odds, in order to return glory to our ancient nation' (Pan 1930: 45). The next day, Gan commits suicide in his prison cell.

'Death of an Indian Policeman', along with other Chinese texts in the 1930s, imagines the Indian policeman as gaining a revolutionary consciousness and joining forces with independence movements underway in India.[26] Historically speaking, the notion of Indian policemen as revolutionary anti-colonials is no mere fantasy: Indian policemen were involved in covert Ghadar activities in Shanghai, as well as in the nationalist Indian Independence League and Indian National Army under Subhas Chandra Bose.[27] That such nationalist activities, with violent missions for India's independence from

British rule, were in fact antithetical to Gandhi's non-violent vision likely remained unbeknownst to most Chinese writers and readers. The literary sphere instead allowed an otherwise impossible view of Indian nationalism, one in which the Indian policeman and Gandhi could stand side by side, united against the British.

Beyond Hatred

Noting the derogatory tone that often characterizes Chinese depictions of the Indian policeman, historian Isabella Jackson has argued that 'negative portrayals' of the Indian policeman in Chinese popular culture 'carry political resonance', indicating the Chinese public's hatred of this Indian figure (Jackson 2012: 1674). Indeed, many of the texts discussed in this essay seem to corroborate the widely held view of the Indian policeman as a singularly hated figure in China. Yet, the symbolic and aesthetic functions of the literary Indian policeman far surpass mere expressions of hatred. Reading together the various Chinese texts of the Indian policeman, a different kind of literary relation emerges, one that resists easy fixity and thrives in indeterminacy. The literary Indian policeman embodies an exercise in thinking China and India together beyond the binary poles of solidarity/resistance and friendship/enmity, resisting the tendency to treat the dyad as oppositional ('either/or') and revealing the many textures of relation in between ('neither', 'both').

A final literary example elucidates particularly well the way in which hatred towards and solidarity with the Indian policeman manifest as two sides of the same coin. In a 1936 poem, 'Gei Yindu Asan' (給印度阿三) ['Ode to the Indian Asan'], the poet Bai Yun (白云) opens with the unwanted ubiquity of the Indian policeman in Shanghai:

> On the streets of the flourishing International Settlement,
> At the closely watched doorways of the banks,
> At the bustling entrance of the many shops,
> We can see, we can see,
> Our armed Indian brother.
> Six feet tall; strong, robust limbs,
> A white turban wrapped around his head; black-faced, like soot,
> You have become imperialism's obedient dog,
> Roaming around all over Shanghai. (Bai Yun 1936: 43)

Referring to the policeman sarcastically as 'our armed Indian brother', Bai Yun at once recalls and critiques the cliché of China–India fraternity. The Indian policeman stands simultaneously as a 'brother' and as 'imperialism's obedient dog', evoking the blurred self/other dynamic in an expression of intimacy that is inextricably bound up with enmity. The poem continues:

> Ah! Indian Asan, you are but a guard dog of the world!
> You silly, clueless creature, without embarrassment or shame!
> For whom do you bear arms? For whom do you toil?
> Whom do you work for, whom do you serve?
> You lamentable, pitiful, last descendent of the Sakyamuni,
> You have brought boundless scorn on all of Asia.
> Ah! Indian Asan, you stupid man,
> After all, at whose chest is your pistol aimed? (Bai Yun 1936: 44)

The poem at once upholds and scorns pan-Asianist narratives that laud India as the fount of Buddhist spiritualism. In the same breath, Bai Yun reviles the Indian policeman for his present and reveres him for his past: 'You lamentable, pitiful, last descendent of the Sakyamuni/ You have brought boundless scorn on all of Asia'. Finally, with a line that encapsulates the fraught binds of literary relation, the poem concludes by suggesting that in pointing his gun at his Chinese victim, the Indian policeman only aims the weapon at himself. In the image of the Indian policeman shooting a Chinese protestor who is revealed as none other than the Indian himself, opposing the same enemy and striving towards a shared revolution, oneness between Chinese and Indian comes alive only in the moment of its death.

Over the first four decades of the twentieth century, clashes with the Indian policeman in China's treaty ports fuelled writers' sustained interest in fictionalizing the encounter between Chinese and Indian. The potential and challenge of imagining the Indian policeman enabled writers to play with dominant discourses of their time, from the late Qing 'front-car' rhetoric of India as a cautionary tale, to early Republican-era debates on vernacularizing literature, to preoccupations with revolutionary literature in the late 1920s and 1930s. At each historical juncture, texts of the Indian policeman imbue these ongoing debates not with lofty pan-Asianist ideals of China–India unity but with the everyday anxieties of confronting colonization and reckoning with one's own position in its power-riddled operations.

The story of the Indian policeman in Chinese literature, therefore, doubles as a story of modern Chinese literature's development told from the perspective of China's colonial experience.

Notes

1. Here I use the term 'Indian policeman', with 'India' referring to the geographical entity under British colonial governance, instead of the more commonly used term 'Sikh policeman'. This is because the Chinese texts I examine attribute to the policeman a primarily 'Indian' identity above other identificatory markers. In addition, 'Sikh' in British colonial discourse emerges as a particular category constructed by colonial ideologies of martial races in order to further instrumental purposes of defending and policing the Empire. Although a common term in colonial British parlance, 'Sikh policeman' thus identifies not the men themselves (many of whom, in any event, did not belong to what the British defined as the 'Sikh' community in Punjab) but rather a mythic colonial construct used strategically to homogenize a variegated group of people. On the latter point, see Ballantyne (2006), Rand and Wagner (2012), and Streets (2004).
2. An examination of literature circulating in the other Chinese treaty ports remains beyond the scope of this study. By 'journals', I refer to literary periodicals and magazines that grew in popularity during the late Qing and Republican periods, often associated with a literary society or group. On journal culture in Republican China, see Hockx (2003).
3. On precolonial literary engagements with India, often within the Buddhist-inflected Chinese cultural sphere, see Kieshnick and Shahar (2014).
4. On Kang Youwei's writings on India, see chapters in this volume by Viren Murthy, Zhang Ke, and Kamal Sheel.
5. Kang discusses the following ten commensurable characteristics linking China and India in order to argue that India is the most suitable country to act as China's 'front-car':

   > In comparison to China, is there any nation with a similar location in Asia, of a similar size, a similar ratio of coastal and landlocked territories, a similarly large-sized population; with as advanced an enlightenment, as ancient a civilization; with similar laws and customs, similarly soft-natured peoples; similarly invaded by Northerners, similarly unified, and had a similarly autocratic government? ... Fortunately, there is one nation ... that can act as our mirror, whose example we can learn from.... This is none other than India. (Kang [1902] 1998: 334)

6. In addition to Isabella Jackson's scholarship referenced here, further historiographic research on the Indian policemen in China include Bickers (1999), Cao (2017), and Thampi (2005). See also Chapter 9 by Yin Cao in this volume. For a discussion of the iconography of the Indian policeman in popular culture, see Liu (2018).

7. On Xu's understudied writings published during his time in Japan, see Chen (2016).

8. This earlier penname, literally 'melon seeds', could also be read as 'son of China' since *guafen* or 'cutting up the melon', alluded to in the novel's title, was a common metaphor for the colonial powers' intention to carve up China like a melon (as they did in Africa). On the concept of 'guafen', see Wagner (2017).

9. In late Qing discourse, the Indian's slavishness was perhaps rivaled only by 'black slaves' (*heinu* [黑奴]) (Karl 2002b).

10. Incomplete novels were not uncommon in the late Qing period. Writers' enthusiasm to get new stories into print often left old ones unfinished. Further hindering completion, the serial format of long-form fiction, published over several journal or newspaper issues, added another layer of unpredictability and inconsistency. On reading late Qing fictional incompleteness constructively, see Andolfatto (2019).

11. This novel was *Qixia nüxia* (棲霞女俠) [*The Female Knight: Errant of Qixia*], also by Peng Yu (the author of *Twin Souls*), apparently a translation of a work attributed to a Japanese writer, Iwatani Ranken (巖谷蘭軒). Serialization of the novel was discontinued in *Shenbao* because it had since been published in book form.

12. Although the characters *pofo* (破佛) may suggest anti-Buddhist sentiment (if understood literally as 'destroying the Buddha'), the penname is perhaps better interpreted when *po* is taken in its less common usage to connote exposition or revelation. In this sense, *pofo* may be better translated along the lines of 'exposing the truth of the Buddha'. Such an interpretation would be in line with the author's interest in Buddhist classics and his years spent as a monk.

13. Some scholars have categorized *Twin Souls* as among the works Peng is said to have translated from Japanese but this seems unlikely for at least two reasons. First, scholars disagree on whether Peng was proficient enough in Japanese to be able to translate (Fu 2016: 14). Second, I have found no record of which Japanese source text *Twin Souls* could conceivably be a translation of, and it is difficult to see how a novel steeped in late Qing discourses of Chinese national autonomy could have been translated from Japanese.

14. Snippets of Peng's life as a monk appear in the diaries of Feng Zikai (豐子愷) (1898–1975) and Li Shutong (李叔同) (1880–1942) who over-lapped with Peng at Hupao. For biographical accounts of Peng, see Fu (2016), Liu (1996), and Peng (1981).

15. Such movements of the soul within the body would not have been entirely foreign to the reader. According to Chinese folk medical beliefs, a fright can cause body–soul dissociation with involuntary 'soul-loss' occurring as a common ailment (Harrell 1979).

16. Such scientific approaches are in line with late Qing science fiction explorations of the idea that problems of the soul could be cured through Western scientific techniques (Luan 2006).

17. The story is published in the Shanghai Nanyang Advanced Business School's student association magazine and was authored by Chen Kangtai (陈康泰), likely a student at the school.

18. More specifically, 'Hongtou asan' is written in the style of the early Creation Society, a literary group formed in the 1920s. The writings of the Creation Society, members of which most famously included Guo Moruo and Yu Dafu, often depicted 'a romantic hypertrophied ... expansive, libidinous, and tormented self' (Tang and Hockx 2008: 107). Interestingly, 'Hongtou asan' appeared in the same year that Yu Dafu publicly announced his withdrawal from the Creation Society, suggesting that the short story could have been written as a tribute to the writer.

19. On the trope of national shame and 'Sinking', see Chen (2003), Denton (1992), Hsia (1961), and Lee (1973).

20. On the May Thirtieth Movement, see Clifford (1976), Ku (1979), Rigby (1980), and Wasserstrom (1991).

21. The Sun Society was an offshoot of the Creation Society. Although both were comprised of leftist writers and both societies promoted the practice of revolutionary literature, the writers in Sun Society were cardholding members of the CCP and developed close ties with the Party. On the Creation and Sun Societies, see Tang (2008).

22. Jiang's story is included in Harold Isaacs's *Straw Sandals*, a collection of Chinese short stories (1918–33) curated by Isaacs in conversation with Lu Xun and Mao Dun. In reference to his correspondence with Lu Xun on whether to include Jiang's story in the collection, Isaacs notes: '[I]n one of his letters about this collection, Lu Hsun, who was on record as having scant regard for this writer and, indeed, the whole type he repre-sented [likely referring to members of the Creation and Sun Societies], indicated indifference as to which of his stories might be used, but no objection to including him' (Isaacs 1974: lx). Isaacs mistranslated 'Asan'

as 'Hassan', endowing the Indian policeman with an individualized (and unlikely) name. This has the effect of reframing the story as narrating an extraordinary incident concerning a single policeman, whereas the anonymity of 'Asan' in fact enables Jiang to center a collective revolutionary consciousness shared among the colonized and oppressed.

23. For analyses of the interplay between revolution and love in *Rainbow*, see Chow (1991), Liu (2003), and Wang (1992).

24. See, for example, 'Gandi' (1930) and 'Yindu' (1930).

25. A third Indian figure popular in literary discourse of the time was Nobel Laureate Rabindranath Tagore and a similar strategy of reconciling Tagore with the Indian policeman animated some responses. Much has been written on Tagore's controversial visit to China in April–May 1924. As is well known, his talks were often disrupted by protestors, and according to reports of those present, student protestors used the epithet 'wangguo nu' to refer to Tagore: 'No sooner had the Indian poet finished speaking than a clamoring of voices began on the outskirts of his audience. Young men shouted in Chinese, "Go back, slave from a lost country [wangguo nu]!" "We don't want philosophy, we want materialism!" and waved placards with these same slogans' (Hay 1970: 181). By throwing at Tagore an insult commonly reserved for the Indian policeman, the protestors discursively linked the two figures, transferring to Tagore the label of 'colonized slave' and thereby articulating their objection to the poet in the colonial vocabulary of the time.

26. A second story, 'From Gandhi to Nehru: The Story of an Indian Policeman', published in a youth journal in 1937, similarly attempts to reconcile the politics of the Indian policeman stationed in Shanghai with the competing philosophies of Gandhi's non-cooperation movement and Nehru's socialist approach to Indian independence. Framed as a dialogue between two Indian policemen, the story reads as a pedagogical endeavor to teach its young readers about India's current political landscape. The story ends with the protagonist, an Indian policeman stationed in China, resolving to quit his job and return to India to join the independence movement. The story recalls Ghadarite discourse in its depiction of an Indian policeman switching loyalties from the British to the cause of the Indian nation. See He (1937). On Ghadar activities in China, see Deepak (1999).

27. See Chapter 11 by Madhavi Thampi in this volume.

References

Andolfatto, Lorenzo. 2019. *Hundred Days' Literature: Chinese Utopian Fiction at the End of Empire, 1902–1910*. Leiden: Brill.

Ba Jin (巴金). 1931. *Siqu de taiyang* (死去的太陽) [*The Setting Sun*]. Shanghai: Kaiming shudian.

Bai Yun (白云). 1936. 'Gei Yindu Asan' (給印度阿三) ['Ode to the Indian Asan']. *Shidai zhishi* (時代知識) 1 (7): 43–4.

Ballantyne, Tony. 2006. *Between Colonialism and Diaspora: Sikh Cultural Formations in an Imperial World.* Durham: Duke University Press.

Bickers, Robert. 1999. *Britain in China: Community, Culture and Colonialism 1900–1949.* Manchester: Manchester University Press.

Cao, Yin. 2017. *From Policemen to Revolutionaries: A Sikh Diaspora in Global Shanghai.* Leiden: Brill.

Chen, Eva. 2003. 'Shame and Narcissistic Self in Ya Dafu's *Sinking*'. *Canadian Review of Comparative Literature* 30 (3–4): 565–83.

Chen Kangtai (陳康泰). 1927. 'Hongtou Asan' (紅頭阿三) ['Red-Headed Asan']. *Nanyang gaoji shangye xuexiao xueshenghui jikan* (南洋高級商業學校學生會季刊) 1: 39–41.

Chen Linghong (陳凌虹). 2016. 'Xu Zhuodai liuri jingli ji zaoqi chuangzuo huodong kao' (徐卓呆留日經歷及早期創作活動考) ['Xu Zhuodai's Experiences in Japan and Early Works']. *Zhongguo xiandai wenxue yanjiu congkan* (中國現代文學研究叢刊) 11: 60–9.

Cheng Guan (澄觀). 1923. 'Yindu Asan mingcheng zhi youlai' (印度阿三名稱之由來) ['The Reason Behind the Red-Headed Asan's Name']. *Hongguang* (宏光) 5: 61.

Chow, Rey. 1991. *Woman and Chinese Modernity: The Politics of Reading between West and East.* Minneapolis: University of Minnesota Press.

Clifford, Nicholas. 1976. *Spoilt Children of Empire. Westerners in Shanghai and the Chinese Revolution of the 1920s.* Hanover: University Press of New England.

Deepak, B.R. 1999. 'Revolutionary Activities of the Ghadar Party in China'. *China Report* 35 (4): 439–56.

Denton, Kirk. 1992. 'The Distant Shore: Nationalism in Yu Dafu's "Sinking"'. *Chinese Literature: Essays, Articles, Reviews,* 14: 107–23.

Diedie (喋喋). 1913. 'Chao Yindu xunbu' (嘲印度巡捕) ['Mocking the Indian Policeman']. *Huaji Shici* (滑稽詩詞) 2.

Dongfang zazhi (東方雜誌). 1930. 'Yindu zhi fan Ying yundong' (印度之反英運動) ['India's Anti-British Movement']. 27 (8): 1–3.

Fried, Daniel. 2004. 'A Bloody Absence: Communist Narratology and the Literature of May Thirtieth'. *Chinese Literature: Essays, Articles, Reviews* 26: 23–53.

Fu Jianzhou (付建舟). 2016. 'Wan qing zhe ji zuojia Yadong Pofo shengping zhushu kao' (晚清浙籍作家亞東破佛生平著述考) ['The Life and Writings of Yadong Pofo, a Zhejiang Writer in the Late Qing Dynasty']. *Suzhou jiaoyu xueyuan xuebao* (蘇州教育學院學報) 33 (5): 12–18.

Guowen zhoubao (國文週報). 1930. 'Gandi kang Ying yundong' (甘地抗英運動) ['Gandhi's Anti-British Movement']. 7 (20): 8–9.

Harrell, Stevan. 1979. 'The Concept of Soul in Chinese Folk Religion'. *Journal of Asian Studies* 38 (3): 519–28.

Hay, Stephen. 1970. *Asian Ideas of East and West: Tagore and his Critics in Japan, China, and India*. Cambridge: Harvard University Press.

He Zou (何奏). 1937. 'You Gandi dao Nihelu: Yige Yindu xunbu de gushi' (由甘地到尼赫魯：一個印度巡捕的故事) ['From Gandhi to Nehru: The Story of an Indian Policeman']. *Xin shaonian* (新少年) 3 (9): 54–8.

Hockx, Michel. 2003. *Questions of Style: Literary Societies and Literary Journals in Modern China 1911–1937*. Leiden: Brill.

Hsia, C.T. 1961. *A History of Modern Chinese Fiction*. New Haven: Yale University Press.

Isaacs, Harold (ed.). 1974. *Straw Sandals: Chinese Short Stories 1918–1933*. Cambridge: MIT Press.

Jackson, Isabella. 2012. 'The Raj on Nanjing Road: Sikh Policemen in Treaty-Port Shanghai'. *Modern Asian Studies* 46 (6): 1672–704.

Jiang Guangci (蔣光慈). 1930. 'Asan' (阿三). *Tuohuangzhe* (拓荒者) 1 (1): 57–61.

Jin Xuan (錦軒). 1930. 'Hongtou Asan' (紅頭阿三) ['Red-Headed Asan']. *Qianfeng zhoubao* (前鋒週報) 6: 46–7.

Kang Youwei (康有為). [1902] 1998. 'Yu tongxue zhuzi Liang Qichao deng lun Yindu wangguo youyu ge sheng zili shu' (與同學諸子梁啟超等論印度亡國由於各省自立書) ['A Letter to Fellow Scholar Liang Qichao and Others on India's Colonization due to the Independence of Its Provinces']. In Jiang Yihua (姜義華) and Zhang Ronghua (張榮華) (eds), *Kang Youwei quanji* (康有為全集). Beijing: Zhongguo renmin daxue chubanshe.

Karl, Rebecca. 2002a. '"Slavery", Citizenship, and Gender in Late Qing China's Global Context'. In Rebecca Karl and Peter Zarrow (eds), *Rethinking the 1898 Reform Period: Political and Cultural Change in Late Qing China*. Cambridge: Harvard University Asia Center.

———. 2002b. *Staging the World: Chinese Nationalism at the Turn of the Twentieth Century*. Durham: Duke University Press.

Kieshnick, John and Meir Shahar (eds). 2014. *India in the Chinese Imagination: Myth, Religion, and Thought*. Philadelphia: University of Pennsylvania Press.

Ku, Hung-Ting. 1979. 'Urban Mass Movement: The May Thirtieth Movement in Shanghai'. *Modern Asian Studies* 13 (2): 197–216.

Lau, Joseph and Howard Goldblatt (eds). 2007. *The Columbia Anthology of Modern Chinese Literature*. New York: Columbia University Press.

Lee, Leo Ou-fan. 1973. *The Romantic Generation of Chinese Writers*. Cambridge: Harvard University Press.

Liu Delong (劉德隆). 1996. 'Shuang linghun' (雙靈魂) ['Twin Souls]. *Ming-Qing xiaoshuo yanjiu* (明清小說研究) 2: 231–5.

Liu Jianmei. 2003. *Revolution Plus Love: Literary History, Women's Bodies, and Thematic Repetition in Twentieth-Century Chinese Fiction*. Honolulu: University of Hawai'i Press.

Liu Yongguang (劉永廣). 2018. 'Zhimin chiru yu wenhua xixue: "hongtou Asan" xingxiang de suzao yu chuanbo' (殖民恥辱與文化戲謔: "紅頭阿三" 形象的塑造與傳播) ['Colonial Shame and Cultural Irony: The Portrayal and Circulation of the Image of Red-Headed A San']. *Lishi Jiaoxue* (歷史 教學) 12: 20–30.

Luan Weiping (欒偉平). 2006. 'Jindai kexue xiaoshuo yu linghun: You "Xin Faluo xiansheng tan" shuo kaiqu' (近代科學小說與靈魂——由《新法螺 先生譚》說開) ['Early Modern Fiction and the Soul: Starting from "New Tales of Mr. Braggadocio"']. *Zhongguo jindai wenxue yanjiu congkan* (中國 現代文學研究叢刊) 3: 46–60.

Mao Dun (茅盾). 1930. *Hong* (虹) [*Rainbow*]. Shanghai: Kaiming shudian.

Mittler, Barbara. 2004. *A Newspaper for China? Power, Identity, and Change in Shanghai's News Media, 1872–1912*. Cambridge: Harvard University Asia Center.

Pan Jienong (潘子農). 1930. 'Yinbu zhi si' (印捕之死) ['Death of an Indian Policeman']. *Kaizhan* (開戰) 5: 31–46.

Peng Changqing (彭长卿). 1981. 'Yadong Pofo zhuanlue' (亞東破佛傳略) ['A Biography of Yadong Pofo']. *Qingmo xiaoshuo yanjiu* (清末小說研究) 5: 26–39.

Rand, Gavin and Kim Wagner. 2012. 'Recruiting the "Martial Races": Identities and Military Service in Colonial India'. *Patterns of Prejudice* 46 (3–4): 232–54.

Rea, Christopher. 2015. *The Age of Irreverence: A New History of Laughter in China*. Berkeley: University of California Press.

———. 2019. 'Introduction: "Charlie Chaplin of the East", Xu Zhuodai'. In *China's Chaplin: Comic Stories and Farces by Xu Zhuodai*. Ithaca: Cornell University East Asia Program.

Rigby, Richard. 1980. *The May 30 Movement: Events and Themes*. Canberra: Australian National University Press.

Shenbao. 1907. 'Benbao fuyin' (本報附印) ['Printed in This Newspaper'], 11 March.

Shih, Shu-mei. 2001. *The Lure of the Modern: Writing Modernism in Semicolonial China, 1917–1937*. Berkeley: University of California.

Shi Jiu. 1935. 'Hongtou Asan kao' (紅頭阿三考) ['On Hongtou Asan'], 24 August.

Shiyong Yingwen banyuekan (實用英文半月刊). 1937. 'Hongtou Asan yu lach-eren' (紅頭阿三與拉車人) ['Red-Headed Asan and the Rickshaw Puller']. 2 (4): 49–50.

Streets, Heather. 2004. *Martial Races: The Military, Race and Masculinity in British Imperial Culture, 1857–1914*. Manchester: Manchester University Press.

Tang Xiaobing and Michel Hockx. 2008. 'The Creation Society (1921–1930)'. In Kirk Denton and Michel Hockx (eds), *Literary Societies of Republican China*. Plymouth: Rowman and Littlefield Publishers.

Thampi, Madhavi. 2005. *Indians in China, 1800–1949*. New Delhi: Manohar Publishers.

Wagner, Rudolf. 2017. '"Dividing Up the [Chinese] Melon": The Fate of a Transcultural Metaphor in the Formation of National Myth'. *Transcultural Studies* 8 (1): 9–122.

Wang, David. 1992. *Fictional Realism in Twentieth-Century China: Mao Dun, Lao She, Shen Congwen*. New York: Columbia University Press.

Wang Ruliang (王汝良). 2018. *Zhongguo wenxue zhong de Yindu xingxiang yanjiu* (中國文學中的印度形象研究) [*The Image of India in Chinese Literature*]. Beijing: Zhonghua shuju.

Wasserstrom, Jeffrey. 1991. *Student Protests in Twentieth-Century China: The View from Shanghai*. Stanford: Stanford University Press.

Xu Zhuodai (徐卓呆). 1904. 'Fenge hou zhi wuren' (分割後之吾人) ['My People after Partition']. *Jiangsu* (江蘇): 8–10.

Yadong Pofo (亞東破佛). 1907. 'Yuyan xiaoshuo shuang linghun' (寓言小説雙靈魂) ['Twin Souls: An Allegorical Story']. Published in parts numbered 1–24. *Shenbao* (申報), 12 March–9 April.

Yang Cunren (楊邨人). 1930. 'Hongtou Asan' (紅頭阿三) ['Red-Headed Asan']. *Dazhong wenyi* (大眾文藝) 2 (3): 133.

2

China–India Myths in Xu Dishan's 'Goddess of Supreme Essence'

Gal Gvili

In 1923, Xu Dishan (許地山) (1895–1941), a prominent author of Republican China (1911–49), published a short story titled 'Tihu tiannü' (醍醐天女) ['Goddess of Supreme Essence'] in the widely circulated journal *Xiaoshuo yuebao* (小說月報) [*Fiction Monthly*]. I will explore this story at length here because it provides an entry point to one of the least studied yet most significant elements in Xu Dishan's poetic world, namely, his vision of a China–India literary imagination.

Xu Dishan's fiction has been studied as part of 'Nanyang literature', a corpus of writings by Chinese authors which features the South Sea in its various locations, including Burma (now Myanmar), Thailand, Borneo, Malaysia, Singapore, and India. Other writers who contributed to this body of texts, which Brian Bernards (2015: 30) has convincingly argued 'alludes to and critically diverges from the imperial Chinese worldview of the Nanyang and the "southern barbarian"', include Yu Dafu (郁達夫) (1896–1945), Xu Zhimo (徐志摩) (1897–1931), and Lao She (老舍) (1899 –1966). Given that Xu Dishan's protagonists travel all over the South Seas, reside in different locations in South and Southeast Asia, and often spend a significant amount of the narrative space voyaging by sea,[1] can we think about Xu Dishan's work as a particular instance of China–India connectivity?

This chapter argues to the affirmative for two reasons. First, while he is mostly remembered today as a writer of short fiction, Xu Dishan was much more prolific as a scholar of Sanskrit, Buddhism, Daoism, and comparative religion. He visited India twice, translated Indian folktales, and wrote comparative studies of Chinese and Indian folktales and drama, alongside publishing the first survey of Indian literature in modern China in 1930. Xu Dishan's scholarship is rarely considered something that can provide an entry point into his fiction, but in his case, as I intend to show, we cannot understand how his work forms part of Chinese Nanyang literature without examining his engagement with Indian culture in general, and with comparative work between China and India in particular. Second, a close examination of Xu Dishan's engagement with Indian mythology and religions in his fiction constitutes, I argue, a critique of social Darwinist ideals, which were immensely popular during the Republican era, particularly in the May Fourth literature (Jones 2011). In a similar vein to Zhang Taiyan's 'Asia as Method', which Viren Murthy examines in this volume, and to the pliability of the trope of the Indian policeman that enabled Chinese writers to both identify with and actively resist colonization, as Adhira Mangalagiri notes in this volume, Xu Dishan envisaged a China–India horizon through a literary device I call 'transregional metonymy', that is, tropes that travelled between India and China through cultural exchange of myths.

This chapter begins by situating Xu Dishan and his work within the larger context of Chinese literature in the 1920s so as to provide a background for the reader to understand the author's intervention. The following sections elaborate on the concept of 'transregional metonymy' through a close reading of the short story 'Goddess of Supreme Essence'. The essay shows how a shared China–India figurative domain emerges in the story in order to offer a new understanding of myths and how they function in modern life. Modern Chinese writers often rewrote myths in an effort to sanction a national past through national culture. Xu Dishan presented a radical alternative: Instead of rewriting the past, myths can rewrite the present; instead of using myths to establish a national culture, literature can use myths to imagine a transregional horizon. Focusing on India in order to think about the nature of storytelling and the relationship between myth and reality, Xu Dishan undid the binary distinction between ancient India as a soul brother and colonial India as a cautionary tale. As such, and complementing the other two chapters in this section of the present volume, the following draws our attention to moments when China–India connections were envisaged as a way to challenge existing imperialist paradigms by offering a new way of thinking about knowledge production.

Xu Dishan's Place in Modern Chinese Literature

The 1920s were seminal years in a long process that arguably began in the late Qing era (1644–1912): the creation of a new canon of modern Chinese literature (*xiandai wenxe* [現代文學]) in a fledgling modern vernacular (Hanan 2004; Huters 2005). Literature, especially fiction, spearheaded the sweeping project to reform Chinese culture during the first half of the twentieth century—an endeavour that encompassed government, education, religion, family structure, and the arts. The May Fourth Movement (1919–25)—the best-known manifestation of this era of social and cultural transformation—called for all social and cultural traditions, including religious structures, folk culture, and literature engaging with the supernatural and the mythical, to be abandoned, and instead advocated a scientific outlook, marital freedom, an end to traditional education, and literary realism focused on China-related themes (Chow 1960; Schwarcz 1986).

Within the larger context of 1920s literary production in China, Xu Dishan's short story, 'Goddess of Supreme Essence', merits particular attention for two reasons: the location of the plot in India; and the use of mythical, supernatural elements in modern fiction. The story's publication venue, *Fiction Monthly*, was an official organ of the prolific Literary Research Association (Wenxue yanjiu hui [文學研究會]; established in 1921), a group of writers and critics committed to the task that the majority of Chinese writers shouldered as early as the late nineteenth century: to reform what they perceived to be a creatively bankrupt national culture. Heralding literary realism and calling for socially engaged fiction, *Fiction Monthly* mainly published short stories featuring Chinese characters who dealt with some of the foremost concerns in 1920s China, such as poverty, pressures stemming from urbanization and industrialization, and the collapse of the traditional family household.[2]

Xu Dishan was a founding member of the Literary Research Association, but his short stories take place almost exclusively in Southeast and South Asia. Few of Xu Dishan's plots are situated in India, but many of them make use of Indian mythology, religions, and folklore.[3] Xu Dishan's exploration of Indian literature and culture developed in his early twenties. We know that by 1918, at the age of 25, he was learning Sanskrit. The same year, he introduced the works of the luminary Bengali poet Rabindranath Tagore to Zheng Zhenduo (鄭振鐸) (1898–1958), still known for the translations he made of Tagore's poetry. In 1921, along with Zheng Zhenduo, Xu Dishan formed Tagore Research Society (Taige'er yanjiu hui [泰戈爾 研究會]), which operated under the auspices of the Literary Research Association.[4] Xu Dishan travelled to India twice, in 1926 and in 1933. He spent time at Banaras Hindu University, where he sharpened his Sanskrit and researched Buddhist sources. Xu Dishan managed to meet Tagore, whom he admired, and who encouraged him to compose a Sanskrit–Chinese dictionary (Wang 1998: 200–1). Upon returning to China in 1927, Xu Dishan solidified his position as a scholar of Indian languages and literature, teaching courses on Sanskrit and Indian literature at Yenching University and Peking University, and publishing a slew of studies in which he attempted to map the historical impact of Indian literature and drama on the developments of these arts in China (Xu Dishan 1925, 1929, [1927] 1990). In 'Goddess of Supreme Essence', Xu Dishan mastered his fullest representation of India both as geographical location for the plot and as a tradition with which China has had religious and literary exchanges throughout history and into the modern era.

Transregional Metonymy

'Goddess of Supreme Essence' has received less scholarly attention than works such as 'Zhui wang lao zhu' (綴網勞蛛) ['The Web-Mending Spider'] (1922), 'Chun tao' (春桃) (1934), or *Yu Guan* (玉

官) ([1941] 2005), but it merits revisiting and resituating within Xu Dishan's oeuvre, as this story reveals a vision of a China–India connection, which was created through and reflected upon the medium of literature and its possibilities.

The goddess in the title of 'Goddess of Supreme Essence' is Lakṣmī, the Hindu Goddess of fortune, who also features in different incarnations in Buddhist texts and iconography.[5] 'Goddess of Supreme Essence' opens with the story of Lakṣmī's birth from the Ocean of Milk, and employs Hindu and Buddhist mythical elements to narrate the tale of a young Indian couple who gets lost in a jungle on the borders of Punjab and Kashmir.

In Chinese, *tihu* (醍醐)—which I translate here as 'supreme essence'—literally means ghee, the richest, most refined part of clarified butter. As such, tihu also serves as a well-recognized metonym for the most sublime form of Buddhist teachings. Beginning the title of the story with tihu immediately situates 'Goddess of Supreme Essence' in a China–India figurative domain, an arsenal of shared imagery that emerged through eons of economic, cultural, and religious exchange between the regions that constituted India and China. Tihu, standing for the sublime knowledge of Buddha's teachings attainable only by true believers, can be understood as a case of what I term 'transregional metonymy'. Here and throughout this chapter, I use 'metonymy' as a type of trope, part of what literary scholars term 'figurative language'. Abrams and Harpham's definition is helpful in clarifying what I mean here. They write (2009: 132), 'In metonymy, the literal term for one thing is applied to another with which it has become closely associated because of a recurrent relation in common experience. Thus, "the crown" and "the sceptre" can be used to stand for the king'. As an object standing for something else (often something beyond our immediate grasp, for example, the Bodhi tree that stands for the Buddha), metonyms are very common in religious imagery, both visual and textual.[6] The travels of Buddhist texts and images from India to China facilitated the circulation of many transregional metonyms as early as the first century CE.[7]

A prolific scholar of Buddhism and Daoism,[8] Xu Dishan's true passion was for folk culture. He devoured studies of folktales, myths, and rituals, and his particular interest in India kindled a lasting study of the ways in which popular cultures and religions animate the encounter between China and India. In his translation of Lal Behari Day's *Folk-Tales of Bengal* ([1883] 1912), Xu Dishan included a comprehensive introduction in which he related both myths and folktales to the field of folklore studies and emphasized the importance for Chinese writers of studying Indian folktales (Day 1929: 3).[9] The reason why it is important for Chinese writers to study Indian culture, he claimed, was because China–India networks for exchanging folktales had existed for centuries. Through these networks, Chinese writers could discern oral motifs and recurring themes shared by both cultures. Through India, in other words, Chinese authors could deepen their own understanding of Chinese culture. With its widely known Buddhist connotations, the metonym 'tihu' would very likely have been familiar to a Chinese reader of Xu Dishan's generation (and would probably resonate with many contemporary Chinese readers as well). Opening with this term, and situating his Chinese readers in the known territory of Buddhist tropes, Xu Dishan could then strategically draw his readers into a story that engages with a less familiar mythical tradition of Hinduism.

The story begins as follows:

> As the legend goes, Lakṣmī emerged from the Ocean of Milk [*tihu hai* (醍醐海)]. She is the mother of the God of love,[10] and the wife of Viṣṇu—preserver of the world. Whenever Lakṣmī is brought up in conversation with an Indian person, that person would praise her. In Brahmin[11] imagination [*xiangxiang* (想像)], Lakṣmī's incarnations are too numerous to count. People believe she is omnipresent and everlasting. And yet, being that I am not that young myself, how come I have never seen her image before? I raised this question to some Indian friends when we were travelling in the Indian Ocean. They laughed at my foolishness: having lived this long in the world of sentient beings,[12] how is it possible that I still cannot differentiate the nature of gods from that of men?[13] (Xu Dishan 1923: 13)

Reading the first paragraph of this story, one can already discern the presence of both Hindu and Buddhist elements. The first-person narrator, who is Chinese (as we learn from his distinguishing himself from 'an Indian person'), recapitulates the well-known Hindu myth of *Samudra Manthan* (The Churning of the Ocean).[14] According to the myth, devas (gods) and asuras (demons) churned the Ocean of Milk, one of seven oceans, in order to obtain *amrita*, the nectar of immortality. In the process of churning, several animals and deities emerged. Lakṣmī was one of them. By translating Ocean of Milk— Kṣīra Sāgara—as *tihu hai*, 'sea of ghee' or 'sea of supreme teaching of the Buddha', the Chinese narrator appropriates the Hindu myth and creates a new Hindu–Buddhist notion of a primordial sea of the purest essence. The narrator is fascinated by the survival of Lakṣmī in the popular imagination and by the praise she receives. In fact, the narrator is so enthralled by the power of this myth that he keeps looking for evidence of Lakṣmī's existence in this world because to him, as his friends tease him, the distinction between myth and reality is not clearly drawn.

Placing the Buddhist 'world of sentient being' alongside the Hindu version of Lakṣmī's birth, Xu Dishan charted a map for a China–India shared imagination. This hybrid figurative domain, epitomized in the conflation of Buddhist and Hindu traditions, invites further enquiry. For example, how is 'transregional metonymy' different from any type of synthesis? How is Xu Dishan's work different from his contemporaries such as Guo Moruo, whose celebrated poetry collection, *Shennü* (神女) [*Goddess*] ([1921] 1958), employed a rich tropology that drew upon mythological traditions from Greece to India?[15] That May Fourth writers explored literatures, religions and cultures from around the world during the 1920s is well known, and indeed these investigations have been often understood as syncretistic and eclectic (Shih 2001). Yet, Xu Dishan did not delineate a China–India figurative terrain indiscriminately. His use of Hindu–Buddhist imagery emerged from years of study in original languages, and he must have been aware of the coexistence of these two traditions in Southeast Asian art, architecture and religious worship (Hammond 2001; Lien 2014). Given the accelerated movement of migrants across Southeast Asia in the nineteenth and twentieth centuries, religious exchanges increased. Burma under British rule witnessed the arrival of many Indians and the erection of Hindu temples such as the Shri Kali temple in Yangon established in 1871. Xu Dishan spent 1913 to 1915 in Burma teaching Mandarin in a local school, and it is likely that he encountered the coexistence of Hindu and Buddhist religious practices in temples in Rangoon, such as the Shwedagon pagoda, which appears in his earliest publication, the short story 'Ming ming niao' (命命鳥) ['Birds of the Same Fate'] ([1921] 1996).

While Buddhist tropes were common in modern Chinese literature, Hindu ones were rare. Employing a holistic approach towards myths which privileged cross-cultural connections, Xu Dishan wrote on several occasions that myths, rituals, and superstitions are not remnants of a long-gone past, but continue to inform our lives in the present: how we interact in society, how we handle the challenges faced by current national and international pressures.[16] The Chinese narrator of 'Goddess of Supreme Essence' harbours this naïve desire—a naiveté that he is aware of—for a myth to become reality. Among his fellow travellers, who tease him for his attachment to stories of gods and deities, one friend, Chandra, obliges his request. Chandra means 'moon' in Sanskrit. A popular name in India, it was most likely chosen by Xu Dishan for its connection to the myth of Lakṣmī's birth—like the goddess of fortune, the moon also materialized through the churning of the ocean:

> Chandra [Zhun Tuoluo (準陀羅)] was on the same boat. He didn't say anything at that time, only gazed fixedly at the auspicious clouds taking shape on the horizon. That evening he instructed me to accompany him to the top of the helm, near the engine. We looked down at the white billows stirred by the propeller. Chandra said: 'Only a small fraction of this vast ocean resembles the colour of the Ocean of Milk'. His words prompted my curiosity to learn more about Lakṣmī. Chandra always was an avid storyteller, so I implored him to tell me a story about Lakṣmī. Gazing upon the boundless ocean, he happily exclaimed: 'That is my mother!' ... I stood up, surprised. 'You find it strange?' he said. 'Here, let me explain.' I sat down and listened to my friend, the self-proclaimed son of Lakṣmī, narrate the story of his parents. (Xu Dishan 1923: 13)

The aforementioned scene concludes the exposition of the main narrative—the story of Chandra's mother. It is a detailed vignette, vividly painted: the vast ocean, the sea foam connoting the Ocean of Milk, auspicious clouds forming on the deep horizon. Like tihu, 'auspicious clouds' (jixiang haiyun [吉祥海雲]) also serve as a transregional metonym. China has a long tradition of depicting colourful clouds in wall paintings and classical poetry. Buddhist and

Daoist cave paintings in China abound in representations of colourful, shape-changing clouds. In the Buddhist and Daoist traditions, clouds forming on the horizon such as those the Chinese narrator mentions in this vignette point to heavenly spheres—the abodes of gods and deities. Daoist myths depict devotees stepping on clouds on their way to be received in heaven, and deities are often depicted as riding on clouds on their way to visit the mundane world (Reiter 1991). Mocked by his friends for failing to distinguish between the world of gods and the world of men, the narrator nevertheless insists on creating a space that maintains this obliteration—a space in between the earthly and the heavenly. What enables the formation of this narrative space is the transregional metonym of auspicious clouds. Signposting the entrance to the heavenly realm, shape-shifting clouds carry powerful symbolic power in Hinduism (Zimmer 1972), Buddhism, and Daoism. Together with the milky foam, which 'resembles the colour of the Ocean of Milk', the stage is set for a new incarnation of Lakṣmī as the protagonist in the story Chandra is about to tell. It is thus apt that the territory where Chandra tells his story, beneath the transregional metonym of auspicious clouds—between the mundane and the earthy, the Chinese and the Indian—is the ocean.

Imperial Routes

There is a common narrative in Chinese literary studies that tells how modern thought travelled from Europe to Japan and then arrived in China. According to this consensus, realism—the privileged form of writing throughout the Republican era—was introduced to China through Japanese translations of Emile Zola, Balzac, Victor Hugo, Tolstoy, and other European authors. From these works, Chinese authors derived the basic ideals of European realism, which relied heavily upon the emerging doctrine of social Darwinism. Darwinism-based realism centred on protagonists from the lowest rungs of society, whose path towards untimely death is predetermined by their physical and mental weaknesses. Counter to the argument that knowledge of literary modernity travelled on a one-way route from Europe to Japan to China, Xu Dishan offers a new perspective on Chinese literary modernity by critiquing Darwinism-based realism through what has been termed his 'Nanyang Narrative' (Li and Sun 2015; Wan 2016; Yan 2013).

Reflecting, perhaps, shades of the author's biography—Xu Dishan was born in Taiwan on the verge of its colonization by Japan; his father refused to serve the new regime, and as a result the family spent his childhood as refugees, moving between Taiwan, Thailand, Singapore, Guangdong, and Fujian—the characters in Xu Dishan's short stories are constantly on the move between destinations in the South Sea.

One thing that has gone unnoticed is that the South Sea is often portrayed in Xu Dishan's fiction as a gateway, a path leading from India to China both literally and metaphorically. In another short story, 'Shangren fu' (商人婦) ['The Merchant's Wife'] (1921), he tells of a woman who is travelling in the South Sea between China and India. She was born and raised in a poor family in Fujian, in southern China. As a young married woman, her husband gambles away the family fortune and decides to try his luck earning money in Singapore. He promises to send for her. Ten years later, having received no word from him, the woman travels to Singapore on her own to find her husband. She finds him remarried and running a successful business. The husband, who is not too happy about this unexpected visit from his first wife, sells the woman to an Indian Muslim merchant of woolen textiles, who takes her with him from Singapore through the straits of Malacca and the Bay of Bengal to Madras (now Chennai), India. The merchant's wife, who is travelling from China to India, takes the British imperial route, through which soldiers, opium merchants, indentured, and missionaries moved between China and India from the mid-nineteenth until the mid-twentieth centuries, in numbers that were recently estimated by Sunil Amrith (2013) as more than 28 million.

Locating his stories in the colonial South Sea was Xu Dishan's way of staking a claim to the significance of a new, distinctly modern terrain in his fiction. His characters are not imperially sanctioned eminent monks journeying to India through the Silk Road to collect Buddhist *sutras*, but ordinary men and women, who traverse imperial routes as immigrants, labourers, refugees, or, in the case of 'Goddess of Supreme Essence', travellers.

Breaking Ground

It is no coincidence that the narrative of 'Goddess of Supreme Essence' takes place aboard a ship. Xu Dishan wrote this story in 1923 during a sea voyage when travelling from Shanghai to New York City to pursue a master's of arts degree at Columbia University's Department of Indo-Iranian Languages. Xu Dishan and fellow writers who travelled with him, such as Bing Xin and Xiong Foxi, composed short stories and poems and collected them in a short anthology they entitled *Haixiao* (海嘯) [*Tsunami*], published in *Fiction Monthly* later that year (Wang 1998). Mirroring the moment of its own creation, 'Goddess of Supreme Essence' also contains an instance of telling a story on board a ship. On deck, in the interim space of the Indian Ocean, a second narrative—the story Chandra tells—begins to unfold in India proper:

> My family home is on the border between Punjab and Kashmir. There is a lush jungle there. My mother was married at thirteen. My father was not even fourteen at the time. Every day she would venture into the forest with my father because she loved the towering trees, the uninhibited songs and dances of wild birds and insects. These truly were the heart of the jungle. Because my parents would often go into the woods, the wild animals all knew them very well. Parrots holding fruit in their mouths would drop their food upon seeing them to sound excited greetings. Peacocks would follow, spreading their feathers wide to welcome them. Deer and elephants would approach, leisurely chewing their food and letting my mother and father stroke them. Most of the paths in these woods were created by my parents. They loved opening up new paths. Whenever a certain path became well-trodden, they would venture to clear a new one, sweeping aside thistles and thorns of wisterias to break new grounds. Walking through these wild forests was, of course, extremely dangerous. My parents risked a great deal, and danger, indeed, chanced upon them. My father would hack his way forward with a big stick and mother would follow. They were making their way under a banyan tree heavy with aerial roots when a small stream appeared, flowing through the wild grass. (Xu Dishan 1923: 14)

The story that Chandra shares with the narrator straddles both truth and fiction. Told beneath auspicious clouds—a transregional metonym of a realm between the mundane and the divine—Chandra portrays a highly visual scene endowed with divine sensibilities: a young couple—we never learn their names and they are referred to as simply 'mother' and 'father'—surrounded by layers of flora and fauna, with wild animals drawn to them, eating from their hands. The fondness of the parents for breaking new ground in the jungle provides the story with a myth-like quality. Creating order out of chaos by carving a path and describing an unusual encounter with the forces of nature are scenarios depicted in many myths.

The banyan tree under which the couple walks contributes to the mythical atmosphere. The banyan is linked with longevity and immortality in several Indian traditions (Haberman 2013). In Hinduism, the banyan is a metonym for the Trimūrti, the three supreme principles: the roots stand for Brahmā the creator, the bark for Viṣṇu the preserver, and the branches for Śiva the destroyer. The banyan leaves are said to be the place where Kṛṣṇa resides. The banyan is also referenced in several Buddhist sources, most notably in the Pāli canon, where it appears in one of the most important episodes in the Buddha's life. A shepherdess named Sujātā asks the spirit of a banyan tree (yakṣa) for a son. When she finally gives birth to a boy, she resolves to make an offering of rice milk to the spirit. On the day of the offering, Bodhisattva Siddhārthā is sitting under the Banyan tree, emaciated and practicing austerities to no avail. Sujātā offers him the rice milk she has prepared, and the strength he regains from the milk enables him to focus and achieve enlightenment. Sujātā's character and the notion of the divinely nourishing milk will appear once again in 'Goddess of Supreme Essence'. We will return to it later.

As Chandra's story continues, the young couple sits down by the stream and enjoys a welcome respite. After a while, however, the restless father wanders off and, when he fails to return, the mother's suspicions arise. From that moment on, the story moves exclusively to the mother's point of view:

> Dusk fell, welcomed by the songs and howls of birds and animals. Hastily, mother waded through the stream in search of father. She looked through broken wisteria branches, thick muddles of grass and winding trees. It darkens much faster in the thick greenery. Just a few fireflies and the rays of the evening sunlight through the leaves were lighting the way in the forest for this woman. Though mother was frail,

she was courageous. As soon as she spotted father lying on the ground bleeding, she rushed over there. She saw that blood was still pouring from father's leg, and so she took off her outerwear and used it to bandage his leg. The bleeding stopped but father was, by then, standing outside the doors of the netherworld. (Xu Dishan 1923: 14)

Chandra's mother decides to search for help. She picks up Chandra's father and puts him on her back, but quickly realizes that she must continue on her own, as her strength will not carry both of them very far. She covers the father with branches and leaves to keep him warm, and continues walking until she finds a nearby village. Chandra's mother knocks on doors to no avail. She locates three men sitting around playing cards and begs for their help, but no one is willing to help her. Though the mother exerts all her remaining energy to use 'the words a good laywoman would use' to explain her situation, the men remain steadfast in their refusal to help (Xu Dishan 1923: 15). 'A good laywoman' (shannü [善女]) is a Buddhist designation for laywomen in the audience for Buddhists sermons, who are able to grasp Buddhist teachings fully as the result of the good deeds they carried out in their former existences. Calling Chandra's mother a good laywoman connotes once again the story of the shepherdess Sujātā—an archetypal good laywoman. The mother is at once a real person—her son is narrating her real historical past—and a mythical figure connected to the shepherdess Sujātā and to generations of female believers. This amalgam of the real and the fictional in Xu Dishan's stories has often been studied under the rubrics of 'exotic literature' or a 'literature with religious colour' (zongjiao secai [宗教色彩]) (Chen 1984; Yang 1997). But if we situate this story within Xu Dishan's focus on Indian myths and folktales, as well as within the larger picture of the approach taken by Republican Chinese writers to mythology, we will arrive at a much more nuanced understanding of 'Goddess of Supreme Essence'.

Myth-Making in Modern Chinese Literature

The 1920s in China witnessed profound engagement with mythologies and the relationship between myth and literature. Chinese intellectual circles comprising historians, literary critics, poets, and fiction writers were engrossed in the myths of different cultures, as well as in research into and the construction of a Chinese mythology. As early as the first years of the twentieth century, Chinese intellectuals urged their peers to study mythology (*Shenhua xue* [神話學]). Ancient myths were believed to be the first accounts of human storytelling, a proto-literature. For this reason, Chinese writers perceived myths to be a means for understanding the origins of human creativity. Only by tapping into the very essence of creativity, they believed, could China launch a new vernacular literature that would turn its back on the stifling, dogmatic classical language and literature. From its inception, creating a Chinese mythology was part of the project of building a new national culture. It is no coincidence that in the same year—1902—the renowned political and cultural reformer Liang Qichao wrote his call to write new fiction, which famously began: 'If one intends to renovate the people of a nation, one must first renovate its fiction', he also revisited the ancient myths of sage kings (*sheng wang* [聖王]) and Chinese progenitors in an attempt to rewrite a history of the Chinese nation from its origins to modernity (Liang Qiacho 1902a).[17]

Literary paragons such as Lu Xun (魯迅) (1881–1936), Zhou Zuoren (周作人) (1885–1967), Mao Dun (茅盾) (1896–1981), and Guo Moruo (郭沫若) (1892–1978) researched Greek, Nordic, and Chinese myths, and incorporated mythical themes and tropes into their literature. Mao Dun was engrossed in studying Chinese myths in the 1920s,[18] as was Zhou Zuoren, who translated Jane Harrison's *Our Debt to Greece and Rome* (1924) in the late 1920s (Daruvala 2000). Lu Xun's *Zhongguo xiaoshuo shilüe* (中國小說史略) [*A Brief History of Chinese Fiction*], originally published in 1926 as a volume of lectures he gave at Peking University, devoted its second chapter to discussing myths as the origin of fiction. In 1935, Lu Xun published perhaps the most celebrated mythopoeic work of Republican China, *Gushi xin bian* (故事新編) [*Old Tales Retold*], a collection of short stories he wrote between 1922 and the early 1930s, which retell and often parody Chinese myths, from the creation of man to the deluge and the early philosopher sages.

Incorporating myths into modern literature was certainly not a uniquely Chinese phenomenon. Indeed, preoccupations with mythical heroes and cosmogonies in modern literature were popular from the nineteenth century until the post–World War II era, from Europe to North America to Asia. Much has been written on why the modern era occasioned such a dramatic return to the mythological past.[19] Studies of the engagement of Chinese writers with mythology during the Republican era in both literary works and literary criticism have emphasized the evolutionary approach that informed their undertakings. In other words, the Republican Chinese construction of a new mythology and the employment of myths in literary works have been understood as an offshoot of European cultural anthropology, folklore studies, and comparative religion—all new disciplines at the time that emerged during the nineteenth century as explorations of the origin of man and the development of human societies from savagery to primitivism to civilization (Daruvala 2000; Jones 2011: 156–60).

This evolutionary view of human society and culture, inspired by the almost coterminous development of life sciences and social Darwinism, acquired much popularity in Asia towards the end of the nineteenth century. Foundational texts which shaped cultural anthropology, comparative religion, and folklore studies in Europe, such as *Anthropology: An Introduction to the Study of Man and Civilization* (1881) by Edward Tylor (1832–1917) and *The Golden Bough: A Study in Magic and Religion* (1890) by James Frazer (1854–1941), were first introduced to Chinese readers through Japanese translations. These works inspired several May Fourth writers, including Zhou Zuoren (周作人) (1885–1967), whose encounter with Andrew Lang's *Custom and Myth* (2016) propelled him to explore the notion of the 'savage mind' as the source of oral myths, which in turn inspired literature and art in the age of civility (Daruvala 2000: 86).[20] From Liang Qichao to Lu Xun, numerous Chinese authors and historians attempted to study myths in order to reach the so-called 'primordial sources' of what would become their national culture. Chinese writers were convinced that the analytic tools employed by mythographers and anthropologists in the study of ancient Greece and Rome would prove essential not only in separating 'myth' from 'history' for a better understanding of their past, but also in defining the limits and boundaries of 'literature', which was to shoulder the task of transforming the national future (McNeal 2012).

A scholar of comparative religion and folklore studies, Xu Dishan was well versed in such scholarship. He read some of these works with his students at Yenching University in courses such as 'Advanced Social Anthropology', 'Primitive Societies', and 'Problems of Religion'.[21] However, unlike several of his peers, such as Zhou Zuoren and Mao Dun, Xu Dishan did not turn to Greek or Nordic mythologies to explore myth-making in his fiction, nor did he understand the development of human societies as a Darwinian evolution from myth to science. Through his knowledge of Indian cultures and traditions, Xu Dishan defined the human engagement with the supernatural not as a stage to evolve away from, but as something which is as relevant in modernity as it was in antiquity. For this reason, he did not adapt myths into modern fiction, as Lu Xun did in the *Old Stories Retold* ([1935] 1957) mentioned earlier. Instead of using fiction to retell myth, Xu Dishan allowed mythical elements to rupture the veneer of his fiction. In 'Goddess of Supreme Essence', mythological figures and elements constantly undermine the reader's 'suspension of disbelief'. From the Ocean of Milk to the good laywoman and the banyan tree, the presence of numinous tropes laces the narrative with the supernatural. This process reaches a climax towards the end of the story, as Chandra's mother exhausts all attempts to reach help in the village.

The Supreme Essence

After Chandra's mother is repeatedly refused help, she wanders aimlessly about, scared and confused. At this moment, the good laywoman receives help from a surprising source:

> She walked by a vegetable garden, where she saw an empty stool. Helpless and out of her wits, she sat down. Shortly afterwards, a seven- or eight-year-old boy appeared. He stared at her as if in astonishment. Mother knew he was the landlord's son, and so she explained her situation to him with great respect. The little boy was much kinder than the men she had met earlier. He told mother: 'I will sneak out and come with you. We also have a white cow in the shed: we milk it every day. Now I will lead it along. Wait a little while, and I will instruct it to carry you, because you are so tired'. And so he led the cow with my mother on it, and the three of them went into the woods again under the moonlight. (Xu Dishan 1923: 16)

The encounter with the small child echoes several myths from both Hindu and Buddhist traditions. I mentioned earlier that the Samudra Manthan, the churning of the Ocean of Milk to create the elixir of immortality, released many things into the world. Along with Lakṣmī, other deities and supernatural animals, including a divine white cow known as Kāmadhuk, emerged. This cow is considered the mother of all cows, and the ghee made from her milk is the supreme food offered to the gods in sacrifices. When the churning was done, a lethal poison burst fuming from the ocean, which turned the milk into salt water. Śiva swallowed the poison to protect the universe. From then on, only cows possessed the divine ability to produce milk (Buck 2000).

In addition to alluding to Samudra Manthan, Xu Dishan is also referencing a famous parable from the *Lotus Sutra*, one of the most highly venerated sutras in Chinese Mahayana Buddhism.[22] In a chapter titled 'Simile and Parable' (Watson 2002), a story often referred to as 'the parable of the burning house' mentions a white ox. In the parable, a wealthy man's house catches fire, and he must make his sons leave the house to get to safety. But the sons are busy playing their games and refuse to come out. The man is forced to resort to 'expedient means' to convince them to leave the burning house. He tells them that three carts loaded with toys and jewellery are waiting for them outside: a deer cart, a goat cart, and a white ox cart. His sons excitedly heed his request and leave the burning house. Outside, they find three decorated carts brimming with playthings and driven by white oxen. The moral of the story is this: The burning house is a metonym for 'the world of sentient beings'—the deluded world of desires and emotion. The three carts (*san che* [三車]) that the father promises to give his sons represent three practices of Buddhist learning in the path towards enlightenment: the goat cart represents the voice-hearer (*śrāvaka* [聲聞]), the deer cart represents the self-enlightened Pratyekabuddha (緣覺), and the ox cart represents the Bodhisattva (菩薩)—a being on its way to achieving enlightenment and Buddhahood. One of the accepted interpretations of this parable is that, while all vehicles are ways of achieving the same enlightenment, the compassionate Buddha will return the practitioners to the true single Buddha vehicle: the white ox.[23]

The 'Goddess of Supreme Essence' story thus presents an interesting inversion of the *Lotus Sutra*: here the child saves the man and not vice versa. Like the white ox that represents the road to enlightenment, the white cow harbours the supreme essence—divine milk which will save the dying man. When the child and the mother reach the place where the mother left Chandra's father, she cannot find him. But the young child, who miraculously appeared from darkness with his white cow, spots the father lying on the ground and points to him:

He pointed to a tree branch on top of which a man was sitting and asked: 'Is this him?' Mother hurried to him, overjoyed: 'When did you wake up? How come you didn't say anything when you saw us approaching?' Father just said: 'I'm so thirsty.' 'I will milk the cow for him,' the boy said and rushed over. He plucked a shiny leaf, filled it with milk he had taken from the cow, and gave it to father. Father slowly regained his vitality. 'An elephant nudged me,' he told mother. 'When I woke up I didn't see you, only saw the elephant chewing leaves. Where did these leaves come from? It is you who piled them here last night. I remember when I was hurt, but it wasn't here.' Mother told him what transpired and asked him how he got hurt in the first place. Father said he got a venomous sting and didn't want to scare her, so he decided to treat himself, even though the more blood he drew, the more kept pouring out. Who knew that the more he would try treating the bleeding the more blood he would lose? When he woke up, he knew it was mother who stopped the blood. Father knew the cow belonged to the little boy and thanked him and mother profusely: 'If you hadn't brought the cow, I wouldn't have made it.' Mother answered wholeheartedly: 'Stream water would have sufficed. If I had known you would wake up, I wouldn't have left you. I'm so sorry.' 'Who among us can tell the future? The milk that you gave me is better than the heavenly supreme essence [*tianshang tihu* (天上醍醐)]. Luckily, you found it for me!' (Xu Dishan 1923: 16)

The transregional metonym of tihu—the first ghee that was offered in sacrifice to the Hindu gods and the supreme essence of Buddhist teaching—materializes in this scene: The milk given to the father echoes offerings to the gods, as well as the rice milk that the shepherdess Sujātā offered the Buddha, saving his life. After the rice milk resuscitates the emaciated Buddha, he achieves enlightenment and Sujātā becomes a follower of the Buddha's teachings, also known as a 'stream-enterer' (*srota-āpanna* or *ruliu* [入流]). Similar to Sujātā's transformation, Chandra's mother, once her husband is rescued, becomes 'a Lakṣmī:

> Father praised mother's loyalty and said she is even better than Lakṣmī who emerged from the Ocean of Milk. Mother appreciated father's words, especially after the humiliation she endured the night before. Elated, she concurred: 'Just call me Lakṣmī then!' Since then, father always called her Lakṣmī. (Xu Dishan 1923: 17)

The mother's 'rebirth' as Lakṣmī is the final line of the story—this is how it ends. Chandra both did and did not deliver on his original promise: to tell the story of Lakṣmī, whom he describes earlier as his mother. On the one hand, the mother is fondly called Lakṣmī by her family, and in that sense Chandra did tell the narrator a story about Lakṣmī. On the other hand, it almost goes without saying that this was not the story the narrator expected to hear. But, while the narrator did not listen to a story about the goddess emerging from the Ocean of Milk, by telling the story of his mother—a narrative that spans truth and fiction, myth and reality—Chandra is teaching the narrator a valuable lesson. Lakṣmī, the narrator learns, is not just the goddess of the Ocean of Milk. She is also a shepherdess called Sujātā, a frightened young woman seeking help, and a good lay-woman. In Chandra's story, 'Lakṣmī' becomes a metonym as well, standing for a myriad of meanings and layers of myths. Through the figure of Lakṣmī, Xu Dishan encourages his readers to think about myths broadly, in terms of time and space. In 'Goddess of Supreme Essence', myths are not limited to an ancient past, but accumulate layer upon layer of meaning to shape different 'Lakṣmīs'. In a similar vein, myths do not belong to one tradition or one national culture, but are constantly recreated in the process of transcultural exchange. Replete with transregional metonyms, and told to a Chinese listener by an Indian storyteller, 'Goddess of Supreme Essence' unfolds in the South Sea between China and India, enabling the creation of a narrative tapestry of cross-cultural allusions which invites readers to explore the possibility of a China–India mythology.

***

While many other authors of the Republican era turned to myths to rediscover a long-buried source of passionate creativity, Xu Dishan believed that myths do not just belong to a stage of our past but are an element of human life at every point in history. Adopting a cyclical view of history—an understanding which owes much to his training in Buddhist and Daoist texts—Xu Dishan challenged the evolutionary logic which dominated many of China's literary circles. Instead of comparing Chinese gods to Greek or Roman deities, he set out a different methodology, one that sought not to compare or contrast, but to reveal continuities, connections, and networks. In India, Xu Dishan found a shared imagination of a mythical past, present, and future. Using transregional metonyms formed through a history of shared tropes, images, and religious texts was his way of activating this imagination in his texts. In this sense, his engagement with India in his short fiction should be understood not only as broadening the geographical boundaries of May Fourth themes and aesthetics beyond China, but also as an opening up of new vistas of figurative thinking by envisaging not a strictly Chinese, but a transregional literary horizon that opens up the past to understand the present and that uses myth to approach reality.

Notes

1. Some more familiar examples include stories such as 'Ming ming niao' (命命鳥) ['Birds of the Same Fate'] ([1921] 1996), which takes place in Burma; 'Shangren fu' (商人婦) ['The Merchant's Wife'] (1921), which takes place in Chennai, Singapore, Fujian, and the Indian Ocean world in general; and 'Zhui wang lao zhu' (綴網勞蛛) ['The Web-Mending Spider'] (1922), which sees its protagonist leaving for Malaysia, as does the novella, *Yu Guan* (玉官) ([1941] 2005), in which the protagonist embarks on a ship en route to Borneo at the end of the story.

2. Variations of this argument have characterized scholarly works on modern Chinese literature since the 1970s. In the past few years, scholars have begun to question the paradigm of China-centred literature both in the Republican era and after 1949 (see Bernards 2015; Volland 2017). This essay joins these efforts in redrawing the map of cultural exchange during the formative period of modern Chinese literature.

3. Most notably in 'The Merchant's Wife', where the story also takes place in India, as well as in the short story 'Birds of The Same Fate' and the collection *Kongshan lingyu* (空山靈雨) [*Timely Rain in the Empty Mountain*] ([1925] 2008), which contain many references to Sanskrit sources. For a comprehensive list of works by Xu Dishan where India features thematically or where Indian languages and sources feature as intertexts, see Xue (2010).

4. On Tagore's visit to China and his reception in Chinese literary circles, see Gvili (2018).

5. According to Charles Muller's *Digital Dictionary of Buddhism* (1995), Mahāśrī is identified with Lakṣmī. She is the goddess of fortune and beauty who sprang from the ocean with a lotus in her hand. For this reason she is also called Padmā (lotus).

6. According to Robert DeCaroli (2015: 26), metonyms were replete in early Buddhist representations. The earliest stone monasteries, for example, tend to eschew direct representations of Buddha and replace them by an image of the Bodhi tree, the parasol, or the empty throne. These images, which lack a direct representation of the Buddha, have been classed by scholars as belonging to an aniconic phase.

7. While scholars generally concur that Buddhism was first introduced in China through the mediation of Indo-Scythian and Parthian merchants and was not directly transmitted from India, the first Chinese encounter with Buddhism involved the spread not of doctrine but of tropes, in the form of cave paintings, roadside storytellers and images (Sen 2012). According to Victor Mair, Buddhism also deeply informed narrational strategies of Chinese fiction as early as the Six Dynasties period (2013).

8. Wang Sheng provides a detailed list of Xu Dishan's studies of Buddhism and Daoism, most of which were conducted in the late 1920s to mid-1930s. See Wang Sheng (1998: 200–6).

9. Alongside *Folk-Tales of Bengal*, which was originally composed in English by Lal Behari Day and emerged as a global bestseller, Xu Dishan translated two more short volumes of Indian myths from English. These collections were compiled by Francis William Bain ([1898] 1955, [1903] 1956), and were most likely composed by him rather than retold to him in India, as he has claimed.

10. According to the Puranic literature, Kāma, the God of love, was incarnated in Pradyumna, who was the son of lord Krishna and Rukmini—an incarnation of Lakṣmī.

11. Xu Dishan used Brahmin and Hindu interchangeably.

12. *You qing shi jian* [有情世間]. The meaning is of this world: the world of all beings subjected to transformation by the Buddha.

13. Translations are all mine unless otherwise stated.

14. The story appears in several Hindu sources such as the *Bhāgavata Purāṇa*, the *Mahābhārata*, and the *Viṣṇu Purāṇa*.

15. On Guo Moruo's employment of India-related themes and tropes in his writings, see Rawat (2006).

16. See the introduction to Day (1929) as well the introduction to Xu Dishan (1941).

17. The essays on ancient myths and sage kings were published in Liang Qiacho (1900, 1902b). On Liang Qichao's establishment of a new approach to history and his employment of myths for this purpose, see Zarrow (2003).

18. See, for example, Mao Dun ([1929] 1989). In this essay, Mao Dun discusses the evolutionary processes of myths. In his depiction, myths are transferred from generation to generation, and in this process they are refined and improved (*gaixiu* [修改]). He juxtaposes and compares, as case studies, the character of the Queen Mother of the West (Xi wang mu [西王母]) and of Aphrodite, as well as others.

19. Andrew Von Hendy provides an astute exploration of the different approaches that came to 'invent' myths in modernity, from romantic poetry to empirical mythography (2002).

20. Mao Dun conducted many such studies. In *Yanhua yu jieshi* (演化与解释) [*Evolution and Interpretation*] ([1929] 1989), to give just one example, Mao Dun discusses the evolutionary processes of myths. In his depiction, myths are transferred from generation to generation, being refined and improved (*xiugai* [修改]) in the process. This evolutionary methodology is accompanied by a comparative approach that compares Chinese and Greek mythologies. One case study compares the character of the Queen Mother of the West and of Aphrodite. Like Lu Xun, Mao Dun adapted biblical stories for modern fiction. See, for example, Mao Dun ([1941] 1985: 371–9, [1942] 1985: 315–30).

21. Descriptions of the courses Xu Dishan taught can be found in the Yenching Archives, Beijing, China, Files Yj 1929022, Yj 1930023, Yj 1931022.

22. I am grateful to Yang Zhaohua at the Department of Religion at Columbia University for his gracious help in pointing out the connection with the *Lotus Sutra* and the parable of Sujātā here, and for his generosity in discussing other Buddhist references in this story.

23. See *san che* (三車) (the three vehicles) in Charles Muller's *Digital Dictionary of Buddhism* (1995).

References

Archival Material

Yenching Archives, Beijing, China

File Nos Yj 1929022, Yj 1930023, Yj 1931022.

Other Sources

Abrams, M.H. and Geoffrey Falt Harpham. 2009. *A Glossary of Literary Terms*. Boston: Wadsworth Cengage Learning.

Amrith, Sunil S. 2013. *Crossing the Bay of Bengal: The Furies of Nature and the Fortunes of Migrants*. Cambridge MA: Harvard University Press.

Bain, Francis William. [1898] 1955. 'Digit of the Moon' ('Ershi ye wen' [二十夜問]). Translated by Xu Dishan. Beijing: Zuojia chubanshe.

———. [1903] 1956. 'The Descent of the Sun' ('Taiyang de xiajiang' [太陽的下降]). Translated by Xu Dishan. Beijing: Zuojia chubanshe.

Bernards, Brian. 2015. *Writing the South Seas: Imagining the Nanyang in Chinese and Southeast Asian Postcolonial Literature*. London: University of Washington Press.

Buck, William. 2000. *Mahabharata*. London: University of California Press.

Chen Fuchuan (陳福川). 2016. 'Xu Dishan wenxue chuangzuo de Fojiao yiyun' (許地山文學創作的佛教意蘊) ['Buddhist Connotations in the Works of Xu Dishan']. *Can hua (xia)* (參花[下]) 11: 123–6.

Chow, Tse-Tsung. 1960. *The May Fourth Movement: Intellectual Revolution in Modern China*. Cambridge MA: Harvard East Asian Series.

Daruvala, Susan. 2000. *Zhou Zuoren and an Alternative Chinese Response to Modernity*. Cambridge, MA: Distributed by Harvard University Press.

Day, Lal Behari, Rev. [1833] 1912. *Folk-Tales of Bengal*. London: MacMillan.

———. 1929. *Mengjiala minjian gushi* (孟加拉民間故事) [*Folk-Tales of Bengal*]. Translated by Xu Dishan, p. 3. Shangahi: Shangwu yinshuguan.

DeCaroli, Robert. 2015. *Image Problems: The Origin and Development of the Buddha's Image in Early South Asia*. Seattle: University of Washington Press.

Frazer, James. 1993. *The Golden Bough: A Study of Magic and Religion*. Hertfordshire: Wordsworth Reference.

Guo Moruo (郭沫若). [1921] 1958. *Shengnü* (聖女) [*Goddess*]. Renmin wenxue chubanshe.

Gvili, Gal. 2018. 'Pan-Asian Poetics: Tagore and the Interpersonal in May Fourth New Poetry'. *The Journal of Asian Studies* 27 (1): 181–204.

Haberman, David L. 2013. *People Trees: Worship of Trees in Northern India*. New York: Oxford University Press.

Hammond, Kenneth J. 2001. 'Beijing's Zhihua Monastery: History and Restoration in China's Capital'. In Maria Smith Weidner (ed.), *Cultural Interactions in Later Chinese Buddhism*, pp. 189–208. Honolulu: University of Hawaii Press.

Hanan, Patrick. 2004. *Chinese Fiction of the Nineteenth and Early Twentieth Centuries: Essays by Patrick Hanan*. New York: Columbia University Press.

Harrison, Jane. 1924. *Our Debt to Greece and Rome: Mythology*. London: George Harrap and Co. Ltd.

Huters, Theodore. 2005. *Bringing the World Home: Appropriating the West in Late Qing and Early Republican China*. Honolulu: University of Hawaii Press.

Jones, Andrew F. 2011. *Developmental Fairy Tales : Evolutionary Thinking and Modern Chinese Culture*. Cambridge, MA: Harvard University Press.

Lang, Andrew. 2016. *Custom and Myth*. CreateSpace Independent Publishing Platform.

Liang Qiacho. 1900. 'Zhongguo shi xulun' (中國史敘論) ['Introduction to Chinese History']. *Qingyi bao* 90: 1–5.

———. 1902a. 'Lun xiaoshuo yu qunzhi zhi guanxi' (論小說與群治之關係) ['On the Relationship between Fiction and the Government of the People']. *Xin Xiaoshuo* 1 (1): 24–31.

———. 1902b. 'Xin shixue' (新史學) ['New Historiography']. *Xinmin congbao* 1: 52–61

Lien, Le Thi. 2014. 'Hindu-Buddhist Sculpture in Southern Vietnam: Evolution of Icons and Styles to the Eighth Century'. In John Guy (ed.), *Lost Kingdoms: Hindu-Buddhist Sculpture of Early Southeast Asia*, pp. 118–121. New York: The Metropolitan Museum of Art.

Li Meng (李朦) and Sun Lianghao (孫良好). 2015. 'Xu Dishan bi xia de Nanyang xingxiang yi "*Ming ming niao*" "*Zhuiwang laozhu*" wei zhongxin' (許地山筆下的南洋形象——以命命鳥綴網勞蛛為中心) ['The Nanyang Imagery in the Works of Xu Dishan: Focusing on *Birds of the Same Fate* and *The Web Mending Spider*']. *Wenzhou daxue xuebao* (shehui kexue ban) (溫州大學學報 [社會科學版]) 28 (5): 14–19.

Lu Xun (魯迅). [1935] 1957. *Gushi xinbian* (故事新編) [*Old Stories Retold*]. Xianggang: Shenghuo, dushu, xin zhi sanlian shudian.

———. [1926] 2006. *Zhongguo xiaoshuo shilüe* (中國小說史略) [*A Brief History of Chinese Fiction*]. Shanghai: Shanghai guji chubanshe.

Mair, Victor. 2013. 'Transformation as Imagination in Medieval Popular Buddhist Literature'. In John Kieschnick and Meir Shahar (eds), *India in the Chinese Imagination: Myth Religion and Thought*, pp.13–20. Philadelphia: University of Pennsylvania Press.

Mao Dun. [1941] 1985. 'Sansun de fuchou' (參孫的復仇) ['Samson's Revenge']. In *Mao Dun quanji* (茅盾全集), Volume 9, pp. 371–9. Beijing: Renmin wenxue.

———. [1942] 985. 'Yesu zhi si' (耶穌之死) ['The Death of Jesus']. In *Mao Dun quanji* (茅盾全集), Volume 9, pp. 315–30. Beijing: Renmin wenxue.

———. [1929] 1989. 'Yanhua yu jieshi' (演化與解釋) ['Evolution and Interpretation']. In *Mao Dun quanji* (茅盾全集), Volume 28, pp. 207–18. Beijing: Ren min wen xue.

McNeal, Robin. 2012. 'Constructing Myth in Modern China'. *Journal of Asian Studies* 71 (3): 679–704.

Muller, Charles (ed.). 1995. *Digital Dictionary of Buddhism*. Available at http://www.buddhism-dict.net.ezproxy.cul.columbia.edu/ddb/; last accessed 23 June 2017.

Rawat, Devendra Singh. 2006. 'Guo Moruo and India'. In P.A George (ed.), *East Asian Literatures: Japanese, Chinese and Korean: An Interface with India*, pp. 200–7. New Delhi: Northern Book Centre.

Reiter, Florian C. 1991. '"Auspicious Clouds": An Inspiring Phenomenon of Common Interest in Traditional China'. *Zeitschrift der Deutschen Morgenländischen Gesellschaft* 141 (1): 114–30.

Schwarcz, Vera. 1986. *The Chinese Enlightenment: Intellectual and the Legacy of the May Fourth Movement of 1919*. Berkeley: University of California Press.

Sen, Tansen. 2012. 'The Spread of Buddhism to China: A Re-examination of the Buddhist Interactions between Ancient India and China'. *China Report* 48 (1–2): 11–27.

Shih, Shu Mei. 2001. *Writing Modernism in Semicolonial China, 1917–1937*. Berkeley: University of California Press.

Volland, Nicolai. 2017. *Socialist Cosmopolitanism: The Chinese Literary Universe 1945–1965*. New York: Columbia University Press.

Von Hendy, Andrew. 2002. *The Modern Construction of Myth*. Bloomington, IN: Indiana University Press.

Wan Jie (萬杰). 2016. 'Shenfen rentong yu guishugan: jiedu Xudishan Nanyang beijing xiaoshuo de ling yige shijiao' (身份認同與歸屬感——解讀許地山南洋背景小說的另一個視角) ['Identity Affirmation and a Sense of Belonging: Another View of the Interpretation of Xu Dishan's Nanyang Fiction']. *Mingzuo xinshang* (名作欣賞) 36: 38–40.

Wang Sheng (王盛). 1998. *Luohuasheng xintan* (落花生新談) [*New Research on Luohuasheng*]. Nanjing: Nanjing daxue chubanshe.

Watson, Burton. 2002. *The Essential Lotus: Selections from the Lotus Sutra*. New York: Columbia University Press.

Xu Dishan (許地山). 1921. 'Shangren fu' (商人婦) ['The Merchant's Wife']. In *Xu Dishan lingyi xiaoshuo* (許地山靈異小說), pp. 22–40. Shanghai: Shanghai wenyi chubanshe.

———. 1922. 'Zhui wang lao zhu' (綴網勞蛛) ['The Web-Mending Spider'].
In *Xu Dishan lingyi xiaoshuo* (許地山靈異小說), pp. 56–78. Shanghai:
Shanghai wenyi chubanshe.

———. 1923. 'Tihu tiannü' (醍醐天女) ['Goddess of Supreme Essence'].
Fiction Monthly (*Xiaoshuo yuebao* [小說月報]) 14: 13–17.

———. 1925. 'Zhongguo wenxue suo shou de Yindu Yilan wenxue de yingx-
iang' (中國文學所受的印度義蘭文學的影響) ['On the Impact of Indian
and Persian Literature on Chinese Literature']. *Fiction Monthly* (*Xiaoshuo
yuebao* [小說月報]) 16 (7).

———. 1929. 'Jin sanbai nian lai Yindu wenxue gaiguan' (近三百年來印
度文學概觀) ['A General Survey of Indian Literature of the Last Three
Hundred Years']. *Tianjin yi shi bao* (天津益世報) (12, 13, 16, 17, 18, 19, 20,
23 December).

———. 1934. 'Chun Tao' (春桃). In *Xu Dishan lingyi xiaoshuo* (許地山靈異小
說), pp. 151–75. Shanghai: Shanghai wenyi chubanshe.

———. 1941. *Fuji mixin de yanjiu* (扶乩迷信的研究) [*A Study of the Superstition
of Spirit Writing*]. Taipei: Commercial Press.

———. [1927] 1990. 'Fanju tili ji qi aai Hanju shang de diandian didi' (梵
劇體例及其在漢劇上的點點滴滴) ['The Stylistic Rules of Sanskrit Drama
and Their Gradual Sipping into Chinese Drama]. In Li Xiaobing, Huang
Tianji, Yuan Hexiang, and Xia Xieshi (eds), *Zhongguo wenxue yanjiu* (中國
文學研究) [*The Origins of Chinese Drama*], pp. 86–118. Shanghai: Shangwu
yinshuguan.

———. [1921] 1996. 'Ming ming niao' (命命鳥) ['Birds of the Same Fate'].
In *Xu Dishan lingyi xiaoshuo* (許地山靈異小說), pp. 1–21. Shanghai:
Shanghai wenyi chubanshe.

———. [1941] 2005. *Yu Guan* (玉官). Beijing: Jinghua chubanshe.

———. [1925] 2008. 'Kong shan ling yu' (空山靈雨) ['Timely Rain in the
Empty Mountain']. In *Kongshan lingyu: Xu Dishan suibi* (空山靈雨：許
地山隨筆) [*Timely Rain in the Empty Mountain—Informal Essays of Xu
Dishan*]. Beijing: Beijing daxue chubanshe.

Xue Keqiao (薛克翹). 2010. 'Xu Dishan, Zheng Zhenduo and Ji Xianlin
yu Yindu minjian wenxue' (許地山鄭振鐸和季羨林與印度民間文學)
['Xu Dishan, Zheng Zhenduo, ji Xianlin and Indian Folk Literature'].
Heilongjiang shehui kexue (黑龍江社會科學) 1: 110–113.

Yan Min (颜敏). 2013. 'Yiyu huayu de chongxin jiangou: Xu Dishan de
Nanyang xushi ji qi yiyi' (異語話語的重新建構：許地山的 南洋敘事及
其意義) ['Constructing Anew a Discourse on Foreign Languages: Xu
Dishan's Nanyang Narrative and Its Meaning']. *Zhongguo bijiao wenxue*
(中國比較文學) 3: 96–107.

Yang Jianlong (楊劍龍). 1997. *Kuangye de husheng: Zhongguo xiandai zuojia yu jidujiao wenhua* (曠野的呼聲：中國現代作家與基督教文化) [*A Cry in the Wilderness: Modern Chinese Writers and Christian Culture*]. Shanghai: Shanghai jiaoyu chubanshe.

Zarrow, Peter. 2003. 'Old Myth into New History: The Building Blocks of Liang Qichao's "New History"'. *Historiography East and West* 1 (2): 204–41. doi:10.1163/157018603774004502.

Zimmer, Heinrich Robert. 1972. *Myths and Symbols in Indian Art and Civilization*. Princeton: Princeton University Press.

3

Rethinking Pan-Asianism through Zhang Taiyan

India as Method

Viren Murthy

Zhang Taiyan (章太炎) (1869–1936) is perhaps most famous for his role as a radical anti-Manchu propagandist, as well as being a major proponent of national learning (*guoxue* [國學]). However, he was many things to different readers: a scholar, a revolutionary, a Buddhist, and a pan-Asianist. Recently, scholars have turned to his pan-Asianist writings and his Buddhist critique of capitalist modernity.[1] Continuing the above trend, I bring India and China together through Zhang Taiyan by examining his writings on India, which are often embedded in his works on anti-colonialism. Then, complementing the themes of Gal Gvili and Adhira Mangalagiri in this volume, I turn to his writings on Buddhism, through which he constructs a critique of imperialist epistemologies and specifically deconstructs the Hegelian idea of history as progress. The critique of colonialism and linear narratives of history are two sides of Zhang's use of India in his writings.

Zhang associated Buddhism with India, but did not always stress Buddhism's relationship to India, especially if we think of India as merely a geographical entity. To grasp the theoretical and political significance of Zhang Taiyan's India, I draw on the famous idea of 'Asia as Method' (hōhō to shite no Ajia [方法としてのアジア]) by the prominent post-War Japanese intellectual Takeuchi Yoshimi (竹内好).[2] Recently, Lin Shaoyang (林少陽) has suggested that, for Zhang Taiyan writing in the early twentieth century too, India was method,[3] a theme I develop further in this essay. As I explain in the first section, Takeuchi devised the concept of 'Asia as method' to de-reify the idea of Asia and turn it into a method for fighting imperialism. Asia captures the struggles for decolonization and for a world beyond the material and epistemological constraints of global capitalist modernity. I contend that Zhang anticipates Takeuchi's agonistic conception of Asia and places India at the centre of his strategy.

Zhang Taiyan wrote much before the idea of 'India as method' or even 'Asia as method' emerged, but his letters and essays concerning India express a similar attempt to resist a theory of development modelled on the West and to muster support for the Indian independence movement. Zhang continues this critique of linearity in his Buddhist writings, where he draws on Buddhist categories to develop a critique of Hegel. As a result, therefore, India is again in the background. Using Buddhism to confront Hegel could be construed as using India as a method to overcome the linear time. Hegel himself might be more closely connected with India than we had previously thought. In a recent text, Aakash Singh Rathore and Rimina Mohapatra (2017) contend that India was one of the major nemeses of Hegel, which is why he devoted a huge amount of space to developing a critique of Buddhism and especially Hinduism. The reason for this was partly because of something like the logic of what Homi Bhabha (2004: 132–45) calls 'sly civility'— Hegel found parts of Indian philosophy to be quite close to his own ideas and, therefore, had to dismiss it in order to affirm the superiority of his own system. In the early twentieth century, we find Zhang going back to a part of Indian philosophy[4] and finding similarities with Hegel while developing a different conclusion. From this perspective, there is an India hidden in both Hegel and Zhang Taiyan's critique of him. This hidden India is methodologically significant because it represents a critique of a linear history that places the Orient at the immature beginning of history. Indeed, Hegel's writings on India and Indian philosophy were usually written in the context of attempting to understand the Orient or Asia as the 'other' of modernity. Consequently, Zhang Taiyan's turn towards India and Buddhism has both geopolitical and philosophical significance.

In what follows, I begin by outlining Takeuchi's concept of Asia as method, followed by a brief discussion of linear visions of time in China, before turning to Zhang Taiyan's writings on India and his Buddhist critique of evolutionary history. The various sections together should give us a sense of the historical and philosophical significance of India as method in Zhang's political philosophy.

Takeuchi Yoshimi, Mizoguchi Yūzō, and the Problem of 'Asia as Method'

In 1961, Takeuchi inaugurated a new concept with the title of his essay 'Asia as Method' (Takeuchi [1961] 2005). His essay defended the idea of Asia against detractors who sought to dismiss it because of the vast diversity among the peoples of Asia in terms of cultures, practices, history, and ethnicities. In the post-War Japanese context, the scholar who launched this attack most forcefully was the cultural anthropologist Umesao Tadao (梅棹忠夫) (1920–2010). Between 1956–7, Umesao published a series of essays outlining an 'Ecological Conception of Civilizations'[5] in which he stressed that Japan and other countries in Asia belonged to different ecological zones and that this partially explained the similarities between Japan and Western nations. He explained that when he went to places such as India, he felt little in common with the people there, but found great parallels with Japan when he went to France. In a dialogue with Takeuchi in the early 1960s, Umesao attacked Takeuchi's idea of Asia by underscoring the differences within Asia, which tended to make the concept meaningless. Takeuchi's response encapsulates his concept of Asia as method:

> The power of Western Europe came in [to non-Western nations] and many ancient and medieval practices collapsed from the inside. This

power was perhaps that of the mode of production, perhaps spirit, but in any case, this movement began with modernity or the establishment of capitalism. If we follow Arnold Toynbee and others, we can say that this was a response to a challenge. The specifics change based on the nature of the challenge, also based on the particular elements connected to the conditions in various countries. However, I wonder whether we can stipulate the meaning of Asia based on the form of response. Speaking generally, perhaps we can call Asia the form in which there is an internal movement in the countries colonized by Western Europe or imperialism to become independent and form a nation-state. Even if a country is in Asia geographically ... if this movement is not present, we should perhaps not call such a country Asian ... If one gives recent example, a country such as Israel might be geographically in Asia, but is not Asian. But a country like Cuba is in the Americas, but in terms of form it approaches Asia. (Takeuchi Yoshimi 1970: 146)

There had been much discussion about Arnold Toynbee's famous theory of challenge and response after his visit to Japan in 1956. Takeuchi mobilizes the concept of challenge to discuss the formation of a concept of Asia that begins as geographical, but eventually turns it into the ideal movement for national self-determination. From this perspective, he provocatively claims that even Cuba could represent Asia.

In Takeuchi's discourse, Asia acts at the level of geopolitics and history, rather than merely geography. From this perspective, we can understand the concept of 'X as method' as implying de-linking a region from its immediate geographical identity and mobilizing it for a larger theoretical and political struggle. At the level of geopolitics, Asia names those nations that are victims of uneven global development and colonization and that move to resist them. However, this resistance is not just spatial; it is also temporal in that it confronts the vision of civilization that has dominated Japanese intellectual history since the Meiji period. Although Umesao's works, to some extent, served to relativize civilization by linking it to geography, his enterprise lent itself to interpretations that suggest that Japan was ahead of other Asian nations because it had followed a path similar to the West. This suggested in turn that the West was the standard according to which other nations, such as India and China, would be measured.

This leads us to the classic postcolonial situation in which nations that have broken free from colonialism continue to be under the yoke of the temporality of colonialization, where a more advanced nation shows the way to those lagging behind.

In 1980, about three years after Takeuchi's death, a fellow sinologist, Mizoguchi Yūzō (溝口雄三) (1932–2010), continued his project by formulating his own concept of 'China as method', which places the emphasis on multiple historical trajectories and on breaking free from the idea of taking the West as a goal. Mizoguchi (1989: 137–8) writes:

> A world that takes China as method would be a world in which China is a constitutive element. In other words, it would be a pluralistic world in which Europe is also one of the constitutive elements.

In Mizoguchi's vision of a world in which China is method, the various countries of the world are not normatively wedded to one trajectory of development. In this way, he anticipates Dipesh Chakrabarty's (2000) famous phrase, 'provincializing Europe'. In the above passage, the world is not given in advance and represented by Western values; rather, it is constituted by various elements of which each European nation is just one element. In other words, values that make up a world will be constituted by the practices of the various particular nations that constitute the whole. The world becomes an agglomeration of singular nations and the whole is greater than the sum of its parts. 'China as method' thus follows 'Asia as method' in stressing decolonization, but further posits a world in which there is no hegemonic power and where universality does not obliterate particularity, but is constituted by it.

We shall see later that Zhang Taiyan incorporates these two elements in his engagement with India and Buddhism. His writings on Indian freedom fighters are intimately connected to his vision of pan-Asianism, which aimed at national independence for colonized peoples. India becomes the symbol of self-determination and of breaking free from taking the West as a telos. His Buddhist writings, which he published around the same period as his works in support of Asian unity, tackle the problem of progressive history at a philosophical level, where he formulates a Buddhist critique of Hegel.

The background to this critique concerns a general trend to endorse evolutionary theories of history in China, which would put Asia, and India in particular, in an early or underdeveloped position.

India and Linear Time in Late Qing China

We do not need to rehash the events around the late Qing period, but some version of Toynbee's stimulus–response paradigm, along with the introduction of related new concepts, might be used to understand how late Qing intellectuals began to shift their overarching view of history. Given the numerous defeats that China faced at the hands of foreign countries in a series of wars and invasions after the Opium War of 1842, Chinese intellectuals had to both recognize their presence in a world beyond their tribute system and rethink Confucian visions of history which presupposed a golden age and seemed obsolete. In particular, many of the places that were formerly part of the tribute system began to be colonized by foreign powers. Kang Youwei (康有為), the famous reformer, expressed the situation as follows: 'Now our country is in a period when countries mutually struggle; it is not the time when the empire is closed off. During the period when countries mutually struggle, knowledge about politics, technology, literature and crafts can all be set up side by side, and those who are behind will become extinct' (cited in Wang [2004: 741], from Kang Youwei [1981: 301]). These words introduce a social Darwinist vision of the world in which China is no longer the centre and numerous nations compete. There is also a temporal element to this perspective, which suggests that the world progresses through stages such that nations at earlier stages will become extinct unless they catch up with the political and technological structures of the modern period. There is something Hegelian about this vision in that what was appropriate at an earlier stage becomes obsolete because of a historical logic.

After China lost the Sino-Japanese War of 1895, Kang Youwei, Liang Qichao (梁啟超), and other reformers formulated plans for China to become strong and competitive in the global capitalist system of nation-states. With the aid of a young and seemingly sympathetic emperor, Guangxu (光緒), the reformers planned to ameliorate the Qing government from within. However, a number of conservatives within the government, including the famous Empress Dowager Cixi (慈禧太后), staged a coup, putting Emperor Guangxu under house arrest and executing many of the reformers. Kang and his protégé Liang Qichao fled for their lives to Japan and elsewhere. They each at times saw the Meiji restoration as model for China eventually to emerge victorious in global competition.

Kang took the West as an ultimate model because it was technologically and militarily advanced, but at the same time, he was interested in understanding countries, such as India, as they struggled to become modern. While it would be wrong to say that his vision of India was completely negative, we can see a certain temporal logic at work in his text.

In 1899, during his period of exile, he ventured to visit India, giving the following explanation:

> First, after residing in Penang for years, my health has been badly affected by the heat and humidity. I would like to move to the snowy mountain in India. Second, India is the most ancient nation in the world. Its long history and its mixture of India's old system and the British new system may serve as a good reference for China. (Cited in Liu 2012: 174–5)

The second part of the above citation concerns India's hybridity. It embodies the situation of other nations in Asia such as Japan, which also characteristically straddled old and new temporalities. Despite his admiration for India, its significance stems from its being a path that one should not travel. Kang made the following comment about India before his trip to the country, which encapsulates a certain vision of history:

> Formerly, India was a celebrated nation in Asia, but she stuck to her traditions without changing and so during the Qianlong [乾隆] reign (1736–1795) the British organised a company with capital of 120,000 ounces of gold to carry on trade with India and eventually subjugated the five parts of India. (Liu 2012: 177)

In this passage, Kang argues that the British were able to colonize India because it had clung to its past or tradition without implementing reforms. In his later writings, India continues to be a negative example but for different reasons. In a letter to Liang Qichao, Kang (Liu 2012: 176) compares India and Japan to explain why China should follow the Japanese path and not opt to give local autonomy to provinces. From this perspective, while for Kang the goal is still modernization, he stresses the historical specificity of Asia, which, unlike the West, would not be conducive to a federal model.[6] In this case, India was chosen as a representative of a situation similar to China's and the threat of possible colonization.

Note that the emphasis on the similarity between China and India does not amount here to a call to unite with India; rather, following Fukuzawa Yukichi (福澤諭吉) (1835–1901) (2009), Kang warns that China must not take the path that India has. Implicit in the concept of a path is a movement towards a future, a view of time eventually developed by Yan Fu's extremely influential translation of Thomas Huxley's *Evolution and Ethics* [*Tianyan lun*][7] in 1897, in which he outlines a theory of progressive history. I will not go into Yan Fu's theory here, but will briefly give an example of how Zhang's revolutionary comrade Zou Rong (鄒容) articulated this concept with great clarity.

After the failure of the Hundred Days' Reform in September 1898, and especially after the Boxer Rebellion, an increasing number of people opposed Kang's proposal to reform the Qing government and planned to replace the Manchu dynastic system with a modern republic. Zou Rong and Zhang Taiyan were two of the most famous anti-Manchu propagandists. In 1903, Zou penned a famous tract proposing the overthrow of the Manchu government, titled *Geming jun* (革命軍) [*The Revolutionary Army*], which also broached the issue of the temporality of the revolution. We can see how Zou brings together ideas of revolution, evolution, and an emphasis on the West. Indeed, references to Western thinkers pervade Zou's pamphlet. In his self-written preface, Zou (1968: 56, 2002: 5) notes that he believes 'in the great thinkers, Rousseau, Washington and Walt Whitman'. Moreover, it is perhaps strange to find that one of the most famous revolutionary tracts of early Chinese nationalism begins with a sentence that advocates cleansing 'ourselves of 260 years of harsh and unremitting pain, so that ... the descendants of the Yellow Emperor will all become Washingtons' (Zou 1968: 56, 2002: 5). Given that Zou (1968: 58, 2002: 8) speaks here of a becoming, he presupposes a concept of time, which comes out clearly when he discusses revolution:

Revolution is the universal principle of evolution. Revolution is a universal principle of the world [*shijie zhi gongli* (世界之公理)]. Revolution is the essence of the struggle for survival or destruction in a time of transition. Revolution follows heaven and responds to human needs. Revolution rejects the corrupt and keeps the good. Revolution is the advance from barbarism to civilization. Revolution turns slaves into masters.

Here Zou connects revolution to a universal principle of evolution, which implies a sequential development of events and structures. Moreover, crucial to this view of history is the problem of transition from one epoch to another. One moves from barbarism to civilization, from being slaves to becoming masters. Both of these tropes suggest a global movement from tradition to modernity, which is encompassed in the universal principle of evolution.

Zhang endorsed Zou's pamphlet and the anti-Manchu enterprise, but *The Revolutionary Army* was considered a dangerous text, and Zhang and Zou were both charged with sedition and sentenced to three years in prison. These three years could be considered similar to what Takeuchi Yoshimi later describes as *kaishin* (回心) or conversion in the case of Lu Xun (魯迅). It is not that Zhang formally converts to a religion, but his thinking undergoes a fundamental change, which encourages him to push his thinking about revolution and national independence into a new framework, which he develops using Buddhist concepts. Zhang read about Buddhism seriously in jail, and by examining his post-jail writings, we can grasp his new style of thinking in writings from 1906 to 1911, within which we should understand his writings on India.

Zhang Taiyan's Pan-Asianism and Critique of Modernity: Rethinking Japan and India

Zhang Taiyan was released from jail in 1906, and Sun Yat-sen (孫中山) and other revolutionaries helped him flee to Tokyo. This was a period in which there was a pan-Asian boom in Japan, and Japanese intellectuals were critical of the deleterious effects of capitalism and began searching for alternatives in both Asian traditions and Western forms of socialism. Zhang thrived intellectually in this milieu, going to Tokyo and becoming the chief editor of the Chinese revolutionary journal *Minbao* (民報). During this time, he engaged in numerous activities with intellectuals from various parts of Asia, including Japan and India. In various writings from 1906 to 1911, Zhang rethought nationalism in a manner that ran counter to progressive temporality, which overlapped with his vision of pan-Asianism, which also resisted the ideology of progress. During this period, he brings four ideas together: anti-imperialism, nationalism, pan-Asianism, and socialism or anti-capitalism. In this context, Zhang made a distinction between radical and imperialist nationalisms. Within this distinction we could further highlight a link between radical anti-imperialism and socialism. Within this period, he would slowly turn his gaze from Japan to India as a centre of anti-colonialism and potentially of socialism.

Shortly after Zhang came to Japan, he participated in the Socialist Study Group and the Asian Solidarity Society. The fact that he participated in these two together already suggests that there might have been a connection between socialism and pan-Asianism: The former is considered as being opposed to capitalist modernity, while the latter's target is Western modernity and colonialism. During Zhang's time, the question of capitalism is not posed with the same force as it would by later intellectuals, but, as we shall see below, his project dealt with capitalism implicitly.

We catch a glimpse of how he and the founder of *Minbao* regarded economic equality and anti-imperialism by looking at how the journal described its basic ideology from its inception in 1905 until Zhang Taiyan stopped being its editor in 1908: 'The ideology of this company [*benshe* (本社)] is as follows: overthrow all evil governments, establish a republic, maintain world peace, nationalize land, unite the Japanese and Chinese people, ensure that the various countries in the world approve of the Chinese revolution.'[8] Partly because this ideology was written in Japan, the Chinese revolution is placed in a global perspective. The first principle calls for the general overthrow of unjust governments and the establishment of republics, thus placing China in part of a global movement connected to the final principle. People will approve of the Chinese revolution precisely because it is a movement towards a republic. There is, of course, a temporality embedded in this movement from the past to the future, with more modern republican governments replacing the older evil regimes. On the other hand, there is also a mild gesture towards pan-Asianism in the emphasis on the unity of Japan and China. This could, of course, be because the journal was being published in Japan, but Zhang ([1897] 1977) and others had previously spoken of the importance of friendship between China and Japan, and here there are wider concerns about world peace and recognition by other nations. The Asia Solidarity Society already replaces Japan with India, as we shall see below. Finally, the idea of the unification of land gives us a sense of how Zhang and other revolutionaries hoped to overcome capitalism. To some extent, we see a resistance to the ordinary temporality of economic development, where feudalism was to be replaced by capitalism. This was a period when Adam Smith and others were being translated into Chinese, and the impulse of many Chinese intellectuals, and especially pan-Asianists, was connected to the idea that China could move along a different path by drawing on earlier traditions. The critique of imperialism is in the background of this claim, since the ideology of the imperial powers was often seen as trying to recreate Asian nations in their own image. For this reason, the above principles were premised on regaining national independence.

Perhaps the most important political activity related to Zhang's pan-Asianism and his concept of India was his participation in the Asia Solidarity Society. At meetings of this group, Zhang exchanged ideas with a number of radical intellectuals from China, Japan, Burma (now Myanmar), the Philippines, and Vietnam at India House. The Society was established in 1907, the same year in which Japan occupied Korea, and this might be a reason why Koreans refused to participate. The Japanese intellectuals who attended, however, were sympathetic to anti-imperialism, and many would become famous radicals in the future. Among the illustrious left-wing Japanese activists who attended were the founder of Japan's first socialist party in 1906, Sakai Toshihiko (堺利彦) (1871–1933), the anarchist Ōsugi Sakae (大杉栄) (1885–1923) and the future founder of the Japanese Communist Party, Yamakawa Hitoshi (山川均) (1880–1958). Through these radicals, it is more than likely that Zhang was exposed to a mixture of anti-imperialist, anti-statist, and anti-capitalist thought.

As Japan was slowly being seen as increasingly imperialist in its own right, however, the symbolic value associated with India became crucial. The Society was located in India House, a transnational institution where a huge number of Indian freedom fighters in exile from India would gather. For example, by 1910, there were India Houses in London and Vancouver, places where exiles who were part of the independence movement met. Tokyo's India House belonged to this larger conglomeration, but perhaps this particular venue was perhaps significant because it was in Asia and could potentially be a meeting place for Asian radicals.

Zhang Taiyan and Zhang Ji (張繼) drafted a type of manifesto or basic principles in Chinese, which was then translated into English. The first section reads:

> Among the various Asian countries, India has Buddhism and Hinduism; China has the theories of Confucius [孔子], Mencius [孟子], Laozi [老子], Zhuangzi [莊子] and Yangzi [楊子]; then moving to Persia, they also have enlightened religions, such as Zoroastrianism. The various races in this region had self-respect and did not invade one another. The various islands in the south are influenced by Indian culture. The people from the eastern seas are all influenced by Chinese culture. They rarely invaded one another and treated each other respectfully with the Confucian virtue of humanity. About one hundred years ago, the Europeans moved east and Asia's power diminished day by day. Not only was their political and military power totally lacking, but people also felt inferior. Their scholarship deteriorated and people only strove after material self-interests. India fell first and then China was lost to the Manchus. The group of Malaysian islands (including Malaysia, Indonesia, and so on) was occupied by the whites. Vietnam and Burma were subsequently swallowed up. The Philippines were first ruled by Spain; they got independence for a while, but then America annexed them. Only Siam and Persia remain independent; however, they are also in the process of declining.[9] (Zhang 1981: 428)

Although Okakura Tenshin (岡倉天心) was not part of this group, we can see that he paved the way for these developments in pan-Asianist thought.[10] Like Okakura, Zhang constructed a counter-discourse against a progressive vision of history with Europe at the centre by invoking the civilizational or cultural unity of Asia. Note that at the beginning of the description, Zhang identified Asia only in terms of culture, philosophies, and religions. He did not stress any sense of regional unity with respect to trade or political relations.

He only underscores that in the East, people treated each other with Confucian benevolence and rarely invaded one another. On this latter point, he echoes Okakura's idea that there were numerous 'states' (*guo* [國]) in Asia which had separate boundaries, but they did not invade one another and were relatively peaceful before the arrival of Western dominance (Okakura 1903: 4). In Zhang's discourse this original utopia became an important part of his temporal narrative of return. In other words, rather than a progression, Zhang affirmed that nationalism was a type of return to a past before colonization. Consequently, colonialism appears as a rupture that makes pan-Asianism necessary.

Zhang explains that about a hundred years ago, Europeans moved eastwards and changed the way Asians thought of themselves. European invasion affected Asian nations objectively from a military perspective, but perhaps more importantly their vision of themselves was now mediated by the West, and consequently Asian nations began to feel inferior, as we have seen above in Kang's work. Zhang describes feeling inferior (*zibei* [自卑]), which could also imply looking down on oneself. The reason for this feeling is contained partially in the next sentence: 'Scholarship declined, and people strove after material interests' (Zhang 1981: 428). Here we have Okakura's classic opposition between the East connected with morality and scholarship and the West as implying material and selfish interests. In other words, with the mediation of the West, Asian nations also began to take material wealth as a standard, but failed to measure up to the imperialist countries from this perspective.

Zhang is criticizing a culture that becomes dominant in capitalism. I question the interpretation of scholars such as Hazama Naoki (Hazama and Matsumoto 1990: 249) and Lin (2014: 208), who claim that Zhang's critique of imperialism did not attack capitalism. Zhang does not explicitly use the word for capitalism as later Chinese and Japanese intellectuals would do. However, it is difficult to understand the world of imperialism without thinking about capitalism. Consequently, Zhang attacks the effects of capitalism without always naming it. He describes above a transition from a world where scholarship dominates to one which is based on self-interest. In the beginning of Zhang's text, we see that by scholarship he means Confucianism, Buddhism, and other religions that were connected to morality and self-respect. However, as Western imperialism encroaches on Asia, scholarship declines and is replaced by self-interest, where, as Marx would say, all holy shrines are washed in the cool waters of egoistic calculation.[11] We could say that Zhang does not separate capitalism from imperialism and analyse them or their connections. He does, however, describe the shift that takes place as capitalism becomes global through imperialism. Moreover, in his own way, he attacks both capitalism and imperialism. His criticisms of capitalism are fewer, but he is conscious of this problem as he tries to revive tradition. For example, in a speech given to Chinese exchange students in Tokyo shortly after he arrived in 1906, he makes the following point about the Imperial Examination System:

> Because of such a system, even poor people had hopes of becoming officials. Had this not been the case, study to gain official positions would have to have been left exclusively to the rich. The poor would have sunk to the bottom of the sea, and the day when they participated in political power would not come for a long time ... Our present reverence for our own tradition is nothing less than a reverence for our own socialism. (Cited in Shimada 1990: 41)

Zhang does not mention capitalism here, but if one stopped at this level, one would fail to understand the significance of Zhang's re-evaluation of tradition. By using the term 'socialism' (shehui zhuyi [社會主義]), Zhang engages in a strange type of trans-lingual practice (Liu 1995). He translates the Chinese historical experience of the examination system into the political project of socialism. From this perspective, given that socialism was and is generally regarded as a goal towards which one should strive, the Chinese past (the tradition, the examination, and so on) become the future. This is a 'back to the future' effect in which the significance of temporal distinctions has changed. The unsaid present in Zhang's discourse is capitalism, which he associates with the West and is something to be overcome or avoided through the future, which is socialism. He articulates this same point by discussing China and the West earlier in the same speech when dealing with the equitable field system. He notes:

> What China has been particularly superb at, something the countries of the West can absolutely not approach, is the equitable-field [juntian (均田)] system; this institution conforms to socialism, to say nothing

of the well-field [*jingtian* (井田)] system of the Three Dynasties of high antiquity. From the Wei and Jin eras through the Tang, the equitable field system was in effect. (Cited in Shimada 1990: 40)

Zhang legitimates the Chinese nation by elevating the Chinese past. However, how he does this again gestures toward socialism, and by making the contrast with the West, he implies an opposition to capitalism. One of the reasons that the West will not be able to overcome its chronic inequalities is because it has become capitalist. It is almost as if, in Zhang's discourse, the opposition between China and the West is an opposition between socialism and capitalism. The mediation of the West enables the Chinese past to be reinterpreted as something that points beyond the present. The problem is that the discourse of imperialism and Eurocentrism block this movement to the future because such theories assert that Asian pasts remain mired in stifling traditions that can never gesture to a different future.

Zhang attempts to counter the feeling of inferiority mentioned in the Constitution by opening a space of Asian traditions to be used in the future. This gesture dislocates Asia from the spatio-temporal matrix that places it in the past and forms the basis for a possible future. Zhang's concern is to liberate the Chinese and Indian pasts and by extension the Asian past. But such a liberation is inextricably connected to the actual liberation of Asian nations. After all, it is because of Western invasions that the Asian past became a problem in the first place, and if there is not sufficient resistance, certain Asian nations could disappear. He recounts how various nations in Asia have either come under the yoke of colonialism or have faced this threat in some way.

In his description of successive colonialism, the sequence is important. India has a special significance because it was the first to be colonized and, as for Kang, Zhang notes a similarity between India and China. However, in Kang's view, China represented the not-yet colonized, which placed it in a similar but better situation than India, that is, China and India were similar in that they both faced the threat of colonization, but China was better because it avoided colonization by Western powers. So, rather than helping India liberate itself, the aim was to ensure that China takes a different path and follows the

Western model of development, even if the strategy to do so would be different. In Zhang's case, because he viewed the Manchu takeover of China as an instance of colonialism, India and China were in even more analogous situations. In addition, Zhang's pan-Asian position posits that until Asian nations are liberated, they are all already and always under the gaze of colonization and must unite to overthrow the imperialist system. He made this point in another essay, 'On the Five Negations', where he set out a path to go from a world of nation-states to a world without nation-states, a type of nation as method. In light of this goal, Zhang (1996a: 255) distinguished between two types of nationalism:

> As long as people establish nation states, we must hold to nationalism. But there are broader nationalisms. We uphold a nationalism that is not limited to the Han race. If we have enough power, we must also help other weak nations, nations that have been conquered by other nations, whose governments have been stolen and made into slaves. Alas, India and Burma were destroyed by England. Vietnam was destroyed by France. The wise and benevolent races will be eliminated. Our nation must counter this trend. Except for our nation, which wise and ancient state still bears to let its people fall into slavery? If one wants a complete nationalism, one must extend our hearts to help people suffering from the same ailment, and make their land totally independent.

Zhang continued to explain that the imperialists used advanced technology to expand their borders and enforced harsh laws on the colonies. From the earlier discussion, we can see that Zhang looks at the nation-state on a variety of different levels. Given the reality of the nation-state system, he stressed the importance of states and nations for protection. Within this system of states, Zhang separated imperialist from imperialized regions, and Asia came to represent a conglomeration of countries facing imperialism.

In an essay on the Indian national essence movement written during the same period, he emphasized the consciousness of time in relation to anti-imperialist nationalism. He claimed that 'what separates humans from animals is that humans have the idea of the past' (Zhang 1982–6, Volume 4: 366). In another essay, he argued that love and desire are strongest for the past and future, rather than something we possess in the present.

This is because human consciousness moves in and out of existence like a long continuous flowing stream; it can imagine the past and long for the future. Since all things come into the realm of consciousness and conform to its rules, we express love not for what we have at present, but for that which is absent, in the past or future. Hence patriotism involves loving a country's history. (Zhang 1982–6, Volume 4: 463)

However, this love for the past leads to two different types of action when linked to the future.

In Zhang's view, although strong countries may use various discourses to glorify their actions, patriotism and the emphasis on the national essence lead to imperialism. Hence, he concluded that it is appropriate to criticize their patriotism. However, with Asian countries, things were not the same. He asserted that countries such as China, India, and Korea 'had only been trampled on by other countries and only want to get back what was originally theirs' (Zhang 1977: 367).

The second part of the Constitution presupposes the above problematic and addresses the question formulated by Lenin in 1902: 'What is to be done?' The answer is now conceived not only in terms of cultural commonalities, but also strategically in terms of uniting to combat imperialism. Here India becomes central:

In the past, the thirty-six countries of Tianshan [天山] met with the invasions of the Tujue [突厥] and Huihu [回鶻] barbarians; as the result the various races of Tianshan were destroyed. It appears that at a later time, China, India, Vietnam, Burma, the Philippines and other Asian countries will suffer a fate similar to the thirty-six countries of Tianshan. Learning from the experience of Tianshan, we establish the 'Asia Solidarity Society' in order to resist imperialism and protect our nation states. In the future, we hope to drive away the foreign races and stand mighty. The various groups of the Southeast will mutually help each other and form a web of resistance. We must unite the various clans and resuscitate old, but broken friendships. We must revitalize our Hinduism, Buddhism, Confucianism and Daoism and develop our compassion in order to squeeze out the evil Western superficial morality. We will lead the sages to avoid being conquered by the whites. We will not follow separatism and we shall not bow to form. All of our close friends of several different types have not completely united. First India and China must unite to form a group. These two old countries

of the East are huge and if they can be fortunate and obtain independence, they will form a shield for the rest of Asia. The remaining dozen
neighbouring countries can therefore avoid being bullied. All nations
of Asia who support independence, if you want to take this precious
step and take an oath to unity, pray that such unity arrives. (Zhang
1981: 429)

Zhang draws on older periods in China's history and then advocates placing India and China at the centre of the Asian resistance.
He compares the international situation of his time to that of the
Qin and Han dynasties and suggests that the Western invasion of
Asia is similar to the barbarian invasion of the thirty-six countries
of the Tianshan. Kang Youwei had already made such an analogy
between the Chinese past and the late Qing present. Like Kang,
Zhang hopes to resist a full repetition, since the first time the
barbarians invaded they transformed society. However, while Kang
ultimately aimed for global unity, Zhang stresses on diversity.
Zhang laments that after the barbarian invasion the variety of races
decreased and the country was unified. Zhang fears that this would
happen again with respect to contemporary Asian states, such as
Burma, India, and China. The West could annihilate the cultural
plurality of Asia through force.

Zhang describes an Asia that is united because each individual state
has become an object of invasion. However, to resist this invasion, he
suggests that the various Asian nations must become self-conscious of
this unity and resist European expansion. In other words, he affirms
the diversity that exists in terms of races in Asia, but unites them at a
higher level through the process of struggling for independence. Part
of the strategy here returns to reviving earlier teachings and religions
to combat the morality of egoism, as we saw earlier. The war must
be fought simultaneously culturally and militarily. The moral ideology is, of course, imbricated in the military battle, since it allows a
type of transcendence. The constitution states that we should not bow
to form, which suggests both the physical power of the imperialists
and their ideology of focusing on the outer form of material goods.
The teachings of Hinduism, Buddhism, Confucianism, and Daoism
emphasize a transcendence of material goods, which can ensure that
pan-Asianists are not seduced by the lure of the West, as well as giving
them the power to resist against the odds.

As in the case of listing nations that were colonized, the sequence is important in the naming of religions. In the first part of the constitution, Zhang (1981: 428) notes that 'India has Buddhism and Hinduism' before naming numerous Chinese teachings. This shows that he clearly considered Buddhism to be an Indian religion and yet one that was also central to Asia. However, Buddhism was, of course, central to China and Japan as well and could be the bridge that links India culturally to East Asia, or at least to China. For this reason, it is crucial to see how Zhang mobilizes Buddhism against the West in works from around the same period as part of his overall plan of resistance. Throughout the constitution, Zhang uses Buddhist terms to discuss the difference between Asia and the West. For example, he uses the Buddhist term *zhantuoluo* (旃陀羅) (Sanskrit: *cendala*) or 'evil' to describe Western morality, advocating countering this evil morality through a new alliance with India.

Zhang's emphasis on the relationship between India and China indicates a shift from a previous discourse on Asia which placed Japan at the centre. After the Sino-Japanese war of 1895, a number of Chinese intellectuals, including Zhang Taiyan, avoided following the Japanese model and uniting with Japan. In an essay written in 1897, Zhang also stressed uniting with Japan, but now the geopolitical situation had changed, and Zhang's perception of this change was partially mediated through his interactions with Indian intellectuals.

Zhang's Geopolitical Vision of Nation and Unity with India

Partly in connection with the Asia Solidarity Society, Zhang came into contact with Indian freedom fighters while in exile in Japan. One of the best testaments to Zhang's support for an India–China alliance during this time is his essays on the Indian National Essence Movement and the Indian Commemoration of Shivaji in Tokyo in 1907. These essays express the idea of India as method or as a symbol of anti-colonialism. In one of his essays on the Indian National Essence Movement, Zhang (1982–6, Volume 4: 366–7) asserted that, while a national essence movement might have negative effects on Western countries, these movements were essential for countries such as China and India.[12] He noted that just as bullies will dominate a person who is not self-aware, other nations will bully a nation that is not self-aware (Zhang 1982–6, Volume 4: 367). In Zhang's view, a nation's self-awareness was intimately linked to recognizing its national essence and history; therefore, by rejecting its national essence, one would eventually weaken national self-awareness, and this would enable other nations and races to invade. One of the examples Zhang looks at concerns Indians gathered in Japan to honour Shivaji.

In 'The Commemoration of Shivaji', Zhang begins by mentioning two Indians who organized the event. He writes:

> Mr. Bo Luohan had come to Japan from the United States, and he visited me at the *Minbao* editorial offices. He said: 'The treatment meeted [*sic*] out to Indians by the British government was far worse than that of the Mogul dynasty of earlier times. Those who set their minds on learning have been unable to study politics and law, and, even if they go overseas to pursue their studies, they still feel under a strict prohibition in this area.'... He granted this interview with the interpreting help of his friend Mr. Bao Shen, who speaks Japanese quite well. (Cited in Shimada 1990: 78)[13]

The main point in Zhang's writing about the meeting in which Bo Luohan and Bao Shen (Surendramohan Bose) participated was to show that China had to move away from Japan and to unite with India. This is different from Taraknath Das's argument that India, Japan, and China must all unite. Zhang continues his earlier argument in favour of China and India uniting, but explicitly argues against including Japan. In an essay on Indians in Japan, he provides another interpretation of the Russo-Japanese war and points out:

> Since the Russo-Japanese War, the Japanese have become extremely proud and believe that they are the great dragons of the East! ... They see India already gone, they defeated China in a war and they annexed Korea without a fight. They are extremely proud of this ... All the Japanese who were previously ethical now believe this ... Before Japan rose, although there were minor skirmishes in Asia, it was relatively peaceful. Now it is the opposite. (Zhang 1908: 3156–7)

Although the Russo-Japanese War to some extent provided an impetus for the pan-Asianism of many members of the Asia Solidarity

Society, Zhang continues to turn away from Japan. This is also connected to the Japanese support for British imperialism. After describing the way in which the Japanese politician Ōkuma Shigenobu (大隈重信) praised British rule of India, he notes the problems of imperialism and racism, which he connects to the development of civilization.

To counter Ōkuma, Zhang invokes an argument about the two-sided nature of evolution. In another essay from this period using Buddhist concepts, he contends that as society evolves, good and bad increase in tandem, and consequently society becomes more brutal.[14] In his account of the Commemoration for Shivaji, he explains:

> We should know that the more civilization advances, the more it tramples humanity under foot. It has already taken our children and destroyed our homes ... Generally speaking, civilized countries clog up people's eyes and ears with false morality. The French treat the Vietnamese people like domesticated animals; the English treat the Indians like beggars. (Cited in Shimada 1990: 81)

Through this direct critique of the British, he attacks not only Ōkuma, but also the larger trend to support evolutionary thinking. He further contests Ōkuma's comparison of India and the colonies of the Global North, such as USA and Australia. By pointing out the difference between India and these places, Zhang highlights the unevenness and racial differences in imperialism:

> Autonomy in Australia was given primarily to the English, not to the native population. Autonomy in Canada was given to Englishmen and other Caucasians, not to the native population. Even if the British government were to release India to independence, the blessing would be bestowed only on white men ... Take the American black man, who, although he possesses the franchise in name, is in fact not the equal of other citizens. He cannot escape being lynched and burned ... Do you think the kingdom of Great Britain will make common cause with the Indian people? (Shimada 1990: 82)

Zhang points to a dimension of pan-Asianism that goes beyond merely struggling against imperialism in Asia and tends towards the universal liberation of oppressed peoples, including aboriginals, blacks, and American Indians. These are precisely the people who have been trampled on by capitalist civilization and who are then forgotten. This is an early impulse towards a broad-based anti-imperialist coalition, where Asia and India represent resistance to various forms of oppression.

Moreover, Zhang points out the resistance of Indians, which indicates a critique of capitalism:

> Indians have been thinking about Independence for almost 4 or 5 years ... Their strategies start from organizing strikes and boycotting commodities. Those who strike agree that they will not be employed by the English. Those who boycott commodities agree not to buy English commodities. When the first village engaged in such a boycott, the British fined them, but a neighbouring village helped them pay the fine, so they incurred no loss. (Cited in Kai-wing Chow 1999: 220)

By invoking strikes and boycotts, Zhang clearly connects anti-imperialism to frustrating capitalist production and consumption. In this manner he suggests that, rather than wait for the generosity of the English, the Indian people have relied on themselves and resisted British imperialism by refusing to participate in their capitalist ventures. This is not yet a Marxist position that rejects both foreign and national capital, but Zhang gestured towards this position in other essays in which he stressed equality. Indeed, I believe we can find a conceptual critique of capitalist imperialism in his creative combination of Chinese and Indian philosophies.

Philosophical 'Chindia'[15] vs Hegel

We saw that in the constitution of the Asia Solidarity Society, Zhang stressed that Buddhism came from India and then mentioned various religions of China, including Confucianism and Daoism. After fleeing to Japan in 1906, he began drawing on Yogācāra Buddhism intensely to formulate a critique of modernity and in particular of the concept of linear time. He unfolded a synthesis of Buddhism and Daoism, specifically in the works of Zhuangzi, to formulate an alternative theory of equality and difference. In these writings, he moves towards what Mizoguchi calls China as method, since he rejects the universality of the West, which is often presupposed by progressive visions of history, and aims instead to realize a universality that is reconciled with particularity.

Some would argue that the aim of Hegel's philosophy was also to reconcile the universal with the particular. Indeed, Hegel's own critique of Indian philosophy, and Oriental philosophy more generally, was precisely that it did not allow for particularity but drew everything into an undifferentiated ontological substance. For this reason, Indian philosophy becomes one of Hegel's favourite others. Recently, Rathore and Mohapatra (2017: 4–5) have shown that Hegel wrote about Indian philosophy and religion in almost all his major works. Hegel himself points out the similarity between the concept of the absolute in Indian thought and his own work, but says that there are two problems with it. First, Indian thought does not have a developed conception of freedom. Second, it is static: There is no progressive mediation. The lack of progression and mediation account for why the absolute in oriental philosophy becomes a nebulous annihilation of difference.

Zhang attacks both of these claims by drawing on Buddhism and finally claiming that Hegelian philosophy and evolutionary theory eclipse that which is different. But before we come to Zhang's critique, we should note that during the late Qing period, a prevalent interpretation of Hegel involved seeing his thought as eclipsing difference, even by proponents of his philosophy. Guan Yun (觀雲), a student of Kang Youwei, made the following statement in 1905.

> From Hegel's discussion of ethics, and according to the principle that his philosophy establishes, the world is an expression of a great spirit, and the individual is just a small part of this great spirit ... Hence all things such as states, families, societies and countries do not have the goal of developing the individual, but only that of developing the great spirit of the world. According to Hegel's theory, the myriad things of the world are equal as one. It appears that there are differences, but in actuality there are none ... Socialism and cosmopolitanism both take equality as their moral foundation and thus they both can be deduced from Hegel's theory. (Kang 1977: 21)

From this perspective, the whole is greater than the parts. Equality signifies sameness, an example of what Mizoguchi would call a vision that 'takes the world as method' and measures particular nations based on this standard. This vision perhaps accounts for why, a couple of years later, Zhang would begin to focus on issues related to Hegel, Indian/Chinese thought, evolution, equality, and difference.

One of the first places where Zhang outlines a critique of Hegel is in his critique of evolutionary history, which he develops using Buddhist terminology. He does not doubt the validity of something like a process in which change occurs and technological mediation increases, but questions the moral overtones that Hegel, as he was read in China, bestows on such developments. In Zhang's view, technological change and modern political apparatuses are inextricably connected to imperialism and an increase in general human suffering. In short, with evolutionary development, pleasure and suffering increase together. While we need not to delve into the details of Zhang's critique here, the following passage from an essay published in 1907 outlines the main thrust of his argument:

> Some steal Hegel's theory of being, non-being, and becoming and believe that the universe emerged because of a goal and hence only things that accord with this goal are correct. If we take the universe not to have any knowledge/consciousness then there is originally no goal. If we take the universe to have knowledge/consciousness then it is as if this peaceful and happy self suddenly created the myriad things to bite into itself. It is as if it eats without stop and in the end the harms of a parasitic worm emerge, and so the universe repents [creating]. Sometimes one thinks of how one can use laxatives such as lilac daphne and croton to get rid of these things.[16] So the goal of the universe is perhaps precisely this repentance about its 'becoming'. How can one be happy about 'becoming'? The person who manages the world must be the person who repents about the universe. This person should not be the one who floats around with the universe. If one speaks from the perspective of humans limited by their physical form, then both purity and contamination stem from one's will. What use is it to make loyalty and filiality the goals of the universe? If one speaks from the perspective outside of form and matter, then the universe originally does not exist, so how can there be a goal? (Zhang 1996b: 264)

The aforementioned passage is a direct attack on Hegel's teleological vision of history. In short, rather than narrating a series of stages through which Spirit (*Geist*) becomes increasingly conscious of itself,

Zhang counters with a scenario in which history or becoming leads to increasing disaster. The situation is similar to Walter Benjamin's (1968: 257) 'angel of history', which is pushed by a storm and is unable control itself as it faces the debris of history. In this mode, Zhang anticipates later critics of what would be called modernization theory by uncovering the dark side of progress. He also underscores the manner in which tropes such as progress and civilization are used to justify and beautify imperialist aggression, reinforcing his sympathy for India and other colonized regions. When one makes this realization about the trajectory of history, one repents and attempts to find a way to end history as it now exists and create a new world. The transformation of the world is simultaneously philosophical, dealing with 'form and matter', and political, as indicated by his revolutionary practice. But, as we saw in the passage on Indian boycotts, he also advocates a rejection of existing form and matter, which Indians exemplified by withdrawing from Britain's political economy.

However, the above passage leaves an important question unanswered, namely, what type of ideal did Zhang oppose to the Hegelian? As I suggested earlier, one could say that Zhang applies Hegel's criticism to himself and contends that Hegel is unable to account for difference. Consequently, Zhang draws on Zhuangzi and Buddhism to outline a world that affirms difference. He outlines this position with reference to Zhuangzi's concept of 'equalization' in an essay published in 1908 also attacking Hegel. He notes that, according to Zhuangzi's idea of the equalization of things:

> [T]here is no correct place, no correct taste, no correct colour; it lets each thing be what it wants ... As Zhuang Zi says, 'all things are so and all things are permissible [*wu wu bu ran, wu wu bu ke* (無物不然，無物不可)]'. The literal meaning of this phrase is the same as Hegel's 'all events are in accord with principle and all things are virtuous and beautiful [*shi shi jie heli, wu wu jie shanmei* (事事皆合理，物物皆善美)]'.[17] However, the former takes people's hearts and minds to be different and difficult to even out, while the latter posits a final end, which is the process by which things are realized. This is a basic and huge difference. (Zhang 1996a: 304)

Like Hegel, Zhang notes the similarity between the formulations of oriental philosophy, in this case Zhuangzi's and Hegel's own formulations. However, now it is Zhuangzi who is credited with actually grasping difference, while Hegel posits a telos, which evens things out. Note that in Zhang's discussion of Hegel the statement is given in the affirmative: 'Things are rational and beautiful'. From this perspective, the reasonable or the beautiful becomes the absolute standard against which various particulars can be measured. Here we return to the problem of using the world as method or standard, which in Zhang's view is one of the key tropes of imperialism. However, the citation from Zhuangzi reads literally, 'There is no thing that is not so and no thing that is not possible'. In this formulation, there is no principle (*li* [理]) or ideal such as virtue and beauty to which things must conform. Rather, each thing is affirmed in its singularity, and out of it will emerge a new universality. In Roy Bhaskar's (1994) terms, this would be a world in which the concrete singularity of each is the condition for the possible flourishing of all.

Zhang explicates his theory of equality as difference most completely in his long essay, 'Qiwu lunshi' (齊物論釋) ['An Interpretation of an Equalization of Things'], in which he uses Yogācāra Buddhism to read Zhuangzi and thus creates a Chindian philosophy. He was most proud of this work and famously claimed that each character was worth a thousand gold pieces. The opening passage explains the above point further by drawing on a Buddhist text, *Dacheng qixin lun* (大乘起信論) [*Awakening of Mahayana Faith*].[18] He writes:

> 'Equalizing things' refers to absolute equality. If we look at its meaning carefully, it does not refer only to equality between sentient beings, such that there is no inferior and superior. It is only when [dharmas] 'are detached from the characteristics of speech; detached from the characteristics of naming cognition; and detached from of them as objects,' that one understands absolute equality. This is compatible with the 'equalization of things'. (Zhang 1982–6, Volume 6: 4)

Awakening of Mahayana Faith is a controversial text, since it has status as a text translated from India, but scholars believe it to be a forgery created in China. Consequently, it has the liminal status of being in between a Chinese text and an Indian text.[19] The text involves a certain imagination or reconstruction of Indian Buddhism in China, perhaps more than other actually translated texts. In this context, it is significant to note that Zhang does not quote the line immediately

following the above passage, since that would have pushed the text in
the direction of Guan Yun's reading of Hegel. The text reads: 'There is
nothing but this One Mind, and for this reason it is nominally called
Suchness.' This suggests that there is one mind that exists even after
one detaches oneself from objects, cognition, and naming. Zhang
does not cite this passage and constructs a radically negative position,
which affirms radical difference and the new universality to which he
gestures above. The dialectic of difference and universality to which
Zhang alludes has not yet come into being, and consequently he can
only gesture to it through paradoxical expressions connected to the
trace. We find an excellent example of this in the following passage:

> One only uses traces to guide transformations. Without words nothing
> can appear and words have the nature of returning. Thus, one uses
> words to signify things. This is what is said in the following passage
> [from *Zhuangzi*]: 'In speaking there are no words. One speaks one's
> whole life and has never spoken. One does not speak throughout one's
> life and has never stopped speaking [*wei chang bu yan* 未嘗不言].'
> (Zhang 1982–6, Volume 6: 6)

Zhang writes here of a trace that inscribes difference beyond
our usual opposition between the particular and the universal. He
posits a world in which there is no overarching dominant principle
that determines a priori the nature of universality and is then grafted
on to particulars. The problem is that one cannot merely affirm the
particular as it exists at present because such a particular is always
mediated already by a false universal. Consequently, Zhang speaks
of a future always to come because it must be constructed out of
singularities; one can only use traces to guide transformations.
Moreover, reified terms can never grasp what is always emerging as
a totality constantly reconstituted by the emerging particulars. For
this reason, Zhang develops a new dialectical language by bringing
Yogācāra and Zhuangzi together. This dialectical language engages in
a play between signification and silence, gesturing to what Mizoguchi
outlined with his concept of China as method, namely, a world that
is not determined a priori by an ideal forced on to beings from the
outside. Mizoguchi took the nation as his unit of discussion, but by
drawing on a synthesis of Buddhism and Zhuangzi, Zhang attempts
to discuss the problem of difference more fundamentally and opts for

something like a metaphysics of democracy or a metaphysical democracy, which he believes would point the way to an ideal politics in the future. In other words, even in terms of what exists, one must begin from the singular, but this only has a provisional identity because it is ultimately contingent upon the whole that does not exist yet. When applied to politics, this view—where the concrete singularity of each is the condition for the flourishing of all and the flourishing of all is the condition for the singularity of each—requires a world with institutions different from the modern nation-state. For this reason, Zhang also wrote against the reality of the state. However, as his activities with Indian intellectuals show, at the level of realpolitik, he also saw the necessity of anti-colonial nationalism as long as the world remained imperialist. From this perspective, his problematic anticipated that of postcolonial thinkers who affirmed anti-colonialism, but were concerned that colonial structures might be reproduced without more fundamental transformations in one's consciousness and practice.

***

We have seen how Zhang Taiyan engaged with India at two different levels, which were connected but did not completely overlap. However, we can understand both engagements with India under the two 'as method' constructions of Takeuchi and Mizoguchi respectively. Takeuchi's 'Asia as method' underscored the link between a regional imagination and anti-colonial nationalism by redefining the idea of Asia. The key to this project involved battling progressive visions of history, which translated space into time by placing colonizing regions ahead of the colonized in a narrative of development. Asia was a matter of dismantling this temporal trajectory. Mizoguchi's 'China as method' continued this line of thinking by affirming the particular histories of each region or nation and attempting to constitute a new universality out of these particulars. Zhang's engagement with Indian intellectuals and his identification with India against both Japan and the West anticipates Takeuchi's version of Asia as method, but with India playing a crucial role with China. By invoking India, Zhang counters the prevailing ideology in Japan and China that would relegate India to the lost countries, a fate China should avoid.

In Zhang's view, China had to unite with India and the colonized to create a world beyond imperialism.

But according to Zhang, the engagement with India and the struggle with imperialism did not stop at formulating a geopolitical strategy. He also grappled with issues of subjectivity and consciousness by synthesizing Indian and Chinese classical texts and mobilizing them for use in the present. In this way, Zhang brought Yogācāra Buddhism and Zhuangzi to attack what might be called the late Qing version of Hegel, which posited a progressive vision of history with the West by showing the way to those states that were less developed. However, his critique did not stop there. In his 'An Interpretation of an Equalization of Things', he gestured to a world where singularities are liberated from conceptual violence and combine to recreate what universality and particularity mean. This would be a process in which the telos is inseparable from the movement itself and such a purposive movement is not separate from particulars. In short, Zhang like Hegel aims to overcome subject–object duality, but does so in a manner that does not privilege Europe or oppose the particular to the universal. Recall that on Guan Yun's interpretation of Hegel (cited earlier in this chapter), equality or the universal took precedence over the particular. Similarly, on many interpretations of Hegel, the teleological movement presses against individuals. While Hegel definitely believed that Europe was more advanced that Asia, he held a more dialectical view of universal and particular. From this perspective, Zhang liberates this dialectical vision from Eurocentrism, to create a world where telos and universality are constituted out of the movement of particulars.

Hegel himself gestures towards this point in the preface to his *Science of Logic* and it will be helpful to outline the subtle differences between Zhang and Hegel's respective positions. Hegel writes:

> [A] given particular is not subsumed under this universal but, on the contrary, it has already been determined together with the determining of the difference and the dissolution of this determining. This spiritual movement, which in its simplicity gives itself its determinateness, and in this determinateness gives itself its self-equality (*Gleichheit mit sich selbst*)—this movement, which is thus the immanent development of the concept, is the absolute method of the concept, the absolute method of the concept, the absolute method of cognition and at the same time, the immanent soul of the content. (Hegel 2015: 17)

Hegel explains that the universal does not oppress the particular; rather the two are co-determining in a movement that has a goal embedded in the various particulars. He speaks of an equality, which, as in Zhang's case, is one that encapsulates particularity and difference. The key difference between Zhang and Hegel's respective positions lies in the next few phrases, which deals with the immanent development of the concept. It would appear at first glance that there is no analogous concept in Zhang's philosophy of equality, which would in turn imply indeterminacy or no telos. Indeed, he explicitly writes that the universe has no goal. However, note that, when Zhang writes of blind development, he is describing the alienated world governed by karmic seeds, which needs to be overcome in order to realize the goal of equalization. The state of equalization then acts as a goal, which requires the negation of our present alienated condition. In other words, Zhang does not affirm blind development as a normative condition; rather, purposeless movement is a state of unfreedom, which we ourselves have created through karmic action. Consequently, Zhang articulates a negative teleology towards equalization (qiwu). Within the state of equality of qiwu, the telos would be unalienated and itself emerge out of the movement of the particulars. This returns us to the earlier point about the dialectic between concrete singularity and general flourishing and vice versa, which would be the model for real democracy.[20]

In continuing Zhang's project, aspects of both Zhang's attempt to revive Buddhism to confront Eurocentrism and his vision of Asia, namely, of weak countries uniting, are relevant, even if they need to be rethought in a new context. Today, Zhang's attempt to bring India and China both geopolitically and philosophically together is especially important, given the resurgence of visions of progressive history and of a neoliberal world, where China and India's respective success is often measured in terms of their productive output. Both India and China today are confronting demands for self-determination in Kashmir and Hong Kong, respectively. In each case, the lack of real democracy that entails people having a say in the conditions that govern their lives is one of the main causes for the discontent and the respective states have responded with different degrees of violence. Following Zhang's analysis, we could say that such conflicts and demands will constantly emerge unless we solve the more fundamental problem of an alienated system of nation states misrepresenting the people. These problems were of course exacerbated in each case by specific policies, but Zhang's theory helps us to uncover the structural conditions that continuously undermine the self-determination of particulars in both Asia and the world.

The situation in Asia is, however, specific. Given that the global capitalist world is also imperialist, we should not be surprised to find the major imperialist power, USA, often mediating relations between Asian nations, especially between China, India, and Japan. In this international context, it is important that we continue Zhang's project of imagining different political and philosophical possibilities concerning India and China. Moreover, it is precisely in the contemporary context that the unity of India and China could be endowed with a new anti-imperialist significance.

Notes

1. See Karl (2002) and Murthy (2011).
2. Richard Calichman has translated a selection of Takeuchi Yoshimi's works. See Takeuchi Yoshimi ([1961] 2005). 'Asia as Method' is also the title of an essay by Takeuchi, which Calichman has translated in the above volume. I have dealt with Takeuchi's conception of Asia along with other, related concepts in Murthy (2012, 2016, 2017).
3. See Lin (2018: 177–224), who uses the 'India as method' formulation (p. 210). See also Lin (2014: 201–27) for an earlier version of the same argument.
4. Zhang Taiyan, at times, discusses other Indian philosophies, such as *Samkhya* and *Advaita*, but dealt most extensively with Buddhism. Therefore, at times, he seems to use Buddhism to stand in for India.
5. Some of Umesao Tadao's essays have been translated in Umesao (2003).
6. See Adhira Mangalagiri's contribution in this volume for a brief discussion of Kang's vision of India as having an analogous situation to China's.
7. For Yan Fu's preface and notes to this translation, see Yan ([1897] 1996).
8. This was printed in all of issues of *Minbao* from 1905–8. See Lin (2014: 205).
9. Translation mine.
10. See Okakura Kakuzo (Tenshin) (1903).
11. The metaphor comes from Marx and Engels (1978: 475).
12. Zhang (1982–6, Volume 4: 367) noted that some Western scholars criticized National Essence because it affirmed everything a country did,

even though some of a country's actions might go against humanism. He explained that this theory emerged because Westerners were worried about the state stifling the rights of the individual. However, Zhang shows that this is not necessarily the case. He claimed that one needed to separate a subjective and objective attitude towards national history. In the objective moment, one records what has happened, and in the subjective one, one evaluates.

13. For a long time we were not sure who these two Indian freedom fighters were, but Lin (2014: 215–16) has recently suggested that their names were Muhammad Barkatullah (d. 1928) and Surendramohan Bose. Bao Shen is clearly Surendramohan Bose. However, in most accounts, Barkatullah only came to Japan in 1909, so I am not certain that Bo Luohan is Barkatullah. Barkatullah was involved in organizing pan-Islamic and pan-Aryan movements. Bose founded the Indo-American Association in USA with his fellow freedom fighter Taraknath Das, who was a supporter of Japanese pan-Asianism.

14. This is his argument in his essay 'On Evolution', which I discuss in detail in Chapter 4 of *The Political Philosophy of Zhang Taiyan* (Murthy 2011).

15. 'Chindia' is a combination of 'China' and 'India'. As business relations between the two countries increase, this term has increased in popularity. See Tan (2007).

16. Zhang mentions two traditional Chinese herbal medicines, *yanhua* (芫華) and *badou* (巴豆)), the latter being especially used to remove poison from the body.

17. This must be Zhang's rendition of 'the real is the rational and the rational is real'.

18. As *Awakening of Mahayana Faith* states:

> Therefore all the dharmas since the very beginning are detached from the characteristics of speech; detached from the characteristics of naming cognition; and detached from of them as objects. They are absolutely undifferentiated, devoid of any [capacity to] become otherwise, and are indestructible. There is nothing but this One Mind and for this reason it is nominally called Suchness'. [是故一切法從本已來,離言說相、離名字相、離心緣相,,畢平等、無有變異、不可破壞。唯是一心故名真如,以一切言說假名無實。]

Translated by John Makeham, John Powers, and Mark Strange. Available at https://www.cbeta.org/node/4977; accessed on 22 June 2020.

19. A number of scholars in the late Qing and early Republican periods regarded *Dasheng qixin lun* as closely aligned with *Yogācāra*, if not an actual Yogācāra text. Doctrinally, this is a problematic position, the roots of which can be traced to developments in sixth-century China, and it is

complicated by the fact that traditionally its translation was attributed (again problematically) to Paramārtha (499–569 CE), a scholar-monk closely associated not only with Yogācāra, but also with *Tathāgatagarbha* thought. Zhang himself believed that *Dasheng qixin lun* was a Yogācāra text written by Aśvaghoṣa. See Zhang ([1908] 1978). With respect to the text I am discussing, 'An Interpretation', it is also clear that Zhang cites *Dasheng qixin lun* with other texts that are uncontroversially considered to be Yogācāran, such as the *Yogācārabhūmi-śāstra*. However, as I shall show, he has a unique interpretation of the text.

20. Here I am attempting to unpack the implications of Zhang's formulations and not suggesting that Zhang was explicitly promoting democracy.

References

Benjamin, Walter. 1968. *Illuminations*. Translated by Harry Zohn, edited by Hannah Arendt. New York: Schocken Books.

Bhaba, Homi K. 2004. *The Location of Culture*. London: Routledge.

Bhaskar, Roy. 1994. *Dialectics: The Pulse of Freedom*. London: Verso.

Chakrabarty, Dipesh. 2000. *Provincializing Europe: Postcolonial Thought and Historical Difference*. Princeton: Princeton University Press.

Fukuzawa, Yukichi. 2009. *An Outline of a Theory of Civilization*. Translated by David Dilworth and G. Cameron Hurst III. New York: Columbia University Press.

Hazama Naoki (狭間直樹) and Matsumoto Kennichi (松本健一). 1990. 'Shō heirin to meiji no ajiashugi' (章炳麟と明治のアジア主義) ['Zhang Binglin and Meiji Pan-Asianism']. *Chishiki* (知識) (August).

Hegel, G.W.F. 2015. *Science of Logic [Wissenschaft der Logik]*. Translated by George Di Giovanni. Cambridge: Cambridge University Press.

Kai-wing Chow (周佳榮). 1999. *Xinmin yu fuxing: Jindai Zhongguo sixiang shilun* (新民與復興：近代中國思想史輪) [*New People and Revival: Interpreting Modern Chinese Intellectual History*]. Xianggang: Xianggang jiaoyu tushu gongsi.

Kang Youwei (康有為). 1977. *Xinhai geming qian shinian jian shilun xuanji* (辛亥革命前十年間時論選集) [*Selected Commentations during the Decade before the Revolution of 1911*], Volume 2, Part 1. Beijing: Sanlian chubanshe.

———. 1981. *Kang Youwei zhenglunji* (康有為政論集) [*A Collection of Kang Youwei's Political Writings*], Volume 1. Beijing: Zhonghua shuju.

Karl, Rebecca. 2002. *Staging the World: Chinese Nationalism at the Turn of the Twentieth Century*. Durham, NC: Duke University Press.

Lin Shaoyang (林少陽). 2014. 'Zhang Taiyan "zizhu" de lian Ya sixiang' (章太炎 「自主」的連亞思想) ['Zhang Taiyan's Ideas of Independence and Asian Unity']. *Quyu* (區域) 1 (3): 201–27.

———. 2018. *Dingge yi wen: qingji geming yu Zhang Taiyan "fugu" de xinwenhua yundong* (鼎革以文：清季革命章太炎與章太炎「復古」的新文化運動) [*Revolution by Means of Culture: Zhang Taiyan's New Culture Movement and "Returning to the Ancient Past"*]. Shanghai: Shanghai renmin chubanshe.

Liu, Lydia H. 1995. *Translingual Practice: Literature, National Culture and Translated Modernity—China, 1900–1937*. Berkeley: University of California Press.

Liu, Xi. 2012. 'Kang Youwei's Journey to India: Chinese Discourse on India during the Late Qing and Republican Periods'. *China Report* 48 (1–2): 171–85.

Marx, Karl and Frederick Engels. 1978. 'Manifesto of the Communist Party'. In Robert C. Tucker (ed.), *The Marx-Engels Reader*, pp. 469–501. New York: W.W. Norton Company.

Mizoguchi Yūzō (溝口雄三). 1989. *Hōhō to shite no chūgoku* (方法としての中国) [*China as Method*]. Tokyo: tokyodaigaku shuppansha.

Murthy, Viren. 2011. *The Political Philosophy of Zhang Taiyan: The Resistance of Consciousness*. Leiden: Brill.

———. 2012. 'The 1911 Revolution and the Politics of Failure: Takeuchi Yoshimi and Global Capitalist Modernity'. *Frontiers of Literature in China* 6 (1): 19–38.

———. 2016. 'Resistance to Modernity and the Logic of Self-Negation as Politics: Takeuchi Yoshimi and Wang Hui on Lu Xun'. *Positions: Asia Critique* 24 (2): 513–54.

———. 2017. 'Imagining Asia and the Chinese Revolution: Takeuchi Yoshimi and His Transnational Afterlives'. In Joyce H. Liu and Viren Murthy (eds), *East Asian Marxisms and Their Trajectories*, pp. 195–215. London: Routledge.

Okakura Kakuzo (Tenshin). 1903. *Ideals of the East: With Special Reference to the Art of Japan*. London: John Murray.

Rathore, Aakash Singh and Rimina Mohapatra. 2017. *Hegel's India: A Reinterpretation with Texts*. New Delhi: Oxford University Press.

Shimada Kenji. 1990. *Pioneers of the Chinese Revolution*. Translated by Joshua Fogel. Stanford: Stanford University Press.

Takeuchi Yoshimi (竹内好). 1970. *Takeuchi Yoshimi taidanshū* (竹内好対談集) [*A Collection of Takeuchi Yoshimi's Dialogues*]. Tokyo: gōdō shuppansha.

———. [1961] 2005. 'Asia as Method'. In *What Is Modernity*. Translated by Richard Calichman, pp. 149–67. New York: Columbia University Press.

Tan Chung (譚中) (ed.). 2007. 'Zhongyin datong: Lixiang yu xianshi' (中印大同：理想與現實) ['Chindia: Idealism and Realization']. Ningxia: Ningxia renmin chubanshe.

Umesao Tadao. 2003. *An Ecological View of History: Japanese Civilization in the World Context*. Melbourne: Transpacific Press.

Wang Hui (汪暉). 2004. *Zhongguo xiandai sixiangshi de xingqi* (中國現代思想史的興起) [*The Rise of Modern Chinese Thought*]. Beijing: sanlian shudian.

Yan Fu (嚴復). [1897] 1996. 'Tian Yan Lun xu yu an yu' (天演論序與案語) ['Preface and Annotations to Huxley's Evolution and Ethics']. In Lu Yunkun (ed.), *Shehui jubian yu guifan chongjian: Yan Fu wenxuan* (社會劇變與規範重建：嚴復文學) [*Social Change and the Reconstitution of Norms*], pp. 317–40. Shanghai: Shanghai Yuandong chubanshe.

Zhang Taiyan (章太炎). [1897] 1977. 'Lun Yazhou yi zi wei chunchi' (論亞洲宜自為唇齒) ['A Discussion of Asian Nations Being Dependent on One Another Like Teeth and Lips']. In *Zhang Taiyan zhenglun xuanji* (章太炎政論選), Volume 1. Beijing: Zhonghua shuju.

———. 1908. 'Indu ren zhi guan Riben' (印度人之觀日本) ['Indian's Visions of Japan']. *Minbao* (民報) 20 (April).

———. 1977. 'Guojialun' ['On the State']. In *Zhang Taiyan zhenglun xuanji* (章太炎政論選), Volume 1, pp. 359–70. Beijing: Zhonghua shuju.

———. [1908] 1978. 'Dasheng qixin lun bian' (大乘起信論辯) ['Disputing the Awakening of Mahayana Faith']. Reprinted in *Xiandai Fojiao xueshu congkan* (現代佛教學術叢刊) [*Collection of Modern Buddhist Scholarship*], Volume 35, pp. 9–12. Taipei: Dasheng wenhua chubanshe.

———. 1981. *Zhang Taiyan Xuanji: zhushiben* (章太炎選集—註釋本) [*Zhang Taiyan: Selected Works, with Notes*]. Edited by Zhu Weizheng and Jiang Yihua. Shanghai: Shanghai renmin chubanshe.

———. 1982–6. *Zhang Taiyan quanji* (章太炎全集) [*The Complete Works of Zhang Taiyan*], Volumes 4 and 6. Shanghai: Shanghai renmin chubanshe.

———. 1996a. *Gegu dingxin de zheli Zhang Taiyan wenxuan* (革故鼎新的哲理：章太炎文選) [*The Philosophy of Reform and Improvement*]. Shanghai: Shanghai Yuandong.

———. 1996b. 'Wu wu lun' (五無論) ['On the Five Negations Zhang Taiyan']. In *Gegu dingxin de zheli Zhang Taiyan wenxuan* (革故鼎新的哲理：章太炎文選) [*The Philosophy of Reform and Improvement*]. Shanghai: Shanghai Yuandong.

Zou Rong (鄒容). 1968. *The Revolutionary Army: A Chinese Nationalist Tract of 1903*. Translated by John Lust. Paris: Mouton.

———. 2002. *Geming jun* (革命軍) [*The Revolutionary Army*]. Beijing: Huaxia chubanshe.

SECTION II

ENCOUNTERS AND IMAGES

4

Through the 'Indian Lens'

Observations and Self-Reflections in Late Qing Chinese Travel Writings on India

ZHANG KE

Monks and merchants have been travelling between various regions of China and India for several centuries. From tenth century, maritime connections between these two parts of the world witnessed significant growth, and by the late Qing period (1840–1911), the sea route became the most usual way to travel from southern China to India. For instance, Kang Youwei (康有為), a renowned Confucian reformist who travelled to India in 1901, noted that there were six steamboats sailing from Guangzhou to Calcutta (now Kolkata) every month. According to him, thousands of Chinese businessmen, carpenters, and shoemakers, among others, travelled by this route (Kang [1902] 2007: 509). This upsurge in maritime connections was also associated with the colonization of several regions of Asia by Western powers. In fact, the exchanges between the Qing Empire and India were intertwined with the presence of the British in the region. This included the Qing concern over a possible military confrontation with the British (Mosca 2013: 222) and the expanding opium trade. It was against this historical backdrop that various Chinese writings on India emerged in the late Qing period.

These late Qing Chinese writings on India reveal new types of connections, concerns, and perceptions compared to the content of past Chinese writings, especially those written by Buddhist monks. Whilst Section II examines the mutual perceptions of Indians and Chinese in the nineteenth and early twentieth centuries, the current chapter focuses on the Chinese views on India as revealed in the analysed late Qing Chinese travel writings. There are two distinct modes of observation and critical reflection. On the one hand, by observing and analysing India, the Chinese authors tried to gain knowledge of British rule and the Western culture it represented. On the other hand, seeing a reflection of China in India, they pondered China's own international crisis through these writings. Often these two modes were intertwined, with India and Britain alternately becoming the 'other' in the Chinese imagination.

It should also be noted that these writings, which were mostly travelogues written by Chinese in India, mixed old perspectives and new experiences in what the authors considered exotic places. They were the intellectual products of a mixture of the ethnical, religious, and cultural background of each and every author. During the late Qing period, different Chinese writers, although travelling to the same place and sometimes part of the same delegations, felt and recounted their experiences in totally different manners. This indicated the diversity of people's awareness, understanding, and expectations of their travels.

In the decades following the Opium War (1839–42), several Chinese representatives travelled to India and wrote detailed reports and diaries (see Table 4.1). However, ignoring these people and their accounts, Kang Youwei claimed that he was 'the fourth person' in China to have travelled to India,[1] after the famous historical figures of Qin Jing (秦景),[2] Faxian (法顯), and San Zang (that is, Xuanzang [三藏]) (Kang [1902] 1995: 1). His claim was made despite the fact that Kang had actually read the work of Huang Maocai (黃楙材), who visited India in the late 1870s. In Kang's opinion, only those who visited India and left detailed accounts of Indian religions, politics,

Table 4.1   List of Late Qing Chinese Travelogues on India

Title	Author	Year of Travel
Journal of the Journey to the West (西輶日記)	Huang Maocai (黃楙材)	1878
Notes of the Journey (遊歷芻言)	Huang Maocai (黃楙材)	1878
Notes on India (印度箚記)	Huang Maocai (黃楙材)	1878
Notes of the Journey to the South (南行記)	Ma Jianzhong 馬建忠)	1881
Notes of the Journey to the South (南行日記)	Wu Guangpei (吳廣霈)	1881
Notes of the Journey to India (印度遊記)	Kang Youwei (康有為)	1901
Notes of the Journey to India (印度遊記)	Kang Tongbi (康同璧)	1901
Journal of the Journey to India and Ceylon to Investigate Tea Production in 1905 (乙巳考察印錫茶土日記)	Zheng Shihuang (鄭世璜)	1905
Journal of the Journey to India and Ceylon to Investigate Tea Production in 1905 (乙巳年調查印錫茶務日記)	Lu Ying (陸溁)	1905

Source: Compiled by author.

languages, arts, and contemporary developments with China's well-being in mind should count as 'travellers to India'. This not only reflects Kang's arrogance, but also the fact that some writers in late Qing China believed that travelogues were not merely descriptive records of the places they visited. Contrary to Kang's assertion, and as this chapter will demonstrate, some nineteenth-century Chinese writings on India contain detailed accounts and imaginings regarding the nature of the modern state and civilization in the context of the respective authors' encounters with India. These writings are important for understanding India–China connections in the late nineteenth century because they are rare first-hand accounts revealing Chinese perceptions of India in the aftermath of the Opium War.

Huang Maocai's Idealized India

Since the fifteenth century, Europeans have travelled by sea to South
Asia and been active in various coastal regions. The earliest record of
European activities in India can be found in the Chinese-language
work *Zhifang waiji* (職方外紀) [*Record of Foreign Lands*], an atlas compiled in 1623 by Giulio Aleni, a Catholic missionary who served at
the Ming imperial court (Aleni [1623] 1985: 16). This and other such
writings formed sources on India for Chinese text such as *Haiguo
wenjian lu* (海國聞見錄) [*Record of Things Seen and Heard about the
Maritime Countries*], compiled in 1730 (Chen Lunjiong [1730] 1991),
and *Hai lu* (海錄) [*Travels of the Seas*], composed in 1820 (Xie Qinggao
[1820] 2016).[3] These works provided basic details about South Asia
and pointed to the fact that the British had occupied many areas along
the coast.

Shortly before and, in particular, after the Opium War, the Chinese
began to seek information about India for more strategic purposes.
This is reflected in works such as *Sizhou zhi* (四洲志) [*Record of the
Four Continents*], compiled by Lin Zexu (林則徐) in 1839, and later
Haiguo tuzhi (海國圖志) [*Records with Maps of Maritime Countries*],
compiled in 1852 by Wei Yuan (魏源). In *Haiguo tuzhi*, Wei Yuan
described how the various ethnic groups in South Asia resisted British
rule. He suggests that the Qing government could exploit indigenous
resistance to the British to its own advantage and that of the Indian
minorities as well. He famously calls this strategy *yiyi zhiyi* (以夷制
夷), that is, to play off one group of foreigners against another (Wei
[1852] 1998: 773).

Although Wei Yuan had never visited India, his work was popular
and often carried by Chinese travellers to Southeast Asia and India.
By the 1860s, the Qing government had begun to dispatch officials
abroad on investigative tours, trying to find inspiring models for its
reform programme in China. Most of these officials were tasked to
keep and send home detailed records of what they had seen and heard
overseas. These records widened and deepened the Chinese understanding of foreign countries. In 1878, the Qing government sent
its first official delegation to India. The governor of Sichuan, Ding
Baozhen (丁寶楨), appointed Huang Maocai to head this delegation
in order to collect military information and study the geography of

India and the area that connected Sichuan to South Asia (Sen 2017: 265). Huang was born in Jiangxi Province and had excelled in his studies of European languages and cultures at the Tongwen School in Beijing.

Under the Sino-British Treaty of Yantai, signed in 1876, the British were allowed to send travellers into Tibet from either the Chinese mainland or India. Many Chinese officials such as Ding Baozhen were worried that the British would take advantage of this concession to establish a route from India through Darjeeling to Tibet, thus posing a threat to the Qing's defence on the Tibetan border and at the same time providing a gateway into the province of Sichuan. Therefore, Ding suggested that the central government appoint Huang to lead a delegation to India and collect intelligence on political and military affairs, as well as geographical information on British India.

From the start of his mission, Huang kept a detailed account of the route to India, Indian geography, and the various goods its regions produced. Prior to this mission, Huang had already travelled to Shanghai in 1866 and written *Huyou cuoji* (滬遊脞記) [*Notes of the Journey to Shanghai*] ([1886] 1994). In his book, Huang described the international situation in Shanghai and the Western presence in the city, including that of the British, French, and Russians. He praised the military and economic strengths of the British and described Britain as the strongest power in Europe. He also knew that most of India was already under British rule (Huang [1886] 1994: 164). Thus, Huang was well aware of the geopolitical situation in Asia and determined to examine British rule carefully in India.

In 1879, Huang first travelled to Rangoon and from there took a ship to Calcutta. During his journey and after his arrival in Calcutta, Huang was stunned as he noticed various things that Qing China did not have. He was full of admiration for British rule in India, which is reflected throughout his travelogue. On his way from Rangoon to Calcutta, for instance, Huang praised the British vessel that he boarded for being 'gorgeous, neat, and tidy'. The picturesque birch walls were particularly impressive to him. When he arrived in India, the first thing he took note of was the convenience of the railway system (Huang 1886a: 40). In his earlier book on Shanghai, Huang had already mentioned the usefulness of the British railway system, but this time, he was able to experience it. He took a train from Calcutta to Darjeeling, which he vividly described in his travelogue. In fact, during the rest of his journeys in India, he repeatedly travelled in trains, including to Delhi and Bombay (now Mumbai), and marvelled at the experience.

In addition, there were many material objects which Huang admired during his travels in India. For example, he talked about the speed of the telegram service. When the viceroy of India left Calcutta and went on holiday elsewhere, he explained, 'telegrams served as a means of communication if there was a major incident'. Similarly, the use of tap water in India drew his attention. He witnessed the construction of a water plant, noting that the 'water pumped from the bottom of the pool is clear and clean. It is brought to Calcutta by a large iron pipe and supplied to millions of people'. He was most impressed with the gas streetlamps in Calcutta, which were kept shining all night long. Huang mentioned the streetlamps several times in his travelogue, at one point noting that because of these lamps 'thieves find it difficult to escape, leading to few robberies'. Huang also reported meticulously and admiringly on the gardens, museums, zoos, and other public places in the capital of British India (Huang 1886b: 2–4).

Huang's perceptions of British India were driven by his curiosity about the new things he was seeing in a foreign land. Moreover, what he reported in his travelogue was highly selective and intended to serve a particular purpose. His eagerness to imitate Westerners, his preference for Westernization, and his exaggerated descriptions of the exotic were quite usual among late Qing Chinese travellers in foreign lands. Similar accounts and descriptions can be found, for example, in the works of Guo Songtao (郭嵩焘) and Wang Tao (王韬), both of whom visited European countries (Tian 2011).

Huang also praised the administrative efficiency of British officials in India, especially the proficiency of the police and judicial systems. Moreover, Indian politics is described as just, Indian society as orderly, and Indian industries as highly developed. It is evident, however, that Huang's praises were more about British rule in India than India itself. Lin Chengjie (林承节) (1993: 26), who discussed Huang Maocai's travelogue in his book on India–China relations after the Opium War, acknowledged that Huang focused too much on the new things brought to India by the colonial power and showed his envy of the British in his account. Indeed, in Huang's work, India is portrayed as a country dependent on the British and a model representative of British governance in Asia. Most of his narratives are written from the perspective of the British rulers and feature very few views of Indians themselves. Huang and his entourage travelled in different parts of India for six months and met a lot with ordinary Indians. Indeed, local customs and food habits are rarely discussed in Huang's work, suggesting that he was not interested in observing the native Indians.

Most notably, Huang failed to distinguish between Britain and India, often confusing the political structures of Britain with India to compare them with China. For example, he argued that 'China's political structure benefits the poor first, while the Western government supports the rich. Perhaps in the Western tradition being poor is shameful, and so Western people are all working hard to get rich' (Huang 1886b: 5). He then noted that the Indians were also devoted to working as hard as the British.

Similarly, while Huang acknowledges that the taxes imposed by the British are heavy, he comments that 'there is no complaint from the people' about this. He adds, 'Perhaps the previous local (Indian) governors were too cruel and mean. The British government, instead, uses taxes to develop the local infrastructure. Most people benefit from these and are thus pleased' (Huang 1886b: 3). It is clear that these views reported by Huang originated from his discussions with the British in India, which he accepted uncritically.

Although Huang sometimes described the British upper class in India as people 'pursuing pleasure without any restriction', this was not a critique of colonialism, but merely a curiosity about the lifestyle of the people he seemed to admire (Huang 1886b: 5). It was also part of his overall positive portrayal of British colonial rule that he wanted to convey to his Chinese readers. Huang was neither an experienced official nor a seasoned diplomat when he was commissioned to visit India. While he was one of the first Chinese to witness, experience, and record British rule in India, Huang did not explore the impact of the colonial administration on the local people. His meticulous account of British India turned out to be one-sided and did not provide a comprehensive picture of Indian society and culture. Huang's travelogue was published some years later. Although his travelogue did not have much direct impact on his contemporaries, it represented an idealized view, not altogether rare among Qing officials, of British rule in India.

India as an Enslaved Country

In 1881, two years after Huang's visit, Li Hongzhang (李鴻章) sent Ma Jianzhong to India tasked with meeting with the viceroy of India and discussing the exportation of opium from India to China. Wu Guangpei, Ma's close friend, was part of the mission. Neither knew of Huang's earlier trip to India and thus they compiled their own travelogues without any knowledge of the descriptions of India that had been written two decades ago.

There are several differences between the writings of Huang, Ma, and Wu concerning India. This includes a difference in writing styles because the objectives of the two missions were not the same. Huang Maocai travelled to India to collect general information about the region and wrote a work that was primarily a travelogue. Ma Jianzhong, however, had a specific mandate related to the opium trade. Ma's writings focus on the negotiations he had with officials and friends in Hong Kong, Southeast Asia, and India. Much of his writing dealt with issues of production, transportation, marketing, and tariffs of opium based on his discussions with the governor general, provincial governors, and other British officials. Everything, including relevant data, was recorded by Ma. In this regard, Ma's reporting was similar to that of Zheng Shihuang (鄭世璜), who visited India in 1905 to examine tea production in India. These two works are written in the form of official reports rather than accounts of places visited.

There are also differences between the works of Ma Jianzhong and Wu Guangpei. Wu notes in his journal that he had 'expurgated and polished' Ma's work (Wu 1890: 11). This indicates that Wu was Ma's assistant and secretary during the mission. It also suggests that Ma's original work may have been revised in the format of an official report. In contrast, Wu's record of his visit to India appears to be more casual and richer in content. Wu wrote meticulously during his trip. He had also read extensively prior to his visit. A comparison of the itineraries of Ma and Wu reveals that Wu did not always accompany Ma to official visits and meetings, so he had more private time to wander around and observe India and, at the same time, express more insightful views and thoughts.

Unlike Huang, Wu did not have a favourable opinion of India. Wu's knowledge about India prior to his visit came from Buddhist classics and legends, and his impression of the appearance of Indians derived from Buddhist portraits and statues. In the afternoon of the day after his arrival in Calcutta in 1881, Wu walked around his hotel and remarked that 'the natives are as dark as mud. The men and women are all ugly.' He felt that people did not have the 'good and solemn' appearance that was described in the Buddhist classics. He described as 'noisy and repugnant' a group of people who were smoking together on the street. The people of India, he concluded, had been enslaved by the British (Wu 1890: 15).

Distinctions in skin colour played an important role in the conceptualization of race in ancient China. Since the Song dynasty, with the increase in interactions with foreign regions, racial awareness had become more prominent, skin colour coming to be linked to the respective qualities of different cultures. As Dikötter points out, this can be seen in the sinicization of Buddhist divinities, who were transformed from darker and semi-naked Indian figures into gods with fair complexions and regal forms of dress (Dikötter 2015: 12).

Chinese scholars who went to Southeast Asia and India in the late nineteenth and early twentieth centuries, therefore, discovered that the local people looked very different from what they had imagined through textual knowledge. As a result, these scholars labelled the cultures of these regions as 'inferior'. During his trip to India in 1901, for example, Kang Youwei ([1902] 2007: 539) made several references to the dark skin and short stature of the 'lower classes' in India. From these physical observations, he concluded that they were unintelligent, lacked in self-assertion, and deserved to be enslaved by the Westerners. Similarly, when Xue Fucheng (薛福成) (1985: 86) travelled to Southeast Asia and India on his way to Europe in 1890, he remarked that the people in these regions 'are all dark and short. Compared with them, the Chinese people look gentle and pretty. And there are significant differences between these people and the white and strong Europeans.'

With regard to British rule of India, both Ma and Wu seem to support the legitimacy of the colonial government. When they passed through Agra after visiting the Taj Mahal, Ma commented on the Indian Mutiny of 1857. In his view, the Mughal ruler of India had 'spread rumours and incited the hearts of the people'. Ma claimed that the uprising of Indian soldiers was a 'betrayal' and the British troops were 'pacifying' the rebels (Ma 1896: 16). And while Huang praised British governance in India, Wu focused on Indian nationalism and argued that the British were able to rule India because the Indians were preoccupied with their cultural achievements.

In general, Wu's perspective on the Indian nation was starkly different from Huang's. Huang had described India's rapid development under the administration of the British; Wu saw an India that had been enslaved by the British. Later, after the Sino-Japanese War (1894–5), Wu Guangpei (1898: 6) wrote another book in which he criticized previous scholars who had travelled abroad only to be shocked by the 'Western cars, buildings and other physical things without any insights of the enemy'. Although he did not know of Huang's writings on India, it is evident that Wu was criticizing a common perception of the West among Chinese travellers in the second half of the nineteenth century.

On his arrival in Calcutta, Wu lamented that 'such a rich country with such a vast territory was ruled by another nation. Dependent on others, the [Indian] people live on in degradation'. Wu was repelled by seeing Indians sitting and smoking, and kneeling to worship in the morning. Noting the brilliance of ancient India, the recent decline of ancient religions and the colonization of the region, he remarked that the Indians 'are ignorant and simple ... destined to be slaves when another nation conquered India after the sea route became accessible'. He also asked, 'How do the Indian people remain so content as if nothing had happened? Don't they feel sad and ashamed?' (Wu 1890: 17).

Since Qing China faced a similar threat from Britain's military encroachment into East Asia, and because of the increasing addiction to opium among Chinese people, Wu did not appreciate the 'good governance' of the British as Huang did. Taking the opposite position, he raged at the meekness of the Indian people. When he travelled to Rajasthan to study the battlefields where Indians had fought against the British Army, he commented that it was not enough to defend territory simply by relying on bravery in battle—a good strategy was also crucial (Wu 1890: 18).

Wu placed India on the same level as China and saw it as containing lessons for his country. In fact, Wu often compared India with China, calling India 'affluent and prosperous': '[W]ith only a third of the Chinese territory, India can generate an annual expenditure of sixty trillion gold pounds, which is more than seven times the amount of China's. Thus, we get to know how rich India is' (Wu 1890: 14). Wu's understanding of the modern history of India came only from Chinese geographical records such as *Haiguo tuzhi*, which did not contain many details about the country. In his view the fact that India, a wealthy and prosperous land, was conquered so easily by the British indicated the meekness of the Indians. This view shaped his narrative and analysis of India.

Prior to his travels in India, Wu had worked in the Chinese embassy in Japan. In addition, he had had discussions with Ma Jianzhong and other acquaintances who were knowledgeable about foreign affairs and geopolitics of the late nineteenth century. Within this context, Wu, like Ma, did not perceive the West favourably and held it in contempt. For example, in considering the defence of the Qing Empire and the 'overall situation in Asia', Wu (1890: 16) expressed concern about the inroads Europeans were making in the region. Unlike Huang, who praised the convenience of the railway system, Wu worried that the British wanted to build a railroad through northeastern India to the Yunnan region. In other words, Wu thought that the British had an ulterior motive in building the railways, which was to help Britain expand its colonies, resulting in a 'monstrous disaster' for China (Wu 1890: 18).

Wu also had more serious concerns about the international situation. He said:

> In a situation in which every nation in the world is competing fiercely with every other and only the strongest survive, an old nation has to change its traditional way of ruling and act aggressively 'like a beast'. Only in this way will the nation not lose out in international competition so that we can truly preserve the inner 'benevolence'. (Wu 1890: 15)

Rare for his time, Wu already had a strong pan-Asian perspective. He also said, 'Looking around Asia, India and Turkey are the other big countries apart from China. Now that India has been destroyed, it should be regarded as a lesson for other countries' (Wu 1890: 15).

Invoking the collapse of India and Turkey as a warning for China became common at the turn of the century, but Wu was one of the first Chinese writers to refer to this in the early 1880s.

Wu's views are associated with changes in general Chinese perceptions of India during the late Qing dynasty. The perception changed from India as a strategic middle zone between the British and Qing empires to India as an Asian country which was similar to China in also being at the critical juncture of 'modern transformation'. The differences in the writings of Huang and Wu about India reflect this shift. This change in the Chinese people's concept of India was closely related to the spread of Western learning and the increase in 'crisis awareness' among Chinese intellectuals. More broadly, it was also associated with the process of China's gradual integration into the global system, as well as changes in China's self-understanding in a world dominated by nation-states (Esherick 2006). In Wu's travelogue, India as the object of observation started to become more prominent than the British 'other' in the region.

In the late Qing period, other officials were also sent to visit India. In 1905, Zhou Fu (周馥), the viceroy of Liangjiang, appointed Zheng Shihuang to lead a delegation to India and Ceylon to study tea production and trade. The whole journey lasted more than four months. Zheng Shihuang and the secretary of the delegation, Lu Ying, both wrote about their visits. Tea was one of the most important of China's exports. However, since the mid-nineteenth century, the sale of Indian tea had grown rapidly in the international market. By the 1880s, the Indian tea industry had become more competitive than China's. One of the objectives of Zheng's mission was to learn about the experience of tea cultivation and production from India, Ceylon (now Sri Lanka), and other regions. After returning to China, he wrote a detailed report on the production of tea in India and Ceylon in which he advised the viceroy on how to improve the tea industry in China.

As with the writings of Ma Jianzhong and Wu Guangpei, the reports of Zheng Shihuang and Lu Ying overlapped with each other substantially and, in many cases, the sections were exactly the same. It is possible that a considerable part of Zheng's report was written by Lu. Zheng's report dealt mostly with the tea industry and economy in a very simple and straightforward fashion without offering any personal opinions. In contrast, Lu's report is much richer in content, the detailed observations, and records found in his work making it a valuable historical text. Lu had much sympathy for Indians, both labourers and well-educated intellectuals. Shortly after he arrived in Calcutta in July 1905, he met Lu Yunqiu (陸雲秋), a Chinese person living in the city's Chinatown who brought him to visit the local Indian (Bengali) elites. From these Indians, Lu came to know about the Indian independence movement. He noted, 'I learned that in recent years, the Indian people have thought quite a lot about autonomy. They said that Asia used to be integrated. Unfortunately, India was invaded by the West, which stopped India from interacting with China. What an extraordinary claim! How intelligent the Indian people are!' (Lu 1905: 53).

It is clear that the Indian concept of 'an integrated Asia' was new to him. Like the other Chinese visitors, Lu Ying also analysed the reasons for India's decline and concluded that they were deeply rooted in the caste system and in vulgar customs like child marriage and opium consumption, both of which, he believed, made social reforms difficult to implement. In his opinion, the plethora of religions, languages, and cultures throughout South Asia was hindering the revival of a unified Indian nation.

Among his contemporaries, Lu shows rare optimism about the prospect of Indian independence and claimed that India 'will certainly become independent' in the future. He argued that there were two reasons why Indian independence was a likely prospect: 'inspiration from Japan, and the Indians' eagerness to learn' (Lu 1905: 53). Lu meant that externally, many Japanese exchanged ideas with Indians and disseminated nationalist ideals in India. Internally, the number of educated people in India continued to increase, many of whom were daring to criticize the British administration openly. Lu Ying (1905: 53) added the following comments:

So far, the Indians have never forgotten the decay of their nation. They do not have enough knowledge and capability, and thus have borne shame until today. How could an ancient civilization with thousands of years of history and three hundred million people be degraded to be the domain of slaves and darkness? Today, the Commonwealth of Australia has gained her autonomy, and Canada has set up her parliament. Their influence can reach almost every corner of the world. The British people had better change the way they rule India.

At the beginning of the twentieth century, a strong awareness of the crisis associated with Western colonialism spread among the Chinese intelligentsia. Many scholars compiled and published treatises explaining the decline of ancient civilizations. By narrating these episodes, they endeavoured to cultivate the idea of national salvation among their own people (Karl 2002; Yu 1996; Zou 2012: 390). Within this context works were written describing the decline of Indian civilization. The familiarity with the Indian situation found in Lu Ying's work indicates that he was aware of this broader discourse. Furthermore, the aforementioned quotation echoed Liang Qichao's (1899: 2) lament and warning to his 'four hundred million compatriots' who had been enslaved by the Westerners in his popular article 'Aiguo lun'. Obviously, Lu Ying seemed to be expressing his own feelings for China's suffering in the post–Opium War period through the imagination of the Indian nation.

In the travelogues of Wu Guangpei and Lu Ying, the anxiety over China's own destiny forced them to view India from a nationalist perspective. India was not simply a vassal of the British, but an independent entity that needed to be observed. Lu was arguably the first Chinese to take note of India's nationalist independence movement. He was also among the first Chinese scholars to write about the changing British policy on India.

Kang Youwei: India as the 'Other'

Prior to travelling to India in 1901, Kang Youwei had been to Canada, Britain, and other foreign countries. In the aftermath of the failed Hundred Days' Reform in 1898, Kang escaped to Penang, where the 'heat and malaria' made him sick. It took him several months to recover from his illness. He was subsequently advised that relocating to the snow-capped mountainous parts of northern India would benefit him. From Penang he took a ship to India along with his daughter Kang Tongbi, arriving in Calcutta on 12 December 1901. In the following several weeks, Kang travelled throughout northern India, arriving early in 1902 in Darjeeling, in the foothills of the Himalayas, where he stayed there for more than a year. He left India in 1903.

Unlike the other Chinese travellers to India mentioned previously, Kang and his daughter were not on an official mission to the country.

Rather, Kang's visit to India was decided in a hurry and was not well planned. In the preface to his travelogue, *Yindu youji*, Kang discussed the development of the ancient Indian civilization. He remarked that during the past several thousand years few people had travelled to India and no one had studied the religions and politics of ancient India or their recent history. He noted that 'there must be something worth learning from India for China', thereby hoping to justify his decision to move to India (Kang [1902] 2005: 509).

It should also be noted that many of Kang Youwei's overseas travelogues have attracted scholarly attention. However, his writings on India are rarely examined, even though they are rich in content. When Kang was in Canada, he called on the Chinese people to support the last Qing emperor and save the country. In India, he wrote about his loneliness and seclusion, which essentially framed his narrative. The changes in Kang Youwei's thoughts during his stay in India are important aspects of his travelogue on the country.[4] Here only a brief analysis of what he observed on India and Britain can be provided.

According to Kang, when he read the Buddhist scriptures in 1884, he began to learn about Brahmanism as well. Then, in 1890, he wrote a book titled *Poluomenjiao kao* (婆羅門教考) [*An Examination of Brahmanism*], but the work was lost after the Hundred Days' Reform (Kang [1898] 1992: 22). Regardless of whether or not this book about Brahmanism ever existed, Kang seldom elaborated on the ancient Indian civilization until 1900. For the first time in his assessment of India in 1895, he talked about India and Turkey together and regarded them as the examples of 'declining ancient powers'. He said that India had 'few wise men' and that 'Turkey, with the best army, had been weakened and India, by advocating the doctrine of laissez-faire, had been destroyed. That is the clear manifestation of the lack of wise people' (Kang [1895] 2007: 42). He also thought that India was too conservative. In between this article and his trip to India in 1901, Kang held to this view of India.

Since Kang had been to London and had lived in Canada for more than a year, he already had an in-depth understanding of Western societies. Therefore, his perceptions of the British in India differed from those of Huang Maocai. When Kang was in India, he became acquainted with members of the upper class in the British-Indian government. He was also a keen observer of the system of government.

For example, he said that 'The British employ lots of ceremonial rituals to awe their subjects. In India, the governor general's parade [in India] is grander than the Queen's procession in London. In other respects, how the British rule India is far different from how they govern their own country' (Kang [1902] 2007: 520). This kind of comparative analysis is rarely found in earlier Chinese writings on India. In addition, Kang also often compared Indian and Chinese civilizations and considered the British 'outsiders'.

Generally, Kang praised the ancient civilization of India. In his preface, he notes that 'the cultural relics, religions, the writing systems, the palaces, and the utensils in Europe and America originated in India. These civilizations are related closely' (Kang [1902] 2007: 513). Kang was aware of ancient Europe, as well as of the Egyptian and Mesopotamian civilizations, but he grouped European and American civilizations under Indian civilization as both originate from Indian civilization, to help him compare Indian and Chinese civilizations (Kang [1902] 2007: 509).

Kang also complimented India for preserving its historical artefacts. Like Kang, Huang Maocai, Ma Jianzhong, and Wu Guangpei had also visited the Taj Mahal and various museums in India, only to mention how finely they had been built, but Kang ([1902] 2007: 530) noted that, 'in preserving historical artefacts, China has done far worse than India'. Kang visited many sites in India and was impressed with their magnificence and gorgeous decoration. He further noted that the ancient Chinese palaces built of wood could not be preserved for long, whereas the Indian and European palaces were built of stone and could thus 'last for thousands of years' because the material was 'strong and enduring' (Kang [1902] 2007: 530).

However, a careful examination of Kang's travelogue reveals his contempt for present-day Indian society. During his travels around northern India he saw filthy streets, lazy people, strange customs, and 'unsavoury food'. He also described in detail the difficulties and inconveniences he encountered during his travels, as well as the incomprehensibility of present-day Indian customs and practices.

From the aforementioned criticisms, it is clear that Kang initially did not have a good impression of India. The reason for this is twofold. First, because of his visits to London and Canada, Kang, unlike Huang Maocai, was able to identify India's shortcomings when juxtaposed to Britain and North America. Kang exaggerated and magnified these shortcomings, commenting that British rule in India had not changed anything. Second, similar to Wu, Kang arrived in India expecting to see a Holy Land depicted in Chinese Buddhist sources. This was evident from the poems he wrote soon after he reached India. Nearly every poem expressed his disappointment with the failure to find Buddhist monuments. Lines such as 'looking for a Pure Land in Buddhahood', 'Seeking Buddhism around without any results', and 'I came to India to visit Buddhist remains' were repeated in his poems (Kang [1902] 1996: 148–150). Obviously, he was saddened by the decline of Buddhism in India, which seems also to have affected his views of India.

For Kang, Buddhism in ancient India and its role in connecting China and India were key elements of both Indian and Chinese civilizations. It was out of intellectual curiosity that Kang had examined Brahmanism when he read Buddhist scriptures. At the start of his travels in India, he was very interested in the local 'Brahmin temple', but after visiting a few temples, he became disillusioned. When he arrived in Mathura, he visited the 'Great Temple' and found that 'the natives spoke of the great Goddess of Brahmin, but there was nothing about Buddha at all'. Then he turned around and left immediately, saying that he would 'no longer visit Brahmin temples' (Kang [1902] 2007: 529).

Kang's dismay regarding Brahmanism was not merely because of his disappointment at the Mathura temple, but rather resulted from his belief that Brahmanism should be blamed for India's decline. In his view, there were two reasons for its decline. First of all, 'the pioneers of Brahmanism advocated "benevolence" too strongly and were too eager to achieve it' (Kang [1902] 2007: 532). He believed not only that the idea of 'benevolence' had been difficult to disseminate in ancient times, but that it was also untenable in the modern times due to cruelty of the British colonizers. He remarked that the Indians 'cared much more about the things they made, but they failed to protect themselves' and thus were enslaved by others (Kang [1902] 2007: 532). Kang quoted the 'three-stages theory' found in the classical Confucian text Chunqiu (春秋) [Spring and Autumn Annals] (c. 5 BCE) to the effect that a society must go through a 'stage of decay and chaos', then a 'stage of rising peace' before finally reaching 'universal peace'.

He thought that India became weak because what Brahmanism advocated was incompatible with the stage of decay and chaos, though it was more suitable for the two stages of peace (Kang [1902] 2007: 532).

The second reason for the decline of India, according to Kang Youwei, was the caste system advocated by Brahmanism. Initially, Kang did not know much about the caste system. He found it strange that the Indians he saw, regardless of appearance and knowledge, were different from what he had previously imagined. He nonetheless learned something about the hierarchical system in ancient India and concluded that 'what I saw were all the lower-class people. The upper-class people are clever and strong, and thus ancient Indian civilization can lead the world' (Kang [1902] 2007: 540). Lamenting the harm that the caste system had caused Indian society, he remarked that 'the worst thing Indian people do is grade people [according to their birth]'. Perhaps influenced by what he saw, Kang set out to write *Datong shu* (大同書) [*A Book on Great Harmony*] ([1902] 2005) to explain the theory of human equality. This book frequently discussed the suffering of Indians that was caused by inequality. However, Kang was clearly not fully knowledgeable about the caste system. For example, he believed that the upper and lower castes had great differences in both physical appearance and their spirits. The lower castes 'look dark and have glazed eyes', while the upper castes have 'bigger heads, strong bodies and bright eyes'. This physiological distinction, he believed, was hereditary. 'People in the lower castes do not value literature and do not know how to keep healthy. Their stupidity is passed on [to the next generation] and keeps getting worse' (Kang [1902] 2007: 539).

Kang also contrasted ancient Indian civilizations with the modern period based on his incorrect understanding of the caste system. 'On the roads in India', he explained, 'I saw no upper-caste people. The upper-castes can only be seen in cars.' On meeting them one could, he says, understand '[w]hy the pioneers of Indian philosophy were so intelligent' (Kang [1902] 2007: 540). However, in the modern era, because the lower castes are in the majority, the whole nation had become less intelligent. The decline of India, Kang concludes, 'was in effect a result of this inequality among the people' (Kang [1902] 2007: 540). Kang also expressed such views in *Datong shu* and insisted that although there were two hundred million people in India, only ten or twenty million were upper castes. The lower castes, according to him, were 'unable to fight on the battlefield', resulting in the defeat of the country by the British colonizers (Kang [1902] 2005: 105).

Kang's criticism of the lower castes clearly carries with it a tone of racism. For example, he writes that '[t]he Indians I saw are very foolish, dark, short and with very small heads' (Kang [1902] 2007: 539). He also disparaged them, saying that the Indians were lethargic and lacked proper knowledge. When fighting against the intelligent and strong British, they were easily defeated. Conquered by another nation for almost a hundred years, India had not changed a bit. The Indian people were too foolish to understand the world situation and were thus doomed. He also blamed the lower castes for 'first letting the country be destroyed by Muslims, then the Mongols, and finally the British. The Indian people are extremely stupid and weak. Now they are enslaved like sheep and barely able to keep themselves alive' (Kang [1902] 2007: 532).

In addition to criticizing India and the Indians, Kang praised China and the Chinese. When he first arrived in India, Kang delivered a talk at the Tianhou Temple in Calcutta's Chinatown. 'Indians are surely going to destroy their own country,' he told his Chinese audience. In contrast to the lazy and unintelligent Indians, 'the Chinese were quick-witted, diligent and united. Unlike India, China had the aspiration to be independent. In this regard, only Europe could surpass China' (Kang [1902] 2007: 515). When comparing India and China with respect to their respective social hierarchies, he viewed China as a model of egalitarian society and said, 'People enjoy more equality in China, which is really one of Confucius' great achievements' (Kang [1902] 2007: 515).

As noted earlier, Kang's writings on India are much more personal than those of the other travellers because his works were not official reports. He elaborated on the connections and differences between China and India from the perspective of 'civilization', observations, and an analytical framework that are not found in the writings of the earlier Chinese travellers to India. After visiting north India, Kang wrote a preface for his travelogue in which he explained that civilization is a blend of differences and that the more it blended the more civilized society became. Therefore, for him, only mutual exchanges could inspire the growth of civilizations. Kang said that Chinese civilization had benefited from the influences it had received from India. However, it had had no impact on India in return, which had caused India to remain conservative and to lack progress.

In the early 1880s, Wu Guangpei had realized that India provided China with a negative example with respect to modern geopolitics. China should not repeat the mistakes of India. As the situation in China worsened in the aftermath of the Opium War, the Chinese lamented that China was on the same ill-fated path as India. In this depressing atmosphere, Kang took the opposite position and tried his best to inspire national self-confidence by underscoring the strengths of Chinese civilization. He did so by differentiating India and China and by disparaging the former. As a historical text, Kang's travelogue on India was a mixture of sound arguments and extreme bias.

***

These travelogue writers who visited India in the late Qing period neither knew the local languages nor had a comprehensive understanding of Indian religions and cultures. Therefore, even though they had many experiences and their records were detailed, their descriptions were often biased. Regardless of whether they recorded the 'facts', provided analysis of the country through individual perspectives, or reflected the expectations of their own imaginations, these writings are nonetheless valuable historical sources. For scholars in the late Qing period, not unlike their counterparts in present-day China, India was considered a good reference point for understanding the situation in China.

However, the use of such reference points is fraught with problems and complications. Travel often provides a way to reconfirm one's own cultural identity and beliefs, being marked by constant cycles of 'culture shock' and 'cultural adherence' (Guo 2005). The late Qing Chinese observations on India turned out to be more complex than the Indian views on China, discussed in Chapters 5 and 6 in this volume. While Huang Maocai utterly praised British governance in India, the observers after Huang were more eager to find out the reasons why India became colonized by Britain, largely provoked by the crisis of contemporary China. They stood against the Western colonists, but showed some admiration for the Western civilization.

This paradoxical stance was best showcased in the writing of Kang Youwei. In his writings, Kang Youwei sometimes criticized India in order to justify British colonial rule, while at other times he criticized India in order to praise China. He also occasionally used examples from Britain and India to criticize China, which actually reflects shifts in the imagination of the 'other'. During the colonial era this shift is particularly noteworthy, with the 'modern' narrative centring on the West, and the expression of superiority and the ranking of each nation's own culture.

The works by Chinese travellers to India in the late Qing period discussed in this chapter offer different perceptions of a region that had intensive interactions with China in the past. When they visited India in the late nineteenth and early twentieth centuries, however, the region was under British rule and China had been humiliated by the same Western colonial power. After all, they arrived in India, only to find that 'Buddhist India' had long gone and they would have to recast its contemporary story for their Chinese readers.

Notes

1. There are two different existing versions of Kang Youwei's 1901–2 Indian travelogue, the manuscript copy (*shougao ben* [手稿本]) and the mimeograph copy (*youyin ben* [油印本]); the latter was edited by his daughter Kang Tongbi (康同璧) in the 1950s. The manuscript copy appears in Kang ([1902] 1995), while the mimeograph copy is collected under Kang ([1902] 2007). In the mimeograph copy, Kang became 'the fifth person' in China to travel to India, adding Hui Yun (惠云), a Tang Buddhist monk as the fourth traveller prior to Kang himself.

2. In 64 CE, Qin Jing (秦景), an Eastern Han official, was sent on a mission westward by Emperor Mingdi (漢明帝) to study Buddhism. He did not reach India; instead, he met two Indian Buddhist monks in areas inhabited by the Greater Yuezhi (大月氏) and took them back to Luoyang (洛陽). This is regarded as the beginning of Buddhism in China. Kang mistook Qin as the first Chinese to reach India.

3. For a detailed analysis of these books, see Mosca (2013: Chapter 6).

4. For other studies of Kang's Indian travelogue ([1902] 2007), see Lin (2007), Liu (2012), and Wang (2007). Unlike these studies, I regard the formation of Kang's perceptions of India as a more dynamic process.

This chapter focuses on Kang Youwei's 1902 Indian travelogue, while Chapters 1 and 5 in this volume examine Kang's other works.

References

Aleni, Giulio. [1623] 1985. *Zhifang waiji* (職方外紀) [*Record of Foreign Lands*]. Beijing: Zhonghua shuju.

Chen Lunjiong (陳倫炯). [1730] 1991. *Haiguo wenjian lu* (海國聞見錄) [*Record of Things Seen and Heard about the Maritime Countries*]. Beijing: Zhonghua shuju.

Dikötter, Frank. 2015. *The Discourse of Race in Modern China*. Oxford: Oxford University Press.

Esherick, Joseph. 2006. 'How the Qing Became China'. In Joseph Esherick, Hasan Kayali, and Eric van Young (eds), *Empire to Nation: Historical Perspectives on the Making of the Modern World*, pp. 229–59. Lanham MD: Rowman & Littlefield.

Guo Shaotang (郭少棠). 2005. *Lüxing: Kuawenhua xiangxiang* (旅行：跨文化想象) [*Travel: Trans-cultural Imaginations*]. Beijing: Beijing daxue chubanshe.

Huang Maocai (黃楙材). 1886a. *Xiyou riji* (西輶日記) [*Journal of the Journey to the West*]. Shanghai: Menghuaxuan.

———. 1886b. *Yindu zhaji* (印度箚記) [*Notes on India*]. Shanghai: Menghuaxuan.

———. [1866] 1994. *Huyou cuoji* (滬游脞記) [*Notes of the Journey to Shanghai*]. Shanghai: Shanghai shudian chubanshe.

Kang Youwei (康有為). [1898] 1992. *Kang Youwei zibian nianpu* (康有為自編年譜) [*A Self-Edited Chronicle of Kang Youwei's Life*]. Beijing: Zhonghua shuju.

———. [1902] 1995. *Kang Youwei yigao: lieguo youji* (康有為遺稿·列國遊記) [*Unpublished Manuscripts of Kang Youwei: Travelogues*]. Shanghai: Shanghai renmin chubanshe.

———. [1902] 1996. *Kang Youwei yigao: Wanmu caotang shiji* (康有為遺稿·萬木草堂詩集) [*Unpublished Manuscripts of Kang Youwei: A Collection of Poems*]. Shanghai: Shanghai renmin chubanshe.

———. [1902] 2005. *Datong shu* (大同書) [*A Book on Great Harmony*]. Shanghai: Shanghai guji chubanshe.

———. [1895] 2007. 'Shang Qingdi diershu' (上清帝第二書) ['The Second Statement Submitting to the Emperor']. In Jiang Yihua and Zhang Ronghua (eds), *Kang Youwei quanji* (康有為全集) [*The Complete Works of Kang Youwei*], Volume 2, pp. 32–45. Beijing: Zhongguo Renmin daxue chubanshe.

———. [1902] 2007. 'Yindu youji' (印度遊記) ['Notes of the Journey to India'].
In Jiang Yihua and Zhang Ronghua (eds), *Kang Youwei quanji* (康有為全
集) [*The Complete Works of Kang Youwei*], Volume 5, pp. 509–50. Beijing:
Zhongguo Renmin daxue chubanshe.

Karl, Rebecca. 2002. *Staging the World: Chinese Nationalism at the Turn of the
Twentieth Century*. Durham, NC: Duke University Press.

Liang Qichao. 1899 (梁啟超). 'Aiguo lun' (愛國論) ['On Patriotism']. In Liang
Qichao (ed.), *Qingyi bao* (清議報), Volume 7, pp. 1–9. Yokohama: Qingyi
bao she.

Lin Chengjie (林承節). 1993. *Zhong-Yin renmin youhao guanxi shi, 1851–1949*
(中印人民友好 關係史, 1851–1949) [*A History of the Friendship between the
Chinese and the Indians, 1851–1949*]. Beijing: Beijing daxue chubanshe.

———. 2007. 'Kang Youwei lun Yindu he tade Yindu youji' (康有為論印
度和他的<印度遊記>) ['On Kang Youwei's Perceptions of India and his
Indian Travelogue']. In *Clio at Beida* (*Beida shixue* [北大史學]), Volume 12,
pp.164–87. Beijing: Beijing daxue chubanshe.

Lin Zexu. [1839] 2002. *Sizhou zhi* (四洲誌) [*Record of the Four Continents*].
Beijing: Huaxia chubanshe.

Liu, Xi. 2012. 'Kang Youwei's Journey to India: Chinese Discourse on India
during the Late Qing and Republican Periods'. *China Report* 48 (1, 2):
171–85.

Lu Ying (陸漻). 1905. *Yisi nian diaocha Yin-Xi chawu riji* (乙巳年調查印錫
茶務日記) [*Journal of the Journey to India and Ceylon to Investigate the Tea
Production in 1905*]. Shanghai: Nanyang yinshua guanchang.

Ma Jianzhong (馬建忠). 1896. *Nan xingji* (南行記) [*Notes of the Journey to the
South*]. Shanghai: Zhuyishi.

Mosca, Matthew. 2013. *From Frontier Policy to Foreign Policy: The Question
of India and the Transformation of Geopolitics in Qing China*. Stanford:
Stanford University Press.

Sen, Tansen. 2017. *India, China, and the World: A Connected History*. Lanham,
MD: Rowman & Littlefield.

Tian, Xiaofei. 2011. *Visionary Journeys: Travel Writings from Early Medieval
and Nineteenth-Century China*. Cambridge MA: Harvard University Asia
Center.

Wang Xiangyuan (王向遠). 2007. *Foxin Fanying: Zhongguo zuojia yu Yindu
wenhua* (佛心梵影：中國作家與印度文化) [*Chinese Writers and the Indian
Culture*]. Beijing: Beijing Shifan daxue chubanshe.

Wei Yuan (魏源). [1852] 1998. *Haiguo tuzhi* (海國圖志) [*Records with Maps of
Maritime Countries*], Volume 2. Changsha: Yuelu shushe.

Wu Guangpei (吳廣霈). 1890. *Nanxing riji* (南行日記) [*Journal of the Journey
to the South*]. Hong Kong: Taoyuan.

————. 1898. *Jianhuatang jiushi yaoce wanyan shu* (劍華堂救時要策萬言書) [*Ten Thousand Words from Jianhua Tang on Rescuing the Nation*]. Shanghai: Zhuyitang.

Xie Qinggao (謝清高). [1820] 2016. *Hai lu* (海錄) [*Travels of the Seas*]. Changsha: Yuelu Shushe.

Xue Fucheng (薛福成). [1892] 1985. *Chushi Yin Fa Yi Bi siguo riji* (出使英法義比四國日記) [*Journals of the Diplomatic Missions to Britain, France, Italy and Belgium*]. Changsha: Yuelu shushe.

Yu Danchu (俞旦初). 1996. *Aiguo zhuyi yu Zhongguo jindai shixue* (愛國主義與中國近代 史學) [*Patriotism and Modern Chinese Historiography*]. Beijing: Zhongguo Shehui kexue chubanshe.

Zheng Shihuang (鄭世璜). 1905. *Yisi kaocha Yin-Xi chatu riji* (乙巳考察印錫茶土日記) [*Journal of the Journey to India and Ceylon to Investigate the Tea Production in 1905*]. Shanghai: Nanyang yinshua guanchang.

Zou Zhenhuan (鄒振環). 2012. *Shutong zhiyi shi* (疏通知譯史) [*A History of Translation Studies*]. Shanghai: Shanghai renmin chubanshe.

5

India–China 'Connectedness'

China and Pan-Asianism in the Late Nineteenth- to Mid-Twentieth-Century Writings in Hindi

KAMAL SHEEL

S tudies of interactions between India and China suffer not only from a lack of materials but also from the absence of the meaningful study of even the few materials that are available. In this context, this chapter introduces popular writings in Hindi from the late nineteenth to mid-twentieth centuries and examines their representations of encounters between India and China. To the extent that these representations evolved in the shadow of tensions between traditional 'civilizational bonhomie' and the modern West-inspired 'nationalism's anxieties', they facilitate our comprehension of the production of contemporary Indian discourse on China in India and its dilemmas and predicaments. As such, I follow the task undertaken in the other two chapters of this section by Anand Yang and Zhang Ke.

In sampling writings on China in Hindi, I have mostly focused on those available in editorials, reportage, introductory descriptions, and news items with extended version of some in English. They have been mostly collected from such major local libraries as the Kashi Nagari Pracharini Sabha, Varanasi; Carmichael Library, Varanasi; Bharat Kala Bhavan Museum and Library, Varanasi; Nehru Memorial Museum and Library, Delhi; and Hardayal (Hardinge) Municipal Public Library, Delhi. Besides these, the Reza Library in Rampur, Uttar Pradesh, and Khuda Bakhsh Library in Patna, Bihar, were also scanned for writings in Urdu/Hindustani.[1] It is evident that reporting on China in Hindi newspapers and magazines is pretty limited until the First World War. Their numbers, however, increase several times over from the 1930s.

Of all the Hindi-language magazines, perhaps the most important was *Saraswati*, which commenced publishing in 1900 and continued until the 1980s at different frequencies of publication. It was initially edited by Mahavir Prasad Dwivedi, a journalist and such a stalwart of Hindi prose that a whole age in the history of Hindi literature is named after him. *Saraswati* periodically reported on China and expressed opinions and concerns about events there. Other periodicals that sporadically covered China were *Kavivachansudha, Bharat Jeevan, Hindostan, Hindi Bangvasi, Hindi Pradeep, Maryada, Madhuri*, and *Hans*. Balmukund Gupta was another key figure in the development of Hindi journals and prose, being editor of *Hindostan. Aj*, established by Shiv Prasad Gupt, and *Abhyudaya* by Pandit Madan Mohan Malaviya, published in Varanasi and Allahabad (now Prayagraj), respectively, were influential Hindi newspapers that reported and remarked on China's flirtations with modernity.

My forays into the archives of Urdu and Persian materials, namely, the Khuda Bakhsh Library in Patna and the Raza Library in Rampur, led to Urdu translations of some late nineteenth-century books on China being uncovered. This includes several volumes of translations of George Curzon's 1894 travelogue-based *History of China* [*Tareekh-e Mamalike Cheen*] and an 1867 translation of Lord Elgin's *History of China and Japan* [*Tareekh-e-Cheen-wa-Japan*]. Others relate to early twentieth-century travelogues on China, descriptions of Chinese Muslims and of Islam in China, commentaries on the Communist movement in China, and translations of Chinese stories and anecdotes.

However, in examining writings in native languages, one must be sensitive to the range of sources that influence narratives and produce 'invented' or 'reinvented' descriptions. Popular literature more often than not legitimized or delegitimized prevailing ideas and values through their selective appropriation of news items and reports in 'formal' or 'official' literature. It borrowed concepts and frameworks from writings in English produced from the perspective of empire and colonies and presented them as part of a 'civilizing', 'progressive', or 'modern' agenda. In the burgeoning literature in Hindi, obvious examples are writings by missionary societies such as the Christian Literary Society or the North Indian Christian Tract and Book Society in Allahabad. These compared nations and their characteristics on the basis of their self-introduced or devised yardsticks. So great was their influence that the first Indian travelogue on China (*Cheen Mein Terah Maas* [*Thirteen Months in China*] 1902),[2] written by Thakur Gadadhar Singh in 1900–1, ends an otherwise very balanced and sympathetic account of China from the Indian perspective by describing similarities and differences between India and China, using quotations from a missionary's description in the book *Cheen-Desh-Chitra-Mala: Pictures of China and Its People* , published by the Christian Literary Society in 1895.[3]

The first half of the twentieth century was a period of the large-scale proliferation of mass literature and the development of Hindi writing. Nonetheless their scope was limited by the state's restrictive monitoring of publications. Journals combining literary works and informative news items with social comments and political observations survived better because of their varied content. Linking local voices with national and international developments, they played major roles in spreading new ideas and issues in the context of contemporary debates on modernity and progress for building their respective nation-state.

Contemporary discourses in Hindi or other local languages shared a common perception of the enslavement of two similar civilizations under Western dominance and a yearning to evolve their own paths to emancipation and modernity. Scholars looking at both countries from long historical and civilizational perspectives find much that naturally connects them.[4] Many early Hindi writings highlight these contexts when introducing China to local intellectuals and the masses. With the rise of the Western-induced concept of the nation-state and its links with particular views of modernity and progress as the twentieth century progressed, the display of intrinsic differences between the two countries also entered contemporary Hindi-language discourses on China. The pros and cons of the Chinese Communist and Republican models and their viability for India became matter of discussion. Not surprisingly nationalist sensitivities and agendas thus began to distort civilizational sensibilities. This sometimes made discussions of interactions or connectedness highly contentious,[5] thus contributing to contemporary configurations or reconfigurations of strains of Sinophilia, trends in pan-Asianism, and notions of civilizational affinity and connectedness between the monist East and the dichotomous West.[6] The coinage of some broadly and loosely defined terms and concepts such as 'Oriental wisdom', 'Asian values', and 'Confucian or Hindu ethic' arose in reaction to the Western-inspired notions of progress, culture, and modernity that treated Asian civilizations as static and as incapable of development or progress.

Samples of Hindi Writings on China

In our sampling of Hindi-language materials, we mostly found four types of subject matter. The first type relates to the introduction of China through travelogues, snippets of information on Chinese life and society, stories, and illustrations. The second pertains to essays, editorials, reviews, analyses, and detailed comments on contemporary events in China. The third concerns contemporary Indian intellectuals' discussions, mostly addressing points of convergence and difference between India and China in the context of searching for and formulating Asian ideas and values with respect to pan-Asianism or of the unity of the East against the Eurocentrism of the West. The fourth consists mostly of news items taken from English newspapers on domestic politics, as well as internal political movements and activities. To be sure, these subjects are not distinct and often overlap.

Most of the introductory, informational, and popular writings by Indian authors on China praise the achievements of Chinese civilization and are sympathetic to the country's contemporary crisis. Ranging from the first substantive Hindi-language works on China by Gadadhar Singh and Mahendulal Garg of 1901–2 to a variety of later writings, there has been almost constant recognition of China's rich ancient cultural traditions and its links to India. These often also attempt to demonstrate myriad similarities in social rituals and practices between India and China. To be sure, the idea of civilizational connectedness that we encounter in popular writings and have highlighted here must not be seen as a process of manufacturing coherent methods to produce a linear story of India–China relations. Rather, our attempt is to comprehend articulations and silences in historical studies of this relationship arising out of the separation of popular civilizational perceptions and the anxieties of nationalism. This method of study makes it possible to interrogate both similarities and differences.

Chin Darpan [*Mirror on China*] by Mahendulal Garg and *Cheen Mein Terah Maas* [*Thirteen Months in China*] by Thakur Gadadhar Singh were published in 1901 and 1902, respectively.[7] Mahendulal Garg was a middle-school graduate who later did a diploma in hospital assistantship at a medical college in Agra. Proficient in Urdu, Hindi, and English, he joined the Seventh Rajput Regiment in 1891 at the age of twenty-one. He wrote his observations of China in the form of serial items for a Hindi newspaper in Kolkata, which was later published as a book titled *Chin Darpan* in 1901.

Gadadhar Singh was a matriculate who also joined the Bengal Seventh Rajput Regiment in 1886 at the age of seventeen following his family tradition. Well versed in both Hindi and English, he was a good reader and writer. Because of his sound educational background, in 1894, he was also assigned the duties of a teacher in the army. In 1896, he was promoted to the position of subedar major, that is, a viceroy's commissioned officer in the British Indian Army, a position equivalent to full major, though with authority confined to Indian troops, and until 1866, the highest rank an Indian could achieve in the British Indian Army. When the Boxer Rebellion broke out in China in 1900, the Seventh Rajput Regiment was one of several British units sent to China to join the Foreign Joint Expeditionary Force fighting the Boxers. Gadadhar Singh accompanied his regiment to China and spent thirteen months there. His travelogue-cum-memoir of his visit to China during the Boxer uprising was published as *Cheen Mein Terah Maas* and provided what was probably the first detailed modern account of China in Hindi.

In spite of being in the service of the British and having acquired a first-hand background knowledge of Chinese history and culture from contemporary popular English books by western authors, both Singh and Garg presented powerful narratives highlighting the closeness between India and China. This is remarkable when viewed in the context of the plethora of counter-narratives coming from the West.

Gadadhar Singh's reading of Chinese history reinforced his enchantment with the country. He writes that, in terms of its progress and the maturity of its civilization, China was far ahead of any other civilization in the world. He was impressed by the teachings of Confucius and Laozi, which highlighted the strains in what he conceived as Vedic as well as popular 'ideal' Hinduism. He proudly noted that China has 'long been a neighbour, co-religionist, and brother of Aryavarta and hence, in that time too, the kings of Aryavarta did not forget about China. Buddhist preachers were first sent to China in 216 B.C. Buddhism rapidly became widespread' (Yang 2017: 211).[8]

To be sure, Singh did not find the Boxers' ideology at all preposterous or bizarre. Growing up in an Indian milieu, he was familiar with the subaltern belief in 'mystical' or 'super power' and esoteric rituals connected with ordination in secret societies. For him, there was nothing surprising or new in it. Everybody, he writes, knows about the 'super power' of Hazarat Mohammad, Christ, the Supreme Being, and Guru Nanak. The wondrous sword of Badshah (Emperor) Govind Singh was no less miraculous than the swords of the Boxers. Various stories about 'master' and 'half-master' Boxers' abilities to climb trees, walk on straight walls, ward off bullets through their swift movements of heavy swords, perform stupendous tasks and make their bodies impregnable and indestructible by chanting mantras were thus probable and plausible to him (Yang 2017: 115–20). He quotes the words of Sir Robert Hart and of a priest he met to prove his point.[9]

For Singh, indignant Boxers' invocations of mystical power were a legitimate weapon with which to counter the threats of foreign and Chinese Christian missionaries, as the latter had begun to wield power in local areas. After all, it was on the pretext of suppressing the anti-Christian Boxer movement that the British, French, Germans, and Russians gradually grabbed China's most important cities one after the other, which enraged the ordinary people. What went wrong for the Boxers was their greater reliance on mystics alone and their lack of emphasis on the realistic organization and training of forces of the sort that had ultimately brought the country to its present state of destruction. Should we, he asks, then call Boxers ruffians and evil-doers? It is a natural law of the world to condemn the 'weak' as miscreants and scourges. Condemning the Boxers, therefore, required better judgement (Yang 2017: 119).

In the same vein, and knowing that Buddhism had come from India, Mahendulal Garg (1901: 21–2) writes that the Chinese often call themselves Hindus. However, they do not have any distinctions of caste or sect as Indians have, nor do they believe in differentiating human beings as touchable or untouchable, nor food as auspicious or inauspicious. He finds the average Chinese to be smarter than anybody else in knowledge and skills (Garg 1901: 11–12). They can tell the time by looking at the movement of the sun and they know all the four cardinal points as well as cooking, sewing, purchasing, rowing, drawing water, and harnessing various animals very well. Their business skills are so fine that they could never be mastered by outsiders in hundreds of years. Their examination system is the most difficult in the world. Westerners, he notes, have been learning Chinese for several years, but still none of them could answer all the questions in that language. On the other hand, while there are hundreds of Chinese doctors, engineers, graduates, and postgraduates, not a single Westerner could pass the prestigious Chinese examinations (Garg 1901: 12). There are Chinese dentists whose knowledge and skills are so high that, compared to Western medical professionals, many westerners go only to them for the treatment of complex dental problems (Garg 1901: 12–13).

Whatever the Chinese have achieved, Garg emphasizes, is due to education and manners, as it is these that have kept the essential unity of Chinese culture intact. It is indeed a difficult task for such a large nation, with many dialects and regional differences, to have a unified value system. That the Chinese have been able to do this reflects the powerful role of education. In the nineteenth-century Chinese education system, he writes, children are taught to memorize words for morality and ethics. They then spend another four to five years writing and recognizing characters. After that, they are taught idioms and their meaning. The Chinese have very sharp memories, being able to memorize a whole book easily. He also quotes some of the common folk idioms that Chinese children learn and that resonate with similar sayings in India: better late than never; all work is difficult in the beginning; easy to say, difficult to do; a stick is stick, whether it

is long or short; five desirables: healthy body, honesty, wealth, long
life and respectful death, and so on. He praises the power of the written word and the respect for paper and notes such that the Chinese
condemned anybody placing their feet on them. Moreover, he attests
to their self-sufficient nature, their ability to face crises, and their difficult yet skilful works, which are praised world-wide.[10]

Westerners, Garg says, consider them liars and greedy. But after
meeting with hundreds of Chinese, he writes: 'I find that once they
are sure of your intention they become too honest. In fact, as far as
honesty is concerned they are not at all thieves except what is custom-
arily practised as gift or bribe' (Garg 1901: 11–12). Different cultural
premises for gift-giving in Chinese and Indian culture as compared to
the West also come to surface in his description.

Garg (1901: 13–14) in fact notes how the lack of cultural understanding often leads to violent quarrels between Chinese and foreigners. For example, he relates how, once, on a narrow footpath, an old
person was walking with a heavy load. Six to seven foreigners were also
passing by. Seeing these foreigners, the old person did not move away
from the footpath. Taking this as an insult, they pushed the old person
in the back, scattered his load and caned him several times. In fact, as
he explains, the old person had not done any crime. It is customary
that those carrying heavier loads are given the right of way over those
with lighter loads or none at all. The old person was thus correct in
exercising his right, and he was also among the oldest persons in the
locality to command respect because of his age. Therefore, once the
villagers learnt of his ill-treatment, they caught hold of the foreigners
and beat them up. Such incidents mattered locally and influenced the
psyche of the local people. Garg uses the incident to demonstrate how
closely akin were the practices of Indians and Chinese.

However, the adulation of China that one finds in Hindi writings
was not all one-sided. For example, while expressing his disappointment with colonial India, Kang Youwei considered his trip there to
be very significant. His enchantment with the country owed much to
the civilizational affinity that both China and India shared over a long
period of history. In a public letter to Liang Qichao, he rhetorically
asks, 'Which country is so similar to our country? That is indeed India'
(Kang 2007b: 334).[11] He saw India as the source of civilization, having had impacts over most of the world civilizations in both east and

west. Its links with China are now more than 2,000 years old. India introduced bamboo products and medicinal betel nuts and leaves to China. Further, after the arrival of 'Buddhist scriptures in China on the white horses' (Kang 2007a: 509) and their translation into Chinese, the Buddha dharma, along with its religious and cultural artefacts, such as bells, drums, and cymbals, abundantly enriched the spiritual life and culture of the Chinese people. 'The mind, soul, precept and temple are the treasures that entered China' (Kang 2007a: 509). Thus, Indian and Chinese civilizations are intimately entwined, so much so that making any comparison between India and China is difficult, and finding differences is even more challenging. Using a Confucian locution that 'Lu and Wei are brothers, it is difficult to compare them', Kang (2007b: 343) asks how India and China can be compared as brothers. In his narratives, statements about India are constantly followed by references indicating analogies with historical Chinese experiences. More frequently, similarities or near similarities between India's and China's respective situations are indicated. His use of terms such as *tong lei* (同類) ('same as') or *lei/leisi* (類似) ('similar to/ same kind') is unlike his descriptions in his European travelogue, where differences galore are identified.[12]

To be sure, it is difficult to ignore certain basic similarities in the pristine religions of both India and China which led to the development of seemingly common customs and rituals. For example, unlike the Abrahamic religions, those in these two countries lacked a founder-prophet, a divinely authorized book for purposes of initiation or conversion, or a specific historical origin point. Instead, both emphasized the primacy of the text and its divine characteristics in binding human beings to the cosmos. Powered by texts, rituals such as *li* (禮) in China and dharma in India acquired significance. Both were supposed to emanate from heaven and concerned heaven's relations with human beings, including the moral and social management of hierarchies. Li and dharma thus represent the normative principles of Chinese and Indian culture and traditions, respectively.[13] Such mutually comprehensible premises underlying the normative order accounted for popular expressions of connectedness and indignation over the defiling of legitimate rituals and cultural practices perpetrated by foreigners in travel narratives.

Unlike Gadadhar Singh's and Mahendulal Garg's informative people-centric descriptions of China, a few 'fake', 'invented', or 'sensational' narratives appeared in the mushrooming local journals of the early twentieth century. For example, the description of China by the novelist Gopalram Gahmar, published in 1916 in the Hindi journal *Maryada*, which was based in Prayāg (Allahabad), appears to be based more on hearsay and is an example of fragmented knowledge (Gahmar 1916: 158–60). He notes that China is the most exceptional country in the world in terms of its size, population, and civilization. Besides mainland China, it also covers Korea, Manchuria, Mongolia, Tibet, and the Tatars. Chinese people do not call their country *Cheen desh* (China) but the 'middle country' in Chinese. This he relates to Qin, the first great unifier-ruler of China, and also to the ancient biblical name 'Sinim'. He mentions that the Chinese people are very hard-working, practising intensive agriculture and producing almost all kinds of crops, including commercial crops such as tea, tobacco, indigo, and jute. Among various varieties of trees, those of bamboo, camphor, and varnish (lacquer) are also to be found, and both precious and other minerals are excavated. The Chinese rear many varieties of colourful fish, duck, swan, and so on. Not many animals are seen, though, as dense population covers most of the area. Raising cattle is less popular. The Great Wall of China is one of Seven Wonders of the World. So are Chinese lanterns, with prices ranging from a few *annas*[14] for an ordinary one to several hundred rupees for something exquisite.

The dress of Chinese mandarins is different from that of other people, with its extraordinarily long sleeves, that worn by civil officials having pictures of varieties of birds, while that worn by military commanders is adorned with drawings of ferocious animals. Food ordinarily consists of fish and vegetables, though the meat of 'black dogs' and cats is also appreciated. Sometimes they also eat frogs and grasshoppers. Consumption of opium is prevalent. Tea is a favourite drink throughout the country. However, Gahmar adds that many religious Chinese do not eat meat because they believe that if they do so their own flesh will be eaten similarly in the next birth cycle. This observation may actually have resulted from the author's own sense of imagery in his effort to find similarities with certain Indian superstitions or beliefs.

Gahmar (1916) finds the practice of foot-binding among women barbaric. He says that both civilized and barbaric peoples like to beautify themselves. While civilized peoples use their minds and knowledge to obtain 'true beauty', barbaric peoples beautify themselves by deforming their physical attributes through painting, tattooing, and poking or pricking. The practice of keeping women's feet small by encasing them in iron boots to make them look like a 'beautiful lotus' is thus most brutish and uncivilized. Further, based on a French narrative about Chinese hospitality, he concludes that Chinese etiquette is just empty rhetoric.[15] The practice of such rhetoric and of excessive 'self-glorification' in dealing with foreigners may have caused China's downfall. The lack of ancient temples except for those to the Buddha surprises him. Yet, he enthusiastically approves of Chinese marriage practices, ancestor worship, respect for parents and elders, belief in ghosts and the supernatural, and reasons for keeping 'queues' (braids), all of which he found to be more or less similar to India.[16]

But such descriptions are few. Our eclectic gleanings from local accounts indicate an overwhelming preference for demonstrating 'connectedness' with China. Ram Lal Sarkar's eyewitness account of the 1911 Revolution in Yunnan, published originally in *Probasi* and later translated into English in the *Modern Review* (Sarkar 1912) on the one hand lauds the revolution's effect in blocking superstitious practices while on the other hand lamenting the end of India-like religious festivals. He writes:

> It is wonderful how this ancient, superstitious and conservative race effected a revolution in religion *pari passu* with the political revolution ... Only recently the much-revered images of Yamaraja (Pluto) have been destroyed, and pieces of gold and silver having been found in them, the soldiers have been eagerly destroying them ... In some of my former contributions to the '*Prabasi*', writing on the 'Spring festival' or on the festival of 'Yama's (Pluto's) journey to his father-in-law's house' celebrated on the third month of year I mentioned how pompously these festivals were celebrated, how processions were to parade the streets, and how in autumn the officials used to worship Lakshmi the goddess of the harvest at her temple. But those days are gone forever and are counted as past history. (Sarkar 1912: 492–3)

Ram Lal Sarkar (1912: 485) found that after the Revolution there was a marked change in the attitude of the Chinese: 'The courteous and gentlemanly demeanour which formerly marked their behaviour towards foreigners was changed into arrogance'. While demonstrating an 'inimical tendency towards the English in their conversation', officers of the revolutionary troops distinguished Indians from foreigners (Sarkar 1912: 485). Having confirmed his Indian origin, they treated him sympathetically, saying that he belonged to the yellow race. However, they also wondered why the English were the rulers of the people of India and why Indians did not drive them out. In contemporary Chinese discourses on India, these questions crop up quite often.[17]

An article in the Hindi magazine *Madhuri* enthusiastically demonstrates similarities in social custom with respect to the treatment of guests (Shukla 1925: 6). With regard to Chinese religion, it confirms that 'Mahatma' Confucius was not the founder of a specific religion but was a preacher of the Dharma of rituals, etiquette, and social relationships on the basis of certain principles. He was like Manu Maharaj in India, and his ideas had the same kind of impact as Mahatma Ramdas had in Maharashtra. Religion in actual terms relates to Buddhism only. Attention is also drawn to the procession that accompanies the dead, which he relates to the *hansa-tamasha* (graceful spectacle) custom of Kshatriyas living in western India. It is also practised in central India, including Chhattisgarh. Like Indians, the Chinese do not always consider the dead inauspicious. Rather, it is considered auspicious if one encounters a dead body wrapped in red cloth during a journey. Marriages in both countries require match-making by trained astrologers, the only difference being that the marriage gift is given to the bride in China, while the groom has the priority in India. Most lifecycle rituals and practices nonetheless have many similarities, so much so, the author emphasizes, that they appear to have come from India.

Commenting on the dawn of a new age in China, an article by Kamalapati Shastri (1927: 637–44) in the Hindi magazine *Madhuri* begins with a laudatory account of the East's historical contribution to civilizing the world and its role as 'teacher of the world'. Among the countries of the Eastern civilization, China occupies a highly respected position. Its religious and business connections with India are evidence of a high level of achievement. Like India, China lived in self-glorification and self-pride regarding its ancient culture and civilization. Confronted with the onslaught of new youthful and more aggressive currents, their deeply rooted traditions thus enabled them to sustain themselves, though they barely kept them alive. They nonetheless avoided the fate of ancient Western civilizations, which, in similar situations, simply disappeared. But, the author avers, in order to remain vigorous, Eastern civilization must welcome change according to the requirements of the time. The belief that they are the greatest because their rulers have divine sanction as the 'Son of Heaven' could no longer be maintained. This is evident from the continuous expansion and control of foreign powers over China since the Opium Wars. Now China is rising. The contemporary East is anxiously looking at China's struggle to regain its premier status because it knows that the rise of China would elevate its own status. Very sympathetic to the original social and moral values of the region, and in admiration of the great civilizations that these produced, these writings find the lapse into self-glorification and the inability to foresee changes as the primary reasons behind their contemporary lack of dynamism.

There is also strong criticism of the Western/European imperialist forces and their social and economic exploitation of China, which is seen as contrary to their professed faith in democracy. It is these injustices, perpetrated through the brute force of guns and cannon, that are making proud young Chinese 'anti-foreigner'. The editorial in the first issue of the Hindi magazine *Sudha* (1927–8: 477–8) thus rejects European accusations that 'Bolshevism' is responsible for all China's contemporary problems as preposterous and untenable.[18] Instead this was seen as a ploy to divert attention from the contemporary crisis originating in their own exploitation of China. The great injustice to China becomes apparent when one interrogates the history of the Opium, Boxer and other wars in or against China. To prove this point, the editorial even quotes a progressive former prime minister of Italy, Francesco Saverio Nitti, who said that although the seeds of the present revolution in China may have been sown by Russian Bolsheviks, it is undeniable that Chinese indignation against the Western powers is the result of the latter's treacheries, destructive policies and widespread looting. The Chinese are usually tolerant and are not quarrelsome. Their anger against European injustice is natural.

Given such references, it cannot be denied that the East as a significant category, with India, China, and Japan as its three pillars, has
overwhelming ideological acceptance in competition with Western
notions.[19] The East mattered, as did Asia. It was not an empty rhetoric but an idea that blurred differences and was becoming more and
more real with the power to move people and countries against the
West's intrusion in both society and culture. This ideology overshadowed the representation of various contemporary issues in China in
Hindi writings. Its search for points of convergence between India
and China also increased sinophilia in the Hindi belt.

Reactions to the 1911 Revolution in China

An example of the reporting on the 1911 Revolution in Hindi-
language newspapers is interesting in terms of the feeling that there
were larger connections between these two countries struggling for
emancipation and modernity. The 1911 Revolution and the establishment of a republic in China created euphoria in intellectual circles in
India. Examining articles in Hindi, two reasons for this enthusiasm
emerge. First, this development was seen as the first successful victory in the East for a republican movement and the end of monarchy.
Second, it marked the beginning of Asia's resurgence in response to
Western hegemony. For many intellectuals, this was far more important than the idea of republicanism it promoted.

Contemporary local newspapers came out with special editorials
and followed the subsequent progress of these events. The Hindi
magazine *Maryada* ran a biography of Sun Yat-sen by a writer using
the pseudonym 'Narayana' (1916). This article highlighted Sun's
exceptional rise to power as a national leader from a poor background,
his impeccable character, and his ability to bring major sections of
China's population together against the Manchus. There were also
interesting discussions on the advisability of selecting Yuan Shikai
as emperor because of Sun being a Christian. Also, for some, the
support that Sun garnered from Japan made China susceptible to
Japanese occupation, while others felt that Japanese intervention
would be better than the control of several Western countries over
China, or believed that, in order for Japan to be powerful, she had to
have a friendly and independent China.

Bhikshu Uttam, who taught Pali and Sanskrit at a Buddhist university in Kyoto between 1907 and 1910, describes his first meeting with Sun Yat-sen in Japan in 1910 in his 'Cheen ke Kuch Sansmaran' ['Reminiscences of China'] in the Hindi magazine *Vishal Bharat* (Uttam 1934: 707–13). He was greatly impressed by Sun's personality, commitment, and passion for liberating China from Manchu rule. A member of the Indian National Congress (INC), Uttam was jailed by the British in 1924 for three years for his participation in the independence movement. After his release in 1927, he went to Taiwan, Japan, and other Buddhist-dominated countries in Southeast Asia to garner support for the INC's Madras Conference resolution on full independence of India. After Sun's death, an official ceremony was held to entomb his body in a beautifully constructed mausoleum in Nanjing. Uttam was deputed to go to Nanjing by the then INC president, Pandit Motilal Nehru, to represent the Party and India in this ceremony, to be held on 1 June 1928. He reached Nanjing on 27 May and was shown full hospitality and honour, in spite of representing a colonized country. His article is full of praise for the love and affection that Chinese from all walks of life showered on him. In the light of the 1911 Revolution, he called Sun the 'priest of awakened Asia' (Uttam 1934) and a powerful messenger for the independence of Asia, finding the whole experience of being in independent China electrifying. His lecture there emphasized age-old brotherly relations between the two countries and promoted the innate 'connectedness' and unity of the countries of the East against divisive agenda of the West. This is how the East could regain its ancient glories.

Writing about the 1911 Revolution, Pandit Madan Mohan Malaviya, one of the most eminent early Indian nationalists and the chief editor of the newspaper *Abhyudaya*, emphasized in an editorial that 'if an unchanging, old, and autocratic country [China] could take a bold step for progress and modernity, how could India remain behind' ('Samsara-sankat' ['World Crisis'], *Abhyudaya*, 11 February 1912, p. 2). Another editorial by Padmakant Malaviya ('Cheen ki Jagriti' ['Reawakening of China'], *Abhyudaya*, 8 February 1912, p. 2) commented that:

> Western countries always thought that democracy is impossible to be established in eastern countries. But recent historical events have rejected their assumptions. Sometime back Turkey surprised

everybody by establishing a democratic state system without much bloodshed and if selfish European powers do not interfere it would successfully reform its domestic conditions ... Persians too struggled hard for democracy but before they could succeed Russians intervened and trapped them ... But compared to the above-mentioned countries the awakening of China is most surprising. The rapid awakening of such a huge country and acceptance of this [democratic] kind of state system is really inexplicable ... Many reasons for such incredible changes are offered or cited ... [what is however important is that] it has suddenly awakened from its delusive sleep and has started experiencing new life, new hope and new strength. It believes that under the light of democracy everybody will have equal relief, freedom and rights and enjoy peace and prosperity ... China has succeeded in doing what was always considered impossible for the eastern countries.

Analyses of the 1911 Revolution in Indian newspaper reports squarely blame the Manchus for derailing the process of modernity in China.[20] They are often referred to as indomitable Tartars and considered in the same light as all-powerful colonizers such as the British in India. As such, they blocked all efforts to introduce modernizing reforms and suppressed the yearnings of intellectuals for a modern political system and for new knowledge and science, as shown by their overturning the 1898 reform movement and the crushing of the southern rebellion in 1907. Finally, migrant Chinese intellectuals trained and settled abroad in countries such as Japan, England, and USA secretly conspired to overthrow the monarchy and succeeded. People who often said that East is East and West is West to accentuate irreconcilable differences between Eastern and Western ideas or who argued that Japan is different from other eastern countries were now startled to find China treading on the path to progress and modernity according to the requirements of the time.

The Hindi newspaper *Abhyudaya* also warns about Western attempts to create a wedge between India and China. It refers to a report from a *London Army Review* that warns, 'If we are not careful China and India will join boundaries without any buffer territory at all, and foreign railway enterprise from Europe will strike in at the shoulders of India' ('Cheen' ['China'], *Abhyudaya*, 11 February 1912, p. 2). Contradicting this assumption, *Abhyudaya* writes that this was a ploy to create a threat scenario to scare people into agreeing to build a large army and throw out the Liberal Party out in favour of the Conservatives and Unionists in Britain ('Cheen' ['China'], *Abhyudaya*, 11 February 1912, p. 2). In fact there was no such danger, and Indians were not naïve. They would vigorously resist intrusion by any foreign power. With China likely to be busy with internal reforms, the *Army Review*'s suspicions of a threat were only imaginary.

The achievements of the 1911 Revolution in the social, political, and economic fields were highlighted and much lauded. To emphasize and support these developments, foreign writers were often quoted. For example, in a 1927 Hindi article by Thakur Chhedilal in *Madhuri* (1926–7: 316), W.R. Manning was quoted as saying, 'Could the Sage Confucius have returned a decade ago he would have felt almost as much at home as when he departed twenty-five centuries before. Should he return a decade hence he would feel himself almost as much out of place as Rip Van Winkle, if the recent rate of progress continues.'[21] Similar words came from Hardan P. Bach: 'Those, who like myself, compare China of 25 years ago with China of this year, can hardly believe our senses' (Chhedilal 1926–7: 316).

Ramesh Verma (1938: 443) in *Madhuri* explains that China is the first country to adopt democracy in Asia. Even today, in 1938, except for Turkey, all other Eastern countries still had monarchy. Japan, in spite of having achieved modern economic and industrial progress surpassing Europe and USA, has not experienced such a revolution and is still ruled by an emperor. The Japanese have always been the slaves of feudal samurai warriors. That is why Japan is an imperialist country with fascist military control. As imperialism requires ample 'legroom', it is showing its teeth to China. It kept quiet even when there was a call for peace and democracy all over the world after the Great War. Unlike the above remarks, most contemporary Indian articles express ambivalence regarding the political aspirations of Japan in Asia when compared to their overall approval of China's progress on the path towards modernity.

Certainly Japan's successful transition to the path of modernity after the Meiji Restoration, as well as her impressive victory over Russia in 1904, fascinated Indian modernists. A 1907 editorial in the Hindi newspaper *Abhyudaya* by Pandit Madan Mohan Malaviya congratulated the Empress Dowager Cixi for establishing parliamentary government in China and thus paving the way for the country's resurgence ('Cheen mein Parliament' ['Parliament in China'], *Abhyudaya*, 19 March 1907, p. 1). It linked this transformation to the example provided by the good deeds of the Japanese Empress Mikado. However, Japanese forays into China and its colonial-imperialist designs on the country proved to be embarrassing for Indian intellectuals and confused them.

Writing in the Hindi magazine *Maryada*, Lala Lajpat Rai (1919: 205), an eminent early Indian nationalist, notes that Japan has established herself in the world as a self-reliant and independent country. Its status is now accepted by the contemporary Western civilization, which is based on *pashubala* (referring to physical or bestial as opposed to spiritual strength). There are, however, still various myths and false imaginaries about Asia and Asians among Europeans and Americans. Western schoolbooks perpetuate these idiosyncrasies further. In theatre and drama, Asians are portrayed as laughing stocks. It is therefore encouraging and most welcome that native Asian scholars are writing more and more about their civilization and courageously presenting the true picture of both it and themselves. In this context, Rai found the work of a Japanese scholar, Mr Kawakami,[22] praiseworthy primarily because of his bold acceptance of all the acts of Japan in Korea and China as being contingent on Japan's adoption of 'Western' modernity and self-defence in the current situation. If Japan had not acted, the European powers would have intervened. Kawakami notes growing contacts between Indian and Japanese intellectuals and the fruitful visit of Rabindranath Tagore and hopes that Japan will not let itself be made a party to the suppression of India's struggle for self-rule and independence under the Anglo-Japanese Friendship Treaty. Yet, modern Indian intellectuals' 'anti-foreignism' or 'anti-West' beliefs compelled them to defend their biases towards Japan.

Beyond the 1911 Revolution: Benoy Kumar Sarkar and Rabindranath Tagore

For some modern Indian scholars and intellectual commentators, the significance of the 1911 Revolution went beyond republicanism to show signs of Asian revival and unity and the triumph of the East over the West. Among them, the earliest and most prolific were Benoy

Kumar Sarkar[23] and Rabindranath Tagore,[24] who profoundly influenced Hindi writings on China. Both Tagore and Sarkar elaborated on the natural affinity between India and China and wrote strong critiques of the West, though their quests for modernity differed.

Tagore's transcendental nationalism was then considered anachronistic. Yet, his message to China about the essential connections between the Indian and Chinese civilizations was appealing. He asks what it is in China 'which we who come from another land feel at home in this land of ancient civilization' (Tagore 2002: 14). This is neither materialism nor brute physical strength. 'I cannot', he answers, 'bring myself to believe that any nation in this world can be great and yet be materialistic. I have a belief [that] no people in Asia can be wholly given to materialism. There is something ... which somehow gives to us an understanding of the inner music of existence' to which none of us are deaf' (Tagore 2002: 76).[25] This is the moral strength or dharma that acts as a 'normative principle' to sustain civilization and leads to perfection. This is what legitimizes and reinforces 'civilizational bonhomie' in popular perceptions of China in Hindi writings.

Sarkar's conservative nationalism was different from Tagore's 'transcendental-nationalism' or 'internationalist-nationalism'. It sought to confront the predicaments arising out of Western-inspired nationalism with the virtues of civilizational states. This had more supporters, as it resonated with conservative-nationalist modernizers such as Pandit Madan Mohan Malaviya and others. In 1916, this maverick and little-studied Indian scholar[26] wrote an article in Hindi titled 'Cheeni Saamraajya kaa Bhavishyat' ['Future of the Chinese Empire'] in *Maryada* (Sarkar 1916: 78–84). Discussing his assessment of the contemporary Chinese situation, he refers to his talks with two eminent foreign-trained Chinese intellectuals, Yan Fu[27] and Gu Hongming.[28] Yan is often regarded as one of the most influential Chinese intellectuals of the early twentieth century because of his avowed faith in Western notions of modernity and scientism, though he abhorred republicanism. Gu Hongming, on the other hand, was a Confucianist whose supporters hailed him as a 'Chinese Tagore' and his modernist critics as 'reactionary' and 'conservative'.

Writing about his conversations with both Yan and Gu, Benoy Kumar Sarkar (1916: 82–4) mentions that they were already more than fifty years old when he met them. Long before China's intellectual awakening in the twentieth century, they had sought knowledge in the West and were renowned for their literary and philosophical works. While Yan exerts himself in translating Western literature and introducing it to the Chinese, Gu takes pains to do the same for the dissemination of Chinese culture and philosophy to Westerners. They are thus diametrically opposed in their assessments and interpretations of 'modernity' in China. Yan, a pioneering modernist, favoured Yuan Shikai and his group and was a member of the consultative council of the government. Gu, a Manchu loyalist, was opposed to both Yuan and Sun Yat-sen. Unlike Yan, he sported a long snake-like black queue to demonstrate his allegiance to the Manchus.

Sarkar tells us about his discussions of Thomas H. Huxley's *Evolution and Ethics* (1893) with Yan Fu. Yan's Chinese translation of Huxley's work had provided the Chinese with their first introduction of Western science and knowledge and had great impact on the growth of modernist trends in China. When it was published, however, its radical interpretations of religion and society shocked the people, and Yan was branded an enemy of Chinese culture and country. Yan also told him about his translation of Herbert Spencer's *The Study of Sociology* (1876), Montesquieu's *The Spirit of Laws* (1748), and Adam Smith's *The Wealth of Nations* (1776). Translations of Western scientific works into Chinese, he stated, were made very difficult by the paucity of phonetic sounds in the language. Even when new words are coined, appropriate Chinese characters with matching meanings need to be selected and explained to make them comprehensible to ordinary Chinese readers.

Sarkar, however, appears to be more impressed by Gu Hongming. He likened his status and position in Yuan's government in contemporary China to Vibhishana at Ravana's court. In the popular Indian epic, the Ramayana, Vibhishana is the noble-hearted brother of the demon king Ravana. A pious and conscientious person of high morals among the demons, he opposed his own brother for kidnapping Sita, the wife of the divine prince Rama. On Ravana's refusal to return Sita, he helped Rama kill Ravana and thus restored just order. In contemporary Chinese disavowals of Confucian thoughts, Sarkar found Gu's single-minded effort to restore Confucianism and thus 'Eastern glory' admirable. This was very much in tune with the culturally and religiously inspired notions of nationalism that were evolving in contemporary India at that time.

Sarkar writes that he found Gu's book, *The Spirit of the Chinese People* (1915), on sale in his hotel bookshop. Gu had met scholars from Russia, Germany, France, England, and many other countries but so far had had no chance to interact with an Indian scholar. So when he learnt about Sarkar's arrival, he immediately went to his hotel to interact with him.

Gu talked about his life's mission to translate the true thoughts of Confucius and disseminate them throughout the world. Foreign scholars' translations of Chinese literature were often complex and confusing, so it was important that the true spirit of Confucius be presented through correct renditions of the classical texts. Even those young Chinese who knew English were not adept at reading the ancient classical Chinese literature. Those who could did not know English. This was the reason for the failure of outsiders to comprehend the real China.

Further, according to Gu, Confucianism was China's own discovery and was her primary philosophy. However, it gradually lost its vigour and significance. This provided an opportunity for Buddhism to enter China and exert its influence, reinvigorating Chinese philosophy and contributing to the beginning of a new cultural era in China. Confucius originated in the sixth century BCE, Buddhism was introduced in the first century CE, and the Chinese renaissance began in the eighth century CE. He emphasized that, without the introduction of Buddhism, China would have not reached such heights in art and aesthetics. It is a truism that a serious knowledge of India was necessary to comprehend China properly. He lamented that China was quite ignorant of India.

Sarkar writes that Gu is a staunch swadeshi. He approvingly quotes Gu from the latter's article in Paul S. Reinsch's book, *Intellectual and Political Currents in the Far East* (1911). 'Confucianism, with its way of the superior man, little as the English man suspects, will one day change the social order and break up the civilisation of Europe' (Sarkar 1916: 84). While many in contemporary China did not support Gu, Sarkar hoped that the new China would soon comprehend the essence of his thoughts and accordingly re-establish the nation.

In Gu's vision, Sarkar (1922: 184–8) found affirmation of his own belief in a rising and radical East. The 1911 Revolution in China demonstrated the empowerment of Asia and the emergence of Asian unity. 'In overthrowing the Manchus the Chinese intelligentsia has sought simply to rebel against Occidental exploitation and to emancipate Eastern Asia from Eur[o]-American vassalage—political, economic and cultural' (Sarkar 1922: 188). Like Gu, Sarkar finds difficult to defend the 'nation' in terms of one race, which would have made his concept of 'unity of India' and 'unity of Asia' fragile. He therefore writes,

> China like India is, in realpolitik, a geographical expression. It is a 'pluralistic universe', in spite of the 'fundamental unity' of 'cultural ideals' pervading the entire area. China is one country only in the sense in which Europe is one. But neither in ancient and medieval ages nor in modern times has it been possible to postulate the 'unity of Europe' for purposes of international politics. 'The unity of China' and 'the unity of India' are equally unreal terms in the diplomatic history of Asia. There have been many Chinas and many Indias at the same time during almost every century. (Sarkar 1922: 192)

Pluralism and the essential unity of Indian and Chinese society were thus highlighted. The essential 'unity' of India, as of China, existed in spite of several territorial fragmentations or division over the long course of their history. The present crisis was essentialized as exceptional and as threatening both life and culture. He thus avows: 'The wars of medieval India were thus neither racial nor religious but fundamentally territorial or provincial ... Mohammedan rule in India was in no respects the government of one people by the other' (Sarkar 1922: 197). It was not alien rule like that of the Hohenstaufens, and later the Habsburgs, in Italy, nor like that of the Americans in Philippines. The rule of the Mongols and Manchus was likewise not a foreign rule.

After the 1930s, substantive descriptions of China began to appear in Hindi with strong strains of nationalist anxieties or nationalist-socialist agendas within the context of civilizational bonhomie. The World Wars, the Civil War, the struggle of the Chinese Communist and Nationalist parties, and other internal developments in China received much attention. The writings of Rahul Sankrityayan, Rambriksh Benipuri, Lala Sundarlal, Ram Manohar Lohia, and many others developed the modern discourse with their nuanced writings in Hindi on China. Works and reports by Agnes Smedley, Edgar Snow, and other foreign observers on China were also regularly translated and published in the Hindi media, keeping their readers informed about developments there.

In avowing the meta-concept of Asianism, the themes of Asian unity/Asian wisdom/'Grand East' and other such cultural or civilizational specificities were thus formulated and invoked by intellectuals in Asia in the early twentieth century. Contemporary intellectuals in both India and China expressed a sense of disappointment with the culture of the West and emphasized the essential importance of involving Indian and Chinese patterns and ideas in modern change (Isay 2014: loc 6443). Writings in Hindi and other Indian languages to a large extent reflect the invocation of commonality in respect of certain comparable and enduring features associated with their respective cultures that produced affinities and connections. Their adherence to Asianism may have different connotations, specificities and sources of invention, but it was invoked to fit into the ideological framework that was being raised as a bulwark against the West and Western intervention. This coexisted with contemporary political currents characterized by nascent nationalism, Marxism, liberalism, republicanism, and many others. The proliferation of such sentiments in Hindi writings is indicative of their powerful influence. Yet, nation state-inspired discourses that highlighted fundamental differences in state–society relations in the two countries, driving them along their own characteristic historical paths, received less attention in India, at least until the two countries had both been established as independent nation-states.

Notes

1. An excellent overall review of published literary journals in various Indian languages has been provided in Das ([1991] 2008).
2. This work has now been translated into English; see Yang (2017). Except where noted otherwise, all the translations from Hindi into English are the author's.
3. See Christian Literary Society (1895) for a comparison of India and China. This Society published several books on many aspects of Indian society with its own interpretations and judgements. It may be noted that the ascendancy of the West created a dominant narrative that projected its own vision or markers of modernity and progress based on the values

and ethics of the Enlightenment. This led to 'modern' native intellectuals developing aspirations to steer their countries away from 'so-called' traditional, static, and moribund pasts and build 'modern' nation-states instead, mimicking the West. This produced a variety of 'national' histories highlighting distinct markers of modernity and progress that were compatible with those associated with the 'Enlightenment spirit'.

4. See Lin (1993), Tan (1998), Tan and Geng (2005), Sheel (2006), and Sen (2017) for extensive discussions of these civilizational connections. Also see Public Diplomacy Division, Ministry of External Affairs, Govt. of India (2014) for brief introduction of many prominent persons who were active in India–China interactions.

5. Scholarly debates on the issue of cultural borrowings have been contentious due to difficulty in separating the wheat from the chaff after lapse of long historical time, so much so that even Indian monkey-sage god Hanuman is found to be appropriated in the main cultural stream of both the countries. Was the Chinese monkey-sage god Sun Wukong an imagination based on similar Indian tales of monkey god Hanuman of the Ramkathās? See Mair (1989). In fact, nationalist inspired narratives further distract our attention from the fact that both the cultures could have shared a common belief and faith through appropriation and absorption. For excellent discussions in this area, see Duara (1988, 2001), Yu (2000), Lutgendorf (2007), and Kieschnick and Shahar (2014).

6. See Tan (1998) for various sources on the rise of 'affection' or natural affinity with China. Sen (2017) provides a more comprehensive and fresh analysis of the historical connections between India and China. For the evolution of nation-state-centric views, see Philips (1954a, 1954b, 1954c, 1954d) and Taylor (1989). Rejecting Sardar K.M. Panikkar's famous observation about the civilizational unity of Asian countries from Japan to India and 'a community of thought and feeling between the common peoples of India and China', in a radio talk in 1954, Cyril Philips (1954a: 325) argued that the mere identification of similar primitive responses to the challenge of nature does not confirm 'that the two civilizations have developed in the same way'.

7. For the English translation of Singh (1902), see Yang (2017). Anand Yang's discussion of vernacular writings in Chapter 6 in this volume further illuminates the strong sympathetic concern of Indian intellectuals towards China as they felt that the collapse of China 'meant the end of an Asia that they had envisaged themselves being a part of, with ties particularly to China because both countries were bound together by geography, history, civilization and the shared experience of western imperialism and colonialism'.

8. The last chapter of Gadadhar Singh's travelogue, titled 'Miscellaneous Accounts', looks at India–China connections at various levels in an interesting manner using popular perceptions and beliefs. This ranges from descriptions of Chinese society, religion, rituals, customs, and practices to music, art, and architecture and its connecting thread with those of India. Not surprisingly, the emphasis is on seeking civilizational affinities, not on demonstrating the 'differences' or 'otherness' characteristic of emerging modern nation-state discourses.

9. See Yang (2017: 116–20) for Singh's very sympathetic account of the Boxers and his attempt to justify their movement.

10. See Garg (1901) for a description of many such sensible and rational features of Chinese culture, life, customs, and practices. Meant specifically for native Indian readers of the Hindi belt, it emphatically presents the idea of 'the connectedness of civilization' with China.

11. See Kang (2007a, 2007b). Unlike earlier Chinese travel narratives, Zhang Ke, in this volume, aptly notes that Kang's was the first one to analyse connection and difference between India and China from the perspective of 'civilization'. Yet, Zhang's description somewhat ignores the differences that Kang makes between colonized and pre-colonized India. In fact, Kang's letter to Liang Qichao presents a persuasive argument that India, in spite of having a very old and rich civilization comparable to China's, perished because Indians allowed their country to be fragmented by the colonial power. Kang makes a strong plea to a radical group of Chinese intellectuals to reject support for provincial autonomy in China arising out of the die-hard belief in Western notions of nationalism, modernity and progress and thus save the country from falling to the fate of India.

12. Roland Felber (1997: 76–7) notes that Kang borrowed this locution from Sima Qian's *Shiji* (史記) [*Records of the Grand Historian*] to express the notions of the 'harmonious organism' and the 'homogeneous continuum'.

13. See the special issue on li and dharma in *Philosophy: East and West* (McDermott 1972: 127–220), and especially Gimello (1972). See also Gier (2014), Theodor and Yao (2014), Matilal and Ganeri (2002), Mohanty (2000), and Schwartz (1985), whose discussions of li and dharma facilitate comprehension of various similarities and points of connection between Indian and Chinese philosophical discourses. These render substance to the argument that as Zhouli in China attributed 'indwelling law' or 'li' to every aspect of human life, and so did the Vedas in India imbue to dharma all ethical rules of action and moral virtues of human beings, indicating underlying connections between the two cultures.

14. Old monetary unit of India equivalent to 1/16th of a rupee.

15. He describes an incident where an outside guest in the house of a Chinese family, after being earnestly requested several times to take food in their house, finally stays for the meal; the house owner feels cheated and becomes angry at the fact that the guest did not reciprocate properly in terms of etiquette by vehemently refusing to take the food.

16. There were also brief comments about the decline of the 'rice-eating' races, which included both the Chinese and Indians. Experimenting to make potato bread to replace the rice diet in Japan, one Mr Matsumura declares in *Jitsugyō no Nihon* (実業之日本) [*Business Japan*], one of the first Japanese business journals, starting publication in 1897 in Tokyo, that the 'lack of the proper amount and variety of vitamins in the food, needed for the proper growth of brain power', have brought about the retrogression and decadence of the Hindu race (*Modern Review* 1928: 578).

17. Indians' enlistment in the British Army and their participation in the Opium War and other wars as part of the British imperialist army and state were discussed often in contemporary Chinese writings as evidence for the capitulation of the national spirit. In Chinese debates, India thus figures as a 'lost' or 'dead' country lacking the essential characteristics that a 'modern/Western' model of the nation-state requires. Some of these issues are discussed in Wang (2003), Karl (2002), and Van Der Veer (2014). Philips (1954c: 416–17) too raises this issue and links it to the lack of political consciousness in India, as opposed to China's continual contriving to hold itself together. China, he writes, did not contribute to her own break up. In India, the Western powers, especially England, had easily persuaded Indians to do their fighting for them. Indians had no concept of a political India and could have no loyalty to it. In the main, it was an Indian Army that conquered India for Britain. However, no European power could do that in China: European political supremacy would have been resisted as spelling the end of Chinese culture. The sense of national consciousness there was too deep and strong.

18. Also see Shastri (1927–8: 362–8) in the same issue of *Sudha*.

19. Japan often appears in the context of East in these writings and is seen as a saviour that restored the glory of eastern civilization and culture, though its attack on China also perplexed promoters of the East.

20. For the full editorial, see 'Cheen' ['China'], *Abhyudaya*, 11 February 1912, p. 2.

21. This probably refers to W.R. Manning, whose writings include 'China and the Powers since the Boxer Movement' (1910). The quotation in English referred to was not legible in the copy available to me, so it has been paraphrased.

22. Lala Lajpat Rai is probably referring to Otojirō Kawakami (川上音二郎) (1864–1911), who drew peoples to civil rights and freedom by staging anti-government popular theatrical performances. But irked at the Western yellow press's caricature of Orientals and Japanese, he turned to creating an exotic, extravagant, farcical, 'un-Japanese' drama for European and American audiences, with his characters performing Orientalist stereo-types on themes adapted from stories glorifying Western imperialism and colonialism. He thus chose to challenge and subvert contempo-rary imaginaries that were based on the East–West dichotomy. It was also symptomatic of tensions arising out of the contradiction between Japanese tradition and the demands of Western 'modernity'. See Sarkar ([1916] 1988, 1922) for comprehension of intellectual basis for the idea of 'Asian unity'.

23. Benoy Kumar Sarkar was closely associated with emerging national-ist universities in the Hindi belt, like Kashi Vidyapeeth in Varanasi. A good friend of Shiv Prasad Gupt, the owner of the nationalist Hindi newspaper *Aaj*, he was tagged with conservative Hindu nationalists. Gupt even funded his trip to Europe to learn more about Western and modern nationalism and the nation-states of the world. Besides writing in English and Bangla, he also wrote in Hindi journals and espoused the idea of Asian unity. Sarkar spent a year in 1915 as visiting professor and fellow at the North China Branch of the Royal Asiatic Society in Shanghai.

24. Tagore first visited China in 1924. Before Sarkar and Tagore, soldiers, petty officials, merchants, traders, and fortune seekers had interacted with the Chinese as part of the British Imperial network. They were fol-lowed by a number of activists, revolutionaries and scholars like M.N. Roy, Jawaharlal Nehru, and S. Radhakrishnan, as well as leaders and members of Ghadar and other revolutionary parties. See also Chapter 7 by Yu-Ting Lee in this volume.

25. For a detailed explanation of Tagore's anti-materialism, see Tagore (1922). Also see Webb (2008).

26. For an illuminating discussion of Benoy Kumar Sarkar's ideas, see Sen (2015).

27. The best work on Yan Fu is still Benjamin Schwartz's (1964) *In Search of Wealth and Power: Yen Fu and the West*.

28. A good introduction to Gu is provided by Du (2011). Like many early Chinese Confucian modernists, such as Zeng Guofan, Zhang Zhidong, Li Hongzhang, and others, he too has been resurrected in contemporary China and received positive appraisals of his contribution.

References

Chhedilal, Thakur. 1926–7. 'Vartamaan Cheen' ['Contemporary China']. *Madhuri* 5 (1, 3): 314–17.

Christian Literary Society (ed.). 1895. *Cheen-Desh-Chitra-Mala: Pictures of China and Its People*. Allahabad: Mission Press.

Das, Sisir Kumar (ed.). [1991] 2008. *A History of Indian Literature*, 3 Vols. New Delhi: Sahitya Academy.

Du, Chunmei. 2011. 'Gu Hongming as a Cultural Amphibian: A Confucian Universalist Critique of Modern Western Civilization'. *Journal of World History* 22 (4): 715–46.

Duara, Prasenjit. 1988. 'Superscribing Symbols: The Myth of Guandi, Chinese God of War'. *The Journal of Asian Studies* 47 (4): 778–95.

———. 2001. 'The Discourse of Civilization and Pan-Asianism'. *Journal of World History* 12 (1): 99–130.

Felber, Roland. 1997. 'The Use of Analogy by Kang Youwei in His Writings on European History. *Oriens Extremus* 40 (1): 64–77.

Gahmar, Gopalram. 1916. 'Cheen Desh Ka Vivarana' ['Accounts of China']. *Maryada* (12): 158–60.

Garg, Mahendulal. 1901. *Chin Darpan* [*Mirror on China*]. Mathura: Sukhsancharak Press.

Gier, Nicholas F. 2014. 'Li and Dharma: Gandhi, Confucius, and Virtue Aesthetics'. In Ithamar Theodor and Zhihua Yao (eds), *Brahman and Dao: Comparative Studies of Indian and Chinese Philosophy and Religion*, pp. 67–78. New York: Lexington Books.

Gimello, Robert M. 1972. 'The Civil Status of Li in Classical Confucianism'. *Philosophy East and West* 22 (2): 203–11.

Isay, Gad C. 2014. 'The Poet and the Historian: Criticism of the Modern Age by Rabindranath Tagore and Qian Mu'. In Ithamar Theodor and Zhihua Yao (eds), *Brahman and Dao: Comparative Studies of Indian and Chinese Philosophy and Religion*, pp. 263–76. New York: Lexington Books.

Kang Youwei (康有為). 2007a. 'Yindu youji' (印度遊記) ['Records of Travel to India']. In Jiang Yihua and Zhang Ronghua (eds), *Kang Youwei quanji* (康有為全集) [*The Collected Works of Kang Youwei*], Volume V, pp. 509–50. Beijing: Beijing renmin chubanshe.

———. 2007b. 'Yu tongxue zhuzi Liang Qichao deng lun guo yindu wang-guo youyu gesheng zili shu' (與同學諸子梁起 超等論印度亡國由於個省自理書) ['Discussing Records on India's Extinction and Its Association with Independence of Provinces with Colleagues, Followers and Liang Qichao']. In Jiang Yihua and Zhang Ronghua (eds), *Kang Youwei quanji* (康有為全集) [*The Collected Words of Kang Youwei*], Volume VI, pp. 334–49. Beijing: Beijing renmin chubanshe.

Karl, Rebecca E. 2002. *Staging the World: Chinese Nationalism at the Turn of Twentieth Century*. Durham, NC: Duke University Press.

Kieschnick, John and Meir Shahar (eds). 2014. *India in the Chinese Imagination: Myth, Religion, and Thought: Myth, Religion, and Thought*. Philadelphia: University of Pennsylvania Press.

Lin Chengjie (林承節). 1993. *ZhongYin renmin youhao guanxi shi* (中印人民友好關係史) [*History of the Friendly Relations between the Peoples of China and India*]. Beijing: Beijing daxue chubanshe.

Lutgendorf, Philip. 2007. *Hanuman's Tale: The Message of a Divine Monkey*. New York: Oxford University Press.

Shukla, Matadin. 1925. '*Prithvi Pradakshinaa*: Samalochanaa' ['A Critical Appraisal of *Circumambulation of the Globe*']. *Madhuri* 1 (6): 779–99.

Mair, Victor. 1989. 'Suen Wu-kung = Hanumat? The Progress of a Scholarly Debate'. In *Proceedings of the Second International Conference on Sinology* (Section on Literature), pp. 659–752. Taipei: Academia Sinica.

Manning, W.R. 1910. 'China and the Powers since the Boxer Movement'. *The American Journal of International Law* 4 (4): 848–902.

Narayana. 1916. 'Mahapurush Sun Yat-sen' ['Sun Yat-sen: The Great Man']. *Maryada* 10–11 (January–February): 106–8.

McDermott, Robert A. 1972. 'On Dharma and Li'. *Philosophy East and West* 22 (2): 127–9.

Matilal, Bimal Krishna and Jonardan Ganeri (eds). 2002. *The Collected Essays of Bimal Krishna Matilal: Ethics and Epics*, Volume II. New Delhi: Oxford University Press.

Modern Review. 1928. 'Gleanings'. XLIII (1): 578.

Mohanty, J.N. 2000. *Classical Indian Philosophy*. Lanham, PA: Rowman & Littlefield Publishers.

Philips, Cyril. 1954a. 'Tradition and Experiment in Asia'. Talk no. 1, in *The Listener*, 25 February: 325–7.

———. 1954b. 'Tradition and Experiment in Asia-II: The Heritage of India and China'. Talk No. 2, in *The Listener*, 4 March: 355–7.

———. 1954c. 'Tradition and Experiment in Asia-III: China: New Version of an Old Society'. Talk No. 3, in *The Listener*, 11 March: 416–18.

———. 1954d. 'Tradition and Experiment in Asia-IV: The Indian Experiment'. Talk No. 4, in in *The Listener*, 25 March: 511–13.

Public Diplomacy Division, Ministry of External Affairs, Govt. of India. 2014. *Encyclopaedia of India-China Cultural Contacts* (EICCC), Vols I and II. New Delhi: MaXposure Media Group.

Rai, Lajpat. 1919. 'Samsaar ke Rajnaitik-Kshetra mein Japan kaa Sthaan' ['The Place of Japan in World's Political Configuration']. *Maryada* 5 (November): 205.

Sarkar, Benoy Kumar. 1916. 'Cheeni Saamraajya kaa Bhavishyat' ['Future of the Chinese Empire']. *Maryada* 11 (11): 78–84.

———. [1916] 1988. *Chinese Religion through Hindu Eyes: A Study in the Tendencies of Asiatic Mentality*. New Delhi: Asian Educational Services.

———. 1922. *The Futurism of Young Asia: And Other Essays on the Relations between the East and the West*. Berlin: Julius Springer.

Sarkar, Ram Lal. 1912. 'The Revolution in China'. *Modern Review* XII (8, 10, 11, 12): 155–66, 349–56, 485–96, 613–18.

Schwartz, Benjamin I. 1985. *The World of Thought in Ancient China*. Cambridge. MA: Harvard University Press.

Schwartz, Benjamin I . 1964. *In Search of Wealth and Power: Yen Fu and the West*. New York: Belkknap Press.

Sen, Satadru. 2015. *Benoy Kumar Sarkar: Restoring the Nation to the World*. New Delhi: Routledge India.

Sen, Tansen, 2017. *India, China and the World: A Connected History*. Lanham: Rowman and Littlefield.

Shastri, Devavrat. 1927–8. 'Cheen ka Kuomintang Dala' ['Kuomintang Part of China']. *Sudha* 1 (1): 362–68.

Shastri, Kamalapati. 1927. 'Cheen mein navayuga ka aarambh' ['Beginning of New Age in China']. *Madhuri* 5 (2): 637–44.

Sheel, Kamal. 2006. 'Some Observations on Chinese Discourses on India'. Presidential Address (Countries Other Than India), 66th Session of the Indian History Congress, Visva-Bharati, Santiniketan.

Singh, Gadadhar, 1902. *Cheen mein terah maas* [*Thirteen Months in China*]. Lucknow: Dilkusha.

Sudha. 1927–8. 'Sampaadikiya Sammati' ['Editorial Comments']. 1 (1): 477–8.

Tagore, Rabindranath. 1922. *Creative Unity*. New York: Macmillan.

———. 2002. *Talks in China; Lectures Delivered in April and May 1924*. New Delhi: Rupa Publications.

Tan, Chung (ed.). 1998. *Across the Himalayan Gap: An Indian Quest for Understanding China*, Indira Gandhi National Centre for Arts. New Delhi: Gyan Publishing House.

Tan, Chung and Geng Yinzeng. 2005. *India and China: Twenty Centuries of Civilization Interaction and Vibrations*. Project of History of Indian Science, Philosophy and Culture, Centre for Studies in Civilizations, New Delhi.

Taylor, Romeyn. 1989. 'Chinese Hierarchy in Comparative Perspective'. *Journal of Asian Studies* 48 (5): 490–511.

Theodor, Ithamar and Zhihua Yao (eds). 2014. *Brahman and Dao: Comparative Studies of Indian and Chinese Philosophy and Religion*. New York: Lexington Books.

Uttam, Bhikshu. 1934. 'Cheen ke Kuch Sansmaran' ['Reminiscences of China']. *Vishal Bharat* 13 (January–June): 707–13.

Van der Veer, Peter. 2014. *The Modern Spirit of Asia: The Spiritual and the Secular in China and India*. Princeton and Oxford: Princeton University Press.

Verma, Ramesh. 1938. 'Cheen ka Sanghursh' ['China's Struggle']. *Madhuri* 315 (November): 441–9.

Wang, Gungwu. 2003. *Anglo-Chinese Encounters since 1800: War, Trade, Science, and Governance*. London: Cambridge University Press.

Webb, Adam K. 2008. 'The Countermodern Moment: A World Historical Perspective on the Thought of Rabindranath Tagore, Muhammad Iqbal, and Liang Shuming'. *Journal of World History* 19 (2): 189–212.

Yang, Anand A. (ed.). 2017. *Thirteen Months in China: Subaltern Indian and the Colonial World*. Translated by Anand A. Yang, Kamal Sheel, and Ranjana Sheel. New Delhi: Oxford University Press.

Yu, Chün-fang. 2000. *Kuan-yin: The Chinese Transformation of Avalokiteśvara*. New York: Columbia University Press.

6

China in the Popular Imagination

Images of *Chin* in North India at the Turn of the Twentieth Century

ANAND A. YANG

W hat did people in colonial India make of China at the turn of the twentieth century? What were their responses to the Boxer Uprising that produced such upheavals in North China and the frenetic events beginning with the encirclement of the Foreign Legations in Beijing in June 1900, followed by the defeat of the Boxers and the Qing Dynasty by the International Expedition that was mobilized to lift the siege of the Forbidden City? How did they perceive the clash between China and the foreign powers that the British in India and at home characterized as a war to safeguard a morally superior and modern Western civilization from barbarism and superstition? What were their reactions to the ensuing occupation of China by foreign powers that threatened to lead to that country's colonization and division by the Western nations? To what extent were popular understandings, based on peoples' familiarity with a growing body of literature written in English by travellers, journalists, missionaries, and politicians, among others, available and accessible to the educated elite in India, as well as coverage in the vernacular and English newspapers that were increasingly gaining a wide reading public? Many of these elites were products of the primary and secondary schools emerging in the late nineteenth century, where they had, in the third and fourth standards, read geography texts emphasizing the affinity between China and India.

The China-in-crisis story in the initial years of the twentieth century commanded headlines the world over, prompting some Western writers and journalists to travel to China to file stories about the tumultuous events of the Boxer Uprising and the seemingly imminent break-up and foreign takeover of the last major empire left standing in Asia. These momentous events also generated tremendous attention in India, enough so that a small handful from among the several hundred from India who were in China at the time wrote accounts of the country in Hindi and Urdu to share with their fellow countrymen and women. These men were there not as journalists but as sepoys or soldiers, that is, members of the Indian military commanded by British officers who fought in all of Britain's military campaigns in China, beginning with the First Opium War during 1839–42. In fact, Indian soldiers made up the overwhelming majority of the British troops in China in the nineteenth and early twentieth centuries.

My chapter will start by reviewing their writings, as well as those of the great man of letters, Rabindranath Tagore, before turning to the stories that vernacular newspapers in India spun for their growing audience of readers. It focuses particularly on the sources and reasons underlying the highly favourable images of China that circulated in India at the turn of the twentieth century, 'scratches'[1] on the minds of those who portrayed the Chinese as kith and kin. My examples are drawn primarily from east and north India, specifically from Bengal and the United Provinces (UP), two vast, overwhelmingly rural provinces then populated by over 120 million people (undivided Bengal by almost 75 million, the UP by 47 million), and extending today over the areas of West Bengal, Assam, Bihar, Odisha, Jharkhand, and Uttar Pradesh in India and the nation-state of Bangladesh.[2]

Most of the works I have consulted were written in Hindi, Bengali, Urdu, and English around the turn of the twentieth century in 1900 or the years on either side of it. Although literacy levels in India were extremely low at the outset of the twentieth century—according to the 1901 Census, only a little over 5 per cent of the population was literate across the country, with provinces such as Bengal roughly at that level and other areas such as the UP closer to 3 per cent—more and more people were engaging with the medium of print in the late nineteenth and early twentieth centuries. In fact, many more people had access to print culture than is suggested by colonial census data for literacy, not only because of undercounting but also because such statistics do not account for the wider 'reading' public, such as those who gained familiarity with texts through oral performances or by listening to readings performed by their friends and neighbours. Moreover, as publishing expanded, so did the popular reading and listening public for its products, from books and printed texts of one sort or another to journals and newspapers to school textbooks (Dubrow 2018; Orsini 2002; Stark 2007).

Circulation data for newspapers provide one indication of this grow-ing reading and listening public. For instance, although the number of daily newspapers in Bengali fell from six to two in the last decade of the nineteenth century, newspaper circulation rose from 1,088 to 2,400, while weekly newspapers increased in number from 24 to 34, and in circulation from 33,529 to 112,553 (Gait 1902: 303). As with other kinds of publications, newspaper circulation figures—500 to 600 in the case of a large distribution and 100 to 300 on average—did not account for the many who got their news from newspapers 'being read in libraries, bazaars, and schools' (Codell 2004: 113).

I shall begin by culling passages uttered by a well-known poet and a largely obscure soldier. The poet is none other than the polymath and Renaissance man Rabindranath Tagore, the man for all Chinese seasons; the other a man in uniform, Gadhadar Singh, whose remarkable account of his *Thirteen Months in China* I have edited and co-translated with Kamal Sheel and Ranjana Sheel (Yang 2017).[3] Although worlds apart in many ways, the two men had in common an affinity for China, as evidenced by the sentiments Tagore expressed in a number of China-related pieces that he wrote in response to various English-language sources he came across, and the book Singh pub-lished in 1902 based on his experiences as a member of the multina-tional military force in China. Tagore wrote from afar, from Bengal, and as the son and grandson of Debendranath and Dwarkanath, respectively, both of whom had strong ties to China. Singh, from the UP, where his regiment was stationed after it returned from China, wrote from memory first-hand experiences and his perusal of some well-known English-language books on China in circulation in India.

That an Indian soldier should compose a substantial work on China in Hindi or any vernacular language is surprising not only because no other extensive texts of that type exist in any Indian languages prior to the twentieth century, but also because few sepoys, if any, have left substantial textual traces of their military experiences. The soldier's account featured China is less startling because the largest group of people from India who spent any extended period of time in China in the nineteenth century were military men. The only other groups who worked and resided there in any numbers were merchants and traders (Sen 2017: 252–88; Yang 2017). Indeed, the number of sepoys with experience of China totalled hundreds and thousands of people, men mobilized from regiments stationed in India to fight the two Anglo-Chinese wars (1839–42, 1856–60) and to make up a large part of the British contingent in the multinational force that was mobilized to defeat the anti-Christian Boxers in 1900–1 (Harfield 1990).

Singh's *Thirteen Months* is one of three published accounts I have located so far, all penned in Hindi or Urdu, and all seemingly written to inform the growing reading public about the momentous events in China. The other two are Pandit Mahendulal Garg's *Chin Darpan* [Mirror on China] (1901) (discussed in Chapter 5 by Kamal Sheel in this volume), and Abd al-Majid Khan's *Natijah-I shamshir, al-mo'ruff bih M'rakah-I Chin* [Account in Verse of Author's Experiences with the Bengal Lancers in China] (1903), an Urdu account in verse of his experiences as a member of the Bengal Lancers.[4] I am not surprised that at least three writers—there may be more, as some authors may have excerpted their China reminiscences in local newspapers and magazines—sought to capitalize on the attention that the Boxer Uprising and its aftermath generated in India. That it was a global event of great interest in India as well is evidenced by the many headlines and stories devoted to it in the vernacular newspapers.

Long before Tagore set foot on Chinese soil in what has been termed his 'controversial' visit to China in 1924, he wrote several pieces in Bengali about that country and its people. Most of these writings represented his response to articles and books he had read in English, clear evidence of his generation's lively interest in China. Consider, for instance, his 1901 essay entitled 'Samajbhed' (social difference) in the literary magazine *Bangadarshan*, written after he had read E.J. Dillon's piece, 'The Chinese Wolf and the European Lamb' (1901). A PhD in Oriental languages and literature, Dillon wrote about China in his capacity as a correspondent for the *Daily Telegraph*. From the frontlines of the war in China, Dillon provided an eyewitness account of the 'wanton destruction'—the looting, pillaging, killing, and rape—that foreign powers committed in the name of civilization. As Tagore noted, Dillon (1901) describes 'the unspeakable atrocities perpetrated by the Europeans against the Chinese people. Even the names of Genghis Khan and Tamer Lane bow down in the front of the barbarity of civilized Europe' (Majumdar 2011; Tagore 1960). Tagore was also critical of Western missionaries whose intrusions disrupted China's ancient civilization and constituted a brutal assault on its society (Majumdar 2011: 78).

Dillon's recounting of the outrages committed in China by members of the International Expedition elicited a similar response from the Bengali newspaper, *Hindoo Patriot*, which reminded its readers about comparable British representations of Indians involved in the Mutiny or Rebellion of 1857. As the newspaper declaimed: 'When the atrocities of the dark days of the Indian mutiny were told, the cry was raised against the perpetrators, and their horrid crimes were washed in oceans of blood. Who is there who will raise such a cry now for the down-trodden Chinese?'[5]

Tagore also took up his pen on behalf of China the following year in response to a pamphlet he had read titled *Letters from John Chinaman* (Dickinson 1911), purportedly written by a Chinese person fluent in English and originally published in the *Saturday Review* on 12 January 1901. Tagore's essay, which appeared in his magazine *Bangadarshan*, found little to fault in the *Letters* and its critique of Western capitalism, imperialism, and religious hypocrisy. 'Vast China,' Tagore (1960) wrote, 'has not been tamed by the rule of weapons; her discipline comes from the rule of ethics. If that ethos is struck, China would taste death pangs.'

These were not the first occasions on which Tagore broached the subject of China. His interest in and writings on China dated to well before 1900. His 'vision' of China, he once acknowledged, was 'formed when . . . [he] was young' and imagined a 'romantic China' because of his reading of the Arabian Nights (cited in Das 2017: 95). Not until much later, he writes, did he manage a closer look; he 'caught glimpses' of China when he was in Japan for the first time in 1916.

As early as 1881, as a twenty-year old, he wrote 'Chin Maraner Byabasa' ['Death Traffic in China'] in the Bengali magazine *Bharati*. This article, a review of Bonn theology professor Theodore Christlieb's book (1879) originally written in German and translated into English as *The Indo-British Opium Trade*, boldly declared:

> A whole nation . . . has been forced by Great Britain to accept the opium poison—simply for commercial greed. In her helplessness, China pathetically declared: 'I do not require any opium'. But the British shopkeeper answered: 'That's all nonsense. You must take it'.
>
> Both the hands of China were tightly bound. Opium was forced down China's throat with the help of guns and bayonets, while the British merchant cried, 'You have to pay the price of all the opium you take from us.' (Tagore 1925)

While Tagore's affinities for and sympathies with China prior to his visits to Japan in 1916 and to China in 1924 grew out of his textual knowledge of that country, the subalterns who expressed comparable sentiments based their texts on their personal experiences of China. As I have noted elsewhere (Yang 2017: 20–6), Gadadhar Singh expressed deep sympathy with the country and people he had been sent to wage war against as a member of the British contingent of the eight-nation multinational force.

Singh voiced his concern for China, even though he and his fellow soldiers of the Seventh Rajput Regiment were shipped out from India with the parting words that they were heading to China on a civilizing mission. That was the message drilled into them at their send-off in Calcutta (now Kolkata), when their commanding general told them that they were representing the world and the civilized powers against the Boxers, a movement widely perceived in many European writings as dabbling in magic and superstition and as fiercely opposed to Western missionaries, Christianity, and its Chinese converts.

Nevertheless, Singh wears his compassion for China on his sleeve, his affinity for it perceptible almost from the opening lines of his text. He states it—by design, I believe—when his ship first approached Chinese soil at Dagu (Tanggu district), the entry point into Tianjin and Beijing. He remembers that moment as an occasion when he surveyed the nearby landscape and detected many deserted and destroyed villages. On some broken buildings he saw French, Russian, and Japanese flags fluttering, and in some villages, he espied a few people alive, skeleton-like old people standing upright with the help of their walking sticks. The foreign powers stood tall, in other words, while China and its people were battered and broken (Yang 2017: 48–9).

'Even hearts of stone', Yang (2017: 48) declares, 'would [have] be[en] moved ... There was no need for us to feel compassion because we had come to fight the Chinese. But ... seeing people of our same colour generated .... "emotion" for them in our minds if not in actions.' This caring outlook frames his 'eyewitness' account. It permeates his recollections of his regiment's march into Beijing and the subsequent takeover of the capital by the International Expedition, whose military victories he chronicles alongside its brutalization of China and the Chinese. The Allied forces in China, to cite his suggestive metaphor, were engaged in *shikar*, 'hunting', a word that also means 'prey' or 'victim'. In graphic detail, he documents incidents when Allied troops treated Chinese bodies and possessions as game to be hunted down—killed, raped, or plundered, depending on who or what their prey was. He recounts many instances of the Allied soldiers brutalizing the local population. He also reports that everyone, even his fellow Hindustanis, participated in the looting of Beijing (Yang 2017: 48–9, 74–7, 292–9).

Singh's sympathetic representation of China is all the more telling given the overwhelmingly negative attitudes about the country and the Boxers in all the Allied countries, especially Britain. Contrast, for instance, the tenor of his narrative with that of Edwards's *Story of China*, a book he relied on for some of his historical information. The latter's China was portrayed as the 'Asiatic "sick man"' 'hampered and cramped to an extraordinary degree by ... rock-fixed customs, superstitions, and prejudices' (Edwards 1900: 8, 128). Singh's story also differs from that written by Vaughan, his superior officer, who reveals his attitude to the conflict by designating his account, *St. George and the Chinese Dragon*, in short, as a struggle between Christian good and pagan Chinese evil. Based on his diary and published in 1902, as was Singh's book, the two works could not be more dissimilar, even though they focused on the same sequence of events.

Singh's different stance is also evident from his characterization of the Boxer Uprising as a *bidroha*, a revolt, a designation that perfectly matches current historiographical understandings of it. He begins his discussion of the Boxers by issuing a caveat: The term 'Boxers', he points out, is a word of foreign fiction. The Chinese term for them, he states, is 'I ho chuan (Yihequan [義和拳])' or 'Fists of Righteous Harmony', and he attributes its origins to an organization with the same name and to another body known as the Dadaohui (大刀會) [Big Sword Society]. He does not reveal whether he acquired this information from personal knowledge and experience or from his readings of English-language sources (Yang 2017: 22).

Singh's subaltern view of the world, which was partly shaped by a sense of his racial and ethnic difference from the 'white' British who ruled his country and were on the cusp of extending their power over China, colours his eyewitness account and brief history of China and the world. It led to his wholehearted embrace of China, even though he was there to wage war on that country and its people.

He then notes, seemingly in order to process his own feelings, that he realized that the 'Chinese are Buddhists. (I did not know about Confucianism at that time.) They share a religion with Hindustanis.' 'As inhabitants of Asia', he elaborates, 'they are also almost fellow countrymen. In complexion, tradition, and culture, too, they are not dissimilar. Why had God inflicted this distress on them! Did God not want to help them?' (Yang 2017: 48). Thus, he emphatically advances a case for a special relationship between China and India based on geographical contiguity, race, and religious and cultural practices. Furthermore, the two countries were neighbours, both inhabited by people with black skins and sharing Buddhism, in common along with many traditions and customs.[6]

Although far less personal in its outlook, Pandit Mahendulal Garg's *Chin Darpan*, based on knowledge the author had acquired from seeing, listening, and reading ('*ankhe dekha, kano suna*', and '*pustko meh padkar likha*'), expresses similar sympathies for China. According to the author, he composed his book while he was in Shanhaiguan in northern China in 1901 and published earlier extracts in the Calcutta-based newspaper *Bharat Mitra* between

June and December 1900. He saw his work—a first print run of a thousand copies was issued—as addressing all the essential topics relating to Chinese 'life, conduct, religion, crafts, and trade' in as simple a language as possible so that even people who were not highly educated and somewhat illiterate could understand it. For him, as the opening line of the book (Garg 1901) spells out, only the Himalayan mountains divided Hindustan from China, otherwise they might even be part of the same empire.

Singh and Garg—although not Tagore who was primarily home-schooled—were products of a late nineteenth-century colonial education system that catered to a tiny fraction of the overall population, mostly children of upper-caste, middle-class, and urban-based families. By 1899–1901, in Bengal alone, English-language schools enrolled over 107,000 pupils in 471 high schools and over 62,000 in 950 middle schools. In addition, 57,039 students were registered in 1,045 middle vernacular schools, and 177,233 and 1,007,878 students, respectively, in upper primary and lower primary vernacular schools (Bengal 1902: 210–12).

As their primary- and secondary-school geography texts reveal—government-supported schools taught geography in the last year of primary and beginning years of middle schools—these elites grew up learning about the proximity of China to India and their co-location in Asia. Whereas the primary-class books offer little more than a thumbnail sketch listing countries and oceans bordering China, its territorial and population numbers, and the name of the capital, the texts for the more advanced classes generally do more than just provide geographical coordinates: they also identify some of the main cities and often discuss trade, in one case extending that description to refer to the British presence in China and their involvement in the opium trade. In many Bengali textbooks of the colonial era, as one scholar has noted, China was placed on 'a higher pedestal'.[7]

Tagore, Singh, and Garg were three of many voices at the turn of the twentieth century who sought to speak for China to their fellow countrymen and women at a time of chaos and convulsion, highlighting its ties to and similarities with India. In drawing out these connections, these writers, as well as those who broadcast their thoughts in the newspapers, invariably invoked the sense of fellowship and sympathy they felt towards China and its people.

Indeed, contemporary vernacular newspapers wrote of China in crisis with an equal measure of concern and sympathy. In India, as elsewhere in the world, China commanded newspaper headlines in 1900 as the Boxer Uprising erupted across its northern provinces. It generated even more coverage that summer as the Boxers, with the support of the ruling Qing Dynasty, encircled the foreign legations in Beijing in June, a development that prompted the mobilization of a multinational force to raise the siege of the foreign diplomats and community.

Singh and Garg participated in the relief force that marched into Beijing in mid-August, defeated the Boxers and the Qing forces, seized control of the imperial capital, and brought the Chinese Empire to its knees. Their involvement in China and that of hundreds of other Indian sepoys was widely known, and not just in their home villages and towns. Thus, even though the so-called 'native press' sided with China, many of its writers were well aware that their country was deeply implicated in the war. As the *Bharat Jiwan* (13 August 1900) pointed out, it would be 'a mistake to suppose ... that India has little or no concern with the Chinese imbroglio. England being involved in the imbroglio twenty thousand troops have already been sent from India, and many more will be despatched in the future; and there is no knowing how many of them will perish, which will put India to great expense'. Furthermore, India was involved because of the opium trade, and were that to dry up Indian revenues would be down by 'two crores ... The war will [also] inflict heavy losses on the mill owners of Bombay, whose cotton fabrics were largely consumed in China, and also affect the native princes.'[8]

Generally, the vernacular newspapers praised the good conduct of the sepoys in China, particularly in contrast to the widespread savagery, rape, and looting that other foreign troops were reported to have engaged in. The *Bengalee* (30 January 1901), for instance, contrasted the atrocious behaviour of Russian and Japanese soldiers with Indian troops 'against whom not a whisper has been heard of improper conduct'. Thus, it exclaimed: 'Well done, sons of India'.[9]

From the very outset of the Boxer Uprising, however, the vernacular newspapers were also worried that the Boxers were 'courting the ruin of their country', for the 'struggle' between China and 'the combined great European powers will be like that between a jackal and a lion' (*Hindustan*, 20 June 1900). In a similar vein, the Banaras weekly, the *Kalidas*, expressed concern because China was arrayed against not only Japan but also England, Germany, France, Russia, and USA. In its estimation, one did not have to be 'a prophet to predict' the outcome of a war against 'the great powers of the world.... These vultures, which have attacked the corpse of China, will not depart until they have devoured it.'[10]

The Calcutta-based Bengali weekly, the *Hitavadi* (27 July 1900), also characterized the Western powers as vultures flying in 'from all quarters' towards a China

> now somewhat in the condition of a carcass.... The vultures flock to the carcass and try to devour it piecemeal. Even so, the civilized Western Powers, seeing the Boxers opposing foreign aggression and tyranny, are resolved to devour China piecemeal, ignoring all religious and moral considerations. Like vultures flocking to the carcass, European troops and fleets are flocking to China.[11]

Many newspapers elected to elucidate China's plight in 1900 by providing their readers with some historical context. In the words of the *Hitavadi* (27 July 1900), the 'seeds' of its crisis were sown over the previous century. 'China owes her decline to her contact with Europe, and its Christian poison which is now consuming her', the newspaper elaborated. 'There wasn't another country in the world so powerful, so rich and so vast as China, or another nation so skilful in arts and manufactures as the Chinese. It is Europe's contact which has ruined China, and it is the Christian missionaries who were the first to bring about her ruin.'[12]

As the *Hitavadi* (27 July 1900) also informed its readers, China had been 'a very powerful empire' in the eighteenth century when it conquered Nepal, only 60 miles from British-colonized India. It also noted the failures of earlier British missions to China in securing concessions—in particular Lord Macartney's 1793 mission, which was followed by Lord Amherst's in 1816—undoubtedly to recount the changing dynamics in power between China and the West over time. The Opium War, however, exposed its weaknesses, which were caused by Western incursions. Moreover, 'Christian Europe' took advantage of its vulnerability by introducing, as the newspaper sarcastically noted:

[T]hree well-known means of spreading knowledge and civilisation in uncivilised countries.... The first is the brandy bottle, the second is the bayonet, and the third is the Bible. Opium served the purpose of wine in China. The importation of opium into China raised her one step higher in the ladder of civilization. The British bayonet raised her another step. The missionaries finished what was left unfinished by opium and bayonet. The settlement of Christian missionaries in China in 1842 raised China to the highest stage of civilization.[13]

The historical details that many vernacular newspapers often added to their stories were gleaned from the very same English-language sources that circulated widely in Britain and India and that provided English-speaking readers such as Singh and Tagore with up-to-date information about China. However, many of these consumers of articles and books on China written in English, such as Singh, Tagore, and various newspaper editors, read these sources highly selectively, preferring to cite works that were sympathetic to China and critical of the Western presence, or reading them against the grain when they did not agree with the pro-British stance of the writings. For instance, an article in the *Hitavadi* mentions Sir William Butler's book (1889), *Charles George Gordon*, no doubt because it viewed the existing conflict between Britain and China to be, above all, about opium. Quoting from the book, the *Hitavadi* approvingly served its readers Butler's statement that the 'real matter in dispute between the two nations had all the simplicity that lies in the distinction between black and white, between abstract right and abstract right'.[14] Butler (1889: 42) then goes on to say—a line of argument that apparently resonated well with Indian readers—that in

forcing our opium upon China we were reversing the alternative of money or life given by the highwayman to his victim. We were demanding life and money at the same moment. Opium ... was death and worse than death, and in endeavouring to keep this terrible new poison ... from their shores ... China ... [was] only fulfilling the first obligation of rulers—the protection of the lives of their people.

The *Hitavadi* also references another English-language text favourably, namely Lord Curzon's *Problems of the Far East*,[15] not for its analysis of China, Japan, and Korea or its position on India, but for its critique of missionary activities in China. Curzon's book, initially published in the summer of 1894, attracted a considerable readership in Britain, India, and USA because it had perceptively gauged Japan's military superiority over China in advance of the Sino-Japanese War of 1894–5, when the former easily defeated the latter power. Readers in India were also drawn to the book because its author became the viceroy of India in 1899 and remained in that office until 1905.[16]

Neither the *Hitavadi* nor other Indian consumers of the book paid much heed to the opening dedication of Curzon's (1894) book, which was addressed to '[t]hose who believe that the British Empire is, under providence, the greatest instrument for good that the world has seen and who hold, with the writer, that its work in the Far East is not yet accomplished'. Instead what these readers in India seemed to focus on is Curzon's (1894: 287, 297) forthright condemnation of Western missionaries in China for their 'implacable hostility to all native religions and ethics' and their 'presence' that reminded the Chinese of 'the continued ascendency of an alien Power ... originally introduced by force' and 'a policy which has been and is forced upon them in opposition both to the interests of the government, the sentiments of the *literati*, and the convictions of the people'.

Like Tagore and Singh, the vernacular newspapers generally shared a critical attitude towards the role of Christian missionaries in China and their culpability in the events leading up to the Boxer Uprising. In the words of the Moradabad paper, *Jami-ul-Ulum* (14 July 1900), the European powers treated China contemptuously, considering its people 'fit only to black[en] the shoes of Europeans' and the country 'a good tit-bit ... to swallow'. These foreign nations, furthermore, were on Chinese soil in part because of their interest in establishing their 'Heavenly Kingdom' in the 'Celestial Empire' of China. 'They accordingly sent out their missionaries ... who at once took to establishing their churches and making converts of the Chinese at various places ... The native converts received support (in every matter) from the missionaries, and the latter[s'] ... respective governments.' Consequently, in China as in India, everyone feared

> native Christians ... Nobody can utter a word against a native Christian ... When a scavenger or shoemaker [that is, of the so-called untouchable or Dalit caste] becomes a Christian in a village, the zamindar

[landholder] fears to demand rent or extract service from him. In native states, too, native Christians are made much more of than the Hindus and Musalmans.[17]

Christianity, in other words, inverted the structures and practices of Indian society.

Several newspapers also drew connections and parallels between the Boxer campaign against foreigners and the efforts of Europeans and others to expel Chinese from their countries. The Mymensingh newspaper, *Charu Mihir* (26 June 1900), claimed that the Boxers were doing what they had seen Australia and Canada do to Chinese labourers, and the Calcutta weekly, the *Prabhat* (27 June 1900), advanced a similar argument in stating that the Boxers were doing precisely what others had done, namely, 'Cape Colony and Australia ... [driving] out Indians from their towns and America ... prevent[ing] an influx of Chinamen into the United States'. The only difference it saw from these actions was that the Indians and, by extension, the Chinese were 'weak and the Europeans ... strong'. In fact, 'rash and reckless' though the Boxers may have been in confronting the Europeans, their actions were nevertheless 'proof of [their] noble courage'. By contrast, the Europeans who attacked Indians in the British Cape Colony in South Africa were cowards, their 'cowardice' all the more disgraceful because 'Indian assistance was not slighted or refused' when the Cape was 'in serious peril'.[18]

To many observers in India, the International Expedition to China and the subsequent occupation of Beijing appeared to be a prelude to that country's takeover by the Western powers and a follow-up to their recent acquisitions in Asia and their colonization of almost all of Africa. Understandably, some discerned similarities with earlier developments in India that led to its takeover by Britain. Intriguingly, some also saw the events in China in 1900–1 as marking the end of an Asia that encompassed India and other regions into an imagined community of sorts. As the editor of *Kalidas* (10 July 1900) wrote, he could not

view with equanimity the impending destruction of the Chinese Empire ... The occupation of China by the European powers may be considered as an end of the independence of Asia, a fate which has already befallen Africa and America. Japan, which is at the present day helping the European powers in destroying her neighbours, will share the same fate ere long. If Asiatics are born to be slaves, there is no help for it.[19]

In a similar vein, the *Hitavadi* (27 July 1900) conceived of the war in China as critical to the future of Asia:

The issues of the war will decide whether the political independence of this great continent will be preserved—whether the black and yellow races of Asia will or will not be deprived of their liberty by the civilized and warlike nations of Europe. All the Asiatic nations, therefore, have their political interests involved in this war. Japan and China are intimately related.[20]

Such intimate relationships occurring across the different countries and peoples of Asia made it, in the eyes of many writers, a singular and interconnected whole. Geography forged ties across the entire region, as did history and civilization. Furthermore, at the outset of the twentieth century, Asia also shared the experience of Western imperialism and colonialism. As the *Hitavadi* (27 July 1900) bemoaned, European states, fuelled by 'national hunger', were bent on 'extirpating the old and civilised nations of Asia. What little these nations have gained in Asia has, instead of satisfying their hunger, only served to whet it', the newspaper added. 'They are mad with greed ... The white man in Asia, with his uncontrolled greed, has cast all religious considerations to the winds, and is trying to gain his ends by harassing the down-trodden Asiatics with the help of their new civilization.'[21]

In that struggle, Asia only stood a chance if it unified and shook 'off all her infirmities ... But if she is crushed and crippled, Asia will forever lose her independence and will fall into the hands of Europe'. As the *Hitavadi* (29 June 1900) went on to assert: 'That is why we say that this China war isn't a war between sovereigns but a war between Asia and Europe. It is a struggle for the maintenance of Asia's national existence.' Were its 'utter collapse' to occur, China would lose its 'independence', a possibility that, in the estimation of the *Hitavadi*, would cause 'us so much anxiety. The last of the Asiatic Empires is going to disappear. Isn't that matter for sorrow to the people of Asia?'[22]

The Chittagong-based Bengali weekly, the *Jyoti*, also framed its coverage of China in pan-Asian terms. All 'inhabitants of Asia', the newspaper insisted, were troubled by the Western presence in China and the spheres of influence they had carved out. The newspaper reminded everyone that they were indebted to China for what it had contributed 'to promote human welfare' in the world. 'Any good news regarding China', the *Jyoti* noted, 'fills the minds of every Asiatic with joy'. Thus, all Asians, the newspaper concluded, welcomed the news that China was beginning to realize, after having suffered several setbacks, the sources of 'her degraded condition' and the importance of the 'Chinese and the Manchus ... henceforward [agreeing] to sink all their differences and act in union. The Chinese government has sent two hundred Chinese youth to learn arts and science in Japan, and 600 more will be sent to Europe'.[23]

Many newspapers also connected China's present to India's past, that is, they read into the former country's looming predicament parallels between what had happened and what was about to happen with what had already occurred in the latter country. In the opinion of the Calcutta-based Bengali weekly, *Sanjivani*, slavery was 'in store' for China, a country that had created 'some of the principal factors of modern civilization' and was 'the favoured abode of ancient civilization'. As it pointed out, China first manufactured the paper on which its article was published; it also invented the printing press and gunpowder. But it was in 'serious peril' now and about to face a fate that had befallen other nations.[24]

India, as the newspaper noted, once had 'a glorious past', as embodied 'in the historic figures of Asoka and Kaniksha ... [and] Prithwiraj, Pratap Sinha, Ranjit Sinha and Sivaji ... [and] such powerful and heroic races as the Sikhs and the Mahrattas'. However, the 'greatness and glory of India are gone. So it has been with Egypt and Babylon, [and] Persia is in a moribund condition'. And, according to the newspaper, that was about to happen to the great civilization of China too, its fate sealed by the overwhelming might of the Western powers.[25]

China, in the eyes of many in India, appeared on the verge of suffering the fate that had befallen India, namely, succumbing to British or Western rule and domination. Not only was China a neighbour but it was also, in size and historical greatness, on par with India. And, as Singh and Garg and other Indian travellers to China encountered, the two countries shared beliefs and practices in common, in part because of their Buddhist heritage.

Such fears and hopes continued to infuse responses to events in China in the ensuing decade or so. In the aftermath of the Chinese Revolution of 1911, newspapers in India worried about the possibility of Western intervention even as many expressed support for the 'revolutionary outbreak' and optimism about the seeming rise of a 'liberal and progressive' form of government. The *Bharat Mitra* (15 January 1912) pointed out that a 'republic' had been established in a country in an Asia that Europeans did not believe was capable of change. Similarly, the *Bangavasi* (26 February 1912) wrote favourably about the 1911 Revolution and the rise of an 'infant republic' that it anticipated would lead to a revival of the 'ancient greatness of China, till it becomes an object of pride to the Eastern world'.[26]

The crisis in China at the turn of the twentieth century, beginning with the Boxer Uprising, the International Expedition, the latter's defeat of the Boxers and their Qing allies, and the ensuing occupation of Beijing by the multinational force, elicited tremendous sympathy and support for China and the Chinese from people in India. As the works authored by Tagore, Singh, and Garg reveal, China exerted a powerful hold over people's imagination in India because its people saw themselves and their experiences as colonized subjects reflected in the tumultuous events that China was experiencing and was likely to experience as Western powers expanded their authority across the land. Vernacular newspapers in Bengali, Hindi, and Urdu echoed similar concerns and sympathies: Their reports on China also invariably sided with their Asian neighbour and lamented the growing might and influence of Western powers in China and across Asia. To many, China's demise as an independent state seemed imminent, a fate that India had already suffered earlier, much to the chagrin of many a writer. Many voices also expressed concern that its potential collapse meant the end of an Asia that they had envisaged themselves being a part of, with ties particularly to China because both countries were bound together by geography, history, civilization, and the shared experience of Western imperialism and colonialism.

Notes

1. The notion of 'scratches' on the minds of the people, specifically US impressions about China and India, comes from Isaacs (1958). For a view from the other side, see Chapter 4 by Zhang Ke in this volume.

2. See Risley and Gait (1903: 42). Bengal's population, including the so-called 'native states', totalled over 78 million and that of the UP and its native states, over 48 million.

3. Rabindranath Tagore's writings are collected in a multi-volume series entitled *Rabindra-Racanabali*, published by Visva-Bharati, and also available at https://www.worldmets.com/rabindranath-tagore/rabindra-rachanabali-all-volumes/rabindra-rachanabali-all-volumes-27/; accessed on 4 June 2020. See also Tan et al. (2011).

4. There is also *Amar Singh's Diary*, superbly edited by Susanne Hoeber Rudolph and Lloyd I. Rudolph with Mohan Singh Kanota, but it was never meant for publication, was written in English, and spans a forty-four-year period of his adult life and not just his 1900–1 China years.

5. Week ending 16 February, 'Report on Native Papers in Bengal', 1901, L/R/5/27, British Library (BL), London, UK.

6. Tagore and Chinese intellectuals such as Liang Qichao (1873–1929) deployed similar arguments to emphasize the long-standing fraternal relationship between China and India (Bharucha 2006).

7. See Basu (2010) for a discussion of Bengali textbooks that offered a racial understanding of Asian countries and generally placed China 'on a higher pedestal'. For examples of Hindi geography textbooks, see Prasad (1905) and Simha (1879).

8. 'Selections from the Vernacular Newspapers Published in the North-Western Provinces and Oudh' (Confidential), 1900, L/R/5/77, BL, London, UK.

9. 'Report on Native Papers in Bengal', 1901, L/R/5/27, BL, London, UK.

10. 'Selections from the Vernacular Newspapers Published in the North-Western Provinces and Oudh', 1900, L/R/5/77, BL, London, UK.

11. 'Report on Native Papers in Bengal', 1900, L/R/5/26, BL, London, UK.

12. *Hitavadi*, 27 July 1900, in 'Report on Native Papers in Bengal', L/R/5/26, BL, London, UK.

13. *Hitavadi*, 27 July 1900, in 'Report on Native Papers in Bengal', L/R/5/26, BL, London, UK. The reference apparently is to the clashes between Nepal and Qing China in the 1790s in the wake of Nepalese incursions into Tibet. By then, Nepal was unified under one ruler and Qing China had extended its dominance over the 'outer provinces' of Tibet, Central Asia, and Mongolia.

14. *Hitavadi*, 27 July 1900, 'Report on Native Papers in Bengal', L/R/5/26, BL, London, UK.

15. *Hitavadi*, 27 July 1900, 'Report on Native Papers in Bengal', L/R/5/26, BL, London, UK.

16. Amar Singh (2000: 141, 143, 145–6), who joined the British contingent in China as part of the Imperial Cadet Corps, writes of buying Curzon's

Problems of the Far East book in Calcutta prior to his departure and struggling to understand its difficult English en route to China.

17. *Jami-ul-Ulum*, 14 July 1900, in 'Selections from the Vernacular Newspapers Published in the North-Western Provinces and Oudh', 1900, L/R/5/77, BL, London, UK.

18. 'Selections from the Vernacular Newspapers Published in the North-Western Provinces and Oudh', 1900, L/R/5/77, BL, London, UK. The British were careful about not involving non-Europeans in the Boer War because both sides in the conflict were Europeans. Many Indian newspapers noted that their soldiers were not sent to South Africa to fight on behalf of the British.

19. 'Selections from the Vernacular Newspapers Published in the North-Western Provinces and Oudh', 1900, L/R/5/77, BL, London, UK.

20. 'Report on Native Papers in Bengal', 1900, L/R/5/26, BL, London, UK.

21. 'Report on Native Papers in Bengal', 1900, L/R/5/26, BL, London, UK.

22. 'Report on Native Papers in Bengal', 1900, L/R/5/26, BL, London, UK.

23. *Jyoti*, week ending 22 June, in 'Report on Native Papers in Bengal', 1901, L/R/5/27, BL, London, UK.

24. *Sanjivani*, week ending 21 July, in 'Report on Native Papers in Bengal', 1900, L/R/5/26, BL, London, UK.

25. *Sanjivani*, week ending 21 July, in 'Report on Native Papers in Bengal', 1900, L/R/5/26, BL, London, UK.

26. Week ending 2 March, 'Report on Native Papers in Bengal', 1912; Week ending 4 November, 'Report on Native Papers in Bengal', 1911, BL, London, UK. See also Chapter 5 by Kamal Sheel in this volume for Indian impressions of the Chinese Revolution of 1911 and ensuing events in the early twentieth century.

References

Archival Material

British Library, London, UK

'Report on Native Papers in Bengal', 1900, 1901, 1911, 1912.
'Selections from the Vernacular Newspapers Published in the North-Western Provinces and Oudh', 1900.

Other Sources

Basu, Subho. 2010. 'The Dialectics of Resistance: Colonial Geography, Bengali Literati and the Racial Mapping of Indian Identity'. *Modern Asian Studies* 44 (1): 53–79.

Bengal. 1902. *Report on the Administration of Bengal during 1900–1901.* Calcutta: Bengal Secretariat Press.

Bharucha, Rustom. 2006. *Another Asia: Rabindranath Tagore and Okakura Tenshin.* New Delhi: Oxford University Press.

Butler, William F. 1889. *Charles George Gordon.* London: Macmillan.

Christlieb, Theodore. 1879. *The Indo-British Opium Trade and Its Effects: A Recess Study.* Translated by David B. Croom. London: James Nisbet.

Codell, Julie F. 2004. 'Introduction: The Nineteenth-Century News from India'. *Victorian Periodicals Review* 37 (2): 106–23.

Curzon, George N. 1894. *Problems of the Far East.* London: Longmans, Green, & Co.

Das, Sisir Kumar. 2017. 'The Controversial Guest: Tagore in China', in Madhavi Thampi (ed.), *India and China in the Colonial World*, pp. 85–125. New York: Routledge.

Dickinson, G. Lowes. 1911. *Letters from John Chinaman.* London: J.M. Dent.

Dillon, E. J. 1901. 'The Chinese Wolf and the European Lamb'. *The Contemporary Review* 79 (January): 1–31.

Dubrow, Jennifer. 2018. *Cosmopolitan Dreams: The Making of Modern Urdu Literary Culture in Colonial South Asia.* Honolulu: University of Hawai'i Press.

Edwards, Neville P. 1900. *The Story of China with a Description of the Events Relating to the Present Struggle.* London: Hutchinson & Co.

Gait, E.A. 1902. *Census of India, 1901, Volume VI: The Lower Provinces of Bengal and Their Feudatories—Part I, The Report.* Calcutta: Bengal Secretariat Press.

Garg, Mahendulal. 1901. *Mirror on China [Chin Darpan].* Mathura: Sukhsancharak Press.

Harfield, Alan. 1990. *British and Indian Armies on the China Coast 1785–1985.* London: A. and J. Partnership.

Isaacs, Harold. 1958. *Scratches on Our Minds: American Images of China and India.* New York: J. Day Co.

Khan, Abd al-Majid. 1903. *Natijah-I shamshir, al-mo'ruff bih M'rakah-I Chin [Account in Verse of Author's Experiences with the Bengal Lancers in China].* Lucknow: Abd al-Majid Khan.

Majumdar, Swapan. 2011. 'Looking East: China in Tagore's Cosmology of Thoughts'. In Tan Chung, Amiya Dev, Wang Bangwei, and Wei Liming (eds), *Tagore and China*, pp. 74–87. New Delhi: SAGE.

Orsini, Francesca. 2002. *The Hindi Public Sphere, 1920–1940: Language and Literature in the Age of Nationalism.* New Delhi: Oxford University Press.

Prasad, Rameshwar. 1905. *Geography of India with the Outlines of Asia (for the Fifth Class of Anglo-Vernacular Schools)*, Hindi edition. Allahabad: Anwar Ahmadi Press.

Risley, H.H. and E.A. Gait. 1903. *Report on the Census of India, 1901.* Calcutta: Government Printing.

Sen, Tansen. 2017. *India, China, and the World: A Connected History*. Lanham, MD: Rowman & Littlefield.

Simha, Ganapata. 1879. *Chhota Bhugolavarana* [*Elementary Geography of Asia*]. Hughli: Dudhodya Chapkhana.

Singh, Amar. 2000. *Reversing the Gaze: Amar Singh's Diary, a Colonial Subject's Narrative of Imperial India*. Edited by Susanne Hoeber Rudolph and Lloyd I. Rudolph with Mohan Singh Kanota. New Delhi: Oxford University Press.

Stark, Ulrike. 2007. *An Empire of Books: The Naval Kishore Press and the Diffusion of the Printed Word in Colonial India*. Ranikhet: Permanent Black.

Tagore, Rabindranath. 1925. 'The Death Traffic'. *The Modern Review* 37: 504–5.

———. 1960. *Rabindra-Racanabali*, Volume 12. *Worldmets.com*. Available at https://www.worldmets.com/rabindranath-tagore/rabindra-rachanabali-all-volumes/rabindra-rachanabali-all-volumes-27/; accessed on 11 June 2020.

Tan, Chung, Amiya Dev, Wang Bangwei, and Wei Liming (eds). 2011. *Tagore and China*. New Delhi: SAGE.

Yang, Anand A. (ed.). 2017. *Thirteen Months in China: A Subaltern Indian and the Colonial World*. Translated by Anand A. Yang, Kamal Sheel, and Ranjana Sheel. New Delhi: Oxford University Press.

SECTION III

CULTURES AND MEDIATORS

7

'Tagore and China' Reconsidered

Starting from a Conversation with Feng Youlan[*]

YU-TING LEE

Reflection upon Studies on 'Tagore and China'

This chapter seeks to reconsider the relationship between Rabindranath Tagore (1861–1941) and China, a topic that usually belongs to the broad category of 'pan-Asianism'.[1] However, by delving into documents that are rarely referenced in studies of this kind, I hope to reveal some hitherto unexplored nuances, thereby

[*] This chapter has been substantially revised from the previously published article in Chinese: Yu-Ting Lee. 2012. 'Yizhanzhihou wenminglunyuzhong de Taigeer yu Zhongguo: congqiyu Feng Youlan de duihua shuoqi' (一戰之後文明論域中的泰戈爾與中國：從其與馮友蘭的對話説起) ['Tagore and China in the Perspective of Civilizational Discourse: Starting from a Conversation with Feng Youlan']. *Journal of East Asian Cultural Studies* (Special Issue for the Inauguration of the Graduate School of East Asian Cultures, Kansai University): 275–88.

weaving an intellectual web of the modern world that highlights the connections and comparisons between China and India.

Rabindranath Tagore was awarded the Nobel Prize in Literature in 1913. This dramatic event won him tremendous fame, and he became a much sought-after speaker, touring the world in the following decades. Born in colonial India, and having witnessed the unprecedented damage to human society caused by the First World War, one of the fundamental themes of Tagore's lectures was to propose the spiritual civilization of the East as a remedy for the materialistic civilization of the West. In view of this history, when the 150th anniversary of Tagore's birth was celebrated in 2011, a frequent focus was the relevance of his Asian ideals to the contemporary age of globalization and the 'rise of Asia'.

In China, too, Tagore studies reached a peak around this time. A review of relevant studies in the past hundred years shows that there are several phases to this trend. First of all, Tagore's name became widely known to the Chinese after he received the Nobel Prize in 1913. Studies of the poet and translations of his works began in a fragmented manner, but these preparatory works nonetheless paved the way for Tagore studies to gain momentum in the 1920s, reaching a climax when Tagore visited China in 1924. However, his lectures on spiritual civilization displeased many anti-traditionalist and pro-Western activists, thus involving him unwittingly in a cultural debate that began in China in the late 1910s. Under the circumstances, parties both for and against Tagore made emotional statements that obstructed clear understandings of this Indian poet-thinker. Furthermore, since China was then being devastated by foreign imperialist exploitation and by a struggle for power between domestic warlords, not too much interest was shown in Tagore after his trip, let alone any systematic research being carried out. However, with the establishment of diplomatic relations between the People's Republic of China and the Republic of India and several visits by Zhou Enlai (周恩來) (1898–1976) to India in the 1950s, Tagore came into the limelight again as a pioneer of cultural interaction between the two countries. In 1961, while the 100th anniversary of Tagore's birth was being celebrated, some commemorative articles appeared in China as well. Indeed, since the end of the Cultural Revolution in 1976, there has been a veritable stream of Tagore studies. However, it was not until the turn of the twenty-first century that discussions of his work increased in quantity, apparently because Chinese scholars are trying to address the history of the rise of their own country, one of their tasks being to re-evaluate significant cultural events and intellectual resources in the modern era.

One critical conclusion following a brief review of studies on Tagore in China must be that they do not belong to the field of 'Tagore studies' in the strict sense. Instead, they can be better categorized as branches of 'Chinese studies', such as 'Tagore and China', or the relevant topic of 'cultural interaction between China and India'. Accordingly, these discussions come closer to cultural history, with intellectual issues attracting less critical analysis. This orientation is nonetheless rooted in an intriguing historical fact: How the Chinese interpret Tagore has largely been based on the message he delivered in China in 1924. That is to say, when Tagore addressed Chinese audiences and proposed an idealized Eastern civilization, what he repeated time and again was that Chinese culture is fundamentally humane and that cultural interaction between China and India had existed for millennia. Therefore, during the process in which Tagore propagandized 'the East', he 'Easternized', even 'provincialized', his own image without revealing the full spectrum of his multifarious considerations.[2] A more comprehensive grasp of Tagore's life work—literature, music, painting, religion, philosophy, education, politics, village reform, and so on—and a close reading of his conversations with prominent Western intellectuals show how immense and inspiring his thought is. For example, a biography first published in 1995 lays great stress on the versatility of Tagore's mind (Dutta and Robinson 2009). Nonetheless, for many political and personal reasons, Tagore restricted his speeches in China to certain topics. This had the unfortunate result that 'the East' or 'Asia' occupies too large a proportion of his message to China, thus eclipsing other aspects of his thought worthy of attention. It is almost natural that the Chinese people should have long misunderstood Tagore, research on whom therefore suffers from a degree of rigidity.

As previously described, studies on Tagore in contemporary Chinese academia have two principal foci: 'Tagore and China' and 'cultural interaction between China and India', which crystallize into two interrelated research paradigms.[3] Concerning the former, as early as 1961, Ji Xianlin (季羨林) (1911–2009) wrote a long essay, titled 'Taigeer yu Zhongguo: jinian Taigeer dansheng yibai zhounian' (泰戈爾與中國—紀念泰戈爾誕生一百週年) ['Tagore and China: In Memory of the Centenary of Tagore'], one of the earliest articles to reflect upon Tagore's visit to China and its concomitant lessons. As yet the most exhaustive study of Tagore's lectures made in Asian countries (including China, Japan, and India) and their respective responses to his message is Stephen Hay's *Asian Ideas of East and West: Tagore and His Critics in Japan, China, and India*, published in 1970. Drawing on a profusion of primary sources, Hay's perspective has been largely adopted by later Chinese scholars, that is, their focus remains on Tagore's 1924 trip to China and the controversies he aroused there, with varying degrees of precision of detail. Ai Dan (艾丹) (2010) is another, more recent example. Ai traces the history of Tagore studies in China, expanding on the itinerary of Tagore's 1924 visit and on his interactions with several leading intellectuals in early twentieth-century China. While this book is worth referencing, it overlaps with many previous studies, and the sections on intellectual background and future prospects would have benefited from greater insight. The author states that 'for over half a century, studies on "Tagore and China" have produced significant results'; she also points out some of the limitations inherent in existing research (Ai 2010: 15–17). However, in repeating chronological details and some apparent differences between Tagore's thought and that of contemporary Chinese intellectuals, this work is not immune from those very drawbacks.[4]

On the other hand, studies of 'cultural interaction between China and India' must be placed within the context of the rise of Asia, with Tagore being considered a pioneer in reconnecting the two countries in the modern era. There are some representative works in this field, such as Tan Chung's *Across the Himalayan Gap: An Indian Quest for Understanding China* (2006), published in 1998,[5] and *Zhong-Yin datong: lixiang yu shixian* (中印大同—理想與實現) [*CHINDIA: Idealism and Realization*], published in 2007. In August 2010, a conference titled 'Understanding Tagore: New Perspectives and New Research' was convened at Peking University, the collection of papers of which was edited by Tan Chung et al. and published in 2011 under the title *Tagore and China*. The contributors to this volume are the current leading scholars in Tagore studies. Besides continuing to explore the relationship between Tagore and China, some authors have even attempted to establish a new paradigm of civilizational discourse based on the long cultural interaction between China and India. In addition, in Taiwan a research group headed by Shih Chih-Yu (石之瑜), a political scientist at National Taiwan University, has published many studies of Tagore's ideals about Asia and its potential for Sino-Indian relations in the twenty-first century.[6]

All the research mentioned earlier conduces to a better understanding of Tagore, and it provides evidence that the single topic of 'Tagore and China', if thoroughly probed and connected with relevant issues, can demonstrate the complexity of Tagore's mind and activities to a certain degree. Complementing previous research, this essay shifts the focus to the intellectual world of early twentieth-century China through a refraction of Tagore's thought. To achieve this goal, I shall discard the conventional frame of argument and construct an intellectual web that differs from the ideological battle that occurred when Tagore visited China. By referring to a different set of texts, I hope to reveal some hitherto hidden dimensions of this significant cultural event.

The Conversation between Tagore and Feng Youlan

At the end of 1920, Tagore went to USA for several months to raise funds for Visva-Bharati, the university he wanted to establish to promote cultural interaction between the East and the West. During Tagore's stay in New York, Feng Youlan (馮友蘭) (1895–1990), who was studying for a PhD degree at Columbia University and was to become one of the leading philosophers of modern China, went to visit Tagore to ask his opinion about the differences between Eastern and Western civilizations. They conversed in English, but Feng recorded the content in Chinese and published the dialogue in a journal in China in 1921 (Feng 2001a; referred to hereafter as 'Conversation'). The account is not long, but it touches on many philosophical issues. Here, I will summarize 'Conversation' and leave my analyses to the next section.

To begin with, Feng Youlan explained the motivation for his visit:

Since coming to America, I have been interested in comparing every-thing foreign with what is of China. At first I compared only concrete, individual things, which I then extended to abstract, general things. Finally these comparisons crystallized into an overarching comparison, namely one between Eastern and Western civilizations ... In the *Peking University Daily* I received days ago there was a lecture given by Liang Shuming on *East–West Civilizations and Their Philosophies*. Unfortunately only the introduction was given. To my pleasant surprise, Tagore, who is from India, is now in New York. As he is currently a leading figure in the East, what he has to say about this question can represent what a majority of Easterners think. (Feng 2001a: 3)

The record of their conversation follows, starting with Tagore's expression of his long-standing wish to visit China, and his heartfelt welcome of the young Chinese. After exchanging greetings, Feng Youlan opened their philosophical dialogue with the statement:

Although the civilization of ancient China was brilliant, it is now outmoded. In recent years, we have a new movement for reforming everything old in China—philosophy, literature, art, and all social institutions—to adapt the country to the modern world.... (Feng 2001a: 4)

To this Tagore replied:

Adaptation is urgent indeed ... Western civilization prospers because its force is concentrated ... On the other hand, our Eastern countries are scattered, do not study each other, and do not seek cooperation; therefore, Eastern civilization declines day by day. I am in America this time in order to raise funds for a university that will conduct focused studies on Eastern civilization. What to preserve and what to abolish must be decided by our own judgment and through our own research. We cannot be blindly influenced by Westerners. (Feng 2001a: 4)

Afterwards, Feng delved into a deeper philosophical enquiry stemming from the general discussion on civilization:

Recently a question has been lingering in my mind, that is, whether the difference between Eastern and Western civilizations is a *difference of degree*, or a *difference of kind*?[7] (Feng 2001a: 4)

Tagore's response is as follows:

I can answer this question. It is a difference of kind. The purpose of life in the West is '*activity*', whereas in the East it is '*realization*'. Westerners look to activity and progress without a definite aim ahead, so their activities gradually come to be unbalanced ... According to Eastern philosophy, truth is intrinsic to human beings but is temporarily covered over. Once we remove the cover, truth will come to light. (Feng 2001a: 4)

'The way of learning requires daily accruement; the way of the *Dao* requires daily reduction': Feng immediately cited two lines from *Laozi* (老子) to interpret Tagore's views and then asked, 'Western civilization is "daily accruement", while Eastern civilization is "daily reduction". Is that correct?' (Feng 2001a: 4–5). Tagore agreed with the analogy and elaborated further:

The drawback of Eastern life is that it is too *passive*. Isn't it a disadvantage that comes with 'daily reduction'? Being too *passive* is undeniable, but it is also part of *truth*. Truth consists of both *active* and *passive* sides. For instance, voice is passive and singing is active ... The active changes ceaselessly, but the passive remains constant ... Eastern civilization is like voice and Western civilization is like singing, both of which are indispensable ... Now what the East can contribute to the West is '*wisdom*', while the West can contribute '*activity*' to the East. (Feng 2001a: 5)

Then Feng applied conventional Chinese terms to Tagore's remarks: 'So we can call the passive "*capacity*" and the active "*action*"' (Feng 2001a: 5). Tagore approved of this analogy too. Afterwards, the conversation switched to Buddhism. In evaluating the pros and cons of the real world, Tagore said that, if reality is instrumental to mental creativity, then it is good; it is bad if it obstructs such creativity. But what really matters is how the human mind treats material things, which led Tagore to the conclusion that 'creation is not possible without the help of either mind or matter' (Feng 2001a: 6). When Feng asked for advice for the Chinese people, Tagore replied:

I have only one piece of advice for China: 'Learn science quickly'! What the East lacks and badly needs is science ... China has had many inventors in its civilization; I firmly believe that such a great country can learn science and make contributions to it. (Feng 2001a: 6–7)

Finally, Feng politely enquired how to help the establishment of the university, to which Tagore replied briefly, ending the conversation. However, Feng Youlan added two more paragraphs to the record in the form of his own conclusions and self-reflections:

> What Tagore says seems, at first glance, similar to the old Chinese slogan, 'Chinese learning as capacity; Western learning for action'. But actually they are different ... Tagore's proposition is that there is only one truth that contains two sides, with the East inclined to the passive side and the West inclined to the active side. In other words, Tagore's philosophy is monism, while the old view of China was dualism.
>
> I think that whatever Eastern civilization may come to be, it is worth studying. Why? Because its existence is a fact ... After studying facts, we try to describe them in systematic ways and to devise theories to interpret them. Such descriptions and interpretations constitute science ... The East tends to ignore facts and talks vainly about theories, which is incompatible with the spirit of science. Now China is propagandizing those Western principles of democracy and Bolshevism, but very few people are addressing the problem of how to adapt China to them. Is this any different from our dull imperial examinations? We must study facts and devise theories to regulate them, which embodies exactly the spirit of the modern West! (Feng 2001a: 7–8)

There are two reasons why a faithful presentation of the 1920 conversation between these Indian and Chinese thinkers is important. First, the content is full of philosophical depth. Second, references to this conversation are surprisingly scarce. Even when it is mentioned occasionally in some articles, it serves as background for other arguments rather than being treated as an issue in its own right.[8] For example, in his monograph, Stephen Hay includes a brief analysis of the conversation, but his conclusion is misleading. Hay says that Feng 'left the interview unmoved by Tagore's appeal' (Hay 1970: 236), and then goes on to cite Feng's criticism of the Eastern inclination towards empty words, thereby proving his general observation that 'those [students] specializing in academic philosophy proved as sceptical of [Tagore's] ideas as were their elders in this field' (Hay 1970: 234). Stephen Hay denied that there was any depth to this conversation. Nonetheless, the aforementioned citations indicate that Feng Youlan did not reject Tagore, nor show contempt for him. On the contrary, Feng (2001a:7) considered, 'The right or wrong of Mr Tagore's opinion is another matter. What we should know is that such is the view of Eastern and Western civilizations held by the leading figure of the East.' It can be confirmed that Tagore's notion of civilization, his approval of the analogy between *Laozi* and his own thought, and his monist philosophy had at least stimulated the formulation of Feng's idea.

Stephen Hay's treatment epitomizes well general scholarship on 'Tagore and China': The issue is often approached from the perspective of the controversies that surrounded Tagore in China, little attention being paid to discursive structure and intellectual context.[9] As Tagore and Feng's conversation was conducted at an earlier date, it bore no direct relationship to the 1924 event. Furthermore, the philosophy-oriented content was far from the ideological rivalries that characterized early twentieth-century China. Therefore, 'Conversation' failed to appeal to the Chinese public or to enhance their understanding of Tagore, whose complexity was seriously underestimated.

As mentioned in the beginning of this chapter, Tagore was responsible for the biased image of himself in China as an 'ultra-conservative', understood as someone who adheres to tradition. Nevertheless, while it is true that Tagore's speeches were narrowly focused on so-called Eastern civilization, his Chinese critics also filtered his message and found fault with the traditionalist-sounding parts. In any event, Chinese debates became ideology-ridden. Opposing this, the present chapter proposes a new perspective to explore Tagore's interaction with Chinese intellectuals, starting with his conversation with Feng Youlan. The choice of this starting point is justifiable. The fact that Feng was not an active polemicist in the several rounds of debates over culture in China from the 1910s to the 1930s, and that he is not a usual focus of studies of 'Tagore and China', lend this study somewhat greater objectivity in relation to the cultural ambience of the time of Tagore's visit to China as well as to the mainstream research paradigm that developed thereafter. The space of discourse thus created will be different from the current framework of research in terms of both its historical complexity and intellectual depth.

Network of Thought Derived from the Conversation

There is one point worth mentioning before we delve into the conversation between Tagore and Feng Youlan. The only way for later generations to learn of this intellectual intercourse is through Feng's own record in Chinese. Therefore, it is difficult to determine to what degree the content is shaped by Feng's subjective thinking. Structurally speaking, Feng started the account by describing his own motives and ended it with his own philosophical reflections; throughout the conversation he also tended to interpret Tagore's remarks in traditional Chinese terms. It is precisely because of Feng's involvement of Tagore in the formulation of his philosophical system that 'Conversation' brilliantly sketches an episode in modern Chinese intellectual history, with Tagore and his international activities serving to contextualize this episode within a broader current of thought.

Echoing the beginning of 'Conversation' in his last years in 'Sansongtang zixu' (三松堂自序) ['Autobiography of the Sansong Chamber'; referred to hereafter as 'Autobiography'], Feng recalls that the three years spent at Peking University brought him into the real world of knowledge, which was far beyond the realm of learning required by the imperial examination system:

> There is a contradiction between these two worlds, which derives from the contradiction between two cultures. This contradiction is visible throughout the early modern and modern history of China. Some people at that time did not recognize this contradiction to be between ancient and modern, old and new; instead, they considered it to be a contradiction between East and West, China and foreign countries. Eastern and Western cultures are different because their underlying philosophies are different. (Feng 2001b: 171)

Feng stated that in 1919 he received an official scholarship to study abroad and was planning to enter Columbia University in New York: 'I brought with me this problem—namely the reality of China—to [America]' (Feng 2001b: 172). This autobiographical account is very important. Although Feng was not directly involved in the 'debate on East–West cultures' around the time of the May Fourth Movement in 1919 and did not participate in the 'debate on science vs. philosophy of life' in 1923, the contemporary cultural atmosphere in China had not only stimulated his own thinking but also shaped his later intellectual activities. This is why Feng went to visit Tagore when the latter came to USA in 1920. Furthermore, the distinctions between 'ancient and modern, old and new' and between 'East and West, China and foreign countries' mentioned in Feng (2001b) should correspond, respectively, to the differences of 'degree' and 'kind' that appear in Feng's conversation with Tagore. As for the comment that 'Eastern and Western cultures are different because their underlying philosophies are different', Feng points out that one of the representatives of this view was Liang Shuming (梁漱溟) (1893–1988), the scholar whose lecture captivated him so much that he regretted that the whole text was not available, as described at the beginning of 'Conversation'.

In brief, in his *Dongxi wenhua jiqi zhexue* (東西文化及其哲學) [*East–West Cultures and Their Philosophies*], Liang Shuming specifies three different ways of life: 'First, going forward to fulfil one's needs; secondly, changing, harmonizing, or tempering one's needs; and thirdly, turning back to restrain one's needs' (Liang 2002: 68). In his own view, the civilizations of the West, China, and India embodied these three ways of life respectively, which differ from each other not in quality but in the different priorities they give to each phase of cultural development. If a people is seeking to feed and shelter itself and to overcome nature, it will follow the Western way of life. As this pursuit of satisfaction of personal needs inevitably leads to desire, which makes life painful and overly calculating, the Confucian and, hence, Chinese attitude of adapting even to adverse circumstances becomes necessary in order to foster a well-balanced life temperament. Finally, after both material and emotional needs have been met, there remains the ultimate problem of death and the continuity of life, the Buddhist and, hence, Indian way being that which leads to the realization of the final truth (Liang 2002: 249–52).

Feng Youlan's interest in Liang Shuming was purely philosophical. As he states, 'most of the many comments made at that time were mere demonstrations of the contradiction [between the two civilizations]; there were few extensive interpretations of the contradiction itself' (Feng 2001b: 172). Liang elucidated the spiritual and philosophical foundations of Eastern and Western civilizations, which certainly satisfied Feng Youlan intellectually. Feng paid lifelong homage to Liang. The latter's *East–West Cultures and Their Philosophies* was published in 1921, and Feng wrote to him the next year to discuss it. They did not agree upon every point, but Feng's praise of Liang remained extraordinary: '[Whatever the disagreements between us,] there are very few people except Sir [Liang Shuming] in today's China who have real questions in mind ... and dare to answer those questions themselves. The publication of your book has added lustre to Chinese academia' (Feng 2001c: 591). That same year Feng wrote an English review of Liang's book, which ends with the following commendation: 'Whether Buddhist or Confucian thought are exactly as he interprets, I think there is no one who will not feel moved by his creativity and rigorous argumentation. Mr Liang has real insight, which justifies the existence of such a philosophical work' (Feng 2001d: 57). Even though Feng's philosophical and political stances underwent a sea change after 1949, in his later work, he still judged Liang's ideas in highly positive terms (Feng 2001e: 543–52).

Apparently, for Liang, the difference between Eastern and Western civilizations was one of 'kind' rather than 'degree'. He regarded the three ways he had specified as representing fundamentally different views of life. Feng was also inclined to such an interpretation in the 1920s, as is evidenced by his letter to Liang Shuming and the accounts in his 'Autobiography'. However, the most vivid substantiation of this view can be discerned in his conversation with Tagore. In the beginning, Feng said that traditional Chinese civilization failed to meet modern needs and that in recent years Chinese intellectuals had been trying to reform tradition totally 'to adapt the country to the modern world'. Tagore agreed that 'adaptation' was urgently needed, with the proviso that, when it came to Eastern civilization, 'what to preserve and what to abolish must be decided by our own judgment and through our own research'. This verbal exchange constitutes a momentous event in modern intellectual history: While Feng started the conversation by dichotomizing tradition and modernity as perceived by his fellow Chinese, Tagore soon shifted the focus to East vs. West, going on to emphasize that 'perhaps there is something wrong with our civilization, but how can we know that without serious study?' (Feng 2001a: 4). Feng's reference to *Laozi* also prompted Tagore's comment that truth has its active and passive sides, 'both of which are indispensable'. This analysis makes it clear that both paragraphs containing Feng's own self-reflections at the end of 'Conversation' bear a direct relationship to Tagore's remarks: Feng recognized the difference between the monism Tagore believed in and the old Chinese slogan, 'Chinese learning as capacity; Western learning for action'. Besides, Feng's conclusion that Eastern civilization should be studied echoed Tagore's proposition. In any case, Tagore inspired or at least confirmed Feng's own ideas; between the two men there was a resonance that Stephen Hay failed to perceive.

As time progressed, Feng came to adopt a more abstract view to encompass the antitheses between tradition and modernity, the East and the West:

> In the late 1930s I also discussed similar questions [about Eastern and Western civilizations] ... such discussion concerns a philosophical issue, that is, the relationship between the general and the particular. A certain social type is general, but a country or nation is particular ... It is possible as well as necessary to learn the general. In contrast, to learn [that is, to imitate] the particular is impossible and unnecessary. (Feng 2001e: 582)

Nonetheless, around the time Tagore visited China in 1924, Feng Youlan was still obsessed with the question of whether Eastern and Western civilizations differ in 'degree' or in 'kind'. There is one point worth particular attention here. What Feng compared with Tagore's monism was the old theory of late nineteenth-century China ('Chinese learning as capacity; Western learning for action') rather than the new theories that were formulated around the May Fourth Movement. In the 1910s and 1920s, China experienced a fierce, large-scale debate on the differences between Eastern and Western civilizations. The two main groups—the pro-Western side led by Chen Duxiu (陳獨秀) (1879–1942) and the traditionalist or harmonizer side led by Du Yaquan (杜亞泉) (1873–1933)—criticized and even slandered each other in their respective magazines. However, Feng Youlan completely ignored these disputes in 'Conversation'. One probable explanation is that he believed they were lacking in philosophical depth, just as he stresses in 'Autobiography' that 'most of the many comments made at that time were mere demonstrations of the contradiction'. This accounts for Feng's high regard for Liang Shuming's work, although he also indicated that Liang was often too subjective in drawing his conclusions. Unfortunately, Tagore's visit to China in the form of a cultural event was part of the 'contradiction' that resulted in relevant studies on 'Tagore and China' being restricted to the dispute that arose in 1924. One serious consequence of this is that not much historical complexity or intellectual insight has been attempted in this field of research ever since.

Tagore's advocacy of Eastern spiritual civilization in China contains the following statement:

> This age to which we belong, does it not still represent night in the human world, a world asleep, whilst individual races are shut up within their own limits, calling themselves nations[?] ... This age, that still persists, must be described as the darkest age in human civilization. But I do not despair ... Science also is truth. It has its own place, in the healing of the sick, and in the giving of more food, more leisure for life. But when it helps the strong to crush the weaker ... their own weapons will be turned against them ... Let the morning of this new age dawn in the East, from which the great streams of idealism have sprung in the past, making the fields of life fertile with their influence. (Tagore 1996a: 646–7)

This statement encapsulates many critical points in Tagore's civilizational discourse, including the dichotomies between nationalism and universalism, scientism and idealism, and so forth. Nevertheless, the most thought-provoking aspect of his statement is that it upsets the conventional cognition of tradition and modernity. While Tagore firmly believed in the spiritual glory of the traditional East, he regarded the materialistic attainment of the West as less modern than brutal and dark; he predicted that true modernity would only come with revival of the ideals of the East.[10] On this point, a similarity between Tagore's and Liang Shuming's philosophies is discernible, although their conclusions were quite different. From the previous discussion we know that Liang was by no means a simplistic cultural harmonizer. On the contrary, his theory is closer to cultural evolutionism, with the so-called 'evolution' here a counterargument to the Western paradigm. By regarding the material achievements of the modern West as the first step in satisfying the needs of human life, Liang gave the spiritual superiority to Eastern civilization. To him the problem of China and India was not stagnation but precociousness: both prioritized spiritual pursuit over material desire, thus failing to improve their respective cultures in terms of technological progress (Liang 2002: 287–8). Moreover, Liang mentions Tagore several times in his book. In his view, Tagore's philosophy was different from the otherworldly and often passive thought that characterized Indian tradition, so it was inappropriate to consider him as representative of Indian culture (Liang 2002: 84). As Tagore preached the philosophy of love, which encouraged people to take part in human affairs without selfish calculation, Liang states that 'although there is no seeming relationship between Tagore and Chinese philosophy, I would like to argue that he belongs to China, to the Confucian way of life' (Liang 2002: 234). While we do not have to agree with Liang's argument, his observation is certainly provocative.

Judging from the earlier analyses, when we shift the focus of studies away from Tagore's 1924 visit, a stimulating intellectual world behind the barrage of disputes can be unveiled. In the next section, this network of thought will be expanded to encompass sources that are not exclusively Chinese to explore Tagore's relevance to the intellectual history of the modern world.

A Comparison of Tagore with Chinese and Western Thinkers

Naturally, Liang Shuming's daring classification of world civilizations drew many criticisms. As shown in the previous section, although an admirer of Liang, Feng Youlan did not completely agree with his view. Zhang Dongsun (張東蓀) (1886–1973) also pointed out that 'the so-called *East–West Cultures and Their Philosophies* is merely a "discourse of Eastern and Western cultures from a philosophical viewpoint", which is different from the discourse of ethnic psychology' (Zhang 1989: 503). Zhang differentiated between culture and philosophy: while culture contains everything about the attitudes and modes of living of a people or nation, philosophy is the brainchild of a few thinkers; the two should not be mixed.

Of all the critical responses to Liang's book, Hu Shi's (胡適) (1891–1962) 'Du Liang Shuming xiansheng de *Dongxi wenhua jiqi zhexue*' (讀梁漱溟先生的 東西文化及其哲學) ['Reading *East–West Cultures and Their Philosophies* by Mr. Liang Shuming'] (1998a) is the most influential. Hu's comment is satirical and rebuts Liang's overarching philosophical induction with historical observations (Hu Shi 1998a). There is another well-known essay by Hu Shi (1998b: 3) comparing Eastern and Western civilizations, which starts with the following statement:

The most groundless and vicious fallacy in vogue nowadays is the one that dismisses Western civilization as materialistic, and venerates Eastern civilization as spiritual ... In recent years, the great war that ravaged Europe arouses a sense of disgust at the scientific culture of the modern world; that is why we hear oftentimes the eulogy of Eastern spiritual civilization from Western scholars.

This article was written in 1926, after the publication of Liang's book and Tagore's visit to China. Arguably, the targets of Hu's criticism were those who upheld the superiority of Eastern spirituality, including Liang and Tagore. After contrasting Eastern and Western civilizations point by point, Hu concluded that 'here we find an essential difference between Eastern and Western cultures: the former abandons itself by not thinking; the latter seeks truth persistently' (Hu Shi 1998b: 7). Hu reached his conclusion of an East characterized by inertia versus a West characterized by progress by paralleling historical examples that are deliberately culled. Hu's tone was also critical when he claimed that 'such a civilization [Eastern civilization] that is dominated by material environment and that does not seek to break this environmental bondage is a civilization of the indolent, a civilization that is materialistic in the real sense' (Hu Shi 1998b: 12–13). Of course, Hu aimed his poignant remarks at the problems that were plaguing modern Chinese society and culture. However, his criticism of Liang's cultural philosophy as 'general and imprecise' was also based on personal preferences.

During Tagore's visit to China in 1924, as a committed liberal, Hu Shi defended Tagore from blasphemies that were deemed unsuitable to be directed at a foreign guest. When it came to philosophy, however, Hu showed no sympathy at all with Tagore's thought:

When I listen to Tagore's praise of Eastern spiritual civilization, I always feel ashamed ... What American audiences expect from a lecturer from the East is the kind of information given by Tagore; that is, criticism of the materialistic West and eulogy of the spiritual East ... Indeed, Eastern civilization receives much harsher censure from me than from any Western critics, and my appreciation of modern Western civilization is higher than the self-evaluation of Westerners. (Zhou 1998: 56–7)

Hu Shi sided with 'total Westernization' out of practical considerations:

Those propositions of cultural eclecticism and Sino-centrism are nothing but vain talk. For the moment, we have no alternative but to try hard to totally accept the new civilization of this new world. Once it is totally accepted, the inertia of old culture will naturally make it an eclectic, harmonized new Sino-centric culture. (Feng 2001e: 581)

To this claim, Feng Youlan retorted:

It is not surprising that Hu Shi proposes 'total Westernization'. But according to his words quoted here, the reason for his proposition of 'total Westernization' is rather special. It seems to me that he too considered such a proposition to be a little extreme, but he also thought that only an extreme proposition can bring 'Westernization' into balance. What the balance looks like he didn't explain. (Feng 2001e: 581–2)

It is this lacuna—'he didn't explain'—that confines Hu Shi's comparison of Eastern and Western civilizations to historical critique or ideological debate, without raising itself to the level of a philosophical system.

It might be safe to conclude that cultural debates in China in the 1920s consisted of at least two spaces of discourse. Some probed the 'backwardness' of the East from a historical perspective, like Hu Shi, while others attempted to compare the essence of Eastern and Western civilizations, like Liang Shuming. Li Zehou (李澤厚) describes the two major trends ushered in by the May Fourth Movement as the 'duet of enlightening and saving the country', and he regards Hu Shi as the head of those who sought to enlighten China through educational, cultural and scientific works (Li 2008: 37–8). From the analysis earlier, it is clear that as an antithesis to those who followed the principles of class struggle and the proletarian revolution of Marx-Leninism to save China from ruin, there was more than one suggestion for enlightening the country by means of intellectual endeavours.

Another group to express opinions on these issues during the debate was that of the revivalists of Eastern culture headed by Liang Qichao (梁啟超) (1873–1929). Witnessing the catastrophe brought about by the First World War, and echoing the view held by some Westerners, they believed that Chinese civilization could serve as a remedy for a Western civilization that had become bankrupt. However, this idea was not only dismissed by Hu Shi,[11] it was also criticized by Liang Shuming (Liang 2002: 16). Nonetheless, Liang Qichao's *Ouyou xinyinglu* (歐遊心影錄) [*Record of Reflections during the European Trip*], published originally in 1920, contains some keen observations, such as the following:

> During the past century, the material and spiritual changes of Europe both derived from the principle of the 'development of the individual', which is still being followed on a daily basis. A fundamental difference between such a [modern] civilization and the civilizations of ancient times, of the Middle Ages, and even of the eighteenth century is that the latter were aristocratic and passive, while the former is mass-oriented and self-propelled ... Modern civilization is created by each average person in society through their own will. Therefore, although its 'quality' may not equal past achievements at times, its 'quantity' is much greater and the 'force' much more continuous than before. In a word, everything in modern Europe is mass-oriented. (Liang 1989: 16)

The reason for singling out this comment is that it touches on a critical historical juncture, that is, the change from the 'development of the individual' to the 'mass orientation' of European civilization. This observation contradicts that of Chen Duxiu. In an article published in 1915, Chen points out the differences between Eastern and Western civilizations, stating: 'Western races are individual-based; Eastern races are family-based' (Chen 1993: 166). According to him, it is this emphasis on the individual that has propelled development in many fields: 'ethics, morals, politics, laws—all that is desired by a society and pursued by a country is to protect and support the freedom, rights and happiness of its individuals' (Chen 1993: 166). Here Chen Duxiu does not address the way Western societies concentrated and reinforced their power. On the other hand, although Liang Qichao was sensitive enough to grasp the trend, he gave no clear explanations for the phenomenon in the foregoing citation. This mechanism of concentration, that is, the Western-originated system of the nation-state, is what Tagore criticized throughout his life. Tagore (1996b: 906) once said:

> Western civilization came into being because the power to rule was distributed among a whole people. There was an individual dignity, an

individual consciousness of importance. Dictatorships put an end to such individuality.

Here Tagore was referring to the fascist government of Benito Mussolini (1883–1945), which was trying to suppress personal dignity and consciousness. Although the comment is directed at a somewhat extreme form of governance, criticism of Western-originated nationalism is a recurrent theme in Tagore's lectures and writings. In Tagore's view, the mechanism of the nation-state entails nothing but its own functioning and development: It pays no regard to humanity and its ideals. It is nationalism that linked the egoism of individuals and the collective violence of nations (imperialism is the highest form of its development), characterizing what Tagore termed materialistic Western civilization. In a conversation with the British writer H.G. Wells (1866–1946), Tagore expressed his concern that individual cultures would be effaced or made uniform, while Wells seemed optimistic that world cultures would inevitably converge, implying that heterogeneity obstructs this convergence (Tagore 1996c). Although the conversation is too short for us to make a fair representation of Wells's perspective on world history and civilization, it can be said that what worried Tagore was always the egoism and nationalism—standing at the two ends of the same spectrum—of modern Western civilization, both of which Tagore perceived as lacking in love of and empathy with others.[12]

A few examples have been drawn to show that Tagore was not a blind traditionalist; on the contrary, his criticism of modern Western civilization had chiefly humanistic rather than ideological grounds. Furthermore, Tagore was also rational enough to appreciate the merits of Western culture while censuring the parts that disenchanted him. Moreover, in one of his dialogues with the French novelist Romain Rolland (1866–1944), he even remarked that the gravest problem of Indian religious culture is 'an indiscriminate spirit of toleration that all forms of religious creeds and crudities have run riot in India, making it difficult for us to realize the true foundation of our spiritual faith' (Tagore 1996d: 898). Therefore, Tagore considered a purge was necessary before India could return to its true spiritual heritage. As for the means to reform, Tagore believed that the introduction of scientific rationalism into India could probably be effective. Interestingly,

Tagore held a view similar to that of Hu Shi, thinking that although Indians 'can never believe in mere intellectual determination for any long period of time', a temporary emphasis on science could serve to reverse the swing and lead to its final harmonization (1996d: 899). Though this dialogue contained no specifics, Tagore put these ideas into practice through his long-term educational work. Thus viewed, it is clear that Tagore's thought is broad enough to defy any simplification, which was not only well expressed but also acted out.

Unfortunately, what is also obvious is that the richness of Tagore's thought was largely manifested in the context of his interaction with Western intellectuals. As indicated earlier in the chapter, in China, Tagore overemphasized the notion of the East and focused his speeches too narrowly, which also unwittingly involved him in a cultural debate that had long raged in China. Decades later, when researchers look back to the legacy left by Tagore, they are mainly concerned with his 1924 visit, comparing Tagore's lectures with the views of Chinese polemicists, thus disregarding other peripheral but inspiring texts and failing to take Tagore's interaction with the West into consideration.

Studies of 'Tagore and China' beyond Pan-Asianism

In a 1922 letter from Feng Youlan to Liang Shuming, the former observes that, 'although Tagore's books are loved by general readers, very few references to him can been found in philosophical journals and discussions' (Feng 2001c: 590). Liang Shuming was also perceptive concerning the way Tagore had become popular:

[Tagore's] ability lies in his catering to the modern Western psyche. Westerners are suffering greatly from [too much] rationality, and he is able to save them with intuition ... He is good at expressing intuition through literature without resorting to rational arguments, so he talks nothing about philosophy but merely composes poetry ... In this way, people are moved by him, raising their intuition and suppressing their rationality. Thus people do not bother to criticize the fallacies in his philosophy, but admire the sublimity of his thought. (Liang 2002: 234)[13]

Tagore himself, however, always claimed to be a poet rather than a philosopher, not to mention a prophet. It has been shown that, during the 1920 conversation, Tagore's remarks left an impression on Feng Youlan. However, in Feng's own retrospect of his philosophical development, we can see that he assigned no special role to Tagore and regarded him as a mere representative of those who dichotomized spiritual and materialistic civilizations (Feng 2001b: 173). Feng seems to have forgotten his earlier appreciation for Tagore's monism; a close reading of Tagore's works shows that Feng's later characterization is unfair. Admittedly Tagore's aim was not a delicate system of knowledge, but the integration of the human body, mind, and soul, with harmony between the spirit and the material. Nonetheless, Tagore's conversation with Albert Einstein (1879–1955) confirms the coherence of his humanistic thought, which is no less persuasive than the arguments of the great modern physicist (Tagore 1996e). Therefore, when Hu Shi reduced Tagore's thought to 'criticism of the materialistic West and eulogy of the spiritual East', he was engaging in oversimplification.

Unfortunately, Hu Shi's evaluation of Tagore was shared by the majority of Chinese in the 1920s. Indeed, around the time of Tagore's visit to China, some articles appeared in newspapers and magazines introducing his literary ideas and philosophical thought. However, apart from daily reports on Tagore's itinerary and activities, most of what was written about him consisted of either enthusiastic praise or fierce criticism. It is no exaggeration to say that Tagore became a battlefield in the cultural debate in China that started in the mid-1910s. It was only natural that such a controversial event should attract critical attention, but the outcome was far-reaching and profound: Most studies of Tagore conducted in China since then make little reference to other issues than the debates, which leads to an astonishing overlap in research.

As argued repeatedly in previous sections of this chapter, the mere focus on the cultural debate risks depriving Tagore studies in China of both breadth and depth. The major research method employed therein is to compare Tagore's talks in China with the remarks made for or against him by Chinese thinkers, thus omitting both the temporal and spatial dimensions of Tagore's interaction with intellectuals worldwide. This chapter has examined instead the interconnections between the thought of Tagore, Feng Youlan, Liang Shuming, and other Chinese opinion leaders of the early twentieth century. By contrasting these interconnections with Tagore's interactions with contemporary Western thinkers, it is hoped that a new perspective will emerge to reveal the depth of the intellectual exchanges that took place but that have been obscured by visceral debates. This chapter has also attempted to provide a more vivid image of Tagore than that of a repetitive preacher of Eastern civilization. Of course, it is undeniable that Tagore was responsible for China's negative image of him. His Nobel Prize gave him an easy path with which to communicate his thought to the whole world, but this reputation also moulded him into a 'spokesperson of the East', who was first and foremost expected to provide a spiritual remedy to the Western psyche. It was in this atmosphere that Tagore visited China in 1924. As his discourse was based on India's cultural experiences and was intended for Western audiences, it ultimately simplified the political, social, historical, and cultural complexities of China. As a consequence, it was almost inevitable that Chinese intellectuals should have reduced the richness of Tagore's thought to mere cultural conservatism. After the establishment of the People's Republic of China in 1949, Chinese academia was overwhelmed for a long period with political ideology, which produced confusing results: Some articles whose titles apparently refer to Tagore studies are in reality verbal attacks on ideological enemies. Fortunately, reform and the opening up of China from the 1980s have restored some freedom and autonomy to academic research.

Finally, it is worth mentioning is that although the short-term purpose of Tagore's China trip, namely, to propose 'Asian comradeship', ended in failure, his effort to define and enrich the idea of Eastern civilization a century ago appears as an intellectual feat of the modern world, which is becoming all the more relevant in this age of the 'rise of Asia'. Nevertheless, with Tagore's versatility drawing more and more attention, it is to be hoped that new light can also be shed upon his relationship with China—apart from the still prevalent research topics of either his disagreement with Chinese critics during the trip or sentimental praise for his efforts to rejoin China and India in turbulent modern times—thus eliciting more interesting issues concerning modern Sino-Indian interactions and even world history. This chapter, along with others in this volume dealing with figures such as Xu Dishan, Zhang Taiyan, and Tan Yunshan, to name just a few, represents a step towards this goal of revealing fascinating Sino-Indian connections.

Notes

1. As an ideology, pan-Asianism has defied exact definition, but its emergence in the early twentieth century was basically 'used both to express transnational aspirations to Asian regionalism and integration and to legitimize aggression and empire building' (Saaler and Szpilman 2011: xi). Although Tagore never used this term, he was a pre-eminent proponent of Asian amity and cooperation.

2. A critical issue here is how those Chinese intellectuals who were most welcoming of Tagore created a public image of him to meet their own needs. There are many instances of this. For example, the great leftist writer Lu Xun (魯迅) commented in 1934 that 'had our poets not made [Tagore] a living god, our young people should not have been so distant from him' (Lu 2005: 617).

3. It is noteworthy that Tagore's initial influence on China was felt in the New Literature Movement of the 1910s and 1920s. Indeed, literature was the most palpable connection between the Indian poet and his Chinese admirers, a fact that has never failed to draw critical attention. However, given the intellectual milieu of China from the late twentieth century described earlier, literature seems to be explored less in related studies. For a general discussion of this literary connection, see Zhang (2005). Interestingly, a recent article entitled 'Pan-Asian Poetics: Tagore and the Interpersonal in May Fourth New Poetry' by Gal Gvili (2018), one of the authors of this volume, dexterously addresses the topics of both Sino-Indian interaction and the New Literature Movement in China.

4. The limitations specified by Ai Dan include: (*i*) duplication of research; (*ii*) narrowness of research perspectives; and (*iii*) unvarying research methods. After the publication of the book in 2010, a steady stream of works dealing with 'Tagore and China' are still coming out. However, since few differences can be discerned between them and they have mostly been authored by a rather fixed group of researchers, a thorough review is not necessary in this chapter.

5. This book has a later Chinese counterpart edited by Zhang Minqiu (張敏秋) (2006).

6. These works include a master's thesis by Huang Wei-Lin (黃威霖) (2011).

7. Both italicized terms are as such in the original.

8. An example is an article by Qian Gengsen (錢耕森) (2004), whose title is similar to the current chapter. However, it does not deal with intellectual issues.

9. In 'Tagore and China', an article written for the collection *Tagore and China*, Amartya Sen (2011) also criticizes this conventional approach and calls for discussions of greater sophistication.

10. Tagore made the same points in his speeches in Japan in 1916, which I explore in Lee (2014).

11. Hu Shi once commented that 'such a theory derived from a pathetic mentality, but caters to the megalomania of Eastern nations and fuels the fire of the conservative force of the East' (1998b: 3).

12. Tagore's critiques of nationalism are numerous, but the essays collected in *Nationalism* (1917) are the most famous and systematic. It is well known that Liang Qichao was a strong supporter of nationalism to remedy the lack of unification of the Chinese people. Tagore, on the other hand, stressed the specificity of each race but insisted on his opposition to nationalism, which derived from modern Western history. Obviously, the difference in historical backgrounds between China and India obliged intellectuals in respective countries to adopt different views of nationalism. This issue deserves more discussion.

13. In fact, the West as a whole did not receive Tagore in such a simplistic way as Liang Shuming thought. Tagore's lectures on philosophical and political issues drew rebuttals as well, which I have reviewed in Lee (2013). On the other hand, however, since Tagore's worldwide fame was achieved through his mysticism, Liang's observation was not fundamentally wrong.

References

Ai Dan (艾丹). 2010. *Taigeer yu wusishiqi de shixiangwenhua lunzheng* (泰戈爾與五四時期的思想文化論爭) [*Debating and Discussing: Tagore in China*]. Beijing: Renmin chubanshe.

Chen Duxiu (陳獨秀). 1993. 'Dongxi minzu genben sixiang zhi chayï' (東西民族根本思想之差異) ['Fundamental Differences of Thought between Eastern and Western Nations']. In Ren Jianshu, Zhang Tongmo, and Wu Xinzhong (eds), *Chen Duxiu zhuzuoxuan* (陳獨秀著作選) [*Selected Works of Chen Duxiu*], Volume 1, pp. 165–9. Shanghai: Shanghai renmin chubanshe.

Dutta, Krishna and Andrew Robinson. 2009. *Rabindranath Tagore: The Myriad-Minded Man*. London and New York: Tauris Parke Paperbacks.

Feng Youlan (馮友蘭). 2001a. 'Yu Indu Taiguer tanhua: dongxiwenming zhi bijiaoguan' (與印度泰谷爾談話—東西文明之比較觀) ['Conversation with Tagore from India: A Comparative View of Eastern and Western Civilizations']. In *Sansongtang quanji* (三松堂全集) [*Complete Works of the Sansong Chamber*], Volume 11, pp. 3–9. Zhengzhou: Henan renmin chubanshe.

———. 2001b. 'Sansongtang zixu' (三松堂自序) ['Autobiography of the Sansong Chamber']. In *Sansongtang quanji* (三松堂全集) [*Complete Works of the Sansong Chamber*], Volume 1, pp. 3–314. Zhengzhou: Henan renmin chubanshe.

———. 2001c. 'Zhi Liang Shuming' (致梁漱溟) ['To Liang Shuming']. In *Sansongtang quanji* (三松堂全集) [*Complete Works of the Sansong Chamber*], Volume 14, pp. 588–92. Zhengzhou: Henan renmin chubanshe.

———. 2001d. 'Ping Liang Shuming zhu *Dongxi wenhua jiqi zhexue*' (評梁漱溟著東西文化及其哲學) ['Comment on Liang Shuming's *East–West Cultures and Their Philosophies*']. In *Sansongtang quanji* (三松堂全集) [*Complete Works of the Sansong Chamber*], Volume 11, pp. 54–7. Zhengzhou: Henan renmin chubanshe.

———. 2001e. 'Zhongguo zhexueshi xinbian (di qi ce)' (中國哲學史新編（第七冊）) ['A New History of Chinese Philosophy, Vol. VII']. In *Sansongtang quanji* (三松堂全集) [*Complete Works of the Sansong Chamber*], Volume 10, pp. 485–658. Zhengzhou: Henan renmin chubanshe.

Gvili, Gal. 2018. 'Pan-Asian Poetics: Tagore and the Interpersonal in May Fourth New Poetry'. *Journal of Asian Studies* 77 (1): 181–203.

Hay, Stephen. 1970. *Asian Ideas of East and West: Tagore and His Critics in Japan, China, and India*. Cambridge, Mass.: Harvard University Press.

Hu Shi (胡適). 1998a. 'Du Liang Shuming xiansheng de *Dongxi wenhua jiqi zhexue*' (讀梁漱溟先生的東西文化及其哲學) ['Reading *East–West Cultures and Their Philosophies* by Mr. Liang Shuming']. In Ouyang Zhesheng (ed.), *Hu Shi wenji* (胡適文集) [*Complete Works of Hu Shi*], Volume 3, pp. 182–97. Beijing: Beijing daxue chubanshe.

———. 1998b. 'Women duiyu jindai xiyangwenming de taidu' (我們對於近代西洋文明的態度) ['Our Attitude towards Modern Western Civilization']. In Ouyang Zhesheng (ed.), *Hu Shi wenji* (胡適文集) [*Complete Works of Hu Shi*], Volume 4, pp. 3–22. Beijing: Beijing daxue chubanshe.

Huang Wei-Lin (黃威霖). 2011. *Wenmingchayi yu xiandaixing: Taigeer de zhengzhilixiang jiqi dui Zhongguowenming de qipan* (文明差異與現代性—泰戈爾的政治理想及其對中國文明的期盼) [*Civilizational Differences and Modernity: Rabindranath Tagore's Political Ideals and His Perspective on Chinese Civilization*]. Taipei: Taiwan guoli daxue zhengzhi kexue bu.

Ji Xianlin (季羨林). 1996. 'Taigeer yu Zhongguo: jinian Taigeer dansheng yibai zhounian' (泰戈爾與中國—紀念泰戈爾誕生一百週年) ['Tagore and China: In Memory of the Centenary of Tagore']. In *Ji Xianlin wenji* (季羨林文集) [*Complete Works of Ji Xianlin*], Volume 5, pp. 180–213. Nanchang: Jiangxi jiaoyu chubanshe.

Lee, Yu-Ting. 2013. 'Tagore and Orientalism: Tagore Studies as a Focus for East–West Debate'. *Taiwan Journal of East Asian Studies* 10 (1): 219–59.

———. 2014. 'Tagore's *Nihonjinron* in International Opinion on Asia during the Inter-War Period'. *Asian Cultural Studies* (40): 31–44.

Li Zehou (李澤厚). 2008. 'Qimeng yu jiuwang de shuangchong bianzou' (啓蒙和救亡的雙重變奏) ['Duet of Enlightening or Saving the Country']. In *Xiandai Zhongguo sixiang shilun* (現代中國思想史論) [*On the Intellectual History of Modern China*], pp. 1–46. Beijing: Sanlian shudian.

Liang Qichao (梁啟超). 1989. *Ouyou xinyinglu* (歐遊心影錄) [*Record of Reflections during the European Trip*]. In *Yinbingshi heji* (飲冰室合集) [*Collected Works of the Yinbing Chamber*], *Zhuanji* (專集) [*Monograph*] No. 23. Beijing: Zhonghua shudian.

Liang Shuming (梁漱溟). 2002. *Dongxi wenhua jiqi zhexue* (東西文化及其哲學) [*East–West Cultures and Their Philosophies*]. Taipei: Taiwan shangwu chubanshe.

Lu Xun (魯迅). 2005. 'Masha yu pengsha' (罵殺與捧殺) ['Blame to Death and Praise to Death']. In *Lu Xun quanji* (魯迅全集) [*Complete Works of Lu Xun*], Volume 5, pp. 615–17. Beijing: Renmin wenxue chubanshe.

Qian Gengsen (錢耕森). 2004. 'Taigeer de Zhongguo qingjie: cong Feng Youlan yu Taigeer de tanhua shuoqi' (泰戈爾的中國情結—從馮友蘭與泰戈爾的談話說起) ['Tagore's "China Affection": Starting from the Conversation between Feng Youlan and Tagore']. *Study of Sino–Western Culture* 5 (40): 112–19.

Saaler, Sven and Christopher W.A. Szpilman. 2011. 'Preface and Acknowledgments'. In Sven Saaler and Christopher W.A. Szpilman (eds), *Pan-Asianism: A Documentary History, Volume 1: 1850–1920*, pp. xi–xii. Lanham: Rowan & Littlefield Publishers, Inc.

Sen, Amartya. 2011. 'Tagore and China'. In Tan Chung, Amiya Dev, Wang Bangwei, and Wei Liming (eds), *Tagore and China*, pp. 3–10. New Delhi: SAGE.

Tagore, Rabindranath. 1917. *Nationalism*. San Francesco: The Book Club of California.

———. 1996a. 'Talks in China'. In Sisir Kumar Das (ed.), *The English Writings of Rabindranath Tagore, Volume Two: Plays, Stories, Essays*, pp. 641–86. New Delhi: Sahitya Akademi.

———. 1996b. 'Interview with F.L. Minigerode'. In Sisir Kumar Das (ed.), *The English Writings of Rabindranath Tagore, Volume Three: A Miscellany*, pp. 904–7. New Delhi: Sahitya Akademi.

———. 1996c. 'H.G. Wells and Tagore'. In Sisir Kumar Das (ed.), *The English Writings of Rabindranath Tagore, Volume Three: A Miscellany*, pp. 908–11. New Delhi: Sahitya Akademi.

———. 1996d. 'Romain Rolland and Tagore'. In Sisir Kumar Das (ed.), *The English Writings of Rabindranath Tagore, Volume Three: A Miscellany*, pp. 890–9. New Delhi: Sahitya Akademi.

———. 1996e. 'Einstein and Tagore'. In Sisir Kumar Das (ed.), *The English Writings of Rabindranath Tagore, Volume Three: A Miscellany*, pp. 911–16. New Delhi: Sahitya Akademi.

Tan Chung (譚中) (ed.). [1998] 2006. *Across the Himalayan Gap: An Indian Quest for Understanding China*. New Delhi: Gyan Publishing House.

———. 2007. *Zhong-In datong: lixiang yu shixian* (中印大同—理想與實現) [*CHINDIA: Idealism and Realization*]. Yinchuan: Ningxia renmin chubanshe.

Tan Chung, Amiya Dev, Wang Bangwei, and Wei Liming (eds). 2011. *Tagore and China*. New Delhi: SAGE.

Zhang Dongsun (張東蓀). 1989. 'Du *Dongxi wenhua jiqi zhexue*' (讀東西文化及其哲學) ['Reading *East–West Cultures and Their Philosophies*']. In Chen Song (ed.), *Wusiqianhou dongxiwenhuawenti lunzhanwenxuan* (五四前後東西文化問題論戰文選) [*Selected Articles on the Debate of East–West Cultures during the May Fourth Era*], pp. 501–14. Beijing: Zhongguo shehui kexue chubanshe.

Zhang Minqiu (張敏秋) (ed.). 2006. *Kuayue Ximalaya zhangai: Zhongguo xunqiu liaojie Indu* (跨越喜馬拉雅障礙—中國尋求瞭解印度) [*Across the Himalayan Gap: A Chinese Quest for Understanding India*]. Chongqing: Chongqing chubanshe.

Zhang Yu (張羽). 2005. *Taigeer yu Zhongguo xiandaiwenxue* (泰戈爾與中國現代文學) [*Tagore and Modern Chinese Literature*]. Kunming: Yunnan renmin chubansen.

Zhou Zhiping (周質平). 1998. *Hu Shi yu Weiliansi* (胡適與韋蓮司) [*Hu Shi and Edith Clifford Williams*]. Beijing: Beijing daxue chubanshe.

8

When Culture Meets State Diplomacy

The Case of Cheena Bhavana

BRIAN TSUI

I n the sleepy town of Santiniketan, West Bengal, India, lies a two-storey building with a plaque in Chinese. From right to left the four characters read *Zhongguo xueyuan* (中國學院) or, in English, the 'China Academy' (or 'Chinese Hall'). Attributed to the chairman of the Nationalist (Kuomintang [KMT]) government, Lin Sen (林森) (1868–1943), the plaque marks the building's construction, dated the twentieth-sixth year of the Chinese republic (1937). Since its inauguration, the building has hosted Cheena Bhavana, currently the Chinese Studies Department of Visva-Bharati University. The Chinese leader's gesture echoed Mohandas K. Gandhi's (1869–1948) poetic evocation, in a 1937 letter addressed to Rabindranath Tagore, of the then-newly inaugurated building as 'a symbol of living contact between China and India', two traditionally dominant cultures in Asia from which Buddhism and Confucianism originated. 'Yes', the Mahatma wrote in another letter to Cheena Bhavana's founder,

Tan Yunshan (譚雲山) (1898–1983), 'indeed, we want cultural contact between the two nations' (Tan 1957: 16).

However, in the years that followed its foundation, Cheena Bhavana became caught up in the complicated and politically delicate interactions between China, the Indian Independence movement, and the British Raj. Its long-term director, Tan, a peripatetic Buddhist who spent most of his adult life in British colonies and independent India, was a shrewd operator who walked the tightrope between academic pursuits and ideological alignments. At Visva-Bharati, as V.G. Nair (1958: viii) noted, Tan counted among his colleagues the British Anglian priest Charles Freer Andrews (1871–1940) and the Italian Tibetologist Giuseppe Tucci (1894–1984). Like these two other foreigners, Tan had much admiration for Gandhi and his brand of spirituality. Unlike Andrews, but not unlike the fascist-leaning Tucci, Tan established close rapport with the government that ran his own country, which supported his cultural-spiritual pursuits abroad.[1]

However, if there was one theme that was a constant in Tan's career, at least as it was presented to the public, it was his aloofness from politics. The Sino-Indian Cultural Society, which funded Cheena Bhavana until 1949, vowed, as its general constitution (1943) put it, to 'strictly keep away from any political movement' (Tan 1944: 24). '[T]he life of a political movement', Tan (1944: 24) stressed with rhetorical flourish, in a speech marking the inauguration of the Jaipur branch of the Sino-Indian Cultural Society, 'is always short and it changes like a chameleon … [T]he life of our Society and the relationship between our two great countries must be long and permanent.' The society's strategy, which was no doubt also Tan's except where wartime Japan was concerned, was to 'never participate in any work against any State or Race or Government' (Tan 1944: 24). This persistence in staying above the political fray paid off. In 1950, as questions hung over the future of an enterprise that was so financially dependent on the recently deposed Nationalist state, Tan ([1950] 1958: 75) assured his detractors that he was not a politician and that the Sino-Indian Cultural Society was 'entirely a cultural and non-political organisation'. Cheena Bhavana, 'not a Government concern', received the Communist premier Zhou Enlai (1898–1976) during his 1955 visit to India.

The stark dichotomy between culture and politics that Tan held dear does not do justice to the complexities and nuances that characterized the relationship between Cheena Bhavana and the various states and political forces at work across Asia. The Pacific War put Cheena Bhavana in the vortex of great power diplomacy. The open allegiances, simmering tensions, and publicized statements of sympathy traded between Chinese leaders, British-Indian officials, and Indian nationalists could not but affect Cheena Bhavana, an organization that regularly received compliments from the likes of Nationalist elders and senior Indian National Congress members. More pertinently for this chapter, the intrigues that surrounded state leaders, officials, and civil-society activists highlight the convergences and clashes between 'culture' and 'politics', anti-imperialism and an emerging world order, and various nationalisms in a larger regional context. The fact that Cheena Bhavana played unmistakably political functions in Sino-Indian diplomacy was due not primarily to the support it received from senior members of the Chinese state and Indian nationalists, but to the permeability between culture, politics, and diplomacy that was immanent in a conjuncture when the reigning international order—the nation-state, capitalism, Euro-American hegemony—was in disarray.

This chapter echoes many of the themes that underscore this volume. It reflects on the promise, as well as the pitfalls, of China–India interactions at a time before nation-state diplomacy became totally dominant. Tan Yunshan, Cheena Bhavana, and the KMT regime displayed myriad qualities that make it difficult for them to be contained within single categories. Tan was steeped in romantic idealism and his institutional enterprise embodied a radical critique of capitalist modernity, yet the man himself showed hard-nosed pragmatism in securing financial support from the KMT state and accommodated himself to its political agenda. The KMT, while leading an embattled nation-state that was increasingly being drawn into an international system dominated by Britain and USA, also styled itself as a revolutionary movement standing in solidarity with anti-colonial activists in India. The Janus-faced character of the protagonists in this chapter rendered the critical potential of Chinese epistemological engagements with India in respect of colonialism much more ambiguous than the cases examined in Section I of this volume.

The Politics of Culture

In China and beyond, elevating culture and treating it as a lofty pursuit, kept strictly apart from political realities, was a hallmark of modern conservative self-identity. In her pioneering article on modern Chinese conservatism, Charlotte Furth (1976: 30) observed that all Republican Chinese intellectuals were modernizers in one way or another. What distinguished the conservatives among them was their insistence that cultural and moral issues be kept apart from politics and the forces that controlled the power of the state. In other words, conservatives did not resist reforms but saw culture as an autonomous and stable human endeavour insulated from the vagaries and chaos that afflicted early twentieth-century China. More recently, however, Edmund Fung has argued (2010: 96–127) that by working to mobilize cultural heritage in order to buttress national identity and drive social and moral transformation, conservative intellectuals also effected the convergence between cultural and political agendas. 'Politicocultural nationalism', as Fung (2010: 96–127) called this strain of thought, was not partisan but tended to be 'reformist, pro-state, proauthority' and make 'loyal critics' well-disposed to a government that was capable of maintaining social order and introducing reforms. It also enabled morally charged critiques of government systems such as Western liberal democracy. This identification of culture as an 'ethical pedagogy' (Eagleton 2000: 7), healing political differences and producing a common humanity, was not specific to China. Chinese cultural conservatism, particularly its aversion to political struggle, would not be out of place among Europeans such as Matthew Arnold and Friedrich Schiller.

What was, however, peculiar to early twentieth-century China was that culture became the arena from which old politics was discarded and a new one created. The 1910s saw what intellectual historian Wang Hui (2016: 44–5, 59–60) aptly called a 'cultural turn' in Chinese intellectual thought. Radicals and conservatives alike saw cultural transformation as the key to transcending European modernity, whose bourgeois nation-state system and freely competitive capitalist economy were in deep crisis. The Great War, commonly known then as the 'European War' (Ouzhan [歐戰]), along with China's aborted early experiments with parliamentary and party politics, shredded the prestige that Western political, economic, and military systems had heretofore enjoyed in the East. The fairy tale of industrial progress lost its spell for the intelligentsia across Asia in favour of alternative world views arising out of Eastern spirituality and socialisms. While celebrating traditions, figures such as Rabindranath Tagore (1861–1941), Liang Qichao (梁啟超) (1873–1929), and Liang Shuming (梁漱溟) (1893–1988) shared with May Fourth iconoclasts an aversion to liberal capitalism. Appeals to 'culture', 'civilization', and 'thought' were seen as ways of constructing new political subjects to replace discredited ones. By leveraging national cultures into solutions to how the global human community should be organized in the future, Chinese and Asian thinkers and activists worked to reinvent politics and ground it in new ethical commitments.

In many ways, Cheena Bhavana emerged at the tail end of a historical moment that began in the 1910s when numerous publishers, study societies, and editorial boards mushroomed in China. First broached by Tagore with Liang Qichao, the institute was conceived in the midst of many cultural experimentations in both China and India. Its establishment, which almost coincided with the beginning of full-scale hostilities between China and Japan in 1937, was an important addition to Tagore's project to craft an alternative to Western modernity. Founded in 1921 with proceeds from the Bengali savant's Nobel Prize money, Visva-Bharati represented a rebuttal to the bureaucratized, elitist institutions run by colonial educators from modern Indian cities such as Delhi and Calcutta (now Kolkata). Writing in *Dongfang zazhi* (東方雜誌) [*Eastern Miscellany*], an influential Shanghai-based magazine, Tan (1929: 21–30) hailed Visva-Bharati, to which he gave the cosmopolitan moniker 'Indian International University' ('Yindu guoji daxue' [印度國際大學]), as a bastion of egalitarianism and progressive values. On its rural and austere campus, men and women, professors and workers, and people from different countries studied, played, and lived together as one wholesome community. Instead of being trapped in concrete-and-steel buildings and dictated by the ticking of mechanical clocks, 'Eastern education' (*dongfang jiaoyu* [東方教育]) offered students the freedom to engage in deep conversations with their teachers beyond the strictures of the classroom and the urban colonial institutional machine they embodied. Likewise, in the proposal he made to Lin Sen, Tagore (1934: 2) submitted that

Visva-Bharati was conceived 'to promote the spirit of Eastern Culture, of which the Indian and Chinese Cultures are the main pillars'. Culture and spirit, counted upon to bring unity between India, China, and their Asian neighbours, were the antithesis of the myopic materialism and muscular nationalism that energized European countries' conquests of Asia and of one another. Tagore and his associate Tan Yunshan crafted an intellectual response to the crisis of a violent and unjust modernity, with Visva-Bharati and Cheena Bhavana as its institutional embodiments. Paradoxically, the desire to transcend the corrupt and unsustainable global nation-state system attracted the earnest attention of one nation-state, one colonial state, and a nationalist movement working to inject India into the very order about which Tagore and Tan were, to say the least, highly ambivalent.

Tagore and Tan's strategy for engagement with the Nationalist regime, whose financial backing was critical to Cheena Bhavana's establishment, was to treat it not as a formidable state apparatus committed to industrial and military modernization but as a facilitator of civilizational renaissance. In the letter that accompanied Tagore's request for funding for his project, the Nobel laureate recounted learning from 'Prof. Tan Yun-shan of your heroic struggles for the resuscitation and revival of your most ancient and superb nation with its historic and magnificent culture'.[2] The Nationalist state was the custodian of a once glorious culture waiting to be awakened from its long stupor, as if China's resurgence under the Nationalist state was but poetic justice in a world dominated by Euro-America. Likewise, Tan's only extended exposé of contemporary China, published as a series of lectures in 1938, treated the government led by Chiang Kai-shek (蔣介石) (1887–1975) as part of a larger process whereby Chinese civilization recalibrated its once 'stable foundation' against the West. Since the Opium War, Tan (1938b: 67–8) told his audience at Andhra University, China had felt that it had to imitate the expansionist but advanced Western civilization. Initially drawn only to Western technology, China become increasingly beholden to foreign political and moral values. While there was the occasional Cai Yuanpei (蔡元培) (1868–1940) who worked to reconcile the East and the West, the bulk of the New Culture Movement 'proved very destructive of Chinese Culture'. Fortunately, 'the Chinese culture movement ha[d] entered into a new phase' on the Nationalists' watch

(Tan 1938b: 67–8). Chiang's New Life Movement, launched in 1934, redressed the nihilist tendencies of the New Culture Movement by carrying on Cai's project. The state-sponsored initiative aimed 'to take Chinese philosophy and ethics as the foundation of Chinese culture and then to assimilate the Western scientific spirit' (Tan 1938b: 67–8). That the 'culture movement' followed on the heels of a bloody campaign against the Chinese Communists and was thus deeply implicated in an extended political feud between two militarized parties did not warrant even a single mention.

To be sure, Tan's identification with the New Life Movement and the Nationalist state as cultural projects was not without historical basis. The KMT was keen on promoting its movement as an expression of Chinese spiritual and ethical values, which, along with Eastern cultural practices such as Buddhism and Confucianism, were set to liberate humankind from the West's materialism and moral nihilism. For Nationalist China, as for Japan, celebration of Eastern civilizational superiority was tied to nation-state building with imperialist hues. For many members of civil society, the East's spiritual wisdom transcended national boundaries (Duara 2003: 99–103). Tan mostly belonged to the latter group, although his pan-Asianism was by no means anathema to the Nationalist party-state. Likewise, senior Nationalists were adept in navigating the ambiguity of Tagore and Tan's ideological commitments, freely exploiting pan-Asianist, anti-colonial, and internationalist discourses in their diplomatic manoeuvres. These shifts illuminate the convergence and tensions between, on the one hand, the KMT's anti-imperialist and even prophetic identity vis-à-vis a rapacious Western-dominated global order, and, on the other hand, its increasingly embedded role in the geopolitical power play that was the modus operandi of the nation-state system.

Uneasy Convergence of Nationalisms

The years leading up to Cheena Bhavana's establishment until the beginning of the Second World War saw the coming together of Chinese nationalism and Indian anti-colonialism. For different reasons and with varying degrees of enthusiasm, the KMT and the Indian National Congress were both open to collaboration with movements in other countries that challenged the dominance of European powers in Asia. In its diplomacy and management of centrifugal frontier regions inherited from the Qing Empire, Nationalist China partook in an Asianist discourse to affirm China's own civilizational superiority, seek allies among other Asian societies, and appeal to non-Han populations. Tan, a lay Buddhist, offered to be a link between the KMT's stronghold in southeastern China, Tibet, and India. As a pan-Asian religion, Buddhism was a promising platform enabling China's search for regional allies in its affirmation of the East's moral import. It was no coincidence, then, that the main theoretician of Asianism in the Nationalist government, Examination Yuan President Dai Jitao (戴季陶) (1891–1949), was a devout Buddhist adept in blending his faith with state and military agendas (Xue 2005: 110–14).

Tan's religiosity easily played into the nationalist politics of India and China, while his career also bridged the two societies in a practical sense. A native of Hunan province, Tan spent most of his life outside China. During his four-year stay in British Malaya, Tan established himself as an educator and editor in the Southeast Asian Chinese community, from which he initially hoped to draw funds for Cheena Bhavana. In 1928, at Tagore's invitation, he joined the faculty of Visva-Bharati to teach Chinese. Soon enough, Tan became a keen observer of the Congress movement. In December the same year, he travelled to Calcutta to attend the Indian National Congress session, at which a resolution was passed demanding that Britain grant India dominion status. Tan portrayed his involvement in this highly political event as a religious pilgrimage, a chance to meet Gandhi. In the end, he only secured what he recalled in 1948 as a 'distant darshan' (Tan 1948b: 26). His choice of the Indic word for sight of a deity to describe his encounters with Gandhi—the two men finally met in April 1931 at Sabramati Ashram, where they discussed the Congress's strategy for dealing with the British and Sino-Indian collaboration—resonated with the premium that Tan's Chinese-language publications put on the Mahatma's sagely or saintly (*sheng* [聖]) qualities. Analogously, his visit to the Dalai Lama, who governed Tibet as a de facto independent state, as part of a Chinese government mission was described as a disciple seeking an audience with the 'Living Buddha'.

The fact that Tan's religious pursuits were so regularly translated into engagement with political figures and organizations worked to his advantage and that of the two leading nationalist movements in

China and India. Shortly after his putative darshan of Gandhi, Tan travelled to Nanjing and Shanghai to relaunch Tagore's Cheena Bhavana project, which was first mooted in 1924.[3] He was warmly received by prominent Buddhists such as the reformist monk Taixu (太虛) and philosopher Ouyang Jingwu (歐陽竟無) (1871–1943). More significantly, Tan secured the blessing of powerful Nationalists such as Dai Jitao and, according to British intelligence reports, Chen Lifu (陳立夫) (1900–2001).[4] The latter headed a major clique within the party and commanded a sophisticated network of spies, party and government officials, publishers, and journalists. In 1933, the Sino-Indian Cultural Society was founded in the Chinese capital. Despite his access to the corridors of power, Tan consistently wrote of organic, bottom-up support. 'The Chinese people', he recalled ([1950] 1958: 73), 'generally regard[ed] Gurudeva Tagore and Mahatma Gandhi as modern Buddhas or Bodhisattvas in India'. Popular enthusiasm, along with the historical connections between the two countries, led naturally to Tan's good fortune. Tan's wish was for a new stream of pilgrims traversing the Himalayas that would transcend state politics. This was intended, as he explained in a magazine run by the secretive Blue Shirts, to fashion the 'future of world culture' (*shijie weilai wenhua* [世界未來文化]) and to overcome global crises brought about by Western culture. Tan's description of culture, it bears stressing, subsumed political and economic issues and referred to to Sun Yat-sen's maxim that China should ally itself with weak nations in the East (Tan 1935: 1–3). Twentieth-century Sino-Indian enmity enlisted the help of politicians even as it drew on Liang and Tagore's critique of the modern socio-political order. Tan's appeal to culture was put to good use by Chinese Nationalists when they asserted their own self-identity as anti-colonialists coming to the rescue of fellow Asians.

If the 'cultural turn' in 1910s China cast a shadow of intellectual doubt over the nation-state system and gave rise to new political movements, the synergies between intellectual and political experimentation against the reigning world order began to unravel in the 1930s. The First World War, significant as an intellectual event, was a conflict in which the Chinese state participated on the margins. What eventually became the Second World War, however, engaged the Nationalist political machinery fully as not only a defender against encroaching enemies but also a power broker in the beleaguered capitalist nation-state system. This system, dominated by Britain and USA, was precisely the status quo against which friendship between China and India was projected. As Tagore hoped, Cheena Bhavana was built with funding injected by none other than Chiang Kai-shek himself through the Sino-Indian Cultural Society, an India chapter of which was founded in 1934. At its inauguration in April 1937, the poet spoke of 'old friends' coming together again after centuries of isolation. However, Sino-Indian amity was not just about the two nations but about 'defend[ing] our humanity against the insolence of the strong' and refusing to remain 'hypnotised and dragged by the prosperous West behind its chariot' (Tan 1957: 43–4). Simply put, Cheena Bhavana was the harbinger of a moral, reciprocal human commons freed from the barricades that divided nation-states. Congress President Jawaharlal Nehru (1889–1964), represented by his daughter Indira (1917–84), saw the comradeship between China and India as embodying the indomitable 'spirit of man' resisting fascism and imperialism (Tan 1957: 16). From Nanjing, Dai Jitao's congratulatory telegram (*Xin xinyuebao* (新新月報) [*New New Monthly*] 1937)—hoping that the school would contribute to human well-being and world unity (*datong* [大同])—echoed the generous spirit expressed by Indian leaders. On the eve of the Marco Polo Bridge Incident, Nanjing and Santiniketan recalled post–Great War interrogations of Euro-American civilization, a position Tagore had presented to a suspicious audience on his visit to China thirteen years earlier.

Yet, by 1937, any appeal to culture as a realm untainted by political strife had become compromised, as organized nationalism in both China and India turned both countries into sophisticated geopolitical players. Nationalist China's credentials as the custodian of an alternative global order to the rapacious one dominated by Western civilization was, to say the least, long in doubt. The Indian National Congress itself noted that the KMT regime under Chiang Kai-shek had relied on 'the support of feudal and bourgeois interests and understanding with foreign imperialisms' (Lohia 1938: 39–40). It was only after the 1936 Xi'an Incident that China, with a more inclusive political climate, returned to 'the front-line of world anti-imperialism', and it was on account of this new development that the Indian nationalists threw their support behind Chiang's government (Lohia 1938: 39–40). Nanjing's interest in the Indian nationalist movement ran deep; it hosted the eccentric

Raja Mahendra Pratap (1886–1979) and funded Ghadar activists.[5] Its engagement with the Congress since the late 1930s was marked by a mix of anti-colonial idealism, Asianist sentiments, and cool-headed geopolitical calculation. While the Congress was assembling a medical mission at Communist general Zhu De's (朱德) (1886–1976) request, Tan met Nationalist top brass, including Chiang Kai-shek in Wuhan, to discuss Sino-Indian cooperation. In August 1939, Nehru flew into the Nationalist wartime capital Chongqing to pledge solidarity with China in its fight against Japanese imperialism. Emerging from the visit was a tacit agreement that the two nationalist parties would work together by synchronizing their propaganda and avoiding any possible rapprochement between Britain and Japan. The KMT and Congress would 'liaise with one another discreetly' (anzhong miqie lianxi [暗中密切聯繫]) in the form of cultural cooperation, making use of existing cultural, educational, and religious organizations. The Sino-Indian Cultural Society was named specifically as a body capable of presenting an uncontroversial guise to collaboration between China's ruling party and a movement opposed to the British colonial government.[6] Much as Tan claimed that his role as a bridge between Indian freedom fighters and Chinese leaders transcended politics, both sides were deeply cognizant of the political sensitivities involved the convergence of two Asian nationalist parties. British India's scrutiny of Tan's activities, as I show later, proved them right.

Putting Culture to Work

The fact that culture segued naturally into realpolitik and vice versa is well illustrated by the 'Outline of Sino-Indian Cultural Collaboration', a statement of intent tasking the Sino-Indian Cultural Society, led by Chen Lifu's ally Zhu Jiahua (朱家驊) (1893–1963), to coordinate 'cultural cooperation enterprises' (wenhua hezuo shiye [文化合作事業]) between the two countries. 'Cultural cooperation' in the document was broadly defined; it included, unsurprisingly, exchanges between religious figures (primarily Buddhists but also Muslims) and academics, translations of major published works into Chinese and Indian languages, and the gifting of books. The Education Ministry, the Chinese Buddhist Association, and Dai Jitao's New Asia Society were to plan study tours and goodwill missions along with China's major universities and research institutes. Yet, cultural exchange also encompassed industry and agriculture. Industrial development was a major concern for Nehru (1942: 6–9), who showed great interest in the cooperative movement sponsored by left-leaning foreigners in China to spur production in the largely agrarian hinterland. In addition, under the umbrella of culture, China was to receive intelligence (*qingbao* [情報]) from the Congress through the state-run Central News Agency's new bureaus in Calcutta and Bombay (now Mumbai). Even more revealingly, the KMT was also to send observers, under other guises, to the next session of the Indian National Congress. All these connections were to be managed by the Sino-Indian Cultural Society.[7]

As it transpired, Sino-Indian or, more precisely, KMT–Congress engagement departed slightly from the original plan. In February 1942, during his visit to India, Chiang Kai-shek enquired about implementation of the outline with Zhu Jiahua, who reported that the Sino-Indian Cultural Society had yet to be reorganized on a scale that allowed it to steer the wheel of diplomacy between the two countries. Various ministries and the KMT's propaganda department, Zhu added, were supposed to follow up on the outline, but progress was slow. The Central News Agency bureaus were still on the drawing board. Planning for exchanges between academics, students, and industrialists had likewise stalled because, among other reasons, Congress leaders such as Nehru were in prison. He urged Chiang to put pressure on relevant ministries to expedite implementation of the 1939 outline, taking advantage of renewed interest in improving Sino-Indian relations stimulated by Chiang's visit. The Sino-Indian Cultural Society, Zhu assured Chiang, would be reinforced with Dai Jitao's contributions.[8] The society, and particularly its India chapter, was finally reorganized in 1943; Nehru and Gandhi became honorary presidents along with Chiang, his wife, and Dai. It is not clear, however, if the organization's capacity received a real boost. The revamped society, British India's China Relations Officer Humphrey Prideaux-Brune (1886–1979) observed, was 'doubtless little more than the usual paper scheme—"name without substance"'. Apparently, Tan had nominated the career diplomat to the Society's Central Committee without the latter's knowledge.[9]

The 'cultural' exchanges the KMT did put together were significant and had Tan's fingerprints all over them. In 1939, leading Buddhist monk Taixu visited India on a trip organized by the KMT's propaganda department (*xuanchuan bu* [宣傳部]) to garner support for the anti-Japanese war. In appearance, however, the tour was a Chinese Buddhist Association initiative. 'It is likely', according to historian Tansen Sen (2016: 308), 'that Taixu's itinerary in India and his meetings with Indian political leaders, visits to Buddhist sites and lectures may have all been arranged by Tan, who had recently returned from China where he was involved in organizing anti-Japanese propaganda activities. It is also possible that Tan was the one who instigated the Goodwill Mission in the first place.' What is clear is that Tan accompanied Taixu, of whom the lay Buddhist was a discipline, throughout the trip and hosted him at Cheena Bhavana. Choosing Buddhism to channel communications between the Chinese elite and Indian anti-colonialists was provided with a convenient guise, as anticipated during Nehru's Chongqing trip. The Sino-Indian Cultural Society, after all, was supposed to 'strictly keep away from any political movement' (Santiniketan Press 1943: 5). Buddhism, in addition, was one of the society's core concerns and led to conduits of funding for Cheena Bhavana (Sen 2017: 309). While its teaching and research programmes encompassed history, philosophy, literature, and other religions, Buddhism—in particular, translations of the canon into Chinese, Sanskrit, and other Indian languages—took pride of place (Tan 1957: 20–1). The fact that Buddhism spread from the Indian subcontinent through Tibet and took root in China and northeast Asia gave concrete expression to pan-Asian values. It exemplified the ecumenical, morally profound spiritualism that Tagore and his Chinese admirers had, since the Great War, held to be Eastern civilization's timely contribution to a rapacious modernity. It was 'the urgent duty of our Buddhistic [*sic*] countries', Tan declared (1938a: 16–18), with India also in mind, 'to make more efforts than ever for a universal propaganda and for a cosmopolitan salvation.' It was crucial for Westerners, cognizant of 'the frailty of modern life', to appreciate 'the great wisdom, learning, virtue, courage, charity, and the great mercy of Buddhism' (Tan 1938a: 16–18). Tan took a swipe at suave Japanese who were capable of claiming Chinese Buddhism as their own. Despite the universalism that Buddhist civilization implied, Chinese Buddhist leaders such as Taixu complained that Japanese Buddhists were too tolerant of, if not complicit in, their country's encroachment into the Asian continent (Sen 2016: 307; Xue 2005: 77–82). War against Japan meant that Asianist civilizational discourse was no longer just an intellectual movement or the basis of anti-colonial solidarity but a contested terrain between two nation-states.

The most ardent advocate of pan-Asianism in the Nationalist government, lay Buddhist Dai Jitao, was unsurprisingly embroiled in the highly politicized religious exchanges between China and India. In late 1940, he followed Taixu in making what Tansen Sen (2016: 307) has aptly called a political pilgrimage on a trip 'under Chiang Kai-shek's personal planning and direction'. Billed as a 'distinguished Buddhist scholar', Dai visited famed religious sites such as Bodh Gaya, Kusinara, Lumbini, and Rajgir, as well as Allahabad (now Prayagraj), where the Indian National Congress was headquartered. The Congress's message welcoming Dai to Swaraj Bhavan appealed explicitly to common, if less than obvious, cultural ties between China and India: 'Today though the majority of our people are not officially called Buddhists but Hindus, yet they have incorporated this great doctrine in their ancient faith.' Responding to Dai's 'endorsement to the movement of non-violence as a basis for permanent world peace', Congress looked forward to bringing about 'in the east a bloc of free nations and thus bring about a new order'.[10] The reciprocal Asianist sentiments were palpable. Equally obvious was Tan Yunshan's role in mediating Dai and the Congress leadership. Tan partook in Dai's pilgrimage to Buddhist sites and to Allahabad, ostensibly as an interpreter, but he oversaw the latter's itinerary, at least insofar as it involved the Congress.[11] Dai's visit, in Tan's recollection, followed the model of seamless fusion between politics and cultural pursuits that the Cheena Bhavana director had established. The main purpose of Dai's trip, according to Tan (1948a: iv–v), was innocuous, being intended merely to 'pay a cordial visit to Gurudeva Tagore ... and to specifically enquire about his illness'. Writing in 1947, however, Tan did not hesitate to highlight Dai's politics, which was opposed to 'Marxian materialism' and 'based on the traditional values of Chinese philosophy and culture'. Dai's intellectual, heavyweight role as a party 'draftsman' was compared to Nehru's role in the Congress (Tan 1948a: iv–v).

Chiang's Landmark Visit: Blending Pan-Asianism and Geopolitics

Daï's India visit anticipated Chiang's in February 1942, although the latter was undoubtedly made not in any semi-official basis but as representative of China and the Allied powers. Historian Yang Tianshi (2010: 324) wrote that Chiang Kai-shek, due to his sympathy for the Indian freedom movement, had been consistent in adopting a 'pro-Indian, anti-British' (*fu Yin fan Ying* [輔印反英]) policy. The generalissimo's position was, in fact, more complicated. Chiang's visit followed hard on the heels of the beginning of the Pacific War in December 1940, under which China's war of resistance against Japan was subsumed. The Great East Asian War (Dai Tōa sensō [大東亜戦争]), as the Japanese called its military crusade to supplant Anglo-American dominance in Asia, was embraced by some beyond Japan as a showdown between 'Yellow' and 'White' races (Saaler and Szpilman 2011: 26–7). The Nationalist government's challenge was to come up with an alternative to the Japanese empire's anti-Western rhetoric without actively challenging the interests of its more powerful allies. It appealed to Sino-Indian solidarity, drawing on historical ties and the anti-colonial nationalism that the KMT cadres shared with their Congress counterparts. At the same time, Chiang was wary of giving credence to Indian activists who wanted an immediate end to British rule and might allow Japan to expand into South Asia.

The civilizational romance that Cheena Bhavana forged between India and China featured prominently during the visit. It was, as Tan (1957: 32) boasted, the only place on the generalissimo's itinerary aside from those in New Delhi. In fact, Chiang, his wife, and entourage also went to India's boundary region with Afghanistan, reviewing military facilities there and meeting indigenous leaders. He was also meant to pay a visit to Gandhi in his base at Wardha but decided to change this plan due to opposition from British Prime Minister Winston Churchill and Viceroy of India Lord Linlithgow (Zhou 2011: 299–300).[12] It was remarkable nonetheless that the Chinese leader should drop by an institution with such solid ties to the Congress elite. The symbolism attached to this particular leg of Chiang's itinerary, the only one Nehru joined, was difficult to miss. More important, though, was the discursive ground that had been laid by the

Sino-Indian Cultural Society and Cheena Bhavana, which Chiang exploited in his engagement with Congress leaders. On his way to Santiniketan, Chiang called on Gandhi at his Calcutta residence, where the Chinese visitor stayed for five hours. Early on in their talk, Chiang tapped into Tan's assertion that the Chinese public had an intense emotional connection with Gandhi and Tagore. 'The concern revolutionary comrades at the Chinese Nationalist Party have for your health', Chiang confided to his interlocutor, 'is no less earnest than that shown toward our late Premier', that is, Sun Yat-sen.[13] It was only after this expression of affection that Chiang got down to business and asked Gandhi if he was waiting for Japanese and German intervention to free India from colonial rule. Responding to Gandhi's complaint that Anglo-American democracy was deceptive and no more trustworthy than the Japanese, Chiang launched into a long defence of Asianist solidarity:

> We yellow people must seek liberation with our own methods ... Japan is predatory by nature; we would be repeating previous mistakes if we placed hope on it to liberate Eastern nations. For the many centuries since the Tang dynasty, each Chinese dynasty had seen invasion by Japan. However, while the boundary between China and India is as much as three thousand kilometers and exchange between us two countries had lasted for more than two thousand years, there was only cultural and economic connections without any incidence of mutual aggression.[14]

Chiang's eulogy to Sino-Indian unique commitment to peace could well have been delivered by Nehru or Tagore. At Cheena Bhavana's opening ceremony, both men celebrated the amity between the two ancient civilizations and compared them to Western and Westernized nation-states. Amidst 'this modern world of head-hunting and cannibalism', Tagore maintained that Indians and Chinese led human civilization in the altruistic exchange of spiritual and cultural gifts (Tan 1957: 44).

In Santiniketan, Chiang meticulously rehashed the idealized communion of peoples as projected on to Cheena Bhavan and, by extension, China and India. This gesture echoed the first thing Chiang did on arrival at Visva-Bharati on 19 February 1942—pay homage to the recently deceased Tagore (Zhou 2011: 347). At the reception, Chiang compared Sun Yat-sen to Tagore, suggesting that the professional revolutionary was somehow as committed to spiritual uplift of the nation and humankind as the Nobel laureate. He then alluded, not too subtly, to Tagore's characterization of Sino-Indian relations as disinterested and uncorrupted by material calculations: 'I have brought nothing from China to offer you but the warmth of my heart and the good wishes of our people' (Tan 1957: 49). As it transpired, however, along with his people's good wishes Chiang presented INR 50,000 for a Tagore memorial and another INR 30,000 for Cheena Bhavana. Tinged with monetary transaction or not, the Protestant statesman was, of course, not in India as a religious pilgrim but to garner support for China's war efforts from the British colonial authorities and anti-colonial nationalists alike. As he told his underlings, the meeting with Gandhi the day before was a great disappointment:

> [Gandhi] languished under British rule, and his heart became as hard as iron and rock [*tieshi xinchang* (鐵石心腸)]. He only loves India and cares not about the world and the rest of humankind. He is most hardhearted [*renxin ji* (忍心極)]! This attitude is probably informed by Indian philosophy and traditional spirit and not worthy of revolutionary leaders. Yet, only Gandhi and his heart were appropriate for dealing with the British and the British alone. (Zhou 2011: 349–50)

On the Calcutta-bound train from Santiniketan, Chiang complained to Nehru that the latter did not pay enough attention to diplomacy and developments outside India (Zhou 2011: 350). Instead of universalism, India's cultural traditions were leading to insularity at the Allies' expense. Chiang's anxiety over the Congress's unwillingness to aid China's defence by tempering its anti-British campaign showed shrewd geopolitical calculations behind public confessions of mutual love and beautifully articulated visions of a conflict-free world.

The tension between Chiang's realism, typical of politicians presiding over established nation-states, and his professed sympathy for nationalist movements outside China was well appreciated by the Chinese commentariat, or at least that part of it that was close to the state. On 16 February, the Central News Agency reported that India was critical because its unexploited industrial capacity could be transformed into the British Empire's arsenal and become a reliable supplier of arms to China as well (Anonymous 1942: 8). The famed writer and translator Liang Shiqiu (梁實秋) (1903–87) warned, while also echoing the point about India's growing industrial prowess, that the Japanese were already on the doorstep of South Asia after the fall of Singapore. Yet, Indians were not predisposed against Japan. Tagore's *Nationalism* (1917) was popular in Japan, and Japanese pan-Asianism was music to many Indian ears. 'If in response to the Japanese threat the Indians were to practise Ahimsa', Liang (1942: 3–5) warned, 'India could well see a new master.' In the context of wartime geopolitics, the non-violent philosophy that Tan saw implied in Chinese Buddhism and Gandhism and touted as beaconing an alternative to Western colonial exploitation turned into a tacit embrace of Japanese aggression. The differences between Chiang's wartime strategy and Nehru's were laid bare in the two men's conversation after their brief stay in Santiniketan. Nehru confessed that if the Congress were to actively contribute to the Allies' war efforts, the Indian populace could see it as collaborating with the British colonizers. The best China could hope for in the event of Japanese encroachment onto India would be non-violent resistance on Congress's part. Chiang was not at all impressed by a non-violent response to Japan and explicitly urged Nehru to reject this Gandhian strategy. Only by fully cooperating with China in the global strategy against the Axis powers could India secure its own national liberation. As for Nehru's concern for the Congress's popularity in India, Chiang responded tartly, 'We who committed ourselves to revolutions would not care to sacrifice ourselves as long as we could help others.'[15] Yet, it was precisely the actual processes of revolution-making and nation-building that began to pull Chinese nationalists and their Indian counterparts apart. Whatever convergence the ideals of Tagore and Nehru might have enjoyed with Sun and Dai could not be neatly hypostatized as diplomacy.

'Culture' under Scrutiny

With more frequent interactions between the KMT and Congress leadership, Tan's claim that his activities in India were above politics came under even greater scrutiny by Raj officers in both New Delhi and Calcutta. An intelligence report in 1940 observed that 'Censors in Calcutta' had kept a close eye on the communications between

Tan, Dai Jitao, and Chen Lifu. Tan's activities, the report found, were subsidized by the KMT's propaganda department.[16] The latter stage of the Pacific War saw the China chapter of the Sino-Indian Cultural Society raise funds for flood relief in Bengal, while scholars in India extolled the virtues of the New Life Movement and translated Chiang's 1943 treatise, *Zhongguo zhi mingyun* (中國之命運) [*China's Destiny*] into Hindi (Nair 1942: 42–3; Tan 1957: 24). While culture for Tan no doubt encompassed the thoughts and even actions of politicians— nationalist leaders did not just embody partisan ideologies but were sages propelling civilizational renaissance in the East and even the entire humankind—others saw culture as no more than a front for political activism. Colonial officials in New Delhi struggled to situate Tan Yunshan and the Sino-Indian Cultural Society within the context of Nationalist Chinese manoeuvres in India. In 1943, as a result of Chiang's prompting and at the British Raj's invitation, an educational mission was dispatched to India. The mission focused Delhi's attention on previous Chinese visitors. Remarkably, none of the British-Indian officials who dealt with China were heretofore familiar with what Olaf Caroe (1892–1981), the top diplomat in the Raj, called China's 'Shantiniketan connection'.[17] In a note dated 18 February, Humphrey Prideaux-Brix (1886–1979), who had just taken up the position of China Relations Officer in India after various diplomatic appointments in China, confessed that he had had no knowledge of Tan Yunshan or the Sino-Indian Cultural Society until recently. Apart from noting the sponsorship of Dai Jitao ('a rather shadowy personage') and Zhu Jiahua ('not popular'), the old China Hand drew attention to the society's non-political self-identity. If the society were genuinely apolitical, Delhi might well consider leveraging it to its own advantage.[18]

Soon enough, the Raj realized that culture and politics were not separable, or at least not in a way that colonial officials felt reassuring, in Santiniketan. A September 1942 letter that Tan sent to Dai was understood by the Intelligence Bureau as indicating that the Society was, for some Chinese officials, at least, 'a cover for political activity'.[19] Tan himself, Prideaux-Brune found out, had 'strayed from the straight and narrow path', presiding over a gathering at Visva-Bharati in support of Gandhi's fast on 11 February 1943.[20] The fifteen-day ordeal, which the Mahatma launched as a protest in the aftermath of the Quit India Movement, proved too sensitive for Tan to be associated with, albeit marginally. At the end of the fast, Tan travelled to Pune, where Gandhi had been placed under house arrest, to attend a thanksgiving meeting. He was at the multi-faith event as a Buddhist, in which tradition he offered prayers, while the British Quaker Horace Alexander (1889–1989) read from the Bible.[21] For colonial officials, Tan's well-advertised sympathy for Gandhi was clearly provocative. Their frustration stemmed from the impression that Tan's actions were those not only of a pious Buddhist but of the leader of a body backed by the Chinese government. It is for this reason that New Delhi requested the Chinese commissioner Shen Shihua (b. 1900) to, as the 'demi-official letter' put it, 'fortify [Tan] ... to eschew all political activity'.[22] The fact that Shen agreed to ask the head of the educational mission to India, a vice minister of education, to admonish Tan no doubt confirmed suspicions that the Sino-Indian Cultural Society was connected to, if not a front for, the Nationalist regime.[23]

The Santiniketan connection, External Affairs Department officials quickly concluded, was anathema. Tan's broad definition of culture, with its repudiation of Euro-American modernity and vision for a universal order drawn from Asian historical experiences, translated easily into sympathies for political figures. Imaginings of Eastern civilizational renaissance were potentially useful for Chiang's government, which had to juggle its identity as a nationalist revolutionary movement with its commitments to the established international system. For British-Indian bureaucrats, however, Tan's dabbling in oppositional politics was undesirable, if not downright subversive. Cultural relations organized out of Chongqing and Santiniketan were too much based on the 'Kuomintang–Congress Axis'.[24] Tan Yunshan, Cheena Bhavana, and the Sino-Indian Cultural Society were thus situated in the context of Nationalist cosiness with the Congress. The secretary to the Raj's envoy in China suggested in 1942 that

The Chinese ... appear to be very sentimental. The equation of the Congress party with the Kuomintang, and suggestions that the Congress is revolutionary tend when taken together to intensify their feeling for the Congress. They are very proud of their own revolutionary history although they would not care for flattering references to the revolutionary spirit of the Chinese communists![25]

Misguided affection for the Congress, he continued, stemmed from Chinese anti-foreignism—their relish in embarrassing the British—and 'from this it [was] an easy step to a sort of pan-Asiatic feeling'.[26] Chiang Kai-shek and the China he led, British-Indian officials observed, without a shred of irony, had an imperialistic impulse.[27] British understanding of Nationalist outreach to the Congress was almost a mirror image of how Chiang portrayed Japanese pleas to pan-Asianist sentiments in Tokyo's attempt to appropriate Indian nationalism (Zhou 2011: 341).

To be sure, Tan was not exactly a threat to British rule. Prideaux-Brune concluded, after accompanying the Chinese educational mission to Santiniketan, that Cheena Bhavana was 'a dead-or-alive affair' and that the Sino-Indian Cultural Society, which apparently included him in its stellar list of central committee members, was 'little more than the usual paper scheme'.[28] As for Tan, Prideaux-Brune attributed his political involvement to difficulties in sustaining meaningful Sino-Indian cultural intercourse, given his low intellectual calibre and unfavourable location.[29] Prideaux-Brune's portrayal of Tan demonstrated an inadequate grasp of either Tan's long-standing association with Indian nationalist leaders or the ways in which his devotion to cultural communion between China and India naturally intersected with nationalist politics. Regardless, the consensus among British-Indian diplomats was that the Santiniketan connection should be sidelined. A proposal calling for the establishment of Sino-Indian institutions, managed by the New Delhi-based Inter-University Board (of which Visva-Bharati was not a part), to coordinate cultural exchanges between the two countries, was mooted. Yet, probably due to its sensitivity, the idea was not raised with the Chinese educational mission.[30] The delegation was already confronted with the possibility that the donations Chiang committed to Cheena Bhavana during his 1942 visit might not result in new facilities because of the Indian government's wartime policy of withholding steel and cement from non-essential projects.[31] The agent general for India in China, K.P.S. Menon (1898–1982), communicated with Prideaux-Brune and agreed that the latter should ignore the invitation to join the central committee of the Sino-Indian Cultural Society in India. Menon himself showed 'polite but no means undue interest' when meeting with the society's president,

Zhu Jiahua, and other officers such as the 'Oxford man' and budding translator Yang Xianyi (楊憲益) (1915–2009).[32]

***

In terms of its capacity for training Sinologists, Cheena Bhavana would perhaps soon be eclipsed if similar departments were sponsored by the Raj at the universities of Calcutta or Delhi. Prideaux-Brune described Cheena Bhavana—occupying 'the only quite unattractive building in Shantiniketan—as a sorry place where Tan and his associates conducted amateurish teaching and research in Chinese language and Buddhism with very limited resources'.[33] In fact, according to Tansen Sen (2017: 307), Cheena Bhavana remained until the late 1950s 'the leading global center for India-China studies'. Its scholarly achievements regardless, the primary significance of Cheena Bhavana lay not in its academic prowess, nor even in that of its director. The experiment was important, instead, for being an institutional articulation of a civilizational ideal, a vision of Asianist unity that was supposed to overcome the violence, avarice, and mutual suspicion that beset humanity carved up into nation-states and divided into subjects pursuing material interests. Even as both Rabindranath Tagore and Tan Yunshan assiduously sought financial support from the Chinese state, there is no reason to suggest that Santiniketan was designed to become a base for political agitation.

Nonetheless, it was also true that Cheena Bhavana was embroiled in wartime nationalist politics and great power diplomacy, despite its transcendental vision. First, the Sino-Indian Cultural Society, which originated as the conduit of funds for the new Sinological unit, was identified as a front for collaboration between the Nationalists and the Congress. Second, Tan actively helped organize the visit of Dai Jitao and contributed to that of Chiang Kai-shek. On the latter occasion in particular, appeals to humanistic culture coexisted with unsentimental realpolitik calculations. Finally, even as he insisted on being above politics, Tan's admiration for Gandhi rendered Cheena Bhavana an anathema to the British colonial officials, who already harboured suspicions of Chinese support for the Congress movement. Tan did not ask to be involved in political machinations, but his cultural agenda eased him into the political realm.[34] As an institution, wartime contingencies brought Cheena Bhavana attention and new injections of funds. Convergence, as I argue elsewhere (Tsui 2018: 157–9), was the modus operandi of how Nationalist government and Chinese liberal intellectuals interacted with one another. While Tan had never embraced liberalism and was attracted more to Gandhism, he most probably shared with contemporaries, such as Hu Shi (胡適) (1891–1962), Jiang Tingfu (蔣廷黻) (1895–1965), and Zhu Guangqian (朱光潛) (1897–1986), discomfort with the strictures the Nationalist government imposed on society. The Nationalist approach to governing China was anathema to the free-wheeling informality that characterized Visva-Bharati. Yet, there was enough common ground between intellectuals such as Tan and the Nationalist state, given their common animosity to class struggle, foreign threats, and a shared desire to craft a world freed from colonial capitalism, to bind them together. That Tan more than welcomed funding from China to keep Cheena Bhavana afloat and that the Nationalist state appreciated Santiniketan as an unofficial but highly symbolic diplomatic site rendered academic culture and state politics inextricable.

It was also the dynamics of the Pacific War that brought into sharp relief the limitations besetting Tan's notion that Sino-Indian amity was based on exchange not of strategic interests between political actors but of goodwill between cultures. In spite of what they professed publicly, Nationalist leaders in China saw their Congress counterparts as, at best, difficult allies. Despite sharing the predicament of being threatened by imperialist powers, the two nationalist parties obviously had different views on how to deliver their countries from colonialism. While partaking in the desire to refashion an Asia-centric future, Chiang effectively asked Congress leaders to suspend India's struggle against British colonialism. Finally, given Cheena Bhavana's increasing involvement mediating the interactions between the Nationalists and the Congress, its claims to be a body set above state politics became increasingly untenable, and its catholic definition of culture was questioned, not the least by the British colonial state governing India. This last dilemma was not to be resolved with British colonizers' withdrawal in 1947; instead, Cheena Bhavana became ever more entangled in state diplomacy with India becoming an independent nation-state and China soon being torn between two governments in Beijing and Taipei, locked in Cold War confrontation. Tan Yunshan's decision to befriend the Chinese Communist government was probably informed by the same optimism that culture could transcend the state power that be, but it was definitely not brought about by any cosmopolitan, humane order that inspired Chinese intellectuals disillusioned with European-style geopolitical rivalries in the aftermath of the Great War.

Notes

1. For Tucci, see Bevavides (1995). Recent works on Andrews include Visvanathan (2007: 62–80).
2. Rabindranath Tagore to Lin Sen, 28 September 1934, Nationalist Government Collection, 001000006256A, Academia Historica, Taipei, Taiwan.
3. The original proposal called for an exchange of scholars, including Liang Qichao, between Visva-Bharati and Beijing-based universities. Funding for a guest house was to come from Jugal Kishore Birla (1883–1967), an industrialist who supported Gandhi and the Congress (Tan [1942] 1998).
4. Intelligence Bureau note, 'Sino-Indian Cultural Society or Association', 22 February 1943, External Affairs Department Collection, 135(8)-X/43, National Archives of India, New Delhi, India; 'Report of a Secret Agent dated 13.7.40', 13 July 1940, File no. 468/39(4), Serial no. 628-40, West Bengal State Archives, Kolkata, India. See also Tan (1957: 18–19).
5. 'Bolata jiang "Yindu geming shi"' (勃拉塔講「印度革命史」) ['Pratap on the "Indian Revolution"'], 25 November 1927, general files, 436/119.9, Kuomintang Archives, Taipei, Taiwan; see also Deepak (2001: 78).
6. Chen Lifu and Zhu Jiahua to Chiang Kai-shek, 6 October 1939, special files, 13/1.2, Kuomintang Archives, Taipei, Taiwan.
7. Zhu Jiahua to Chiang Kai-shek, 17 February 1942, Nationalist Government Collection, 001000006307A, Academia Historica, Taipei, Taiwan; 'Zhong-Yin wenhua hezuo dagang' (中印文化合作大綱) ['Outlines on Sino-Indian Cultural Cooperation'], 6 October 1939, special files, 13/1.3, Kuomintang Archives, Taipei, Taiwan.
8. Zhu Jiahua to Chiang Kai-shek, 17 February 1942, Nationalist Government Collection, 001000006307A, Academia Historica, Taipei, Taiwan.
9. Humphrey Prideux-Brune to Hugh Weightman, 17 April 1943, External Affairs Department Collection, 329-X/43 (Secret), National Archives of India, New Delhi, India.
10. Dai's speech in Allahabad, 3 December 1940; Congress's message on Dai's visit, undated, All India Congress Committee (AICC) Collection, G40/1940, Nehru Memorial Museum and Library, New Delhi, India.

11. Tan to Nehru, 10 October 1940; J.B. Kripalani to Congress Provincial Committees, 28 October 1940, G40/2075; Nehru to Kripalani, 28 October 1940, Nehru Memorial Museum and Library, New Delhi, India.

12. Churchill to Chiang, 12 February 1942, Nationalist Government Collection, 001000000375A, Academia Historica, Taipei, Taiwan.

13. Transcript of Chiang's conversation with Gandhi, 18 February 1942, Nationalist Government Collection, 002000000375A, Academia Historica, Taipei, Taiwan.

14. Transcript of Chiang's conversation with Gandhi, 18 February 1942, Nationalist Government Collection, 002000000375A, Academia Historica, Taipei, Taiwan.

15. Transcript of Chiang's conversation with Nehru, 20 February 1942, Nationalist Government Collection, 002000000375A, Academia Historica, Taipei, Taiwan.

16. 'Report of a Secret Agent dated 13.7.40', 13 July 1940, File no. 468/39(4), Serial no. 628-40, West Bengal State Archives, Kolkata, India

17. Olaf Caroe's comments on education adviser to the Government of India's report on the Chinese educational mission's visit to India, 15 June 1943, External Affairs Department Collection, 329-X/43 (Secret), National Archives of India, New Delhi, India.

18. Prideaux-Brune's response to Hugh Weightman, 18 February 1943, External Affairs Department Collection, 329-X/43 (Secret), National Archives of India, New Delhi, India.

19. 'Sino-Indian Cultural Society of Association,' Intelligence Bureau, Government of India, undated, External Affairs Department Collection, 329-X/43 (Secret), National Archives of India, New Delhi, India.

20. Notes written by Prideaux-Brune, 22 February 1943, External Affairs Department Collection, 329-X/43 (Secret), National Archives of India, New Delhi, India. Intelligence agents in West Bengal were much blunter in describing Tan as someone working for the Chinese government under the innocuous guise of cultural activities (Sen 2017: 320).

21. Intelligence Bureau newspaper clipping, 'Thanksgiving Day for Mr Gandhi', 5 March 1943, External Affairs Department Collection, 329-X/43 (Secret), National Archives of India, New Delhi, India.

22. Weightman to Shen, 24 February 1943; Weightman to Prideaux-Brune, 24 March 1943, External Affairs Department Collection, 329-X/43 (Secret), National Archives of India, New Delhi, India.

23. Weightman to Shen, 24 February 1943; Weightman to Prideaux-Brune, 24 March 1943, External Affairs Department Collection, 329-X/43 (Secret), National Archives of India, New Delhi, India.

24. Olaf Caroe's comments on the education adviser to the government of India's report on the Chinese educational mission's visit to India, 15

June 1943, External Affairs Department Collection, 329-X/43 (Secret), National Archives of India, New Delhi, India.

25. H.E. Richardson to A.S.B. Khan, undated, External Affairs Department Collection, 159X(P)/1942 (Secret), National Archives of India, New Delhi, India.

26. H.E. Richardson to A.S.B. Khan, undated, External Affairs Department Collection, 159X(P)/1942 (Secret), National Archives of India, New Delhi, India.

27. H.E. Richardson to A.S.B. Khan, undated; Appendix written by P.D. Butler, 17 September 1942, External Affairs Department Collection, 159X(P)/1942 (Secret), National Archives of India, New Delhi, India.

28. Prideaux-Brune to Weightman, 17 April 1943, External Affairs Department Collection, 329-X/43 (Secret), National Archives of India, New Delhi, India.

29. Prideaux-Brune to Weightman, 17 April 1943, External Affairs Department Collection, 329-X/43 (Secret), National Archives of India, New Delhi, India.

30. Extract from notes of discussions between the educational adviser to the Indian government and members of the Chinese Educational Mission during their visit to India in 1943, 3 June 1943, External Affairs Department Collection, 329-X/43 (Secret), National Archives of India, New Delhi, India.

31. Release of certain materials for the completion of buildings of the Cheena Bhavana, External Affairs Department Collection, 135(8)-X/43, National Archives of India, New Delhi, India.

32. Menon to Weightman, 1 December 1943, External Affairs Department Collection, 329-X/43 (Secret), National Archives of India, New Delhi, India.

33. Prideaux-Brune to Weightman, 17 April 1943, External Affairs Department Collection, 329-X/43 (Secret), National Archives of India, New Delhi, India.

34. The only evidence suggesting that Tan had political ambitions is a 14 May 1940 letter, intercepted and translated into English by censors in Calcutta (File no. 468/39[4]), Serial no. 628–40, West Bengal State Archives), in which Chen Lifu responded to Tan's request to be involved in unspecified 'political work'.

References

Archival Material

West Bengal State Archives, Kolkata, India

'Report of a Secret Agent dated 13.7.40', 13 July 1940, File no. 468/39(4), Serial no. 628–40.

File no. 468/39(4), Serial no. 628–40.

National Archives of India, New Delhi, India

'Sino-Indian Cultural Society of Association,' Intelligence Bureau, Government of India, undated, External Affairs Department Collection, 329-X/43 (Secret).

Appendix written by P.D. Butler, 17 September 1942, External Affairs Department Collection, 159X(P)/1942 (Secret).

Extract from notes of discussions between the educational adviser to the Indian government and members of the Chinese Educational Mission during their visit to India in 1943, 3 June 1943, External Affairs Department Collection, 329-X/43 (Secret).

H.E. Richardson to A.S.B. Khan, undated, External Affairs Department Collection, 159X(P)/1942 (Secret).

Humphrey Prideux-Brune to Hugh Weightman, 17 April 1943, External Affairs Department Collection, 329-X/43 (Secret).

Intelligence Bureau newspaper clipping, 'Thanksgiving Day for Mr Gandhi', 5 March 1943, External Affairs Department Collection, 329-X/43 (Secret).

Intelligence Bureau note, 'Sino-Indian Cultural Society or Association', 22 February 1943, External Affairs Department Collection, 135(8)-X/43.

Menon to Weightman, 1 December 1943, External Affairs Department Collection, 329-X/43 (Secret).

Notes written by Prideaux-Brune, 22 February 1943, External Affairs Department Collection, 329-X/43 (Secret).

Olaf Caroe's comments on the report by the Indian government's education adviser, on the Chinese Educational Mission's visit to India, 15 June 1943, External Affairs Department Collection, 329-X/43 (Secret).

Prideaux-Brune to Weightman, 17 April 1943, External Affairs Department Collection, 329-X/43 (Secret).

Prideaux-Brune's response to Hugh Weightman, 18 February 1943, External Affairs Department Collection, 329-X/43 (Secret).

Release of certain materials for the completion of buildings of the Cheena Bhavana, External Affairs Department Collection, 135(8)-X/43.

Weightman to Prideaux-Brune, 24 March 1943, External Affairs Department Collection, 329-X/43 (Secret).

Weightman to Shen, 24 February 1943, External Affairs Department Collection, 329-X/43 (Secret).

Nehru Memorial Museum and Library, New Delhi, India

Congress's message on Dai's visit, undated, All India Congress Committee (AICC) Collection, G40/1940.

Tan to Nehru, 10 October 1940.

J.B. Kripalani to Congress Provincial Committees, 28 October 1940, G40/2075.

Nehru to Kripalani, 28 October 1940.

Dai's speech in Allahabad, 3 December 1940, All India Congress Committee (AICC) Collection, G40/1940.

Kuomintang Archives, Taipei, Taiwan

'Bolata jiang "Yindu geming shi"' (勃拉塔講「印度革命史」) ['Pratap on the "Indian Revolution"'], 25 November 1927, general files, 436/119.9.

'Zhong-Yin wenhua hezuo dagang' (中印文化合作大綱) ['Pratap on the "Indian Revolution"'], 6 October 1939, special files, 13/1.3.

Chen Lifu and Zhu Jiahua to Chiang Kai-shek, 6 October 1939, special files, 13/1.2.

Academia Historica, Taipei, Taiwan.

Rabindranath Tagore to Lin Sen, 28 September 1934, Nationalist Government Collection, 001000006256A.

Churchill to Chiang, 12 February 1942, Nationalist Government Collection, 001000000375A.

Zhu Jiahua to Chiang Kai-shek, 17 February 1942, Nationalist Government Collection, 001000006307A.

Transcript of Chiang's conversation with Gandhi, 18 February 1942, Nationalist Government Collection, 002000000375A.

Transcript of Chiang's conversation with Nehru, 20 February 1942, Nationalist Government Collection, 002000000375A.

Other Sources

Anonymous. 1942. *Jiang weiyuan zhang fangwen Yindu jiyao* (蔣委員長訪問印度紀要) [*Description of Major Events during Generalissimo's Visit to India*]. Chongqing: Duli chubanshe.

Bevavides, Gustavo. 1995. 'Giuseppe Tucci, or Buddhology in the Age of Fascism'. In Donald S. Lopez (ed.), *Curators of the Buddha: The Study of Buddhism under Colonialism*, pp. 161–96. Chicago: The University of Chicago Press.

Deepak, B.R. 2001. *India–China Relations in the First Half of the Twentieth Century*. New Delhi: A.P.H. Publishing.

Duara, Prasenjit. 2003. *Sovereignty and Authenticity: Manchukuo and the East Asian Modern* Lanham, MD: Rowman & Littlefield.

Eagleton, Terry. 2000. *The Idea of Culture*. Oxford: Blackwell.

Fung, Edmund S.K. 2010. *The Intellectual Foundations of Chinese Modernity: Cultural and Political Thought in the Republican Era*. Cambridge: Cambridge University Press.

Furth, Charlotte. 1976. 'Culture and Politics in Modern Chinese Conservativism'. In Charlotte Furth (ed.), *The Limits of Change: Essays on Conservative Alternatives in Republican China*, pp. 22–55. Cambridge, Mass.: Harvard University Press.

Liang Shiqiu (梁實秋). 1942. 'Jinri zhi Yindu wenti' (今天之印度問題) ['Today's India Problem']. *Zhongyang zhoukan* (中央週刊) [*Central Weekly*] 4 (34): 3–5.

Lohia, Rammanohar. 1938. *India on China*. Allahabad: All India Congress Committee.

Nair V.G. (ed.). 1942. *Generalissimo and Madame Chiang Kai-shek in India*. Calcutta.

———. 1958. *Professor Tan Yun-shan and Cultural Relations between India and China*. Indo-Asian Pub.

Nehru, Jawaharlal. 1942. 'Foreword'. In Nym Wales (ed.), *China Builds for Democracy: A Story of Cooperative Industry*, pp. 6–9. Allahabad: Kitabistan.

Saaler, Sven and Christopher W.A. Szpilman. 2011. 'Introduction: The Emergence of Pan-Asianism as an Ideal of Asian Identity and Solidarity, 1850–2008'. In Sven Saaler and Christopher W.A. Szpilman (eds), *Pan-Asianism: A Documentary History, Volume 1: 1850-1920*, pp. 1–41. Lanham, MD.: Rowan & Littlefield.

Santiniketan Press. 1943. 'General Constitution of the Sino-Indian Cultural Society'. *The Sino-Indian Cultural Society*, pp. 4–6. Santiniketan.

Sen, Tansen. 2016. 'Taixu's Goodwill Mission to India: Reviving the Buddhist Links between China and India'. In Nayanjot Lahiri and Upinder Singh (eds), *Buddhism in Asia: Revival and Reinvention*, pp. 293–322. New Delhi: Manohar.

———. 2017. *India, China, and the World: A Connected History*. Lanham, MD.: Rowan & Littlefield.

Tagore, Rabindranath. 1934. *A Scheme for Building a Chinese Hall at Shantiniketan*. Santiniketan: Visva-Bharati.

Tan Yunshan (譚雲山). 1929. 'Yindu guoji daxue gaishu—Dongfang jiaoyu zhi techan' (印度國際大學概述——東方教育的特) ['A Brief Introduction to Visva Bharati—A Special Product of Eastern Education']. *Dongfang zazhi* (東方雜誌) [*Eastern Miscellany*] 26 (5): 21–30.

———. 1935. 'Zhong-Yin wenhua zhi lianluo—Yindu gailun xu' (中印文化之聯絡——《印度概論》序) ['Cultural Connection between China and

India—Preface to *An Overview of India*']. *Qiantu zazhi* (前途雜誌) [*The Future*] 3 (2): 1–3.

———. 1938a. *Buddhism in China Today*. Nanking: The Sino-Indian Cultural Society.

———. 1938b. *Modern Chinese History: Political, Economic and Social*. Madras.

———. [1942] 1998. 'The Visva-Bharati Cheena-Bhavana'. In *Sino-Indian Culture*, pp. 85–94. Calcutta: Visva-Bharati.

———. 1944. *The Visva-Bharati Cheena-Bhavana and the Sino–Indian Cultural Society*. Chungking: The Sino–Indian Cultural Society.

———. 1948a. 'His Excellency Dr. Tai Chi-Tao (A Biographical Introduction)'. In Dai Jitao, *Goodwill Messages to India*, pp. i–vi. Shantiniketan: The Sino–Indian Cultural Society in India.

———. 1948b. 'My First Visit to Gandhiji'. *The Sino–Indian Journal* 1 (2): 26–37.

———. [1950] 1958. 'Sino-Indian Relationship'. In V.G. Nair (ed.), *Professor Tan Yun-shan and Cultural Relations between India and China*, pp. 71–6. Madras: Indo-Asian Publication.

———. 1957. *Twenty Years of the Visva-Bharati Cheena-Bhavana 1937–1957*. Santiniketan: The Sino–Indian Cultural Society of India.

Tsui, Brian. 2018. *China's Conservative Revolution: The Quest for a New Order, 1927–1949*. Cambridge: Cambridge University Press.

Visvanathan, Susan. 2007. *Friendship, Interiority and Mysticism: Essays in Dialogue*. New Delhi: Orient Longman.

Wang Hui. 2016. *China's Twentieth Century: Revolution, Retreat and the Road to Equality*. London: Verso.

Xin xinyuebao (新新月報) [*New New Monthly*]. 1937. 'Yindu Zhongguo xueyuan luocheng juxing kaimu' (印度中國學院落成舉行開幕) ['Cheena Bhavana in India Completed and Inaugurated']. 3 (6): 6.

Xue Yu. 2005. *Buddhism, War, and Nationalism: Chinese Monks in the Struggle against Japanese Aggressions, 1931–1945*. New York: Routledge, 2005.

Yang Tianshi (楊天石). 2010. *Zhaoxun zhenshi de Jiang Jieshi—Jiang Jieshi riji jiedu* (找尋真實的蔣介石──蔣介石日記解讀) [*Search for the True Chiang Kai-shek—Decoding Chiang Kai-shek's Diaries*], Volume 2. Hong Kong: Sanlian shudian.

Zhou Meihua (周美華) (ed.). 2011. *Jiang Zhongzheng zongtong dang'an: Shilue gaoben* (蔣中正總統檔案──事略稿本) [*The Chiang Kai-shek Collections: The Chronological Events*], Volume 48. Taipei: Academia Historica.

9

Erecting a Gurdwara on Queen's Road East

The Singh Sabha Movement, the Boxer Uprising, and the Sikh Community in Hong Kong

YIN CAO

In early 2014, I received an email enquiring about the detailed origins of a gurdwara (Sikh temple) in Hong Kong. Although I had read some articles in historical newspapers that mentioned the gurdwara, my knowledge did not go beyond the information provided by Wikipedia. In July 2014, however, I was given the opportunity to stay at the University of Hong Kong, which was close to the location of the gurdwara, and so I decided to visit it myself (Figure 9.1). The secretary of the gurdwara warmly welcomed me into his office. When I enquired about the gurdwara's early history, however, he became very quiet. Worse still, this gurdwara did not have any archives from before 1945. I left the office empty-handed and decided to go to the langar for a free meal.[1] As I approached the langar, I saw a foundation stone on the very corner of the sidewall.

Figure 9.1   The Hong Kong Gurdwara on Queen's Road East

Source: Photographed by the author.

Figure 9.2   The Foundation Stone of the Hong Kong Gurdwara

Source: Photographed by the author.

On the stone was written '1901', the year the gurdwara was first built (Figure 9.2). My interest was stimulated even further.

This chapter therefore investigates the trans-local background of the establishment of the gurdwara in Hong Kong. In the process, new perspectives are introduced to explore the Singh Sabha Movement in the context of imperial history. Another aim of this chapter is to present an experiment in narrating local history, which often has global outlook.

The Imperial and Transnational Turn of Sikh Studies

In the past few decades, most scholars have employed two approaches to examining the Sikh past—the impact–response approach and the Punjab-centred approach. Among Western scholars who have an interest in Sikh history, there is a long tradition that highlights the colonial regime's impact on the socio-economic structure cultural identity of Punjabi Sikhs. For example, Bernard Cohn (1996) has conducted excellent research into the relationship between the British colonial powers and Sikh clothing. In an effort to strengthen their assumption that the Sikhs were a specific 'martial race', the British authorities supported and promoted the turban to distinguish Sikhs from other ethnicities in Punjab (Cohn 1996). Richard Fox has a similar position to Cohn's. In his analysis of the formation of the Khalsa identity, Fox argues that it was the British colonial authorities rather than the Sikhs who played the central role. On the one hand, the British Indian Army's preference for 'authentic' Sikhs (Sikhs who were loyal to their community and religion) cultivated a strong commitment to religious requirements and rituals by them. On the other hand, the British authorities continuously supported the institutionalization of Sikhism in an attempt to use the religion to discipline their Sikh soldiers (Fox 1987). For both Cohn and Fox, modern Sikh history is therefore explainable through an impact–response model. It was the colonial state that first initiated or brought about changes, to which the Sikhs then made their various responses.

However, the impact–response approach attracted scepticism and criticism from the very beginning. Its overemphasis on the role of the colonial authorities and neglect of local dynamics have been interpreted as Eurocentric. Critics contend that this approach fails to take the continuity of Sikh traditions into account. Precolonial social customs, economic structures, and cultural identities were not static but in a state of constant transformation. During the colonial period, these traditions continued to dominate all aspects of the Sikh community, to which the colonial regime had to make adjustments (Ballantyne 2006: 18).

An alternative to the impact–response approach is the Punjab-centred approach. Most scholars using this approach put place the development of Sikh culture, society, and politics within Punjab at the centre of the debate. However, W.H. McLeod adopted the Rankean method in his interpretation of Sikh history, suggesting that scholars should go more deeply into the classic Sikh texts in exploring Sikh tradition and culture (McLeod 1989). Eschewing McLeod's textual-based research, N.G. Barrier used colonial archives to examine the local institutions, power structures and modes of mass mobilization of the Sikh community in Punjab during the colonial period (Barrier 1968: 523, 2000: 33–62). Some scholars also take Punjab's environmental landscapes and economic structures into account in charting transformations of the Sikh community over history (Banga 1978; Grewal 1998).

Research into the Singh Sabha Movement has been influenced by both the impact–response and Punjab-centred approaches. Some studies focus on the colonial policies that facilitated the rise of the movement and that transformed its development, while others maintain that the roots and main characters of the Singh Sabha Movement could be traced back to the precolonial Sikh intellectual tradition. Nevertheless, both schools agree that the Singh Sabha Movement was a regional movement that merely had its genesis in Punjab (Barrier 1998; Jones 1973).

In recent years, some scholars have tried to resolve the dichotomy of the impact–response and Punjab-centred approaches. Their solution is to take modern Sikh history as a diasporic formation (Ballantyne 2006: 20). This diasporic approach suggests that the Sikh communities overseas not only maintained reciprocal linear interactions with the Sikh homeland in Punjab, but were also interconnected themselves (Tatla 2005). The circulation of the Sikh population, institutions, and knowledge across the globe largely shaped the economic, political, and cultural landscapes of Punjab (Dusenbery 1995). It is even argued that the very concepts of Punjab as the Sikh homeland and Sikhs as a nation have origins in the diaspora (Axel 2001).

Inspired by the diasporic approach, Tony Ballantyne goes a step further by relating the Sikhs' diasporic network to the British imperial network. He contends that by examining the mobility of Sikh emigrants within the latter, we could not only improve our understanding of the development of Sikhism but also deepen our knowledge of the way the British Empire worked. For Ballantyne, the two networks are intertwined. The imperial expansion facilitated the flow of Sikh subjects and the formation of the Sikh diaspora, while the Sikh diaspora, in its turn, contributed much to the empire-building process (Ballantyne 2006; Ballantyne and Burton 2014).

This chapter echoes Ballantyne's appeal for an 'imperial turn' to Sikh studies. Taking the construction of the Hong Kong gurdwara in 1901 as a case study, it argues that the Singh Sabha Movement was by no means a regional movement, but rather that it spread to Southeast and East Asia and shaped the cultural landscape of the Sikh settlements in these regions by the turn of twentieth century. The infrastructure of the British imperial network played a significant role in the dissemination of the Singh Sabha reformers, institutions, and ideologies. The Singh Sabha reformers, in their turn, collaborated with the British colonial authorities to strengthen colonial rule and discipline the Sikh emigrants. This article also demonstrates that the mobility of Sikh emigrants (most of whom worked as policemen in British colonies), the outflow of the Singh Sabha reformers, and the deployment of Sikh soldiers overseas were largely interrelated phenomena. It is these seemingly irrelevant but essentially imbricated circulations that gave birth to the gurdwara in Hong Kong. In this sense, this article is therefore about a local event with a global outlook.

When the Singh Sabhas Went Abroad

The Singh Sabha movement was a Sikh religious movement that existed from the 1870s to the early twentieth century, initiated by a group of Sikh notables and intellectuals to create homogeneity and a corporate identity among Sikhs living in Punjab and beyond. This movement was one of the most influential socio-religious events in modern Sikh history, as it dramatically transformed the outlook of the Sikh religion and Sikh identity (Singh 2012: 90).

The first Singh Sabha was established in Amritsar in 1873, a reaction to a crisis that erupted when four Sikh students studying in a Christian missionary school in Amritsar publically announced their conversion to Christianity. This move greatly unsettled the local Sikhs, pushing them to respond. A resolution was soon reached by Sikh gentry and scholars in Amritsar that a society (Singh Sabha) should be founded to promote religious as well as secular education among Sikhs (McLeod 1989: 70). It was hoped that the traditional and 'authentic' Sikh philosophy, way of life, and loyalties to their religion could be restored and revitalized through the education programme initiated by the Singh Sabha movement (Grewal 2009: 275).

The work of Christian missionaries, however, was just one of several causes of the establishment of the Singh Sabha movement. Before colonial rule, most Sikhs showed little interest in distinguishing themselves from local Hindus. Due to the lack of a centralized religious institution, a plurality of religious rituals and a diversity of lifestyles were widely acknowledged by people living in Punjab. In other words, the religious identity of the individual in nineteenth-century Punjab was rather ambiguous (Oberoi 1988: 136–41).

After Punjab was annexed by the British in the 1840s, the region underwent a dramatic transformation under the influence of the colonial regime. The British authorities in Punjab taxed peasants not in kind, as the Sikh monarchy used to, but in cash, a move that led to the commodification of the local economy (Khilnani 1972: 179). With cash in hand, rich families began to settle down in urban areas such as Lahore and Amritsar. In these provincial centres, a professional class emerged. Members of this class attended Western schools, received their education in English, and worked as civil servants, lawyers, and doctors. These classes soon came to monopolize the public debate over social values, thus becoming the cultural elites of the region. With their Western education, moreover, they incorporated the Christian concept of religion as monotheistic and exclusive into their understanding of Sikhism and Hinduism (Oberoi 1988: 136).

In the 1860s and 1870s, a Hindu religious movement that was later known as the Arya Samaj [Noble Society] gradually gained momentum in Punjab. The original aim of this movement was to purify

Hinduism by promoting values and practices based on the teachings of the Vedas. The leaders of Arya Samaj denied that Sikhism was an established religion and insisted that Sikhs were Hindus. Under the influence of the Arya Samaj, accordingly, many Punjabis abandoned their Sikh identity (Grewal 1990: 132).

In the face of claims of the Arya Samaj, a counterattack organized by a well-disciplined organization might have seemed imperative. In fact, the chosen methods of defence employed by the Singh Sabha movement against the influence of the Arya Samaj were very similar to the latter's own practices of asserting Hindu authenticity.[2] In the last three decades of the nineteenth century, the Singh Sabha Movement, like its Arya Samaj counterpart, made good use of modern print technology to produce newspapers and large quantities of scholarly as well as propaganda literature on Sikh traditions. In addition, the Singh Sabhas also built schools, opened orphanages, and established historical societies to promote secular and religious education among the Sikhs (Barrier 1988: 171).

The recruitment policy of the British Indian Army also aided the Singh Sabha movement. The bravery and bellicose character of the Sikh fighters had deeply impressed the British officers as early as the two Anglo-Sikh wars (from 1845 to 1849), and thus earned them the reputation of being excellent soldiers with a strongly martial spirit (Allen 2000; Cook 1975). Nonetheless, the Sikhs were not widely deployed outside India before the Indian Mutiny (Kaur 2009: 13–14; Roy 2008: 98; Streets 2004: 65).[3] During the Mutiny of 1857, Sikhs demonstrated their loyalty to the Raj by not only fighting against the mutineers along with their British officers but also actively joining the government army (Ballantyne 2006: 72; David 2002; Omissi 1994: 6).[4] By combining perceptions of the bravery and loyalty of the Sikhs with social Darwinist racial theory, the British thus tagged the Sikhs as a 'martial race' and enlisted them extensively into the Indian Army.[5] The British believed that the valour and loyalty of their Sikh soldiers came from their religion and therefore equated 'martial race' Sikhs with Sikhs who strictly followed Sikhism. All Sikhs in the army were required to maintain their religious identity by wearing the 'five K's', the external symbols of Sikhism.[6] Separate religious sites were also provided to Sikh soldiers in an attempt to differentiate them from Hindus (Grewal 1990: 138).

Enforcement of the army's policy dovetailed perfectly with the mission of the Singh Sabha movement, giving it legitimacy and momentum. After the first Singh Sabha was inaugurated in 1873, almost a hundred Singh Sabhas were set up across Punjab in the following thirty years, with Lahore and Amritsar as their centres. These Singh Sabhas worked hard in villages and towns to replace Hindu rites with new Sikh rites by circulating newspapers and tracts and holding lectures. Singh Sabha reformers also asked ordinary Sikhs to follow 'authentic' Sikh lifecycle rituals, which in fact had been designed by the reformers (Oberoi 1988: 150). For the Singh Sabha reformers, the gurdwara was a crucial site to exchange information and make plans. As a public space of the Sikh community, the reformers usually used the gurdwara as a centre to propagate their resolutions and educate the Sikh public. In this sense, to take control of old gurdwaras or to build their own ones often became a priority of the reformers (Grewal 2009: 276). By the early twentieth century, the Singh Sabha movement had achieved impressive success. Most Punjabi Sikhs had come to agree, more or less, with the movement's interpretation of the Sikh tradition and adopted an exclusively Sikh identity (McLeod 1989: 62).

The Singh Sabha movement also coincided with the unprecedented outflow of the Sikh population from Punjab to Southeast and East Asia by the turn of the twentieth century. It is significant here that the Sikhs had been tagged by the British as a martial race and were extensively enlisted into the Indian Army. Their martial reputation soon spread to other British colonies and settlements, in particular the Straits Settlements, Hong Kong, and the Shanghai concession. The British overseas authorities, therefore, rushed to recruit Sikhs to strengthen their own police forces. Since the salary of a policeman in the overseas colonies and settlements was much higher than that of a soldier or a farmer in India, tens of thousands Sikhs emigrated in the late nineteenth and early twentieth centuries (Cao 2014: 331).[7] Gradually, Sikh communities sprang up in Southeast and East Asia. For example, by 1896, there were 122 Sikh policemen in Singapore, 78 in Penang, and 18 in Malacca.[8]

In addition to joining the police force, some Sikh professionals also emigrated to Southeast Asia in pursuit of other job opportunities. As W.H. McLeod observes, the Singh Sabha movement was initiated by Sikh intellectuals and professionals who had received a Western education in either Lahore or Amritsar (McLeod 1989: 70). When these educated Sikhs went abroad, they took their reform ideas with them.

Sunder Singh was one such person. Sikh by origin, he graduated from the Lahore Veterinary College in the 1890s ('A Sikh Veterinary', *The Straits Times*, 17 April 1896). Although he studied veterinary medicine in college, he showed great interest in the religious movement that was taking place in Punjab at that time. Like contemporary Singh Sabha leaders such as Baba Sir Khem Singh Bedi and Bhai Kahn Singh, Sunder Singh appreciated the work done by Max Arthur Macauliffe, who was the pioneer in introducing Sikh scriptures to the English-speaking world. By corresponding with Macauliffe and other Singh Sabha leaders, Sunder Singh became an enthusiastic supporter of the Singh Sabha movement. He strongly insisted that Sikhism should be modernized and that the Sikh population needed to be educated (Macauliffe 2013: 3–28).

In April 1896, Sunder Singh was employed by the colonial authorities in Penang as the local veterinary inspector. Once he arrived in Penang, he found that local Sikhs were living in ways that were in total opposition to the precepts of the Singh Sabha movement. Most of these men were illiterate and few observed the rites of Sikhism. Furthermore, there was no public place where Sikhs could perform religious practices or hold events ('A Sikh Veterinary', *The Straits Times*, 17 April 1896). To improve the situation, Sunder Singh made a plan to set up a gurdwara in Penang and use it as the stronghold of the Singh Sabha movement in the Straits Settlements and British Malaya. He unveiled his plan during the Diamond Jubilee celebrations of Queen Victoria's reign in June 1897. Explicitly trying to obtain the support of the British, Sunder Singh announced in the Sikh police barracks that the Penang Sikhs had decided to construct a gurdwara specifically in commemoration of Queen Victoria's Diamond Jubilee ('Diamond Jubilee Permanent Memorial', *The Singapore Free Press and Mercantile Advertiser*, 20 July 1897). He further appealed to the British authorities to provide a plot of land on which the gurdwara could be built on the grounds that of all those living in Penang, only the Sikhs did not have their own place of public worship. The authorities subsequently approved the application and granted a site for its fulfilment ('Sikhs in Penang', *The Straits Times*, 1 September 1899).

In August 1899, the Sikhs in the Straits Settlements and Malaya held a large meeting in Penang at which a committee was set up to raise funds and take charge of the process of building the gurdwara. Sunder Singh was appointed the secretary of this committee ('Untitled', *The Straits Times*, 31 August 1898; 'Diamond Jubilee Permanent Memorial', *The Singapore Free Press and Mercantile Advertiser*, 20 July 1897). After two years of preparation, in June 1901, the gurdwara's foundation stone (known as the Diamond Jubilee Sikh Temple) was laid along Brick Kiln Road, Penang, in the presence of almost 400 Sikhs ('Untitled', *The Straits Times*, 8 June 1901). After the gurdwara was completed in 1903, it played a crucial role in providing a public space for local Singh Sabhas to organize religious activities, collect relief donations, and promote education among young people. Through these efforts, the Singh Sabha movement's aim of strengthening Sikh identity was largely achieved.

The case of the gurdwara in Penang shows that the Singh Sabha Movement was by no means a local movement. The emigration of the Sikh population in late nineteenth century facilitated the ideas of the Singh Sabha reformers flowing from Punjab to other parts of the world. The Diamond Jubilee Sikh Temple in Penang was not the only product of the activities of the Singh Sabha movement. The Sikhs in Hong Kong, one of the most popular destinations for Sikh emigrants in the late nineteenth and early twentieth centuries, closely watched the gurdwara plan of their Penang counterparts ('Sikh Temples', *The China Mail*, 14 June 1901). Once the news that Penang's gurdwara foundation stone had been laid reached Hong Kong, the Hong Kong Sikhs immediately set out to construct their own gurdwara ('Untitled', *The Singapore Free Press and Mercantile Advertiser*, 17 June 1901; 'Untitled', *The Straits Times*, 18 June 1901).

Disciplining Sikh Emigrants in Hong Kong by Religion

The history of the Sikhs in Hong Kong can be traced back to the 1860s. Most of these pioneers worked in the Hong Kong Police Force. In the early 1860s, the governor of Hong Kong, Sir Richard MacDonnell, castigated the Hong Kong Police Force as the most corrupt and least efficient police force he had known throughout his entire career.[9] Frustrated by the poor performance of the police and concerned about social unrest, MacDonnell proposed alternative ways to protect the colony.[10] As the governor was haunted by the deficiency of his police force, Charles Creagh, the deputy superintendent of police in Sind, was transferred to Hong Kong to act as the deputy superintendent of police in 1866.[11] Since Creagh had formed a positive view of the highly disciplined character of the Sikh policemen in his unit while he had been in India, he immediately recommended that the governor recruit some Sikhs from Punjab to police the troubled colony.[12]

MacDonnell approved this proposal in 1867. From 1867 to 1868, Creagh returned to Punjab twice to recruit suitable Sikhs, from whom he eventually recruited approximately 200.[13] Since the Hong Kong authorities offered relatively higher salaries than those offered by the Indian Army and the Straits Settlements authorities in late nineteenth century (as shown in Table 9.1), more and more Sikhs made their way to Hong Kong to seek a better livelihood.

In the years that followed, the size of the Sikh branch of the Hong Kong Police gradually grew. As shown in Table 9.2, the number of Sikhs serving in the Hong Kong Police doubled between 1875 and 1900.

Table 9.1.   Comparison of Salaries for Sikh Recruits

Straits Settlements[*]	Hong Kong[**]	Indian Army[***]
INR 200/year	INR 237/year	INR 84/year

Source: [*] Civic Establishments, 1885, pp. L50–L51, CO 277/20; [**] Hong Kong Blue Book, 1905, p. J118, Civil Establishments of Hong Kong; [***] Tan Tai Yong (2005: 79).

Table 9.2.   Number of Sikhs in the Hong Kong Police Force

Year	Sikhs in the Hong Kong Police
1875[*]	174
1880[**]	174
1890[***]	211
1900[+]	351

Sources: [*] Civil Establishment of Hong Kong for the Year 1875, Hong Kong Government Reports Online, p. 97; [**] Civil Establishment of Hong Kong for the Year 1880, Hong Kong Government Reports Online, p. 46; [***] Civil Establishment of Hong Kong for the Year 1890, Hong Kong Government Reports Online, p. 70; [+] Civil Establishment of Hong Kong for the Year 1900, Hong Kong Government Reports Online, p. 82.

Early Sikh settlers were managed like paramilitaries; they were accommodated in barracks and trained as soldiers. Although they were also assigned to metropolitan-style beat duty, such as directing traffic and checking minor offences, the result was often unsatisfactory. For example, in July 1869, a Sikh policeman was assigned to direct traffic on a street. When he saw an aged Chinese man collecting paper and rags in the middle of the street, he kicked the man's head and seriously injured him ('Sikh Brutality Again', *Hong Kong Daily Press*, 10 July 1869). In another case, a Sikh who had been patrolling a neighbourhood in July 1871 was subsequently charged with attempting to rape a Chinese girl ('A Valuable Sikh', *Hong Kong Daily Press*, 15 July 1871). However, Hong Kong authorities insisted that the Sikhs were very skilful in quelling riots, deterring secret societies, and resolving local disputes.[14] In addition, the government kept the Sikhs operational in duties such as patrolling the hill roads at night, guarding prisons and watching government buildings.[15]

In the 1870s, the Hong Kong government was notably satisfied with the service of the Sikhs.[16] When addressing the police in 1878, the Hong Kong governor, Pope Hennessy, asserted that it was one of the best in the British Empire and that the Sikh corps was a credit to the colony.[17] The character and performance of Sikhs in Hong Kong were even cited in handbooks and guides for young colonial officers (Barstow 1941; Bingley 1899). As a result, the Sikhs in Hong Kong 'acquired a reputation amongst the British officers for their loyalty and martial prowess in service to the Empire' (Kaur 2009: 19). Subsequently other colonies and settlements also attempted to establish their own Sikh police units, modelling them on Hong Kong's experience.[18]

However, as more and more Sikhs were enlisted into the police force, the colonial authorities in Hong Kong gradually lost their positive view of their Sikh policemen. Sikh misconduct was widely reported in the 1890s: In 1895, for example, there were 162 negative reports about the behaviour of Sikh policemen. Given that there were about 200 Sikh policemen in Hong Kong at that time, this figure shows that more than half of them were likely to have been guilty of misconduct in that year alone.[19] The situation worsened even further in the following years, with 320 reports being made against Sikhs in 1899.[20] It was reported that many Sikhs consumed excessive amounts of alcohol, indulged in gambling while not on duty, and frequently caused disorder in public ('Inspector Caught Two Sikh Constables Gambling with Chinese', *China Mail*, 20 August 1892). They were often blamed for either sleeping or idling on duty. Some of them even defied the orders of their officers and slipped away from their positions.[21] Furthermore, in order to earn extra money, many Sikh policemen entered the moneylending industry. This not only distracted them from their police work but also brought them into conflict with civilians ('Local and General', *Mid-Day Herald*, 13 August 1895; 'Local and General', *The Hong Kong Telegraph*, 8 October 1897; 'Hindoo Money Lending', *The Hong Kong Telegraph*, 11 June 1898).

Although the Hong Kong authorities repeatedly insisted that the Sikhs could fit well into any foreign environment, reality challenged this assumption. Depression was widely observed among the Sikhs. In February, 1894 a twenty-year-old Sikh policeman shot himself dead while on duty ('Suicide of a Sikh Constable', *Hong Kong Daily Press*, 20 February 1894). Just ten months later, another Sikh policeman lost his mind in a police station and committed suicide after killing a Chinese colleague ('Murder and Suicide at the "Central"', *The Hong Kong Telegraph*, 11 December 1894).

The British explanation for the frustrated behaviour of their Sikh policemen was that the Sikhs had lost their militant spirit in foreign lands. Most Sikh policemen working in Southeast and East Asia were from rural Punjab. Before joining overseas police forces, they had been peasants. The British, therefore, assumed that the loyalty, discipline, and bravery of the Sikh race was cultivated by the harsh living conditions in Punjabi countryside (Streets 2004). Once the Sikhs were taken to urban centres such as Singapore, Hong Kong, and Shanghai, they were exposed to urban evils such as alcohol, gambling, and prostitution. In the view of the British, these vices polluted the militant spirit of the Sikhs and reduced them to this disappointing condition ('The Sikh Gurdwara: Opening Ceremony', *The North China Herald*, 4 July 1908).

Since the Hong Kong authorities did not trust Chinese policemen and could not afford to increase the European proportion of the police force, they had no other choice but to help their Sikh staff regain their militant spirit (Cao 2015; Miners 1990). The solution was to resort to religious influence. The British held the idea that by introducing Sikhism and the teachings of Guru Nanak, who firmly forbade Sikhs from excessive drinking, smoking, and gambling, the discipline and martial spirit of their Sikh policemen could be restored ('Decrease of the Militant Spirit among the Sikhs', *The Straits Times*, 14 November 1887; 'Our Sikh Auxiliaries', *Straits Times Weekly Issue*, 22 November 1892).

The British proposal, therefore, dovetailed perfectly with the aims of the Singh Sabha movement, which was also struggling to promote religious learning among the Sikh population in order to bolster Sikh identity. The Singh Sabha reformers, in their turn, had already set out to transform Hong Kong into a stronghold of their movement.

Bhai Raga Singh was born into a rich Sikh family in a village near Ludhiana, Punjab, in the 1860s. During his childhood, he received systematic education in the Sikh classics. He was then sent to a missionary school in Amritsar to learn English and obtained Western knowledge. While at the missionary school, however, he witnessed the conversion of large number of Sikh students to Christianity. This experience stimulated his commitment to Sikhism. While still at school, he took part in the Singh Sabha movement and worked hard to establish codes of conduct and lifestyle in the local community in accordance with the teachings of the Sikh classics. He also wrote articles arguing against the Arya Samaj's conviction that all Sikhs were Hindus.[22]

In the 1890s, Bhai Raga Singh saw many Sikhs in his village migrating abroad. However, few Sikh priests and scholars were willing to follow the flow of emigration to promote the cause of the Singh Sabha movement overseas. Bhai Raga Singh then decided to reverse this trend. His first stop was British Malaya, where he spent three or four years teaching emigrants Sikh traditions and religious precepts.

As he had heard that a big Sikh community was forming in Hong Kong, Bhai Raga Singh headed to this colony in 1895. Once he arrived there, he found that the Sikhs there were doing everything contrary to the teachings of Guru Nanak. In order to improve the situation, Bhai Raga Singh made contact with Subadar Teja Singh, the leader of the Sikhs in the Hong Kong–Singapore Royal Artillery, which was then based in Hong Kong. Subadar Teja Singh agreed with Bhai Raga Singh that a Singh Sabha should be set up in Hong Kong to promote education, welfare and religious identity among local Sikhs.[23]

While Subadar Teja Singh and Bhai Raga Singh were planning the inauguration of the Hong Kong Singh Sabha in 1899, news of Sunder Singh's request to build a gurdwara in Penang and the formation of a committee of the Gurdwara Sahib in that colony spread to Hong Kong ('Sikh Temples', *The China Mail*, 14 June 1901). Incentivized by the actions of their Penang counterparts, Subadar Teja Singh persuaded local Sikh notables to found a similar gurdwara committee to request a gurdwara for Hong Kong. The committee soon materialized, and Subadar Teja Singh was elected its president. Unlike the Penang gurdwara committee, which was supported by Sikhs across Malaya, the Hong Kong gurdwara committee could not obtain sufficient help from the outside. A shortage of funds, therefore, became the most serious challenge to this initiative on the part of Bhai Raga Singh and his colleagues ('The New Sikh and Hindu Temple', *The Hong Kong Telegraph*, 12 May 1902).

Opportunity Provided by the China Field Force

During the opening ceremony of the Sikh temple in Hong Kong in May 1902, Subadar Teja Singh announced that, although the Sikh community in Hong Kong had been very enthusiastic about building a gurdwara in the past few years, the heavy cost had seriously slowed the progress of this project. However, he added that the arrival of the China Field Force had relieved that financial burden and greatly facilitated the building ('Opening of a Sikh Temple in Hong Kong', *The Hong Kong Weekly Press*, 19 May 1902). But what was the China Field Force, why did it come to Hong Kong, and why did it help with the building of the gurdwara?

In 1899 and 1900, the Boxer Uprising plunged northern China into chaos (Bickers and Tiedeman 2007; Cohen 1998; Esherick 1988). As thousands of foreign civilians, soldiers, and Chinese Christians were besieged in the diplomatic compound and the North Cathedral in Beijing, an international coalition was created to break the siege. The coalition was composed of troops mainly from eight powers: Japan, Russia, the British Empire, France, USA, Germany, Italy, and Austria-Hungary. The British Empire dispatched about 10,000 soldiers to take part in this campaign, among them the First Sikh Infantry Regiment, mainly composed of Sikh soldiers. This unit became the China Field Force mentioned in Subadar Teja Singh's address.

The First Sikh Infantry Regiment was a unit of the British Indian Army. It had long been affiliated to the Punjab Frontier Force and had been assigned to defend and maintain order along Punjab border with Afghanistan (Condon 1962). In early 1900, the regiment was in Kohat, south of Peshawar, to fight against some Afghan tribes along the border.[24] On 28 June 1900, the regiment received orders to join the expedition to break the siege in Beijing. The whole unit, with 8 British officers, 61 native officers, and 647 Indian soldiers (most of them Sikhs), was transported to Calcutta (now Kolkata) on 6 July 1900.[25]

The ship that took the regiment to China stopped at Hong Kong on 19 July 1900, and the soldiers were given one day to relax. Upon landing in Hong Kong, they found that they were welcomed by the local Sikh community. Nevertheless, they failed to find a gurdwara in the colony that could meet their religious needs, provide them with Punjabi cuisine and entertainment, or give them a public space in which they could acknowledge the generous treatment they received in Hong Kong. Instead, they were told of the financial difficulties of constructing a gurdwara in the colony. A call for donations was immediately made, and all Sikh soldiers in the regiment eventually donated a month's salary to the cause. In total, a sum of 1,461 Mexican silver dollars was collected from the First Sikh Infantry Regiment ('The New Sikh and Hindu Temple', *The Hong Kong Telegraph*, 12 May 1902).

The First Sikhs left Hong Kong a few days later and arrived in Tianjin at the end of July 1900. It fought against the Boxers and Chinese troops in Tianjin and Beijing until the Chinese capital fell to the international forces on 15 August 1900 (Yang 2015).[26] The regiment camped in the neighbourhood of Beijing for another ten months until it had completed its mission, and sailed back to India in May 1901 (Thacker, Spink and Co. 1903: 83–6). In the same month, the foundation stone of the Hong Kong gurdwara, to which the Sikh soldiers in the First Sikh Infantry Regiment had contributed so much, was laid ('Untitled', *The Straits Times*, 18 June 1901).

On the morning of 10 May 1902, a procession consisting of colonial officials and local Indians and headed by the Band of the Hong Kong–Singapore Royal Artillery marched towards a site behind

Figure 9.3   The Hong Kong Gurdwara in 1902

Source: Courtesy of Sri Guru Singh Sabha, Hong Kong.

Morrison Hill on Queen's Road East, Wanchai, Hong Kong Island. On the site stood a two-storey building, a gurdwara named after Sri Guru Singh Sabha (Figure 9.3). The first floor of the gurdwara was designed to accommodate visitors, with a space big enough for forty people to stay there at the same time. This floor was also used for preparing food and dining. The second floor housed the main offices of the priests and secretaries, with a hall just beside the offices. The Sikh Holy Book (the Adi Granth) was placed at the innermost end of this hall, and believers practiced religious rites in front of it. It was at the front of this hall that Subadar Teja Singh announced the opening of the gurdwara ('Opening of a Sikh Temple in Hong Kong', *The Hong Kong Weekly Press*, 19 May 1902).

Since its inauguration, the gurdwara had served as the centre of the Singh Sabha movement in Hong Kong. The work of the Singh Sabha reformers was paid off as the Sikh identity was strengthened in the early twentieth century. Religious teachers from Punjab were accommodated in the gurdwara for organizing Sikh festivals such as Vaisakhi (celebrating the birth of the Khalsa brotherhood by offering respect to the Guru Granth Sahib in the gurdwara), Bandi Chhor Divas (celebrating the release from prison of Guru Hargobind by going to the gurdwara to listen to the preaching), and Guru Nanak Gurpurab (celebrating the birthday of Guru Nanak by reading the Guru Granth Sahib and singing hymns in the gurdwara). The Singh Sabha reformers also used the gurdwara as a school to provide both secure and religious education to Sikh youths. Local Sikhs were asked to donate money to the gurdwara to establish a charity fund to help the destitute and homeless. To fully discipline the local Sikhs, the Singh Sabha reformers set up the Khalsa Diwan Board in the gurdwara to watch over the behaviour of local Sikhs. Disputes among Sikhs were brought to the gurdwara to be settled, instead of being taken to court directly (Batra 2005; Kwok and Narain 2003; Viad 1972; White 1994).

Contrary to the expectation of the British authorities that the Singh Sabha movement could help them better discipline the Sikh population in Hong Kong, the strengthened Sikh identity echoed the Indian nationalist movement instead. Between 1910s and 1940s, the gurdwara was also used by Indian revolutionaries as a meeting place to organize and plan anti-British struggles in Asia. Seditious publications were brought into the gurdwara from abroad before being distributed to local Sikhs (Cao 2015).

During the Second World War, the gurdwara was bombed by the Japanese and suffered extensive damage. However, it still played a significant role in accommodating Sikh and other Indian refugees. When the War ended, the gurdwara was repaired and even extended. The post-War economic boom made Hong Kong an ideal destination

Figure 9.4   The Main Hall of the Hong Kong Gurdwara

Source: Photographed by the author.

for Sikh migrants: The Sikh population in Hong Kong increased from around 700 in the early twentieth century to more than 8,000 a century later. Over the course of its development, the gurdwara served more social functions. A kindergarten was built in the basement of the gurdwara to cater to Sikh children, and language, music, and even computer classes were held in the gurdwara to provide local Sikhs with a better education (Figure 9.4). Through these initiatives, the primary aims of the Singh Sabha reformers to strengthen the specific Sikh identity and increase the cohesion of Sikh communities overseas have been generally achieved (Batra 2005; Chuek 2008).

***

The story of the Sri Guru Singh Sabha Gurdwara does not end in Hong Kong. The donation list of the Hong Kong gurdwara indicates that the Sikh constables in the Shanghai Municipal Council (SMC) donated some 600 Hong Kong dollars to it ('New Sikh and Hindu Temple', *The Hong Kong Telegraph*, 12 May 1902). In fact, the SMC badly needed to improve its Sikh constables' morale and efficiency in the first decade of the twentieth century. The SMC believed that the Singh Sabha-based gurdwara could greatly facilitate its administration of all Sikhs in Shanghai, including policemen, watchmen, and the unemployed. With the help of the Singh Sabha reformers, the authorities wanted to impose religious teachings on their Sikh subjects and thus prevent serious misconduct. Because of these considerations, the SMC had a growing interest in the work of the Hong Kong gurdwara ('Late Telegraphs', *North China Herald*, 9 August 1907).

After years of consideration and observation, the SMC sanctioned a plan to build a gurdwara in their city in 1906 (Shanghai Municipal Council 2001). Agents were soon dispatched to Hong Kong to learn the details of the building. Blueprints and plans of Hong Kong's gurdwara were also obtained and taken back to Shanghai.[27] Based on the Hong Kong model, a gurdwara was erected in North Sichuan Road in the International Settlement of Shanghai in June 1908 ('The Sikh Gurdwara: Opening Ceremony', *North China Herald*, 4 July 1908).[28]

The connections between the gurdwaras in Penang, Hong Kong, and Shanghai demonstrate the mechanism of the Sikh diasporic network. What sustained this network was actually the circulation of Sikh policemen, professionals, and soldiers across the globe by the turn of the twentieth century. These agents in motion were by no means unrelated to each other, but closely intertwined. It was their coming together in Asian port cities such as Penang, Hong Kong, and Shanghai that facilitated the outflow of the Singh Sabha movement.

The cross-boundary mobility of the Singh Sabha reformers and institutions also reflects the multifaceted nature of the British Empire. For quite a long time, scholarship on the British Empire was dominated by the dichotomy between metropole and colony. On the one hand, historians highlight how the imperial centre influenced and transformed almost all aspects of the colonies and its colonized subjects. On the other hand, revisionists contend that the British imperial system was a process of mutual interaction and that the social, economic, and cultural landscapes of the metropole were subjected to constant influence from the colonies (Ghosh 2012; Hall 2002; Hall and Rose 2006; Thompson 2005, 2013).

The rise of global history in recent years, with its emphasis on concepts such as networks and circulation, has provided imperial historians with a chance to review the metropole–colony dichotomy. A growing number of scholars have been willing to see the British Empire not as a vertical structure only concerned with the linear interaction between the metropole and the individual colonies, but as a horizontal structure that connected different parts of the Empire and beyond (Crosbie 2011; Grant, Levine, and Trentmann 2007; Hillemann 2009; Lambert and Lester 2006; Lester 2006).

It is in this context that some scholars have come to take India, not Britain, as the metropole of the British Empire. From Cape Town to Shanghai, Indian soldiers were deployed to put down uprisings and defend newly conquered territories, Indian policemen were employed to maintain social order, and Indian indentured workers were contracted to construct the railways. Furthermore, colonial officers who had received their training in the Raj transplanted their experience and knowledge of India to other parts of the Empire (Aiyar 2015; Metcalf 2007). In this sense, the British Empire had an Indian face (Jackson 2012).

By exploring the stories behind the gurdwara in Hong Kong, this chapter echoes the argument that focus of the British Empire should be shifted to India. It further contends that Indians were not exclusively employed, enlisted, indentured, or manipulated by the British in this India-centred British Empire. Instead, some Indians made good use of imperial infrastructures to facilitate their own businesses, seek better livelihoods, and set up religious institutions by negotiating and collaborating with the British colonial authorities. In so doing, they ceased to be the subjects of the British world system and became its engineers.

Notes

1. Langar is a Punjabi term meaning 'canteen'. According to Sikhism, all gurdwaras are required to have a langar to provide free meals for all visitors regardless of their religion, ethnicity, or social status.
2. J.S. Grewal (1990: 133) argues that communal consciousness took shape among Hindus, Muslims, and Sikhs in Punjab almost spontaneously in the late nineteenth century. All groups adopted more or less similar techniques to promote their communal identities.

3. One main reason why the British had no interest in recruiting the Sikhs into the Indian Army was the very fact that they had fought so well in the Anglo-Sikh wars, making the British afraid of a possible Sikh mutiny in their own army in the future.

4. Reportedly, 23,000 Sikhs joined the British in fighting to suppress the Mutiny.

5. Other typical 'martial races' in South Asia were the Gurkhas in Nepal and Muslims in northwest India.

6. The Five Ks' symbolize the five articles of faith and are worn by Sikhs at all times. They are Kesh (uncut hair), Kangha (a wooden comb), Kara (a metal bracelet), Kachera (a cotton undergarment), and Kirpan (a sword).

7. In 1900, while a Sikh soldier in the Indian Army could earn INR 84 a year, a Sikh policeman in Singapore could earn INR 272 a year.

8. Annual Report on the Straits Settlements Police and on the State of Crime for the Year 1896, Colonial Office Records (CO) 275/53, p. 47.

9. MacDonnell to Colonial Office, 7 January 1867, CO 129/120, pp. 42–6.

10. MacDonnell to Colonial Office, 7 January 1867, CO 129/120, pp. 42–82.

11. *Hong Kong Government Gazette*, no. 87, 8 June 1867. In this document Creagh's name was wrongly given as Giles Creagh, but in the erratum of the Government Gazette, 15 June 1867, his name was corrected as Charles Creagh.

12. MacDonnell to Colonial Office, 7 January 1867, CO 129/120, pp. 42–82.

13. *Hong Kong Government Gazette*, no. 2, 23 May 1868, p. 198; MacDonnell to Duke of Birmingham & Chandos, 8 June 1868, CO 129/122, pp. 135–40.

14. *Hong Kong Government Gazette*, no. 44, 17 April 1869, p. 210; Whitfield to Colonial Office, 28 September 1870, CO 129/145, pp. 414–22; *Hong Kong Blue Book*, 4 February 1873.

15. *Hong Kong Government Gazette*, no. 40, 16 April 1870, p. 188.

16. India Office to F. Roger, 20 March 1868, CO 129/134, pp. 631–6; *Hong Kong Government Gazette*, no. 44, 17 April 1869, p. 210; *Hong Kong Government Gazette*, no. 40, 16 April 1870, p. 188; *Hong Kong Government Gazette*, no. 90, 24 June 1871, p. 282.

17. *Hong Kong Government Gazette*, no. 43, 9 March 1878, p. 89.

18. One example was the Bahamas. When the Bahamas government proposed to reorganize its police force in the 1880s, they took Sikhs into account, based on the information that Sikhs behaved well in Asia, especially Hong Kong. See Shea to Knutsford, 7 November 1890, CO 23/2322.

19. Report of the Acting Captain Superintendent of Police for 1895, *Hong Kong Government Reports Online*, p. 110.

20. Report of the Captain Superintendent of Police for the Year 1899, *Hong Kong Government Reports Online*, p. 200.

21. Report of the Captain Superintendent of Police for the Year 1898, *Hong Kong Government Reports Online*, p. 135.

22. In its early years, Arya Samaj leaders in Punjab appreciated the works and thoughts of Sikh gurus, thereby attracting a large number of Sikh followers. Nevertheless, when it had been established firmly in Punjab, Arya Samaj leaders came to preach that Sikhism was simply a branch of Hinduism and asked their Sikh followers to convert to the Hindu mainstream.

23. The life and travels of Bhai Raga Singh was told to me by Mr Sukha Singh Gill, the President of Khalsa Diwan Hong Kong, whom I interviewed in May 2016.

24. Thacker, Spink and Co. (1903: 82).

25. Thacker, Spink and Co. (1903: 83).

26. The war experience of Indian soldiers in China during the Boxer uprising has been well researched by Yang (2015).

27. Report for the Year 1906, U1-1-918, pp. 22–4, Shanghai Municipal Archives, Municipal Council of Shanghai.

28. Report for the Year 1908, U1-1-921, pp. 13–14, Shanghai Municipal Archives, Municipal Council of Shanghai. On the Sikh policemen in Shanghai, see also Mangalagiri's chapter in this volume.

References

Archival Material

Colonial Office Records

Annual Report on the Straits Settlements Police and on the State of Crime for the Year 1896, CO 275/53, p. 47.

MacDonnell to Colonial Office, 7 January 1867, CO 129/120, pp. 42–82.

MacDonnell to Duke of Birmingham & Chandos, 8 June 1868, CO 129/122, pp. 135–40.

Civic Establishments, 1885, pp. L50–L51, CO 277/20.

Whitfield to Colonial Office, 28 September 1870, CO 129/145, pp. 414–22.

India Office to F. Roger, 20 March 1868, CO 129/134, pp. 631–6.

Shea to Knutsford, 7 November 1890, CO 23/2322.

Shanghai Municipal Archives, Municipal Council of Shanghai, China

Report for the Year 1906, U1-1-918, pp. 22–4.

Report for the Year 1908, U1-1-921, pp. 13–14.

Hong Kong Government Gazette, The University of Hong Kong Libraries, Hong Kong

Nos 2, 40, 44, 87, 90, 43.

Hong Kong Government Reports Online, The University of Hong Kong Libraries, Hong Kong

Civil Establishment of Hong Kong for the Years 1875, 1880, 1890, 1900.
Reports of the Acting Captain Superintendent of Police for 1895, 1898, 1899.

Hong Kong Blue Book, The University of Hong Kong Libraries, Hong Kong

1873, 1905.

Other Sources

Aiyar, Sana. 2015. *Indians in Kenya: The Politics of Diaspora*. Cambridge, MA: Harvard University Press.

Allen, Charles. 2000. *Soldier Sahibs: The Daring Adventurers Who Tamed India's Northwest Frontier*. New York: Carroll & Graf.

Axel, Brian Keith. 2001. *The Nation's Tortured Body: Violence, Representation, and the Formation of a Sikh Diaspora*. Durham: Duke University Press.

Ballantyne, Tony. 2006. *Between Colonialism and Diaspora: Sikh Cultural Formations in an Imperial World*. Durham, NC: Duke University Press.

Ballantyne, Tony and Antoinette Burton. 2014. *Empires and the Reach of the Global*. Cambridge: Harvard University Press.

Banga, Indu. 1978. *Agrarian System of the Sikhs*. New Delhi: Manohar.

Barrier, N.G. 1968. 'The Punjab Government and Communal Politics, 1870–1908'. *Journal of Asian Studies* 27 (3): 523–39.

———. 1988. 'Sikh Politics in British Punjab Prior to the Gurdwara Reform Movement'. In Joseph O'Connell, Milton Israel, and Willard Oxtoby (eds), *Sikh History and Religion in the Twentieth Century*, p. 171. Toronto: University of Toronto Center for South Asian Studies.

———. 1998. 'The Singh Sabhas and the Evolution of Modern Sikhism, 1875–1925'. In Robert Baird (ed.), *Religion in Modern India*, pp. 129–223. New Delhi: Manohar.

———. 2000. 'Competing Visions of Sikh Religion and Politics: The Chief Khalsa Diwan and the Panch Khalsa Diwan, 1902–1928'. *South Asia: Journal of South Asian Studies* 23 (2): 33–62.

Barstow, A.E. 1941. *Handbooks for the Indian Army: Sikhs*. New Delhi: The Manager Government of India Press.

Batra, Gulbir Singh. 2005. *Sikhs in Hong Kong*. Hong Kong: Sri Guru Singh Educational Trust.

Bickers, Robert, and R.G. Tiedeman (eds). 2007. *The Boxers, China, and the World*. Lanham, MD: Rowman & Littlefield.

Bingley, A.H. 1899. *Caste Handbooks for the India Army: Sikhs*. Shimla: Government of India Printing.

Cao, Yin (曹寅). 2014. 'The Journey of Isser Singh: A Global Microhistory of a Sikh Migrant'. *Journal of Punjab Studies* 21 (2): 325–54.

———. 2015. 'Quanqiushi shijiao xia de zhimin diguo shi yanjiu: Yi Xinjiapo he Xianggang de xike jingcha wei zhongxin de tantao' (全球史視角下的殖民帝國史研究：以錫克警察為中心的探討) ['Colonial Empire and Global History: A Study on the Sikh Police Units in Hong Kong and Singapore']. *Ershiyi shiji* (二十一世紀) [*Twentieth-First Century*] 147 (1): 82–100.

Chuek, Ka Kin. 2008. 'Transnational Connections, Local Life, and Identity: A Study of the Sikhs in Hong Kong'. MPhil Thesis, Chinese University of Hong Kong.

Cohen, Paul. 1998. *History in Three Keys: The Boxers as Event, Experience, and Myth*. New York: Columbia University Press.

Cohn, Bernard. 1996. *Colonialism and Its Forms of Knowledge: The Birth of India*. Princeton: Princeton University Press.

Condon, Brig. 1962. *The Frontier Force Regiment*. Aldershot: Gale & Polden.

Cook, Hugh. 1975. *The Sikh Wars: The British Army in Punjab, 1845–49*. New Delhi: Thomson Press.

Crosbie, Barry. 2011. *Irish Imperial Networks: Migration, Social Communication and Exchange in Nineteenth-Century India*. Cambridge: Cambridge University Press.

David, Saul. 2002. *The Indian Mutiny: 1857*. London: Viking.

Dusenbery, Verne. 1995. 'A Sikh Diaspora? Contested Identities and Constructed Realities'. In Peter Van der Veer (ed.), *Nation and Migration: The Politics of Space in the South Asian Diaspora*, pp. 17–42. Philadelphia: University of Pennsylvania Press.

Esherick, Joseph. 1988. *The Origin of the Boxer Uprising*. Berkeley: University of California Press.

Fox, Richard. 1987. *Lions of the Punjab: Culture in the Making*. Berkeley: University of California Press.

Ghosh, Durba. 2012. 'Another Set of Imperial Turns?'. *The American Historical Review* 117 (3): 772–93.

Grant, Kevin, Philippa Levine, and Frank Trentmann (eds). 2007. *Beyond Sovereignty: Britain Empire, and Transnationalism, 1880–1950*. New York: Palgrave MacMillan.

Grewal, J.S. 1990. *The New Cambridge History of India, Volume 2.* Cambridge: Cambridge University Press.

———. 1998. *The Sikhs of the Punjab.* Cambridge: Cambridge University Press.

———. 2009. *The Sikhs: Ideology, Institutions, and Identity.* New Delhi: Oxford University Press.

Hall, Catherine. 2002. *Civilising Subjects: Metropole and Colony in the English Imagination 1830–1867.* Chicago: The University of Chicago Press.

Hall, Catherine and Sonya Rose (eds). 2006. *At Home with the Empire: Metropolitan Culture and the Imperial World.* Cambridge: Cambridge University Press.

Hillemann, Ulrike. 2009. *Asian Empire and British Knowledge: China and the Networks of British Imperial Expansion.* New York: Palgrave Macmillan.

Jackson, Isabella. 2012. 'The Raj on Nanjing Road: Sikh Policemen in Treaty-Port Shanghai'. *Modern Asian Studies* 46 (6): 1672–704.

Jones, Kenneth. 1973. 'Ham Hindu Nahin: Arya Sikh Relations, 1877–1905'. *Journal of Asian Studies* 32 (3): 457–75.

Kaur, Arunajeet. 2009. *Sikhs in the Policing of British Malaya and Straits Settlements (1874–1957).* Saarbrucken: VDM Verlag Dr. Muller.

Khilnani, Niranjan. 1972. *British Power in the Punjab, 1839–1858.* Bombay: Asia Publishing House.

Kwok, Siu-tong and Kirti Narain. 2003. *Co-Prosperity in Cross-Culturalism: Indians in Hong Kong.* Hong Kong: Chinese University Press.

Lambert, David and Alan Lester (eds). 2006. *Colonial Lives across the British Empire: Imperial Careering in the Long Nineteenth Century.* Cambridge: Cambridge University Press.

Lester, Alan. 2006. 'Imperial Circuits and Networks: Geographies of the British Empire'. *History Compass* 4 (1): 124–41.

Macauliffe, Max Arthur. 2013. *The Sikh Religion: Its Gurus, Sacred Writings and Authors,* Volume 1. Cambridge: Cambridge University Press.

McLeod, W.H. 1989. *Who Is a Sikh? The Problem of Sikh Identity.* Oxford: Clarendon Press.

Metcalf, Thomas. 2007. *Imperial Connections: India in the Indian Ocean Arena, 1860–1920.* Berkeley: University of California Press.

Miners, Norman. 1990. 'The Localization of the Hong Kong Police Force, 1842–1947'. *The Journal of Imperial and Commonwealth History* 18 (3): 296–315.

Oberoi, Harjot. 1988. 'From Ritual to Counter-Ritual: Rethinking the Hindu-Sikh Question, 1884–1915'. In Joseph O'Connell, Milton Israel, and Willard Oxtoby (eds), *Sikh History and Religion in the Twentieth Century,* pp. 136–57 Toronto: University of Toronto Center for South Asian Studies.

Omissi, David. 1994. *The Sepoy and the Raj: The Indian Army, 1860–1940.* London: Macmillan.

Roy, Kaushik. 2008. *Brown Warriors of the Raj: Recruiting and the Mechanics of Command in the Sepoy Army, 1859–1913*. New Delhi: Manohar.

Shanghai Municipal Council (ed.). 2001. *The Minutes of the Shanghai Municipal Council: 1920–1921*, Volume 16. Shanghai: Shanghai Gujichubanshe.

Singh, Nazer. 2012. *Modern Sikh Studies and Historiography*. New Delhi: K.K. Publications.

Streets, Heather. 2004. *Martial Races: The Military, Race and Masculinity in British Imperial Culture*. Manchester: Manchester University Press.

Tan Tai Yong. 2005. *The Garrison State: The Military, Government and Society in Colonial Punjab, 1849–1947*, pp. 79. New Delhi: SAGE.

Tatla, Darshan Singh. 2005. *The Sikh Diaspora: The Search for Statehood*. London: Routledge.

Thacker, Spink and Co. 1903. *History of the 1st Sikh Infantry, 1887–1901*, Volume 2. Calcutta.

Thompson, Andrew. 2005. *The Empire Strikes Back? The Impact of Imperialism on Britain from the Mid-Nineteenth Century*. Harlow: Person Education.

——— (ed.). 2013. *Writing Imperial Histories*. Manchester: Manchester University Press.

Vaid, K.N. 1972. *The Overseas Indian Community in Hong Kong*. Hong Kong: Center of Asian Studies, University of Hong Kong.

White, Barbara-Sue. 1994. *Turbans and Traders: Hong Kong's Indian Communities*. New Delhi: Oxford University Press.

Yang, Anand. 2015. 'China and India Are One: A Subaltern's Vision of "Hindu China" during the Boxer Expedition of 1900–1901'. In Eric Tagliacozzo, Helen Siu, and Peter Perdue (eds), *Asia Inside Out: Changing Times*, pp. 207–25. Cambridge: Harvard University Press.

10

Mecca between China and India

Wartime Chinese Islamic Diplomatic Missions across the Indian Ocean

JANICE HYEJU JEONG

The travels, settlements, and cartographic imaginations of diverse Chinese Muslim (Hui) populations have unfolded in and around the Indian Ocean from as early as the eighth century, when merchants and soldiers from Arabia, Persia, and Central Asia arrived in the coasts and cities of China's empires.[1] Ports on the South China Sea and the Indian Ocean, centres of which changed at different times, mediated the commercial and religious journeys of Muslims between China and the rest of Eurasia. The pilgrimage to Mecca was a constant factor that facilitated the mobility of a limited number of Muslims from China's different geographies. Until air travel was popularized in the second half of the twentieth century, both Turkic- and Chinese-speaking Muslims constituted a pilgrimage traffic that utilized a combination of maritime and overland routes.

The Second Sino-Japanese War (1937–45) or the War of Resistance radically politicized the activities of Chinese Muslims in Mecca and its interconnected sites across the Indian Ocean. Four months after the outbreak of the War in July 1937, a Chinese Islamic Goodwill Mission to the Near East consisting of five members set out on its diplomatic travels. For the heterogeneous group of Chinese Muslim writers and entrepreneurs who had developed a political conscious-ness and actual partnerships with the emerging states of post-Qing China, transit points in the Indian Ocean represented an external arena that they could expediently mobilize in order to undertake diplo-matic propaganda on behalf of the Nationalist state. Imperial Japan's uses of Islam as a foreign policy—attracting Turkic exiles from Soviet territories to Tokyo, sending its Muslim agents as surveyors of the Middle East and Southeast Asia, and propagandizing among Muslim populations in China to resist Chinese oppression—aroused heated criticisms from Nationalist-affiliated Chinese Muslims, but they also offered a precedent to follow and a model to emulate.[2]

Representatives of the Goodwill Mission combined pilgrimage routes with projects of diplomatic outreach, thereby establishing a practice for both the Nationalist Party and the Communist Party that would outlast the Second Sino-Japanese War itself. Arranging diplo-matic travel around the pilgrimage meant that the delegates could achieve their agendas in multiple locales in one go. Participation in the pilgrimage enabled not only encounters with dignitaries present at the largest religious congregation in Mecca, but also brief transi-tions and extended sojourns in the wide-ranging geographies that lay between China and Arabia.

Among the locations where the Goodwill Mission disembarked and stayed for lengthy periods in 1938 were cities and ports in India. Equipped with the language of Islamic solidarity and transnational anti-imperialism, Chinese Muslim cultural ambassadors who were endorsed by the Nationalist Party forged connections with a sec-tion of political and religious dignitaries who represented India's Muslim populations, and later established the new state of Pakistan. Simultaneously, the delegates undertook propaganda activities among diaspora communities who had hailed from within China's tenuous borders, including those from the present-day Xinjiang Province. In this way, the Goodwill Mission and subsequent Islamic delegations offered the Nationalist state an extra arm in building relations with political leaders who could be approached though the rhetoric of shared Islamic brotherhood—however tenuous that may be—and in concurrently attempting to appeal to Chinese and Turkic Muslim diasporas. As Brian Tsui shows in this volume and elsewhere (Tsui 2018: 195–228), the divisions between culture, politics, and diplomacy were by no means clear at this juncture when the contradictory forces of Euro-American imperial hegemony, claims to anti-imperial pan-Asianist solidarity, and the ideals of a sovereign nation undergirded the dynamics of the international order. While China was wedded to military and material support from Britain and USA, a critical strategic alliance that Liao Wen-shuo unearths in this volume, senior Nationalists exploited 'pan-Asianist, anti-colonial, and international discourse in their diplomatic manoeuvres'.[3] If leading Buddhist figures and organizations offered the Nationalist Party flexible outlets to forge linkages with the non-Han Tibetan populations and socio-political associations in India, wartime Chinese Islamic missions provided bridges to another geographic nexus of the expansively defined Islamic world.[4]

Building on existing surveys of the Goodwill Mission, this chapter explores its previously unexamined activities in India, which involved interactions with prominent local figures and simultaneously with diaspora communities from western and southeastern China.[5] On the level of the state, Chinese Islamic delegations between 1937 and 1947 carried messages of goodwill between Nationalist China, the Indian National Congress, and the future founders of the state of Pakistan, potentially catalysing the establishment of official diplomatic relations between Nationalist China and Pakistan upon the latter's founding. The delegations' encounters with and outreach towards émigré from within China's borders, on the other hand, reveal an existing traffic of travellers, traders, escapees, and labourers between ports in India and China that had long preceded the Chinese Islamic delegations.

Since the founding of the People's Republic of China (PRC), Muslim populations have been categorized into ten out of fifty-five non-Han 'minority nationalities'. Scholarship within the PRC tends to portray the Chinese Muslim Goodwill Mission as an exemplar of the patriotic resistance of an ethnic minority against the Japanese Empire, a narrative produced through a politics of its own.[6] The Mission, however, had a much more flexible understanding of Muslims as a group cutting across ethnic or national categories. Prior to the Second Sino-Japanese War, they had already formed part of a circle of writers, religious scholars, entrepreneurs, politicians, and translators who had constructed social spaces across the Indian Ocean and imaginations on the Islamic world including India that far exceeded the confines of an ethnic minority bounded within a nation-state.

These universalist languages and transnational networks were both a symbolic and a real resource that the pilgrim-cum-delegates of the Mission and those who followed them continued to reformulate, even while performing their roles as diplomatic representatives of the Nationalist state. Following their dispersal to places outside mainland China after the victory of the Communist Party in 1949, including Pakistan, Malaysia, and Taiwan, members of the Goodwill Mission reknitted networks of religion, politics, and kinship. Their colourful biographies and itineraries unravel both the ethnic minority paradigm and the physical and conceptual confines of the nation-state and area studies. Instead, we see the dynamic worlds that Chinese Muslims constructed and occupied as they traversed the wide-ranging geographies within which South Asia was situated.

Chinese Islamic Associations and the Goodwill Mission

On the cracked and termite-bitten pages of the notes of Ibrahim Ma Tianying (馬天英) (1900–82) from 1937 and 1938, pressed hard with pencil and pen are the names and addresses of several persons in Calcutta (now Kolkata), Lahore, Karachi, and Bombay (now Mumbai). The scribbles include a list of local English-language newspapers such as the *Eastern Times* in Lahore, the *Sind Sentinel* in Karachi, the *Bombay Chronicle*, and *Patrika* in Calcutta. On a sheet or two, Ibrahim Ma practised writing 'good morning' and the numbers one to four in Arabic with great care. On another page designed for recording daily expenditures, he wrote down his own calculations of the number of Muslims in Egypt (2 million), China (50 million), India (84.7 million), Turkey (20 million), France (200,000), England (30,000), Asia, and finally the world. Several of the persons he encountered left their signatures or remarks in the said notebook.[7]

Ma jotted down these notes as he travelled across the South China Seas and the Indian Ocean as one of the main leaders of the Chinese Islamic Goodwill Mission to the Near East (16 November 1937–25 January 1939). Leading the Mission was his colleague Jelāl al-Dīn Wang Zengshan (王曾善) (1903–61), who had studied in Istanbul in the 1920s. Wang Zengshan's own notes outlined the team's mission in two succinct sentences: 'On the surface: to conduct visits as China's Muslim believers. In reality: to proclaim Japan's violence perpetrated in China and sell nation-saving bonds'.[8] Wang Zengshan's draft plan, which included expected fees of 17,323 yuan and a duration of seven months, proposed to visit seven countries and twenty-six cities. According to the schedule, the itinerary would start with departure from Shanghai, followed by a transition in Hong Kong; the delegation would then enter India and proceed to Iran, Iraq, Palestine, Arabia, and Egypt, returning to Shanghai via the 'South Seas' (*Nanyang* [南洋]).

The Chinese Islamic Goodwill Mission to the Near East represented the first-known instance in which an organized group of Chinese Muslims assumed roles as diplomats across the oceans by drawing explicitly on their religious background and discourse. During the fourteen months from the time of their departure from Nanjing to their return to Chongqing, the five members of the delegation transited through or sojourned in a dozen cities including Hong Kong, Singapore, Suez, Jeddah, Mecca, Cairo, Alexandria, Haifa, Beirut, Damascus, Baghdad, Isfahan, Bushehr, Bombay, Karachi, Istanbul, Ankara, Djibouti, Aden, Colombo, Pondicherry, Madras, Haiphong, Hanoi, and Laoka. They arranged the schedules of their travels according to the timing of the annual hajj or the pilgrimage to Mecca (Wang 1997: vii). Throughout their visits, the members delivered lectures to propagandize Japanese aggression in China, attended meetings and receptions, visited mosques, museums, and zoos, and conversed with more than sixty religious and political dignitaries. The list included Muhammad Ali Jinnah (1876–1948) of the Muslim League.

When Wang Zengshan assumed the position of the Mission's leader, he had been serving in the Legislative Yuan as a representative of Muslims in China and was a professor at Shanghai's Jinan University. To make his case for the Goodwill Mission, Wang Zengshan combined overlapping strands of universalisms between East and West Asia to appeal to the idea of solidarity between 'weak nations', to which China and countries in the Islamic world belonged. Wang Zengshan reasoned in his draft proposal:

> The world's weak nations [*minzu* (民族)] are dispersed in the two con-
> tinents of Africa and Asia. What is most important to me is tying those
> in Asia together with our nation [minzu] to form relations that are tight
> as lips and teeth. Their struggles have already produced fruitful results,
> and hope lies in the future. For instance, Turkey, Iran, Afghanistan
> and Arabia and Africa's Egypt are all weak nations but are now break-
> ing away from the yoke of imperialism. One after another they are
> annulling consular jurisdiction and are seeking to acquire complete
> autonomy.[9]

Wang Zengshan stressed that whereas conventional diplomats regarded Europe and America (Oumei [欧美]) as the most important parts of the world for conducting productive propaganda work, the more promising and important actors resided in countries in the Near East. This vast arena, he stressed, could not be overlooked.

His major example of the power of Islamic solidarity was the post–First World War Khilafat movement linking the now defunct Ottoman Empire and South Asia two decades earlier. Wang Zengshan continued:

> In 1918, when Turkey sought for independence yet was consumed
> by warfare, there was no one in the whole country who did not take
> it upon themselves to save country and nation [*jiuguo jiuzu* (救國救
> 族)]. The most important thing I noticed is that during the period
> of the most severe fighting, representatives were dispatched to go to
> every Islamic country to disseminate propaganda through unofficial
> means. Due to the bonds of shared faith and sentiments [*tongyi xinyang
> ganqing zhi weixi* (同一信仰感情之維繫)], it aroused the sympathies
> of every country. India, where Muslim populations reach 90 million,
> donated 500,000 rupees. As for the material support from people of
> other countries where a majority were Muslim believers, [one would]
> know even without asking.[10]

The Turkey of the present existed, he argued, thanks to its power to draw assistance from Islamic countries at such a tremendous pace. The tight links between the countries of the Near East were like 'a structure made of solid iron' (*jiantie zhi jigou* [堅鐵之機構]), which made even Soviet Russia hover between them. 'Imperialism cannot dare look at them lightly' (*diguozhuyi bugan qingshi zhi ye* [帝國主義不敢輕視之也)], he concluded.[11]

The next step, then, was to bring together Muslim notables and intellectuals in China and dispatch them to Islamic countries under the name of an Islamic organization, which would enable them to visit various countries in the east to conduct propaganda work and sell nation-saving bonds. Ibrahim Ma Tianying, Wang Zengshan believed, could visit Ceylon, Bombay, Hyderabad, Delhi, Calcutta, Karachi, and others and sell at least 5,000,000 yuan's worth. The original plan was to have five members in the delegation: Imam Ha Decheng (哈德成) (1888–1943), Zhang Zhaoli (張兆理) (1906–97), and Xue Wenbo (薛文波) (1909–84), in addition to Wang Zengshan and Ma Tianying. Yet because Ha Decheng could not resign from his responsibilities as leader of the Muslim communities in Shanghai, he could not participate in the Mission. Instead, Wang Shiming (王世明) (1910–97), who had studied at al-Azhar University in Cairo, joined them in Suez (Wang 1997: 442).

Indeed, much had changed since the rise of the Khilafat movement that Wang Zengshan referred to. Shortly after Indian Muslims had mobilized moral and financial support for the Turkish War of Independence, the Ankara government dissolved the Ottoman Empire and abolished the caliphate, shattering the imaginations of pan-Islamic solidarity that the caliphate had symbolized (Aydin 2017: 124–6).

The changed circumstances, however, mattered little for the materialization of the Chinese Islamic Goodwill Mission and the idea of the Muslim world that it staunchly propagated. As the Nationalist state desperately searched for international allies following the Japanese aggression, religious figures with political connections strengthened their ties with the state, as well as with their co-religionists abroad. The wartime travels to India of the Buddhist thinker Taixu (太虛) (1890–1947) following Dai Jitao's (戴季陶) outreach to Buddhist leadership well exemplifies how the Republican state sought to utilize a transnational religious community for its diplomacy (Bulag 2010: 81; Sen 2016). The Goodwill Mission on the other hand could cling to another ideology—that of the Republic of Five Races. Post-Qing states in China vacillated between the Han-centric conception of China and 'state transnationalism' as promoted by Sun Yat-sen's pan-Asianism and his promise of a Republic constituted of Han, Hui, Mongols, Manchus, and Tibetans (Han 2015: 28). Here, 'Hui' classified as such was a religious-ethnic category that also implicated post-imperial China's territorial claims to Xinjiang (Brophy 2012). Ever since the establishment of the Republic, the ambiguity of the concept had stirred confusion and intense controversies among Chinese Muslims in eastern urban centres about the definitions and boundaries of the Hui, or Huizu (Hui ethnicity [回族]) more specifically (Cieciura 2016). The Mission members adopted an ambivalent approach, using the term Hui as an all-encompassing pan-Islamic imagery that referred to all of Muslims in China's tenuous territories and worldwide, thus positioning themselves as the linkage between the diverse groups of Muslims across China and the Indian Ocean world on both societal and state levels.

Who, then, were the Mission's members as individual actors and a social group? The members of the Mission represented the amorphous class of mobile cosmopolitans that emerged in urban locations in China on the eve of the fall of the Qing Empire. While accessing imperial institutions and infrastructure within and outside the country's tenuous borders, they grafted new meaning on to them by constructing translocal Islamic networks, building internal and external ties of religion, scholarship, philanthropy, commerce, as well as interpersonal contacts.

The Mission's two leaders Wang Zengshan and Ma Tianying, for instance, both traced their native place to Linqing (臨清) in Shandong Province, yet ceaselessly relocated themselves between different cities. As his colleague explained in Wang Zengshan's obituary in 1961, Linqing was a transport hub that connected the north–south axis due to its proximity to the Grand Canal prior to the construction of the Tianjin–Pukou railway, which was completed in 1912. Wang's family had thus engaged in both agriculture and commerce. As Linqing gradually declined due to the obstruction of its waterways, Wang Zengshan's father Wang Baoqing (王葆卿) migrated to Beijing together with his family and became the leader of the Linqing Commercial Association in Beijing (Wang 1997: 507).[12] He also presided over Beijing's Sheep Association and served as an elderly manager of the Dongsi mosque (Dongsi Pailou Qingzhensi [東四牌樓清真寺]) where the Chengda

Normal School (Chengda Shifan Xuexiao [成達師範學校]), a pivotal Islamic educational institution in Republican China (Matsumoto 2006), was housed (Wang 1997: 1). From a relatively affluent background, in 1924, Wang Zengshan graduated from Yenching University, which had been founded by Christian missionaries, and subsequently studied at Turkey's National Istanbul University between 1925 and 1930, funding himself. Upon his return from Istanbul, he served in the Legislative Yuan and represented Muslim populations in China between 1932 and 1946.

Ibrahim Ma Tianying, like his colleague Wang Zengshan, did not come from a land-owning family but took opportunities that arose from a multiplicity of positions. Ma Tianying also traced his native place to Linqing. Amidst the political turmoil of the Taiping Rebellion, Ma Tianying's grandfather Ma Yukui (馬玉奎) moved to and settled in Wanping (宛平) in Hebei Province (now corresponding to Fengtai District [豐台區] in Beijing) with his whole family. Ma Tianying's father Ma Baolong (馬寶龍) ran a halal meat shop for a living. Ma Tianying was born in 1900, the same year as the outbreak of the Boxer Uprising, and attended a private old-style school in his youth. Having witnessed his family's economic hardships, Ma Tianying decided to enter a school run by the French; with his father's arduous support, he finished his studies in seven years. In 1917, he had an opportunity to go to France as an interpreter for Chinese mineworkers in the country. He divided his time between work and study, learned different French dialects, and practised public speech-making and writing, thus developing his skills as a future diplomat. Upon his return to China in 1922, he came back to Beijing where he got married, and moved to Zhengzhou in Henan Province to work as a manager of materials for Longhai Railway for seven years. In 1929, he returned to Beijing and worked as a secretary of the Belgian Bank (Huabi yinhang [華比銀行]) for one year before moving to Shanghai in 1930 and taking up the position as a secretary at the Turkish Embassy in Shanghai. He also worked as an interpreter at a police station in the French Concession area, from where he resigned after witnessing the ill treatment of Chinese residents (Jia 2005: 150).

In Shanghai, Ma Tianying actively engaged with the city's vibrant community of Muslims who had migrated to it from surrounding areas such as Nanjing, Suzhou, and Yangzhou as seekers of

opportunities following the Opium War or as refugees in the aftermath of the Taiping Rebellion. Ma Tianying acquainted himself with
Muslim scholars and leaders such as Ha Decheng, Da Pusheng, and
Wu Tegong. He would also join the protest against *Nanhua wenyi*
(南華文藝) [*Nanhua Literature*] and *Beixin shuju* (北新書局) [*Beixin
Book Bureau*], which published derogatory articles against Muslims
in 1932 (Jia 2005: 151; Wan 2017). While sojourning in Shanghai,
Ma Tianying taught at and wrote for the Shanghai Islamic School
which had been established in 1928 inside the Xiaotaoyuan mosque
(Xiaotaoyuan Qingzhensi [小桃園清真寺]). The mosque itself had
been constructed in 1917 through a donation from the merchant Jin
Ziyun (金子雲) (1869–1937), who had originally come from Nanjing
and specialized in the jade and pearl business.

The Mission's members thus emerged out of new groups of Chinese
Muslim urban elites who, while inheriting the legacies of old gentry
and scholars, came to assume much more diverse public positions in
the commercial, religious, and political realms. Like revolutionaries,
intellectuals, and independence fighters throughout Asia at the turn
of the twentieth century, whose successes and survival depended on
transnational diaspora networks (Schulz-Forberg 2015: 9), this circle of
Chinese Muslims collectively constituted and constructed a capacious
'cultural nexus' (Duara 1988) that was not confined to any one city or
province in China, but was extended to far-flung locations across the
Islamic world.[13] 'Progressive' religious leaders emerged in Nationalist
China who could 'enter into constructive negotiation with the government and, in exchange for political support and endorsement of the
state's anti-superstitious policies, were rewarded with some autonomy'
(Goossaert and Palmer 2012: 62). Likewise, Chinese Muslims from different social and geographical backgrounds could build alliances on
levels that transcended the local village, city, province, or countries,
thereby accruing resources not necessarily available to popular religions that faced anti-superstition campaigns and the confiscation of
temple properties (Nedostup 2009).

The outbreak of the Second Sino-Japanese War immediately
tightened the links between Chinese Muslims at different levels and
brought them close to the leadership of Chiang Kai-shek through
both personal connections and the mediation of a national religious
association. Chinese Islamic delegations were organized under the

tutelage of the Chinese Islamic National Salvation Association, and as mentioned earlier, were a reaction against Japan's use of Islam in its diplomatic strategies. For imperial Japan, Mecca and pilgrimage routes represented a space that could be utilized for political purposes, long before its invasion into China. Thinkers, politicians, and military circles of imperial Japan had developed partnerships with Muslim notables from Russian/Soviet Central Asia since the turn of the twentieth century. As Japan's ideologues refined pan-Asianist thoughts on the wake of its imperial expansion, observers in the Ottoman Empire, in turn, were shocked and amazed at post-Meiji Japan's victory against the Ottoman archrival Russia in 1904–5 (Worringer 2014). The event instigated travels of streams of Russian Tatar intellectuals to travel to Japan, who developed ties with Japan's political and military circles and performed critical roles in the founding of pan-Asianist Islamic study circles in Tokyo (Aydin and Wen 2014).[14]

Onto the early inter-War period, Japanese Muslims—who had converted through contacts with exiles and refugees from Russian Central Asia—utilized pilgrimage channels to create contacts with political and religious authorities in Arabia. A parallel aim was to survey new markets in West Asia for Japan to export cotton and light industrial products, a task that gained increased urgency following the Great Depression (Koyagi 2013: 862–7). Japan's strategy of cultivating its own Muslim networks and befriending those of rival powers reached its height during the 1930s following its occupation of Manchuria in 1931 and the exit from the League of Nations in 1933. In Manchuria, Japan nominally sponsored the 'Muslim state' (Huihuiguo [回回國]) as a strategy of penetration into China. From mid-1937, Japan immediately established branches of the Chinese Muslim United Association (Zhongguo huijiao zonglian hehui [中國回教總聯合會]) in northern China to win the support of Muslims, informed by active learning on histories of Germany's alliances with the Ottoman Empire and Italy's engagements with Libya and Imam Yahya of Yemen (Hammond 2015: 55–69). Japan would adopt a similar approach and propaganda in Southeast Asia, portraying itself as a liberator of Muslims from British and Dutch colonial rule during the brief number of years of its occupation (1941–5) (Ahmad 2003; Benda 1958). When the Goodwill Mission reached Mecca in 1938, the members were alarmed at Japan's outreach to Egypt and Arabia that relied on Japanese pilgrims and a Chinese Muslim from Manchuria. In particular, the Mission noted with alarm Japan's penetration into the community of some 6,000 refugees from Xinjiang in Mecca who had suffered under the oppression of regional governments in Xinjiang. The Mission warned that Japan was luring these wanderers with the prospects of Xinjiang's independence, and disseminating propaganda that criticized the encroachment of communism in China as evidenced by the Sino-Soviet alliance. Japanese commercial goods were also flooding the markets in Arabia.[15]

Although multiple Islamic cultural and educational associations already existed throughout China in the Republican period, the Chinese Islamic National Salvation Association that aimed to counter Japan quickly rose to prominence as the first all-national Islamic federation that carried the backing of the central government. With the outbreak of the War, scholar-politicians such as Shi Zizhou (時子周) (1879–1969) and Wang Jingzhai (王靜齋) (1879–1949) initially organized the Chinese Muslim Anti-Japanese and National Salvation Association (Zhongguo Huimin kangri jiuguo xiehui [中國回民抗日救國協會]) in Zhengzhou, Henan Province, in 1937. The Association relocated to Hankou several months later and changed its name to the Chinese Muslim National Salvation Association (Zhongguo Huimin jiuguo xiehui [中國回民救國協會]).

A combination of militarists and educators led the Association. Its president was Bai Chongxi (白崇禧) (1893–1966), the minister of defence under the Nationalist government from Guangxi. Figures such as Ma Buqing (馬步青) (1901–77), the younger brother of Qinghai Provincial Governor Ma Bufang (馬步芳) (1905–75), and Shi Zizhou served on the board of trustees. The Association's headquarters later moved to the war-time capital of Chongqing in 1939 and changed its name to the Chinese Islamic National Salvation Association (Zhongguo Huijiao jiuguo xiehui [中國回教救國協會]), in 1942 becoming the Chinese Muslim Association (Zhongguo Huijiao xiehui [中國回教協會]) (Zhu 2011: 197).

By December 1945, the Association had 381 branches in the wartime capital Chongqing and twenty provinces—Anhui, Qinghai, Hunan, Sichuan, Henan, Jiangxi, Hubei, Guizhou, Guangxi, Gansu, Guangdong, Ningxia, Xikang, Shaanxi, Shanxi, Suiyuan, Zhejiang,

Yunnan, Fujian, and Hebei. It could not, however, establish branches in Xinjiang Province, although plans to do so were discussed (Ding 2015: 8). After the Association moved to Taipei in 1949 following the victory of the Communist Party, General Bai Chongxi continued his role as its president until 1959. The same Chinese Muslim Association has maintained its functions in the Taipei Central Mosque up to the present day.

The precise organizational structure of the Association and its operations in different local contexts is a topic that requires more research. It seems, however, that the Association occupied an ambiguous status as a semi-governmental religious organization that also undertook socio-religious projects according to local circumstances. The records of the branch in Shaanxi, for instance, show that several members were affiliated to the Nationalist Party, while most, predominantly men, were not. The Shaanxi branch depended on monetary support not only from the Executive Yuan and contributions from General Bai Chongxi, but also on numerous private donations from individuals, such as other sub-branches of the Association, noodle companies, banks, and even the Xi'an branch of the Red Swastika Society.[16] Besides countering the Japanese Empire's invasion by mobilizing Muslims in and outside China—an explicit aim of the organization as reflected in its very name—the tasks of the Association were as diverse as counting and managing mosques around China, delivering relief aid to refugees and the poor, improving agricultural productivity, promoting education amongst Muslim communities, and facilitating the logistics for pilgrims or diplomatic delegations including the Goodwill Mission.

Journeys and Encounters in India

The Goodwill Mission to the Near East was the first diplomatic delegation to be officially organized under the auspices of the Chinese Islamic National Salvation Association. Xue Wenbo, who served as the secretary, composed comprehensive records of its travels as diary entries, which were published in 1943 in Chongqing and republished in 1997 in Kuala Lumpur by Wang Zengshan's son. According to the account, the delegates departed Nanjing in November 1937 and returned to Chongqing in January 1939. Wang Zengshan, Zhang

Zhaoli, and Xue Wenbo travelled to Hong Kong from Nanjing; Ma Tianying was scheduled to depart from Shanghai and met them later in Hong Kong, while Wang Shiming joined the team in Cairo.[17]

Before reaching ports in South Asia, as they transited through different places, the delegates encountered persons whom they described as Indian Muslims. In Hong Kong, the gateway to the Mission's journeys abroad, they met an imam at Molimiao (摩理廟), a mosque built and operated by Indian Muslims (Wang 1997: 6). After departing from Hong Kong and arriving in Saigon onboard the ship *Dartangnan*, they dined at the Royal Restaurant Bombay, run by an Indian Muslim by the name of Amir Hassan Haji, who had come from London and served chicken and lamb dishes. Although the business seemed to be deserted, there was another person from Xinjiang dining at the restaurant 'Habibullah', who had travelled from Afghanistan (Wang 1997: 15). They also participated in Friday prayers at a mosque in Saigon, where Muslim believers from different ethnicities, Indian and Malay, Westerners, Chinese-looking Malays, and Africans wearing different costumes gathered. At their next destination, Singapore, they held meetings with members of the all-Malaya Islamic Association, leaders of the Arab diaspora and Indian Muslim communities, as well as reporters. A few days later, while transiting through Colombo, they stayed at the Paris Hotel, which was run by Indian Muslims, and visited the Indian Muslim Association. They conversed with Syed Raof Pasha, a Muslim activist, on the need for the Islamic and Indian worlds to connect and ally with one another in order to fight imperialism (Wang 1997: 45).

The cohort's full-scale activities in British India began in July 1938, after their pilgrimage to Mecca and sojourns in Jeddah, Cairo, Alexandria, Haifa, Beirut, Damascus, Baghdad, and Isfahan. The Mission departed from Bushire on 26 June and arrived in Karachi three days later after a difficult sail due to the high winds. After touring Karachi briefly, they returned to the ship and arrived in Bombay on 2 July. Vice Consul Chen Leshi (陳樂石), with whom they had exchanged letters twice, as well as a group of *qiaobao* (僑胞), literally 'sojourning siblings from the same womb', greeted them onshore (Wang 1997: 296).

The five members of the Mission persistently held conversations with prominent religious and political leaders in Bombay, Lucknow,

Lahore, and Calcutta. Inter-dispersed between such meetings were lectures and meetings with diaspora populations from different parts of China and Xinjiang, whom they referred to collectively as *qiaobao* or when referring to persons from Xinjiang, *jiaobao* (教胞), or 'siblings of the same religion'. The delegates arrived in the heat of Bombay on 2 July, where they were reunited with Imam Da Pusheng (達浦生), who had been on a pilgrimage-cum-diplomatic mission of his own. The very next day, the Mission met Muhammad Ali Jinnah in the morning accompanied by Consul Chen and, in the afternoon, attended welcome parties held by overseas Chinese communities, most of whom were merchants from Guangdong and Shandong. A couple of days later, they also encountered two persons from Xinjiang. One was a manager of a local mosque, another, a merchant, who spoke about the hardships facing Xinjiang Muslims after the takeover of the province by Jin Shuren and the flight of people abroad whose connections with their homeland had now been lost. Upon hearing this, the delegation promised to deal with the issue after winning the War of Resistance (Wang 1997: 298).

In Bombay, despite the different positions taken on the future of national construction and nationalism, the Goodwill Mission found support from the Muslim League under the broad framework of transnational Islamic solidarity. A few days after arriving in Bombay, the cohort attended a tea gathering with the Muslim League hosted by Muhammad Ali Jinnah, with about 400 people participating. Jinnah made a speech pointing out that: (*i*) every Muslim should have passionate religious sentiments, as Muslims had originally constituted one family, and that the Mission were not only esteemed guests from afar but [our] brothers; (*ii*) Indian Muslims maintain unbounded sympathy for China's Muslims' fighting in the resistance war against Japan for the peace and survival of the minzu; and (*iii*) Indian Muslim delegations of representatives would visit China in the future to build connections between Muslims in the two countries. Jinnah further encouraged the delegation to visit Muslim districts in northern India, upon which the members decided to revise their itinerary despite the fact that they had long since exceeded the original plan that the Mission would last six months. The three of them, Ma Tianying, Zhang Zhaoli, and Wang Zengshan (Figure 10.1 [A, B]), would thus travel to Lahore, Lucknow, and Calcutta for about seventeen days (Wang 1997: 300).

(A)

(B)

Figure 10.1 (A, B)   The Goodwill Mission to the Near East
Above (left to right): Ma Tianying, Xue Wenbo, Wang Zengshan, Zhang
Zhaoli, Wang Shiming.
Below (top to bottom; left to right): Ma Jian, Sha Rucheng, Xue Wenbo, Zhang
Zhaoli, Wang Shiming; Ma Tianying, (Ibrahim) al-Jibali of al-Azhar University,
Da Pusheng, Wang Zengshan, Mustafa al-Maraghi of al-Azhar University.

Source: Wang Zengshan Private Collection, Courtesy of Rosey Wang Ma. Reproduced
by Special Collections, National University of Singapore Libraries.

The three delegates resumed their meetings in these cities with Muslim dignitaries and diaspora communities. In Lahore, where they stayed for about three days, they met princes Shah Nawaz Khan (Nawaz of Mamdot) and Aslam Khan, and were greeted by other princes in the region. They then toured the Badshashi mosque, where they explained the Mission's aims and reported garnering sympathy from the audience. The next day, they visited the Red Cross, where they conversed with the organization's secretary, Bashir Ahmad Khan, and observed the organization mostly run by Muslims. Among the guests who attended their speeches at the Red Cross were persons by the names of Soofi, Bashir, and Hakim, who had come from Qadian and represented the Ahmadiyya Community. In Lucknow, they had more meetings with the members of the Muslim League and local religious scholars. They first met Amir Ahmad Khan of the Muslim League, whom they characterized as knowledgeable, original in thought, and passionate for religious affairs (Wang 1997: 308). They also had discussions with a local scholar, Moulana Jasmaluddin, and the imam, Syed Ghulam Imam, who explained the movement for an independent Pakistan. Jinnah had introduced them to Syed Abdulazziz, the head of the Muslim League branch, but because he was away at that moment, they had a meeting with the secretary, Jafar Imam. Wang Zengshan and Ma Tianying delivered lectures at the League's welcome reception (Wang 1997: 303–9).

During their visits, *Diaries of the Chinese Islamic Goodwill Mission to the Middle East* (henceforth, Diaries) noted that, 'in the present, there is no lack of supporters for the movement [for Pakistan] amongst India's Muslim youth' (Wang 1997: 309). The idea of Pakistan as a sovereign Islamic state and a successor to the lost Ottoman caliphate had garnered enthusiastic popular support in the public sphere before it was realized in the form of a state (Dhulipala 2015).

Yet, as representatives of the Nationalist Party, the Mission by no means shared the separatist agendas of the Muslim League in India. The Mission's members endeavoured to distance Muslims in China from the course of events in British India as much as possible. The Diaries emphasized that China's inland Muslims (*neidi Huimin* [內 地回民]), unlike those in India, regarded themselves as 'guests' (*keju* [客居]) living under, or surrounded by, a non-Islamic state. Their viewpoints were thus very different from those of India's Muslims, to whom Islamic law was applied in aspects of civil law, and who had 'once ruled India for seven hundred years' (Wang 1997: 332). At other points, Wang Zengshan blamed the imperialists for 'deliberately erecting barriers and instigating fights to consolidate their own position' (Wang 1997: 297).

The idea of unified Muslim world, which arose in the Mission's meetings with the League, served as the platform through which the two parties could connect with one another, despite its contrasting evolutions, visions, and goals. The delegates and the League's leaders each appropriated the rhetoric of trans-Islamic solidarity between the Muslim populations of China and India according to their different agendas in their home societies.

While building relations with the League, the Mission also interacted with the Indian National Congress Party in Bombay. This included Gunottam (Raja) Hutheesing in Bombay, the secretary of the party (Wang 1997: 297). The Indian Congress Party in Bombay organized a 'China Fund Day' for three days to commemorate the outbreak of the war and to collect funds and supplies for displaced refugees in China. Two flags, that of the National Congress Party and that of the Republic of China, were displayed at the event (Wang 1997: 299). The Congress Party also arranged medical teams to be sent to war-stricken parts of China. Reportedly, the Mission's lectures on the Sino-Japanese War and relations between the 'two great nations' (*liang da minzu* [兩大民族]) of India and China attracted much attention from the Indian public, and the Chinese community in Bombay contributed donations to the cause (Wang 1997: 477).

In Calcutta, as in Bombay, the Mission socialized with the city's Muslim and Chinese circles. Greeting them upon their arrival in Calcutta on 22 July was Abdul Rahman Siddiqui, whom the Diaries noted as having studied in England and was now serving as a member of the provincial Legislative Assembly. The Diaries also described him as a remarkable person of talent in Calcutta who was passionate about religious affairs, ran an insurance company and was able to speak French, English, Turkish, and Arabic (Wang 1997: 315).[18] Ibrahim Ma Tianying's personal notebook carries Siddiqi's signature and a brazen statement that reads: 'If there are dozen men like Ibrahim in China, Japan will be drowned in the Pacific Ocean, and China will become the leader of Asia and the whole world'.[19] The signature is telling of the anti-imperialist sentiments to which the Mission could appeal and mobilize.

Besides Siddiqi, the Mission met a series of other personalities in Calcutta. For instance, they attended a party held by Adamjee Hajea Dawood, a philanthropist who used his private money for social work. The purpose of the party was to celebrate the British granting a knighthood to Adamjee. They also held a three-hour conversation with Aclam Khan, the editor in chief of the *Ajad* newspaper published in Bengali, who asked about China's war situation and the history of Islam (Wang 1997: 317). Welcoming them as well was Mohammed Abdul Momin, the manager of endowments of Calcutta's Muslims. The Committee for overseeing the waqf was composed of seven persons, and the endowments were managed by local property holders. Momin's family was already wealthy and had endowed a part of their property. Afterwards the Mission attended a reception held by Calcutta's Muslims at which about 3,000 people participated and purportedly showed respect for Chinese Muslim representatives.

Simultaneously, as Calcutta had had historical links with Guangzhou through British commercial enterprises that led to the formation of diaspora populations in the city, the Mission devoted a significant amount of time collecting relief aid from and conducting propaganda with Chinese diasporic communities. For the six days of their stay in Calcutta, the Mission alternated between visiting Chinese districts and Muslim enclaves. Accompanied by the Consul Feng Zhizheng (馮執正) in Calcutta, the delegation visited sites such as the branch of the Chinese Nationalist Party in India; the seat of *Yindu bao* (印度報); Zhi gong tang (至公堂); Jiaying (嘉應), Siyi (四邑), Dongan (東安), and Nanshun (南順) huiguans; and the Overseas Chinese Union (Huaqiao zonggonghui [華僑總工會]). The account estimated the number of Chinese in Calcutta at about 5,000, many of them from Canton and some from Shandong, who formed a district called 'Tangrenjie' (唐人街) or the Chinatown of central Calcutta (Zhang and Sen 2013). The Diaries noted that the Nationalist Party India branch was established in the early years of the Republic, whereas the newspaper *Yindu Bao* was about ten years old. It had been changed from a weekly to daily paper and represented the only Chinese language paper in India. Managed by a person from Henan called Zhai Xiaofo (翟肖佛), the agency published 700 copies daily (Wang 1997: 316).

The Chinese population in Calcutta offered the Mission avenues where they could undertake surveys, propaganda, and appeals for support. At the evening welcome party held at Meiguang School (梅光學校) on 23 July, Wang Zengshan delivered a lecture titled 'The Delegation's Missions and China's Muslims' and Ma Tianying another talk titled 'Islam and the War of Resistance'. About 500 people attended the gathering (Wang 1997: 317). Many of the overseas Chinese had positions in industry and commerce. The Chinese Consulate was less than a year old, but over the course of the year, Calcutta's Chinese community reportedly donated about 200,000 yuan to the War of Resistance, despite the fact that some were without jobs. There were several Muslims among the community who were originally from Guangzhou, who came up to them and happily exchanged greetings (Wang 1997: 318). The Mission also attended the welcome reception and toured the Chinatown in central Calcutta. On 26 July, the delegates again attended an evening party with Chinese communities; a dozen people from the Nationalist Party branch in India, the Meiguang School, the Min Xin Bookstore, and *Yindu Bao* were present (Wang 1997: 322).

The delegates were not as successful in comprehending or gathering sympathy from the émigrés from Xinjiang whom they kept coming across, first in Mecca during their pilgrimage and now in Bombay. The Mission spent two months once again in Bombay after the visit to Calcutta, waiting for additional funds to arrive from Hankou and logistical problems to be resolved so they could move on to Turkey. As they did so, they encountered imams, traders, pilgrims, and escapees from Xinjiang who had come to settle in Bombay. On 2 August, a Xinjiang person by the name of Hutbinddin, a muezzin for a local mosque, introduced them to the Xinjiang Native-Place Association. The delegates then had a conversation with Muhammed Salih at the mosque, who discussed the community's doubts about the Chinese government, the painful realities in Xinjiang and their hopes of returning home (Wang 1997: 331). A few days later the delegation ate lunch with about twenty people from the Xinjiang Native Association. Many, the delegates realized, were engaged in the business of sharpening and honing knives. A young man called Abdul Hak had already become an imam at a mosque. The next day another person from Xinjiang called Abdul Cader came to visit them. Abdul Cader had studied in Nanjing in the past but following the War, had come to India to pursue trade (Wang 1997: 333–4).

Some individuals from Xinjiang had become stuck in Bombay unintentionally on their way home from Mecca. A person by the name of Ma Guohua (馬國華) from Xinjiang's Changji (昌吉) came to visit them with four or five others to seek assistance. After completing the pilgrimage, they had been delayed in Bombay. Now it was time to board the ship, but one of them had lost gold on the way. The group asked whether the Chinese Consulate could intervene. The Mission, however, could not see a clear solution, and the pilgrims themselves were divided as to whether they should stay in India or return to Xinjiang. Some of them did not have passports that needed to be presented at the port. The delegation encouraged them to return home and promised to introduce them to the Xinjiang Native Association, who might be able to aid them (Wang 1997: 331).

A story the Mission repeatedly heard from persons who traced their origins to Xinjiang was the depressing plight of the province. Close to the date of the delegation's departure from Bombay, on 2 October, a person from Xinjiang reportedly visited the members to discuss how local governmental officials in the province were provoking conflicts among Muslims in order to stay in power. The Diaries noted that the brutalities were sufficient to make even a bystander depressed and resentful (Wang 1997: 366). The Mission, as well as other pilgrimage delegations that succeeded them, endeavoured to convey the precarious situation while also being careful to frame the predicament as a regional rather than a national one.

Almost a decade later, in the autumn of 1947, a Chinese Islamic delegation again came across Xinjiang émigré in Calcutta, Karachi, and Mecca. Amidst the ongoing war between Nationalists and Communists, the Chinese Muslim Association had dispatched another pilgrimage delegation, led by Li Tingbi (李廷弼).[20] Pilgrimage delegations sponsored by the Nationalist Party in these years made a rhetorical shift from proclaiming anti-imperialist to anti-communist Islamic solidarity. This time, in 1947, the delegation boarded an aeroplane from Shanghai, transited through Hong Kong and Kunming, and arrived in Calcutta, where it stayed for one week. It again boarded a plane to Karachi, stayed for five days, and continued to travel to Mecca on board ship to partake in the pilgrimage. It returned to Shanghai by ship, and on the way back, made short transits to Singapore and Hong Kong.[21] In Singapore, they conducted meetings with overseas Chinese populations and Malaysian independence fighters.

The delegation was still more or less unable to access the Xinjiang diaspora networks that had been dispersed between the western borderlands of China, South Asia, and Arabia. It could only take down its observations and attempt to portray itself as having transmitted the central government's stance. In Calcutta, the delegation joined gatherings that the Xinjiang community in the city had prepared for pilgrims from Xinjiang. Karachi, on the other hand, was now the base where the delegation met pilgrims who had arrived through overland routes. Besides forty pilgrims who had travelled with it all the way from Shanghai, thirty-three pilgrims from Tibet and southern Xinjiang reached Karachi overland. Among them, eighteen from southern Xinjiang had failed to purchase tickets for a pilgrimage liner in time. The delegation reportedly arranged their safe passage by asking Pakistan's Ministry of Foreign Affairs for special assistance, which made it possible for the Xinjiang pilgrims to onboard the liner.[22] In Mecca, the delegation would attempt to advertise the Nationalist central government's favourable treatment of the borderlands to some 2,000 people who had escaped from Xinjiang to the holy city under the rule of regional warlords Jin Shuren and Sheng Shicai.[23]

Interactions with leaders of the state that had by then become Pakistan indeed seem to have been more fruitful for the delegation compared to its communications with the Xinjiang diaspora. When the pilgrimage delegation undertook its journeys to Mecca in 1947, Karachi and Calcutta belonged to different nation-states. Although the composition of the pilgrimage mission was now different, it advocated for the same strategy of leveraging Islam to build foreign relations in India and Pakistan. The delegation reported having utilized 'religious relations to conveniently visit [Muslim leaders in various circles] and engage in national diplomatic work, which prompted Muslim peoples in India and Pakistan to have correct awareness on China's current situation.'[24] The report suggested that since the new state of Pakistan that neighbours China is a new Muslim ally and since a great number of Muslims are concentrated in China's own northwestern provinces, delegations could be dispatched back and forth to strengthen relations.

The delegation's actual activities appear to have been more extensive in Karachi than in Calcutta. It visited Muhammad Ali Jinnah, who is said to have expressed his desire to establish diplomatic and commercial relations with China in the near future. It also reported meeting other personalities, including Jinnah's younger sister Fatima Jinnah, Minister of Education Fazlur Rahman, the mayor of Karachi, and the president of the University of Sind.[25] The end of the report proposed establishing official diplomatic relations with Pakistan.

In Singapore, on the way back to Shanghai, the delegation leader Li Tingbi told the *Singapore Free Press* that the mission's main task had been to 'tender felicitations on behalf of Chinese Muslims to the new Muslim nation on the occasion of its founding' ('Pakistan Seeks Ties with China', *Singapore Free Press*, 13 December 1947). He announced that: 'We met a number of Pakistan officials, including Mr. Jinnah the Premier of Pakistan, who expressed the hope that China and Pakistan would soon establish diplomatic relations to promote better understanding between the two nations' ('Pakistan Seeks Ties with China', *The Singapore Free Press*, 13 December 1947). Also in Singapore, the delegation conducted meetings with Malay's politicians and with Chinese diaspora populations. The organizers of the independence movement for Federation of Malaya were reported as wanting to collaborate closely with the 2.5 million Chinese populations in Malaya, but did not have in-depth relations with them due to religious divisions; they expressed hopes that China's central government would send a Muslim Consular staff in order to advance such cooperative ties between the Malays and the Chinese.[26] Perhaps as a result of the delegation's relays of messages, between 1947 and 1951, Pakistan indeed maintained official diplomatic relations with the Republic of China. In 1948, as if to respond to the report, Ma Tianying who had been a member of the Goodwill Mission in 1938 was sent to Ipoh as the consular-general with the specific task of facilitating interactions between the Chinese diasporas and local Muslim communities ('First Chinese Muslim Consul to Malaya', *Malaya Tribune*, 26 August 1948).

***

Chinese Muslim writers and entrepreneurs who assumed roles as wartime diplomats constituted an exclusive strand among diverse

Chinese Muslim populations, with targeted goals and destinations. Nevertheless, they reconfigured open narratives of Islamic unity in order to claim their place in dispersed localities, while accelerating the pace and volume of interactions with the local Muslim scholars, businessmen, philanthropists, politicians, and journalists who introduced them to a wider public. Simultaneously, the pilgrimage missions deliberately approached the overseas Chinese and Uighur diaspora communities in South Asia, which consisted of refugees, traders, and sailors, often outside their own social orbits. The Islamic delegations thus extended twin wings to Islamic and diasporic networks, at times successfully mediating relations between state entities and funnelling funds from diaspora populations.

The Second Sino-Japanese War not only mobilized internal populations but left the Republican state desperately seeking external allies. With access to the external space of the Islamic world in the Indian Ocean, as well as to dispersed overseas Chinese diaspora communities, the Chinese Islamic Goodwill Mission to the Near East in particular built relationships on behalf of the state, but on an intermediate level, through unofficial channels that differed from diplomacy between state leaders as conventionally understood.[27]

The Mission members' physical and conceptual journeys did not stop with the end of the Second World War. The former leader Wang Zengshan and his family undertook the perilous journey across the Pamir and Himalayas from Urumqi, where he had become the minister of civil affairs in 1946, to flee the Communist victory. When he fled Xinjiang Province in September through Gilgit, he brought one pistol and one revolver with the permission of the consul-general of Pakistan in Kashgar, which were registered in his and his brother's passports. During his sojourn in Karachi between 1949 and 1956, Wang Zengshan worked as a teacher and translator in Chinese at the Ministry of Foreign Affairs and Commonwealth Relations of Pakistan. While in Karachi, he kept communications with the former minister of defence, Bai Chongxi, still the president of the Chinese Muslim Association, which, by then, was based in Taipei, on such matters as attending the Islamic Conference in Cairo in 1953 and the Muslim Youth Assembly in Karachi in 1955. He wrote reports on affairs in the Near East and South Asia, as well as the prospects of utilizing Islamic connections to combat communism.

The older webs of commerce, exile, pilgrimage, and scholarship between Xinjiang and northern India that the Mission had tapped into during the war awaits more scholarly attention and research. Yet, when Wang Zengshan sojourned in Karachi, he engaged more deeply than he had in 1938 with the Turkic and Chinese Muslim diaspora populations in what had become Pakistan. His private correspondence in Karachi reveals that he had been communicating with the All Pakistan Eastern Turkistan Association and Free China Association in Taipei to coordinate the distribution of relief aid to the refugees and sent on letters from the Chinese Muslim Ahmadiyya community, who were at risk of being evicted from Pakistan due to passport and visa problems following Pakistan's recognition of the PRC in 1951.[28] In 1956, Wang Zengshan himself relocated to Istanbul with his family. As a resident of Pakistan, which officially recognized the PRC, who carried a passport issued by the Republic of China and had explicit political connections to the Nationalist Party, he feared for the safety of himself and his family. In Istanbul University, he assumed a professorship in Chinese studies.

Of the four members of the Mission other than Wang Zengshan, three followed a similar course and permanently left mainland China. Zhang Zhaoli settled in Taipei and started a business by opening a Middle East trading company; he then became the first secretary of the South Korean Embassy in Taipei, assisting overseas Chinese populations in South Korea and directing money from the Turkish government to the first community of Muslims in South Korea (Jia 2005: 190). Wang Shiming, who had joined the Mission in Cairo, continued his diplomatic career in Egypt, Libya, Kuwait, and Saudi Arabia in the embassies of the Republic of China, and later settled in Honolulu, Hawaii. Ma Tianying, who had led extensive Islamic delegations to the South Seas upon his return from the Mission examined in this chapter, was appointed Consul at Ipoh in 1948. With the Communist victory, he and his family settled first in Singapore, then in Kuala Lumpur. Like Wang Zengshan, Ma Tianying maintained his contacts with the religious and political community in Taipei and disseminated ideas of Islamic solidarity and inter-religious peace through his writings and lectures. The Mission's former two leaders, Wang Zengshan and Ma Tianying, initiated ties of kinship, despite being oceans apart, leading to marriage vows between the former's daughter and the latter's son.

The extensive activities of the Goodwill Mission resulted from a series of collaborations between leading members of pre-existing Islamic organizations and the Nationalist Party, a cooperation that came fully into effect with the Second Sino-Japanese War. The matrix of networks that Chinese Muslims built outlasted the transformative events signalled by the end of the Second World War, metamorphosing into new relations of religion and kinship while continuing to be informed partially by the Republic of China's outreach to the Islamic world during the Cold War. The intertwined conduits of diplomacy, religion, and kinship that Chinese Muslims assembled across long distances amidst unpredictable wars, chaos, and uncertainties in China, India, and elsewhere in Asia become visible not by employing the prism of imperial infrastructure and networks, but only by uncovering the mobility and discourses of the actors who laid claims to the Indian Ocean space by summoning histories, conjuring up imaginaries, arranging journeys, and writing all of it down.

Notes

1. For these vibrant histories of early Islam in imperial China, see Leslie (1986), Schottenhammer (2009), Yasuhiro (2008), Chaffee (2006), Sen (2003: Chapter 4), Park (2012), and Kuwabara (1928, 1935).
2. On Japan's uses of Muslim networks as a strategy for its activities Eurasia, including China, see Esenbel (2004), Koyagi (2013), and Hammond (2015).
3. See Chapter 8 by Brian Tsui in this volume.
4. For global histories of anti-imperial pan-Islamism and the evolution of the concept of the Islamic world, see Landau (1994), Aydin (2007, 2017), Green (2013), and Gelvin and Green (2013).
5. In English, Mao (2011) and Lei (2010) have described the general contours of the Goodwill Mission's travels and aims.
6. On the pressures placed on minority nationalities to prove their loyalty to China by portraying themselves as having resisted 'splittist' impulses and fighting against foreign imperialism, see Bulag (2010: 198).
7. Ma Tianying Papers, 1937–9, Centre for Chinese Studies, Kuala Lumpur, Malaysia.
8. Wang Zengshan Private Papers, 1937–60, National University of Singapore Libraries, Singapore.
9. Wang Zengshan Private Papers, 1937–60, National University of Singapore Libraries, Singapore. The draft proposal is contained in the

collection of Wang Zengshan's private documents, now in keeping of the National University of Singapore Libraries. I am grateful to Rosey Wang Ma for kindly granting initial access to them.

10. Wang Zengshan Private Papers, 1937–60, National University of Singapore Libraries, Singapore.

11. Wang Zengshan Private Papers, 1937–60, National University of Singapore Libraries, Singapore.

12. The biography is outlined in an obituary of Wang Zengshan written by Sun Shengwu (孫繩武), dated 20 March 1961, which was included in the reprinted version of the Diaries.

13. Prasenjit Duara (1988: 40) has conceptualized 'cultural nexus' as a 'matrix within which legitimacy and authority were produced, represented and reproduced', wherein embedded symbols and values such as 'religious beliefs, sentiments of reciprocity, kinship bonds, and the like … were transmitted and sustained by the institutions and networks of the nexus' (Duara 1988: 5). The boundaries of the cultural nexus are not defined by 'a geographical zone or a particular hierarchical system', but by the 'persons and groups who pursue public goals within the nexus', thus making it a 'subject-centered universe of power' (Duara 1988: 16). Supra-village religious organizations were not adversely impacted by the transformative drive of 'state involution' that followed the Boxer Uprising (Duara 1988: 156).

14. The most well-noted and critical person among them was Abduressid Ibrahim (1857–1944), an anti-tsarist Russian activist born in Tara and buried in Tokyo, who became the first imam of Tokyo mosque in 1938. For a fascinating account of his life and journeys, straddling between Russian/Soviet, Ottoman, and Japanese empires, see Algar (2012) and Yamazaki (2014).

15. 'Zhongguo Huijiao Jindong Fangwentuan Baogao' (中國回教近東訪問團報告) ['Report of Chinese Islamic Delegation to the Near East'], 1938, File No. 026000013131A, Neizhengbu, Academia Historica, Taipei, Taiwan. I am grateful to Liao Wen-shuo for referring me to this record. I elaborate further on Chinese Islamic pilgrimage delegations' outreach to Mecca's Xinjiang diaspora populations and Sino-Japanese contestations over winning their support in Jeong (2019: 236–66).

16. 'Xikang Guizhou Shaanxi Sansheng Ji Tianjinshi Huimin Jiuguo Xiehui Fenzhihui Zuzhi Jianzhang' (西康貴州陝西三省及天津市回民救國協會分會組織簡章) ['General Regulation on Establishing Branches of Muslim Association for National Salvation in the Three Provinces of Xikang, Guozhou, Shaanxi, and the City of Tianjin'], 1938–40, Shehuibu, No. 2 Historical Archives, Nanjing, China.

17. In the end, Ma Tianying could not arrive in Hong Kong on the scheduled date because of severe wind and waves in Shanghai. The rest of the team

decided to leave first and meet him later in Cairo to ensure that they could arrive in Mecca in time for the hajj, the crucial component of the delegation's aim of broadcasting Japanese brutalities in China.

18. Abdul Rahman Siddiqui was also a leader of the Muslim League, a member of the Bengal Legislative Assembly (1937–46), and a participant in the Khilafat movement. He initiated the *Daily Morning News* in Calcutta and was elected the mayor of Calcutta Municipal Corporation in 1949. He was elected the mayor of Calcutta in 1940 with the support of Subhas Chandra Bose (Bose 2004: 12).

19. Ma Tianying Papers, 1937–9, Centre for Chinese Studies, Kuala Lumpur, Malaysia.

20. Li Tingbi's background remains unclear. He seems to have relocated to Taipei in the aftermath of the Nationalist–Communist War. In 1985, he published a short recollection of his 1947 pilgrimage in Taipei's Islamic periodical published by the Chinese Muslim Association in Li (1985).

21. 'Zhongguo Huijiao Chaojin Xuanchuantuan Baogaoshu' (中國回教朝覲宣傳團報告) ['Report of Chinese Islamic Pilgrimage Propaganda Delegation'], *Xiezhu Lüwai Xinjiang Qiaomin Fanguo* (協助旅外新疏僑民返國) [*Assistance on Repatriating Xinjiang Subjects Sojourning Abroad*], 1948–9, File No. 020-021904-0002, p. 3, Waijiaobu, Academia Historica, Taipei, Taiwan.

22. 'Zhongguo Huijiao Chaojin Xuanchuantuan Baogaoshu' (中國回教朝覲宣傳團報告) ['Report of Chinese Islamic Pilgrimage Propaganda Delegation'], *Xiezhu Lüwai Xinjiang Qiaomin Fanguo* (協助旅外新疏僑民返國) [*Assistance on Repatriating Xinjiang Subjects Sojourning Abroad*], 1948–9, File No. 020-021904-0002, p. 4, Waijiaobu, Academia Historica, Taipei, Taiwan.

23. 'Zhongguo Huijiao Chaojin Xuanchuantuan Baogaoshu' (中國回教朝覲宣傳團報告) ['Report of Chinese Islamic Pilgrimage Propaganda Delegation'], *Xiezhu Lüwai Xinjiang Qiaomin Fanguo* (協助旅外新疏僑民返國) [*Assistance on Repatriating Xinjiang Subjects Sojourning Abroad*], 1948–9, File No. 020-021904-0002, p. 5, Waijiaobu, Academia Historica, Taipei, Taiwan.

24. 'Zhongguo Huijiao Chaojin Xuanchuantuan Baogaoshu' (中國回教朝覲宣傳團報告) ['Report of Chinese Islamic Pilgrimage Propaganda Delegation'], *Xiezhu Lüwai Xinjiang Qiaomin Fanguo* (協助旅外新疏僑民返國) [*Assistance on Repatriating Xinjiang Subjects Sojourning Abroad*], 1948–9, File No. 020-021904-0002, p. 3, Waijiaobu, Academia Historica, Taipei, Taiwan.

25. 'Zhongguo Huijiao Chaojin Xuanchuantuan Baogaoshu' (中國回教朝覲宣傳團報告) ['Report of Chinese Islamic Pilgrimage Propaganda

Delegation'], *Xiezhu Lüwai Xinjiang Qiaomin Fanguo* (協助旅外新疆僑民返國) [*Assistance on Repatriating Xinjiang Subjects Sojourning Abroad*], 1948–9, File No. 020-021904-0002, p. 4, Waijiaobu, Academia Historica, Taipei, Taiwan.

26. 'Zhongguo Huijiao Chaojin Xuanchuantuan Baogaoshu' (中國回教朝覲宣傳團報告) ['Report of Chinese Islamic Pilgrimage Propaganda Delegation'], *Xiezhu Lüwai Xinjiang Qiaomin Fanguo* (協助旅外新疆僑民返國) [*Assistance on Repatriating Xinjiang Subjects Sojourning Abroad*], 1948–9, File No. 020-021904-0002, p. 7, Waijiaobu, Academia Historica, Taipei, Taiwan. The delegates heard a similar request from pilgrim representatives from Indonesia in Mecca. Indonesia's pilgrim representatives were reportedly headed by the deputy minister of foreign affairs, Rashid, who had also represented Indonesia in the Asian Relations Conference in 1947 convened by Jawaharlal Nehru. Chinese and Indonesian pilgrimage delegates together discussed clashes between the Chinese diaspora and the rest of the Muslim-majority population in Indonesia, which were exacerbated in the course of Japanese occupation of and the revolution in Indonesia. The delegation's report proposed dispatching staff to Indonesia to maintain relations between the government and society. Preferably, the staff would be Muslim, which would smoothen his entry into the arena of civil relations (*minjian* [民間]) and make it easier to mediate conflicts.

27. For the Kuomintang's wartime diplomacy, and with a focus on its top political leaders, see Lary, MacKinnon, and Van de Ven (2015) and Mitter (2013). See also Brian Tsui's contribution to this volume. Conversely, Marsden, Ibañez-Tirado, and Henig (2016) have proposed the concept of 'everyday diplomacy' as a framework for uncovering non-traditional actors' diplomatic mediations beyond the conventional realm of international relations.

28. For the politics of Taipei's outreach to Uyghur refugees in South Asia, Turkey, and Saudi Arabia, see Jacobs (2016).

References

Archival Material

No. 2 Historical Archives, Nanjing, China

'Xikang Guizhou Shaanxi Sansheng Ji Tianjinshi Huimin Jiuguo Xiehui Fenzhihui Zuzhi Jianzhang' (西康貴州陝西三省及天津市回民救國協會分會組織簡章) ['General Regulation on Establishing Branches of Muslim

Association for National Salvation in the Three Provinces of Xikang, Guozhou, Shaanxi, and the City of Tianjin'], 1938–40.

Academia Historica, Taipei, Taiwan

Waijiabo (Ministry of Foreign Affairs) File No. 020-021904-0002, 'Zhongguo Huijiao Chaojin Xuanchuantuan Baogaoshu' (中國回教朝覲宣傳團報告) ['Report of Chinese Islamic Pilgrimage Propaganda Delegation'], 1948–9.

Neizhengbu (Ministry of Interior) File No. 026000013131A, 'Zhongguo Huijiao Jindong Fangwentuan Baogao' (中國回教近東訪問團報告) ['Report of Chinese Islamic Delegation to the Near East'), 1938.

Centre for Chinese Studies, Kuala Lumpur, Malaysia

Ma Tianying Papers, 1937–9.

National University of Singapore Libraries, Singapore

Wang Zengshan Private Papers, 1937–60.

Other Sources

Ahmad, Abu Talib. 2003. *Malay-Muslims, Islam, and the Rising Sun: 1941–1945*. Kuala Lumpur: Malaysian Branch of the Royal Asiatic Society.

Algar, Hamid. 2012. 'Tariqat and Tariq: Central Asian Naqshbandis on the Roads to the Haramayn'. In Alexandre Papas, Thomas Welsford, and Thierry Zarcone (eds), *Central Asian Pilgrims. Hajj Routes and Pious Visits between Central Asia and the Hejaz*, pp. 21–135. Berlin: Klaus Schwarz Verlag.

Aydin, Cemil. 2007. *The Politics of Anti-Westernism in Asia: Visions of World Order in Pan-Islamic and Pan-Asian Thought*. New York: Columbia University Press.

———. 2017. *The Idea of the Muslim World: A Global Intellectual History*. Cambridge, MA: Harvard University Press.

Aydin, Cemil and Wen, Shuang. 2014. 'Changing Modes of Political Dialogue across the Middle East and East Asia, 1880–2010'. *The Asia-Pacific Journal* 12 (20). Available at https://apjjf.org/2014/12/20/Cemil-Aydin/4118/article.html; last accessed 8 June 2020.

Benda, Harry J. 1958. *The Crescent and the Rising Sun: Indonesian Muslims under Japanese Occupation, 1942–45*. The Hague: W. van Hoeve.

Bose, Mihir. 2004. *Raj, Secrets, Revolution: A Life of Subhas Chandra Bose*. Grice Chapman Publishing.

Brophy, David. 2012. 'Five Races, One Parliament? Xinhai in Xinjiang and the Problem of Minority Representation in the Chinese Republic'. *Inner Asia* 14 (2): 343–64.

Bulag, Uradyn Erden. 2010. *Collaborative Nationalism: The Politics of Friendship on China's Mongolian Frontier*. Lanham, MD: Rowman & Littlefield Publishers.

Chaffee, John. 2006. 'Diasporic Identities in the Historical Development of the Maritime Muslim Communities of Song-Yuan China'. *Journal of the Economic and Social History of the Orient* 49 (4): 395–420.

Cieciura, Wlodzimierz. 2016. 'Ethnicity or Religion? Republican-Era Chinese Debates on Islam and Muslims'. In Jonathan Lipman (ed.), *Islamic Thought in China: Sino–Muslim Intellectual Evolution from the 17th to the 21st Century*, pp. 107–46. Edinburgh: Edinburgh University Press.

Dhulipala, Venkat. 2015. *Creating a New Medina: State Power, Islam, and the Quest for Pakistan in Late Colonial North India*. Daryaganj and Delhi: Cambridge University Press.

Ding Mingjun (丁明俊). 2015. 'Bai Chongxi yu Zhongguo huijiao jiuguo xiehui' (白崇禧與中國回教協會) ['Bai Chongxi and Chinese Muslim Association']. *Journal of Hui Muslim Minorities* 3: 5–13.

Duara, Prasenjit. 1988. *Culture, Power, and the State: Rural North China, 1900–1942*. Stanford, CA: Stanford University Press.

Esenbel, Selcuk. 2004. 'Japan's Global Claim to Asia and the World of Islam: Transnational Nationalism and World Power, 1900–1945'. *The American Historical Review* 109 (4): 1140–70.

Gelvin, James and Nile Green (eds). 2013. *Global Muslims in the Age of Steam and Print*. Berkeley: University of California Press.

Goossaert, Vincent and David A. Palmer. 2012. *The Religious Question in Modern China*. Chicago, Ill.: The University of Chicago Press.

Green, Nile. 2013. 'Spacetime and the Muslim Journey West: Industrial Communication in the Making of the 'Muslim World'. *The American Historical Review* 118 (2): 401–29.

Hammond, Kelly. 2015. 'The Conundrum of Collaboration: Japanese Involvement with Muslims in North China, 1931–1945'. PhD dissertation, Georgetown University, Washington, DC, USA.

Han, Inhye. 2015. 'The Afterlives of Korean An Chunggŭn in Republican China: From Sinocentric Appropriation to a Rupture in Nationalism'. *Cross-Currents: East Asian History and Culture Review* (17): 26–57.

Jacobs, Justin M. 2016. 'Exile Island: Xinjiang Refugees and the "One China" Policy in Nationalist Taiwan, 1949–1971'. *Journal of Cold War Studies* 18 (1): 188–218.

Jeong, Janice Hyeju. 2019. 'Between Shanghai and Mecca: Diaspora and Diplomacy of Chinese Muslims in the Twentieth Century'. PhD dissertation, Duke University, Durham, USA.

Jia Fukang (賈福康). 2005. *Taiwan Huijiaoshi* (台灣回教史) [*History of Islam in Taiwan*]. Taipei: Yisilan wenhua fuwushe.

Koyagi, Mikiya. 2013. 'The Hajj by Japanese Muslims in the Interwar Period: Japan's Pan-Asianism and Economic Interests in the Islamic World'. *Journal of World History* 24 (4): 849–76.

Kuwabara, Jitsuzo. 1928. 'On Pu Shou-Keng: A Man of Western Regions'. *Memoirs of the Research Department of the Tokyo Bunko* 2: 1–79.

———. 1935. 'On Pu Shou-Keng: A Man of Western Regions', *Memoirs of the Research Department of the Tokyo Bunko* 7: 1–104.

Landau, Jacob. 1994. *The Politics of Pan-Islam: Ideology and Organization*. Oxford: Clarendon.

Lary, Diana, Stephen R. MacKinnon, and Hans J. Van de Ven. 2015. *Negotiating China's Destiny in World War II*. Stanford: Stanford University Press.

Lei, Wan. 2010. 'The Chinese Islamic "Goodwill Mission to the Middle East" during Anti-Japanese War'. *Dîvân DİSİPLİNLERARASI ÇALIŞMALAR DERGİSİ* 15 (29): 133–70.

Leslie, Donald. 1986. *Islam in Traditional China: A Short History to 1800*. Belconnen, ACT: Canberra College of Advanced Education.

Li Tingbi (李廷弼). 1985. 'Zhongguo Huijiao xiehui di yici chaojin jishi' (中國回教協會第一次朝覲紀事) ['A Record of the First Pilgrimage Delegation [sent by the Chinese Muslim Association']. *Zhongguo Huijiao* 191 (December): 39–42.

Mao, Yufeng. 2011. 'A Muslim Vision for the Chinese Nation: Chinese Pilgrimage Missions to Mecca during World War II'. *The Journal of Asian Studies* 70 (2): 373–95.

Marsden, Magnus, Diana Ibañez-Tirado, and David Henig. 2016. 'Everyday Diplomacy'. *Cambridge Journal of Anthropology* 34 (2): 2–22.

Matsumoto, Masumi. 2006. 'Rationalizing Patriotism among Muslim Chinese: The Impact of the Middle East on the Yuehua Journal'. In Stéphane A. Dudoignon (ed.), *Intellectuals in the Modern Islamic World: Transmission, Transformation, Communication*, pp. 117–42. London: Routledge.

Mitter, Rana. 2013. *Forgotten Ally: China's World War II, 1937–1945*. Boston: Houghton Mifflin Harcourt.

Nedostup, Rebecca. 2009. *Superstitious Regimes: Religion and the Politics of Chinese Modernity*. Cambridge, MA: Harvard University Asia Center.

Park, Hyunhee. 2012. *Mapping the Chinese and Islamic Worlds: Cross-Cultural Exchange in Pre-Modern Asia*. Cambridge: Cambridge University Press.

Schottenhammer, Angela. 2009. 'Transfer of Xiangyao from Iran and Arabia to China: A Reinvestigation of Entries in the Youyang Zazu (863)'. In Ralph Kauz (ed.), *Aspects of the Maritime Silk Road: From the Persian Gulf to the East China Sea*, pp. 117–49. Wiesbaden: Otto Harrassowitz.

Schulz-Forberg, Hagen. 2015. *A Global Conceptual History of Asia, 1860–1940*. London: Routledge.

Sen, Tansen. 2003. *Buddhism, Diplomacy, and Trade: The Realignment of Sino–Indian Relations, 600–1400*. Honolulu: University of Hawai'i Press.

———. 2016. 'Taixu's Goodwill Mission to India: Reviving the Buddhist Links between India and China'. In Nayanjot Lahiri and Upinder Singh (ed.), *Buddhism in Asia*, pp. 293–322. New Delhi: Manohar.

Tsui, Brian. 2018. *China's Conservative Revolution: The Quest for a New Order*. Cambridge: Cambridge University Press.

Wang Zengshan (王曾善), Jelal al-Din. 1997. *Zhongguo huijiao jindong fangwentuan riji* (中國回教近東訪問團日記) [*Diaries of the Chinese Islamic Goodwill Mission to the Middle East*]. Kuala Lumpur: Wang Erli of the Muslim Welfare Organization of Malaysia.

Wan, Lei. 2017. 'Two Scholars and the Hui Protest Movement in China in 1932: The Attitudes of Hu Shih and Lu Xun toward the Hui Minority and Islam'. *Qiraat* (11): 1–31.

Worringer, Renée. 2014. *Ottomans Imagining Japan: East, Middle East, and Non-Western Modernity at the Turn of the Twentieth Century*. New York: Palgrave Macmillan.

Yamazaki, Noriko. 2014. 'Abdürreşid İbrahim's Journey to China: Muslim Communities in the Late Qing as Seen by a Russian-Tatar Intellectual'. *Central Asian Survey* 33 (3): 405–20.

Yasuhiro, Yokkaichi. 2008. 'Chinese and Muslim Diasporas and the Indian Ocean Trade Network under Mongol Hegemony'. In Angela Schottenhammer (ed.), *The East Asian Mediterranean: Maritime Crossroads of Culture, Commerce, and Human*, pp. 73–97. Wiesbaden: Otto Harrassowitz.

Zhang, Xing, and Tansen Sen. 2013. 'The Chinese in South Asia'. In Chee-Beng Tan (ed.), *Routledge Handbook of the Chinese Diaspora*, pp. 205–26. London, New York: Routledge.

Zhu Rongrong (朱蓉蓉). 2011. 'Kangzhan Shiqi Huijiao Shijiede Minjian Waijiao' (抗戰時期回教世界的民間外交) ['Islamic World's Civil Diplomacy during the War of Resistance']. *Xueshu Jiaoliu* 213 (12): 196–9.

SECTION IV:

BUILDING AND CHALLENGING
IMPERIAL NETWORKS

11

Indian Political Activism in
Republican China

MADHAVI THAMPI

D ocuments in the National Archives of India (NAI) in New
Delhi dating back to the early 1910s reveal a concern that had
started to trouble the British colonial government in India.
This was the problem of 'Indian sedition', which had begun to manifest
itself far away from India's shores, in the treaty ports and other cities
of China, including the British colony of Hong Kong. Thereafter, right
up until the mid-1940s, this problem continued to give headaches to
British policymakers, administrators, and diplomats in India, China,
and Britain, more so in some years than in others, but without ever
ceasing to cause some anxiety. What made it more difficult for the
authorities was that the phenomenon of 'Indian sedition' showed a
great capacity to metamorphose and adapt to changing circumstances
both in China and globally, making it that much harder to root out.

How did China become a locus of Indian political activism in
the first half of the twentieth century? Here, we need to distinguish
between two strands of such activism, though the two necessarily
overlapped. One was the phenomenon of radical Indian individuals
and groups, exiled from India because of their anti-colonial activities

or ideas, who were drawn or compelled to take refuge in China. The
other was the radicalization of ordinary Indian working people who
had come to China in pursuit of a livelihood or economic betterment.
Discontent and resentment among Indians resident in China came
together with dedicated political and organizational work by radical
groups and individuals. It was the existence and interaction of these
two strands that strengthened Indian political activism in China and
rendered it particularly troublesome to the British.

It must be noted that it was not just in China but at various other
places around the globe in this period that Indian emigrants and
exiles engaged in political activity directed against British colonial
rule. But, barring perhaps North America, few other places sustained
nationalist activism among Indians for so long as China, especially
in proportion to the size of the community there, which never numbered more than a few thousand at any given time.[1] My aim in this
chapter is to understand the reasons for this phenomenon, a much-
neglected aspect in the history of both the Indian national movement
and modern Sino-Indian relations.

The great currents of nationalism that arose in countries such as
India and China in the early twentieth century went hand in hand
with the spread of *trans*national movements and ideologies such as
socialism, anti-imperialism, and pan-Asianism. It would be correct
to say that nationalist organizations and leaders in India and China
did not view the problem of liberating their nations from foreign
domination in a narrow sense, but embraced larger visions of a new
and more just world order and of the place of their nations within
it. In a more practical sense, they also realized that the nationalist
cause in their own countries would benefit from external support
and alliances. This led them to pay great attention to geopolitical
developments both in the region around them and across the globe,
and they learned to utilize them skilfully for their cause. The inter-
weaving of national and international aspects was particularly con-
spicuous in the political activism of Indians in China. In this chapter,
I shall explore all these diverse aspects of Indian political activism
in China: the national as well as transnational strains within the
movement; conspiratorial aspects as well as mass mobilization; and
the role of various ideologies in this activism, such as nationalism,
pan-Asianism, and socialism.

This chapter is based primarily on archival material in the NAI and the Colonial Office Records in Hong Kong. The Foreign and Political Department proceedings in the NAI contain a large number of reports and correspondence relating to 'Indian sedition' in China. In addition, the Indian National Army (INA) collection of letters, memoirs, photographs, intelligence reports, and records of interrogations of INA prisoners, located in the Special Collections section of the NAI, are particularly revealing, as are the files in the Raja Mahendra Pratap Collection (RMP Coll.) in the same section. Since Hong Kong was an important location of Indian activism in China, as well as a major transit point for Indians going to and coming from China, the colonial authorities there kept a close watch on any signs of disturbance among the colony's resident Indians. Hence, the Colonial Office Records in the former colony (CO 129 series) has also produced important material related to this subject.

Early Disaffection among Indians in China: The Hindustan Ghadar Party and the First World War

The irony of Indian nationalism and political activism in China was that it was rooted in precisely those Indians who were considered the bedrock of British dominance in the region—the members of the police and armed forces. About half or more of the Indians in eastern China belonged to the security services (Thampi 1999: 339–45). In the nineteenth century, service in the British security forces stationed in China was seen as a desirable way of bettering a young Indian recruit's economic prospects, particularly among certain communities in Punjab and elsewhere in the northwest India that had a tradition of military service. However, by the beginning of the twentieth century, discontent over pay and other conditions began to surface among Indians employed in the British police, jail staff, and army regiments stationed in Hong Kong and the treaty ports in China. There was particular resentment over the disparity between their pay and those of their British counterparts, and 1907 saw the first strike by the police force in the Shanghai International Settlement, including the large proportion of Indians who served in it.

Initially, this disaffection found an outlet in secondary migration to other regions, particularly North America, where pay scales and other conditions were much better. The problem faced by the British was thus to find enough Indians to replace those who had left China for greener pastures, and they were eventually compelled to increase the pay of Indians serving in the police and jail staff there. But the safety valve provided by emigration to North America did not last long. From 1908, exclusion laws discouraging Indian immigration began to be implemented in both Canada and USA. By 1911, it was reported that Indian emigration from China's shores to North America was 'practically at a standstill' (Hong Kong Census Department 1965: Table XLI, 103 [56]). The number of Indians compelled to stay on in China while waiting in vain for a chance to go to North America was swelled by those who were forced to return from North America. Few of them had any gainful employment. A Sikh businessman visiting Hong Kong at that time testified to the conditions and mood among these Indians:

> When I came to Hong Kong for some private business in January 1914, I could not bear the grief and hardship of the Vancouver emigrants who had been waiting in the Sikh temple in Hong Kong. It was a matter of injustice and darkness, I thought, because our brethren were passing their days in a miserable state for the hope of arriving at Vancouver while staying here for one year and spending money for their eating from their own pockets.[2]

The Sikh temples or gurdwaras in Hong Kong and Shanghai became seething cauldrons of discontent, and the British even resorted briefly to the extraordinary measure of trying to prohibit army men and policemen from visiting them.[3] Among the officiating priests or *granthis* in the gurdwaras were some radical nationalists who inflamed the passions of their congregations. One of them, Bhagwan Singh, who served for three years as the granthi of the gurdwara in Hong Kong, was dismissed in 1913 for his 'seditious' activities. He made his way to Canada, where he became an influential figure in the recently formed the Hindustan Ghadar Party. Later he came back again to East Asia, where he interacted with Sun Yat-sen and other Asian revolutionaries.[4]

The same social stratum from which Indians in the security services in China came—mainly young men from rural Punjab and northwest India—formed the basis of the militant Hindustan Ghadar Party, which was founded on the west coast of USA in 1913. The Ghadar Party believed in the necessity for an armed overthrow of British rule in India, and a major target of its mobilization efforts was soldiers in Indian regiments, both in India itself and abroad. It is not surprising that its work among Indians in China, a large proportion of whom belonged to the armed forces, began almost as soon as it was founded. As early as September 1913, an activist called Mathra Singh arrived in Shanghai to begin organizing there, while in the same year a committee of four consisting of Hira Singh, Labh Singh, Bhagat Singh, and Hardit Singh was set up in Hong Kong (Deepak 1999: 440, 442). One of the major activities of the Ghadar activists was to persuade Indians to return to India to take part in the planned uprising there. The first *jatha* or detachment of volunteers from Shanghai left for India in August 1914. Another group consisting of Indians from North America and China left Guangzhou in October 1914.

Thousands of copies of the party's literature, including its main organ, *Ghadar* [*Revolt*], were distributed among Indians in China. Various places in China, such as the Hankou post office, also served as distribution points for smuggling the literature into India (Dignan 1983: 32–3). An Indian station master on the Shanghai–Nanjing railway line, M. Kohli, was one of those found to be involved in this activity.[5] The Ghadar Party's literature openly called on Indians not to be pawns in the hands of the British when it came to fighting the Chinese, probably the first such organization to do so. A poem in one of its publications, 'Ghadar ki Gunj' ['Echoes of Revolt'], in those years appealed to them as follows:

> Oh Brother, do not fight in a war against the Chinese. Beware of the enemy. He should not deceptively instigate you to fight your Chinese brothers. The enemy splits brothers and makes them kill each other. The people of Hind, China and Turkey are real brothers. (Josh 1977: 193)

In contrast to the high-flown sentiments of pan-Asianism that began to find expression among intellectuals and others in this period, this early manifestation of Asian solidarity stands out for the simplicity and directness of its expression, and for the fact that it was aimed at ordinary Indian working people, those who had been used to repress other

Asians, with the practical aim of rendering them ineffective as instruments of British aggression against China. The impact of this kind of mobilization was to become even more evident later, in the 1920s.

Indian revolutionaries abroad in this period, at a time when pan-Indian mass nationalism within India was still not strong, were very conscious of the need to mobilize external support for their cause. The outbreak of revolution in China, Britain's preoccupation with the First World War, and the existence of a number of states which were either overtly hostile to Britain (such as Germany) or at least not unsympathetic to anti-British fighters were all favourable circumstances which they were quick to try and use to their advantage.

The revolutionary atmosphere in China in the immediate aftermath of the 1911 Revolution and the heightened mood of anti-imperialism made it particularly suitable for political work by Indian nationalists. A letter written by a member of the Ghadar Party testifies to the support the Party received from various Chinese people, including prominent Chinese leaders such as the then-president of the Chinese Republic, Li Yuanhong (黎元洪), and the foreign minister, Wu Tingfang (伍廷芳). Li, the letter stated, 'is in sympathy with the Indian revolution and would like English power weakened. Some of the prominent people are quite eager to help India directly, and Germany indirectly, without exposing herself [*sic*] to any great risk'.[6] Ghadar Party leaders Satyendranath Sen and V.G. Pingley met Sun Yat-sen in November 1914 when they were on their way back to India from USA, as did the exiled nationalist Raja Mahendra Pratap. At that time, a major effort was underway to procure arms for the uprising that was being planned in India. Since arms were freely obtainable in China in this period, the country was important both as a source of military equipment and a route through which to smuggle it into India. The leaders of the Chinese government were directly approached for their help in this regard, and negotiations were held, but were ultimately unsuccessful. M.N. Roy, who was later active in the Comintern, also met Sun Yat-sen in Tokyo in 1915, but came away disappointed. As he wrote later, 'my faith in racial solidarity was shaken rudely by the refusal of the prophet of Asiatic nationalism to help India against Britain. His reason was purely opportunistic. He could not do anything against the British because Hong Kong was the base of his operations in South China' (Roy 1964: 5–6).

The outbreak of the First World War greatly expanded the possibilities for Indian nationalist activists in China to obtain foreign support. Germany showed great interest in encouraging Indian radical nationalists, not just in Berlin but in China as well. In China, Germany not only influenced those Indians who were directly in its employ, it was also reported to have tried to incite Indians in British service (Dignan 1983: 103–4). This prompted the British ambassador in China to ask the Government of India to send an intelligence officer to China for the first time with the specific purpose of keeping the Indians there under surveillance. In particular, Germany became instrumental in plots to acquire arms and ammunition for the Indian revolution, and it even negotiated with the Chinese government on behalf of the Indian nationalists.

The Colonial Office files in Hong Kong record the testimony of a certain Nawab Khan, an activist of the Ghadar Party who later became an informer. In it, Nawab Khan described in some detail the discussions he and his comrades had held with the German consul in Guangzhou:

> We found him in his office and explained to him at some length of our intention of going to India and stirring up a revolution. We further asked him to make arrangements with some Norway-Swedish Shipping Company for our conveyance to India ... We then asked the Consul whether he could procure us passports from the Chinese Government and thus enable us to buy arms in China and journey unhindered by land to India. In reply he pointed out that the Chinese Government was neutral and that the passports required were not likely to be granted ... We then asked the German Consul whether, in the event of our success in stirring up a revolution in India, whether we could count upon assistance from the German Navy. If such help were given us, we promised to allow Germany free trade with India. The German Consul said that he was not in a position to make us any promises in these matters ... He urged us to proceed to India and guaranteed us safety from the attacks of German cruisers. 'You must,' he said, 'make every effort direct or indirect to raise a rebellion in India.'[7]

What was clear was that the governments and political leaders of China, Germany, and other places were quite willing to see Indian nationalists cause trouble for the British, and were even willing to offer limited assistance, but what they were prepared to offer often did not match the Indians' expectations. In the end, this attempt to stage a revolt in India, led by returning Indians from abroad and with a limited infusion of arms and support from foreign powers, did not succeed. In 1915, the uprising planned by the Ghadar Party in India was betrayed from within and quickly stamped out by the British authorities. Heaving a sigh of relief, the British authorities in China concluded that the circumstances that had given rise to political activism among Indians there 'were unusual, and not likely to be repeated' (Petrie 1927: 190).[8]

High Tide of Anti-imperialist Solidarity in the 1920s

This optimistic British assessment failed to take into account several new factors ensuring that Indian political activism in China did not just survive but grew stronger in subsequent years. Even before Germany had been defeated, the October Revolution in Russia and the spread of 'Bolshevism' began to haunt the British. Although the Ghadar uprising was snuffed out in India, the party remained intact abroad (Deepak 1999: 447–54). Many activists in the Ghadar Party and other Indian nationalists made the journey to the Soviet Union to meet Soviet and Comintern leaders and to receive political and military training in academies set up specifically for the purpose. Raja Mahendra Pratap, the fiery nationalist exile who was later active in China for many years, was one of those who travelled to Moscow, even meeting V.I. Lenin in 1919. The inspiration and support received from the Soviet Union and the Comintern gave a new lease of life to Indian revolutionaries abroad, including in China, and it also helped to broaden their ideological horizons. In addition, the various international anti-imperialist, pan-Asian, and labour conferences organized with the support of the Comintern in the 1920s helped revolutionary individuals and groups form stronger and more enduring transnational links and networks, thus ending the conditions of relative isolation in which they had been compelled to function earlier.

The upsurge of mass anti-imperialist nationalism in China in the 1920s, which also received encouragement from the communist movement, was yet another factor that rekindled Indian political activism in China. In particular, the successes of the campaign led by the Kuomintang to achieve national unification and end foreign domination galvanized Indian activists. The Ghadar Party adopted a resolution in 1927 declaring that 'We the Hindustan Ghadar Party sympathize [with] and endorse in its entirety the national program adopted by the Kuomintang Party of China and its national struggle for freedom from the domination of the foreign powers' (cited in Deepak 1999: 449).

The Ghadar Party and other Indian nationalists were called upon to put their support for Chinese nationalism to the test when the British used Indian soldiers and police to attack anti-imperialist Chinese demonstrators in Hankou, Shanghai, and Guangzhou in 1925, resulting in the deaths of several Chinese. Munsha Singh, secretary of the Ghadar Party, sent a cable to the Kuomintang which bluntly stated: 'The Hindustan Ghadar Party declared any Hindu who fired upon the Chinese a traitor' (cited in Josh 1978: 264). As the British rushed reinforcements from India to confront the Chinese protests against its establishments in China, Indian activists in China swung into action at considerable risk to themselves to stop these Indian soldiers from attacking the Chinese. A report in *China Weekly Review* dated 6 August 1927 described how a detachment of Indian troops arriving in China 'were met, almost at the dock, by certain men of their own nationality, who were working for the cause of Indian freedom among the large groups of Indian police and watchmen already in Shanghai' (cited in Bhargava 1982: 221). In this particular case, the work of the activists was so effective that the detachment had to be quickly transferred back out again. It was also reported that Indian members of units from the Hong Kong and the Hankou police had defected to the Chinese side. There were even rumours that the entire Indian contingent of the Shanghai International Settlement police were preparing to do the same. Intelligence reports on Indians who were later arrested and deported testify to the methods they used to undermine the troops. For example:

> Gulzara Singh ... an ex-watchman with a bad record, spoke to a Mahomedan Lance Naik and three men of the 3/14th Punjab Regiment, and asked them why they came from the Punjab to fight against their Chinese brethren. Gulzara Singh went on to speak in a disloyal strain of the dishonesty of the British Government in paying Indian soldiers

less than British, and ended by attempting to persuade these men to
desert with their arms and equipment to the Chinese Nationalists.
(Petrie 1927: 211–12)

The British intelligence officer David Petrie (1927: 206–7), writing
in 1927, acknowledged that 'the anti-British agitation among Indians
in China is of an extent and intensity that cannot be regarded without
some anxiety'.

Raja Mahendra Pratap testified to how Chinese support for Indian
nationalism grew in the heady environment of the mid-1920s.
Describing a visit to Beijing at that time, he wrote:

> It was very lucky that just then China was in one of her most revolution-
> ary moods. Perhaps you remember that in spring 1925 British troops
> clashed with the Chinese masses at Shanghai. I openly condemned
> British police for killing Chinese! Chinese leaders at Peking welcomed
> me. Dinners were given, meetings were held and I lectured here and
> then there. One great mass meeting before the palace was exception-
> ally fiery. Here Madame Sun Yat-sen and myself spoke from the same
> platform. People wildly cheered us. (Pratap 1947: 102–3)

In this period, Pratap was the recipient of encouragement and
support from a wide variety of Chinese political leaders. On Sun
Yat-sen's son, Sun Ke (孫科), Pratap wrote: 'His knowledge about the
Indian affairs is very extensive, and he takes personal interest in the
Indian problems ... in thought and spirit he is very near to India and
the Indians. He can count several Indians as his personal friends'
(Pratap 1947: 196). Pratap even received support from Chinese leaders for some of his more adventurous schemes, such as an attempt
to visit Lhasa and obtain the support of the Dalai Lama for his plans
to overthrow the British in India. Although this scheme was unsuccessful, he was cordially received by Chinese leaders and administrators and offered assistance throughout his long march to Tibet. The
warlord Feng Yuxiang (冯玉祥) assisted his delegation with passports
and travel documents, as well as guns, ammunition, and money. In
Ningxia, the local strongman, General Ma Hongkui (马鸿逵), went so
far as to casually offer 25,000 of his own soldiers to go and fight the
British. Even Pratap, who never hesitated to ask for all kinds of help
for his cause, was astonished at this proposal.[9]

Thus, despite the setbacks suffered towards the end of the First World War, favourable conditions both in China and internationally during the following decade enabled Indian activists to carry on and extend their work in China, often under the direct protection and support of Chinese leaders and organizations such as the Kuomintang and the Chinese Communists. Ghadar Party branches were established in Shanghai and Hankou, as well as in Guangzhou, Beijing, Tianjin, and Nanjing. A printing press was set up in Hankou to publish the party paper, the *Hindustan Ghadar Dhandora*. Dasawandha (Dasaundha) Singh and Ganda Singh were among the most important leaders in Hankou, although the former later shifted his base to Shanghai, joining Gajjan Singh there. In Shanghai, their headquarters was situated in the office of the General Labour Union in Zhabei. They also ran a club at 19 North Sichuan Road, which had been set up by a Sindhi merchant, Lal Chand. Chinese support was extended to other Indian nationalist groups as well, such as the Indian Youth League, which also had its headquarters in Zhabei. According to one intelligence report, the Indian Youth League had 'some kind of agreement with the Kuomintang and the Bureau of Public Safety, which enabled it to hold meetings and carry on political activity. The leaders were young working men who were literate and intelligent' (cited in Bhargava 1982: 223).

The split in the ranks of the Kuomintang following Chiang Kai-shek's coup in 1927 had an adverse impact on the Indian activists. The headquarters of their operations had to shift out of Shanghai to Hankou, where the government of the 'Left' Kuomintang continued to function, though not for long. Indian groups that had been receiving some monetary help from the Kuomintang found that their funds were reduced, and then eventually cut off, plunging them into considerable difficulties.[10] It was around the same time that the British in Shanghai, using the excuse of the murder of the top Indian police functionary there, Buddha Singh, cracked down on several leading activists, including Dasawandha Singh and Gajjan Singh, and had them deported to India. Using the general climate of political confusion after 1927, the British continued their raids on Indian activists and deportations until 1931. Thereafter, they were discontinued because the British believed that the movement had been sufficiently undermined and no longer posed a significant threat.

Pan-Asianism and the Problem of Japanese Militarism

The spirit of Asian solidarity went beyond mutual sympathy and support between Indians and Chinese for each other's nationalist struggles. Activists such as Raja Mahendra Pratap in particular envisaged an altogether new world in which the divisions between different Asian societies would be overcome, and Asia would form a single 'Golden Land' in a future World Federation.[11] Pratap's obsession with Asian unity within a larger World Federation certainly made him unique among Indian activists in China, but his fascination with such transnational and universalist ideas was not unusual in the global climate of the inter-War period. Pratap was intensely aware of the limitations of having what he saw as a narrow nationalist standpoint. As he was to write in a distinctly utopian vein:

> Why do you not understand this simple thing: If some one loves Japan he can not love India and if some one loves India he can not love Japan. But one who loves Asia he can love Japan, China, India and the other countries of this continent alike. And one who loves Asia he can not love Europe or America. He will sow seeds of bigger struggles of the continents. But one who loves the world will surely love Africa, Europe and Americas all alike. (Cited in Lawson 2010: 9)

From 1931, Pratap devoted much effort to building up his centre in Beijing in order to promote the idea of a World Federation. Apart from bringing out three different language editions of a paper entitled *World Federation*, Pratap seems to have run a free language school where English, Japanese, Persian, and Urdu were taught. However, his timing was unfortunate. Anger among Chinese against the Japanese invasion of Manchuria in September 1931 had an almost immediate effect on his activities. From October and November 1931, Pratap's diary records that there were now very few takers for either his pan-Asia meetings or his World Federation Club, and even the number of students in his language school dwindled. 'Every little more disturbance in Manchuria or Tientsin affects our student body,' he complained (Pratap 1947: 218).

It must be acknowledged that many Indians in this period were profoundly impressed by Japan's rise to a position from which it could challenge the Western powers, as well as by its espousal of the idea of pan-Asianism and by the concrete assistance and protection powerful Japanese figures gave to exiled Indian nationalists.[12] Pratap himself was particularly influenced by advocates of pan-Asian unity in Japan such as Okawa Shumei and Nakatani Takeyo. He also had close ties with other Indian nationalist activists who were closely connected with Japan, such as Rash Behari Bose and Anand Mohan Sahay. As a consequence, he found it hard to take a stand against Japan when it commenced its expansionist drive against China, which he tended to view rather as an unnecessary quarrel between fellow Asians which would benefit Western imperialism. As he put it,

> If any conflict occurs between Japan and China, a third country will probably come in to usurp whatever China has today. It would be suicidal for China and even for all Asia. The greatest problem which faces Oriental peoples today is to promote understanding between Japan and China.[13]

If Pratap had confined himself to maintaining a position of silence or inaction on the issue of Japan's invasion of China, he might not have opened himself to such condemnation as he experienced. However, he insisted on carrying on with his work of forging pan-Asian unity in concert with Japanese of known militarist inclinations. In 1934, he began a drive to recruit Chinese volunteers for his grand 'Asiatic Army' of the World Federation. However, denounced as 'the false servant of conflicting loyalties'[14] and as a Japanese puppet, he found himself literally chased out of Guangzhou, where he had been well received in earlier days. Other Indian organizations such as the Indian Youth League were compelled to condemn his 'treachery' openly. Pratap confessed to being 'a little angry with the unjust people' who denounced him but, remaining unrepentant, he said that he was only 'sorry that many people cannot see the salvation which our programme brings to all humanity'.[15]

Unsurprisingly, therefore, Pratap's public activities in China tapered off, and he appears not to have visited China again after 1941, spending the remainder of the War years in relative obscurity in Japan. 'Seditious' activities by Indians in China nonetheless continued at a low level in the late 1930s. One development was the formation by Anand Mohan Sahay of the Indian National Association of China in 1938. This organization identified itself closely with the programme and aims of the Indian National Congress, which had come to acquire an increasingly dominant profile in the Indian national movement, particularly after the first provincial elections held in 1937 in India. The Congress had, of course, strongly condemned the Japanese invasion of China right from the 1930s. Nevertheless, the Japan factor in Indian political activism in China refused to die out. Rash Behari Bose, Anand Mohan Sahay, and Pratap himself all continued to speak up and organize some activities on behalf of Indian freedom from their base in Japan. Moreover, once Japan had occupied most of eastern and central China, most Indians in China found themselves living under Japanese control, far away from the zone dominated by the Kuomintang or the Chinese Communists. Although they suffered from the general devastation and disruption caused by war and occupation, as a community, they were not targeted by the Japanese in the same way as the Chinese and the British and other Europeans. Therefore, it was not altogether surprising that the Indian community in China was by and large not hostile to Japan, especially when it appeared to them that Japan would help India achieve its independence. In the wake of Britain's crushing defeats at Japanese hands in Asia after 1941, when the standard of armed revolt against British rule in India in alliance with Japan was raised, Indians in China responded to the call virtually en masse.

The Final Phase: The Indian National Army in China

Although political activity among Indians in China seemed to have declined over the course of the 1930s, the Indian community in China was not immune to the growing momentum of the anticolonial movement back home. A six-monthly intelligence report on Indians in China at the end of March 1940 characterized 'seditious activities' among them as 'negligible'. However, the next report, dated 30 September 1940, stated that 'during this period there has been considerably greater activity in the Indian community in Shanghai than normal'.[16] Sahay, for example, was able to hold a well-attended political meeting of Indians in Shanghai on 4 August.

As had happened earlier in the First World War, the difficulties faced by Britain at the start of the Second World War seemed to many Indian nationalists to provide favourable conditions for putting pressure on Britain to relinquish its control of India. In particular, the string of military defeats Britain suffered in its Asian territories at the hands of Japan in 1942 seemed like a 'golden opportunity' to strike the final blow for freedom for India. The Indian National Congress led by Gandhi and Nehru gave the call for Britain to 'Quit India', which drew a huge response from masses of people across India. However, it was the effort by the equally charismatic leader Subhas Chandra Bose to raise an armed force among Indian soldiers in Asia and to march on India's borders in the company of the advancing Japanese armies that drew an overwhelming response from Indians in China. Bose, like other Congress leaders, had been jailed by the British, but unlike the others, he made a successful bid to escape and fled to Germany. In the meantime, the Japanese in Southeast Asia had been working with Indian soldiers and officers who had been captured there to form the nucleus of the INA dedicated to the overthrow of British rule in India. The arrival of Bose in Singapore in 1943 to take charge of the INA had an electrifying effect on Indians in East and Southeast Asia, who felt that they could now play a decisive role in securing India's freedom.

Within a short time, branches of the INA and its political organization, the Indian Independence League (IIL), were set up in Hong Kong, Shanghai, Guangzhou, and other cities in eastern China. With support from the community and protection from the Japanese authorities, the IIL/INA became the dominant political force among Indians in China during the war. The IIL/INA branches raised funds from the community, including from the predominantly Sindhi and Parsi merchants, conducted military camps that provided military training to both men and women, set up community centres such as the Azad Hind Club in Shanghai, broadcast radio programmes, brought out journals in English and Urdu, and in general undertook measures for the relief and welfare of the community. The chairman of the China Territorial Committee of the IIL was Jalal Rahman, while the heads of the Shanghai and Hong Kong branches were Lala Nanak Chand and Colonel Dost Mohammed Khan, respectively.

Key questions with respect to the IIL/INA have concerned the extent to which it functioned as an agent of Japan, as well as the extent to which its support among Indians in China was voluntary. In the climate of recrimination and infighting in the community following the end of the War and the defeat of the INA and the Japanese, accusations of forced donations and coercion were rife. However, League members consistently emphasized their operational and financial independence. The memoirs of Major B. Narayan Singh, who commanded the Shanghai branch of the INA, insisted that 'We were no puppets in the hands of any foreign power' and that Japanese help was always minimal and slow in coming.[17] Harnam Singh, who was the finance member of the League in Shanghai, wrote:

> [T]he local Indians, though poor and small in number have given over $5,000,000.00 for the Indian war-chest. Most of this money comes from the pockets of those poor people who had saved cent by cent during years of their residence in Shanghai and hard labour as watchmen. Some merchants have also followed their suits [sic]. There have been many instances when people have not only given whatever they possessed but have also left their jobs and enrolled as members of the Indian National Army.[18]

While coercion in specific instances cannot be ruled out, there is no doubting the enthusiasm of hundreds of volunteers and their strong conviction that they were fighting only for India. This enthusiasm reached a crescendo when Bose himself visited Shanghai in December 1944. Addressing a packed hall of local Indians at the Grand Theatre, Bose emphasized the importance of the work being done by the Indians in a city which he described as the nerve centre of communications in this part of the world.[19].

However, by this time, the joint Japanese–INA military campaign to march on India's borders had already been halted and reversed at Imphal and Kohima in India's northeast. Japan and the Axis powers had begun to suffer major defeats. Just a few months after Bose's visit to Shanghai, he was reported as having died in a plane crash in Taiwan. With the end of the War in the East following Japan's surrender, Indians accused of collaborating with the enemy were rounded up, jailed, and deported by the Chinese and the British. This time, it was not just a few activists who were deported, but the bulk of the Indian community in eastern China was repatriated. Mass destitution and starvation stared them in the face at the end of the War, and the British made it clear that they would not assume responsibility for their fate if they rejected the offer to be shipped back to India. Left with no choice, hundreds of them clambered aboard ships bound for

India with whatever possessions they could carry with them, uprooting themselves from the country where they had spent decades, even generations. The officially organized repatriations continued until the end of 1946. Less than a year later, the British finally left India, and the two newly independent states of India and Pakistan came into being.

**

An objective history of the anti-colonial movement in India would show that Indian communities and political groups abroad, at times, played a role out of proportion to their size. Certainly, their relative freedom from the oppressive British colonial state apparatus at home and their ability to form alliances and networks with supportive forces and governments abroad had something to do with this. Perhaps even more important was their exposure to new ideas and experiences, which helped to reinforce and sharpen their sense of discontent with their status as a subjugated people.

Exiled Indian nationalists in China made full use of the fluid political conditions in Republican China. The divided political authority in China and its treaty ports gave them considerable freedom of manoeuvre, while the anti-imperialist and revolutionary atmosphere in the country provided them with powerful encouragement and support. During the Second World War, Japanese protection also enabled them to organize openly against British power. Sudden changes in the political tide did affect them, but never succeeded in eliminating their political activity completely until the end of the colonial period. What we can see are waves of activism, with periods of great intensity interspersed with relative quiet, corresponding to the ebb and flow of larger tides of nationalism and anti-imperialism both in India itself and globally.

Admittedly, however, the role of Japan greatly complicated the nature and fortunes of Indian political activism in China in this period. In the first two decades of the twentieth century, Japan was a model to not just Indian anti-colonial fighters but to other Asians as well. The tradition of Japanese providing support and refuge to Indian nationalists in East Asia began at this time. However, from the early 1930s, the role of Japan became an immensely problematic one as far as Indian nationalists in China were concerned. As we can see from the case of Raja Mahendra Pratap, the Japanese connection became a liability for these Indian activists, as the perception of Japan in China changed from that of a champion of pan-Asianism to that of an occupier. The tag of 'collaborationism' was something that many Indians in China who had joined or supported the INA during the Second World War found hard to shake off.

The character of Indian political activism in China was conditioned by the large proportion of soldiers, policemen, and watchmen among them. On the one hand, this stratum was expected to be, and to some extent certainly was, loyal to the colonial master. However, in particular circumstances, these men, who made their living by bearing arms, responded more willingly than other Indians to calls to take up arms against the British. During the First World War, hundreds of them returned home to take part in an armed uprising, while in the late 1920s, scores of them were willing to break ranks and fight alongside the Chinese against the British. In the Second World War, when the dominant forms of protest among Indians in India took the form of the relatively non-violent satyagraha, civil disobedience, and street protests, Indian soldiers in China and Southeast Asia organized themselves into detachments of the INA with the aim of overthrowing British rule by force of arms. While they may not have succeeded in their immediate aims, they certainly contributed to the crisis of British rule in India and, particularly in the last phase, provided one more proof to the British that their hold over India could not last much longer.

The dominant narrative of the interplay of Indian and Chinese currents of nationalism, pan-Asianism, and anti-imperialism in the early twentieth century has tended to focus on luminaries such as Sun Yat-sen, Tagore, Nehru, and Chiang Kai-shek.[20] However, apart from these prominent individuals, there were also hundreds of lesser known, even largely anonymous individuals who also participated in them. An examination of the political activities of ordinary Indian soldiers, policemen, and other Indian residents in China in this period, I argue, provides greater insights into various dimensions of the interactions between Indians and Chinese in confronting imperialist domination. These include the attraction of militant nationalism based on armed force, the multiplicity of networks forged among Indians, Chinese, and other Asian peoples, the influence of communism and other transnational ideologies and movements, and the deeply problematic role of Japan. What emerges from their story is a more nuanced understanding of the complex forces of nationalism, anti-imperialism, pan-Asianism, and great-power rivalry that were played out in China and India in this period.

Notes

1. Don Dignan (1983: 32–3), speaking of the period during the First World War, stated that 'the conditions in neutral and semi-colonial China made it second in importance only to the United States as a source of recruitment for revolutionary activities'. However, even after the end of the War, Indian political activism continued and adopted new forms (Thampi 2005: 191–209).

2. CO/129, 8 April 1914, p. 286. The businessman Gurdit Singh became famous for chartering a Japanese ship, the *Komagata Maru*, to transport Indians from China and Japan to Vancouver in 1914. The fate of its passengers, who were turned back from Vancouver harbour and then persecuted and even killed when they returned to Calcutta, was an important landmark in the Indian anti-colonial struggle.

3. On the Sikhs in China, see Chapter 1 by Mangalagiri and Chapter 9 by Cao in this volume.

4. To see how the British tracked Bhagwan Singh as he moved around Asia and North America, see CO/129, files for the period 1914–15, nos 410, 423, and 427.

5. NAI/For. & Pol./Secret-War/June 1917/1–46.

6. Cited in G.T. Brown, 1989, 'Hindu Conspiracy and the Neutrality of the U.S.A. (1914–1917)', unpublished MA thesis, University of California, Berkeley, California, pp. 67–9, microfilm, NAI, Acc. No. 1241 (Part).

7. CO 129/429, 17 July 1915, pp. 374 –6.

8. Petrie was the officer in the Indian Crime Investigation Department (CID) who was sent to China to monitor the political activities of Indians there.

9. The support Pratap received from the Chinese on his first attempt to visit Lhasa contrasts strongly with the coolness with which his second attempt in 1931 was received (Pratap 1947: 200–1).

10. NAI/For. & Pol./1932/139-X (Sec).

11. For a discussion of Raja Mahendra Pratap's espousal of pan-Asianism and the ideal of a World Federation, see Stolte (2012: 203–23).

12. See Viren Murthy's contribution to this volume for the differences in attitude towards Japan in this period among people from different Asian

countries. The Sino-Japanese War of 1895 and the Japanese annexation of Korea in 1907 had already led to disenchantment with Japan among many Chinese and Koreans. However, among Indian nationalists, Japan's espousal of pan-Asianism, and in particular its defeat of a Western power, Russia, in 1905, continued to be looked upon with admiration.

13. From an article in *The Japan Adventurer*, 18 March 1934, NAI/RMP Coll./ Scrapbook II/S.No.26 [i] .

14. From an article by Hollington K. Tong, 'China Indians Oppose Pratap's Movement', (NAI/RMP Coll./Scrapbook No.II, S.No. 26[ii]).

15. NAI/RMP Coll./Scrapbook No.II/S.No.27.

16. NAI/EAD/Ext Affairs/1940/F.No.424-X [Sec].

17. Major B. Narayan Singh, 1949, 'Memoirs and INA Activities in Shanghai, China', 10 October, NAI/IIL Papers/Acc. No. 205, F. No. 10.

18. Harnam Singh. 1944, *On to Delhi*, Volume 1, No.5, December, p. 12, NAI/ IIL Papers/Acc. No. 205, F.No. 8. A list of about 52 Indian merchants and their contributions to the IIL can also be found in NAI/IIL Papers/Acc. No.205/File no. 9.

19. NAI/IIL Papers/Acc. No. 205/F.No. 8/14–15.

20. See, for instance, Tan Chung et al. (2011), Yang Tianshi (2015), Yang Yun Yuan (1974), and Samarani (2005).

References

Archival Material

Great Britain Colonial Office, microfilm, University of Hong Kong

Hong Kong: Original Correspondence (CO 129), 1842–1951.

National Archives of India, New Delhi

Indian Independence League Papers.
Proceedings, Foreign and Political Department.
Proceedings, External Affairs Department.
Raja Mahendra Pratap Collection (RMP).
Microfilm, NAI, Acc. No. 1241 (Part).

Other Sources

Bhargava, Moti Lal. 1982. *Netaji Subhas Chandra Bose in South East Asia and India's Liberation War, 1943–5*. New Delhi: Vishwavidya Publishers.

Deepak, B.R. 1999. 'Revolutionary Activities of the Ghadar Party in China'. *China Report* (35) 4: 439–56.

Dignan, Don. 1983. *The Indian Revolutionary Problem in British Diplomacy, 1914–1919*. New Delhi: Allied Publishers.

Josh, Sohan Singh. 1977. *Hindustan Ghadar Party: A Short History*, Volume I. New Delhi: People's Publishing House.

———. 1978. *Hindustan Ghadar Party: A Short History*, Volume II. New Delhi: People's Publishing House.

Lawson, Konrad. 2010. 'Pan-Asianism or World Federalism: Raja Mahendra Pratap and the Japanese Empire, 1925–1945'. Accessible on http://muninn.net/papers/2010/pratap/pratap-presentation.pdf; last accessed on 2 June 2012.

Petrie, David. 1927. *Communism in India*. Calcutta: Government of India Press.

Pratap, Mahendra. 1947. *My Life Story of Fifty Five Years (Dec. 1886 to Dec. 1941)*. Dehradun: World Federation.

Hong Kong Census Department. 1965. 'Report of the Census of the Indian Population of Hong Kong Taken on Twentieth May, 1911'. In *Hong Kong Census Reports, 1841–1941*. Hong Kong.

Roy, M.N. 1964. *M.N. Roy's Memoirs*. Bombay: Allied Publishers Pvt Ltd.

Samarani, Guido. 2005. 'Shaping the Future of Asia: Chiang Kai-shek, Nehru and China- India Relations during the Second World War Period'. Working Paper No. 11, Centre for East and South-East Asian Studies, Lund University, Sweden.

Stolte, Carolien. 2012. '"Enough of the Great Napoleons!" Raja Mahendra Pratap's Pan- Asian Projects (1929–39)'. *Modern Asian Studies* 46 (2): 403–23.

Tan Chung, Amiya Dev, Wang Bangwei, and Wei Liming (eds). 2011. *Tagore and China*. New Delhi: SAGE.

Thampi, Madhavi. 1999. 'A Note on the Indian Population in China in the Nineteenth and Early Twentieth Centuries'. *China Report* 35 (3): 339–45.

———. 2005. *Indians in China, 1800–1949*. New Delhi: Manohar Publishers.

Yang Tianshi. 2015. 'Chiang Kai-shek and Jawaharlal Nehru'. In Hans Van de Ven, Diana Lary and Stephen R. Mackinnon (eds), *Negotiating China's Destiny in World War II*, pp. 127–40. Stanford: Stanford University Press.

Yang Yun Yuan. 1974. 'Nehru and China, 1927–1949'. PhD dissertation, University of Virginia, USA.

12

Between Alliance and Rivalry

Nationalist China and India during the Second World War

LIAO WEN-SHUO

Alliance-Building and Security Abroad

As soon as Japan's Hirota Kōki (廣田弘毅) Cabinet passed the Basic National Policy to confirm that the basis of its foreign policy would be the northern continental policy of 1936, the 'Nanshin-ron' (南進論), or 'Southward Expansion Doctrine', was included in policy discussions in Japan for the first time. The Empire's Diplomatic Policy proposed that in order to secure the stability of East Asia, maintain the survival and development of the Japanese Empire, and strengthen its national power, its continental policy towards China should be regarded as crucial. Consequently, a policy of step-by-step external expansion was to be implemented in order to bring Southeast Asia into Japan's sphere of influence. However, after Japan unleashed an undeclared all-out war of aggression against China in

July 1937 because progress with this policy was not as smooth as expected, its primary strategic objective became cutting off the main route China was using to deliver military supplies and equipment back to the battle front through French Indochina and British Burma. In doing so, Japan aimed to sever China's lifeline and undermine its resistance to the Japanese army.

After the outbreak of the Second World War in September 1939, Japan strengthened its alliances with Germany and Italy and then turned to the southern route. In 1940, the Konoe Fumimaro (近衞 文麿) Cabinet passed an Outline of Basic National Policy explicitly addressing the political objective of southward expansion in order to establish 'New Orders in Greater East Asia', followed by the 'Greater East Asia Co-Prosperity Sphere', a colossal empire dominated by Japan and covering the entire area from India to Australia and New Zealand, and all the states in between. In 1941, Japan's Command Headquarters drew up an 'Outline of a Southward Expansion Policy' with the hope of establishing close cooperative relationships with French Indochina and Thailand in military affairs, political relations, and economic activities while shutting out the influence of Europe and USA upon Asia. At that time, USA was already implementing an oil embargo against Japan, and several rounds of Japanese–US negotiation had stalled. Their relationship rapidly deteriorated, and a big war seemed almost unavoidable.

By then, given the ever-changing situation of the Second World War and the Japanese army's proactive preparations for its south-ward expansion, the British authorities in both India and Burma (now Myanmar) were forced to respond. However, while the subject peoples in both states had been experiencing a change of heart from having lived under colonial domination for too long, the Indian National Congress (INC), the largest political party in the British Raj, strongly objected when the viceroy and governor general of India unilaterally declared war on Germany in September 1939 without consulting Indian public opinion. The INC demanded India's imme-diate independence from the British Empire and the establishment of a constitutional convention, but their demands were rejected, and many of its members were arrested and jailed. Burma left India in 1937 to become a so-called semi-dominion with a fully functioning anti-British independence movement. Thakins, the strongest political party led by Aung San, took the initiative to form an alliance with the New Poor Man's Party led by Ba Maw to establish the National League for Free Burma and to demand that Britain grant Burma the freedom to decide its own form of government and to convene a constitutional conference, a demand that resulted in the governor general's office imposing large-scale military repression. The fact that China, India, and Burma were neighbouring states and that the Kuomintang (KMT)-led Nationalist government had already been fighting alone against Japan for some time gradually induced both the ruling and opposition parties in China, Britain, and the British colonies of India and Burma to be concerned with the development of positive regional relations.

The increasing availability in recent years of Nationalist government documents, intelligence materials, and the personal papers and diaries of Nationalist figures from the 1930s to 1940s has allowed historians to refresh their perspectives on the events of these years and acquire a clearer view of how the Nationalist government in Chongqing assessed the war situation both in China and abroad, including the strength and weakness of Japan, China's neighbouring countries, and the rest of the world. Studies in the archives of the Nationalist government and the KMT, especially the Chiang Kai-shek (蔣介石) Collection relating to India during the Second World War, reveal the directions of Chinese Nationalist foreign policy in this critical historical period.[1]

Using military, diplomatic, and intelligence sources may help scholars understand how the changing images of India and Indian politics that arose in Chongqing during China's war against Japan began to shape national policies and international negotiations. Four episodes will be discussed in terms of regional politics and the struggle for dominance in Asia in the turbulent years: the situations in China, India, and Britain on the eve of the Pacific War; the establishment of a wartime intelligence network; the anti-Japanese propaganda campaign during the initial stages of the Pacific War; and China–India relations between alliance and rivalry towards the end of the Pacific War. This chapter aims to probe two aspects in particular. The first aspect is how the Nationalists managed to collect information and intelligence, conduct people-to-people diplomacy, and develop an anti-Japanese propaganda campaign as a response to the

Japanese army's southward expansion, alongside the increase in the geostrategic importance of both India and Burma to China at war. The second aspect is the impact of the Chinese Nationalist government's perceptions of India on its planning to form alliances and exercise diplomacy during the War, and the distinguishing characteristics of international political manoeuvres as reflected by the activities in question.

China, India, and Britain on the Eve of the Pacific War

Upon the outbreak of the War in Europe in September 1939, China was already into its third year of all-out war against Japan. The Nationalist government gradually changed its assessment of the War from negative to positive, and with it, its strategy for an international solution, that is, to integrate the Sino-Japanese War with the war in Europe. In the spring of 1939, the Chinese government proposed principles of military and economic cooperation in the Far East to the British and French governments. China promised to supply fighting forces, manpower, and natural resources to the limits of its capacity while requesting Britain and France to send naval and air forces to participate in joint warfare in the Far East. The vulnerability of the Western powers' colonial possessions and interests in Southeast Asia to Japanese forces moving south were especially emphasized. In the wake of the Japanese capture of Guangzhou, in a foreign press conference, Chiang Kai-shek described Japan's further occupation of Hainan Island in February 1939 as the 'Mukden Incident of the Pacific'.[2] In their determination to receive Western support and commitment, Chinese Nationalist leaders strove to portray Japanese actions as a drive to expel Western influence from the region and as a formidable scheme for dominating East Asia and the western Pacific. Despite disagreements within his government over the benefits or otherwise of a European alliance, in general, Chiang adhered firmly to the position of making Japan 'the sole enemy' while carefully weighing the respective importance of the other countries whose support he needed.[3] After the French and British had replied that they did not deem the present situation in the Far East to have developed to such a stage that they could consider the proposal for cooperation, Hu Shi (胡適), the Chinese Ambassador to USA, was instructed to

communicate the same proposal to Washington, DC, in April in order
to obtain US support. In July 1939, seeing the war in Europe as inevitable, Chiang wrote to President Franklin Roosevelt requesting USA
to press the democratic nations in Europe not to negotiate separately
or compromise with Japan.

In the meantime, Zhu Jiahua (朱家驊), then-head of the KMT's
Organization Department and director of the Sino-Indian Cultural
Society, was approached by the INC leader Jawaharlal Nehru, who
expressed a wish to visit China. At that time, Nehru had been working
with his INC comrades to give the Indian Independence struggle an
internationalist outlook for over a decade. Leading members of the
INC soon showed their sympathy with China after the war against
Japan broke out in 1937, and in the autumn of 1938, they sent a medical mission to China. In the meantime, Nehru's efforts to build an
anti-fascist alliance, mainly with the left wing of the British Labour
Party under Stafford Cripps, was enjoying great success in 1938,
earning himself the following appraisal from the Conservative leader
Winston Churchill: 'communist, revolutionary, most capable and
most implacable of the enemies of the British connection with India'
(cited in Nanda 1995: 253). On returning from Europe, Nehru made
up his mind to visit China. Arriving in late August 1939, he met with
leading Nationalists and expressed sympathy and support of the INC
for China's war with Japan. In his 'A Note on the Development of
Contacts between China and India', drafted during his visit, Nehru
made a series of suggestions in order to enhance contacts and cooperation between China and India, including:[4]

1. the need to organize an efficient system and regulate service of
    information
2. an exchange of experts for studying the development of coopera-
    tive industries and agricultural problems, here including direct
    contacts between China and the All India Village Industries
    Associations
3. the draft of a common outlook and policy on some major interna-
    tional issues.

Nehru's suggestions were substantially shared and approved by
the Chinese authorities. At Chiang's order, Minister of Education

Chen Lifu (陳立夫) and Zhu Jiahua drafted a KMT–INC agreement of 'Measures for Implementation of Cultural Cooperation between China and India'.[5] The plan of cooperation was highly classified, defined as cultural and limited to relations between the KMT and INC. The Nationalists were deeply concerned about Britain's attitude and especially careful not to offend the British government. They also tried hard to avoid the Japanese propaganda machine's attempts to sabotage China's war effort and the already delicate Sino-British relationship.

Top priorities were given to exchanges of professors, students, and publications, as well as the Buddhist Mission led by Master Taixu (太虛), the Buddhist modernist and activist who at that time had been commissioned to visit Southeast Asia and would later make a detour to Burma and India (Sen 2017: 322–32).[6] As far as the Nationalist government was concerned, cultural cooperation was an instrument on the one hand for establishing the foundations of Sino-Indian cooperation, and on the other hand for developing concrete political cooperation further. All the joint activities were planned and carried out by the KMT and INC.[7] At Nehru's earnest invitation, the Nationalists agreed to send a representative to the 1939 INC Annual National Conference held in December. After due consideration, Zhu Jiahua and other leaders suggested that the famous educator and linguist Fu Sinian (傅斯年), then-director of the Institute of History and Philology, Academia Sinica, would be a good choice. First, KMT leaders were deemed unsuitable for being sent to the conference, as this might annoy the British government. Second, Fu was currently not a KMT member, even though he had sympathy for, good knowledge of, and a close relationship with the party. Third, Fu was a distinguished scholar who had studied at University College London for three years. Fourth, in the name of scholarly exchange, it would be easier for Fu to pursue and assist with political work and connections in India.[8] However, in view of the irreconcilable conflicts between the INC and British authorities, the Chinese ambassador to Britain, Guo Taiqi (郭泰祺) (also romanized as Quo Tai-chi), warned of the inevitable complications of the Indian issue and that it would be best for China to drop the idea of sending a representative to the INC conference.[9] The acute reality of the Second World War beginning in 1939 and the INC's refusal to support the War effort until India was first granted independence made the cooperation plan harder to put into practice.

In October 1940, following repeated requests from Chiang Kai-shek firmly backed by USA, London decided to reopen the Burma Road, which had been closed some months before under Japanese pressure. The Burma Road, which linked southern Burma to Kunming and, therefore, to Chongqing, was then one of the few routes through which China could receive foreign aid after the Japanese had created conditions for a blockade of China. On the occasion of the temporary reopening of the Burma Road in 1940, Chiang Kai-shek personally thanked Churchill for his decision. The newly elected British prime minister immediately took advantage of the occasion to raise the question of the possible moderating influence that China might exert on the INC's position regarding Britain. In accordance with Churchill's suggestions, the Chinese government seized the opportunity to advance its relations with Britain and revisit the proposal for cooperation made a year earlier. Accordingly, Ambassador Guo approached Viscount Halifax, the British secretary of state for foreign affairs, to raise the question of the possibility of the Chinese government 'exercising a helpful influence over the INC Party'.[10] Guo also informed Halifax that Dai Jitao (戴季陶), the president of the Examination Yuan and an acclaimed Buddhist scholar, would soon be leaving Chongqing for a visit to India and Burma. Ostensibly, Dai was going on a mission of goodwill (Sen 2017: 332–5), but while in India, he bore in mind Churchill's suggestion. Guo then brought up the report drawn up by Stafford Cripps, the leading Labour left-winger, in April that year, in which Cripps advocated closer cooperation between India and China.[11] In Guo's opinion, it was clear that some practical basis must be found for this cooperation. Although the Chinese government had not yet made any concrete suggestions, he thought that India could give China considerable material help, for example, in providing steel from India and possibly petrol from Burma. This, Guo felt, would be an opportunity for the Indians to give expression to their sympathy and goodwill towards China, enabling them to contribute their share to the common effort. It would also have an excellent effect in USA.

As far as the Nationalist government was concerned, it continued to advocate that 'a victory acquired from China's War of Resistance against Japan is indeed the prerequisite for India's independence movement to be successful' and 'to recall the fundamental recognition of both the Indians and the Burmese upon their political status in this era ... what benefits the welfare of China and its war against Japan can truly benefit them'.[12] On the one hand, Chiang treated the British government's attitude towards the development of relations between India and China with great caution. He instructed Guo Taiqi to consult further with the British government over Cripps's proposal. Chiang asserted that laying the foundations for cooperation between China and Britain was a matter of first priority, in that it would pave the way for the success of proposals of this kind. On the other hand, Chiang had decided to send Dai Jitao to India as his envoy together with the KMT representative without consulting Britain beforehand. Carrying Chiang's letters to Mahatma Gandhi and Nehru, Dai therefore departed for Burma and India in mid-October 1940. As Chiang explained to Guo later on, Dai's visit was at the press's invitation. The purpose of Dai's visit was to mediate between Indian political groups and the British authorities: it was not aimed to define or reach any particular goal of mutual cooperation. Without professionals travelling along with him, it would be impossible for Dai to discuss the agricultural or other economic projects recommended by Cripps. However, Chiang repeatedly instructed Guo that in negotiating Sino-Indian cooperation, he must both confirm the initiative with the British government and ask India to produce a concrete plan. 'Right now our government's guiding principle is to establish a foundation for Sino-British cooperation, and then the establishment of Sino-Indian-Burmese cooperation will naturally be done, since the conditions are ripe'.[13] In other words, as Chiang still hoped to cooperate with Britain, his attitude towards India was rather cautious and passive at this stage.

In his letter to Chiang prior to his departure for India, Dai mentioned that substantial results were unlikely to emerge from this visit for another five to seven years, but nonetheless, the Chinese people's goodwill is sincere and heartfelt. In order not to offend China's Asian friend, Dai gave extra thought to adopting local etiquette and manners, and he carefully specified a suitable dress code. Dai's polite but patronizing tone recalls the contemptuous stereotypes of India as a 'barbarian' part of the world that were current back at the turn of the twentieth century (Dikötter 2015). Contrary to Churchill's vision, Dai found that the idea of a single united India was the shared hope of the Chinese people. As a former KMT propaganda chief, Dai also set out the principles of his propaganda policy towards India, aiming to awaken the Indian people's self-awareness and understanding of their position and surroundings.[14] Overall, Dai (1959: 936) reiterated the idea of limiting mutual cooperation to culture and/or religion in the best interests of both the Chinese and Indian peoples. In the meanwhile, the British government had voiced its own expectations of Dai's visit. At Halifax's suggestion, Ambassador Guo met with the secretary of state for India and Burma, Leo Amery.[15] Amery was keen to involve the Chinese in the British 'balance of power' scheme in India and urged Dai and other Chinese officials to acquaint themselves more with the Hindu–Muslim conflict and the ethno-religious divisions in Indian society, presumably in the hope of justifying Britain's strategy of 'divide and rule' and support for Muslim separatism.

Establishing a Wartime Intelligence Network

Given the KMT's repeated confrontations with their Communist rivals and the Japanese army's rapid advance in northern China from the late 1920s, the Nationalist intelligence services and their activities soon increased in scope. Prior to the well-known Zhongtong (中統) of the KMT Central Committee and the Juntong (軍統) of the Nationalist Government Military Council, both defined as bureaus of investigation and statistics, government and party secret services had become rampant, while human intelligence, bureaucratic data-processing, and, later, a nascent code-breaking capacity came to both serve political ends and facilitate military strategy and operations. Three major organizations, including the Zhongtong, the Juntong, and the Institute of International Relations (IIR; Guoji wenti yanjiusuo [國際問題研究所]), were formally conceived in 1938 and later involved in collaborative projects with the British Special Operations Executive (SOE) and the US Office of Strategic Services (OSS), respectively. The spymaster, IIR director, Wang Pengsheng (王芃生), was described by many of his contemporaries, including his British colleagues, as providing the 'brainwork' for Chiang's own secret service work in enemy territory, while the notorious 'Chinese Gestapo' Juntong under Dai Li (戴笠) undertook the 'hands and foot work'. The archives show that

intelligence gathered by Wang and Dai right after the outbreak of the
Second World War and right before Pacific War, while the Nationalist
government was still trying to determine how to develop regional
relations further, can be divided into three categories: (*i*) the political situation of India and Burma inside the British Empire, (*ii*) the
development of Japanese–Indian relations; and (*iii*) progress in the
Japanese army's southward expansion.

The Political Situation of India and Burma inside
the British Empire

This category holds information mainly about the future of India's
independence movement, as well as how Britain proactively mobilized the entire empire with India as its centre in its preparations for
the Second World War. In March 1940, Wang reported from Rangoon
that as the convention held by the East India Association in London
came to an end, the former lieutenant governor of Punjab, Sir Michael
O'Dwyer, was shot dead by an armed Indian, and both the secretary
of state for India, Lawrence Dundas, and the former governor of
Bombay (now Mumbai), Charles Cochrane-Baillie, were wounded;
the assassin was arrested. Throughout India, however, it was reckoned that this incident would create a direct impact upon the Indians
striving for freedom and independence in the future.[16] In November,
Wang reported from Calcutta (now Kolkata) that in order to mobilize
its Eastern empire, Britain had convened the Eastern Group Supply
Conference in Delhi in late October attended by representatives from
Australia, New Zealand, South Africa, the British Raj, Burma, British
Ceylon, Hong Kong, and British Malaya. The viceroy of India, Lord
Linlithgow, claimed that the conference carried a special message
urging all Britain's dependencies within the area east and south of
the Suez Canal to take on new responsibilities in order to alleviate
the burden on Britain itself during the Second World War. At the
same time, India was experiencing a huge leap in the expansion of
its weaponry in order to, according to the Indian authorities, prepare
its mechanized forces, light tanks, and air force to join Britain in its
wars abroad in the near future. The Indian government also spent a
huge amount of money developing an aviation project, of which the
air route from Calcutta to Bombay had already been surveyed and the

routes between Bombay and British Ceylon had received approval.[17] In November, Wang reported from Rangoon that the prime minister of Burma, U Saw, together with the minister of commerce, were planning to visit India by the end of the month to sign a new Indian–Burmese commercial contract to strengthen trading relations within the British Empire.[18]

Development of Japan–India Relations

This category holds information mainly about the negotiations surrounding a possible India–Japan neutrality pact and trade agreement. In February 1940, Wang reported from Hong Kong that he had intercepted intelligence from Tokyo to the effect that Japan's minister for foreign affairs, Arita Hachirō (有田八郎), had signed neutrality pacts with India and the Philippines as an indirect way of improving relations with both Britain and USA, as he was finding it difficult to resolve the diplomatic deadlock. In fact, Arita had already given orders to Japanese diplomats in India and the Philippines to enquire about the opinions of the local authorities there.[19] In May, Wang reported from Singapore that although the trade negotiations between Japan and India had entered their eighth round, India was insisting on rejecting Japan's requests to reduce the excessively high customs duties, increase imports of cotton clothing from Japan to India, and reduce the percentage of seeded fabric of cotton clothing imported from Japan to India, as the current quantities of imports were jeopardizing the development of India's own clothing industry. As a result, the negotiations broke down, leaving the two sides on bad terms.[20] In September, Wang reported from Rangoon that the cause of the breakdown in the Japanese–Indian business negotiations was Japan's failure to assure India that it would never resell the raw materials it acquired from India to Germany and Italy. In the light of that, the consulate general of Japan in India and the overseas business representative was recalled home by the Japanese government.[21]

Progression of Japanese Army's Southward Expansion

This category holds information mainly about political provocations and military operations regarding the Japanese army's southward expansion. In September 1940, Wang reported from Shanghai that in the beginning of the month, the Japanese army again sent a fifth column of 120 people, this time to Burma, disguised as businessmen, to investigate and encourage the Burmese to act against the British.[22] In October, Wang reported from Rangoon that in the last third of September, numerous women and children from the Japanese diaspora in Rangoon returned to Japan by boat. It seemed that Japan was waiting for War to break out in the Near East because it was planning to do something about the British dependencies, starting with withdrawing the Japanese diaspora living in areas west of the Indian Ocean. Those in the Japanese diaspora who were living in Southeast Asia might be withdrawn altogether before the battle commenced. Wang specifically pointed out that from then on, any movement or activity on the part of Japanese diaspora was worth paying great attention to.[23] While withdrawing the Japanese diaspora, the Japanese army was still carrying out large-scale strategic immigration. Wang pointed out that according to reliable sources, Japan was implementing an immigration policy targeting Southeast Asia. In the first stage of this policy, 5,000 Japanese would migrate to the islands administered by Japan in the South Pacific Ocean. In the second stage, a further 5,000 would go to Vietnam, Thailand, British Malaya, and the Philippines. All immigrants were to receive colonial political training for one month before departing.[24]

During this period, Dai Li was in charge of the Juntong and had already gathered intelligence from Southeast Asia, entering into competition with Wang's IIR in doing so. By May 1940, Dai had already learned from a Japanese military attaché in Singapore that Japan had set up a headquarters in Thailand to control its secret agents' activities in Southeast Asia, and several thousands of Japanese mercenaries were sent to team up with 8,000 Thai royalists, who then hid themselves in Chiang Mai and other places. Street violence and civil unrest were incited in the Dutch East Indies as a starting point. Based on his US sources, Dai pointed out that the Japanese army was quite enthusiastic about the southward expansion: for example, besides setting up an airfield in Thailand, they had purchased an aircraft from a Thai manufacturer, who then sped up its manufacturing process.[25] In June, Dai reported that Ba Maw, the leader of the Burmese opposition party, recently had several of his cadre members raise funds everywhere to support future independence. The governor general's office in Burma then asked the Nationalist government to advise the overseas Chinese not to give any financial aid to Burmese independence activists.[26]

In November, both Dai and Wang had sources indicating the Japanese army's southward military operations. Dai reported that in order to implement its southward expansion policy, the Japanese army decided first to attack Burma through Thailand and threaten British Malaya and Singapore, and second, to wait and sign the Soviet–Japanese Neutrality Pact and then deploy three military divisions from the borders of Manchukuo as the major attack force.[27] Wang followed this up and confirmed that although the Japanese army had determined the procedures for southward expansion, the actual time for action would be after February the following year. This was because on the one hand, they had already moved the navy and army command headquarters from South China to Hainan Island, so their taking Saigon as the front-line command post and expanding the occupation to the whole of Vietnam could be carried out in no time.[28] On the other hand, the Japanese army would encourage Thailand to invade Vietnam and Burma because two Japanese battleships were stationed near Hainan Island waiting for the negotiations between Japan and Thailand to be successfully concluded, after which they would sail to Bangkok to prepare for the policy of southward expansion. As far as the preparations of the British Army in Southeast Asia were concerned, Dai pointed out that Burma had gathered 20,000 people around Lashio and Namhkam waiting to march to the Burma–Vietnam and Burma–Thailand borders. Meanwhile, several transport vessels had arrived in Singapore from Bombay bringing over 6,000 Indian infantrymen and artillerymen and over 400 military motor vehicles, which were waiting to go to Penang in British Malaya to reinforce the defences there. Dai clearly considered that, since Britain had set up the Far East Force General Headquarters in Singapore, the defence of British Malaya had become stronger. However, Britain had dispatched its entire navy in Singapore to the Mediterranean. In other words, the major forces protecting Southeast Asia were the army and the air force, reflecting Britain's belief that Japanese army would not yet dare to attack.

Ever since the Japanese army drew up its operational plans for southward expansion in mid-1940 and stationed itself in French

Indochina, Southeast Asia had become the major battlefield between Japan and USA. Britain especially, in order to control its own territories such as British Malaya, and the Dutch East Indies produced important resources, while Burma was regarded as the major geographical area capable of severing China's lifeline to fight against the Japanese army, as well as it being both a defensive and an offensive zone of operations outside the main strategic areas of Southeast Asia. In February 1941, Colonel Suzuki Keiji (鈴木敬司), who had used the Burmese independence movements to stage armed riots in order to cut off the Burma Road an effective strategy back in 1940, set up the 'Minami Kikan' (南機關) (Minami Agency) in Bangkok. Through this, he aimed to make 'Liberating East Asia' and the political work of supporting Burma's independence the temporary core of the Japanese army's Burma-related strategies both before and after the outbreak of the Pacific War. In November 1941, the Japanese army's headquarters passed a 'plan that promotes an early closure of wars toward China, the United States, Britain, and the Netherlands' and decided to adopt 'helping Burma with its independence and using the outcome to stimulate Indian's independence' as means to force Britain to surrender (Saito 2009). Afterwards, Japan started to advocate the ideas of anti-colonialism and of 'Asia for the Asians', that is, a pan-Asianism for Southeast Asia. In India, furthermore, Japan encouraged exiled nationalists to form an alliance with the Axis, a movement that undoubtedly became a crucial matter for China, USA, and Britain to deal with when they faced India and Burma after forming alliances during the Pacific War. In addition to gathering and analysing Japan-related intelligence and negotiating international transport with French Indochina, British Burma, and China's provincial authorities on its borders, Wang also started his anti-Japan planning and propaganda work and further developed cooperative relations with Britain.

Anti-Japanese Propaganda during the Pacific War

In mid-1941, following the opening of an eastern front in the Second World War and the rising tension among the Pacific islands, US President Franklin Roosevelt denounced imperialism as a major cause of the World War and adopted an anti-colonial policy, proposing the idea of creating a post-War world order by means of a continuous and comprehensive international safety system. His ideas were put into effect when he and Sir Winston Churchill, Britain's prime minister, signed the Atlantic Charter in August proposing several principles such as no territorial expansion, self-determination, giving the peoples of all countries the right to choose their own regime, fair trade, and so on. The Atlantic Charter served as the first bridge among the Allies. When Chiang Kai-shek learned about the Charter, he felt that 'the general trend of events in Europe and Asia have settled', so he came up with certain aspirations, which were, 'since the population of China and India together is 900 million, accounting for more than 60% of the world's population, human beings cannot have real, lasting world peace unless China and India can be totally independent and equal, so that should be the objective of China's revolution'. Also, 'after China is independent and liberated, the first priority is to help India with its liberation and independence and to help Korea with its autonomy; otherwise, no need to mention China's revolution at all'.[29] He then became enthusiastic about the possibilities of China's intervention in the political affairs of British India and Burma.

From December 1941 to January 1942, the expansion of the Japanese army on the Pacific islands was rapid. Singapore was also occupied, and both British Malaya and the Dutch East Indies were in imminent danger. Indochina and Thailand had already fallen into the enemy's hands, and the Japanese army started to speed up its attacks on Burma. Since the Sino-British Joint Defence of Burma Road Agreement was signed in December 1941, China and Britain had become military allies. In January 1942, Chiang Kai-shek reckoned that it was time for him to visit India and Burma, a trip he undertook in the beginning of February after Britain welcomed it. The visit was originally conceived to 'promote mutual understanding between Britain and India and advise India to dispatch more military forces', to mediate the political conflicts between Britain, the metropolitan state, and the society of its colony, and to urge both Britain and India to agree to India adopting the Dominion system, as well as suppressing the anti-war rhetoric of the Indians so that Britain and India could cooperate in fighting against the fascist invasion. According to Chiang, 'The purpose[s] of the visit to India [were]: (1) persuading the British and Indians to cooperate with each other; (2) persuading the Indians to contribute more troops; (3) persuading the British to allow

Indian autonomy; (4) the basis for future cooperation between China and India; (5) Three Principles of the People propaganda'.[30] During his visit to India and Burma, in addition to having wide-ranging and in-depth discussions with officials from both gubernatorial offices on military issues, transport, economic cooperation, and so on, both the viceroy of India, Lord Linlithgow, and the governor of Burma, Sir Reginald Dorman-Smith, highlighted more than once that Japan's political and propaganda activities in India and Burma had greatly affected the ideas of both the Burmese and the Indians about fighting against Japan. In order to facilitate China in establishing concrete relations with the British Raj and British rule in Burma, Chiang agreed to a request from the former British ambassador to China, Sir Archibald Clark Kerr, and the governor of Burma that China should send semi-diplomatic representatives to reside in India and Burma and vice versa. Chiang also promised to consider the suggestion of Kerr that a joint institute between China, Britain, and USA should be set up, led by Wang Pengsheng, to conduct propaganda work against Japan; Chiang also agreed to a request from the governor of Burma that China should send several agents from Chongqing to organize the overseas Chinese diaspora there to assist in discrediting the activities of Japanese fifth columnists.[31]

During this period, the Japanese army started its attack on Burma: Moulmein was stormed, Rangoon reported an emergency, and the Burma Road was in imminent danger. China's Nationalist government, therefore, immediately sent an expeditionary force from Yunnan to Burma. Furthermore, as follow-up measures regarding Chinese troops fighting overseas, in January and February, the Nationalist government published *Outline for Overseas Troops to Implement KMT Affairs* and *Plan for Implementing People-to-People Diplomacy*, respectively. The former was drafted by the KMT's Organization Department regarding the guiding principles, key points, organization, personnel budget, and so on, claiming that sending troops overseas was an unprecedented, heroic action in consolidating the anti-invasion alliance since the outbreak of the Pacific War. Ever since the Wang Jingwei (汪精衛) government was established in Nanjing in the spring of 1940, Zhu Jiahua, head of the KMT Organization Department, received instructions from Chiang Kai-shek to work with Chen Lifu, head of the KMT Social Affairs Department, and Wang Pengsheng, the IIR director, in fomenting anti-war and revolutionary movements in Japan, Korea, and Taiwan to 'encourage people of the enemy states to strive for revolutionary activities, such as going on strike, in order to promote all possible sabotage efforts in occupied and enemy territory against impending invasion', actions that had been going on in Chongqing for some time.[32] The Organization Department was planning to address the liaisons between the overseas combat troops and the revolutionary groups on friendly soil. However, the director of the Second Department of the Office of Aides, Chen Bulei (陳布雷), along with others, suggested deleting this part from *Outline for Overseas Troops to Implement KMT Affairs*, which they considered inappropriately worded, fearing that it might result in improper practices or misunderstandings among countries friendly to China. When the Central Committee conference was discussing the matter in question, another issue, namely, whether or not to admit Korea's provisional government, came up and caused disagreement. As a result, the case was withdrawn by Zhu Jiahua.[33]

As far as *Plan for Implementing People-to-People Diplomacy* was concerned, it was discussed and drafted by Gan Naiguang (甘乃光) (deputy secretary of the Highest National Defence Commission), Xu Enzeng (徐恩曾) (deputy director of Zhongtong), Hang Liwu (杭立武) (chairman of the Sino-British Cultural Society), Zeng Xubai (曾虛白) (director of the International Propaganda Division of the KMT Propaganda Department), and Liu Daren (劉達人) (IIR agent in Burma) under instructions from Chiang Kai-shek and focusing on the new situation created by the Pacific War breaking out. According to the Plan, the first and foremost priority of Sino-Burmese people-to-people diplomacy was military matters; in other words, military administration came first and people-to-people diplomacy second, so that the objective of military cooperation between China, Britain, and Burma could be achieved by cultivating basic Sino-Burmese diplomatic relations without jeopardizing the interests of Britain as an ally. Since the Plan had to be implemented to cope with military needs in conducting any task contributing to military operations in the war zone, the different liaisons between the Chinese expeditionary force, British troops, Indian forces, and Burmese forces became extremely close, though people-to-people diplomacy mainly targeted the Burmese. For purposes of military administration, a general political headquarters was established, though with a lower number of divisions and personnel under the command headquarters in charge of several missions, organizing (political work inside the army), publicizing (maintaining local connections among Chinese, British, Indian, and Burmese soldiers), and collecting information (creating local connections and collecting military intelligence as a follow-up to military developments). All the people-to-people diplomatic activities were hosted by the Burma–China Cultural Association.[34]

While the expeditionary force was being transferred, on 8 March, Rangoon was stormed by the Japanese, cutting off the Burma Road from the outside world. Chiang Kai-shek ordered the Two-Hundredth Division to halt its move into Burma, since he was now considering replacing the original plan of helping British troops relieve Rangoon with a new one involving defensive warfare centred on Mandalay after he realized the limited determination and actual strength of the British troops. However, Chiang's new idea introduced differences with General Joseph Stilwell, the chief of staff who had just arrived in the China–Burma–India theatre and wanted to launch a full-scale counterattack. Chiang eventually agreed to respect Stilwell's command in order to maintain harmonious relations with the US and British forces. At the same time, however, he sent a letter to Sir Dorman-Smith to point out that in light of the close cooperation between China and Burma regarding the struggle against the Japanese army, and in order to enhance the mutual union and connection, he would send Wang Pengsheng, a diplomatic specialist and a special member of the Highest National Defence Commission, who had not only rich experience in political affairs and military operations but also in-depth understanding of the meaning behind the entire Sino-British-Burmese-Indian cooperation, as well as Japan's situation and its army's violent behaviour. Wang would help the Chinese expeditionary force and overseas Chinese groups with the British–Burmese liaison and publicity work, and would exchange opinions with Burmese government officials and military officers to strengthen existing friendship so that the objective of winning the war could be reached (Liao 2019: 18–20).

The reply from Sir Dorman-Smith stated that Wang was the most qualified person for the job due to his promising abilities. In fact, right after Wang's arrival in Burma, he started to initiate thorough discussions with various ministers in Burma's colonial government. Furthermore, the prime minister of Burma, Sir Paw Tun, handpicked some Burmese and went to Lashio to meet and cooperate with Wang in setting up the organization Wang had suggested so that a new page could be turned regarding anti-Japanese propaganda.[35] When Wang submitted his report to Chiang about his meeting with the governor of Burma, he pointed out that Burma agreed to civilians cooperating with the military police, but only subject to actual local needs. Regarding the meeting, four decisions were made to: (*i*) set up an anti-invasion society in Lashio; (*ii*) expand the original Sino-Burmese Cultural Society and relocate it to Maymyo, a hill town east of Mandalay; (*iii*) set up a secret organization in Mandalay and have military police from both China and Burma cooperate in tracking down enemy agents to protect the safety of the Burma Road; and (*iv*) increase the communication of intelligence both within the areas occupied by enemy troops and in Thailand.

Having obtained the participation and support of the prime minister and other officials in Burma, Wang urged Chiang to send Zheng Jiemin (鄭介民), director of the second division, Ministry of Military Commands, to join him on the Burma and India missions.[36] Furthermore, even Britain started to take action. General Harold Alexander, commander-in-chief of the British Army in Burma, the director of the SOE's Far East branch and others all asked Wang to convey the fact that Britain was willing to promise both India and Burma their freedom and other cooperation after the war; they also strongly advised Wang to visit India to persuade members of the INC. The prime minister of Burma also urged Wang to invite Sir Stafford Cripps, who was in New Delhi dealing with India's post-War independence when Wang arrived there, to visit Burma so that in the future the Burmese would not be alienated by Japan saying that Britain valued India more than Burma.[37] However, Mandalay was soon stormed, a defeat for the allied forces in their first battle for Burma, after which they retreated to India after a long and difficult march. During the Burma Campaign in early April, Wang received information from Chiang that the request from Britain had been agreed. Therefore, Wang was to be in charge of cooperating with Britain in producing anti-Japanese propaganda and gathering intelligence in Japan. Against Wang Pengsheng's will, the IIR worked with Britain only in accordance with Chiang's guidance, and hence the idea of a joint China–Britain–USA war propaganda committee championed by Sir Archibald Clark Kerr was ignored. Throughout the War, the British government was supposedly responsible for the IIR's budget and technical support in exchange for anti-Japanese publicity and an intelligence-sharing agreement focused on Japan's military progress and her economic and internal political situation.[38] However, it was the Sino-American Cooperative Organization that naturally took the leading role in Chinese intelligence collaboration with the Western allies and in regional power struggles and configurations with USA, Dai Li's Juntong being Chiang's vital ally and most faithful cadre in this respect.

***

In early 1942, within weeks of Nehru's release from prison, Chiang paid his visit to India and Burma with the main aim of motivating the Allied and Indian forces. However, communication problems and conflicting national interests between the Allies compromised the impact of Chiang's intercession in reconciling Indian leaders to the war effort. Following the outbreak of the Pacific War and Guo Taiqi's abrupt resignation a month earlier, together with the rapid fall of British power in Southeast Asia, USA quickly replaced Britain as China's major partner when it came to Indian issues. In fact, Chiang Kai-shek first revealed his intention to visit India to Churchill through Roosevelt. Chiang sought to adopt a discreet attitude in order to gain an advantage from the fact that China had taken the initiative internationally following the alliance between the Axis powers. During his stay in Delhi, Chiang secured an agreement with the Indian government that provided for improvements in Chinese–Indian wartime cooperation and the construction of a road from Ledo to Longling in Yunnan Province, first mooted in 1941, with a completion date of early 1945. Chiang also met INC and Muslim leaders, including Gandhi, Nehru, and Muhammad Ali Jinnah. Determined to preserve the British Empire, Churchill considered Chinese and Hindu nationalism a threat to Britain's colonial interests. As Chiang explained to the new ambassador to Britain, Vi Kyuin Wellington Koo (顧維鈞), the Nationalist Chinese government's 'policy of favouring the liberation of weak and small peoples was a fundamental one, but there was no intention on her part to take any active steps to realize it, though these countries would themselves look to China as a natural leader and her civilization as a great heritage for Asia' (cited in Liu 1996: 83).[39] Despite the ultimate failure of his diplomacy, Chiang arguably launched his campaign to intervene in the cause of Asia's decolonization and proclaimed China's role in regional and international affairs during the war.

Nationalist China and British India continued their cooperation in fighting the Axis powers in a few other ways. In April 1942, soon after Chiang's return to Chongqing, the Chinese and Indian governments agreed in principle on the enrolment of some 2,000 unemployed Chinese seamen in India as a War service corps trained to support the War and maintain local infrastructure and public services. Chinese officers were dispatched to Calcutta to organize the corps under the detailed arrangement of China's consulates in Chongqing and Calcutta. Work was allocated to the corps by the Indian authorities, while matters of discipline were left to the Chinese officers. In the meantime, trained at special training schools run by SOE and SACO, one of them near Poona (now Pune), India, Chinese agents helped to gather intelligence regarding India and used India as base from which to conduct espionage and aid local resistance movements in occupied China and Southeast Asia. Under Dai Li's command, on the other hand, since 1942, the Juntong had striven to establish a radio propaganda and intelligence network based in India behind the British and US backs, several months before the founding of SACO.[40] Accordingly, Juntong agents were sent to Calcutta and elsewhere in India to work with the Chinese consulate with local assistance.[41] Most of all, as the mission of the first Chinese Expeditionary Force ended, in August 1942, the well-known Chinese Army in India based in Ramgarh was formed, which became the major force in the second Burma Campaign in 1944–5, leading to Allied victory.[42] However, the British also used India as a base from which to communicate with Chinese Communist intelligence agents in connection with subversive activities towards the end of the war, which distressed Chiang and Dai greatly.[43]

Studies in the archives mentioned earlier have further explored networking across geopolitical borders and reassessed the main objectives of China's policy towards India during the Second World War by focusing on both Chinese apprehensions regarding India's policy and the pragmatic decisions made by the Nationalists in light of the objective reality of the World War and its regional environment. Chinese wartime policies in relation to India were determined to a great extent by India's strategic geopolitical situation and by the fact that the de-colonization of India and its independence would enable it to join the War and thus help safeguard Chinese interests. However, Nationalist Chinese Wartime intelligence on India was prone to stereotypical images and traditionalist Sino-centric attitudes that had their roots in the past but really took shape during the Second World War. Opinions on India turned largely on observers' different ideological standpoints, as attitudes towards race and nationalism developed gradually but vehemently in China. The Chinese Nationalist leaders readily regarded Nehru and the INC as their counterparts, while arrogantly overlooking the latter's leftist orientations. Chinese Nationalist leaders tended to undervalue social problems and differences, preferring instead to push the ideas of a united China and a united India. When it came to the pursuit of major power politics, however, the Nationalist Chinese government's Wartime policy toward India was inevitably subordinated to her relations with USA and Britain. The Chinese Nationalist leaders took for granted the value of their own heritage and China's view of itself as a major power, often speaking of it in a tone of superiority. It may be argued that the strategy of alliance-building played a vital role in Nationalist Chinese wartime diplomacy and victory, which would, however, crumble within a few short years when they found the challenges emanating from India seeking to form a union of its own particularly hard to swallow.

Notes

1. Recent studies have revealed China's active participation in power diplomacy and its desire to join the international system in the Republican Era. See, for example, Xu (2005) and Kirby (2000).

2. 'Entry of 11 February 1939', *Shilüe gaoben*, Col. No. 002-060100-00267-011, Chiang Kai-shek Collection (CKSC), Academia Historica, Taipei, Taiwan.

3. Recent research (Lu 2008; Tsuchida 2014) has highlighted the Nationalist government's strategy for an international solution during the Second World War.

4. 'Fazhan Zhong-Yin guanxi yijianshu', 1939, *Fangwen Yindu* I, Col. No. 002-080106-00071-006, CKSC, Academia Historica, Taipei, Taiwan.

5. 'Zhu Jiahua to Jawaharlal Nehru', 31 October 1939, Col. No. te13/1.7, Special Archives, Kuomintang Party Archives (KPA), Taipei, Taiwan. Brian Tsui has argued that cultural cooperation plans of the sort functioned as an uncontroversial guise or natural transition from culture into realpolitik in Nationalist China. See Chapter 8 by Brian Tsui in this volume, especially the heading 'Putting Culture to Work'.

6. See Chapter 10 by Jeong in this volume for details of an Islamic mission that visited India during the War as well.

7. 'Chen Lifu and Zhu Jiahua to Chiang Kai-shek', 6 October 1939, Col. No. te13/1.12, Special Archives, KPA, Taipei, Taiwan.

8. 'Zhu Jiahua to Chiang Kai-shek', 10 October 1939, Col. No. te13/1.5, Special Archives, KPA, Taipei, Taiwan.

9. 'Guo Taiqi to Chiang Kai-shek', 28 October 1940, *Dui Ying Fa De Yi guanxi* II, Col. No. 002-090103-00012-269, CKSC, Academia Historica, Taipei, Taiwan.

10. 'Gov. of India to S/S for India, Repeating Telegram from Chungking', 6 March 1940, L/PS/12/2310 PZ2046/1940, OIOC (Oriental and India Office Collections), British Library, London, UK.

11. 'Viscount Halifax to Sir A. Clark Kerr', 15 October 1940, F4736/43/10, Foreign Office Confidential Print, National Archives, Kew, UK, published in Preston (1997). The Nationalist government had been telling Britain that '[Dai's visit] would be private non-political and in his dealings with Indians and Burmese, importance of Sino-British relations would be his first considerations'. See 'Gov. of India to S/S for India, Repeating Telegram from Chungking', 6 March 1940, L/PS/12/2310 PZ2046/1940, OIOC, British Library, London, UK.

12. 'Extracts from Notes by Dai Jitao before Visit to India and Burma', October 1940, *Fangwen Yindu* I, Col. No. 002-080106-00071-006, CKSC, Academia Historica, Taipei, Taiwan.

13. 'Chiang Kai-shek to Guo Taiqi', 22 October 1940, *Dui Lianheguo guanxi* IV, Col. No. 002-080106-00017-001; 'Chiang Kai-shek to Guo Taiqi', 30 October 1940, *Fangwen Yindu* I, Col. No. 002-080106-00071-004, CKSC, Academia Historica, Taipei, Taiwan.

14. 'Extracts from notes by Dai Jitao before visit to India and Burma', October 1940, Col. No. 002-080106-00071-006, CKSC, Academia Historica, Taipei, Taiwan.

15. 'Gov. of India to S/S for India to H. Ashley Clark, Foreign Office', 9 November 1940, L/PS/12/2310 PZ6017/1940, OIOC, British Library, London, UK.

16. 'Wang Pengsheng to Chiang Kai-shek, Extract', 17 March 1940, *Chengbiao huiji* 104, Col. No. 002-080200-00531-016, CKSC, Academia Historica, Taipei, Taiwan.

17. 'Wang Pengsheng to Chiang Kai-shek, Extract', 2 November 1940, *Chengbiao huiji* 100, Col. No. 002-080200-00527-127, CKSC, Academia Historica, Taipei, Taiwan.

18. 'Wang Pengsheng to Chiang Kai-shek, Extract', 9 November 1940, *Chengbiao huiji* 104, Col. No. 002-080200-00531-097, CKSC, Academia Historica, Taipei, Taiwan.

19. 'Wang Pengsheng to Chiang Kai-shek, Extract', 11 February 1940, *Chengbiao huiji* 101, Col. No. 002-080200-00528-008, CKSC, Academia Historica, Taipei, Taiwan.

20. 'Wang Pengsheng to Chiang Kai-shek, Extract', 14 May 1940, *Chengbiao huiji* 101, Col. No. 002-080200-00528-038, CKSC, Academia Historica, Taipei, Taiwan.

21. 'Wang Pengsheng to Chiang Kai-shek, Extract', 7 September 1940, *Chengbiao huiji* 104, Col. No. 002-080200-00531-072, CKSC, Academia Historica, Taipei, Taiwan.

22. 'Wang Pengsheng to Chiang Kai-shek, Extract', 20 September 1940, *Chengbiao huiji* 104, Col. No. 002-080200-00531-016, CKSC, Academia Historica, Taipei, Taiwan.

23. 'Wang Pengsheng to Chiang Kai-shek, Extract', 26 October 1940, *Chengbiao huiji* 104, Col. No. 002-080200-00531-016, CKSC, Academia Historica, Taipei, Taiwan.

24. 'Wang Pengsheng to Chiang Kai-shek, Extract', 25 October 1940, *Chengbiao huiji* 104, Col. No. 002-080200-00531-016, CKSC, Academia Historica, Taipei, Taiwan. Here 'mandate' has the meaning given to it under the Treaty of Versailles. Thus, in 1922, Japan set up the Nanyō government to manage its South Pacific Mandate, including the North Mariana Islands, Palau Islands, Caroline Islands, and the Marshall Islands.

25. 'He Yaozu and Dai Li to Chiang Kai-shek, Extract', 6 May 1940, *Chengbiao huiji* 104, Col. No. 002-080200-00531-016, CKSC, Academia Historica, Taipei, Taiwan.

26. 'Dai Li to Chiang Kai-shek, Extract', 23 June 1940, *Chengbiao huiji* 104, Col. No. 002-080200-00531-016, CKSC, Academia Historica, Taipei, Taiwan.

27. 'Dai Li to Chiang Kai-shek, Extracts', 20, 21, and 23 November 1940, *Chengbiao huiji* 104, Col. No. 002-080200-00531-016, CKSC, Academia Historica, Taipei, Taiwan.

28. 'Dai Li to Chiang Kai-shek, Extracts' (20 and 22 November 1940), *Chengbiao huiji* 104, Col. No. 002-080200-00531-016, CKSC, Academia Historica, Taipei, Taiwan.

29. 'This Month Introspection Log', 29, 30, and 31 August 1941, Chiang Kai-shek Diaries (CKSD), Hoover Institution, Stanford University, USA. However, the Atlantic Charter shocked the order and colonial interests of the British Empire; Winston Churchill immediately declared in the House of Commons that it was not applicable to India and Burma.

30. Entries of 8 and 30 January 1942, CKSD, Hoover Institution, Stanford University, USA.

31. 'Meeting Minutes of Chiang Kai-shek and Lord Linlithgow', 10 February 1942, Col. No. 002-020300-00021-008; 'Meeting Minutes of Chiang Kai-shek and Sir Archibald Clark Kerr', 15 February 1942, Col. No. 002-020300-00021-052, *Geming wenxian: tongmengguo zuozhan: Jiang zhuxi fang Yin* I, CKSC, Academia Historica, Taipei, Taiwan.

32. 'Chiang Kai-shek's Confidential Message from Chongqing', 30 March 1940, *Tezhong qingbao: Juntong* VI, Col. No. 002-080102-00039-021, CKSC, Academia Historica, Taipei, Taiwan.

33. 'Chen Bulei to Wu Tiecheng and Zhu Jiahua', 14 February 1942; 'Minutes of the 195th Meeting of the Fifth Central Standing Committee', 16 February 1942, Col. No. hui5.3/180.2, Conference Minutes, KPA, Taipei, Taiwan.

34. 'Shangtao dui Mian waijiao shishi fangan' (商討對緬外交實施方案) ['Discussions on the Implementation of the Plan of People-to-People Diplomacy towards Burma'], 21 February 1942; 'Dui Mian waijiao shishi fangan' (對緬外交實施方案) ['The Implementation of the Plan of People-to-People Diplomacy towards Burma'], February 1942, Col. No. te14/13.2;14/13.9, Special Archives, KPA, Taipei, Taiwan.

35. 'Chiang Kai-shek to Sir Dorman-Smith', 17 March 1942; 'Smith Reply to Chiang Kai-shek', 27 March 1942, *Geming wenxian: tongmengguo zuozhan: Yuanzhengjun ru Mian* I, Col. No. 002-020300-00019-025, CKSC, Academia Historica, Taipei, Taiwan.

36. 'Wang Pengsheng to Chiang Kai-shek', 26 March 1942, *Yuanzheng ru Mian* II, Col. No. 002-090105-00007-323, CKSC, Academia Historica, Taipei, Taiwan.

37. 'Wang Pengsheng to Chiang Kai-shek', March 1942, *Mengjun lianhe zuozhan* VIII, Col. No. 002-080103-00063-013, CKSC, Academia Historica, Taipei, Taiwan.

38. 'Wang Pengsheng to Chiang Kai-shek', 17 August 1943, *Tezhong qingbao: Juntong* VI, Col. No. 002-080102-00039-021, CKSC, Academia Historica, Taipei, Taiwan.

39. Liu goes so far as to claim that the anti-colonial rhetoric of Chongqing was a calculated tactic originating in a weak position not to estrange the Western powers but to win its own bargaining chip.

40. India was later the de facto Asian headquarters of USA's OSS. According to Alghan R. Lusey, a US businessman with much experience in China who was recruited, the US Office of the Coordinator of Information, a predecessor of the OSS, found several vague indications that the Chinese and Indians were carrying on 'some kind of undercover skullduggery' against the British (quoted in Yu 1997: 295n33).

41. 'Dai Li to Mao Renfeng', 9 March 1942, *Daigong yimo: qingbao lei* VI, Col. No. 144-010104-0005-058, Dai Li Papers, Academia Historica, Taipei, Taiwan; 'Dai Li to Bao Junjian', 20 April 1944, *Daigong yimo: qingbao lei* III, Col. No. 144-010104-0003-051, Dai Li Papers, Academia Historica, Taipei, Taiwan. As Dai Li pointed out, the consul-general of China to India Bao Junjian played a vital role in their networking. 'Dai Li's warrant', 17 February 1943, *Daigong yimo: yiban zhishi lei* IV, Col. No. 144-010113-0004-104, Dai Li Papers, Academia Historica, Taipei, Taiwan.

42. The Juntong's India Station, according to Dai Li, was nonetheless relatively dysfunctional and costly towards the end of the War. 'Dai Li's Instruction to the India Station' (5 October 1944), *Daigong yimo: yiban zhishi lei* VI, Col. No. 144-010113-0004-106, Dai Li Papers, Academia Historica, Taipei, Taiwan. See also Chapter 14 by Tansen Sen in this volume for Chinese intelligence activities in Kalimpong.

43. 'Dai Li to Bao Junjian', 6 October 1943, *Daigong yimo: yiban zhishi lei* II, Col. No. 144-010113-0002-044, Dai Li Papers, Academia Historica, Taipei, Taiwan.

References

Archival Material

Academia Historica (Guoshiguan [國史館]), *Taipei, Taiwan*

'Mengjun lianhe zuozhan' (盟軍聯合作戰) ['Allies' Joint Operation'] VIII, CKSC, File Col. No. 002-080103-00063.

'Yuanzheng ru Mian' (遠征入緬) ['Expeditionary Force Move into Burma'] II, CKSC, File Col. No. 002-090105-00007.

'Geming wenxian: tongmengguo zuozhan: Jiang zhuxi fang Yin' (革命文獻：同盟國作戰：蔣主席訪印) ['Revolutionary Documents, Allies' Joint Operation: Chairman Chiang Visits India'] I, CKSC, File Col. No. 002-020300-00021.

'Geming wenxian: tongmengguo zuozhan: Yuanzhengjun ru Mian' (革命文獻：同盟國作戰：遠征軍入緬) ['Revolutionary Documents, Allies' Joint

Operation: Expeditionary Force Move into Burma'] I, CKSC, File Col. No. 002-020300-00019.

'Tezhong qingbao: Juntong' (特種情報：軍統) ['Special Intelligence: Military Investigation and Statistics'] VI, CKSC, File Col. No. 002-080102-00039.

Shilüe gaoben (事略稿本) [*Biographical Sketch Manuscripts*], February 1939, CKSC, File Col. No. 002-060100-00267.

Chengbiao huiji (呈表彙集) [*Collected Reports*] 100, 101, and 104, Chiang Kai-shek Collection (CKSC), File Col. Nos. 002-080200-00527, 00528 and 00531.

Daigong yimo: yiban zhishi lei (戴公遺墨：一般指示類) [*Manuscripts of Dai Li: Category of General Instruction*] II and IV, Dai Li Papers, Col. No. 144-010113-0002 and 0004.

Daigong yimo: qingbao lei (戴公遺墨：情報類) [*Manuscripts of Dai Li: Category of Intelligence*] III and VI, Dai Li Papers, File Col. Nos. 144-010104-0003 and 0004.

Dui Ying Fa De Yi guanxi (對英法德義關係) [*Relations with Britain, France, Germany and Italy*] II, CKSC, File Col. No. 002-090103-00012.

Dui Lianheguo guanxi (對聯合國關係) [*Relations with the United Nations*] IV, CKSC, File Col. No. 002-080106-00017.

Fangwen Yindu (訪問印度) [*Visit to India*] I, CKSC, File Col. No. 002-080106-00071.

British Library, London, UK

Oriental and India Office Collections (OIOC), L/PS/12/2310.

Hoover Institution, Stanford University, Stanford, USA

Chiang Kai-shek Diaries (CKSD), 1941–2.

Kuomintang Party Archives (KPA), Taipei, Taiwan

Special Archives, Col. Nos. te13/1.5 and 1.7, te14/13.2 and 13.9.
Conference Minutes, Col. No. hui5.3/180.2.

National Archives, Kew, UK

Foreign Office Confidential Print.
Preston, Paul (ed.). 1997. 'No. 61'. In *British Documents on Foreign Affairs, Part III, Series E: Asia, Volume 5, Far Eastern Affairs.* Bethesda, MD: University Publications of America.

Other Sources

Dai Jitao (戴季陶). 1959. *Dai Jitao xiansheng wencun* (戴季陶先生文存) [*A Collection of Dai Jitao's Writings*]. Taipei: Zhongyang wenwu.

Dikötter, Frank. 2015. *The Discourse of Race in Modern China*. London: Oxford University Press.

Kirby, William. 2000. 'The Internationalization of China: Foreign Relations at Home and Abroad in the Republican Era'. In Frederic Wakeman, Jr. and Richard Louis Edmonds (eds), *Reappraising Republican China*, pp. 179–204. Oxford: Oxford University Press.

Liao Wen-shuo (廖文碩). 2019. 'Qingbao yu waijiao: Cong dangan lun Wang Pengsheng yu Guoji wenti yanjiusuo (1937–1946)' (情報與外交：從檔案論王芃生與國際問題研究所 [1937–1946]) ['Intelligence and Diplomacy: An Archival Study of Wang Pengsheng and the Institute of International Relations (1937–1946)']. *Chengda lishi xuebao* (成大歷史學報) [*Cheng Kung Journal of Historical Studies*] (56): 91–131.

Liu Xiaoyuan. 1996. *A Partnership for Disorder: China, the United States, and Their Policies for the Postwar Disposition of the Japanese Empire, 1941–1945*. Cambridge: Cambridge University Press.

Lu Xijun (鹿錫俊). 2008. 'Guomin zhengfu dui Ouzhan ji jiemeng wenti de yingdui' (國民政府對歐戰及結盟問題的應對) ['The Nationalist Government's Response to the European War and Alliance']. *Lishi yanjiu* (歷史研究) [*Historical Research*] (3): 94–116.

Nanda, Bal Ram. 1995. *Jawaharlal Nehru: Rebel and Statesman*. Oxford: Oxford University Press.

Saito Teruko (齋藤照子). 2009. 'Erzhan shiqi Rijun dui Mian gongzuo jigou Nanjiguan zaikao' (二戰時期日軍對緬工作機構—南機關再考) ['Re-studying the Japanese Army's Work toward Burma during the Second World War: Minami Agency']. *Nanyang ziliao yicong* (南洋資料譯叢) [*Southeast Asian Studies*] (2): 49–56.

Sen, Tansen. 2017. *India, China, and the World: A Connected History*. Lanham, MD: Rowman & Littlefield.

Tsuchida Akio. 2014. 'Declaring War as an Issue in Chinese Wartime Diplomacy'. In Hans van de Ven, Diana Lary, and Stephen R. MacKinnon (eds), *Negotiating China's Destiny in World War II*, pp. 111–126. Stanford: Stanford University Press.

Xu Guoqi. 2005. *China and the Great War: China's Pursuit of a New National Identity and Internationalization*. Cambridge: Cambridge University Press.

Yu Maochun. 1997. *OSS in China: Prelude to Cold War*. New Haven: Yale University Press.

13

Shipping Nationalism in India and China, 1920–52

ANNE REINHARDT

The expansion of ocean steam navigation in the middle of the nineteenth century reoriented both spatial and economic relations between India and China, solidifying a network of steamship ports between Bombay (now Mumbai) and Shanghai and complicating the once tightly connected triangular trade in tea, opium, and textiles between China, India, and Britain with faster communications, new possibilities for investment, and a greater diversity of commodities. This development was part of the British-led 'communications revolution' of the 1860s and 1870s, precipitated by advances in ocean steamship technology, the opening of the Suez Canal (1869), and the extension of direct telegraphic communication between Europe and Asia. The steamships of the Peninsular & Oriental Company (P&O) had carried mail between Europe and Asia since 1845, but after 1869, a new generation of commercial steamship firms entered long-distance ocean routes, regularizing and rationalizing them. Britain, with the world's most prosperous money market, well-developed iron and mechanical industries, and plentiful supplies of steamship coal, became the world's pre-eminent shipping power, its ships both plying through the Suez Canal to Asia and extending across the Pacific Ocean from Asia to the Americas (Headrick 1988: 25–7, 42–4; Hyde 1973: 22–3). The rapid consolidation of this global 'Ocean Railway' shaped the relationship between India and China by providing new possibilities for movement and settlement, as well as new spaces for exchange and resistance within its networks. As a key facet of the British presence in both places, shipping makes clear the historical and structural relationship between India and China that underlay their sense of shared predicament in the first half of the twentieth century. These steamship networks made concrete the integration of India and China into an emerging globality stemming from the expansion of the British Empire in the mid-nineteenth century, but extending well beyond its borders.

British steamship companies dominated the seas as well as inter-regional, coastal and river shipping in India and China, but in the late nineteenth century, other rising shipping powers—most significantly Japan—joined them at all levels of this trade. Since both overseas and domestic shipping routes in India and China were overwhelmingly served by foreign companies, shipping became an important arena of nationalist mobilization in both countries after the First World War. Shipping entrepreneurs from the growing native bourgeoisie in India and China demanded access to foreign-dominated shipping trades. They claimed shares of the traffic as a step towards building a self-sufficient national economy. This 'shipping nationalism', which was evident in both places, combined political and entrepreneurial efforts to build national merchant fleets to challenge British—and, increasingly, Japanese—shipping power.

This chapter compares the leaders of two important Indian and Chinese steamship companies and their respective engagement with shipping nationalism. Walchand Hirachand (1882–1953) was a founder and later the managing director of the Scindia Steam Navigation Company (established 1919). Lu Zuofu (盧作孚) (1893–1952) was the general manager of the Chinese Minsheng Industrial Company (established 1926). The comparison yields strong parallels in Hirachand's and Lu's respective careers: In the period between the two World Wars, both men identified their companies with nationalist goals, and simultaneously pursued both entrepreneurial and political strategies to advance the agenda of shipping nationalism. After the Second World War, these same principles determined their proposals for decolonization and their engagement with new regimes after Indian Independence (1947) and Chinese Liberation (1949).

Given the substance of these parallels, one would expect that, in this period of intensive interaction and consciously crafted solidarities between Indian and Chinese elites, these two men either knew of one another or at least were aware of the two nations' comparable struggles in shipping. There is, however, little trace of any such concrete exchange in their stories.[1] The significance of the comparison, however, is not in its elucidation of a specific instance of contact, but in its ability to put in relief the structural conditions that India and China shared as a result of their respective enmeshments in the British Empire and its global reach. Whereas the potential for solidarity between India and China in this period was often voiced in terms of past civilizational or religious affinities, as Chapter 8 by Brian Tsui demonstrates, these parallels call our attention back to the urgency of their shared predicament in the present. Although there are overwhelming differences in the very conception of the nation and its opponents in each context, the single arena of shipping highlights the limits of such distinctions and the central struggles common to both. Such parallels encourage us—in Arunabh Ghosh's (2017: 700) words—to 'think China through India and India through China' in order to delineate both the specific contexts and the historical shape of the global.

The Shipping System and the Origins of Shipping Nationalism

Hirachand and Lu sought to dismantle a shipping system that had originated with the extension of the British Empire in the mid-nineteenth century. The extension of foreign steam shipping to these spaces was linked to Britain's rise as the pre-eminent steam shipping power in the world in the second half of the nineteenth century. According to Daniel Headrick (1988), the colonization of India underwrote this rise, and the consequent 'communications revolution' refashioned the transport networks between China and India to include the steamship ports of Bombay, Galle, Calcutta (now Kolkata), Penang, Singapore, Hong Kong, and Shanghai, as well as extended British shipping power across the world. The extension of British ocean shipping to China's shores prompted an intensified invest- ment of British capital in steam shipping on the coast and along the Yangzi River. British entry into domestic coastal and riverine steam- ship routes in India and China thus occurred on either end of the 'communications revolution' of the 1870s. The British domination of steam shipping on both internal and overseas routes, which included places in China and India, was held in place by shipping conferences. Conferences were organizations that employed a range of tactics to keep rival shipping companies off of these routes. When Chinese or Indian shipowners entered this field, they had to confront not only the strength of British capital and ships, but also organizations of British shipowners designed to maintain their market share against outsiders.

The development of coastal and river steam shipping in each context makes visible the historical relationship between India and China as each was incorporated into the British Empire: As other historians have noted, developments in colonial India later extended to China (Bickers 2016; Hevia 2003). Following the 1857 Mutiny, the new Indian government began contracting with private shipping companies to meet its transport needs. In 1862, it awarded a mail contract to the British India Steam Navigation Company—a shipping concern run by the Scottish trading firm of Mackinnon, Mackenzie & Company—to carry mails and government supplies along the coast in exchange for an operating subsidy. The support of the mail contract helped the British India Company to edge out its rivals in the Indian coastal trades, many of which were firms backed by Indian merchants or joint ventures between Indians and Europeans. Thus, the British India Company could develop the coastal steam shipping trade in India in conjunction with the construction of the Indian Railways. The strong position it achieved in the 1860s allowed it to anticipate and benefit from the changes brought about by the communications revolution, which, along with renewed mail contracts in the 1870s and 1880s, allowed it to extend its services beyond India to the Indonesian archipelago (1866), the East African coast (1872), Europe (1874, 1876), and Australia (1881). By 1882, the British India Company possessed the largest steam fleet owned by any single company in the world (Munro 2003: 68, 133–4).

The spectacular rise of the British India Company and Britain's extension into overseas steam shipping routes piqued the interest of British investors in shipping ventures on China's Yangzi River and coast. As in India, in China the pre-existing steamship companies were backed by Chinese and foreign investors residing in the treaty ports. Over the 1870s, this type of company was supplanted by British firms such as Butterfield & Swire's China Navigation Company, or Jardine Matheson & Company's Indo-China Steam Navigation Company, which, like the British India Company, were underwritten by tightly knit family and business networks in England and Scotland (Blake 1956: 19–20; Jones 2000: 51; Liu 1964: 65; Munro 2003: 40). A significant difference in the contexts of shipping in China and India was that, whereas the British India Company enjoyed a near monopoly in Indian coastal shipping, the two British firms in China arose alongside and competed against the China Merchants Steam Navigation Company (established 1873), a commercial steamship company initiated by Qing officials and backed exclusively by Chinese capital. Run by merchant managers, the China Merchants Company received some support from the Qing government through preferential contracts and concessions. By the late 1870s, intense competition between the two British firms and the China Merchants Company had eliminated most of the locally financed companies on the river and coast and they became known simply as the 'Three Companies' (Liu 1964; Reinhardt 2018: 74–5).

By the late 1870s, therefore, British shipping was ascendant on both coastal and river routes in India and China, as well as on the overseas lines that connected them to one another and to other parts of the globe. To maintain this position, British shipowners formed shipping conferences, also called cartels or rings, under the newly competitive conditions in steam navigation that accompanied the communications revolution. Conferences were agreements among shipping companies designed to limit competition among participants and to deter newcomers from entering their trades. Conferences employed both internal controls (setting rates, dividing routes, pooling profits) and exclusionary measures (deferred rebates to shippers, fighting ships, slashing rates) to maintain control of a shipping route (Cafruny 1987: 54). The first overseas conference was the Calcutta Conference of 1875, followed by the Far Eastern Conference of 1879, both initiated and dominated by British steamship companies. The conference system derived in part from practices common on China's coast and rivers: John Samuel Swire, head of the China Navigation Company, was persuaded of the importance of conferences through his experience of rate agreements among companies in Chinese waters, and he promoted overseas conferences in his role as agent for Alfred Holt's Ocean Steamship Company (Marriner and Hyde 1967: 135–41). By the turn of the twentieth century most overseas steamship routes were controlled by British-led conferences. In China, the 'Three Companies' concluded conference agreements in 1877 and 1882 for the coast and Yangzi River, some form of which persisted until the outbreak of the Second Sino-Japanese War (1937–45). On the Indian coast, the British India Company concluded conference agreements with the few British firms it permitted to share these routes and participated in conferences on its regional and overseas routes. The effect of the extensive implementation of the conference system was to set a very high barrier for new competitors trying to enter these trades. When faced with a powerful enough newcomer, however, conferences generally responded by incorporating the new company into the conference structure (Marriner and Hyde 1967: 183).

In the 1880s and 1890s, the overseas conferences began to incorporate shipping companies from nations other than Britain. These newer firms, from France, Germany, and Italy, among others, often had the support from home governments eager to expand their national presence in overseas steam shipping that allowed them to sustain competition against the conference firms long enough to win a place within a conference (Cafruny 1987: 52–61). The most significant of these new shipping powers for China and India was Japan, whose shipping business received increased government support and subsidies following Japan's victory in the First Sino-Japanese War (1894–5). The government particularly supported Japanese shipping companies' expansions into overseas routes and into coast and river shipping in China. In China in 1907, the Japanese government mandated the consolidation of all Japanese shipping firms into one subsidized company, the Nisshin Kisen Kaisha (日清汽船会社). In 1913, after years of intense competition with the Three Companies and other newcomers, Nisshin Kisen joined the Three Companies' conference, although in subsequent years, it had difficulty observing conference agreements because of Japanese government mandates for tonnage and routes. As early as 1896, Japanese overseas shipping companies joined conferences on lines to India, and in the 1920s and 1930s these companies began to make forays into certain coastal trades as well (Wray 1984: 388, 393–4, 1989: 53; Zhu 2006: 73–4). Japan was not the only alternative to British shipping power around the turn of the twentieth century, but it was one of the strongest and most aggressive in Chinese and Indian waters.

When a new generation of indigenous Indian and Chinese shipping companies emerged after the First World War, they confronted not an open field of competition but an arena that was tightly controlled by long-established conferences and well-capitalized or well-subsidized foreign firms. Even to participate in this field, they had to seek out gaps in its control, as well as find longer-term means to dismantle this shipping system. Out of this situation came a shared agenda of shipping nationalism, a combined strategy of business and politics. Shipping nationalism had different inflections and dynamics in India and China, yet the basic principles of the agenda taken up by shipping companies in the 1920s and 1930s in both places were the same. Premised on the recognition of India and China as nations, it promoted the importance of a national mercantile marine for the nations' security and their economic prosperity. In order to build such a fleet, a nation had the right to reserve its domestic shipping (coasts and rivers) for ships under its own flag. Finally, governments were expected to offer aid to support the fleet and promote the nation's shipping autonomy. This model of shipping nationalism was based on the example of Japan: Dependent on foreign steamships as late as the 1870s, the Meiji government supported the expansion of private shipping companies to ensure Japan's coastal shipping autonomy. In the 1890s, the Japanese government offered generous subsidies to shipping companies to expand into overseas routes as well as coastal routes in other countries, making Japan a global shipping power that challenged British hegemony on the seas (Wray 1984; Zhu 2006). Indian and Chinese advocates of shipping nationalism aimed to build a national fleet along Japanese lines and to secure their coasts and rivers for ships under their nation's flag.

Shipping Nationalism in the Inter-War Period

In the years between the two World Wars, the shipping national-ism agenda was more than a distant hope for emerging Indian and Chinese shipping firms—it was intimately connected with their business strategies. In trades already controlled by established players in the global shipping system, indigenous firms confronted formidable obstacles to entry, such as conference tactics designed to force their immediate withdrawal. To establish a presence in these markets, entrepreneurs such as Walchand Hirachand and Lu Zuofu needed to put pressure on their foreign competitors that went beyond participating in the shipping business. For both men, intensive political involvement provided the additional leverage they needed to secure stable positions in major shipping trades. The type of involvement differed for each depending on the specificities of each political environment, but in both cases, Hirachand and Lu drew on shipping nationalism to articulate challenges to foreign dominance. Although the goals of shipping nationalism remained unrealized in this period, its discourse was indispensable to insti-tutionalizing the presence of indigenous firms in major shipping trades in India and China.

India

At the end of the First World War, there was almost no Indian capi-tal in the steamship business. In the 1890s and 1900s, some Indian entrepreneurs had tried to set up firms to compete with the British India Company and its allies, but they were quickly crushed by conference tactics (Rao 1965: 71–4). Walchand Hirachand's Scindia Steam Navigation Company was the first sizeable Indian firm to survive long enough to become a lasting presence on Indian coastal routes. Hirachand belonged to a Gujarati Jain merchant family that had migrated to Bombay and Pune in the mid-nineteenth century. He achieved some early success as a construction contractor for Bombay public works. Later in his career, he would diversify into sugar culti-vation and manufacture of construction supplies, automobiles, and aircraft, but Scindia was his earliest departure from the contracting business (Khanolkar 1969).

The rapid and seemingly spontaneous formation of this company in 1919 indicates that there was already considerable support for an Indian steamship company among members of the business elite in Bombay. Hearing of a liner ship available for purchase on a train journey, Hirachand rushed to inspect it immediately after the journey's end. He convinced Narottam Morarjee, of the Goculdas textile-manufacturing family, to join him in the shipping venture, and the two then enlisted other Bombay businessmen, such as Lalubhai Samuldas, who had close ties to the Bombay government, and Kilachand Devchand, the 'rice king' of Bombay, to form a syndicate to purchase the ship (Jog 1969: 18).

From the earliest stages of this venture, Hirachand and Morarjee faced stiff opposition from British shipping interests. Initially they hoped to put Scindia's first ship on the Bombay–London line, which would put it in direct competition with the British India and P&O companies. Just a few years earlier, in 1914, these two storied steamship companies had merged under the leadership of Sir James Mackay, the later Lord Inchcape. Inchcape's interests, therefore, dominated most shipping in India, as well as overseas lines from India to Europe. Inchcape deployed conference tactics to discourage the new firm: Hirachand and his associates found that repair facilities and shipping agents in Bombay would not work for them for fear that they would lose business with the British India Company. Shippers were likewise unwilling to book space on the ship, as they stood to lose both guaranteed space and rebates from the British India and P&O lines. Finding that he could accomplish little in Bombay, Hirachand took the ship to London in the spring of 1919 to repair and refit it, but found repair facilities and brokers there likewise unwilling to alienate Inchcape's companies. It was not until he found help from a partner in a rival British company critical of Inchcape's tactics that he was able to repair the ship and purchase a fleet of six additional steamers (Jog 1969: 18–22; Khanolkar 1969: 75–6).

When the Scindia fleet returned to India in the winter of 1919, the company had already lost so much time and money that its leaders decided to abandon the overseas trade and focus on the cargo trade along the Indian coast. This trade demanded fewer ships and allowed the company to develop a clientele of Indian shippers. Scindia ships began to call at Malabar and Kathiawar ports, as well as Karachi,

Colombo, and Rangoon. This change in strategy did not reduce the opposition that the company faced from British shipping interests. Because the British India Company, P&O, and other members of the Calcutta Liners Conference also participated in coastal cargo trades, Scindia was immediately subjected to conference tactics. The British companies lowered rates precipitously and refused rebates and cargo space to customers known to have sent goods on Scindia's ships. Shut out of existing trades and auxiliary services, the company needed to develop its own. Scindia focused on the Rangoon–Bombay rice trade, which was almost entirely in the hands of Indian merchants. The company made long-term contracts with these merchants and compensated them for half of the losses they suffered through patronage of Scindia. It also began carrying rice and other goods to ports not served by the British companies. Scindia formed its own subsidiary trading company to fill its holds, as well as another company to provide docking services, stevedoring, and bunkering, since other service companies were unwilling to risk the wrath of the British India Company by providing these services to it (Jog 1969: 27–8; Khanolkar 1969: 172–7).

As Scindia struggled to survive in coastal shipping, Hirachand and Morarjee began a protracted campaign to secure the Government of India's support for Indian shipping. The moment was particularly opportune, as the government had resolved to support the growth of Indian industries after the First World War in order to make India more self-sufficient in industry and manufacturing (Mukherjee 2002: 23; Tomlinson 1998: 132–44). In the light of this policy, Hirachand contended that the Government of India should extend the same assistance and protection to Indian industries that it did to British industries, an argument with particular resonance in the shipping field because the government had supported British shipping with mail contracts and other government business in the past. Invoking the central premise of shipping nationalism, he proposed that the government aid in the formation of a merchant fleet comprised of Indian companies—owned by Indian citizens, under Indian control, and staffed by Indian managers and workers. Hirachand and his associates publicized this cause in the press and cooperated with nationalist politicians to advance it, but its primary object was to convince the Government of India to adopt resolutions or pass laws to build an Indian merchant fleet (Khanolkar 1969: 179–80).

Hirachand was the leading advocate for shipping nationalism, as well as the leader of the only Indian steamship company of sufficient scale to be able to compete against British shipping. Gains and losses in the political sphere had a direct impact on the shipping company's fortunes. In 1922, he submitted a memorandum on the formation of a national merchant marine to the Fiscal Commission that proposed coastal reservation for Indian ships, outlawing the conference practice of deferred rebate, and government subsidies for Indian shipping firms. Early next year, the government appointed an Indian Mercantile Marine Committee, which included representatives of Indian and British shipping and commercial interests, as well as experts in navigation and shipbuilding, to study questions associated with establishing an Indian merchant marine and shipbuilding industry. The Indian Mercantile Marine Committee completed a survey of the shipping industry and published a report early in 1924 that, with one dissenting vote from the representative of British shipping firms, endorsed many of Hirachand's proposals. It recommended establishing an Indian mercantile marine, the gradual implementation of coastal reservation, and the banning of practices detrimental to the development of Indian companies, such as the deferred rebate. The report also recommended measures for the training and employment of Indian seamen, the revival of an Indian shipbuilding industry and government subsidies to assist in the development of Indian shipping firms. Although the report affirmed the principles of shipping nationalism, the government took no further action on it, leaving Hirachand and other advocates to pursue their agenda through bills in the legislature (Khanolkar 1969: 200–3).

The report of the Indian Mercantile Marine Committee, therefore, had few concrete results, but debates over the national merchant fleet in the press brought the agenda of shipping nationalism into the public sphere. The story of Scindia's struggle, told in nationalist terms in the media, put pressure on the British shipping firms to resolve their rate war with Scindia. Lord Inchcape tried to end the conflict by making a bid to purchase the company in 1923. Many of Scindia's directors were inclined to cut their losses, but Hirachand refused to sell on the grounds that the demise of Scindia would be too great a setback for Indian shipping in general. He shocked his fellow directors with his combative stance towards Inchcape in negotiations, but Hirachand nevertheless persuaded them to accept an agreement with the British firms. The Scindia directors signed a ten-year agreement that admitted the company as a junior member of the Indian Coastal Conference. The agreement relieved Scindia of the strain of the rate war, but it placed strict limits on the firm's future growth. It set rates and stipulated how many ships Scindia could add to its fleet over the ten-year period. The agreement compelled Scindia to restrict its business to coastal cargo carriage, preventing it from participating in the coastal passenger trade or overseas trades. Inchcape considered this agreement a 'liberal' concession to a new competitor; Hirachand, although he pushed the other directors to accept it, famously called it a 'slavery bond' (Blake 1956: 170; Jog 1969: 32–4; Khanolkar 1969: 186–7, 199–200).

Despite the government's reluctance to implement the recommendations of the National Mercantile Marine Committee, Hirachand and Morarjee continued to press for government support for shipping nationalism. They worked with the Swaraj Party, a branch of the Indian National Congress, in the Central Legislative Assembly to introduce legislation favourable to Indian shipping. In 1924, they formulated and tabled a bill for coastal reservation, but it was later withdrawn because some in the assembly saw it as promoting flag discrimination in contravention of the Imperial Merchant Shipping Act. If that were true, the legislature did not have the authority to pass the bill. In London, Hirachand spent his own resources investigating the legal questions surrounding the bill, but did not find a definitive answer (Jog 1969: 48; Khanolkar 1969: 203–4). In 1926, legislators revived the question of coastal reservation, expressing frustration with the government's lack of response to the National Mercantile Marine Committee report. In response, the government committed itself to introducing programmes to train Indian navigators and engineers, but refused to endorse coastal reservation (Jog 1969: 56; Khanolkar 1969: 218). In 1928, the Swaraj Party and S.N. Haji, a legislator and Scindia employee, presented yet another bill for coastal reservation, having finally received assurances from Crown lawyers that there were no legal obstacles to its passing. The bill precipitated a bitter debate in the Legislative Assembly, in which opponents argued that coastal reservation took away the shipping trade from those who had developed it without adequate compensation, and that Indian companies lacked the capital and management skill to maintain it at the necessary levels. Hirachand mounted a campaign in support of the bill, in which he secured Gandhi's endorsement. Gandhi wrote essays advocating the bill and incorporated coastal reservation into the 'Eleven Points' he submitted to the viceroy in advance of the second civil disobedience campaign in 1930. When Gandhi was arrested in May 1930, S.N. Haji and other nationalist members of the legislature resigned and the bill lapsed (Jog 1969: 67, 82–3; Khanolkar 1969: 222–3).

While the legislative drama was being played out, Hirachand also sought the intervention of government officials in Scindia's ongoing conflict with British shipping interests. Specifically, Hirachand and Morarjee wanted the government to compel or persuade Inchcape to modify the terms of the ten-year agreement between Scindia and the Indian Coastal Conference. They contended that, although Scindia was part of the conference organization, the British India Company continued to subject it to conference tactics such as cutting rates without consultation and offering secret benefits to shippers (Jog 1969: 49). Furthermore, Scindia had failed to secure a modification to the agreement that would allow it to expand its fleet. In 1928, as Haji's coastal reservation bill was debated in the legislature, Hirachand requested full membership of the conference and began asking officials in the Commerce Department and the India Office, as well as the viceroy himself, to persuade Inchcape to modify the terms of the agreement (Khanolkar 1969: 225–8, 230–40). It was a particularly difficult moment for Scindia as there was a shipping recession just when Japanese companies had entered the Burma (now Myanmar) rice trade that was so important to Scindia's business. At first, these government officials refused to intervene, and the agreement remained unchanged. In January 1930, the viceroy held a shipping conference intended to increase cooperation between British and Indian shipping concerns, but it broke down before reaching a resolution. It was not until after Inchcape's death in 1932 that, with the assistance of the first Indian civil service officer in the Commerce Department, Sir Joseph Bhore, Scindia was able to negotiate full conference membership that allowed it to participate in coastal passenger trades and expand its fleet. Under the revised agreement, the British India Company's tonnage limit was still three times Scindia's, and

Scindia was still barred from overseas routes, but the company had secured a more stable position on the Indian coast (Jog 1969: 90–2).

In the political arena, nationalist legislators continued to propose bills and resolutions in support of Indian shipping after 1930, but the Government of India Act (1935) put an end to the drive for coastal reservation. Responding to arguments from British interests that coastal reservation for Indian shipping constituted 'discriminatory legislation', and upholding the idea of 'equality of trading rights', the Act stated that no new laws could discriminate in favour of either Indian shipping or British shipping (Jog 1969: 85–6). However, Walchand Hirachand remained the primary spokesperson for and organizer of Indian shipping interests. After Narottam Morarjee died in 1929 and S.N. Haji's Coastal Reservation bill lapsed, Hirachand founded the Indian National Steamship Owners Association (INSOA) in 1930, drawing together seven shipping companies and four individuals to represent the cause of Indian shipping (Khanolkar 1969: 242). Under his leadership, the Scindia Company published an 'Indian Shipping Series' that publicized the need for and obstacles to the development of an Indian merchant fleet. The company's Scindia House (established 1938) in Bombay maintained a shipping library for research on these questions (Jog 1969: 37–8).

Examining Hirachand's activity in the inter-War period reveals his two mutually reinforcing strategies: striving to secure a wider scope for Scindia's business; and pursuing an agenda of shipping nationalism directed primarily at the Government of India. The greater the publicity and debates about a national merchant fleet or coastal reservation, the greater the pressure on the British firms to change their practices or modify their conference agreements. Scindia's conflicts with the Inchcape interests, such as the 1923 agreement and later requests to modify it, practically coincided with major political actions such as the appointment of the National Mercantile Marine Committee or the pushes for coastal reservation legislation. This strategy was not always successful in the short term, but the gradual improvement in Scindia's position over the inter-War period made arguments for an Indian national marine all the more viable. Of course, the wider agenda of shipping nationalism that Hirachand pursued through his political activities was not realized in this period, but his tireless promotion of it through the press, the nationalist movement, the legislature, and the government made it a fixture of nationalist discourse, as well as being a goal for which he and others would continue to strive after the end of the Second World War.

China

Walchand Hirachand's Scindia Steam Navigation Company was the primary representative of Indian shipping in the inter-War period. Lu Zuofu's Minsheng Industrial Company, in contrast, would not acquire a similar position until after the Second World War. In the inter-War years, it was one of many Chinese shipping companies, and its scope was more regional than national. Chinese participation in coastal and river steam shipping had been continuous through the late nineteenth and early twentieth centuries. The China Merchants Steam Navigation Company, whose ships sailed under Qing and Republican flags and whose owners and managers were all Chinese, had been one of the Three Companies and a regular conference participant since 1877. The Qing government had discouraged the formation of other Chinese firms until 1895, after which it allowed them to proliferate. Most of the new companies could not compete with the China Merchants Company or foreign shipping firms: They were small concerns that operated on inland or tributary routes rather than the network of coastal and river treaty ports dominated by the conference companies (Fan 1985: 300–2, 320–2, 427). As in India, conditions during the First World War aided the growth of Chinese enterprises, thus enabling several Chinese firms to become new competitors on major shipping routes. The Minsheng Company, established in the Chongqing area in 1925, was a latecomer within this generation, but it transformed itself rapidly from a small local firm to one that could compete against the conference companies on major routes. Minsheng was, therefore, neither the progenitor nor even at the centre of Chinese shipping in the way that Scindia was in India, but in its early years, it faced the very similar challenge of breaking into a shipping trade dominated by well-capitalized and well-organized foreign companies. The tactics of its founder, Lu Zuofu, also resembled those of Walchand Hirachand in that the expansion of the shipping company was closely entwined with Lu's engagement in politics.

Shipping nationalism was already a feature of political discourse in China during the Minsheng Company's early years. In the 'scramble for concessions' after the First Sino-Japanese War, shipping—along with railroads and mines—became a target of Chinese elites' 'rights recovery' projects, in which they tried to regain control over railways, mines and shipping routes granted to foreign powers. During and after the First World War, shipping became an important element in calls to revise China's unequal treaties. The fact that these treaties had granted foreign ships the right to navigate China's coast and rivers was cited as an important way in which the treaties violated the principles of international law among sovereign nations. As in India, the idea that the coasts and rivers of a nation should be reserved for the ships of that nation and the economic and strategic necessity of a national merchant fleet were key aspects of Chinese shipping nationalism (Reinhardt 2018: 183–7). After the Kuomintang (KMT) came to power in 1927 and promoted its treaty-revision agenda, Chinese shipowners formed the Shanghai Shipping Association to work with the government to craft their own demands for the treaty revision process. The Association's journal, *Hangye yuekan* (航業月刊) [*Shipping Monthly*], called for the revision of key treaty clauses, elimination of foreign shipping from Chinese waters, and government support for Chinese shipping companies, shipbuilding, and the training of experts in this field (Reinhardt 2018: 221–3).

This activity was centred in Shanghai and the capital of Nanjing when Minsheng was a small concern working on the Jialing River, a tributary of the Yangzi outside the treaty port of Chongqing. Chongqing was not only distant from the KMT centre in geographical terms, it was also under the control of Liu Xiang, a militarist with only nominal allegiance to Nanjing. The context of warlord conflict in Sichuan Province had a profound effect on Lu Zuofu's decision to start the company. Mostly self-educated, Lu worked as a teacher and journalist. In the early 1920s, he served several Sichuan militarist regimes as an education official. Frustrated by the difficulty in building lasting institutions amidst the conflict, Lu returned to his hometown of Hechuan, on the Jialing River, and started a shipping company as a means to improve its economy. The Minsheng Industrial Company originally ran a service connecting Hechuan to the treaty port of Chongqing. In contrast to the redoubtable Bombay industrialists who underwrote

Scindia, Lu had to appeal to friends, classmates, former teachers, and eventually the local gentry to cobble together the funds to purchase Minsheng's first ship. Lu had to negotiate with two different militarist regimes to guarantee the ship's safe passage to Chongqing. As the area also suffered from banditry, he established the Jialing Gorges Defence Bureau, an organization that trained young men to pacify the area. With the route to Chongqing secured, Lu was able to buy more ships and extend Minsheng's services beyond Chongqing to Fuling, a port on the Yangzi that larger steamships bypassed (Tong 1963; Zheng 1983).

Minsheng's route intersected with the major steamship route of the Upper Yangzi River that connected Chongqing—through the scenic but hazardous stretch of rapids and gorges—with Yichang in Hubei Province. The navigational difficulties of this route demanded specially designed steamships of light draught to carry the plentiful goods and products of Sichuan and West China to Yichang, where they could be transferred onto larger ships and carried downriver as far as Shanghai. The richness of the trade—which drew on China's premium opium-producing areas—and the dangers of navigation made this route particularly lucrative for steamships. Before the First World War, the Upper Yangzi was one of the few important routes that Chinese companies controlled, but after the War, foreign companies returned in force to China, and the two British firms (China Navigation and Indo-China) and the Japanese Nisshin Kisen Kaisha entered the Upper Yangzi trade. Using their downriver connections, they initiated a direct service to Shanghai, bypassing the trans-shipment point at Yichang. On this route, the foreign firms were not organized into a formal conference, but maintained agreements on rates and sailings. The Chinese companies on the Upper Yangzi were generally small and, lacking the resources and downriver connections of the foreign firms, they struggled to remain in the trade (Fan 1985: 487).

It is not clear if Lu Zuofu initially intended Minsheng to expand from the tributaries onto the Upper Yangzi route and eventually onto the entire Yangzi River, but when an opportunity to secure a more prominent place for Minsheng arose, Lu took it. As for Walchand Hirachand, the growth of an indigenous shipping company in a foreign-dominated market called for both entrepreneurial and political skill. In the militarist-dominated Chongqing area of the 1920s and

1930s, however, political activity looked different from Hirachand's legislative and lobbying efforts in India. Lu Zuofu negotiated an alliance with Liu Xiang which offered both distinct benefits. After Liu had taken control of Chongqing in 1925, he struggled to collect revenue from its trade. A major treaty port, it was served by foreign-flag steamships, some Chinese-owned ships flying foreign flags of convenience, and various small-scale Chinese shipping companies. Under the treaty regime of extraterritoriality, only ships flying the Chinese flag could be compelled to pay Liu Xiang's taxes. Foreign-flag ships were only required to undergo inspection by and pay duty to the Maritime Customs (stationed in each treaty port); they could, therefore, bypass Liu's checkpoints. As the trade of Chongqing was the main source of revenue for Liu's garrison area, he tried to force Chinese-owned companies flying flags of convenience to revert to the Chinese flag. Finding these companies recalcitrant and the small companies under the Chinese flag fractious and unstable, he planned to consolidate all the Chinese-owned ships in the Chongqing area into a single company under the Chinese flag, thus ensuring that a reliable portion of the steam fleet that served Chongqing would generate revenue for him (Reinhardt 2008: 263–5). On the advice of his officials, who knew about Lu Zuofu's anti-banditry work, Liu chose Lu as the person to oversee the unification of Chinese companies, which in turn would result in a much-enlarged fleet for Minsheng (Liu 1978: 174–6; Zhang 2003: 268–9).

To raise Lu Zuofu's profile in Chongqing, in 1929, Liu Xiang made him the head of the Upper Yangzi Navigation Bureau, an agency of Liu's regime responsible for collecting duties on shipping. In this position, Lu Zuofu worked to organize and coordinate the services of the small Chinese firms. Even more significant was the confrontation he orchestrated between the Navigation Bureau and the Nisshin Kisen Kaisha. By threatening a protracted boycott of the company's ships, Lu persuaded the Japanese firm to allow searches by the Navigation Bureau, a decision that amounted to giving up an extraterritorial privilege. The British companies followed suit without protest. The foreign firms' capitulation to the Navigation Bureau's demands was a coup for Lu Zuofu at that moment, but it was not entirely surprising given that these companies had already endured numerous boycotts on the Upper Yangzi in response to local incidents, such as the accidental sinking of junks, and were all too cognizant of the disruptive power of boycotts. Furthermore, immediately prior to this incident the British consul-general had decided that consuls would no longer enforce the 'principle of immunity from search' across China, and the Chongqing consul had relayed this information to the British companies. In the immediate context of Chongqing shipping, however, this confrontation succeeded in levelling some of the inequities between foreign and Chinese shipping firms, as well as providing a way for Liu Xiang to collect duties on foreign steamship cargoes (Reinhardt 2018: 231–2).

After his successful term at the Navigation Bureau, in 1930, Lu Zuofu returned to the Minsheng Company to oversee the consolidation of the Chinese shipping companies. In some cases, Minsheng purchased ships directly from their owners, while in others, it organized mergers that paid off the original company's debts, hired its former employees, and compensated its owners in Minsheng stock. Liu Xiang consistently supported Minsheng by providing direct financial assistance and granting the company monopoly rights to important shipping routes and trades, such as transporting opium and silver for the regime. By the end of 1932, Minsheng had twenty ships and 1,000 employees. The company used this fleet to dominate shipping routes in the tributaries and above Chongqing, and to challenge the British companies and Nisshin Kisen Kaisha by vying for a share of the profitable Chongqing–Yichang route (Ling 1990: 29, 37–8).

Minsheng's challenge prompted protests similar to those accompanying Scindia's entry into important routes along the Indian coast. The Shanghai-based English-language periodical *Shipping Weekly* criticized Minsheng for its monopolization of the Upper Yangzi traffic. Minsheng's publication *New World* printed a Chinese translation of this article, the central claim of which was that a business fostered by foreign companies had been invaded by a monopolistic Chinese concern under the protection of the Sichuan military, destroying 'free competition'. This article prompted a sharp riposte in *New World*, whose writer denied that Minsheng was part of the military and highlighted the irony of a Chinese company 'invading' a shipping route in China's own interior. 'Who deserved to be called "invader"?' the writer asked (*New World* 1933a). Although some claims in both the *Shipping Weekly* and the *New World* articles were open to dispute, the exchange was nevertheless nearly identical to one between Walchand Hirachand and Lord Inchcape in which Inchcape called Scindia 'pirates' for entering the British India Company's trades and Hirachand responded, 'Who are the pirates—we or you?' (Khanolkar 1969: 190).

Despite these polemics in print, Minsheng did not face the same intractable opposition from the foreign companies that Scindia received from Inchcape. The foreign firms were not pleased to have a new rival on an already competitive route, but they did not resort to the harshest conference tactics, such as rate wars, to undermine Minsheng. There was, of course, the lingering threat of boycott, but China Navigation Company correspondence also revealed appreciation for Lu's efforts at the Navigation Bureau to address foreign companies' concerns and to try and benefit Chongqing shipping overall by limiting military interference and ensuring order on the docks.[2] As the Minsheng Company expanded—particularly when it entered the direct shipment trade to Shanghai in 1932—the British and Japanese companies considered depressing rates, but in the end decided to continue cooperating with Lu Zuofu.[3] Although there was no formal conference agreement on the Upper Yangzi, Lu was not opposed to cooperative arrangements, and he proposed several mutually beneficial rate agreements to the other companies. As Minsheng grew even larger in the mid-1930s, the British and Japanese companies included Lu in their deliberations on the Upper Yangzi route. The four companies did not always agree or honour the agreements they made with one another, but Minsheng had secured a regular place at the table with the British and Japanese firms.[4] In 1937, just prior to the outbreak of the Second Sino-Japanese War, Minsheng had a fleet of forty-seven ships and regularly competed in the direct shipment trade to Shanghai (Ling 1990: 43–6, 48–50).

In comparison to Walchand Hirachand's pursuit of shipping nationalism at the political centre of inter-War India, Lu Zuofu's politics appear significantly more circumscribed. Lu's alliance with Liu Xiang may seem more expedient than a contribution to a broad programme of shipping nationalism. Whereas its importance for local trade and government finance cannot be overlooked, the alliance's outcomes also benefitted shipping nationalism more generally by helping to reduce foreign shipping privileges on the Upper Yangzi and mobilizing a sizable Chinese-flag fleet. Yet perhaps more significant was that, from this foundation, the scope of both Minsheng's and Lu Zuofu's activities widened from the local to the national scale. Between 1932 and 1937, the reach of the Minsheng Company extended beyond the Upper Yangzi route to the entire river, and the company built offices in Shanghai and other downriver ports. Lu registered Minsheng with the Nationalist government's Enterprise Bureau, and it became a member of Shanghai Shipping Association. An outspoken nationalist in print, at this time Lu began to publish essays in national-level journals such as *Dagong bao* (大公報) [*L'Impartial*] and offered advice and assistance to Chiang Kai-shek's New Life Movement (Kapp 1973: 96; Zhang 2014: 419, 442–4, 499).

In inter-War China, as in India, the agenda of shipping nationalism was well-publicized but not realized. Rather than implement the full programme, the achievement of companies such as Minsheng and Scindia in these years was that they carved out spaces for national shipping within the arenas once completely dominated by powerful foreign firms. In both cases, this achievement was the result of both entrepreneurship—the development of the companies and trades—and political involvement. The form that politics took was different in each case, underscoring some of the historical differences between India and China at this time. As the primary representatives of Indian shipping, Walchand Hirachand and Scindia directly opposed British shipping interests and pursued shipping nationalism through both legislation and lobbying directed at the colonial Government of India. The militarist-dominated Sichuan in which Lu Zuofu founded the Minsheng Company had an uncertain relationship with the political centre of the Nationalist government at Nanjing. As such, Lu Zuofu and Minsheng's contributions to shipping nationalism were complicated by this uncertainty and their distance from the centre. Without question, Lu's alliance with Liu Xiang was critical to establishing Minsheng as a company of sufficient scale to compete on major routes and to establish Lu Zuofu as a credible leader with whom the foreign companies would negotiate and cooperate. Yet, from a peripheral position, these victories did not contribute directly to Nanjing's pursuit of shipping nationalism. The Nationalist government's treaty revision process stalled in 1931, leaving both foreign shipping rights and extraterritoriality in place until the final abrogation of the unequal treaties in 1943. The foreign powers' rationale for abandoning treaty revision was the lack of sufficient Nationalist government control over all parts of China to enforce any promises made in the process (Fung 1991: 236–8). Although there were more spectacular examples of insubordination to Nanjing, Lu Zuofu and Liu Xiang's assertion of autonomous authority over both foreign and Chinese shipping at Chongqing could only have added to this negative assessment of Nanjing's power. By the mid-1930s, however, Lu Zuofu had parlayed these local victories into an expansion of Minsheng that made it one of the most important Chinese-owned shipping firms nationwide and a clear advocate of shipping nationalism. Walchand Hirachand and Lu Zuofu carried the aims of shipping nationalism into the post-War era, when they persevered in searching for opportunities to achieve them.

Shipping Nationalism and Decolonization, 1937–52

Walchand Hirachand's and Lu Zuofu's inter-War careers shared broad similarities, but were distinct in their specific challenges and the solutions they proposed. After the Second World War, their trajectories became more evidently parallel: both saw the end of the War as an unprecedented opportunity to expand their companies and call upon states to advance the goals of shipping nationalism. These efforts were not always successful, but the continuity in their respective commitments to shipping nationalism helps to explain their involvement in the processes of decolonization initiated by the post-Independence and post-Liberation regimes in India and China. After 1947 and 1949, respectively, both entrepreneurs gave up considerable autonomy in entering into joint ventures with these regimes in order to build national fleets.

Despite divergent experiences during the Second World War, both Scindia and Minsheng emerged from the War with ambitious plans for expansion. Prior to India's entry into the War in 1939, Scindia had laid plans to capture 50 per cent of the coastal trade, but Wartime conditions halted its progress. Defence of India rules required Scindia to supply ships for the War effort, and it could no longer determine its freights and passenger fares. The company protested at what it saw as government interference in its business, while the government supported British shipping during the War (Jog 1969: 121–5).

Whereas Scindia suffered during the War, the War situated Minsheng at the centre of Chinese shipping. Japan's invasion in 1937–8 had confined Minsheng's activity to the Upper Yangzi, but the Nationalist government's choice of Chongqing as a Wartime capital meant that Minsheng's fleet was best suited to provide for its needs. Lu Zuofu became the assistant minister of communications and personally oversaw the transport of many downriver institutions (such as factories, schools, and hospitals) to Chongqing. Minsheng facilitated the shipment of food to troops on the front lines, opened new shipping routes on the Upper Yangzi and its tributaries, and coordinated transfers of goods and equipment between airplanes and river ships throughout the southwest. The company lost ships during the War, but was able to buy more at low prices, growing its fleet by 75 per cent over the course of the War (Ling 1990: 189–203, 328; Wang 1955: 68). As the War came to an end, both Hirachand and Lu saw chances to enlarge their companies through the economic reconstruction process. Both planned expansions that would help them reach the scale and scope of pre-War foreign firms: both wanted to build new ships, extend domestic services, and expand on to overseas routes (Jog 1969: 135–6; Ling 1990: 328–9; Lu 1943).

Hirachand and Lu renewed their hopes of making Scindia and Minsheng viable national fleets and actively sought the assistance of their respective states in this endeavour. They were negotiating potentially central roles for their companies in domestic post-War reconstruction projects as well as the threats of powerful, worldwide US shipping and the return of British shipping after the War. At such a time, the pre-War programme of shipping nationalism remained compelling. In India, Hirachand put proposals for the support of the Indian merchant marine before the government's Postwar Reconstruction Committee (Khanolkar 1969: 550–60). In 1947, this Committee resolved to commit state resources to building an Indian mercantile marine, implementing a policy of coastal reservation, and granting a share of overseas trade to Indian companies. These resolutions were accepted by the government with only slight modifications. Later in the same year, as the government took the first steps to enact these resolutions, India became independent (Jog 1969: 137–41; Khanolkar 1969: 568–74).

Lu Zuofu was a vocal participant in debates over economic reconstruction in China during and after the War, and he consistently supported state planning. Lu believed that the state would be more effective than the market in serving the interests of the Chinese nation. After the War, Lu expected the Nationalist government to grant Minsheng the task of restoring shipping services on the Upper Yangzi in the reconstruction process. He planned to use that role as the starting point from which Minsheng could expand to the Lower Yangzi, coast, and overseas (Lu 1946; Wei 2002: 284). Despite his unimpeachable Wartime service, Lu was disappointed. Rather than distribute reconstruction work equally among surviving Chinese shipping companies, the Nationalist government channelled its aid and projects to the China Merchants Company, which was rebuilding itself after being nearly decimated in the War. Allies of the China Merchants Company in the government felt that Minsheng posed too great a threat, and manoeuvred to exclude both Lu and the company from reconstruction efforts (Huang 2001: 271–2). In the same years, Lu Zuofu and other Chinese shipowners strenuously protested at the government's plans to allow foreign shipping companies to return to Chinese waters. The government feared that there were simply not enough Chinese-flag ships to meet the needs of reconstruction. It signed a treaty with USA that allowed US ships to work in China in 1946, but backed away from a similar agreement with Britain the following year because of these protests (Ling and Xiong 2012: 514; Zhang, Chen, and Yao 1992: 253–78). Despite the setbacks in his relationship with the state, Lu Zuofu did enact his plan to expand Minsheng's fleet and extend its services downriver and to the eastern coast, as well as on overseas lines to Hong Kong, Bangkok, and Singapore (Ling 1990: 348–9).

The Republic of India and the People's Republic of China—the regimes put in place by Indian Independence (1947) and Chinese Liberation (1949)—were committed to decolonization and economic autonomy, and thus it was under these regimes that the full agenda of shipping nationalism was finally realized. In both India and China, the new regimes quickly established coastal reservation for Indian and Chinese ships and set up programmes for foreign shipping companies to withdraw from national waters: in India by 1952; in China by 1953–4. As this process went on, the regimes also had to address the problem of meeting the country's shipping needs with relatively small national merchant fleets. Scindia and Minsheng both worked closely with the new states to make their fleets available to them, as well as accepting state aid to keep the companies operational under difficult conditions. In the early 1950s, both companies entered into partnerships with the new states to provide crucial shipping services. In 1950, Scindia became the managing agents for a state–private shipping corporation called the Eastern Shipping Corporation, in which it held a 26 per cent share. This venture finally sent Scindia ships overseas, as it was allocated the India–Australia, India–Far East, Malaya, and East Africa routes, while the private Scindia Shipping Company expanded on other routes (Jog 1969: 145–6). In China, the Nationalists had taken most of the China Merchants Company's fleet with them to Taiwan, leaving the fledgling People's Republic of China with almost no commercial fleet. In 1950, government officials persuaded Lu Zuofu, who was in Hong Kong, to return to mainland China to preside over the restoration of a national fleet using Minsheng's ships. The government paid off the company's substantial debts, and, in an arrangement that Lu himself proposed, became a part owner of the Minsheng Company, placing government representatives on its board of directors. This arrangement was known as public–private joint management (*gongsi heying* [公私合營]), and after it was implemented at Minsheng, it became a model for other joint ventures between private companies and the state in the early People's Republic (Ling 1990: 402–26; Wang 1955: 82–3).

Neither Walchand Hirachand nor Lu Zuofu lived long enough to experience much of the post-Independence/Liberation regimes. Hirachand, suffering from complications after a stroke, passed away in 1953. Lu Zuofu committed suicide in 1952, as the Three-Anti and Five-Anti campaigns were carried out within the Minsheng Company. After the deaths of these leaders, the states gradually assumed an increasingly greater role in the joint ventures: Under the Companies Act of 1956, the Eastern Shipping Corporation became a fully-fledged public-sector undertaking, and Scindia had to both surrender its agency and return its share of the capital. In 1961, this corporation merged with the completely state-owned Western Shipping Corporation, forming a single Shipping Corporation of India. The Scindia Company remained the largest private shipping firm in India, but it had to divide trades with the shipping corporations and was subject to government decisions regarding freight rates and cargo allocations (Jog 1969: 144, 152, 165, 177–81). In China, by 1956, the Minsheng Company and all remaining private shipping firms had been completely incorporated into the People's Republic's state-run shipping companies (Ling 1990: 402–26). Some might view enterprises such as Scindia or Minsheng as the casualties of the new regimes' zealous statism, but looking back to their origins in the interwar period, the sustained commitments of Walchand Hirachand and Lu Zuofu to shipping nationalism help to explain their active participation in—and even initiation of—joint ventures with the state in the early 1950s.

***

The trajectories of Walchand Hirachand and Lu Zuofu as leaders of the Scindia and Minsheng shipping companies from the 1920s to 1950s were unquestionably parallel: they faced similar problems and proposed and enacted similar solutions to them. Although the two men had no contact with one another, these parallels were neither uncanny nor coincidental. The parallels resulted from similar structural conditions these shipping entrepreneurs encountered in inter-War and post-War India and China. To claim national political and economic spaces, both challenged the powerful entrenched position of British shipping, and the newer but no-less-threatening expansion of Japanese shipping in both the entrepreneurial and political spheres. Both aspired to extend this struggle, to take their ships beyond India's or China's waters, entering into greater contact and competition with other shipping powers on international routes, but before the 1950s, the contest was confined to the rivers and coast of both countries. In this way, the shipping field provided a condensation of global relations at the time: For Hirachand and Lu, as well as for other shipping nationalists in India and China, the British Empire set the terms, while Japan played the double role of both the clearest model for developing an autonomous national fleet and an aggressively expanding foreign shipping power. This arena, in which Indian and Chinese actors negotiated the tension of potential solidarities with Japan against possible threats from it, resembles the politics of pan-Asianism in the early twentieth century (Sen 2017: 295–300). Yet shipping nationalists never invoked an idealized past of intra-Asian kinship or cultural affinity. Theirs was an urgent *national* struggle against unmistakably concrete conditions in the present, which may explain why Hirachand and Lu's experiences are parallel rather than interconnected.

Nevertheless, the ubiquity of parallels in Hirachand's and Lu's lives and careers suggests that another important way of understanding the relationship between India and China in the early twentieth century is through the shared conditions that each faced. Hirachand's and Lu's pursuits of shipping nationalism through entrepreneurial and political strategies furnish a very clear parallel, but other dimensions of their experiences within the shipping system suggest an even deeper range of concerns they shared. They also had a similar approach to the management of their shipping companies, one that disrupted certain practices prevailing among foreign shipping companies and reinforced nationalist values. Both companies challenged the hierarchies of race and skill for steamship crews, in which Europeans (or Japanese) held positions requiring technical training (such as captains and engineers), whereas the less-skilled positions in the crew were invariably held by Indians or Chinese. Scindia and Minsheng both recruited, employed, and provided advanced training to Indians and Chinese in captains', engineers', and other technical positions, upsetting the racialized hierarchy aboard the ships and contributing to the development of skilled Indian and Chinese navigators (Jog 1969: 61–3; Khanolkar 1969: 218–19; Ling 1990: 116–17; Lu 1943: 552–3). Similarly, both companies also made a point of providing services, amenities and improved hygienic conditions to third-class or deck-class passengers, who were almost always Indian or Chinese and were the most neglected passengers on other companies' ships (Jog 1969: 92, 103–108; *New World* 1933b; Reinhardt 2018: 281–6). For both, the national merchant fleet was a fundamental objective, but they also made their companies conform to and reinforce nationalist values in their daily management.

As central as shipping was to their careers, Walchand Hirachand and Lu Zuofu were involved in many other economic, social, and political activities. In these other realms, their experiences also reveal numerous parallel problems encountered and solutions proposed. Such parallels suggest that shipping was not an exclusive factor connecting India and China in this period, but one of an enormous range of questions about economic development, social change, and modernization that proceeded from India's and China's enmeshments in a global order. Both Hirachand and Lu built networks of industries designed to promote regional and national autonomy. Lu developed a group of integrated regional enterprises—the shipping company, a coal mine, a shipyard, a fabric-dyeing plant, and a printing press, among others. Hirachand's shipping, airline, and construction companies, as well as his sugar, automobile, aircraft manufacturing firms were perhaps less closely linked but more ambitious in scope. In the 1930s, both Lu Zuofu and Walchand Hirachand created communities for their employees that provided housing, medical care, schools, entertainment, and other services, intended to promote 'modernity' in both the work and lifestyles of their employees. Lu established Minsheng 'New Villages', which provided housing and services for employees, in the main ports on his shipping routes, and also modernized the town of Beibei, where several of his other companies were located. Hirachand founded the township of Walchandnagar at the site of his sugar-processing factories near Pune (Khanolkar 1969: 143–70; Ling 1990: 22–9; Lu 1943; *New World* 1937).[5] Such enterprise communities were not unique to China and India at this time, but they suggest similar views of industrial management and a concern to mould their employees into modern subjects. Finally, although both Lu and Hirachand were famously committed and outspoken nationalists, neither is easily classifiable within the prominent political categories of his place and time. Lu Zuofu joined the Nationalist Party when he became assistant minister of communications during the War, but maintained contacts and relationships with a wide circle of associates and political regimes, remaining aloof from the central Nationalist–Communist conflict. Likewise, as Sardar Patel remarked of Hirachand, he 'belong[ed] to every party' in that he supported anything he believed could advance national causes, but unlike other Indian industrial leaders, he was not aligned exclusively with the Indian National Congress (Khanolkar 1969: 342; Markovits 1985: 39). The multiplicity of parallels between Hirachand and Lu suggest a broad milieu of shared concerns that linked India and China in the first half of the twentieth century, even if these concerns are not always acknowledged or articulated as the basis of conscious solidarities.

Notes

1. There are only hints that, more generally, Indian and Chinese industrialists saw one another as engaged in a similar project of building a national

economy, such as an article in an issue of Minsheng's periodical *Xin shijie* (新世界) [*New World*], which examined the Tatas' role in developing India's steel industry *Xin shijie* (新世界) [*New World*] 1944.

2. John Swire and Sons Archives (JSS), III 2/8 13 September 1929, 2/9 16 May 1930, 2/10 8 August 1930, 29 August 1930, SOAS, London.

3. JSS III 2/13 29 July 1932, 9 September 1932.

4. JSS III 2/14 3 March 1933, JSS III 2/17 24 April 1936, 3 July 1936, 14 October 1936.

5. Walchand Hirachand Papers (WHP), 684, Nehru Memorial Museum and Library, New Delhi, India.

References

Archival Material

John Swire & Sons Archives (JSS), School of Oriental and African Studies, London, UK.

Walchand Hirachand Papers (WHP), Nehru Memorial Museum and Library, New Delhi, India.

Other Sources

Bickers, Robert. 2016. 'Britain and China, and India'. In Robert Bickers and Jonathan J. Howlett (eds), *Britain and China, 1840–1970: Empire, Finance, and War*, pp. 58–83. Abingdon Oxon: Routledge.

Blake, George. 1956. *B.I. Centenary*. London: Collins.

Cafruny, Alan W. 1987. *Ruling the Waves: The Political Economy of International Shipping*. Berkeley: University of California Press.

Fan Baichuan (樊百川). 1985. *Zhongguo lunchuan hangyun de xingqi* (中國輪船航運業的興起) [*The Rise of China's Shipping Business*]. Chengdu: Sichuan renmin chubanshe.

Fung, Edmund S.K. 1991. *The Diplomacy of Imperial Retreat: Britain's South China Policy, 1924–1931*. Hong Kong: Oxford University Press.

Ghosh, Arunabh. 2017. 'Before 1962: The Case for 1950s China–India History'. *Journal of Asian Studies* 76 (3): 697–727.

Headrick, Daniel. 1988. *The Tentacles of Progress: Technology Transfer in the Age of Imperialism, 1850–1940*. Oxford: Oxford University Press.

Hevia, James L. 2003. *English Lessons: The Pedagogy of Imperialism in Nineteenth-Century China*. Durham NC: Duke University Press.

Huang Shaozhou (黃紹洲). 2001. 'Zhaoshang ju yu Minsheng gongsi de mingzheng andou' (招商局與民生公司的明爭暗鬥) ['The Open Strife and

Veiled Rivalry between the China Merchants and Minsheng Companies']. In Ling Yaolun (凌耀倫) and Zhou Yong (eds), *Lu Zuofu zhuisi lu* (卢作孚追思录) [*Lu Zuofu Memorial Collection*], pp. 269–74. Chongqing: Chongqing chubanshe.

Hyde, Francis E. 1973. *Far Eastern Trade, 1860–1914*. London: A. and C. Black.

Jog, N.G. 1969. *The Saga of Scindia: Struggle for the Revival of Indian Shipping and Shipbuilding*. Bombay: Scindia Steam Navigation Co., Ltd.

Jones, Geoffrey. 2000. *Merchants to Multinationals: British Trading Companies in the Nineteenth and Twentieth Centuries*. Oxford: Oxford University Press.

Kapp, Robert A. 1973. *Szechwan and the Chinese Republic: Provincial Militarism and Central Power, 1911–1938*. New Haven CT: Yale University Press.

Khanolkar, G.D. 1969. *Walchand Hirachand: Man, His Times, and Achievements*. Bombay: Walchand & Company Private Limited.

Ling Yaolun (凌耀倫). 1990. *Minsheng gongsi shi* (民生公司史) [*A History of the Minsheng Company*]. Beijing: Renmin jiaotong chubanshe.

Ling Yaolun (凌耀倫) and Xiong Fu (熊甫). 2012. *Lu Zuofu wenji: zengding ben* (盧作孚文集: 增訂本) [*Collected Works of Lu Zuofu: Expanded Edition*]. Beijing: Beijing daxue chubanshe.

Liu Hangchen (劉航琛). 1978. *Rong mu ban sheng* (戎幕半生) [*Half a Life in the Inner Circle*]. Taipei: Wenhai chubanshe.

Liu, Kwang-Ching. 1964. 'British–Chinese Steamship Rivalry in China, 1873–85'. In C.D. Cowan (ed.), *The Economic Development of China and Japan*, pp. 49–78. New York: Praeger.

Lu Zuofu (盧作孚). 1943. 'Yizhuang candan jingying de shiye—Minsheng shiye gongsi' (一椿慘淡經營的事業-民生事業公司) ['An Enterprise Dismally Managed—The Minsheng Industrial Company']. In Ling Yaolun and Xiong Fu (eds), *Lu Zuofu wenji: zengding ben* (盧作孚文集: 增訂本) [*Collected Works of Lu Zuofu: Expanded Edition*], pp. 409–23. Beijing: Beijing daxue chubanshe.

———. 1946. 'Lun Zhongguo zhanhou jianshe' (論中國戰後建設) ['On China's Postwar Reconstruction']. In Ling Yaolun and Xiong Fu (eds), *Lu Zuofu wenji: zengding ben* (盧作孚文集：增訂本) [*Collected Works of Lu Zuofu: Expanded Edition*], pp. 448–66. Beijing: Beijing daxue chubanshe

Markovits, Claude. 1985. *Indian Business and Nationalist Politics, 1931–1935: The Indigenous Capitalist Class and the Rise of the Congress Party*. Cambridge, UK: Cambridge University Press.

Marriner, Sheila and Francis E. Hyde. 1967. *The Senior John Samuel Swire: Management in Far Eastern Shipping Trades*. Liverpool: Liverpool University Press.

Mukherjee, Aditya. 2002. *Imperialism, Nationalism and the Making of the Indian Capitalist Class, 1920–1947*. New Delhi: SAGE.

Munro, J. Forbes. 2003. *Maritime Enterprise and Empire: Sir William Mackinnon and His Business Network*. Woodbridge, UK: Boydell Press.

Rao, T.S. Sanjeeva. 1965. *A Short History of Modern Indian Shipping*. Bombay: Popular Prakashan.

Reinhardt, Anne. 2008. '"Decolonisation on the Periphery": Liu Xiang and Shipping Rights Recovery at Chongqing, 1926–38'. *Journal of Imperial and Commonwealth History* 36 (2): 259–74.

———. 2018. *Navigating Semi-Colonialism: Shipping, Sovereignty, and Nation-Building in China, 1860–1937*. Cambridge, MA, and London: Harvard University Asia Center.

Sen, Tansen. 2017. *India, China, and the World: A Connected History*. Lanham, MD: Rowman & Littlefield.

Tomlinson, B.R. 1998. *The Economy of Modern India, 1860–1970*. Cambridge UK: Cambridge University Press.

Tong Shaosheng. 1963. 'Minsheng lunchuan gongsi jilue' (民生輪船公司紀略) ['A Brief Account of the Minsheng Steamship Company']. In *Sichuan wenshi ziliao* (四川文史資料) [*Literary and Historical Materials on Sichuan*], Volume 10. Chengdu.

Wang Guang (王洸). 1955. *Zhongguo hangye shi* (中國航業史) [*A History of China's Shipping Industry*]. Taipei: Haiyun chubanshe.

Wei, C.X. George. 2002. 'Imperialism, Nationalism, and Globalization: The Making of the Nationalist Postwar Reconstruction Policy'. In Roy Starrs (ed.), *Nations Under Siege: Globalization and Nationalism in Asia*. New York: Palgrave.

Wray, William D. 1984. *Mitsubishi and the N.Y.K., 1870–1914: Business Strategy in the Japanese Shipping Industry*. Cambridge, MA: Harvard East Asia Center.

———. 1989. 'Japan's Big Three Service Enterprises in China, 1896–1936'. In Peter Duus, Ramon H. Myers, and Mark Peattie (eds), *The Japanese Informal Empire in China, 1895–1937*. Princeton NJ: Princeton University Press.

Xin Shijie (新世界) [*New World*]. 1933a. 'Dule "longduan chuanjiang huo jian zhi qitu" zhi hou' (读了垄断川江货之企图件之后) ['After Reading "The Scheme to Monopolize the Upper Yangzi Cargo Carriage"']. 13 (1 January): 7–11.

———. 1933b. 'Gailiang dake daiyu de shangque' (改良搭客待遇的商榷) ['A Discussion on Improving Treatment of Passengers']. 17 (3 March): 1–3.

———. 1937. 'Duiyu Yichang Minsheng xincun zhi guanjian' (对于宜昌民生新村之管见) ['A View of Yichang's Minsheng New Villages']. 10 (8): 14–16.

———. 1944. 'Yindu de gongshang wangzu—Tata gongsi' (印度的工商王族—塔塔公司) ['The Royal Family of India's Commerce and Industry—The Tata Company']. (15 September): 29–30.

Zhang Jin (張瑾). 2003. *Quanli, chongtu yu biange: 1926–1937 Chongqing chengshi xiandaihua yanjiu* (與權力衝突變革: 1926–1937 重慶城市現代化研究) [*Power, Conflict, and Change: A Study of Chongqing's Urban Modernization, 1926–1937*]. Chongqing: Chongqing chubanshe.

Zhang Shouguang (張守廣). 2014. *Lu Zuofu nianpu changbian* (盧作孚年譜長編) [*The Chronicle of Lu Zuofu*]. Beijing: Zhongguo shehui kexue chubanshe.

Zhang, Zhongli, Chen Zengnian, and Yao Xinrong. 1992. *The Swire Group in Old China*. Shanghai: Shanghai renmin chubanshe.

Zheng Dongqin (鄭東琴). 1983. 'Minsheng gongsi chuangye jieduan jilue' (民生公司創業階段紀略) ['A Brief Account of the Minsheng Company's Formative Stages']. In *Chongqing gongshang ziliao* (重慶工商資料) [*Materials on Chongqing Industry and Commerce*], Volume 2. Chongqing.

Zhu Yingui (朱蔭貴). 2006. *Zhongguo jindai lunchuan hangyun ye yanjiu* (中國近代輪船航運業研究) [*Studies on China's Modern Shipping Business*]. Taizhong: Gaowen chubanshe.

14

The Chinese Intrigue in Kalimpong

Intelligence Gathering and the 'Spies' in a Contact Zone

TANSEN SEN

In the 1950s, Kalimpong was a prominent site for espionage activity. The US diplomat, John Kenneth Galbraith (1988: 310), who served as the US ambassador to India between 1961 and 1963, wrote that the town had a 'famous reputation as a resort of spies, thieves, smugglers and multipurpose rascals'. Already in 1956, Mao Zedong (1893–1976) had objected to the Dalai Lama (1935–) travelling to India by road through Kalimpong, where, he noted, 'there were spies from various countries' and also 'Kuomintang secret agents' (Mao 1977: 346). When discussing the Tibet issue with Premier Zhou Enlai (1898–1976) of the People's Republic of China (PRC) a year later, the Indian Prime Minister Jawaharlal Nehru (1889–1964) (2006: 598) acknowledged that he had heard 'for a long time that Kalimpong has a nest of spies and the spies are probably more than the population'.

On 10 July 1958, the Chinese Ministry of Foreign Affairs made a formal protest to the Indian government, urging it to stop US and Kuomintang (KMT) agents in Kalimpong from instigating rebellion in Tibet.[1] The geopolitical discourse on Kalimpong as a site infiltrated with spies continued until 1962 when the Republic of India (ROI) and the PRC engaged in an armed conflict.

Kalimpong's proximity to Tibet was a key reason this hill town attracted spies from different regions of the world. It was also a well-connected place conducive to intelligence gathering and dissemination. Located at an elevation of over 1,200 metres, Kalimpong, which was in Darjeeling District until 2017, was linked to Calcutta (now Kolkata) through a broad-gauge train from Siliguri; mule caravans connected it to Lhasa (see Figure 14.1), itinerant traders carried goods to Yunnan in the southwest region of the present-day PRC, and the global geopolitics of the twentieth century connected it with the nearby state capitals of Kathmandu in Nepal and Thimpu in Bhutan, as well as faraway centres of power such as Nanjing, Chongqing, Beijing, Delhi, London, Moscow, and Washington, DC, at different times. People from distant places with various intentions lived in Kalimpong, local Lepchas, European missionaries, Nepali migrants, Tibetan refugees and revolutionaries, as well as Marwari and Chinese traders. In addition, a wide assortment of people passed through the town, including political emissaries and activists, religious pilgrims, smugglers, and, indeed, spies.

Using conceptual framework formulated by Mary Louise Pratt ([1992] 2008), recent studies have highlighted the role of Kalimpong as a 'contact zone' (Viehbeck 2017) and also examined the trading networks that connected the town to Lhasa and Calcutta (Harris 2013).[2] Missing from the existing studies on Kalimpong, however, is an analysis of the tension between individuals and the security concerns of the government authorities over this so-called 'nest of spies'. The same holds true for the intelligence and counter-intelligence activities in the town. The surveillance, policing, and counter-intelligence activities of government authorities are common features in contact zones, especially because many of them are located in border regions or coastal areas. They are often hubs that connect the hinterland to foreign regions. Because of such intersecting internal and external connectivities and the diversity and mixing of residents and

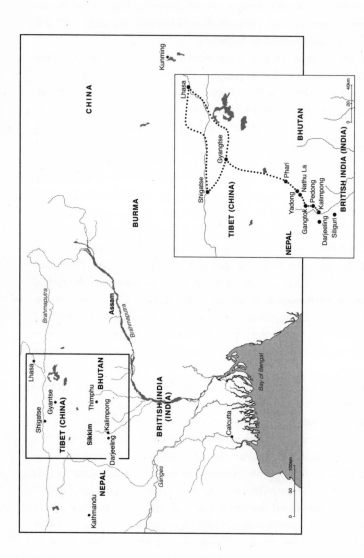

Figure 14.1 Kalimpong's Transregional Connections

Source: Drawn by Inspiration Design House, Hong Kong (© Tansen Sen)

sojourners, contact zones are often strategic sites for espionage and counter-espionage activity. Kalimpong is no exception to this.

One objective of this chapter is to understand Kalimpong as a site of covert and clandestine activity by analysing the confidential reports produced by the colonial and postcolonial Intelligence Branch (IB) of West Bengal, now housed at the State Archives in Calcutta (henceforth WBSA). It specifically examines the intelligence reports on individuals suspected of carrying out espionage activity for the Republic of China (ROC) and the PRC from the 1940s to the 1960s. These individuals were Jampa Wosel (Zhang Fangkun [張方堃]), Pandatsang Rapga (邦達饒噶/邦達饒幹), Shen Fumin (沈福民), Ma Jiakui (馬家奎), Chang Xiufeng (常秀峰), and Yu King Tuck (Yu Jingde [余敬德], also known as A.H. King).

The chapter also aims to grasp the issue of knowledge production and show how such knowledge was used to incriminate suspected foreign agents. The IB files pertaining to the Chinese in Kalimpong and other northern districts of West Bengal illustrate the effects of encroaching nation-states and their concerns about territorial integrity on the lives of individuals residing in or passing through a contact zone. By focusing on several individuals who were identified as 'Chinese agents' in these IB files, the chapter also examines the impact of the changing geopolitical relationship between India and China with respect to Kalimpong and its Chinese residents.

In the context of broader India–China relations, and of the present volume, which deals primarily with the period before the founding of the ROI and the PRC in the second half of the 1940s, this chapter exposes the problems that arise when periodization is based exclusively on political shifts. Covering a period from the 1940s to the 1960s, the chapter illustrates several continuities in Kalimpong that transcended political changes in India and China. Travel and networks of trade across both border regions and merchant groups did not alter dramatically in the early 1950s: The intelligence-gathering methods and structure remained the same, the Indian government's concern over the status of Tibet and the role of the Chinese state in the eastern Himalayan region persisted, and some of the espionage agents continued to practice their craft irrespective of changes of government in the two countries. It was only in the late 1950s that severe restrictions were imposed on cross-border movement and trade. At the same time, the issues of ethnic identities and citizenship started having a serious impact on the daily lives of people residing in Kalimpong. This chapter argues that the watershed moment for the town and its people took place in January 1960, when a memo from the IB in West Bengal acknowledged the 'deterioration in Sino-Indian relations' and ordered the intelligence officials to compile a list of 'adverse' Chinese 'nationals' in their jurisdictions along with recommendations for further action.[3] The execution of this order and the subsequent actions taken against individuals identified as 'adverse' significantly changed the demographic contours and spatial entanglements of Kalimpong. By the end of 1960, Kalimpong had ceased to be a contact zone, and the ROI and the PRC had become adversaries.[4]

The focus on Kalimpong and the intelligence measures instituted there also complicates the use of categories such as 'China' and 'India'. Kalimpong demonstrates the permeability of the borders between the geographic entities of China, India, and Tibet, making it a security concern and a site of interest for several different political regimes. Similarly, the IB reporting on the 'spies' and 'agents' in Kalimpong reveal the arbitrariness of the categories 'Chinese', 'Tibetan', and 'Indian' and how such categorizations could be strategically harnessed in service of a range of political agendas. In other words, the examination of Kalimpong presented here disentangles the 'India–China' premise of existing studies on India–China relations, including this volume, by showing how constructed and in flux these units of connection could be.[5]

The Emergence of Kalimpong as a Security Concern

A series of events in Beijing and Tibet between 1910 and 1913 brought Kalimpong into the limelight. In 1910, when the Qing Manchu troops entered Lhasa, the thirteenth Dalai Lama (Thubten Gyatso [1876–1933]) escaped to Kalimpong. During his residence in the town, he discussed the situation in Tibet with British officials and, at the same time, appointed local Tibetans to represent the interests of Tibet in multilateral negotiations. The defeat of the Manchu troops in Tibet and the fall of the Qing Empire (1644–1911) a year later changed the dynamics of Tibet's political situation in relation to the new government in Beijing. Given that this new government, led at the time by Yuan Shikai (袁世凱) (1859–1916), was militarily weak and unable to assert its control over peripheral regions, Tibet planned to declare its independence (Goldstein 1989: 62; Kobayashi 2014). This possibility not only resulted in an intense round of negotiations involving the representatives of the Dalai Lama, the British government in India and the officials of the ROC, it also led to the establishment of networks of espionage, political support, and propaganda in and around Tibet on all sides. A central figure in all this was Lu Xingqi (Lu Hsing-chi [陸興祺]), a Chinese businessman based in Calcutta who played an important role during negotiations for the Convention Between Great Britain, China, and Tibet, [in] Simla, also known as the Simla Accord of 1913–14. In 1913, Lu was appointed as the associate resident in Tibet by the government in Beijing, but with his office in Calcutta rather than in Lhasa. Since Lu's contacts with Lhasa took place through Kalimpong, the importance of the town in regional geopolitics increased significantly. Already under the viceroy and governor general of India from 1899 to 1905, Lord George Nathaniel Curzon, Kalimpong had emerged as one of the three sites (Beijing and Kathmandu were the other two) that the British government in India utilized as a source of information about Tibet, especially with regard to the Russian activities in the regions (Johnson 2006: 206–8). Lu Xingqi's operations in the town marked the beginnings of Kalimpong as a 'nest' for multicultural espionage specialists.[6]

The Chinese started settling in Kalimpong before the town acquired political significance. The IB file on Yu King Tuck, an individual discussed in more detail later in this chapter, reveals that his father, known as 'Ashing Chinaman', arrived in Kalimpong from Hong Kong in 1895 and married a local Sikkimese woman some time in 1902–3.[7] The political changes in Beijing and Tibet in the early twentieth century triggered the arrival of new Chinese settlers. Yang Twan, who was born in Kalimpong in 1919 to a Sichuanese army official father and a Tibetan mother, reports that his parents and sister were deported from Tibet after the defeat of the Manchu army in Lhasa.[8] Yang also describes his parents' conversion to Christianity after arriving in Kalimpong, his mother's burial in a local Christian graveyard, his father's occupation as a carpenter, his participation in Chinese and Hindu festivities, and his visits to a Chinese temple, which was most likely the Guandi (關帝) temple still existing in the town (Yang 1945: 1–5).[9] By this time, there was also a Chinese cemetery in Kalimpong, where the earliest existing tomb, in which the 'collected bones' of unidentified Chinese are preserved, seems to date from 1920.[10]

After spending several years travelling and working for different 'masters' across India, Yang settled in Calcutta, where he married a Tibetan woman from Darjeeling. Yang returned to Kalimpong several times during his stay in Calcutta. When he visited the town in 1940, he found that it had 'improved' significantly, with 'a big cinema hall', electricity, a bazaar, concrete houses, and people owning radios and telephones (Yang 1945: 187). The transformation of Kalimpong that Yang witnessed was due to the surge in cross-border trade in the late 1930s. This transformation, in addition to the influx of Tibetan revolutionaries (Stoddard 1985), drew the attention of the intelligence officers, who produced several documents, including a report on the findings of Captain A.R. Allen, who was working for the British government's Chinese Intelligence Wing in India. The report, composed in 1944, includes two detailed appendices: a nine-page, single-spaced 'Notes of Kalimpong's Trade with China'; and a similarly long and detailed account called 'Exports Overland to China'. The report stressed that 'Kalimpong's security problem is closely linked up with Sino-Tibetan commercial activities'.[11]

The number of registered Chinese when the report was composed stood at 300, with approximately an additional hundred 'transients', mostly from Yunnan. A detailed breakdown of the composition of the 'Permanent Chinese Residents in Kalimpong' is included in Allen's report (see Table A14.1), which also points to the existence of a Chinese restaurant, one or two small Chinese shops, a Chinese school, and a bank. Most of the Chinese were merchants engaged in the trade in wool, cotton yarn, and piece goods. A list of eleven Chinese firms in Kalimpong, the two 'regular routes' that connected Kalimpong to Yadong, and the volume of trade involved, as well as the suspected sites of Chinese espionage activities in the town, the Homes [Photo] Studio and the bungalow known as 'Morningside', are also described in the report.

The report outlined three problems that the surge in cross-border trade and the influx of new settlers into Kalimpong had created for the security personnel and intelligence officers. First, the inadequacies of border security measures resulted in an increase in smuggling and other illegal activities. Second, it predicted an expanding role for traders based in Kalimpong in the Chinese government's attempts to assert its influence in the region, noting that 'Kalimpong presents a unique centre for such activity'.[12] Third, it highlighted the difficulties in distinguishing between the Chinese and Tibetans entering India through Kalimpong because the latter were exempted from registering as foreigners. This detailed analysis of the situation in Kalimpong resulted in the establishment of new intelligence positions, a quarterly reporting system on suspicious activities and individuals, and the verification of the registration certificates held by the Chinese residents of Kalimpong. The border security and counter-espionage apparatus now in place in Kalimpong generated copious records on the activities of suspicious individuals and organizations that continued well beyond Indian independence.

Intelligence Gathering in Kalimpong

The invention of the telegraph in France in the late eighteenth century and its transcontinental diffusion and commercialization during the nineteenth century resulted in a new and significantly faster means of information gathering and transmission. Telegraphy led to profound changes in news reporting, diplomatic communications and intelligence activity. In fact, according to Christopher Andrew (2018: 421), the use of telegraph 'marked a turning point in intelligence history'. Intelligence gathered at one location could now be transmitted long distances to multiple locations. However, since telegraphic communications were susceptible to interception, electronic intelligence and counter-intelligence activities also became common across the world. Three parallel technological advances in the nineteenth century also facilitated intelligence gathering and sharing activities, namely the invention of the typewriter, the cyclostyle or mimeograph machine, and photography. Typewritten documents gradually replaced handwritten notes and reports, multiple copies of which were made and dispatched to several locations. Photography aided intelligence gathering not only because of the images that were produced of suspected individuals and sites of interest, but also due to its use in making copies of intercepted letters for future translation and analysis. The uses to which these technological tools were put are all apparent in the sources used for this chapter.

C.A. Bayly (1996: 54) has pointed out that the success of East India Company in India was due to its 'effective intelligence', which, he writes, 'was more important than its slender edge of military advantage or its ambiguous capitalist character'. Richard Popplewell (1995) has similarly suggested the crucial role gathering intelligence played in the British colonial enterprise in India. Bayly and Popplewell explain that initially, the British employed the pre-existing intelligence-gathering networks used by the Mughal rulers. Local Indian informants and spies, the *harkaras* (mail runners), *munshis* (accountants/secretaries), and pundits, formed the core of the early British-Indian intelligence network. There were also itinerant traders, such as the *gosains*, and business firms, including those belonging to the Kashmiri Muslims,[13] as well as map-makers, who provided intelligence about foreign and frontier regions.[14] Lord Curzon instituted a thorough reform of the intelligence system, resulting in the establishment of several strategic institutions in charge of collecting and coordinating intelligence from across British India.[15] These included the Department of Criminal Intelligence and various provincial-level Criminal Investigation Departments (CIDs). Popplewell (1995: 52) explains that 'by creating the CIDs and by conferring a high status upon the Director of Criminal Intelligence, Curzon's administration acknowledged the gathering of intelligence as a vital function of good government, and the agencies dedicated to its procurement as legitimate'. An extensive review of the intelligence apparatus in West Bengal took place in 1932, when the issues of intelligence personnel, support staff, and other organizational aspects were discussed in detail.[16] By 1939, an effective system of collecting and transmitting intelligence had become operational in West Bengal.

The IB in West Bengal worked and exchanged confidential information with special branches of police and criminal intelligence in local regions, the Home Department in Delhi, the India Office in London, and British centres of intelligence across the Empire. The basic structure of intelligence sharing within India continued after Indian independence in 1947. And despite the separation from the vast British imperial intelligence network and, in most cases, the replacement of British officers with native officials, the IB files on certain subjects and individuals remained active. Reports were added to these files, some as late as the 1960s. The general concerns of the intelligence officials also endured: local crimes, foreign presence, frontier smuggling, and issues of domestic political concern, cross-border movement, and pro-communist activity.

In 2007, the WBSA made files compiled by the West Bengal IB publicly available. These files date from the early twentieth century to 1950 and cover a variety of topics. Over hundred files in this collection pertain to Chinese and Tibetan communities, organizations, and individuals living in different parts of West Bengal. These files consist of two parts: handwritten communications exchanged among the intelligence officers; and a collection of mostly typewritten documents that include reports by field agents operating in various districts of Bengal, communications from and responses to other IBs, CIDs, and central government, copies of intercepted letters (in English translation), biographical notes on suspects, and so on. A few files also have indexes of names and organizations. Chinese names sometimes include handwritten characters, but frequently, the corresponding character numbers found in Herbert A. Giles's *A Chinese–English Dictionary* are provided.

Material pertaining to Kalimpong and the Chinese either settled in or passing through the town appear in several IB files. Mentions of the town and its Chinese and Tibetan residents and businesses are made in thematic files that have titles such as 'Foreigners: Chinese', 'Chinese Nationals', and 'Chinese Police Security, Control Weekly Survey'. The Chinese authorities also collected intelligence about Kalimpong, its commercial and political significance, and the border policies of the British and Indian governments. In Chapter 12 in this volume, Liao Wen-shuo has briefly noted the use of intelligence organizations by the KMT in British India. Collection of intelligence from Kalimpong by the KMT government seems to have started shortly after the Simla Accord was signed between the British government and Tibet in 1914. The aforementioned Lu Xingqi was actively engaged in Tibetan affairs and frequently communicated information he collected in India to the KMT government. Some Chinese (and Tibetan) businesses and organizations, as well as officials passing through Kalimpong, also gathered intelligence on behalf of the KMT. Many of these communications and reports are preserved in archives located in Nanjing, China, and Taipei, Taiwan.[17]

Together these archival documents provide insights into various aspects of Chinese activities in Kalimpong and about the town itself that are not otherwise available. The documents reveal the methods of intelligence gathering, the ways in which this intelligence was interpreted, and how such interpretations were employed to prosecute the Chinese residents of Kalimpong when relations between the PRC and the ROI deteriorated in the late 1950s. These documents also illustrate the rapid and extensive use of the communication technologies that were introduced in the nineteenth century. At the same time, they demonstrate the shortcomings of some of these technologies. Since British firms such as the Eastern Telegraph Company operated several of the telegraph networks, the Chinese had to use them to transmit their messages related to the activities taking place through Kalimpong. The British intercepted messages transmitted through Calcutta until the KMT installed radiotelegraphy equipment in Lhasa in the latter half of the 1940s, making direct wireless communications between Tibet and Nanjing/Chongqing available.[18]

Information was frequently obtained by intercepting letters sent to or written by people under surveillance in Kalimpong. These letters, often written in Chinese, were photographed and translated, copies of those that were considered to be of significant intelligence value being also mimeographed and shared with relevant intelligence branches, the Home Department, and sometimes the India Office. The contents of intercepted letters ranged from discussions of commercial possibilities and political issues to those that were purely personal in nature. There are also IB files related to the negotiations between the IB and local post offices regarding the interception of mail, as well as concerns about the paucity of skilled translators when dealing with Chinese-language material.

The human network of intelligence gathering is clearly the most fascinating aspect of these documents. Field agents, district police and intelligence officers, superintendents and commissioners at the IB office in Calcutta, the staff at the Home Department in Delhi, and sometimes officials in London were all part of the information and intelligence gathering and analysis. Also included in the network were local informants, police departments, foreigner's registration offices, and British intelligence organizations located outside India. The IB files often include notes requesting clarification of information, orders for additional surveillance and cross-referencing with other relevant files. Many of these methods of intelligence gathering, as noted earlier, continued after Indian independence.

Finally, these IB files reveal the concerns of police departments and intelligence officers about various types of criminal activity, cross-border smuggling, and international security issues in contact zones. The early British apprehensions about Kalimpong related primarily to the smuggling of goods and the infiltration of illegal immigrants, but they were also troubled by the activities of Chinese agents and Tibetan revolutionaries in the town. During the 1950s, the Indian intelligence officers in charge of Kalimpong (and other border regions of West Bengal) were mostly concerned about individuals involved in communist propaganda and their possible links to the PRC. More broadly, for both the British and the independent Indian governments, the intelligence apparatus in Kalimpong related to the security of India's northern frontiers. In the 1950s, Kalimpong had also emerged as one of the main sites for collecting information about the PRC's presence in Tibet. This development brought new groups of foreign agents to the town, many of them working for the US Central Intelligence Agency.[19]

It must be noted that the archival sources, the IB files from India and the documents from China, although providing a wealth of information, also present several problems. These records were compiled and collected by and for the state. As a result, the contents primarily convey the concerns of the state with regard to intelligence activities and analysis, as well as the subsequent public availability of such confidential information. As Nicolas B. Dirks (2002: 58) has pointed out, the colonial archives 'reflect state categories and operations such that the state literally produces, adjudicates, organizes, and maintains the discourses that become available as the primary texts of history'. Employing this critique of the colonial archives by Dirks, as well as Ann Laura Stoler (2009, 2010), Carole McGranahan (2005, 2007, 2017) has questioned the accuracy of the British archival records on an individual called Rapga, a resident of Kalimpong who was branded a Chinese agent and deported in 1946.

Files on Rapga compiled by British intelligence officials are found in London, Delhi, and Calcutta. They contain similar documents because the intelligence reports were often copied to the various British agencies. However, there are also noteworthy differences. While the file on Rapga in the India Office collection[20] contains documents that date from August 1944 to February 1947, the earliest report found in the file in the WBSA[21] is dated August 1943 and the latest 1 February 1957. The National Archives of India (NAI) in Delhi has seven files that have the name 'Rapga' in their titles.[22] In addition, there are about 200 documents related to Rapga in the KMT archives in Taiwan and Nanjing. The analysis of Rapga's activities in Kalimpong in the context of Britain's engagement in Tibet has thus far been based primarily on the lone file in London (Goldstein 1989),[23] later interviews with Rapga and a few others who were associated with his case in the 1940s (Stoddard 1985), and a survey of the books in Rapga's personal collection (McGranahan 2005). The unexplored archival documents detail many of Rapga's networks in China and India and, more importantly, help determine the specific intelligence he was gathering and supplying to the KMT. Indeed, the multi-archival examination undertaken in the next section suggests that Rapga was clearly an agent of the KMT operating from Kalimpong and that, until his deportation, he supported Sun Yat-sen's and Chiang Kai-shek's vision of Tibet under the rule of Nationalist China.

Who Is (Not) a (Chinese) Spy?

The IB files in the WBSA contain reports on hundreds of individuals connected to China living in various districts of West Bengal. Although these records have clear biases, they nonetheless provide insights into the lives and experiences of people that would have otherwise remained unknown. This is true of the individuals discussed in this section of the chapter. These individuals of different ethnic backgrounds were entwined with the intelligence network in Kalimpong as either agents or suspects. While Babu Tharchin, a Tibetan, and Hisao Kimura (aka Dawa Sangpo), a Japanese, rarely appear in these files,[24] possibly because they worked for British intelligence themselves, others have personal files devoted to them in the WBSA. It is evident from the examination of these personal files that the 'conditions of coercion, radical inequality, and intractable conflict' that, according to Pratt ([1992] 2008), defined relationships within the contact zones, were not, as the cases of Ma Jiakui, Chang Xiufeng, and Yu King Tuck outlined later reveal, exclusively an imperial or colonial phenomenon. These conditions persisted or were accentuated by the decolonized states intending to impose clear distinctions between those who belonged to the newly established political entities and those who did not. In Kalimpong, the state-imposed categories of 'Tibetan', 'Chinese', 'citizen', 'stateless individual', and 'agent'; concerns about border security and integrity; and conflicts between nation-states had a tremendous impact on relations among residents, their sense of belonging, and their encounter with the intelligence apparatus. People were forced to choose their group, ethnic, and national affiliations, or were designated foreign 'agents' or 'pro-Chinese'. They were allowed to enter and stay or asked to 'quit' Kalimpong because of such affiliations or classifications. The changes in the internal dynamics of Kalimpong due to such measures took place at the same time as the external links of the town to geographically diverse spaces were being more heavily controlled due to concerns about territorial integrity. By the time India and China went to war in 1962, Kalimpong was no longer a contact zone. Thus, the case studies of the individuals discussed in the next few sections also portray the vicissitudes of Kalimpong linked to its entanglement with state interest and international politics.

Babu Tharchin and Hisao Kimura

In a letter written to Charles Bell, the former British political officer for Bhutan, Sikkim, and Tibet, on 25 December 1937, Babu Tharchin acknowledged his role in supplying intelligence information to the British. 'During many years I did supply much news to Mr. D. Macdonald', wrote Tharchin,

> as well as to Mr. Laden La, also to Rai Bahadur Norbhu Dhondup, and sometimes to the Political Officer ... In 1928, on my way back from Lhasa, I paid my respects to Mr. [Arthur J.] Hopkinson, the British Trade Agent at Gyantse [and later to be the Political Officer], and gave valuable information, and he rewarded me with a sum of Rs. 100/-. (Fader 2002, Volume 3: 330–1)

Born into a family of Christian converts in the village of Pu in the Khunu region of Spiti in the Tibetan borderlands, Tharchin studied at a local missionary school. Before arriving in Kalimpong in 1917, he worked in Delhi, Simla, and Darjeeling. In 1925, he started the first Tibetan-language newspaper titled *Yul phyogs so so'i gsar 'gyur me long* [*Tibetan Mirror*]. This was also when he became an agent for the British. Over the next several decades, he developed an extensive network of sources of information across India and Tibet. He also interacted with European and US scholars, Chinese newspaper editors in Calcutta, members of the local Chinese and Tibetan communities and organizations, and intelligence officers. Eric Lambert, the prolific British intelligence officer in charge of Darjeeling and Kalimpong, declared that Tharchin was his 'most useful source of information on Tibet' (Fader 2002, Volume 3: 357). By 1944–5, when the British started spending significant resources on collecting information in and about Tibet and the KMT government's activities in India, Tharchin had emerged as their main 'spy' in the region.

Tharchin expressed his loyalties to both the British government in India and the independent Indian state that succeeded it. In 1937, he described himself to Charles Bell as 'a loyal British subject' gathering information about Tibet. Then in 1963, he wrote to the Indian political officer in Sikkim, pointing out, 'As regards my loyal services, Your Honour might be aware that there is a large file in Your Honour's office which will relate all about my loyalty and works done for the Government [of India]' (Fader 2002, Volume 3: 332). Tharchin's espionage work is detailed in the three-volume biography written by H. Louis Fader, who concludes that

> so subtly and carefully conducted was Tharchin's undercover network operation, that over the years of its existence none of the Babu's regular associates in the Press nor any of his friends, relatives and family members involved on and off in the publishing work was ever aware that such an ongoing intelligence gathering and disseminating activity had ever taken place. In this respect, at least, Tharchin Babu could be regarded as a spy indeed, and a very good one at that. (Fader 2002, Volume 3: 347)

Fader's description of Tharchin's 'undercover network operation' primarily comes from the writing of Hisao Kimura, a self-acknowledged spy in Kalimpong. Kimura was at first employed by the Japanese in 1939 to collect intelligence in Mongolia and Tibet. In the mid-1940s, when he arrived in Kalimpong disguised as a

Mongolian,[25] Kimura was recruited by Tharchin and Eric Lambert. In his memoir, Kimura provides insights into the intelligence networks based in Kalimpong. 'Like the tree-clad slopes of a dormant volcano', Kimura (1990: 150) writes,

> the calm everyday surface of Kalimpong life disguised feverish under-ground activity. This was mostly Chinese-inspired, with agents sent via Tibet to ferret out what they could about events in India; but there were also anti-government Tibetan exiles and reformers, anti-Chinese Tibetans, White and Red Russians, and a whole medley of other agents working for a variety of causes in this cosy little town.

Kimura's account of the presence of agents from multiple Chinese intelligence agencies in Kalimpong is most revealing:

> To complicate the situation there was a vicious rivalry between three separate Chinese intelligence services under the Defense Department, the Transport Department, and the Tibetan–Mongolian Affairs Commission. These three went at each other with a determination and a savagery that made the well-known jealousies between the British MI5 and MI6 look like a decorous tea party by comparison, and occa-sional mysterious murders in Lhasa or Kalimpong were sometimes found to be the result of this inter-service feuding. (Kimura 1990: 150)

For some reason Kimura does not discuss Rapga, even though he mentions the latter's alleged collaborators, Canglochen Gung Sonam Gyalpo, Kunphel-la (Künpel-la), and Gedun Choephel (Gendün Chömpel) (Kimura 1990: 151).[26]

Rapga and His Chinese Collaborators

Rapga was a member of the wealthy Tibetan Pandatsang family, whose commercial and political influence extended to Tibet, British India, and the ROC.[27] The family was especially close to the thir-teenth Dalai Lama. Rapga and his brother Tobgye were involved in a revolt against the Lhasa government in 1934 that had come to power shortly after the death of the thirteenth Dalai Lama. After the revolt collapsed, Rapga fled to Nanjing and started working for the ROC's Commission on Tibetan and Mongolian Affairs. He frequently travelled between Kalimpong and China, dispatched confidential reports on various aspects of Tibetan affairs in Lhasa and in India, and received support for his political activities from the KMT government.[28] In 1943, he acquired an official ROC passport, with which he returned to Kalimpong (Goldstein 1989: 450–2).

It was also in 1943 that Rapga came to the notice of the IB, which documented his interest in the internal affairs of Bhutan, which was associated with the ROC's larger 'efforts to get her fingers into the N.E. India pie'.[29] Then, in 1944, a Calcutta police raid on a Chinese resident named F.S. Yong (Yang Fuxian [楊富賢]) resulted in the discovery of various letters and documents, including one titled 'The Brief Account of Personal and Family Affairs of P. Rapga of Kalimpong'.[30] From these documents, the IB officials concluded that 'Rapga had joined the Kuomintang and had been asked to get others as well to do so and that China was employing him to contact malcontent Tibetans with a view to getting them start trouble in Eastern Tibet and then back them up with armed forces'.[31] Shortly after this discovery, the IB started intercepting letters addressed to and from Rapga. One of these letters mentioned his intention to start a 'Tibet press in Kalimpong on behalf of the Chungking Government for propaganda work'. For this project, Rapga received INR 70,000 from Shen Zonglian (沈宗濂),[32] the representative of the Mongolian and Tibetan Affairs Commission in Lhasa. By early 1946, the IB had also engaged human sources to extract information directly from Rapga.[33] An intelligence report dated 1 February 1946 pointed out that Gedun Chomphel-la had started working 'as an agent in Tibet for RAPGA and the Chinese Government and that he is sending the latter maps of Tibet and other information' from Lhasa.[34]

The most significant event in early 1946 that resulted in Rapga's eventual deportation may have been a visit to Kalimpong and Calcutta by Shen Zonglian.[35] At a reception hosted by the Pandatsang family at the Zhonghua School in Kalimpong on 28 January, Shen made it clear that 'as long as Tibet was autonomous and *not* independent' China would protect it from other nations.[36] Shen left for Calcutta the following day, and Rapga left on 30 January. A little over a week later, on 8 February, Rapga provided a design for an emblem to a printing company called Thacker, Spink & Co. Later that month, he also made a print order for 4,000 copies of an application form and 2,000 copies of identity cards. These were all for the 'Tibetan Improvement Party'

('Xizang geming dang' [西藏革命黨] in Chinese, that is, 'Tibetan Revolutionary Party') he had established in 1939. The visit by Shen to Kalimpong seems to have precipitated the drive to enrol local members into the party.[37] When the IB officials came to know about the print order, they were no longer able to 'silently tolerate' Rapga's political activities. In June, local police officials launched several raids in Calcutta and Kalimpong, which resulted in the discovery of a large cache of documents and the identification of Rapga's collaborators.[38] On 3 July 1946, an Order of Deportation citing the Foreigners Act of 1940 and the Registration of Foreigners Act of 1939 was issued against Rapga. In a summary report dated 15 July 1946, Lambert listed the evidence gathered against Rapga and concluded that the Chinese government, through the Mongolian and Tibetan Affairs Commission, 'were sponsoring a Tibetan Revolutionary Party to overthrow the existing Government of Tibet. The Chinese were making use of three Tibetan exiles Rapga, Kumhel La and Kung Kusho for the purpose'.[39]

The knowledge that Rapga was an agent of the KMT seems to have been fairly prevalent among Kalimpong's border-crossing itinerants during the 1940s. Abdul Wahid Radhu, a Muslim merchant from Ladakh active in the trade between Kalimpong and Tibet, reports that Rapga's 'association with the Kuomingtang [sic] was notorious' and accuses him of persuading Canglochen, Kunphel-la, and Gedun to undertake intelligence activities and join the 'Chinese orbit'. Rapga, Radhu writes, 'had influence on the leaders of the Kuomingtang [sic] who soon made him a sort of advisor to the Department of Mongol and Tibetan Affairs' (Radhu 2017: 145). Commenting on Rapga's ambiguous political associations after his deportation from India, Radhu (2017: 145) calls Rapga as

> a very cunning man who had certainly laid out elaborate plans to get himself safely out of the predicament in Nanking. But he didn't let anyone know to which side his leanings were and, recalling the political flexibility which he and his brothers had already displayed, I told myself that it wasn't entirely excluded that, after everything, he was thinking of going over to Mao's camp.[40]

Takla Phuntsok Tashi, the brother-in-law of the thirteenth Dalai Lama, also expresses similar views about Rapga and his Tibetan

Revolutionary Party. In the 1940s, when Rapga tried to recruit Takla, the latter turned down the approach because of Rapga's 'connection' to the KMT and his realization that the party he was forming 'was to be a branch office of the Kumingtang [sic] in Tibet' (McGranahan 2017: 87). Carole McGranahan (2017: 87) dismisses Takla's interpretation because it was 'from a distance of almost fifty years'. She explains that 'to be allied with the KMT in the 1930s or the 1940s meant something very different than it did in later decades'. Rather, McGranahan contends that Rapga was a misunderstood figure, a Tibetan nationalist and no 'stooge' of the KMT. However, KMT documents in the PRC and Taiwan on Rapga corroborate the conclusions of British intelligence officers and tally with the views of Abdul Wahid Radhu and Takla Phuntsok Tashi.

Hsiao-ting Lin (2006: 144–5) has cited some of these Chinese documents in the context of the KMT's attempt to secularize Tibet's political structure in the early 1940s within the government's larger objective of recovering the 'lost borderlands'. Lin argues that the ideological formulation and financial support given to the Tibetan Revolutionary Party by the KMT was closely associated with this eventual aim of incorporating Tibet into the Chinese republic. One of these documents records that Chiang Kai-shek, in addition to providing a monthly stipend of 100,000 Chinese yuan to Rapga, 'also instructed his secret service agents in Tibet, Xikang, and India to work closely with Rapga' (Lin 2006: 145).

Similarly, Chen Qianping (2002) has demonstrated a close connection between the KMT and the Tibetan Revolutionary Party based on a study of the Rapga files at Academia Historica, Taipei, Taiwan.[41] These include confidential reports by Wu Zhongxin (吳忠信) (1884–1959), the director of the Mongolian and Tibetan Affairs Commission from 1936 to 1944, replies by Chiang Kai-shek, original and translated letters received from Rapga, and reports on the British case against Rapga and his collaborators written by the Chinese consul-general in Calcutta. A crucial document in this collection is a letter Rapga wrote to Wu Zhongxin on 29 September 1943 in which he volunteered to: (i) join the KMT forces planning to invade Tibet; (ii) organize Khamban forces to attack Tibet; and (iii) organize a Tibetan Revolutionary Party.[42] With regard to the third aspect, he requested advice, permission, and funding from the KMT central government. He proposed that the headquarters of the party be located in Chongqing, with branches in Kangding (Dartsedo) and Kalimpong. Passing on Rapga's request to Chiang Kai-shek, Wu noted that he would leave the decision regarding those of Rapga's proposals that related to military intervention to the central government, but supported Rapga's suggestion to establish a party, especially one that would function as a 'branch' of the KMT.[43] Chiang's financial and organizational support, mentioned earlier, started after this communication and Chiang's subsequent meeting with Rapga. This is also when Rapga acquired his official Chinese passport.

It is evident from these Chinese documents that Rapga's views on Tibet were similar to those of his hero Sun Yat-sen and his paymaster Chiang Kai-shek with regard to the place of Tibet within the structure of the Chinese republic.[44] In his report and a letter to the KMT government in Chongqing, Rapga used the term 'our government' when referring to the KMT.[45] He also emphasized his loyalty to the KMT in a letter to Chiang Kai-shek dated 16 June 1945, where he states, 'After our Government empowers us we are duty bound to render reliable, useful and valuable services to our Government than any other Tibetan has done hitherto-fore'.[46] Similar to Tharchin, who expressed his allegiance to the British and subsequently to the government of independent India, in the 1940s, Rapga, as the documents from the KMT archives demonstrate, considered himself a loyal representative of the KMT in Kalimpong, who not only tried to establish a political unit on behalf of the Chinese government, but also supplied intelligence about activities related to Tibet to the KMT.

Among Rapga's alleged collaborators were two 'Chinese nationals', Jampa Wosel and Shen Fumin, who were characterized by Lambert as 'a spy of quite a high standard' and 'a Chinese agent in Kalimpong', respectively.[47] The two also appear in the KMT documents as informants for the Chinese government. However, the British government handled them differently. A note on Jampa Wosel dated 10 December 1946 states that for a 'yet to be determined' period, Jampa had been working in India for a KMT agency called the 'office of investigation', with 'connections to the Sanmin Chuyi Youth Corps and the Bureau of Statistics'.[48] It anticipated that the documents seized during the raids of places associated with the Rapga case would reveal more details about Jampa's intelligence network in India. Four days later, another report stated that the seized documents were 'very voluminous' and that the analysis might not be completed for 'a very long time'. It recommended that Jampa's case should be adjudicated separately from Rapga's.[49] Perhaps as a consequence of this request, on 31 December 1946, a little over six months after his arrest, an 'Order of Deportation' was issued directing Jampa Wosel to leave India within fifteen days.

The personal file on Jampa Wosel in the WBSA includes summaries from his diary seized by the intelligence officials. The latter deduced from the entries in the diary that Jampa was closely associated with a Lhasa-based intelligence network headed by a person of Chinese-Tibetan heritage called 'Shao Chung Ching' or 'Shao Sung Lin', and a support team that included a Chinese military intelligence officer, a Chinese monk, and a staff member of the Chinese wireless office in Lhasa. Intelligence received from Jampa and other Kalimpong-based operatives was collected by Shao and his team in Lhasa and then transmitted by wireless to Chongqing, then the headquarters of the ROC government. Mention is also made in Jampa's diary of a 'mysterious' figure called 'Wang Pon Chien', who was 'not only spying on Tibet but on officials of the Indian Government concerned with Tibetan affairs, and also on Indian Government activities on the border of Tibet and Nepal'.[50]

The only member of the alleged Rapga intelligence network who escaped jail or deportation was Shen Fumin. He also evaded persecution a decade or so later when many ethnic Chinese like him in India were arrested and/or deported. Shen Fumin's file[51] in the WBSA includes several 'short notes' on him, the earliest dating from 1946. The note dated 5 May 1952 indicates that Shen had fallen under surveillance soon after he arrived in Calcutta in 1940. Shen is alleged to have worked closely with the KMT consulate in Calcutta, as well as the 'Head' of the Mongolian and Tibetan Affairs Commission in Lhasa, who appointed him the 'honorary liaison officer' in Kalimpong in 1942. As the 'Liaison Officer', Shen, then employed as the principal of the Zhonghua School in Kalimpong, was 'entrusted with the following duties':

1) To watch the movement of the overseas Chinese between Kalimpong and Tibet; 2) To watch the Chinese Silver being smuggled to India; 3) To study the control of exports by the Indian Government; 4) To watch political developments in India; 5) To watch developments of

India-China relations; 6) To watch the movements of those Chinese who were suspected to be Japanese spies.[52]

Shen's association with Jampa Wosel and his involvement in the 'Kalimpong Espionage Case' (that is, the Rapga case) are also mentioned in his file. Shen's espionage activities reportedly continued when he went to Bombay (now Mumbai) in 1945, where he maintained contact with a suspected Chinese Naval Intelligence officer called Lai Ning (賴凝).[53] In 1951, Shen was reportedly approached by the PRC general, Zhang Jingwu (張經武),[54] who invited Shen to work in Kalimpong on behalf of the communist Chinese government.

Another note, dated 3 May 1960, acknowledged Shen's previous affiliation with the KMT government, but does not mention his involvement in the Rapga espionage case. Instead, it points to Shen's pro-communist leanings, contending that under his administration of it, the Zhonghua School in Kalimpong had 'become a base of propaganda of the Chinese Communist Party'. The note also remarked that 'after his discharge from the School in 1954 the subject severed his connections with the local pro-Communist Chinese of Kalimpong'.[55] The cover letter to this note, which was compiled in connection with Shen's application to extend his residential permit in India, concluded that there were no adverse reports against Shen, who had been 'usefully employed in establishments which have no concerns with Chinese interests'. As a result, the superintendent of police in Darjeeling wrote to the passport office in Calcutta that he had 'no objection' to the extension of Shen's stay in India. This assessment was confirmed five months later, when the same person noted:

> This is to inform you that the subject does not owe allegiance to the present Government in China and is precluded from approaching them for a Chinese passport and as such he has been treated as stateless person of Chinese origin and registered accordingly.[56]

These endorsements in 1960 are unusual, especially because other ethnic Chinese in India at that time were being denied extensions of stay, arrested, or deported. This included several Chinese residents in Kalimpong, including Ma Jiakui and Chang Xiufeng, whose cases are outlined further in the chapter.

Documents in the Taiwanese archives confirm the British assertion that the Mongolian and Tibetan Affairs Commission in Lhasa had appointed Shen Fumin and tasked him with gathering intelligence in India (Zhu 2016: 315). Despite this knowledge and his involvement with Rapga and Jampa, Shen was not deported in the 1940s. A letter from the Home Department in Delhi, dated 5 March 1947, stated that the External Affairs Department had 'considered the question of F.M. Shen's deportation and have decided that no action against him is necessary at present'.[57] There could be two interrelated explanations for this decision of the British officials and the exemption he received in 1960 from the superintendent of police in Darjeeling. The first relates to Shen's friendship with Tharchin, described by Fader, who writes that the two, both being Christians, quickly 'struck up a professional relationship' in the early 1940s. 'The two of them', Fader (2002, Volume 3: 288–9) points out, were 'collaborating together in printing tax books at the *Tibet Mirror* and in creating a Chinese–Tibetan dictionary. So close had these two become that at the wedding of this Chinese in 1944 the Tibetan publisher gifted him a set of expensive carpets'.

The second explanation is the possibility that Shen was a double agent. This explanation, although speculative, agrees with the fact that Tharchin actively recruited agents for the British in Kalimpong. The firm and quick decision by the British officials not to deport Shen in 1947 and the rare assessment made by the superintendent of police in Darjeeling at the time of an anti-Chinese drive across India indicate that in the view of the intelligence community, he was an exceptional personality among the Chinese in Kalimpong. Indeed, at the same time that Shen received a 'no objection' note from the superintendent of police in Darjeeling, Ma Jiakui and Chang Xiufeng were being asked to leave Kalimpong and eventually India without much evidence of wrongdoing.

The Chinese 'Nationals'

The Ma family was one of the richest among the trading groups from Yunnan who were residing in Kalimpong. This Tibetan Muslim family had been engaged in trade between Kalimpong, Lhasa and Yunnan since 1912. In 1920, Ma Zhucai (馬鑄材) (1891–1963) settled in Kalimpong to trade in brick tea, wool, Chinese medicine, and precious stones. He was a leading philanthropist in Kalimpong, donating money for projects such as the Zhonghua School. He had intimate relationships with the Pandatsangs, the KMT's representatives, especially those passing through Kalimpong, and, after 1949, with the PRC government. In 1960, Ma Zhucai was accused of murdering a Tibetan Buddhist monk, arrested, tried, and eventually found not guilty.[58] Nonetheless, he was deported from India in March 1962. His case was reported in the Indian and Chinese newspapers and mentioned in the official communiqués between the Indian and Chinese governments.[59] Attracting less attention was the deportation of his son Ma Jiakui.

The pro-communist activities of the Chinese residing in India emerged as a major concern for Indian intelligence officials shortly after the founding of the PRC. The entry of the People's Liberation Army into Chamdo (Changdu [昌都]) in 1950 also alerted the intelligence community about the territorial ambition of the new government in China. An 'agent of China' in the 1950s was not just someone collecting secret information or engaged in clandestine activities in the borderlands against India, but also anyone receiving and distributing material relating to communist ideology or participating in communist-related events. Almost every PRC organization in West Bengal, including the Chinese consulate in Calcutta, was suspected of carrying out pro-communist propaganda. In Kalimpong, the intelligence officials identified the Zhonghua School, the Ma family residence and, after 1955, the Chinese Trade Agency (CTA) as centres of pro-communist activity and propaganda. Individuals associated with these organizations or visiting the Ma family residence were placed under surveillance. Ma family members were regular visitors to the CTA and were therefore under constant surveillance. The intelligence reports in the personal file of Ma Jiakui highlight his visits to and connections with the CTA. The file also repeatedly referred to Ma Zhucai and Ma Jiakui as 'well-known pro-communist Chinese in India'.[60]

The file on Ma Jiakui also includes statements he made to the local police and intelligence officials, formal notes and reports compiled by the IB, translated copies of intercepted letters, and a 'précis of watch' kept on Ma. In one of his statements to IB officials, Ma Jiakui admitted his and his family's relationship with the CTA, including the fact that they received medicines and magazines from its representatives.[61] In another statement made in June 1959, he also acknowledged that if he were to 'return' to China, he would go to 'Mainland [China] and not to Taiwan'. But, he added, 'some people say that the People's Govt. of China is good while other hold the view that the Govt. is bad. In this connection I can not [sic] give any opinion as I have not personally seen the present conditions in China. I love Tibet as my mother country and China as my father land'.[62]

The Field Intelligence Office in Kalimpong produced a detailed report on Ma Jiakui based on the latter's statements and its own investigation. It noted the three decades of the Ma family's business in Kalimpong, Ma Zhucai's ill health and the decline in the Ma family's business. Ma Jiakui was described as someone who had come to Kalimpong as a 'young boy', learned several languages and become a 'veteran opium smoker'. The report blames Ma Jiakui for the decline of the family business due to his opium addiction and calls him 'a very suitable man for the Chinese Trade Agent to collect secret informations [sic] of the Tibetans as well as of Indians'.[63] It concluded with vague statements such as 'it is reliably reported that Mr. MA CHIA KUEI of Kalimpong is a paid Secret Agent of the local Chinese Agent' and that Ma 'is reported to be one of the right handmen of Mr. LEE (Trade Agent)'.[64] No evidence to corroborate Ma Jiakui's alleged communist or espionage activities is cited in this report or anywhere in his 150-plus page file.

The deterioration of relations between India and China in 1958–9 resulted in significant changes in how the Chinese were treated by the intelligence community in India.[65] The surveillance, arrests, and deportations of several thousand Chinese, many of whom had been born in India but were declared stateless, became common. The watershed seems to have been early 1960, when a memo from the IB, Calcutta, was distributed to all field offices in West Bengal. Dated 22/28 January 1960, the memo noted: 'In view of deterioration in the Sino-Indian relations it is considered essentially necessary that reference notes should be prepared and kept *up-to-date* of all Chinese nationals who have come to adverse notice'. It continued,

> Among such Chinese Nationals there may be some against whom action should be taken immediately in view of the gravity of information on record. In such cases it would be appreciated if the up-to-date

reference notes are sent to us along with your recommendation so that the matter may be taken up with the State Government at once with a view to terminate their stay in India.[66]

Within three months, a list was compiled of fifty such 'adverse' individuals in Darjeeling District.[67] Ma Jiakui was identified as one of them. In a letter from the Ministry of Home Affairs to the chief secretary of the state of West Bengal, dated 25 June 1960, Ma Jiakui and his wife were asked to leave Darjeeling District within a month. As a result, they moved to and lived in Calcutta thereafter, but were occasionally allowed to visit Kalimpong and tend to Ma's ailing father or to dispose of the family's property. However, in December 1961, the Indian Ministry of Home Affairs decided that, 'since Mr. Ma Chi Kuei has not ceased his pro-communist Chinese activities even after expulsion from Kalimpong, the Government of India consider that it would not be desirable to allow him and his wife to continue their stay in India further'.[68] A formal 'Quit India' notice describing Ma as a 'prominent pro-Communist Chinese' involved 'in the espionage ring of the Chinese Trade Agent, Kalimpong' was served on 6 January 1962. Ma and his wife were given thirty days to leave India. Petitions for extension of stay by Ma and his wife were approved, but finally on 12 April 1962 the two, along with their 'minor daughter', departed Calcutta for Rangoon.[69]

The fate of Chang Xiufeng, the principal of Zhonghua School in Kalimpong, was somewhat similar to Ma Jiakui's.[70] In the 1940s, Calcutta and Santiniketan, like Kalimpong, were important contact zones and also under IB surveillance. Both locations attracted a diverse group of Chinese settlers and visitors. Calcutta housed several thousand Chinese migrants,[71] and it was also a site of frequent visits by KMT officials, some of them transiting through Kalimpong to Lhasa. Santiniketan, a university town established by Rabindranath Tagore (1861–1941), attracted Chinese students, intellectuals, Buddhist monks, and artists such as Xu Beihong (徐悲鸿) (1895–1953). Chang Xiufeng was associated with all three contact zones. He studied at Santiniketan, taught in Calcutta, and eventually became the principal of the Zhonghua School in Kalimpong.

Chang Renxia (常任侠) (1904–96), the famous Chinese artist, poet, and scholar, was Chang Xiufeng's uncle and lived in Santiniketan and Calcutta between 1945 and 1951. It was on Chang Renxia's suggestion that Chang Xiufeng first went to India in 1947. Initially, he worked as a teacher at a Chinese school in Calcutta and then, in 1949, went to study art under the renowned Indian painter Nandalal Bose (1882–1966) at Kala Bhavana in Santiniketan. Chang married a third-generation Chinese woman from Calcutta and later returned to the city to work as an art teacher and an assistant headmaster at the Xinghua School. In 1957, he replaced Shen Fumin as the principal of the Zhonghua School in Kalimpong.

Chang Xiufeng was already under surveillance in 1949, when a report alleged that he was 'secretly carrying on pro-Communist propaganda' under the guidance of Tan Yunshan (譚雲山) (1898–1983), the founder of Cheena Bhavana ('Chinese Hall') in Santiniketan.[72] Two weeks later, another report branded Chang as one of the 'underground leaders' within the overseas Chinese community working for the communist government in China. Both reports were drafted prior to the ROI's official recognition of the PRC. A longer 'Secret Note' on Chang appeared in early 1951, which pointed out his relationship with Chang Renxia, his association with Tan Yunshan, his 'mixing' with the Pandatsangs in Kalimpong, his alleged formation of a youth group in Calcutta to promote communism among the overseas Chinese community in Calcutta, and his secret liaison with Pei Meilong, the second secretary in the Chinese embassy in India. The latter had been sent to India, according to the note, 'to collect political intelligence for the Chinese communist movement'. However, a contradictory report filed on the same day absolved Chang of any political activities.[73] 'The individual', it noted, 'did not stay in Cheena Bhavan and no information regarding his coming in contact with the Indian students and intelligentsia in Shantiniketan to form an Indian Communist Liaison Office there came to our notice during his stay there'.[74]

In 1957 and 1958, when Chang Xiufeng applied for an extension of his stay in India, the superintendent of police in Darjeeling supported his application and reported that there was 'nothing adverse' against Chang and, therefore, he had 'no objection to the extension being granted to him'.[75] The aforementioned memo from 1960 not only changed this assessment but also disrupted the lives of Chang and his family in India. In the list of 'adverse' individuals compiled in response to the 1960 memo, Chang was described as an 'agent of the Chinese Trade Agent in Kalimpong' and someone 'engaged in deeply anti-Indian activities and should be deported early'.[76] The superintendent of police in Darjeeling, who had found no adverse information on Chang two years ago, now rejected Chang's request for an extension of his stay in India. He now submitted the following note:

> In view of the adverse information against Cheng Siu Feng, (headmaster) and his highly objectionable activities especially in a border town like Kalimpong, I do not consider the Foreigner to be a suitable person for grant of further extension of stay in India and recommend that he should be served with notice to leave India within 30 days.[77]

This decision, which is dated 10 May 1960, came less than two weeks after a notice to leave Kalimpong was served upon Chang Xiufeng and his wife. In June, the Ministry of Home Affairs agreed with the superintendent of police in Darjeeling and authorized the order to have Chang and his family leave Kalimpong within one month; 'thereafter, they should be served with a notice to leave the country within a period of one month and made to do so'.[78]

Unlike Ma Jiakui, Chang Xiufeng and his wife refused to leave Kalimpong. In early December, they were arrested, tried in the local court, and sentenced to jail for violating the order of the Indian government.[79] Chang Xiufeng and his wife, who was nursing a child, were first jailed in Kalimpong and then taken to Darjeeling. In his memoir narrating his time in Darjeeling jail, Chang Xiufeng (1999: 59) noted how one of the jailers comforted him. 'Even if you are in the prison, don't I still see you as a friend?' asked the jailer, explaining that the Indian people were still friendly towards China and that it was the Indian government and industrialists who were responsible for the country's anti-Chinese policies. Chang (1999: 59) responded by saying that he too saw the jailer as a friend and that he had great appreciation for Indian art and artists. In fact, throughout most of his stay in India, Chang Xiufeng produced various paintings and other art forms, including bamboo flowers and vases, made during his time in Darjeeling jail. It was only after Chang Xiufeng and his wife agreed to leave India that they were released from jail. Within one month, on 2 June 1961, they left India with their five children.

The case of Yu King Tuck is significantly different. Like the individuals mentioned earlier, Yu was also branded a Chinese agent. However, his torment was related to the ambiguities of his nationality and emblematic of the problems created by nation-states insisting on categorizing and separating citizens from non-citizens.[80] Yu's father, as noted earlier, settled in Kalimpong in 1895 and married a local Sikkimese woman. Yu had been born in Darjeeling District in 1906, where he also received his early education. Later, he seems to have studied architectural engineering in Bombay. A newspaper report in 1950 described him as a 'well-known Sino-Indian Buddhist architect' who designed the Chinese temples in Sarnath and Bodhgaya ('Over "Quit India" Order on Mr. King Rule Issued on Central and W. Bengal Govts', *Nation*, 20 August 1950). In 1945, he went to Lhasa to work at the Chinese Residency, the site where the Chinese officials resided. In 1949, he, his mother, and his wife were part of a group of a hundred evacuees from the Lhasa Chinese Residency who (re-)entered India. The group was allowed to enter India 'without valid travel documents' and was also 'exempted from the provisions of the Indian Passport Rules of 1921' by the Government of India.[81]

On entering India, however, Yu, a person of mixed heritage, had to register himself as a Chinese. A year later, shortly after the ROI recognized the PRC, Yu was one of the evacuees from Lhasa who was served notice to leave India. This decision to deport the evacuees originated in concern in the Indian Ministry of Home Affairs at the 'embarrassment' the Indian government might face because of its decision to accept the Lhasa evacuees in the aftermath of the official recognition of the PRC. The notice from the Ministry of Home Affairs to the chief secretary of the West Bengal government also suggested that:

> So far as the Chinese colony in Kalimpong is concerned, earnest efforts should be made to weed out the undesirable and deport them from India as quickly as possible, preferably before the arrival of diplomatic and consular representatives of the Peking Government.[82]

In response to the notice to leave India, Yu claimed that, since he had been born in India and because his mother was an Indian, he was a '100% Indian citizen'.[83] Court litigation ensued, resulting in the Indian government referring to him as 'a Chinese ineligible for Indian citizenship', but allowing him to stay in India as a registered foreigner.[84] When relations between the ROI and the PRC deteriorated, Yu was designated a 'stateless person', which most likely allowed him to stay on in India. Then, in 1964, when Yu returned from Bhutan after working there for about a year, he was arrested along with many other 'stateless' Chinese. He was moved from a jail in Siliguri to one in Jalpaiguri and eventually to the Alipore Jail in Calcutta. Yu remained incarcerated until January 1968, when the Indian government decided to release all ethnic Chinese remaining in Indian jails. While some of these Chinese were served 'Quit India' notices at the time of their release, a few such as Yu were permitted to reside in India but were 'restricted' from going to five northern districts of West Bengal. Although Yu was allowed to visit Kalimpong after his release in order to visit his ailing mother, his request for permanent residence in the town was rejected. The last entry in Yu's file, dated 24 October 1969, noted his return to Calcutta after this rejection.

Yu's claim for Indian citizenship and his assertion of his family's affinity with India was supported by a number of local government officials, businessmen, and religious institutions in 1950. However, intelligence officials and subsequently the Indian government remained fixated on his 'Chinese' ethnicity, noting at one point that, by virtue of her marriage, his Indian mother was also Chinese. Yu's petition to the Indian courts did not yield any results in his favour. He was not given Indian citizenship but was 'allowed to remain in India for other reasons'.[85] This ambiguity in Yu's status was not uncommon. Many Chinese residents in India of mixed parentage encountered similar struggles. Some were deported, while others remained in India as stateless people. Very few were allowed to return to their hometowns near the India–China border because they continued to be perceived as potential Chinese agents.

***

Concerned with the security of the borderland areas and the clandestine activities of suspected foreign agents, the colonial and postcolonial intelligence officials and their local recruits kept watch over a wide range of people and organizations in Kalimpong. The intelligence apparatus in the town focused on illicit cross-border trade, the political and espionage activities of both Chinese governments (ROC and PRC), and the activities of suspicious Tibetans. Arrests and/or deportations were recommended when individuals allegedly engaged in 'anti-India' activities or against friendly foreign government. In some cases, as with Rapga, concrete evidence instigated such actions. The justifications for interventions in the cases of others, such as Ma Jiakui and Chang Xiufeng, were much less well substantiated. There were also instances, as with Shen Fumin, for example, when no action was taken despite adverse evidence.

Intelligence officials collected a significant amount of information on their subjects through surveillance, interrogation, and the interception of letters and telegraphic messages. Local organizations, communities, and individuals could be branded 'adverse' to the interests and security of the state or empire and become targets of the intelligence apparatus. They were often classified as 'suspects', 'agents', or 'spies'. Intelligence records and communications kept by the British and later Indian officials reveal many problems with the classification of suspects and the recording of mostly incriminating statements and evidence. A few of these records on those classified as 'Chinese agents' can be verified by examining the KMT's archival materials. The roles of Rapga, Jampa Wosel, and Shen Fumin as representatives of the KMT in India, for instance, are confirmed through such cross-analysis. These are voluminous records, distributed in both Mainland China and Taiwan, with unknown numbers not made public. Still, they need to be explored in detail for a proper understanding of the pre-1947 intelligence reports on suspected Chinese agents in British India.

Examination of similar materials for the post-1947 period is significantly more problematic because of the lack of access to a majority of IB files in India and the almost complete inaccessibility to the PRC archival material concerning India.[86] The available material from the WBSA indicates that the concerns about communist activities in India during the 1950s and the changing nature of India–China relations had a significant impact on how intelligence officials designated certain individuals as agents of the PRC operating in India. The mass arrests and deportations of ethnic and mixed-heritage Chinese from India on the eve of and subsequent to the India–China war of 1962 without firm evidence of espionage or anti-India activity were extreme interventions in the lives of these people.[87] Indian policy-makers decided to take pre-emptive steps at the time of the national crisis, instead of finding incriminating evidence against these individuals. Yu King Tuck was one among numerous such individuals who were caught up in the ambiguities of citizenship, the targeted persecution of a migrant community, and the conflict between the two nation-states. The intelligence apparatus, the IB files suggest, was fully complicit in these interventions. The intelligence reports and government actions dramatically reduced the number of ethnic and mixed-heritage Chinese in India, with long-term impacts on how the Indian state, the intelligence apparatus, and even ordinary people perceived the Chinese more generally.[88]

Despite their shortcomings, archival materials provide valuable insights into the lives of those who live in a contact zone and the concerns the mobility of both people and goods create for security and intelligence officials. Within this context, the importance of the documents in the State Archives must be emphasized. The files in the WBSA clearly demonstrate that not all documents generated in local areas by the police and intelligence departments reached or were preserved by the colonial authorities in London. In fact, the State Archives in Calcutta are a key resource for examining the activities of both Chinese and Tibetans residing in various districts of West Bengal. They also provide detailed information about local organizations, 'subaltern' individuals, and regional security directives that often do not appear in the archives in London. Furthermore, the IB files in the WBSA are also noteworthy because of the post-1947 additions made by officials working for the independent Indian state. These additions, particularly those related to places such as Kalimpong and Calcutta, demonstrate the ways in which the establishment of a new, post-Independence nation-state resulted in greater state jurisdiction over contact zones and over the categorization of the population that did not reflect the complexity and fluidity of these sites.

Notwithstanding its notoriety as a nest of spies, Kalimpong has been neglected in studies dealing with India–China relations, inter-actions, and exchanges. Yet the small hill town was a microcosm of broader India–China relations as these changed with the transition from colonial to postcolonial rule and eventually entered a phase of territorial conflict. The archival material in the WBSA, the NAI in Delhi, the British Library, Taiwan, and Nanjing are central to understanding the strategic importance of Kalimpong in the 1940s and 1950s, the networks of trade and communications with several regions of India and China that traversed the town, the ways in which the Chinese and Indian intelligence apparatuses functioned in this contact zone, and how individuals and families were caught up in the dispute between the two nation-states. Small places, as the anthropologist Thomas Eriksen (2015) suggests, can become entangled with large issues and therefore deserve our attention.

Appendix

Table A14.1   Permanent Chinese Residents in Kalimpong, 1944

	Place of Birth	Male	Female	Total
W. China, Tibet,	Yunnan	34	12	46
Sinkiang	Sikang (Xikang)	3	1	4
	Szechuan (Sichuan)	14	NA	14
	Tibet	8	1	9
	Sinkiang (Xinjiang)	5	2	7
N.& E. Central China	Hopei (Hebei)	12	NA	12
	Shantung (Shandong)	11	NA	11
	Kiangsu (Jiangsu)	NA	1	1
South China	Chekiang (Zhejiang)	3	2	5
	Kiangsi (Jiangxi)	2	NA	2
	Fukien (Fujian)	2	NA	2
	Kwangtung (Guangdong)	21	13	34
	Hupeh (Hubei)	3	2	5
	Hunan	NA	2	2
Overseas Chinese &	Burma & Malaya	2	2	4
Others	India	9	9	18
	Unknown	NA	NA	NA
Total		129	47	176

Source: 'Foreigners: Chinese Nationals. Chinese Activities in Kalimpong, Darjeeling',
WBSA File No. 955/44, Serial No. 234: 36–5.

Table A14.2   A List of Reports and Letters Exchanged between Rapga and the
KMT in January–March 1945

Month	Document Title	File No.
January	Report from Pandatsang Rapga on the nineteen issues about Tibet raised by the Secretary of the Chinese Consulate General in Calcutta (邦達饒乾關於中國駐加爾各答總領事館秘書提出有關西藏十九個問題報告)	141-3736

(Cont'd)

Month	Document Title	File No.
	Report from Pandatsang Rapga on the specific course of events surrounding the closing of the British school in Lhasa and other matters (邦達饒乾關於拉薩英國學校停辦具體經過等事報告)	141-3736
	Report from Pandatsang Rapga on the conflicts between the monk-officials and secular-officials within the local governments in Tibet (邦達饒乾關於西藏地方政府僧俗官員間矛盾情形報告)	141-3736
	Report from Pandatsang Rapga on the animosity between Daza and Razheng and the improbability that Razheng would reassume regency (邦達饒乾關於達扎與熱振不睦熱振無機會復攝政之職報告)	141-3736
	Report from Pandatsang Rapga on the conflict between the pro-China lamas and the pro-British non-lama officials in Tibet (邦達饒乾關於西藏親中央喇嘛與親英非喇嘛官員間矛盾情況報告)	141-3736
	Report from Pandatsang Rapga on the negotiations between the Tibetan local governments and merchants with the representatives of the British authorities about the resumption of commerce after the interruption in transportation (services) (邦達饒乾關於自西藏運輸停頓後西藏地方政府和商人與英方代表接洽要求恢復商務情況報告)	141-3736
	Report from Pandatsang Rapga on the connections between Bhutan, Sikkim, and India and their relationship with Britain (邦達饒乾關於不丹錫金印度之聯繫及與英國關係情況報告)	141-3736
	Report from Pandatsang Rapga on the current situation in Tibet (邦達饒乾關於西藏現狀報告)	141-3737
February	Report from Pandatsang Rapga on Tibet's plans to print currency in Zhashi and to purchase and build up its own gold reserve (邦達饒乾關於藏方在扎什城準備印行鈔票並購儲黃金情況報告)	141-3736

Month	Document Title	File No.
	Report from Pandatsang Rapga that the real intention of British intervention in Tibetan affairs lies in invading Nepal through Tibet (邦達饒乾關於英人干預藏事之真實企圖在於越過西藏侵犯尼泊爾報告)	141-3736
	Letters in lieu of telegram to the Executive Yuan from the Mongolian and Tibetan Affairs Commission on Pandatsang Rapga's claim that the Tibetan authorities undertake military action on the basis of the Simla Accord (Three documents) (蒙藏委員會為邦達饒乾稱藏方根據西姆拉草約採取行動事致軍委會行政院等代電[共三件[)	141-3737
	Report from Pandatsang Rapga on the recent movement of Awangjianzan (*Ngag-dbang rgyal-mtshan*), the Tibetan representative stationed in Chongqing (邦達饒乾關於西藏駐重慶代表阿旺堅贊近來行蹤等事報告)	141-3736
	Report from Pandatsang Rapga on the explanation of the map of Tibet and the distribution of cloth and other such commercial matters (邦達饒乾關於對西藏地圖解釋布疋分配等商務情形之報告)	141-3736
	Brief report from Pandatsang Rapga on the roads in Tibet (邦達饒乾關於西藏道路簡介報告)	141-3736
March	Letter to Pandatsang Rapga from the Mongolian and Tibetan Affairs Commission in reply to his request for using his salary towards the preparation of the Tibetan newspaper and for the granting of operation subsidies (蒙藏委員會為答復請求薪俸匯兌籌辦藏文報及補助經費等事致邦達饒乾函)	141-3736
	Report from Pandstsang Rapga on the discussion of the new Panchen's Enthronement Ceremony at a Shigatse conference with participation of the officials and people of the former Panchen in Shigatse (邦達饒乾關於前班禪所屬官民於日喀則舉行大會討論新班禪坐床等事報告)	141-3736

Source: Zhongguo di'er lishi dang'anguan and Zhongguo Zangxue yanjiu zhongxin (2002).

Notes

1. 'Notes, Memoranda and Letters Exchanged and Agreements Signed between the Governments of India and China 1954–1959', *White Paper*, Volume 1, p. 70, Ministry of External Affairs, India. The note detailed several individuals and organizations that the Chinese Ministry of Foreign Affairs alleged were 'special agents and reactionaries in Kalimpong'. In a formal response to the note, the Indian government stated that it had 'no evidence' of either USA or the KMT was 'using Kalimpong as a base for disruptive activities against China's Tibetan region' (Bhasin 2018: 1908).

2. In her work on colonial South America, Pratt ([1992] 2008: 8) defines a 'contact zone' as a 'space of imperial encounters, the space in which peoples geographically and historically separated come into contact with each other and establish ongoing relations, usually involving conditions of coercion, radical inequality, and intractable conflict'. The contributors to the volume entitled *Transcultural Encounters in the Himalayan Borderlands: Kalimpong as a 'Contact Zone'*, although intending to 'construct the history of Kalimpong as a prime example of a "contact zone"', wanted to 'go far beyond a mere literal interpretation of Pratt's concept' and 'a (simplistic) usage of the concept found in the literature of a wide range of disciplines' (Viehbeck 2017: 19).

3. 'Ma-Chia-Kuei s/o Ma-Chu-Tsai of Jedong, China', WBSA File No. 2300/49(1), Serial No. 273: 72.

4. 1960 and 1961 also witnessed the arrival in Kalimpong of the Kaches (the so-called 'Kashmiri Muslims'), who, after intense arguments between the ROI and the PRC governments, were recognized by the latter as 'Indians' and allowed to leave Tibet. See David Atwill's (2018) excellent study of the Kache and their torments. John W. Garver (2001) has the most detailed discussion of the political relations between the ROI and the PRC in the 1950s and 1960s.

5. On the problems with these terms and the tendency to impose nation-state framework on subregional connections and exchanges, see Sen (2017: 14–18).

6. On Lu Xingqi and his activities in India, see Mehra (1976) and Zhu (2016).

7. 'Yu King/Tuck s/o Late Thien Sing of Kalimpong', WBSA File no. 2876/50, Serial No. 336/3: 1–3, 7a. In 1906, according to the Scottish missionary John Anderson Graham, there were 'a few Cantonese carpenters in the town'. Ashing may have been one of these Cantonese carpenters (Minto 1974: 95; Poddar and Zhang 2017: 164).

8. The arrival of Chinese soldiers in Kalimpong and Darjeeling in the aftermath of the defeat of the Manchu armies is confirmed in the IB

files. *Intelligence Branch, C.I.D., Bengal. Weekly Reports, 1911* (pp. 3, 5), for example, reports that some of these Chinese officers from Lhasa sought protection from the British commercial agent in Yadong, who then helped them travel to Sikkim and India.

9. Yang Twan frequently wrote for *The Himalayan Times*, which was published in Kalimpong, and he seems to have been an acquaintance of Babu Tharchin, the publisher of the *Tibetan Mirror* and an informant of British intelligence in India (see under 'Who Is [Not] A [Chinese] Spy?' in this chapter). The collection of Tharchin's documents held in Columbia University's C.V. Starr East Asia Library includes two black-and-white negatives of Tharchin and Yang Twan (Tharchin Family Photo Album, Sub-subseries 2: Other Photographs, Box 9).

10. The Chinese year engraved on the tomb is Minguo 9 (民國九年), which corresponds to 1920. Poddar and Zhang (2017: 164) have identified another (?) tomb, which according to them dates from 1918.

11. 'Foreigners: Chinese Nationals. Chinese Activities in Kalimpong, Darjeeling', WBSA File No. 955/44, Serial No. 234: 41–24. Another document titled 'A Brief Report on Smuggling into China via Kalimpong' was also drafted at this time. See 'Foreign Countries: China. Publication. A Report on Smuggling into China via Kalimpong', WBSA File No. 955/44, Serial No. 301.

12. 'Foreigners: Chinese Nationals. Chinese Activities in Kalimpong, Darjeeling', WBSA File No. 955/44, Serial No. 234: 46.

13. On the case of the Kashmiri merchant Ahmad Ali, arrested by the Qing authorities in 1830 on charges of spying, see Bray (2011) and Mosca (2015).

14. These pundits, who mapped the frontier regions of British India and Tibet, included Nian Singh and Sarat Chandra Das. For detailed studies of this group of 'spies', see Stewart (2006) and Waller (2015).

15. For the intelligence network and personnel set up in the border regions of India under Curzon, and especially the British cadre involved in Tibetan affairs through to the Indian independence, see McKay (1997).

16. 'Organization of an Improved Secret Service for Bengal', WBSA File No. 202/1932, Serial No. 60/1932.

17. Although documents in Nanjing are not easily accessible, some of the KMT materials have either been selectively published by the respective archives or citied by Chinese scholars when they were briefly made available. The Second Historical Archives of China at Nanjing is in the process of publishing KMT documents related to Tibet. Fifty volumes in this collection have been published thus far. There is also a two-volume index to the entire collection. See Zhongguo di'er lishi dang'anguan and Zhongguo Zangxue yanjiu zhongxin (2002, 2009–).

18. See, for example, the file 'Tibet, Intercepted Telegrams, Indian Office Records' (IOR): L/PS/10/393, which contains intercepted messages between the Chinese government and their representatives involved in the Simla Accord.

19. For an excellent study of CIA activities in Kalimpong, see McGranahan (2010).

20. 'Tibet, Chinese Intrigues (Rapga)', IOR: L/PS/12/4211.

21. 'Pu Rapga @ Bhu Rapga @ Panda Rapga', WBSA File No. 453/46, Serial No. 71.

22. See the list of references for all files listed under National Archives of India.

23. An exception to this is Chen Qianping's (2002) study of the Tibetan Revolutionary Party that Rapga founded.

24. Tharchin and Kimura appear in a report dated 1949 in which the latter is described as a Japanese who joined the Japanese Military Intelligence Service in 1939 and after his arrival in Kalimpong in November 1948 worked for Tharchin. See 'Publication/Official: Internal Interception Report (Weekly Interception), Issued by Chinese Intelligence Wing, Calcutta', WBSA File No. 1398/43, Serial No. 116: 1837–1835.

25. The aforementioned IB file incorrectly gives November 1948 as the year of his arrival at Kalimpong. Kimura seems to have reached the hill town in 1945.

26. For a detailed study of Gedun Choephel, which includes an interview with Rapga, see Stoddard (1985). A section of Stoddard's French work has been summarized in English in Stoddard (2013).

27. On the Pandatsang family's role in Tibetan politics, see Goldstein (1989: 177–85).

28. Several of these reports are in the Second Historical Archives of China in Nanjing, while the Academia Historica has others. See Table A14.2 for a selection of Rapga-related documents in the Second Historical Archives of China.

29. 'Pu Rapga @ Bhu Rapga @ Panda Rapga', WBSA File No. 453/46, Serial No. 71: 1.

30. Rapga is said to have resided with Yong when he travelled between India and China.

31. 'Pu Rapga @ Bhu Rapga @ Panda Rapga', WBSA File No. 453/46, Serial No. 71: 14.

32. 'Pu Rapga @ Bhu Rapga @ Panda Rapga', WBSA File No. 453/46, Serial No. 71: 2.

33. A report from this 'new' source, dated 8 January 1946, is found in the WBSA File No. 453/46, Serial No. 71: 6–5.

34. This report confirms the views of Melvin Goldstein's Tibetan sources, who believed that Geldun 'erred by sending the maps and notes to Rapga through the British-run postal service between Gyantse and India, instead of using a personal messenger'. However, Goldstein (1989: 453–4) doubts this claim because Hugh Richardson did not recall any such incident and because the 'records in British and British Indian archives make no mention of such a letter or maps'. This brief report seems to suggest otherwise.

35. See Chang (2014) for a detailed analysis of Shen's activities in Tibet.

36. 'Pu Rapga @ Bhu Rapga @ Panda Rapga', WBSA File No. 453/46, Serial No. 71: 16; emphasis in original.

37. This 'Top Secret' note, written by W.A.B. Gardener, the additional deputy commissioner of police in Calcutta, and dated 5 April 1946, appears in all the personal files on Rapga. See, for example, 'Pu Rapga @ Bhu Rapga @ Panda Rapga', WBSA File No. 453/46, Serial No. 71, and 'Tibet, Chinese Intrigues (Rapga)', IOR: L/PS/12/4211.

38. Stoddard (1985: 97) writes that Rapga burnt many documents two to three days before the raid after the Chinese consulate in Calcutta warned him about the pending action by the British authorities. The list of evidence found in the report dated 15 July 1948 seems to indicate otherwise. The report records of thirteen items, including Rapga's diary covering the period from 1943 to 1945, that were recovered from the raid ('Pu Rapga @ Bhu Rapga @ Panda Rapga', WBSA File No. 453/46, Serial No. 71: 58).

39. 'Pu Rapga @ Bhu Rapga @ Panda Rapga', WBSA File No. 453/46, Serial No. 71: 58–57.

40. On Rapga's post-1949 activities in China, see Garver ([1997] 2015: 168, 170–1). Rapga's file at the WBSA also has entries about his eventual return to India. There is also a CIA document on Rapga dated 19 November 1951, where, in an interview, he expressed his willingness 'to join the Greater China family' and noted, referring to the entry of the PLA into Tibet, that 'I have not experience that any of my rights as the governor has been infringed by the Chinese advisors, nor has any such report come from other departments. The same is the report of other provinces of Tibet and I am happy at that' ('Report of Rapga Pangdatshang on Chinese Communist Occupation of Ch'angtu', CIA File no. 25X1A).

41. Chen (2002: 90) also points out that on one of the membership forms seized by British intelligence the Chinese characters (unlike the Tibetan or the English) mention enrolment of the individual in the KMT. This document appears in 'Tibet, Chinese Intrigues (Rapga)', IOR: L/PS/12/4211: 70. Stoddard (1985: 95) has explained that the first version of the application form that Rapga drafted concurrently enrolled the

applicant as a member of the KMT. The second draft did not include such wording. With regard to the Chinese term 'revolutionary' (that is, *geming*) in the name of the party, she writes (1985: 95),

> Tenant compte de l'anglais, il est indéniable que Rabga cherchait à la grande majorité des Tibétains qui ne lisaient pas le chinois. Peut-être voulait-il également se distinguer du Kuomintang en choisissant le terme geming qui pouvait convenier aux autorité tout en lui permettant d'expliciter les aspirations de son parti.

42. Rapga wrote that he was also making these three proposals on behalf of Canglochen, Kunphel-la, and Gedun.

43. 'Proposals on Tibetan Affairs', AH 001000005050A/000.

44. Several documents in both the English and Chinese archives mention Rapga's interest in translating Sun Yat-sen's *Sanmin zhuyi* (*The Three Principles of the People*), in which the latter's ideas of a united China encompassing the five major ethnic groups are presented.

45. 'Proposals on Tibetan Affairs', AH 001000005050A/003.

46. 'Proposals on Tibetan Affairs', AH 001000005050A/003.

47. While Jampa is described as a 'Chinese national' of 'Tibetan race' born in 'Ta Tsian Lu' ('Jampa Wosel @ Chang Fan Kun', WBSA File No. 595/46, Serial No. 4: 41), Shen Fumin, a Han Chinese, is reported to have been born in Shanxi province ('Shen Fu Min, Kalimpong, Darjeeling. Interception of Correspondence Addressed to:', WBSA File No. 816/46, Serial No. 261: 2). A report on Shen Fumin states that Jampa was sent to India in 1942 'to learn English and continue espionage at Kalimpong, particularly with regard to the British attitude towards Tibet, to watch troop movements in the area which might possibly be directed towards Tibet and to report on the Indian political movement' ('Shen Fu Min, Kalimpong, Darjeeling. Interception of Correspondence Addressed to:', WBSA File No. 816/46, Serial No. 261: 3). Jampa's deportation is reported in 'Deportation of Jampa', IOR: L/PJ/7/12155.

48. The latter organization, the report correctly points out, was headed by the KMT spymaster Dai Li (戴笠). On Dai, see the detailed study by Wakeman (2003).

49. 'Tibet, Chinese Intrigues (Rapga)', IOR: L/PS/12/4211: 7–8.

50. 'Foreigners: Chinese Nationals. Chinese Activities in Kalimpong, Darjeeling', WBSA File No. 955/44, Serial No. 234: 127.

51. 'Shen Fu Min, Kalimpong, Darjeeling. Interception of Correspondence Addressed to:', WBSA File No. 816/46, Serial No. 261.

52. 'Shen Fu Min, Kalimpong, Darjeeling. Interception of Correspondence Addressed to:', WBSA File No. 816/46, Serial No. 261: 40.

53. A document in Academia Historica (0200499990018) indicates that Lai Ning was the principal of the Huaqiao Primary School in Bombay.

54. Zhang subsequently served as the secretary of the Communist Party of China in Tibet from 1952 to 1965.

55. 'Shen Fu Min, Kalimpong, Darjeeling. Interception of Correspondence Addressed to:', WBSA File No. 816/46, Serial No. 261: 94.

56. 'Shen Fu Min, Kalimpong, Darjeeling. Interception of Correspondence Addressed to:' WBSA File No. 816/46, Serial No. 261: 96.

57. 'Jampa Wosel @ Chang Fan Kun', WBSA File No. 595/46, Serial No. 4: 51; 'Decision not to take any action against F.M. Shen, a Tibetan Improvement Party member. 2. Reports regarding activities of Phu Rapga, Jampa Wosel, Kumphel La and Abdul Wahid Ladakche and other Tibetan Party members. 3. Kamchung Thubten Sangpo and Lodza Jampa Ngawang are the recognised Tibetan representatives at Nanking in China. 4. Return to Tibet of Kumphel La and Phinjo who were deported from India in 1948', External Affairs, NAI File No. 7(2)-NEF, 1947 (Secret).

58. The *Himalayan Times* on 9 October 1960, in an article titled '"Chinese Spy Chief" Arrested in Kalimpong', reported that Ma Zhucai was arrested because he was the 'spy Chief' of the Chinese in Kalimpong.

59. Several books and articles have been published on Ma Zhucai, including an article by his son Ma Jiakui (1993). See also Mu et al. (2013) and Xu and Li (2015).

60. 'Ma-Chia-Kuei s/o Ma-Chu-Tsai of Jedong, China', WBSA File No. 2300/49(1), Serial No. 273.

61. 'Ma-Chia-Kuei s/o Ma-Chu-Tsai of Jedong, China', WBSA File No. 2300/49(1), Serial No. 273: 32.

62. 'Ma-Chia-Kuei s/o Ma-Chu-Tsai of Jedong, China', WBSA File No. 2300/49(1), Serial No. 273: 43.

63. 'Ma-Chia-Kuei s/o Ma-Chu-Tsai of Jedong, China',WBSA File No. 2300/49(1), Serial No. 273: 33–5.

64. 'Ma-Chia-Kuei s/o Ma-Chu-Tsai of Jedong, China', WBSA File No. 2300/49(1), Serial No. 273: 33–5.

65. The deterioration in their relations also had an impact on how the Chinese government treated the Kache in Lhasa and elsewhere in Tibet. See Atwill (2018).

66. 'Ma-Chia-Kuei s/o Ma-Chu-Tsai of Jedong, China', WBSA File No. 2300/49(1), Serial No. 273: 72.

67. 'Foreigners: Undesirable Chinese Nationals in Darjeeling', WBSA File No. 2782/50, Serial No. 320.

68. 'Ma-Chia-Kuei s/o Ma-Chu-Tsai of Jedong, China', WBSA File No. 2300/49(1), Serial No. 273: 137.

69. 'Ma-Chia-Kuei s/o Ma-Chu-Tsai of Jedong, China', WBSA File No. 2300/49(1), Serial No. 273: 158.

70. Chang Xiufeng's ordeal is discussed in more detail in Sen (2017).

71. On the presence of Chinese migrants in South Asia and Calcutta, see Oxfeld (1993), Liang (2007), and Zhang and Sen (2013).

72. Tan was also a target of intelligence surveillance. On Tan Yunshan and Cheena Bhavana, see Sen (2017). See also Chapter 8 by Brian Tsui in this volume.

73. 'Chang Hsui Feng @ Chang S.P. @ Chang, Shu Feng @ Hsui Feng @ Chang Siu Fen s/o Gang Chiu Hsiang of China Bhavan, Santiniketan, Birbhum, Hd. Master Chung wah School, Kalimpong',WBSA File No. 2312/49 (1), Serial No. 274: 9.

74. 'Chang Hsui Feng @ Chang S.P. @ Chang, Shu Feng @ Hsui Feng @ Chang Siu Fen s/o Gang Chiu Hsiang of China Bhavan, Santiniketan, Birbhum, Hd. Master Chung wah School, Kalimpong', WBSA File No. 2312/49 (1), Serial No. 274: 11.

75. 'Chang Hsui Feng @ Chang S.P. @ Chang, Shu Feng @ Hsui Feng @ Chang Siu Fen s/o Gang Chiu Hsiang of China Bhavan, Santiniketan, Birbhum, Hd. Master Chung wah School, Kalimpong', WBSA File No. 2312/49 (1), Serial No. 274: 16.

76. 'Chang Hsui Feng @ Chang S.P. @ Chang, Shu Feng @ Hsui Feng @ Chang Siu Fen s/o Gang Chiu Hsiang of China Bhavan, Santiniketan, Birbhum, Hd. Master Chung wah School, Kalimpong', WBSA File No. 2312/49 (1), Serial No. 274: 22, 36.

77. 'Chang Hsui Feng @ Chang S.P. @ Chang, Shu Feng @ Hsui Feng @ Chang Siu Fen s/o Gang Chiu Hsiang of China Bhavan, Santiniketan, Birbhum, Hd. Master Chung wah School, Kalimpong', WBSA File No. 2312/49 (1), Serial No. 274: 38.

78. 'Chang Hsui Feng @ Chang S.P. @ Chang, Shu Feng @ Hsui Feng @ Chang Siu Fen s/o Gang Chiu Hsiang of China Bhavan, Santiniketan, Birbhum, Hd. Master Chung wah School, Kalimpong', WBSA File No. 2312/49 (1), Serial No. 274: 47.

79. Chang Xiufeng and his wife were not the first Chinese family to be arrested for refusing to leave Kalimpong. *The Himalayan Times* (9 October 1960), in an article titled 'Chinese Leave Kalimpong', reported that a person named Yu-Chen-Shieu and his wife were the first to be prosecuted under the Foreigners' Act. Reports of Chang and his wife's arrests appeared in the article 'Chinese Arrested in Kalimpong' on 11 December 1960.

80. David Atwill's (2018) study of the Kache in Tibet is pertinent here with regard to the complexity of categorizing people. Invoking the PRC's argument that

the Chinese in Indonesia should be able to choose their citizenship, the Indian government argued that the same option must also be available to the Kache, who were claiming Indian citizenship. However, the Indian government itself was denying citizenship to the Chinese migrants and their descendants in India, such as Yu, who claimed Indian nationality.

81. 'Yu King/Tuck s/o Late Thien Sing of Kalimpong', WBSA File No. 2876/50, Serial No. 336/3: 45.

82. 'Foreigners: Undesirable Chinese Nationals in Darjeeling', WBSA File No. 2782/50, Serial No. 320: 3.

83. 'Yu King/Tuck s/o Late Thien Sing of Kalimpong', WBSA File No. 2876/50, Serial No. 336/3: 11.

84. 'Yu King/Tuck s/o Late Thien Sing of Kalimpong', WBSA File No. 2876/50, Serial No. 336/3: 109.

85. 'Yu King/Tuck s/o Late Thien Sing of Kalimpong', WBSA File No. 2876/50, Serial No. 336/3: 109.

86. Documents dating from 1949 to 1966 from the Foreign Ministry Archives of the PRC were made public in 2004. However, from 2012, access to these documents has been restricted. Several scholars were able to collect India-related material prior to 2012. This includes Sulmaan Wasif Khan (2015), who cites the foreign ministry reports on a Kalimpong resident named Sangzheng Duojie Pamu. Pamu, according to these reports, informed the Chinese officials about the Indian government's support for Tibetan rebels. Pamu eventually went to China.

87. On this episode, see the detailed study by Cohen and Leng (1972).

88. An editorial titled 'Chinese Spy Rings' in *The Himalayan Times* on 4 September 1960 supported the government's 'Quit India' notices issued against the alleged Chinese spies in Kalimpong. It also called on the government to 'see that the orders issued are carried out and those who are served with quit notices actually quit Kalimpong or India'. Moreover, on 21 January 1962, an article titled 'Chinese School in Kalimpong Raided' carried by the same newspaper reported that 'KMT Chinese and Tibetans' had raided the Zhonghua Chinese school 'shouting anti Communist slogans'.

References

Archival Material

Academia Historica (AH), Taipei, Taiwan

001000005050A. 'Zangzheng jianyi' (藏政建議) ['Proposals on Tibetan Affairs'].
129000093794A. 'Bangda Raogan' (邦達饒幹) ['Panda Rapga'].

0200499990018. 'Ouzhou siza juan' (歐洲司雜卷) ['Miscellaneous Europe [-Related] Folder'].

Central Intelligence Agency, https://www.cia.gov/library

File No. 25X1A. 'Report of Rapga Pangdatshang on Chinese Communist Occupation of Ch'angtu'.

India Office Records (IOR), British Library, London, UK

L/PJ/7/12155. 'Deportation of Jampa'.
L/PS/10/393. 'Tibet. Intercepted Telegrams'.
L/PS/12/4211. 'Tibet. Chinese Intrigues (Rapga)'.

National Archives of India, New Delhi, India

External Affairs, File No. 174-C.A., 1944: 'Correspondence between one P. Rapga and Chinese of Mongolian and Tibetan Affairs in Chungking on Affairs in Tibet intercepted in censorship information relating to Rapga and his brother application from Rapga to set up a press at Kalimpong for Producing a Tibetan paper'.
External Affairs, File No. 166-C.A., 1945 (Secret): 'Correspondence of one P. Rapga a Tibetan intercepted in Censorship'.
External Affairs, File No. 229-C, 1946: 'Tibetan Improvement Party deportation of P. Rapga and question of action against his accomplices'.
External Affairs, File No. 7(2)-NEF, 1947 (Secret): 'Decision not to take any action against F.M. Shen, a Tibetan Improvement Party member. 2. Reports regarding activities of Phu Rapga, Jampa Wosel, Kumphel La and Abdul Wahid Ladakche and other Tibetan Party members. 3. Kamchung Thubten Sangpo and Lodza Jampa Ngawang are the recognised Tibetan representatives at Nanking in China. 4. Return to Tibet of Kumphel La and Phinjo who were deported from India in 1948'.
Sikkim Agency, File No. 3(7)-L, 1946: 'P Rapga's activities with Tibetan Improvement Party'.
Sikkim Agency, File No. 23(14)-P, 1947: 'Rapga'.
Sikkim Agency, File No. 7(8)-P, 1946: 'Printing of secret documents by P. Ragpa under the heading of Tibetan Improvement Party'.

Second Historical Archives of China, Nanjing, PRC

Zhongguo di'er lishi dang'anguan (中國第二歷史檔案館) and Zhongguo Zangxue yanjiu zhongxin (中國藏學研究中心) 2002. *Zhongguo di'er lishi dang'anguan suocun Xizang he Xizang shi dang'an mulu* (中國第二歷史檔案館所存西藏和西藏 事檔案目錄) [*Catalogue of the Collection of Archival Documents on Tibet and Tibetan Affairs Preserved in the Second Historical Archives of China*], 2 Vols. Beijing: Zhongguo Zangxue chubanshe. (See Table A14.2 for a select list of documents.)

————. 2009–. *Zhongguo di'er lishi dang'anguan suocun Xizang he Xizang shi dang'an huibian* (中國第二歷史檔案館所存西藏和 西藏事檔案彙編) [*Collection of Archival Documents on Tibet and Tibetan Affairs Preserved in the Second Historical Archives of China*], Volumes 1–50. Beijing: Zhongguo Zangxue chubanshe.

West Bengal State Archives (WBSA), Intelligence Branch (IB) Records, Calcutta, India

File No. 202/1932, Serial No. 60/1932. 'Organization of an Improved Secret Service for Bengal'.

File No. 1398/43, Serial No. 116. 'Publication/Official: Internal Interception Report (Weekly Interception), Issued by Chinese Intelligence Wing, Calcutta'.

File No. 955/44, Serial No. 234. 'Foreigners: Chinese Nationals. Chinese Activities in Kalimpong, Darjeeling'.

File No. 955/44, Serial No. 301. 'Foreign Countries: China. Publication. A Report on Smuggling into China via Kalimpong'.

File No. 453/46, Serial No. 71. 'Pu Rapga @ Bhu Rapga @ Panda Rapga'.

File No. 595/46, Serial No. 4. 'Jampa Wosel @ Chang Fan Kun'.

File No. 816/46, Serial No. 261. 'Shen Fu Min, Kalimpong, Darjeeling. Interception of Correspondence Addressed to:'.

File No. 2300/49(1), Serial No. 273. 'Ma-Chia-Kuei s/o Ma-Chu-Tsai of Jedong, China'.

File No. 2312/49(1), Serial No. 274. 'Chang Hsui Feng @ Chang S.P. @ Chang, Shu Feng @ Hsui Feng @ Chang Siu Fen s/o Gang Chiu Hsiang of China Bhavan, Santiniketan, Birbhum, Hd. Master Chung wah School, Kalimpong'.

File No. 2782/50, Serial No. 320. 'Foreigners: Undesirable Chinese Nationals in Darjeeling'.

File No. 2876/50, Serial No. 336/3. 'Yu King/Tuck s/o Late Thien Sing of Kalimpong'.

Intelligence Branch, C.I.D., Bengal, Weekly Reports, 1911.

Government Documents

'Notes, Memoranda and Letters Exchanged and Agreements Signed Between the Governments of India and China 1954–1959', *White Paper*, Volume 1. Ministry of External Affairs, India.

Other Sources

Andrew, Christopher. 2018. *Secret World: A History of Intelligence*. New Haven: Yale University Press.

Atwill, David. 2018. *Islamic Shangri-La: Inter-Asian Relations and Lhasa's Muslim Communities, 1600 to 1960*. Berkeley: University of California Press.

Bayly, C.A. 1996. *Empire and Information: Intelligence Gathering and Social Communication in India, 1780–1870*. Cambridge: Cambridge University Press.

Bhasin, Avtar Singh (ed.), 2018. *India–China Relations, 1947–2000: A Documentary Study*. New Delhi: Geetika Publishers.

Bray, J. 2011. 'Trader, Middlemen or Spy? The Dilemmas of a Kashmiri Muslim in Early Nineteenth-Century Tibet'. In Anna Akasoy, Charles Burnett and Ronit Yoeli-Tlalim (eds), *Islam and Tibet: Interactions along the Musk Routes*, pp. 313–37. Farnham: Ashgate Publishing.

Chang, Jui-te. 2014. 'An Imperial Envoy: Shen Zonglian in Tibet, 1943–1946'. In Hans van de Ven, Diana Lary, and Stephen MacKinnon (eds), *Negotiating China's Destiny in World War II*, pp. 52–69. Stanford: Stanford University Press.

Chang Xiufeng (常秀峰). 1999. *Dajiling zhi qiu: Chang Xiufeng lü Yin huiyi lu* (大吉嶺之 秋：常秀峰旅印回憶錄) [*The Autumn in Darjeeling: Memoirs of Chang Xiufeng's Sojourn in India*]. Beijing: Zhongguo wenlian chubanshe.

Chen Qianping (陳謙平). 2002. 'Xizang gemingdang yu Zhongguo Kuomintang guanxi kao' (西藏革命黨與中國國民黨關係考) ['An Examination of the Relationship between the Tibetan Revolutionary Party and the Kuomintang']. *Lishi yanjiu* (歷史研究) [*Historical Research*] 3: 89–97.

Cohen, Alan Jerome and Shao-chuan Leng. 1972. 'The Sino-Indian Dispute over the Internment of Chinese in India'. In Alan Jerome Cohen (ed.), *China's Practice of International Law: Some Case Studies*, pp. 268–320. Cambridge, MA: Cambridge University Press.

Dirks, Nicolas B. 2002. 'Annals of the Archive: Ethnographic Notes on the Sources of History'. In Brian Axel (ed.), *From the Margins: Historical Anthropology and Its Futures*, pp. 47–65. Durham, NC: Duke University Press.

Eriksen, Thomas. 2015. *Small Places, Large Issues: An Introduction to Social and Cultural Anthropology*. London: Pluto Press.

Fader, H. Louis. 2002. *Called from Obscurity: The Life and Times of a True Son of Tibet, Gergan Dorje Tharchin*, 3 Vols. Kalimpong: Tibet Mirror Press.

Galbraith, John Kenneth. 1988. *Ambassador's Journal: A Personal Account of the Kennedy Years*. London: Houghton Mifflin.

Garver, John. 2001. *Protracted Contest: Sino-Indian Rivalry in the Twentieth Century*. Seattle: University of Washington Press.

———. [1997] 2015. *The Sino–American Alliance: Nationalist China and American Cold War Strategy in Asia*. London: Routledge.

Goldstein, Melvin. 1989. *A History of Modern Tibet, 1913–1951: The Demise of the Lamaist State*. Berkeley: University of California Press.

Harris, Tina. 2013. *Geographical Diversions: Tibetan Trade, Global Transactions*. Athens: University of Georgia Press.

Johnson, Robert. 2006. *Spying for the Empire: The Great Game in Central and South Asia, 1757–1947*. London: Greenhill Books.

Khan, Sulmaan Wasif. 2015. *Muslim, Trader, Nomad, Spy: China's Cold War and the People of the Tibetan Borderlands*. Chapel Hill: The University of North Carolina Press.

Kimura, Hisao. 1990. *Japanese Agent in Tibet*. London: Serindia Publications.

Kobayashi, Ryosuke. 2014. 'Tibet in the Era of 1911 Revolution'. *Journal of Contemporary East Asian Studies* 3 (1): 91–113.

Liang, Jennifer. 2009. 'Migration Patterns and Occupational Specialisations of Kolkata Chinese: An Insider's History'. *China Report: A Journal of East Asian Studies* 43 (4): 397–410.

Lin, Hsiao-ting. 2006. *Tibet and Nationalist China's Frontier: Intrigues and Ethnopolitics, 1928–49*. Vancouver: UBC Press.

Ma Jiakui (馬家奎). 1993. 'Huiyi xianfu Ma Zhucai jingying ZhongYin maoyi' (回憶先父馬鑄材經營中印貿易) ['Remembering (My) Late Father Ma Zhucai's China–India Trading Business']. In *Yunnan wenshi ziliao xuan* (雲南文史資料選) [*Selection of Literary and Historical Documents from Yunnan*], Volume 42, pp. 198–207. Kunming: Yunnan renmin chubanshe.

Mao Zedong. 1977. *Selected Works of Mao Tse-Tung*, Volume 5. Beijing: Foreign Languages Press.

McGranahan, Carole. 2005. 'In Rapga's Library: The Texts and Times of a Rebel Tibetan Intellectual'. *Cahiers d'Extrême–Asie* 15: 253–274.

———. 2007. 'Empire Out of Bounds: Tibet in the Era of Decolonization'. In Ann Laura Stoler, Carole McGranahan, and Peter Perdue (eds), *Imperial Formations*, pp. 173–209. Santa Fe: School of American Research Press.

———. 2010. *Arrested Histories: Tibet, the CIA, and Memories of a Forgotten War*. Durham NC: Duke University Press.

———. 2017. 'Imperial but Not Colonial: Archival Truths, British India, and the Case of the "Naughty" Tibetans'. *Comparative Studies in Society and History* 59 (1): 68–95.

McKay, Alex. 1997. *Tibet and the British Raj: The Frontier Cadre, 1904–1947*. Richmond: Curzon Press.

Mehra, Parshotam. 1976. 'Lu Hsing-Chi, the Simla Conference and After'. *Journal of Asian History* 10: 49–71.

Minto, James R. 1974. *Graham of Kalimpong*. Edinburgh: William Blackwood.

Mosca, Matthew W. 2015. 'Kashmiri Merchants and Qing Intelligence Networks in the Himalayas: The Ahmed Ali Case of 1830'. In Eric Tagliacozzo, Helen F. Siu, and Peter C. Perdue (eds), *Asia Inside Out: Connected Places*, pp. 219–42. Cambridge MA: Harvard University Press.

Mu Jihong (木霽弘), Li Baoping (李葆萍), He Qiang (和強), and He Gang (和剛). 2013. *Dianyu Zangshang: Ma Zhucai zhuan* (滇域藏商：馬鑄材傳) [*Tibetan Traders in the Borderlands of Yunnan: Biography of Ma Zhucai*]. Kunming: Yunnan renmin chubanshe.

Nehru, Jawaharlal. 2006. *Selected Works of Jawaharlal Nehru, 1 December 1953–21 February 1957, Second Series, Volume 36*. New Delhi: Jawaharlal Nehru Memorial Fund.

Oxfeld, Ellen. 1993. *Blood, Sweat, and Mahjong: Family and Enterprise in an Overseas Chinese Community*. Ithaca: Cornell University Press.

Poddar, Prem and Lisa Lindkvist Zhang. 2017. 'Kalimpong: The China Connection'. In Markus Viehbeck (ed.), *Transcultural Encounters in the Himalayan Borderlands: Kalimpong as a 'Contact Zone'*, pp. 149–174. Heidelberg: Heidelberg University Publishing.

Popplewell, Richard J. 1995. *Intelligence and Imperial Defence: British Intelligence and the Defence of the Indian Empire, 1904–1924*. Farnham: Routledge.

Pratt, Mary Louise. [1992] 2008. *Imperial Eyes: Travel Writing and Transculturation, Second Edition*. New York: Routledge.

Radhu, Abdul Wahid. 2017. *Tibetan Caravans: Journeys from Leh to Lhasa*. Delhi: Speaking Tiger Publishing.

Sen, Tansen. 2017. *India, China, and the World: A Connected History*. Lanham: Rowman & Littlefield.

Stewart, Gordon T. 2006. *Journeys to Empire: Enlightenment, Imperialism, and the British Encounter with Tibet, 1774–1904*. Cambridge: Cambridge University Press.

Stoddard, Heather. 1985. *Le Mendiant d'Amdo*. Paris: Société d'Ethnographie.

———. 2013. 'Progressives and Exiles'. In Kurtis R. Schaeffer (ed.), *The Tibetan History Reader*, pp. 583–608. New York: Columbia University Press.

Stoler, Ann Laura. 2009. *Along the Archival Grain: Epistemic Anxieties and Colonial Common Sense*. Princeton: Princeton University Press.

———. 2010. 'Archival Dis-Ease: Thinking Through Colonial Ontologies'. *Communication and Critical/Cultural Studies* 7 (2): 215–19.

Viehbeck, Markus (ed.). 2017. *Transcultural Encounters in the Himalayan Borderlands: Kalimpong as a 'Contact Zone'.* Heidelberg: Heidelberg University Publishing.

Wakeman, Jr, Frederic. 2003. *Spymaster: Dai Li and the Chinese Secret Service.* Berkeley: University of California Press.

Waller, Derek. 2015. *The Pundits: British Exploration of Tibet and Central Asia.* Lexington: The University Press of Kentucky.

Xu Min (許敏) and Li Wanjia (李婉佳). 2015. *Aiguo Qiaoling Ma Zhucai* (愛國僑領馬鑄材) [*Ma Zhucai: The Patriotic Leader of Overseas Chinese*]. Kunming: Yunnan renmin chubanshe.

Yang Twan. 1945. *Houseboy in India.* New York: The John Day Company.

Zhang, Xing and Tansen Sen. 2013. 'The Chinese in South Asia'. In Tan Chee-Beng (ed.), *Routledge Handbook of the Chinese Diaspora,* pp. 205–26. London: Routledge.

Zhu Lishuang (朱麗雙). 2016. *Minguo zhengfu de Xizang zhuanshi, 1912–1949* (民國政府的西藏專使, 1912–1949) [*The Republican Government's Envoys to Tibet, 1912–1949*]. Hong Kong: Zhongwen daxue chubanshe.

Epilogue

PRASENJIT DUARA

The China–India field of study is a now a booming industry. Both comparisons and connections between the two giants are being researched and commented upon; more recently the relationship is being viewed in terms of their regional and global impact (Sen 2017). Why this is happening seems obvious enough, even if there are protests that such a procedure may be methodologically unsound. While population size (including the combined population), long histories, and broadly parallel modern developments are often cited to validate the study, the critics invoke the Himalayan barrier over millennia, entirely different political and social systems, and, not least, the vastly greater size of the contemporary Chinese economy compared to the Indian one.

Nonetheless, I believe that the China–India relationship, in its different historical and contemporary configurations, remains very significant, not only because of the two nations' size, growth rates, and impact on the world, but also because it reveals interesting methodological insights from a non-Western (though not anti-Western) global perspective. This is sometimes called a South–South perspective, though there is no definitive understanding of that perspective either. The essays in this volume reveal different dimensions outlined later that lead to new pathways of studying connections, comparisons, and convergences between the two societies.

In the first place, the essays diverge significantly from the tradition of intra-Asian studies called pan-Asianism since the early twentieth century. That tradition was pioneered and centred on the Japanese schools of thought that tended to consider the positive and high cultural connections between Asian societies in opposition to forms of Western imperialist domination. It is well known how this thought was hijacked by Japanese militarists to serve as an ideology of imperialist domination; it became a kind of imperialism of anti-imperialism. While in the post-War era, such extreme forms of 'Asian values' were eschewed in the scholarly world, the quest for an alternative framework to study Asian connections has revived.

The most radical of these formulations was the work of the Japanese scholar of China, Takeuchi Yoshimi (1910–77) who coined the enigmatic phrase, 'Asia as method'. Since Asian historical traditions had been wiped out by Western domination, post-War Asian leaders, especially in revolutionary China, were able to chart new and more genuinely enlightened paths for the world from a relatively clean palate. This conception has been recently picked up by several Asian scholars particularly with the economic rise of Asian countries in the late twentieth and twenty-first centuries.[1]

By and large, beyond the study of Japanese pan-Asian imperialism, there has been little analysis of on-the-ground relations between modern China and India. Partly because of the blinding effects of the Sino-Indian Border Conflict of 1962, India–China studies of the modern period have been largely confined either to the study of ancient civilizational exchanges or to contemporary realpolitik competition. Yet what is not mentioned in these formulations is the extent to which these obscuring strategies are themselves an effect of postcolonial Asian societies participating in and even dominating the capitalist nation-state system for control of global resources. To cite the well-known postcolonial intellectual position: While protesting and resisting Western forms of imperial domination, these new nation-states have adopted the institutions of competitive capitalism with equally serious consequences for society and the environment both nationally and globally.

In this context, the essays in this volume can be seen to assess the extent to which the postcolonial critique holds in the India–China configuration. As mentioned, these essays avoid a rose-tinted and high-cultural perspective associated with the Japan–India centred pan-Asianism. Several of the authors fold in the historical actors' various visions of pan-Asianism, but go beyond them analytically. In this regard, they are not necessarily counter to ideologies of pan-Asianism, but they are always at an angle and sometimes opposed to these ideologies. More importantly, the authors work with new empirical materials grounded in a practical and complex reality during the historical period under consideration. The tensions, contradictions as well as the harmonization of different views and interests of pan-Asian ideologies are well researched in their work.

The essays deal with a wider spectrum of historical actors and materials than we have seen before. There are studies here of fiction writers, philosophers, soldiers, policemen, travel writers, journalists, investigative officers, and spies, among others. They portray a mosaic of different interactions in heterogeneous capacities and spaces such as borderlands, public spaces, imaginative writings, and government institutions, where they negotiate attitudes and projects. A few trends—or hypotheses—that I observed may be worth considering. First, the situation in China and India in the colonial period generated a mirror effect for each of the countries among their compatriots. This was especially pronounced among Chinese observers who saw a split image in the Indian mirror. While they, like Kang Youwei and others, discussed by Zhang Ke, saw parallels in the historical and contemporary conditions, they also saw it as a condition to be avoided at all costs as Indians had become 'enslaved' by the British. Adhira Mangalagiri discusses the popular fiction writer Peng Yu's novel, *Twin Souls*, which explores double personas in a single person: the back and forth between the identity of a Sikh policeman—an iconic image of the Indian in Republican China—and a Chinese student focuses acutely on this problematic identification. The Sikh policeman, also discussed here by Yin Cao, represents the dual figuration as an enslaved employee who is also the most proximate oppressor of the Chinese populace.

The split is also noticeable in the one-sided view of Tagore in the Chinese majority intellectual perspective of the May Fourth era, which saw this complex figure as representing only Eastern civilization in opposition to the West. Yet as Yu-Ting Lee argues, this slice of Tagore's views became the centre of a debate on modernity in China that propelled certain ideological trends. The study of Zhang Taiyan by Viren Murthy reveals a different type of split that Zhang needed to manage: his identification with Chinese nationalism and sympathy for the anti-imperialist nationalism of the Indians, even while he developed a philosophical critique of Hegelian ideal of progress embodied in the nation-state (and backwardness of non-Western societies). Zhang developed a novel position by melding Buddhist and Daoist ideas for a new universalism. Gal Gvili recounts the fascinating project of the Nanyang scholar, Xu Dishan who sought to blur the binary of two sides through his recovery of the networks of folktales—their concepts and imagery—that seeped into China based on Buddhist Hindu conceptions. As such, he created a mirror that was not split but rather one in which the ancient and folk other could be seen in the self.

On the Indian side, the experiences and writings of Indian observers, whether it be the celebrated diary of the Indian soldier Gadadhar Singh who served during the Boxer Uprising, the vernacular press in north India and Bengal, or Tagore himself, were reflected in a smoother and brighter mirror. There is considerable admiration and sympathy for China and its contemporary plight. Indians saw in China a great civilization as they once had been, and the struggles in China to overthrow Western domination were very significant for the cause of Indian and global anti-imperialism. Indeed, it may be hard for Indians after the 1962 war to imagine that such a positive view of China existed in the previous half century.

The collection also represents significant historical shifts in attitudes and activities over the first half of the twentieth century. In China, the rise of leftist mass movements and reportage and the simultaneous rise of the Gandhian movement in India generated a more positive view of the Indian cause. Indian nationalist activities among the diaspora found important spaces of refuge and inspiration in China. At the same time, however, the rise of the Kuomintang (KMT) regime generated a strategic vision of Asia and India guided by state interests (what in diplomatic jargon is known as 'reasons of state'). Liao Wen-shuo and Brian Tsui document the strategic concerns and activities of the KMT state as it manoeuvred through its various intelligence agencies and networks between Japanese imperialism, the British colonial state (whose support it needed), and Indian nationalism. This segment is complemented on the Indian side for a later period in the 1950s by Tansen Sen's fascinating account of Kalimpong as a 'nest of spies' which the Indian state managed to break up by asserting the sovereignty claims of the nation-state in the contested Himalayan borderlands.

An important dimension of diasporic Indian nationalist activity in the Sinosphere (for example, Shanghai, Hong Kong, Singapore) is the extent to which the Japanese ideology of pan-Asianism became a thorn between Chinese and Indian nationalists. This was especially the case in East and Southeast Asia where Indians were more favourably treated and lured by Japanese pan-Asian propaganda than in India itself where the Indian National Congress denounced Japanese imperialism but simultaneously denounced British imperialism which was problematic for the KMT. The triadic relationship between China–India–Japan, which continues to be relevant today, is worthy of a fuller study.

The segment in the volume about cultural brokers between China and India also generates novel ways to look at this phenomenon particularly with the rise of nationalism and the nation-state. Cultural diplomacy on the part of the KMT discussed by Brian Tsui and Janice Hyeju Jeong through the medium of Tagore's Santiniketan scholar Tan Yunshan and Jeong's Chinese Islamic Diplomatic Missions, respectively, were both cultural and political. In the age of nationalism, the cultural and national became difficult for these mediators to separate. Yet their activities could not be reduced to the political or national alone. In both cases, personal and cultural relationships survived regime change and generated new relationships as Tan and his family became recognized anew as cultural ambassadors between China and India. Similarly, the Islamic missions to British India also generated friendships that created a basis for the China–Pakistan relationship in the post-War era.

Finally, I believe a number of these essays can be viewed through the methodological lens I have dubbed convergent comparison. The concept is based on the idea that histories are circulatory and not necessarily shaped by linear national processes. The method suggests that although there may be many different factors and institutions in different societies, they can often be understood comparatively through their responses to the common factor that impacts them.

Circulatory processes, ideas, and forms may develop in Society A and travel to Societies B and C where they are reshaped and travel elsewhere in those forms. They may sometimes even to return to Society A, though they may be recognized as something else. These processes are institutionalized in different societies but nonetheless reveal how national institutional processes often resemble each other often more than their past processes. What I call the zone of convergence is the impact space of circulatory forces that elicit or demand a response; the responses of various social formations, in turn, form the basis of convergent comparison. It is a method that allows us to account for differences even while recognizing that there are processes and forces that link them in a common future.

We could consider various processes in Sino-Indian historical flows over the last millennium, whether they be Buddhism, popular culture, astronomy, or technologies of silk and sugar production. Here let us consider one of the most important forces in the twentieth century. The impact of imperialism, particularly British (and later Japanese) imperialism, was experienced in both societies as domination or monopoly of economic and political power. Elsewhere I have argued that in broad terms, we can see parallel movements in the emergent forms of nationalism in the two societies all the way from the 1880s to the present. The essay by Anne Reinhardt on shipping nationalism draws remarkable parallels in the techniques and resources used by nationalist Chinese and Indian shipping magnates to overcome the similar imperialist monopolies and control they confronted in the two societies. In this case, the magnates did not seem to be aware of the similarity of the conditions and means available to them and which they utilized most effectively. In the other essays of the volume, there was much greater awareness of their common condition during this period. The advent of the nation-state and the logic of nationalism appear to have pushed this awareness to fair oblivion as they pushed for the exclusive greatness of the nation at the cost of our common planetary belonging.

Note

1. For studies that build upon Takeuchi's idea of 'Asia as method', see Chen (2010), Sun (2005), and Murthy (2016). The concept is also discussed in the introduction to this volume.

References

Chen Kuan-hsing (陳光興). 2010. *Asia as Method: Toward Deimperialization*. Durham, NC: Duke University Press.

Murthy, Viren. 2016. 'Resistance to Modernity and the Logic of Self-Negation as Politics: Takeuchi Yoshimi and Wang Hui on Lu Xun'. *positions: asia critique* 24 (2): 513–54.

Sen, Tansen. 2017. *India, China, and the World: A Connected History*. Lanham: Rowman and Littlefield.

Sun Ge (孫歌). 2005. *Zhunei Hao de beilun* (竹内好的悖論) [*The Paradox of Takeuchi Yoshimi*]. Beijing: Beijing daxue chubanshe.

Index

Editors and Contributors

Editors

Tansen Sen is professor of history and director of the Center for Global Asia at NYU Shanghai, China, and Global Network Professor at NYU, New York, USA. He received his MA from Peking University, China, and PhD from the University of Pennsylvania, Philadelphia, USA. He specializes in Asian history and religions and has special academic interest in India–China interactions, Indian Ocean connections, and Buddhism. He is the author of *Buddhism, Diplomacy, and Trade: The Realignment of Sino-Indian Relations, 600–1400* (2003, 2016) and *India, China, and the World: A Connected History* (2017). He has co-authored (with Victor H. Mair) *Traditional China in Asian and World History* (2012), edited *Buddhism Across Asia: Networks of Material, Cultural and Intellectual Exchange* (2014), and co-edited (with Burkhard Schnepel) *Travelling Pasts: The Politics of Cultural Heritage in the Indian Ocean World* (2019). He is currently working on a book about Zheng He's maritime expeditions in early fifteenth century and co-editing (with Engseng Ho) *The Cambridge History of the Indian Ocean, Volume 1.*

Brian Tsui is associate professor in the Department of Chinese Culture at The Hong Kong Polytechnic University, China, and is interested in the intersection between revolutionary politics and mobilization of cultures on both the left and the right in China's twentieth century. His first book, *China's Conservative Revolution: The Quest for a New Order, 1927–1949* (2018), studies mass politics under the Kuomintang, the dilemmas confronting Chinese liberal intellectuals caught between an authoritarian state and a supposedly untamable populace, and the Nationalist Party's appeal to pan-Asianism as a strategy to garner international support. His current research focuses on the advent of 'New China' as an Asia-wide event, zeroing in on how the early People's Republic of China was interpreted by Indian nationalists and Asian Christians in the 1950s.

Contributors

Yin Cao is associate professor and Cyrus Tang scholar in the Department of History, Tsinghua University, Beijing, China. His research interest lies in modern Indian history, global history, and India–China connections in the twentieth century. He is the author of *From Policemen to Revolutionaries: A Sikh Diaspora in Global Shanghai, 1885–1945* (2017). His other publications can be found in academic journals such as *Britain and the World*, *Indian Historical Review*, *Frontiers of History in China*, and the *Journal of World History*. He is currently working on a project of exploring how India became the home front for China's war with Japan in the 1940s.

Prasenjit Duara is the Oscar Tang Chair of East Asian Studies at Duke University, Durham, USA. He was born and educated in India, and received his PhD in Chinese history from Harvard University, Cambridge, USA. He was previously professor and chair of the Department of History, and chair of the Committee on Chinese Studies at the University of Chicago, USA (1991–2008). Subsequently, he became Raffles Professor of Humanities, and director of Asia Research Institute at National University of Singapore (2008–2015). In 1988, he published *Culture, Power, and the State: Rural North China, 1900–1942*, which won the Fairbank Prize of the American Historical Association and the Levenson Prize of the Association of Asian Studies. Among his other books are *Rescuing History from the Nation* (1995), *Sovereignty and Authenticity: Manchukuo and the East Asian*

Modern (2003), and *The Crisis of Global Modernity: Asian Traditions and a Sustainable Future* (2014). He has edited *Decolonization: Perspectives from Now and Then* (2004) and co-edited (with Viren Murthy and Andrew Sartori) *A Companion to Global Historical Thought* (2014). His work has been widely translated into Chinese, Japanese, Korean, and some European languages.

Gal Gvili is assistant professor in the Department of East Asian Studies at McGill University, Montreal, Canada. She received her MA degree from Hebrew University in Jerusalem, Israel, and her PhD from Columbia University in New York, USA. She researches and teaches modern and contemporary Chinese literature, literary and cultural theory, and South–South connections.

Janice Hyeju Jeong received her PhD degree in history from Duke University, Durham, USA, in 2019. Her manuscript 'Between Shanghai and Mecca: Diaspora and Diplomacy of Chinese Muslims in the Twentieth Century' combines textual and ethnographic data to investigate Chinese Muslim diaspora networks that have revolved around Mecca, and their periodic mobilizations as channels of informal diplomacy. Her broad research and teaching interests include inter-Asian connections and migrations, historical anthropology, Sino-Islamic relations, and religious diplomacy.

Yu-Ting Lee currently teaches at the Graduate Institute of National Development, National Taiwan University, Taipei, Taiwan. He received his BA degree in business administration at National Taiwan University; MA degree in comparative literature at the University of Edinburgh, UK; and PhD degree in cultural interaction at Kansai University, Osaka, Japan. His research and teaching topics include East Asian history, modern Chinese and Japanese thought and civil society, among others. He is currently exploring the pan-Asian intellectual network that connected China, India, and Japan.

Liao Wen-shuo is associate researcher at Academia Historica, Taipei, Taiwan. She is the author of a dozen peer-reviewed journal and conference papers delivered through outlets such as *Twentieth-Century China*, *Humanitas Taiwanica*, and annual meetings of European

Association of Taiwan Studies and Association for Asian Studies. Her research spans cultural diplomacy, international relations, and comparative politics with an emphasis on Nationalist Chinese foreign policies and intelligence in South and Southeast Asia. She is currently working on a manuscript on China's intelligence networks in South and Southeast Asia in the 1940s.

Adhira Mangalagiri is lecturer in the Department of Comparative Literature at Queen Mary University of London, UK. In 2019–20, she was the Victor and William Fung Foundation Postdoctoral Fellow at the Harvard University Asia Center, Cambridge, USA. Her book project, 'States of Disconnect: China–India Literary Relation in the Twentieth Century', examines aesthetic and material intersections between the Chinese and Hindi/Urdu literary spheres, with a focus on the task of China–India comparison. Her work has appeared in the *Yearbook of Comparative and General Literature* and the *Journal of World Literature*, and is also forthcoming in *Comparative Literary Studies*.

Viren Murthy teaches transnational Asian History and researches Chinese and Japanese intellectual history in the Department of History, University of Wisconsin–Madison, USA. During the academic years 2016–18, he was a fellow at the Berggruen Institute, Los Angeles, USA, for philosophy and culture. He is the author of *The Political Philosophy of Zhang Taiyan: The Resistance of Consciousness* (2011), and has also co-edited (with Axel Schneider) *The Challenge of Linear Time: Nationhood and the Politics of History in East Asia* (2013), (with Prasenjit Duara and Andrew Sartori) *A Companion to Global Historical Thought* (2014), (with Joyce Liu) *East Asian Marxisms and Their Trajectories* (2017), and (with Fabian Schäfer and Max Ward) *Confronting Capital and Empire: Rethinking the Kyoto School of Philosophy* (2017). He has published articles in *Modern Intellectual History*, *Modern China*, and *Frontiers of History in China* and *Positions: Asia Critique*, and is currently working on a project tentatively titled 'Pan-Asianism and the Legacy of the Chinese Revolution'.

Anne Reinhardt is professor of history at Williams College, Williamstown, USA. She is the author of *Navigating Semi-colonialism: Shipping, Sovereignty, and Nation-Building in China, 1860–1937* (2018), a study that uses the steamship and steam navigation as means to interrogate China's experience of Euro-American and Japanese imperialism. Her current research focuses on modes of decolonization in China in the immediate aftermath of the Second World War and the early years of the People's Republic of China.

Kamal Sheel retired as professor of Chinese studies from Banaras Hindu University, Varanasi, India, and is now an adjunct fellow of the Institute of Chinese Studies, New Delhi, India. He is the author of *Peasant Society and Marxist Intellectuals in China: Fang Zhimin and the Origin of a Revolutionary Movement in the Xinjiang Region* (1989, 2014). He has co-edited (with Lalji 'Shravak' and Charles Willemen) *India on the Silk Route* (2009) and (with Charles Willemen and Kenneth Zysk) *From Local to Global: Papers in Asian History and Culture* (2017). He was a co-translator of *Thirteen Months in China* (2017) with Anand Yang and Ranjana Sheel. Presently, he is also translating Kang Youwei's travelogue to India and preparing a manuscript on Fang Zhimin for the Jiangxi People's Publishing House, Nanchang, China. His present research interest focuses on comparative studies of Indian and Chinese intellectual discourses in the context of nationalism and modernity.

Madhavi Thampi is an honorary fellow of the Institute of Chinese Studies, New Delhi, India, and, until recently, editor of the journal *China Report*. She taught in the Department of East Asian Studies, University of Delhi, India, until 2014. Her major publications include *Indians in China, 1800–1949* (2005) and *China and the Making of Bombay* (2010, co-authored with Shalini Saksena). She also edited the volume *India and China in the Colonial World* (2005). Her area of interest has been the less-studied aspects of the interactions between India and China in the colonial era. She has also been involved in initiatives to catalogue materials related to modern China at the National Archives of India.

Anand A. Yang is the Walker Family Endowed Professor of history and professor of international studies at the Henry M. Jackson School of International Studies, University of Washington, Seattle, USA. Among his publications are *The Limited Raj: Agrarian Relations in*

Colonial India (1989), *Bazaar India: Peasants, Traders, Markets and the Colonial State* (1999), and a forthcoming book, *Empire of Convicts: Indian Penal Labor in Southeast Asia.* He is also the editor and co-translator (with Kamal Sheel and Ranjana Sheel) of *Thirteen Months in China* (2017), editor of *Crime and Criminality in British India* (1985), and co-editor (with Jerry H. Bentley and Renate Bridenthal) of *Interactions: Transregional Perspectives on World History* (2005). He is currently researching Indian and Chinese global labour migrations in the nineteenth and twentieth centuries.

Zhang Ke is associate professor in the Department of History, Fudan University, Shanghai, China. He also serves as associate director of the International Center for Studies of Chinese Civilization (ICSCC) and the Asia Research Center (ARC) at Fudan University, China. He received his PhD from Fudan University, China, in 2009. His research interests include modern Chinese intellectual history and global history of cultural exchange. He is the author of *Zhongguo renwenzhuyi de gainianshi 1901–1932* [*The Conceptual History of 'Humanism' in Modern China, 1901–1932*] (2015; in Chinese), the editor of *Jindai Zhongguo de zhishi yu guannian* [*The Transformations of Ideas and Knowledge in Modern China*] (2018; in Chinese), and the co-editor of *Jindai Zhongguo de zhishi shengchan yu wenhua zhengzhi* [*The Production of Knowledge and the Politics of Culture in Modern China*] (2014; in Chinese) and *Stray Birds on the Huangpu: A History of Indians in Shanghai* (2018; in English and Chinese). He has published more than thirty articles, and is currently working on a book project on the cultural relations between India and China during the late Qing period.

Other Titles in the Series